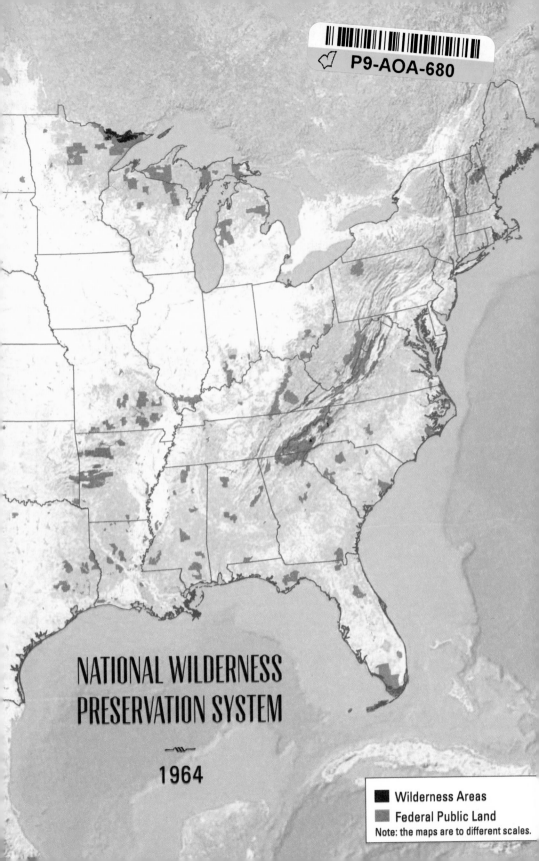

NATIONAL WILDERNESS PRESERVATION SYSTEM

1964

Wilderness Areas
Federal Public Land
Note: the maps are to different scales.

WEYERHAEUSER ENVIRONMENTAL BOOKS

William Cronon, Editor

Weyerhaeuser Environmental Books explore human relationships with natural environments in all their variety and complexity. They seek to cast new light on the ways that natural systems affect human communities, the ways that people affect the environments of which they are a part, and the ways that different cultural conceptions of nature profoundly shape our sense of the world around us. A complete list of the books in the series appears at the end of this book.

JAMES MORTON TURNER

FOREWORD BY WILLIAM CRONON

////

THE PROMISE
OF WILDERNESS

AMERICAN ENVIRONMENTAL POLITICS SINCE 1964

UNIVERSITY OF WASHINGTON PRESS

SEATTLE AND LONDON

The Promise of Wilderness: American Environmental Politics since 1964
is published with the assistance of a grant from the Weyerhaeuser Environmental
Books Endowment, established by the Weyerhaeuser Company Foundation,
members of the Weyerhaeuser family, and Janet and Jack Creighton.

UNIVERSITY OF WASHINGTON PRESS
PO Box 50096, Seattle, WA 98145, USA
www.washington.edu/uwpress

LIBRARY OF CONGRESS
CATALOGING-IN-PUBLICATION DATA
Turner, James Morton, 1973–
The promise of wilderness : American envi-
ronmental politics since 1964 / James Morton
Turner. — 1st ed.
p. cm. — (Weyerhaeuser environmental books)
ISBN 978-0-295-99175-7 (hardback)
1. Environmental policy — United States —
History — 20th century. 2. Environmental protec-
tion — United States — History — 20th century. 3.
Wilderness areas — Law and legislation — United
States — 20th century. 4. Wilderness areas —
United States — 20th century.
I. Title.
HC110.E5T87 2012   333.78'20973 — dc23
2011050149

The paper used in this publication is acid-free and
meets the minimum requirements of American
National Standard for Information Sciences —
Permanence of Paper for Printed Library Materials,
ANSI Z39.48–1984.∞

Printed and bound in the United States of America
Maps by James Morton Turner
Landscape photography by George Wuerthner
Design by Ashley Saleeba
Composed in Minion Pro, Univers, and Tommaso

COVER: Satellite image of Rancho Cucamonga,
California, San Bernardino National Forest,
and Cucamonga Wilderness. Courtesy GeoEye,
Herndon, Virginia, www.geoeye.com.

CONTENTS

PART ONE

WILDERNESS AND THE ORIGINS OF MODERN ENVIRONMENTALISM, 1964–1976

PART TWO

THE POLARIZATION OF AMERICAN ENVIRONMENTAL POLITICS, 1977–1994

PART THREE

WILDERNESS AND A NEW AGENDA
FOR THE PUBLIC LANDS, 1987–2009

FOREWORD

THE SUBLIME AND PRAGMATIC POLITICS
OF AMERICAN WILDERNESS

William Cronon

When the University of Washington Press first launched the Weyer-haeuser Environmental Books series in the early 1990s, none of us had any idea that one of its most enduring intellectual contributions would be to recruit and publish some of the most important recent scholarship on the history of American wilderness. Perhaps because one of the first books we brought out was Nancy Langston's path-breaking *Forest Dreams, Forest Nightmares*, which explored controversies surrounding old-growth forests in the Pacific Northwest, environmental historians brought to the Press a remarkably wide-ranging collection of wilderness manuscripts. The series published David Louter's *Windshield Wilderness*, about the efforts of the National Park Service to accommodate automobiles while trying to protect the wilderness experience of visitors; Kevin Marsh's *Drawing Lines in the Forest*, about the complex political and managerial processes whereby individual wilderness areas are designated; and James Feldman's *A Storied Wilderness*, about the rewilding of an archipelago in Lake Superior that made it possible for lands once viewed as "degraded" to be protected a few decades later as wilderness. These and other studies in the series make signal contributions to a rich scholarly tradition in environmental history reaching back to Roderick Nash's classic *Wilderness and the American Mind* in 1967.

Perhaps the most surprising of the books we have published on this subject, though, are three that with no advance planning by the authors or editors constitute one of the most comprehensive and sophisticated histories of American wilderness politics in the twentieth century. This accidental trilogy began in 2002 with Paul Sutter's *Driven Wild: How the Fight against Automo-*

biles Launched the Modern Wilderness Movement, which explored how a small group of conservationists, disturbed by the construction of high-elevation roads in the national parks and forests, came together in 1935 to found an organization called the Wilderness Society, one of the most effective and influential environmental advocacy groups in the United States. Sutter's book was followed in 2005 by Mark Harvey's *Wilderness Forever: Howard Zahniser and the Path to the Wilderness Act*, which offered a biography of the Wilderness Society leader who was more responsible than any other individual for drafting and promoting the legislation that Lyndon Johnson eventually signed into law as the Wilderness Act of 1964. What the founders of the Wilderness Society had dreamed of accomplishing in 1935—forever protecting the wildest of America's public lands by making it illegal to build roads on or otherwise develop them— seemed finally to have been achieved.

Now, with the publication of James Morton Turner's extraordinary new book, *The Promise of Wilderness: American Environmental Politics since 1964*, we complete the trilogy we did not at the outset even know we were publishing. Turner begins his history of American wilderness politics where most historians are content to end it: with the passage of the Wilderness Act. Until that year, it is easy enough to narrate this history as if the crucial debate was *whether* wilderness should be protected in the United States. The new law seemed to answer that question decisively in the affirmative, which is probably why it is so often treated as the climax of the wilderness story. And yet the decision to protect wilderness was really just the beginning of a much longer, more complicated, and interesting process. Activists, managers, and politicians—along with communities and citizens—would now focus their attention less on *whether* to protect wilderness than on *how* best to do so. No scholar before Turner has tackled this question with anything like the depth and rigor that are apparent on every page of this magnificent volume, which will surely become a standard work on the post-1964 politics of wilderness. But its implications in fact extend much further, since debates over wilderness protection contributed to far-reaching discussions of logging, mining, and grazing on the federal lands, all of which would redefine federal land politics during the 1980s and 1990s.

Like Sutter and Harvey before him, Turner relies on the Wilderness Society—whose records have been deposited in the archives of the Denver Public Library and whose leaders have continued to play central roles in wilderness advocacy right down to the present—to provide the narrative spine on which he hangs his broader history. Whereas wilderness politics before 1964 had concentrated to a considerable degree on getting that statute passed, the very fact of its success meant that activism had to shift significantly across the United States to those federal lands that were suitable for wilderness designation. The remark by Speaker of the House Tip O'Neill that "all politics is local" was now equally true of wilderness.

The Wilderness Act and its successors created elaborate institutional mechanisms for studying potential wilderness areas to determine whether they deserved to be protected. Activists seeking wilderness protection needed to be continuously present throughout this process, which meant that organizations like the Wilderness Society had to reinvent themselves to engage the very legislation they had helped create. New staff had to be hired, both to work on the ground in local wilderness campaigns and to muster the science and legal advocacy that were needed back in Washington. New partnerships had to be forged with the many local organizations that sprang up wherever lands were being considered for wilderness designation. New relationships had to be created with the federal agencies responsible for stewardship of wild lands, from the Forest Service to the National Park Service to the Bureau of Land Management. And new members and funders had to be recruited to provide the financial support that made all these other activities possible.

Turner's deft discussion of these many changes demonstrates that the Wilderness Act has been as much about complex political processes as about definitions of wild land. These processes have involved myriad transformations not just for the Wilderness Society and the broader environmental movement, but for American politics more generally. I cannot do justice to the depth and subtlety of Turner's interpretation in the brief scope of this foreword, so instead I want to emphasize an argument that he places at the very center of his book. One way to do this is to ask how a book about the implementation of a single federal statute dealing with obscure federal lands that most Americans have never even heard of, let alone seen, could be important enough to merit the ambitious subtitle of this volume: *American Environmental Politics since 1964.* Surely the years since 1964 have revealed a host of environmental problems—pollution, toxic wastes, public health, energy shortages, climate change, environmental justice—that many would say are more important than protecting wilderness. Faced with reforming modern civilization to make it more sustainable, isn't there something a little romantic, even nostalgic, about setting aside wilderness areas that are likely to be profoundly altered by climate change no matter how hard we try to protect them? To use a word much favored by activists in the 1960s, are wilderness politics still relevant to the environmental challenges of the twenty-first century?

Turner's answers to such questions—and I very much agree with him about this—is that one cannot understand the most heated environmental controversies of the past fifty years if one ignores the politics of wilderness. They are far more central to the political history of the environment than a naive observer might imagine. A key moment in his story occurs during the 1980s, when the Wilderness Society (along with federal agencies like the Forest Service) found itself suddenly attacked from both the Left and the Right. From the Left, radical environmental groups like Earth First! mounted high-profile media campaigns arguing that what came to be called "mainstream" environmental organizations were so mired in the inside-the-Beltway politics of Washington, D.C., that they had lost touch with their own activist roots. Only by taking direct action in defense of wild nature, these radical environmentalists argued, could one hope to defend wilderness from the forces arrayed against it. A little later, and from a rather different leftward direction, environmental justice activists would argue that wilderness politics were too indifferent to the demands of social justice, especially the oppression of working-class people and people of color. As a result of these challenges, groups like the Wilderness Society would struggle for years to strike the right balance of national with local politics, professional expertise with citizen activism, and wilderness advocacy with other environmental concerns.

From the Right, the 1980s saw the election of Ronald Reagan and his appointment of cabinet secretaries like James Watt who were deeply out of sympathy with the Wilderness Act and all that it stood for. Although Watt's controversial tenure at the Department of the Interior is a familiar story, Turner mounts a much broader and more suggestive argument that federal lands and wilderness were emerging as one of the great dividing lines of American politics, especially in rural areas where wilderness became a symbol of excessive state power intruding on the lives and freedoms of property owners and local communities. To appreciate the force of this claim, look at any electoral map from recent presidential elections and ask how liberal and conservative voters array themselves relative to federal lands containing wilderness. Many of the most conservative states, especially in the West, are precisely those that contain the greatest wilderness acreages. Although this is hardly a simple cause-effect relationship, it does suggest the importance of wilderness, the federal lands, and the American West in national politics in ways that are not nearly as well understood or appreciated as they should be.

This is just one of the many insights that James Morton Turner provides for us in *The Promise of Wilderness*. He is a scholar's scholar, and we are unlikely any time soon to see a book about the twentieth-century history of American wilderness that is so deeply researched, so carefully thought out, and so gracefully argued. But because he is himself committed to the environmental politics that he explores so successfully in this book, he also goes out of his way to offer explicit lessons from this history for those concerned about wilderness protection and federal lands management today. The result is that rare work of scholarship that speaks as powerfully to activists and engaged citizens as it does to professional historians. If your goal is to understand why wilderness remains such a compelling feature of American public life and how it continues to shape contemporary politics, this is a book to savor and ponder carefully. The sublime and pragmatic politics it illuminates so well will be with us for a very long time to come.

ABBREVIATIONS

AFL-CIO	American Federation of Labor and Congress of Industrial Organizations
ALPS	Alpine Lakes Protection Society
ANCSA	Alaska Native Claims Settlement Act (1971)
ANILCA	Alaska National Interest Lands Conservation Act
ANWR	Arctic National Wildlife Range (1960–1980)
ANWR	Arctic National Wildlife Refuge (1980–present)
AUM	animal unit month (unit for calculating grazing fees)
BLM	Bureau of Land Management
COSCC	Colorado Open Space Coordinating Council
DORS	Development Opportunity Rating System
EIA	economic impact analysis
ESA	Endangered Species Act (1973)
FBI	Federal Bureau of Investigation
FLPMA	Federal Land Policy and Management Act (1976)
LASER	League for the Advancement of States' Equal Rights
NEPA	National Environmental Policy Act (1969)
NFMA	National Forest Management Act (1976)
NMWC	Northern Michigan Wilderness Coalition
NRDC	Natural Resources Defense Council

NREPA   Northern Rockies Ecosystem Protection Act

PRIA   Public Rangelands Improvement Act (1978)

RARE   Roadless Area Review and Evaluation (1973)

RARE II   Roadless Area Review and Evaluation II (1979)

REI   Recreational Equipment Incorporated

RP&E   Resource Planning and Economics Department, the Wilderness Society

SEACC   Southeast Alaska Conservation Council

SUWA   Southern Utah Wilderness Alliance

TAP   Trans-Alaska Pipeline

WARS   Wilderness Attribute Rating System

ACKNOWLEDGMENTS

T his book would not have been possible without the many people who have worked to manage and protect the public lands. There are now more than 757 wilderness areas nationwide, none of which would have been protected without the involvement of citizens, interest groups, industry, and government agencies. For every Alpine Lakes or Dolly Sods—two of the places I focus on in this book—there are dozens of other wilderness areas equally compelling and worthy of attention. For every professional wilderness advocate, such as Ernie Dickerman or Melyssa Watson, there are many others who have also been instrumental in national wilderness politics. And for every local activist, such as Helen McGinnis or Bob Hanson, there are thousands of others who have worked to make individuals and local organizations a powerful force in wilderness advocacy. My hope is that the individuals who have worked for and against wilderness and public lands reform will find echoes of their individual experiences in these pages as I unfold the story of wilderness, the public lands, and American environmental politics.

Many of the individuals I write about in this book have been kind enough to speak with me about their work, including Jim Eaton, Bert Fingerhut, George Frampton, Michael Francis, Scott Groene, Kirk Johnson, Tim Mahoney, Mike Matz, John McComb, Clif Merritt, Reed Noss, Brian O'Donnell, Mike Scott, Julie Wormser, and Ed Zahniser. I especially appreciate the support of the individuals who went out of their way over the years—speaking with me, suggesting new avenues for research, or providing photographs and documents from their personal collections—including Ben Beach, Stewart Brandborg, Chuck Clusen, Brock Evans, Dave Foreman, Eric Forsman, Bill Meadows, Debbie Sease, Ken Rait, and Melyssa Watson. From the start of this project, Rupert Cutler and Doug Scott have been especially generous and helpful. Rupert's stories of working for wilderness in the 1960s raised questions I've been trying to answer ever since. Doug helped me appreciate the importance of legislative language, the evolution of citizen organizing, and the complexities of wilderness history. Not only is he an effective advocate, he is a skilled historian too.

While those individuals often helped me fill in the details of this project, much of the information upon which this book is based came from archival research. That research would not have been possible without the help of archivists and librarians at Wellesley College, Princeton University, Gettysburg College, Cornell University, the Bancroft Library, the University of Montana-Missoula, the University of Washington, the American Heritage Center at the University of Wyoming, and the National Archives and Records Administration. An Alfred D. Bell, Jr., travel grant from the Forest History Society made my research at the Forest History Society possible. Of all the archives, I spent the most time in the Western History Collection at the Denver Public Library, which is home to the Conservation Collection and, most importantly for my purposes, the Wilderness Society's records. The Western History Collection at the Denver Public Library is a true gem. I am grateful to the entire Western History and Genealogy staff, all of whom made this research possible, but especially Claudia Jensen. Many other individuals and organizations have contributed to this project in important ways too, including Chris Beeson, Kira Bingemann, Amy Casamassa, Bob Dickerman, Ecoflight, Steve Greenberg, Chris Mammen, Shireen Parsons, Wilson Porterfield, Herbert Ragan, Debbie and Bob Sawin, Zandy Smith, Ralph Swain, Lindsay and Matt Weissberg, the Wilderness Society, and George Wuerthner.

I've been at work on this book for ten years, which has given me the chance to work on it at several different institutions. This book began as my dissertation at Princeton University, where it benefited greatly from the support of students and faculty in the Department of History, the History of Science Program, and the Science, Technology, and Environmental Policy Program. Drew Isenberg was a model advisor: generous with his time, challenging in his criticism, and unfailing in his support. It was his teaching and scholarship that inspired my interest in environmental history. Dan Rodgers helped me to situate this project, and my own thinking, in broader currents of American history. Dan's attention to the powerful place of language and ideas in history has been both a challenge and an inspiration. Other scholars provided crucial advice at important moments, including David Wilcove, Kevin Kruse, and Karen Merrill. I finished this book at Wellesley College as a faculty member in the Environmental Studies Program. The college supported my research with funding from the Frost Fund for Environmental Studies and the Helen S. French Fund. Wellesley students, especially Blair Edwards, Halae Fuller, Mackenzie

Klema, Rebecca Sher, Anli Yang, and Jane Zhou, played important supporting roles researching, fact-checking, and proofreading this book. And I could not ask for a more stimulating or enjoyable group of colleagues than the faculty and staff affiliated with the Environmental Studies Program. I especially appreciate the assistance that Sammy Barkin, Beth DeSombre, Alden Griffith, Jess Hunter, Nick Rodenhouse, and Marcy Thomas provided with this project.

Much of this book has been published in journals or presented at conferences over the past decade. I am grateful to the editorial staff and reviewers at *Conservation Biology*, *Environmental History*, *The Journal of American History*, and *Wild Earth*. Publishing articles in those venues did much to inspire and improve this book. When presenting my research, most often at the American Society for Environmental History, I have found myself among a welcoming crowd of historians who share an interest in the complex place of wilderness and environmental politics in American history. I especially appreciate the help of those who have discussed, read, and commented on portions of this manuscript at various stages, including Pete Alagona, Jim Feldman, Michael Lewis, Christopher Klyza, Kevin Marsh, Daniel Nelson, Adam Rome, Tom Robertson, Jamie Skillen, Darren Speece, Jennifer Thomson, and Laura Watt. Mark Harvey and Paul Sutter have been most generous with their time. Mark helped me rethink how wilderness activism mapped onto the Great Society in the 1960s. Paul Sutter urged me to give more attention to the conservative turn in American politics during the 1970s and 1980s. Their careful and constructive comments shaped this project in invaluable ways. I was fortunate that Bill Cronon took an interest in this project early on, helping me expand the scope of this book and strengthen its narrative. His broad challenges and insightful comments have done the most to give this book its final form. Through Bill, I've worked with the University of Washington Press. Marianne Keddington-Lang, Mary Ribesky, Julidta Tarver, Amanda Gibson, and Ashley Saleeba have helped shepherd this project from manuscript to book with incredible patience, attention to detail, and skill.

Some people have been waiting for this book longer than I've actually been working on it. Nancy Ruth Patterson, Louise Clark, Tina Weiner, Jim Warren, Tyler Lorig, and Eduardo Velásquez—at different points in my education, each set me on my way. Tim and Susie Williams provided a quiet cabin in the woods to begin this project and that is only the first of a long list of thank yous I owe them for their support and generosity. My family has been steadfast in their support of my endeavors. My parents, Suzi and Jay, helped encourage my love of the outdoors, literature, and big projects early on in my life. My first memories of the West are looking out of a Volkwagen pop-top camper on the landscape between Cody, Wyoming, and Yellowstone National Park. I have other such memories, many of which include my siblings, Stafford, Margaret-Hunter, and Catherine. It was quite something to take my own children to visit their first national park in the summer of 2010. As Cole and Liam strike their own paths in the years to come, I look forward to sharing the trail with them in many a wilderness area along the way. My wife, Darcy, and I were married about the time I took up this project. At first, the project promised summers exploring the West. More often, it has meant dinnertime conversations about legislative histories, late nights proofreading, and long working weekends. She has helped make this project a reality in so many ways, both small and large. We have been lucky to visit wilderness areas from West Virginia to Alaska together. Those are some of my most favorite memories. In the wilderness and at home, I would be lost without her. I dedicate this book to Darcy.

THE PROMISE OF WILDERNESS

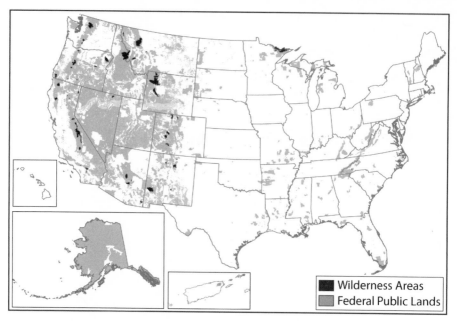

Map I.1 National Wilderness Preservation System, 1964. When Congress established the wilderness system in 1964, it protected 54 wilderness areas encompassing 9.1 million acres, all in the national forests. *Note: maps of Alaska, Hawaii, and Puerto Rico not to same scale.*

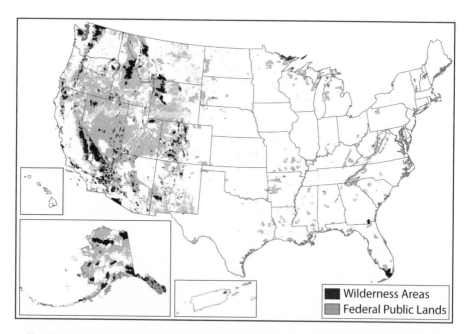

Map I.2 National Wilderness Preservation System, 2009. By 2009, Congress had expanded the wilderness system to 757 areas encompassing 109.5 million acres (57.4 million acres of which are in Alaska). *Note: maps of Alaska, Hawaii, and Puerto Rico not to same scale.*

INTRODUCTION

This land is your land, this land is my land

From California, to the New York Island

From the redwood forest, to the gulf stream waters

This land was made for you and me.

—WOODY GUTHRIE, "THIS LAND IS YOUR LAND"

Woody Guthrie's lyrics evoke powerful ideals about America, democracy, and the land. He penned those words in 1940. He would be pleased to know that today much of America's land is still federally owned: one in four acres nationwide; 620 million acres more or less.[1] What does that mean? It means that every American has a stake in an expanse of land that measures more than six times the size of California. These are the public lands. They include national parks, forests, and wildlife refuges, and quite a bit of other land in between. To put it most optimistically, those lands are as much yours as they are mine. It is not just the melody that made Guthrie's song so catchy.

Few ideas have been more important than wilderness in shaping how Americans have viewed, debated, and managed the landscape Guthrie celebrated. Considered narrowly, protecting wilderness is a straightforward decision to save a portion of the nation's wild lands for the future rather than develop it for its resources today. But viewing wilderness so narrowly would be like mistaking Guthrie's song for a simple patriotic anthem. Debates over wilderness, like the song, are as much about American society and politics as they are about the land. How Americans have debated wilderness and public lands reform more generally has raised questions not just about environmental protection, but about the power of the federal government, who speaks for the public interest, and the rights of individuals. Those questions have been important to modern American environmental politics more broadly too.

This book is about the political meanings of wilderness and the public lands from the origins of the modern environmental movement in the early 1960s to the present day. Recently some scholars have dismissed concern for wilderness as a dead end for environmentalism: it gives no attention to the issues that strike closest to home, like polluted waterways or hazardous waste sites; it does little to challenge the nation's consumer culture and its far-reaching environmental consequences; and it distracts environmentalists from more pressing issues, such as climate change.[2]

But to dismiss the significance of wilderness is to overlook one of the most important and sustained arenas of debate in American environmental politics. Viewed through the lens of wilderness, the history of American environmental politics looks different: it explains the importance of the public lands to the rise of environmental opposition and radical environmentalism, it reveals the changing relationship between local and national environmental advocacy organizations, and it helps explain why Democrats and Republicans often appear on opposite sides of environmental reform. Other environmental issues are important to these changes too, but wilderness offers a crucial barometer for considering the history of mainstream American environmentalism and its place in American political life.

What Is Wilderness?
A Place, an Idea, and a Process

What is wilderness? Wilderness is a place. Wilderness areas are among the best-protected wild landscapes in the United States. In 1964, Congress passed the Wilderness Act, which created the National Wilderness Preservation System. Today, that system protects nearly 5 percent of all the land in the United States, including wilderness areas in forty-four states and Puerto Rico. Wilderness areas are off-limits to logging, mining, roads, motorized vehicles, and all forms of development. As the Wilderness Act promises, "A wilderness, in contrast with those areas where man and his works dominate the landscape, is hereby recognized as an area where the earth and its community of life are untrammeled by man, where man himself is a visitor who does not remain."[3]

What places deserve such protection? Consider Denali National Park and Preserve in Alaska. Mount McKinley, at the center of the park, towers over postcard pictures of central Alaska. On a clear day, the mountain's knife-edge ridges cut skyward. Glaciers fall like a cloak from its shoulders. The summit trails wisps of cloud. Measuring 20,320 feet, Mount McKinley reaches to the sky. Beneath its ramparts of rock and ice unfolds a landscape of mountains, foothills, wide-open river valleys, and the endless tundra of central Alaska. Along the park's northern slopes, wide rivers make real the Alaska Range's awesome dimensions. The flows of the Sanctuary, Teklanika, Toklat, and McKinley rivers run in sweeping braids through streambeds that measure miles across. The grey, green, and even pink hues of the cobblestone bars hint at the geological history of the mountains beyond. It is through this landscape that Denali's wildlife parades: wolves, grizzlies, elk, fox, lynx, and caribou in the lowlands; Dall sheep, mountain goats, and marmots along the foothill crests. Golden eagles soar above it all. Congress further protected Denali and the surrounding plateau as a wilderness area in 1980.

But not all wilderness areas are so majestic. Consider the lesser-known, but impressively named, Great Swamp in central New Jersey. The Great Swamp was scoured out by glaciers and has slowly been reclaimed by swamp and forest. During the twentieth century, central New Jersey's network of roads, neighborhoods, and towns encroached on its borders. But inside the alders and willows that guarded its periphery, the Great Swamp remained a tangle of swampy lowlands and shallow forested ridges. Stunted stands of red maple, elm, swamp rose, alder, and willow populated the wetlands. Grand beech trees, oaks, sugar maples, and hickories anchored themselves along the dry ridges. Like breaks in the clouds, the forest occasionally gave way to acres of open swamp swathed with grasses. Within its boundaries, a visitor might spot a fox, coyote, or beaver and a birder could identify dozens of species of birds. The Great Swamp staked out a small patch of wild land less than thirty miles west of New York City. That distance did not protect the Great Swamp from all human incursion— abandoned homesteads, old drainage ditches, and the occasional apple tree marked a long history of human use. But all that disappeared into the folds of the swamp's vegetation. Congress designated the Great Swamp National Wildlife Refuge a wilderness area in 1968.

Today, the National Wilderness Preservation System protects a wide sweep of America's federal lands that extends far beyond these two places. Wilderness areas range from the mountains and dunes of the California deserts to the peaks of the Rocky Mountains to the rounded knobs and valleys of the Appalachians. The smallest wilderness area is six acres; the largest is more than 9 million acres. Not surprisingly, more than half of the nation's designated wilderness is found in Alaska. Some areas are iconic landscapes, like Denali or

Mount Rainier; some are little known, like the Great Swamp or the Allegheny Islands. Some areas are so remote that one might disappear into them forever, like Gates of the Arctic in Alaska; in other areas, the lights of urban metropolises, such as Denver, Las Vegas, and Tampa, brighten the evening sky. Such an array of wilderness suggests the variety of meanings that we have applied to wilderness and, equally important, that wild lands have cultivated in us in return. All of these places are wilderness.[4]

What is wilderness? It is among the most powerful and troublesome ideas in American environmental thought. For many Americans, it was America's wild lands, tall forests, and spectacular mountains that distinguished the nation from Europe in the nineteenth century. Thomas Cole, the pioneering landscape painter, suggested that "the most distinctive, and perhaps the most impressive, characteristic of American scenery is its wildness."[5] Henry David Thoreau asked, "Why should not we, who have renounced the king's authority, have our national preserves, where no villages need be destroyed, in which the bear and panther and some even of the hunter race, may still exist, and not be 'civilized off the face of the earth'?"[6] The historian Frederick Jackson Turner argued that it was wilderness that had been essential to the creation and renewal of America's democratic institutions.[7] In the 1920s, Aldo Leopold called wilderness "the very stuff that America is made of."[8] In 1960, writer Wallace Stegner described wilderness as the "geography of hope."[9] For Americans, wilderness has been a patriotic inspiration, a primitive recreational retreat, a place of sublime beauty, a countercultural ideal, and a reserve for biodiversity. Wilderness has powerfully informed the American environmental imagination.

Of course, not everyone values wilderness in the same way. The idea of permanently protecting wild places has always sparked controversy, but the scope and intensity of the debate escalated after the Wilderness Act became law. Opponents of wilderness protection argued that such withdrawals ignored the rights of individuals and dismissed the interests of rural communities. To them, wilderness represented an overextension of governmental authority. As the wilderness system grew, they argued, it threatened the public interest, and they began to organize effectively and publicly to let their views be known. Some Native Americans supported wilderness protection in some instances, but in others they opposed it, or worked to ensure it was implemented in ways that respected their tribes, communities, and traditions. Most recently, wilderness provoked debate within the academic community, with some scholars arguing that idealistic notions of protecting wild nature have kept the environmental movement from expanding its political constituency and focusing on more pressing environmental issues, such as environmental justice or climate change. Success has only made wilderness more contested, not only among its opponents, but among environmentalists themselves.

What is wilderness? Although this book is about the many answers to that question, at the heart of this book is one central argument: wilderness is not simply a place or an idea; it is also a political process. Since 1964, the size of the wilderness system has grown more than tenfold to 109.5 million acres of land. That success does not represent a retreat from pressing realities, as some critics have argued; instead, the work of designating wilderness has been an effective vehicle for engaging local citizens as political advocates and leveraging the resources of local and national groups toward a common goal. And such efforts to protect wilderness, both in their successes and failures, have helped launch a much broader set of campaigns to manage the nation's public lands more sustainably for logging, grazing, and mining. Such campaigns can be a lightning rod for anger over issues such as government regulation, extreme liberalism, and elitist environmentalism. Yet environmentalists have not only weathered such opposition and controversy, at times they have turned it to their advantage. At their best, wilderness advocacy and public lands reform have brought together diverse groups of citizens, from ranchers and hunters to wildlife enthusiasts and hikers, in common cause to manage the federal lands in the public interest. This book tells their story.

Wilderness, the Public Lands, and American Environmental Politics

Saving wilderness is not going to resolve our environmental challenges—that was not true in the 1960s and it is not true today.[10] What distinguishes wilderness as an environmental issue is that it, more than many other issues, has been a topic of constant debate since the birth of modern environmentalism in the 1960s. Consider other issues that have appeared on the environmental marquee: population control and nuclear power galvanized the early environmental movement in the 1960s and early 1970s, but then faded from the political scene; new environmental concerns, such as ozone depletion and endocrine disruptors, emerged in the 1980s and 1990s and have since reframed public environmental debate. But the public lands have drawn a disproportionate and, at times, commanding portion of the mainstream environmental movement's attention and energies for five decades. For that reason, wilderness and the public lands can teach us much about the evolution of modern environmental advocacy and American environmental politics.

Why has wilderness been so important to American environmentalism? Answers to this question have often generated more criticism than explanation. Some scientists have faulted environmentalists for focusing on wilderness and overlooking its limits as a tool to protect biodiversity: often the most important habitat is located on non-federal lands or requires active restoration and management. Others argue that wilderness is an artifact of romanticism; the nature that wilderness enthusiasts seem to care the most about saving is the type of wild land depicted in an Ansel Adams photograph.[11] Other critics emphasize that because mainstream environmental concern is a product of leisure—often the leisure of white Americans and the upper-middle class—it tends to emphasize places such as national parks rather than urban areas where most people work and live.[12] For that reason, environmentalism has failed to engage issues of importance to urban communities, people of color, and the poor.[13] Some scholars suggest the longtime emphasis on wilderness is indicative of the misguided priorities of modern environmentalism in general. One critic summed up such concerns when she argued that wilderness was a product of the "uncritically 'preservationist' political culture from which much mainstream environmental thinking has developed."[14]

There is merit in all of these critiques and each demands the careful reflection of those who care about wild lands and environmental advocacy.[15] But none of these critiques explains why wilderness has remained central to mainstream American environmentalism. Simply dismissing wilderness as a problematic preoccupation of some environmentalists makes it easy to avoid taking that question seriously. A whole set of reasons—social, political, economic, cultural, and environmental—has made wilderness important to national conversations about the environment. First, the wilderness movement is ostensibly about protecting "public" lands, which has generally allowed wilderness advocates to avoid challenging the private property rights of landowners or corporations and the historical claims of Native Americans. Second, wilderness has been a concern of national interest around which popular political campaigns could be organized; witness the long-standing debates over the Arctic National Wildlife Refuge or national forest roadless areas. Third, environmentalists often have found it easy to publicize threats to wild lands; logging, mining, and dams pose a recognizable and seemingly more immediate threat than climate change or fisheries depletion. Fourth, the land that wilderness advocates have focused on has often been of secondary economic importance, which has helped defuse the opposition of industry and local communities. And fifth, unlike other environmental policy issues that have devolved into bureaucratic management and regulatory oversight, wilderness advocacy has had a well-defined legislative goal—that is, designating more wilderness.

The point here is that environmentalists who worked for wilderness did so not because they were confused about the realities of the environmental crisis or because they were ignorant of or insensitive to urban issues or claims of environmental justice advocates, conservation biologists, or other critics. A more useful explanation is that the environmental community has been pragmatic. Protecting a public resource of marginal economic value that commands national interest, is clearly threatened, and has significant ecological value has been easy compared to addressing environmental concerns that more directly challenge the social or economic structure of modern America, consumer culture, or private property rights.[16] When wilderness advocates did begin to more aggressively use wilderness as a vehicle to advance a broader public lands reform agenda—such as logging reform, biodiversity protection, and ecosystem management—they faced more sustained opposition and greater challenges.

Surprisingly, historians of the modern environmental movement have given little attention to the recent history of the modern wilderness movement and public lands reform. Instead, as the story of modern environmentalism is often told, wilderness was secondary to the politics of environmentalism, which focused more on a new generation of issues, such as air and water pollution, toxics and hazardous waste, and other threats to human health. In the usual narrative, the modern environmental movement began not with the Wilderness Act of 1964, but with Rachel Carson's *Silent Spring* in 1962, which drew national attention to the threat of persistent organic pesticides and other man-made chemicals.[17] To many scholars, these new issues, which posed an immediate threat to the quality of life and health of Americans, appeared to galvanize the modern environmental movement.[18] But drawing a distinction between an "old" generation of conservation issues focused on wilderness, resource management, and the public lands and a "new" generation focused on pollution, toxins, and threats to human health raises an important question: What place did the wilderness movement, with its focus on the public lands, occupy in relation to the emerging American environmental movement, with its broad sweep of new environmental laws and regulations and popular concern for the environment?[19]

I argue that the wilderness movement was not left behind by a new generation of environmental concerns. Even as the emerging environmental movement made crucial advances in raising public awareness, enacting policies such as the National Environmental Policy Act (1969) and pursuing legal action on behalf of environmental protection to address a new generation of environmental issues, equally important, wilderness advocates aggressively adapted some of those tools and strategies—legislative, scientific, and legal— to make advances for old conservation issues such as wilderness and public lands issues. This is important because the major shifts in modern American environmental politics emerged not just in reaction to a new generation of environmental issues, as many scholars have supposed, but also in response to the changed debates over these old conservation issues, which are the focus of this book. Reconsidering the place of wilderness and the public lands in the history of American environmentalism highlights three crucial questions that shaped American environmental politics in the past and continue to shape it today.

Who holds the reins in American environmental advocacy? Is American environmentalism dominated by the big mainstream groups, such as the Wilderness Society and the Sierra Club, or has the real engine behind environmental reform been grassroots groups, such as the Montana Wilderness Association and the Wildlands Project? Following the interest groups that have done the most to shape public lands debates offers a surprising set of answers to these questions. While national groups have often been at the center of public lands politics, understanding the pivotal role of local and regional groups and ad hoc coalitions is essential to understanding the history of American environmental politics.

To tell this story, I follow the evolution of the Wilderness Society most carefully. Although this strategy highlights the Wilderness Society's work, even in instances when other groups or individuals played a more important role, it is useful because the Wilderness Society and its relationship to other wilderness and public lands advocacy groups are illustrative of important changes in American environmental politics. In the 1960s, the Wilderness Society invested its resources in cultivating local wilderness organizations, educating citizens and leaders, and involving people in the political process. Its goal was not simply to protect wilderness areas, but to inspire a new generation of citizen leaders to advocate for the protection of the public lands. By the 1980s, the Wilderness Society was a very different organization. While the organization gave rhetorical emphasis to citizen activism, the new Wilderness Society emphasized careful economic and scientific analyses, well-orchestrated fundraising campaigns, political lobbying, and media outreach—tactics that marked the mainstream American environmental movement's reinvention as a professional lobby. Since the mid-1990s, the Wilderness Society has worked to harness its professionalism to a resurgent citizens' wilderness advocacy movement.

This is not just a story of national groups gaining more power and influence at the expense of local groups, although at times it appeared that way. It is also a story about the proliferation of local activism in American environmentalism. At times, the relationship between local and national groups has been competitive, but it has often been synergistic and has played a crucial role in the greatest successes for the protection of the public lands. This book also follows the rise of a more distributed model of environmental advocacy—in which the agency and initiative for environmental reform emerged from local groups, ad hoc coalitions, foundations, and national groups. To understand that shift, which occurred in the 1980s and 1990s, requires giving careful attention to the most volatile organizations in American environmental politics, such as Earth First!, more ambitious organizations, such as the Wildlands Project and the Native Forest Council, and some of the wealthiest foundations in American history, such as the Pew Charitable Trusts.

Why has environmental reform become such a divisive issue in American politics? "The environment may be the gut issue that can unify a polarized nation in the 1970s," announced *Time* magazine.[20] Such a claim seemed reasonable at the time, considering the widespread support for the nascent environmental movement. It had attracted support from a wide range of politicians, such as Democrats Lyndon Johnson and Gaylord Nelson and Republicans Richard Nixon and Pete McCloskey, and groups, such as the United Autoworkers of America and the Garden Club of America; and environmentalists could speak with confidence on the importance of protecting the environment for the national interest, whether arguing for the Wilderness Act or the National Environmental Policy Act. On the first Earth Day in 1970, Congress recessed for the day to take part in festivities nationwide that attracted over twenty million Americans, from Girl Scouts marching in front of the Department of the Interior to college students overturning cars in Washington state.[21]

Even if *Time* was optimistic in its observations, something had clearly changed by the early 1980s with Ronald Reagan's election, the backlash against big government, and the mobilization of conservatives nationwide. Although a bipartisan tradition has been important to American environmental politics, when examined carefully, environmental issues have always been divisive, pitting region against region, urbanites against rural Americans, and resource industries and their workers against environmentalists. Often, on issues ranging from petroleum exploration in the Arctic National Wildlife Refuge to clean energy and climate change reform, the most important dividing line has been that between Democrats and Republicans. Debates over the public lands can teach us much about both how partisan politics has changed with respect to environmental issues and, just as important, how environmentalists have successfully negotiated those challenges to generate powerful moments of widespread and bipartisan support for environmental reform.

To understand the more recent partisanship requires first reconsidering the political origins of modern American environmentalism in the early 1960s. If the environmental movement's trajectory had been that of Lyndon Johnson's Great Society, which reached its apex in the mid-1960s, then the environmental movement would have crested with the Wilderness Act of 1964 and then reached a slow denouement. But that is not what happened. Instead, during the same years that the Great Society lost momentum, both the wilderness movement and the larger environmental movement gained strength and began building toward some of the most outstanding legislative accomplishments of the 1970s. This suggests the enduring power of a liberal political formula that emphasized the ability of the federal government to protect the public interest, which was the claim at the heart of much of 1960s and 1970s environmental reform. I argue that the mainstream environmental movement adopted the philosophy and rhetoric of a formulation of "reform liberalism," which emphasized the public good and the role of the federal government, rather than the emerging language of "rights-based liberalism" important to a changing Democratic Party, which emphasized the rights of people to a healthy environment or the rights of nature itself.[22] In those origins are clues to the political challenges environmentalists faced in the 1980s and 1990s as well as clues to how environmentalists can effectively advance their political claims today.

Carefully situating modern environmentalism in the political context of the postwar years also helps explain the mixed successes of the environmental opposition. Starting in the 1970s, some of the most popular manifestations of the environmental opposition, such as the Sagebrush Rebellion and the Wise Use Movement, emerged most forcefully and publicly in response not to new environmental issues, but to changed debates over the earlier conservation issues, such as the public lands and wilderness. And, between the late 1970s and the early 1990s, this opposition evolved in ways that shaped and reflected broader shifts in conservative politics, as critics of public lands protection moved away from the reactionary opposition to the federal government and environmental reform grounded in states' rights claims characteristic of the Sagebrush Rebellion, toward the more positive assertions of individual property rights and liberties characteristic of the Wise Use Movement. That meant it was not only logging or mining companies lobbying against wilderness designations, but their employees and their families marching in the streets, with banners such as "People for the West!—Fighting to Keep America Strong by Keeping Public Lands Open."[23] In doing so, the Wise Use Movement and its conservative allies succeeded in unsettling the wilderness movement's confidence in its ability to speak for the public interest and the role of the government in public life in ways that the Sagebrush Rebellion and resources industries never did in the 1960s or 1970s.[24]

The debates over the public lands and environmental politics thus played a supporting role in a central transition in postwar American politics: the decline of liberalism and the rise of modern conservatism. Scholars, however, have generally agreed that, although Americans consistently rank environmental issues as important, historical polling data and election analyses show that in the voting booth they rank environmental issues low relative to other political concerns. For that reason, scholars have generally considered the environment a secondary issue, commanding insufficient attention from political candidates or parties to play a formative role in national politics. But at important moments, debates over wilderness and the public lands have not only been shaped by the polarization of American politics, they have also contributed to it.[25]

Which policy strategies have been most important and successful in environmental politics? To understand the strategies wilderness advocates have pursued to achieve their goals, we must first consider how dramatically the goals for public lands protection have changed since the 1960s. Contrary to some assessments of American environmentalism more broadly, in the case of public lands advocacy the story is not one of retreat from idealistic and ambitious origins in the 1960s and 1970s to a more modest and watered-down agenda in the 1980s and 1990s.[26] The story line runs in the opposite direction. In the 1960s, wilderness advocates aimed to protect a relatively small amount of land, bargained with key resource industries, and avoided systematic challenges to the nation's industries or economy. In the 1980s and 1990s, however, new scientific concerns, economic analyses, and environmental and political values all played important roles in challenging and reshaping wilderness advocates' strategies and ambitions. In response, public lands advocacy began to move in two directions. More ambitious wilderness advocates envisioned larger, scientifically justified wilderness areas as part of large-scale networks of habitat protection and other public lands advocates focused new attention on the basic rules by which the public lands were managed, arguing that activities such as logging, grazing, and mining should either be banned or managed much more strictly. In both cases, environmentalists aimed to promote more sustainable resource management and conserve biological diversity and ecosystem processes. And in both cases environmentalists did something earlier wilderness advocates had not: they directly challenged the fundamental role of resource development on the nation's public lands.

That shift in goals from wilderness to a broader agenda for public lands reform helps explain a key shift in American environmental policy between the 1970s and the 2000s: the uneven turn from a legislative strategy in Congress toward alternative policy pathways that run through all branches of government. To many observers, American environmental politics seemed to have collapsed into a state of gridlock in the late 1980s and early 1990s, as congressional action on environmental reform ground to a near halt. In the face of a whole range of pressing issues—from climate change to public lands protection—the government seemed plagued by inaction. But that interpretation makes sense only so long as you focus on Congress. Political scientists Christopher McGrory Klyza and David Sousa made this argument most carefully in their book *American Environmental Policy, 1990-2006: Beyond Gridlock*. In response to deepening congressional gridlock, as Klyza and Sousa explain, environmentalists and their opponents increasingly turned to alternative policy pathways, such as executive action, congressional appropriations, administrative rulemaking, and administrative and judicial review, to pursue their goals. It was this turn that has helped make environmental politics such a volatile and creative arena of policy action since the 1990s. Some of the most important issues in public lands politics—protecting national forest roadless areas, reforming mining and grazing regulations, and protecting western canyon lands—often followed policy pathways that went around, not through, Congress. What is evident in the case of the public lands is that this shift toward alternative policy pathways was more than just a response to congressional gridlock; it was also very much a product of those new ambitions for public lands protection that informed both wilderness advocates' policy goals and the political opposition to public lands reform starting in the 1980s.[27]

These changes—in the structure of environmental advocacy, the partisanship of environmental politics, and the shifts in policy strategy—all slowed the wilderness movement at times, but they never derailed it. Despite the seesaw of American politics, a community of wilderness advocates has diligently worked to protect the nation's public lands for their aesthetic, recreational, scientific, and public values. There is no single individual who has orchestrated this campaign. Some individuals stand out—such as Howard Zahniser, Doug Scott, Debbie Sease, and Brian O'Donnell—but it is as much the story of a group of people, some professionals, some volunteers, who have made this their careers and their avocation. This is not a story dominated by those with the most money or the best political connections. Groups such as the Wilderness Society may have multi-million-dollar budgets and a strong presence in Washington, D.C., but small groups with fewer resources, such as the Alliance for the Wild Rockies and the Nevada Wilderness Coalition, have played a pivotal role in changing the direction of public lands politics at key moments. Nor is this just a story about playing by the rules, lobbying Congress, appealing to agencies, and filing suits in court. It is also about people putting their bodies on the line, blockading logging roads, sitting in trees, and marching through the streets of rural towns and the thoroughfares of cities. All of these people, these organizations, and these strategies have made the public lands central to American environmental politics. And at key moments, wilderness advocates have advanced their agenda: the Wilderness Act of 1964, the Alaska National Interest Lands Conservation Act in 1980, the California Desert Protection Act in 1994, the contested Clinton roadless rule, and, most recently, the Omnibus Public Land Management Act of 2009. For every legislative victory, there are dozens, even hundreds, of lesser-recognized administrative and judicial victories that have been won behind the scenes. And, as important as these policy successes, wilderness advocates have also played a crucial role in changing the ways Americans understand, value, and debate the future of the nation's public lands. Indeed, few environmental issues have drawn more attention at the local, regional, and national levels, among radicals and moderates, Democrats and Republicans, and environmentalists and their opponents, than wilderness. If we wish to tell a story of modern American environmental politics, wilderness is an important place to begin.

PART ONE

WILDERNESS AND THE ORIGINS OF MODERN ENVIRONMENTALISM, 1964–1976

1 / WHY A WILDERNESS ACT?

Howard Zahniser carried a heavy burden the last eight years of his life. It was not just that he was the executive director of the Wilderness Society, the chief author of the Wilderness Act, and the legislation's most faithful champion. It was his coat. Zahniser had two long overcoats into which extra pockets had been sewn that he filled with copies of wilderness legislation, maps of the public lands, transcripts of congressional testimony, the writings of Thoreau, and more. He was a walking library, ready to educate the nation about wilderness, one person at a time. As he saw it, everyone should be in favor of wilderness. Who could oppose protecting the nation's heritage? Those who opposed the legislation, he believed, did not object to wilderness in principle; they misunderstood the particulars of the proposed law. The only way to fix that problem was to listen to their concerns, explain the aims of the legislation to them, and convince them of the reasonableness and importance of the Wilderness Act to the American people.

Zahniser had long been enamored of wilderness. He spent his youth exploring the Allegheny National Forest in Pennsylvania near his hometown of Tionesta. He and his wife, Alice, honeymooned in Yellowstone and Grand Teton national parks. And during much of his life, he and his family found retreat at a family cabin in the Adirondacks. He did not look the part of a wilderness champion. He was a bookish man, slightly round, who wore owlish eyeglasses and had an imposing forehead. He was often busy with correspondence or had his nose buried in a book or manuscript. But he reveled in wilderness, in language, and in his family. Zahniser was idealistic, but practical, and his commitment to both the values of wilderness and the political process made him a persistent and effective advocate for the nation's wild lands. The magic of Zahniser's wilderness advocacy lay in his patriotism and spirituality, his faith in the government and the political system, his commitment to the values of wilderness, and, as his biographer Mark Harvey explained, "his essential decency and the unfailing respect with which he treated everyone he encountered." Drawing on those beliefs and values, Zahniser played a pivotal role in shaping the campaign for the Wilderness Act of 1964.[1]

The work of Zahniser, the Wilderness Society, and the national coalition that championed the creation of the National Wilderness Preservation System has assumed symbolic importance in American environmental history. The *New York Times* editorialized that the legislation was a "landmark," and later historians have affirmed that assessment. One historian described the new "appreciation of wilderness [as] one of the most remarkable intellectual revolutions in the history of human thought about the land."[2] The Wilderness Act is often regarded as the culmination of a campaign that began with people such as John Muir and Theodore Roosevelt. The Wilderness Act succeeded not just because it was rooted in long-standing concerns for conservation and preservation, however, but also because it aligned with the political priorities important to mainstream American liberalism in the early 1960s. It was one of many laws passed during Lyndon Johnson's Great Society that invested the government with responsibility for protecting the public interest in a clean and healthy environment and established the foundations for the American environmental regulatory state.

This confidence that the Wilderness Act met a public interest propelled Zahniser, his allies, and the legislation forward. "We are advocating a program for the people of the United States of America," explained Zahniser. "The significance may not be how far we can move with [the Wilderness Act] but in the fact that so many people take that step."[3] It is tempting to dismiss such rhetoric as political posturing and to assume that the legislation was of significance only to a fraction of Americans—nature lovers, scientists, and those who tromped in the nation's wilderness—but that does not explain why the legislation commanded such broad political support. When the Wilderness Act became law in 1964, the Senate approved it 73 to 12 and the House approved it 373 to 1. Its congressional champions included leading Democrats and Republicans, and its coalition of supporters included not just the national and local conservation organizations, but also the General Federation of Women's Clubs, the American Planning and Civic Association, and the AFL-CIO, the nation's leading labor organization. Knowing how environmental reform has often been paralyzed by partisan politics since the 1980s, it is worth considering how the Wilderness Act galvanized such a broad constituency in the 1960s. The campaign was not won with careful research briefs on the state of the nation's timber or petroleum supply or the diversity of wildlife in wilderness. Instead, it appealed to national values—patriotism, spirituality, outdoor recreation, and a respect for nature—and the responsibility of the people and the government to protect them. In its aims, its rationale, and its compromises, the Wilderness Act reflected a pragmatic political formula that laid the foundations for what has become an expansive wilderness system. That success offers clues to the political origins of an environmental movement that came to be a powerful force in American politics.

The Threat to the "Public" Lands

The story of the modern wilderness movement begins with how the public lands became "public." Consider headlines such as these: "Bush Is Asked to Ban Oil Drilling in Arctic Refuge." "Tempers Rise over Desert Conservation." "U.S. Judge Upholds Clinton Plan to Manage Northwest Forests." "Feuds with Feds Make West Wild." "Obama to Sign Major Public-Lands Bill."[4] Behind these headlines is a basic assumption: the American people have a vested interest in the future of the nation's public lands. Remember Woody Guthrie's refrain: "This land was made for you and me." That the public lands are "public" is a contested claim, however.[5] What are now the "public" lands could have been dispensed with or managed in other ways. Native Americans, for example, could have been given a larger share of their homelands. In the late nineteenth century, at the same time the federal government established national parks and forests, it pushed Native Americans in the West off their homelands and onto reservations.[6] Congress could have given the western states more of the land within their borders when they entered the union. In many western states, however, the federal government remains the largest landholder, which is a point of frustration in states such as Nevada, Utah, and Wyoming, where the federal government owns 86 percent, 64 percent, and 49 percent of the land.[7] The public lands also could have been managed by the federal government with little involvement of citizens, industry, or other organizations. At the heart of the wilderness movement was the basic assertion that all Americans have a stake in the future of the nation's public lands.

What are now considered to be the "public" lands are the legacy of the nation's conquest of the American West. Between 1803 and 1867, the United States staked firm claims to much of the nation's western territory that now makes up the United States of America. Significant events in that expansion included President Thomas Jefferson's Louisiana Purchase in 1803 and Secretary of the Interior William Seward's acquisition of Alaska in 1867. Those agreements meant little without the will to back them up with force. By the end of the nineteenth century, by treaty, purchase, and conquest, the United

States had defended its claims from Europeans, wrested California and the Southwest from Mexico, and marginalized Native Americans. Then, in the mid-nineteenth century, Congress began giving those lands away. Westward-moving settlers were given 160-acre parcels of land under the Homestead Act, with Jeffersonian hopes of fostering a nation of independent farmers. Railroads and speculators made off with tracts of land best measured in hundreds of square miles. Loggers, miners, and cattle ranchers moved west, too. Loggers began felling the forests of the Great Lakes, Pacific Northwest, and the northern California coast. Mining companies staked claims to gold, silver, and copper lodes across the West. And cattle ranchers began to run their herds, and soon their fences, on lands that a generation before had been home to herds of buffalo and nomadic Indians.

Although such policies helped integrate the West into the United States—by encouraging settlement and the building of railroads and reducing the threat of Native Americans and foreign powers—some observers began to worry that such policies were shortsighted. Instead of supporting a nation of yeoman farmers, the government's policies seemed to encourage the exploitation of the nation's natural resources: the slaughter of the bison on the Great Plains, the clear-cutting of forests in the Great Lakes, and destructive mining practices, such as the hydraulic mining that followed the California Gold Rush. George Perkins Marsh, an early conservationist, was among the first to warn that while America had been blessed with extraordinary natural resources—minerals, forests, and waterways—such riches were not limitless. John Muir, who helped found the Sierra Club, echoed such concerns in 1897. He warned that although God had long saved these lands from "drought, disease, avalanches, and a thousand straining, leveling tempests and floods . . . he cannot save them from fools,—only Uncle Sam can do that."[8] Some westerners also began to realize that they needed the government to protect the mountains that supplied their cities with water and to oversee the grazing lands they depended on for their cattle and sheep. As America became an increasingly urban nation, dominated by growing cities such as New York, Chicago, and San Francisco, some Americans began to worry that the nation was losing touch with the wilderness from which the nation's institutions had been forged.[9]

At the turn of the twentieth century, the federal government began to take new responsibility for managing the western lands. Drawing on these many concerns—materialistic, romantic, and nationalistic—a group of prominent Americans, among whom president Theodore Roosevelt, Forest Service chief Gifford Pinchot, and John Muir are best remembered, advocated placing a portion of the nation's lands in permanent government ownership—a policy shift that meshed with a new commitment to a strong federal government during the Progressive era.[10] Consequently, Congress began to establish what eventually became four federal land agencies: the Forest Service (1905), the National Park Service (1916), the Fish and Wildlife Service (1940), and the Bureau of Land Management (1946). Starting in the 1910s, the federal government also began to purchase logged and mined lands in the East; some of those lands became national forests and others became national parks such as Shenandoah in Virginia and the Great Smokies in North Carolina and Tennessee. Thus, by the 1950s, the federal government still oversaw about one-third of the nation's land—some of it in the East, more of it in the West, and much of it in Alaska. These were the federally owned public lands, and the four federal land agencies were charged with managing those lands in the public interest.[11] The nation has been debating what that meant ever since.

After World War II, that debate gained new urgency as the nation's economy and western settlement accelerated. Historians have described the 1950s as the "supreme period of development" for western resource industries, such as mining, lumber, and energy—what scholars have described as the industries of the "Old West."[12] Bernard DeVoto, an iconoclastic historian and columnist, described the American West of those years in a different way. He called it "the plundered province." Writing for *Harper's Magazine*, DeVoto warned Americans that special interests in the West were raiding the nation's public lands for their own private benefit—they were overrunning the public lands with cattle, planning to build dams on scenic rivers, and calling for logging in the national parks. Whose land was he talking about? DeVoto did not mince words: "This is your land we are talking about."[13] It was a new way of looking at the western lands. DeVoto, like a growing number of conservationists, worried that the federal land agencies were more likely to manage the western lands in accordance with local wishes, which usually gave priority to economic development activities, than with national concerns, which he believed gave more attention to long-term protection of the land. For wilderness advocates, DeVoto's central argument came to define postwar debates over the public lands. The nation's public domain did not belong to resource industries, federal land agencies, or western states. Instead, the public lands were a national heritage in which all Americans had an interest and should have a say.

DeVoto's claims upset many westerners. While the West's industries and politicians often acted as if the public lands were most important as a resource for the region's economy, many westerners also cared passionately for the western landscape. Hunting and fishing were important pastimes, and some saw wilderness as a way to protect their favorite hunting grounds. Rod and gun clubs, sporting groups, and hiking and saddle clubs all provided important support for protecting the public lands in the 1950s and 1960s.[14] For instance, Michael McCloskey, who led the Sierra Club between 1969 and 1985, got his start organizing horsepackers in rural western Colorado in support of the Wilderness Act in 1963.[15] Those who lived in the urban West were more likely to agree with DeVoto's claims. Since the end of World War II, metropolitan areas around Seattle, Phoenix, and San Francisco had grown rapidly, as workers moved west to work in new industries, such as technology and defense.[16] Unlike the industries of the "Old West," which relied on natural resources, these new industries represented what scholars later described as the "New West," which valued the public lands for recreation and tourism more than for natural resources.[17] Thus, while many interests and industries in the West remained committed to developing the public lands, many westerners also wished to see them protected. The West, whether "old" or "new," has had a conflicted relationship with the public lands.[18]

The controversy over the future of the West and the public lands converged dramatically in northwest Colorado in the 1950s. The federal government announced plans for ten new dams to reengineer the upper Colorado River watershed to provide flood control, irrigation water, and electricity to the growing Rocky Mountain West. Such plans were representative of many large-scale projects the federal government undertook in the 1940s and 1950s that accelerated the region's postwar development. But one of the proposed dams was slated for Echo Park, a remote canyon located inside Dinosaur National Monument. Wilderness advocates worked to block the proposal for six years. And, as a half century before, when the government proposed a controversial dam at Hetch Hetchy in Yosemite National Park, the threat to Echo Park thrust the future of the nation's public lands into the national spotlight. With the leadership of two young and rising environmental leaders—the brash and spirited David Brower of the Sierra Club and the steadfast and eloquent Howard Zahniser of the Wilderness Society—two small organizations led what became a national campaign that rallied conservation organizations in coordinated action to stop the dam and maintain the integrity of the park system. Notably, the conservationists did not oppose all dams on the Colorado, only a dam within the boundaries of the park system. Over the strenuous objections of lawmakers from the Rocky Mountain West, the wilderness movement succeeded in persuading Congress to remove the Echo Park dam from the project in 1956. It was a telling victory. While wilderness advocates failed to stop the dam in Yosemite National Park in 1913, they were able to stop the dam in Echo Park in 1956. That turnabout suggested the growing political might of an organized wilderness movement and the claim that these were, in fact, lands of national importance.[19]

Echo Park taught wilderness advocates two lessons, one old and one new. The old lesson they had learned many times before across the West, at places such as Three Sisters Primitive Area in Oregon, the Upper Selway in Idaho, and Olympic National Park in Washington. All of those places were ostensibly protected as "wilderness" or parks by the federal land agencies. But as the postwar western economy boomed, the Forest Service and Park Service were increasingly willing to open wild areas for development, tourism, and the interests of local communities.[20] Those who cared about wilderness were constantly fighting a losing battle to protect the nation's public lands from dams, logging, mining, and roads, one place at a time. They could not keep up. But the success at Echo Park suggested a new lesson. That victory marked the growing power of an organized wilderness movement that could command national political and media attention and galvanize conservationists across the nation. In this respect, Echo Park foreshadowed an emerging environmental movement that viewed Congress and the federal government as the best vehicle for advancing a public interest in the environment. Now was the time, wilderness advocates realized, to launch a campaign to protect the nation's wilderness. Since 1947, Zahniser had been contemplating legislation to establish a wilderness system to permanently safeguard at least some of the nation's public lands. With the outpouring of national concern for Echo Park, such a legislative initiative seemed possible. Making it reality would take eight years.[21]

The Origins of the Wilderness Society

We often think of environmentalists working from outside government to affect policy. Today, for example, the Wilderness Society is one of the largest environmental organizations in the country, with nearly 400,000 members, $37 million in annual revenues, a large office in the heart of Washington, D.C., nine regional offices, and a staff of approximately 170.[22] It remains one of the leading non-governmental organizations working from outside government to advance public lands protection. But in the mid-1930s, the Wilderness Society was a small organization dedicated to quietly working through the federal government to protect wilderness. Many of its eight founders were current or former employees of federal land agencies. Robert Marshall, Aldo Leopold, Benton MacKaye, and Bernard Frank of the Forest Service and Robert Sterling Yard of the National Park Service became the formative thinkers and founders of the Wilderness Society. They were joined by private citizens Harvey Broome, Ernest Oberholtzer, and Harold Andersen, each of whom had a long-standing interest in wilderness preservation. It was a small organization made up of like-minded individuals who intended to "battle uncompromisingly" for "the defense of wilderness in its various forms." With such strong ties to the government, the Wilderness Society generally held the federal land agencies and the government in high esteem.[23]

Surprisingly, the founders of the Wilderness Society did not band together because they opposed logging and mining on the public lands. They were driven by a new threat—the automobile. In the early twentieth century, when Henry Ford put the Model T into mass production, the American "road trip" was born. Each summer, tourists loaded up their new automobiles and drove into the great outdoors, camping by roads, streams, and high mountain meadows, and they set their sights on national parks and forests. In the 1920s, the Park Service and Forest Service began to cater to the auto-tourists in hopes of attracting more visitors and funds from Congress. Often, the two agencies competed with each other to promote their lands. The Forest Service, in particular, feared that new parks would be carved out of the national forests. Thus, the agencies built roads, laid out new campgrounds, and established mountain resorts. During the Great Depression, these development activities accelerated when the federal government raised an army of domestic labor through the Civilian Conservation Corps to continue such public works projects.[24] That is why so many of the lodges, rest areas, and entrance gates in the nation's parks and forests date to the 1930s. In 1928, a government report forewarned of the growing threat. The nation's wilderness is in "grave jeopardy," it reported. "[It is] disappearing rapidly, not so much by reason of economic need [such as logging or mining] as by the extension of motor roads and the attendant development of tourist attractions."[25]

The Wilderness Society's founders drew on many arguments to explain the value of protecting wilderness in the 1930s. Reflecting their strong ties to the Forest Service, they often framed their argument for wilderness in the language of Progressive-era conservation: for some land, particularly that which was remote and of little economic value, its highest use was as a "wilderness" protected from logging and mining and roads and tourism—language that would reappear in the Wilderness Act. Behind that sentiment there were many different ideas about what wilderness meant. Robert Sterling Yard, reflecting his long-standing concerns for the national parks, emphasized that the preservation of "primitive" or pristine lands was the imperative. Robert Marshall described wilderness as "the environment of solitude," as important to the nation's mental health as timber and gold were to its material health.[26] Benton MacKaye, the visionary who first proposed the Appalachian Trail in 1921, saw wilderness as an escape from the consumerism of modern life that distanced Americans from their roots in the land.[27] And Aldo Leopold prized wilderness because it allowed Americans to re-create the primitive pioneer experience that he, like many others, believed had shaped the nation's identity.[28] Leopold asked: "Shall we now exterminate this thing that made us American?"[29] The founding of the Wilderness Society in 1935 reflected as much a set of social concerns— regarding the economy, consumerism, and recreation—as a narrow focus on protecting pristine wild lands alone.[30]

Despite their foresight, the Wilderness Society's founders never anticipated the organization's future role at the helm of public lands advocacy. Initially, the Wilderness Society worked behind the scenes, with some success, to convince the Forest Service and Park Service to adopt policies to protect wilderness; but it was these administrative achievements that seemed so tenuous in the 1950s.[31] Beginning with Echo Park and then with the campaign for the Wilderness Act, wilderness began to emerge as a popular cause. Under Zahniser's leadership, the organization gained a respected place in the nation's capital, established strong ties to conservation groups across the country, and attracted a growing membership (16,000 members by 1962). Although Zahniser was the organization's executive director, the society's direction was generally set by its Governing Council. In the late 1950s, some on the Governing Council remained wary of a national campaign for the Wilderness Act. Might such a political campaign violate the organization's tax-exempt status? Did such a centralized campaign for wilderness make sense? Could the society sustain such an effort? Ultimately, the Wilderness Society's council rallied around Zahniser and his vision. Building on the momentum of Echo Park, the campaign for the Wilderness Act thrust the Wilderness Society into the forefront of an emerging environmental movement. In the early 1960s, the Wilderness Society poured all of its resources into the Wilderness Act. Zahniser gave his life to it.[32]

Wilderness and the Public Interest

The Wilderness Act emerged out of a crucial moment in American politics. Often, when we think of the 1960s, it is the anti-war protests, the Black Power movement, women's liberation movement, and the counterculture that draw our attention to the hopes, frustrations, and protests that spilled over onto the nation's streets in the later years of that decade. But to understand the Wilderness Act, we have to consider an earlier political moment. In 1964, America looked very different than it did at decade's end. The star of Lyndon Johnson and the Great Society was rising. Hope for the Civil Rights Movement was growing. Democrats held commanding political majorities in the House and Senate and touted their party's liberal tradition. Many Americans looked to the federal government with faith and pride.[33] Despite the angst of the Cold War and the injustice, inequities, and racism that still divided the nation, the early 1960s marked a moment of hope for many Americans.[34] The Wilderness Act did not challenge these hopes for the nation or its political system. It captured them.

"To establish a National Wilderness Preservation System for the permanent good of the whole people, and for other purposes."[35] That sentence is the formal title to the Wilderness Act, and it is the key to the law's place in the politics of the 1960s. The advocates and politicians who penned the Wilderness Act believed wilderness was a matter of importance to all Americans. In 1960, Wallace Stegner, the Pulitzer Prize–winning western author, wrote confidently of what wilderness meant to Americans "as a people."[36] Senator Clinton Anderson (D-NM) described the Wilderness Act as a "national objective."[37] And Zahniser expressed his faith that "when the wilderness law is enacted it will be the whole nation who will be for it."[38] In part, this conviction was founded on a belief that wilderness was central to the American experience—a sentiment that dated back to nineteenth-century frontier mythology, Theodore Roosevelt, and the founding of the Wilderness Society. Stewart Udall, President Johnson's secretary of the interior, described wilderness as the "mother of resources" from which "has come the raw material with which Americans have fashioned a great civilization."[39] Today, such deterministic assertions of the American experience sound hollow in a nation that rightly gives attention to the diversity and plurality of the American experience. But in the context of the Cold War and the optimism of the early 1960s, such patriotic statements did much to explain the value of wilderness and to justify the Wilderness Act.

That confidence points toward an important assumption for those who championed wilderness: protecting wilderness was more about its value to American society than it was about the intrinsic value of wilderness itself. Consider the purpose of the law: wilderness areas "shall be administered for the *use and enjoyment* of the American people in such manner as will leave them unimpaired for future *use and enjoyment* as wilderness, and so as to provide for the protection of these areas, the preservation of their wilderness character, and for the gathering and dissemination of information regarding their *use and enjoyment* as wilderness."[40] As Zahniser noted, all of the nation's public lands would be put to some use. In his view, wilderness was one of those important uses: for aesthetic enjoyment, camping and horsepacking, hunting and fishing, protecting watersheds, and spiritual retreat. Of these many uses, the most pressing was recreation. Concerns about recreation ran deep in 1950s America—demand for outdoor recreation seemed to be growing faster than the supply, some Americans worried the nation was growing "soft," and concerns were rising about American youth and delinquency. How could a nation steel a youth mesmerized by rock and roll and the Beatles for the challenges ahead?[41] In 1962, a national Outdoor Recreational Resources Review Commission provided important affirmation for wilderness.[42] And when the Wilderness Act became law, it read: "wilderness areas shall be devoted to the public purposes of recreational, scenic, scientific, educational, conservation, and historical use."[43] From the very first draft of the Wilderness Act, recreation enjoyed prominent attention.

Neither the Wilderness Act nor its champions aimed to challenge the nation's basic commitments to developing resources on the public lands, the institutions that oversaw them, or the nation's commitment to economic growth. This was not just careful politics; it reflected a genuine belief among many, notably Zahniser, that as the nation's economy expanded it could afford to both develop its natural resources and protect wilderness. Just as wilderness advocates had not opposed all dams on the Colorado River in the debate over Echo Park, they did not oppose all development on the public lands. In this respect, the confidence of wilderness advocates aligned neatly with Great Society liberals, who believed it possible for the nation to provide health care, address poverty, protect the environment, and build the economy—all at the same time. Zahniser himself acknowledged that Americans liked their beef from public lands, abundant energy from hydroelectric dams, and motoring in their cars to visit national parks. Such a vision would have generated much discussion among the Wilderness Society's founders, who were deeply concerned by the rise of modern consumerism, but Zahniser's pragmatism became a defining feature of the Wilderness Society.[44] In the 1990s, a new generation of environmentalists would propose ending all logging, grazing, and mining on the public lands—posing a fundamental challenge to the western resource economy—but that comes later in our story.

The emphases on the values of wilderness, its role in American culture, and its uses were joined by a common theme: community. One of the dominant strains of early wilderness thought was the role of wilderness in forging American independence and respecting the rights of the minority. By promoting individualism, hardihood, and self-reliance, wilderness contributed to the nation's democratic origins.[45] Proponents also emphasized that protecting wilderness was consonant with a democratic government that respected the interests of a minority. For instance, Bob Marshall, the Wilderness Society's leading founder, emphasized in the 1930s that the majority should respect the minority's wish to protect wilderness.[46] Supreme Court Justice William Douglas, one of the most illustrious of the Wilderness Act's supporters in the early 1960s, claimed Americans had a "right" to wilderness.[47] In the campaign for the Wilderness Act, however, this emphasis on the interests of the minority or wilderness "rights" was overwhelmed by a focus on the nation's collective interest in protecting wilderness as a national good. As Udall explained, "We are learning . . . that we are not outside nature, but in it; that it is not a commodity which we can exploit without restraint, but a community to which we belong."[48] Stegner wrote of seeing ourselves as "part of the environment" and of our brotherhood with animals and the natural world.[49] Zahniser turned to these ideas frequently to explain the value of wild lands: "In the wilderness it is thus possible to sense most keenly our human membership in the whole community of life on Earth."[50] It was this focus on community that cultivated the value that Zahniser prized most: a sense of humility.

This concept of community reflected the lessons of the developing science of ecology. No one did more to popularize such concerns than Rachel Carson in her 1962 book, *Silent Spring*, which sounded the alarm over the dangers that pesticides and other synthetic chemicals posed to human health and the natural world. At the heart of *Silent Spring* was a belief that the natural world was balanced, harmonious, and vulnerable. Notably, Carson never emphasized wilderness. She began *Silent Spring* by idealizing a pastoral landscape—a town "where all life seemed to live in harmony with its surroundings."[51] That sense of harmony fits closely with Zahniser's vision of community. They shared a belief that society needed to find a balance that respected nature. In explaining the value of wilderness, advocates also emphasized its scientific uses. But in lobbying for the Wilderness Act, scientists and advocates gave less attention to the value of wilderness as habitat for wildlife (although this was a well-established precept) and more attention to its value as a benchmark and a source of knowledge. That is to say, instead of emphasizing the intrinsic value of nature, they emphasized the value of undisturbed wilderness as a source of knowledge for human benefit—an argument consistent with the anthropocentric and prag- matic approach that characterized the campaign for the Wilderness Act.[52]

Thus, for those who championed the Wilderness Act in the early 1960s, the legislation was about relationships, community, and interdependency— indeed, the nation's shared interest in wilderness. And that belief reflected the wilderness movement's confidence that its strongest argument for envi- ronmental protection was an appeal to the national interest, not an appeal to the intrinsic value of nature, the scientific imperative of protecting wilder- ness, or a minority's right to enjoy wilderness. That emphasis on the role of the federal government in protecting the nation's shared interest in wilderness aligned closely with the liberal Democrats' agenda more broadly, and generated widespread support for the Wilderness Act. By the late 1950s, the Wilderness Act enjoyed the support of a dozen leading conservation organizations, such as the Nature Conservancy, the National Wildlife Federation, and the Sierra Club; sixty local and regional groups, such as the Montana Wilderness Asso- ciation and the Federation of Western Outdoor Clubs; and, most importantly, other civic organizations, such as the General Federation of Women's Clubs, the American Planning and Civic Association, and labor unions, notably the AFL-CIO.[53] Such support was grounded in a belief that the Wilderness Act was for the good of the "whole"—people and nature.

A Pragmatic Approach to Politics

Opposition to the Wilderness Act was substantial.[54] Meeting the concerns of the federal land agencies, rural westerners, resource industries, and their rep- resentatives in Congress required eight years of negotiation. The federal land agencies viewed the Wilderness Act as unnecessary or hampering their man- agement discretion—a position that shaped how they implemented the Wilder- ness Act after it became law. Many rural Americans who lived near the public lands, both in the East and West, depended on them for logging, mining, and livestock grazing, and they used them for hunting, picnicking, fishing, and off- road driving as well. Not surprisingly, some of the most powerful opponents of wilderness were the resource industries, which valued the public lands for tim- ber, minerals, and grazing lands, the rights to which they either purchased or leased from the federal government. While such opposition was considerable, it was uncoordinated—there was no orchestrated national campaign against the Wilderness Act, such as those that would rise with the Sagebrush Rebellion in the late 1970s or the Wise Use Movement in the 1990s. Nevertheless, these opponents, who had the ear of their western congressional delegations, played a crucial role in shaping the Wilderness Act. And wilderness proponents like Zahniser understood they had to address their concerns.

While Zahniser is celebrated as the visionary behind the Wilderness Act, no one did more to shape the final legislation than its staunchest congressional opponent, Representative Wayne Aspinall (D-CO). A crusty and iron-willed lawmaker, Aspinall was as tough and unforgiving as the arid region of western Colorado he represented. He carefully guarded the West's ability to develop its natural resources. As a veteran congressman, beloved by his constituents, and chair of the House Interior Committee, with oversight of the public lands, he was in a uniquely powerful position to do so.[55] Zahniser and Aspinall are often seen as rivals of symbolic stature, Zahniser representing a nascent environmental community, Aspinall the forces of development. But that characterization misses the importance of their personal relationship. The Wilderness Act was a product of negotiation that engaged Congress across party lines and resulted in legislation of national scope. Zahniser and Aspinall were representative of such good will. When Aspinall was hospitalized in 1962, shortly after blocking the Wilderness Act, Zahniser sent him a handwritten note offering "best wishes and my prayers." Aspinall responded that although "we may be divided on a piece of legislation [that] does not, I hope, cause any strain on a friendship that is very valuable to me."[56] This respect characterized much of their negotiations.

The most persistent criticism of the Wilderness Act was that it "locked up" the public lands. This was an argument wilderness advocates knew well. Many westerners had a deep sense of pride and ownership in the public lands near their homes. The property value of a ranch might be contingent on access to grazing leases on nearby public lands. Rural counties close to the national forests received 25 percent of national forest revenues to support rural schools and roads (such payments grew from $17.4 million in 1952 to peak at $361 million annually in 1989).[57] Some logging companies and timber towns depended almost entirely on the national forests to keep their mills running. These rural Americans, and the companies they owned and worked for, had a vested interest in any public lands legislation. They often argued that wilderness preservation amounted to a "lockup" that wasted natural resources such as timber and minerals, left lands vulnerable to fire and insect infestations, and made parks and forests inaccessible to most Americans.[58]

Conservationists countered that the Wilderness Act was not a lockup. Even in its earliest drafts, the Wilderness Act included provisions to meet the concerns of rural Americans and the mining, timber, and grazing industries. For

instance, Zahniser knew he needed to address the concerns of ranchers, especially those who depended on the public lands for summer pasture. Thus, existing levels of livestock grazing were permitted in wilderness areas indefinitely.
A chief concern for Aspinall was potential mineral reserves, and he succeeded
in including a compromise to allow mineral prospecting in wilderness areas
through 1983. The Wilderness Act did effectively bar commercial logging, but,
as the timber industry knew, most of the lands then proposed for the wilderness
system lay high up in the mountains where little valuable timber grew. In more
controversial areas, where there was more timber, decisions regarding wilderness designation were delayed pending future reviews. The most far-reaching
compromise concerned the privileges granted to the president. In cases where
wilderness conflicted with the national interest, the president could authorize
dams, utility corridors, roads, and other projects—prerogatives that have never
been exercised. For these reasons, it was difficult for opponents to make the
charge of a "lockup" stick.[59] As wilderness advocates argued in 1962, "For every
lock, [the Wilderness Act] provides a key."[60]

Another familiar criticism was that wilderness protection was elitist.
Aspinall and others often described it as "class legislation" and argued that the
law served the "interests of a small minority of well-endowed citizens," not
the general public.[61] Wilderness restrictions, they argued, made some of the
most beautiful public lands unavailable to families, the elderly, and others who
could not hike or boat into such remote places without assistance. As one critic
put it, wilderness "exclud[ed] from its vaunted recreational delights the great
number of citizens who probably need it most."[62] Such charges would resur-
face repeatedly in the years to come. Yet such arguments seemed misplaced,
considering the support for the Wilderness Act among hunters, fisherman,
and other outdoor enthusiasts in the West. Udall argued, "there is no place
more democratic than wilderness."[63] Anyone could visit wilderness. Little special equipment or support was needed. (This was before the era of Patagonia,
Lowe Alpine, and The North Face.) Visitation to such areas was growing rapidly; between 1960 and 1965, visitation to wilderness areas increased fivefold
to 3.5 million visitor days per year.[64] Wilderness advocates routinely cited the
increasing use of wilderness as a reason for the Wilderness Act. And for those
who never visited wilderness, it was part of what Stegner eloquently described
as the "geography of hope."[65] Just knowing it was there was valuable.

Other critics argued that the Wilderness Act disregarded the interests of
Native Americans. This concern arose during debates over the Wilderness Act
and has been made pointedly in recent years. Did the Wilderness Act push

Native Americans off the western lands? One scholar put the argument this way: by defining wilderness as a place where man is but a visitor, the Wilderness Act "reads" Native Americans "out of the homelands they had managed for centuries with fire, gathering, and hunting."[66] There is validity in that argument, but it represents more a general reaction to the injustices of the nation's imperial expansion during the nineteenth century and its treatment of Native Americans in the twentieth century than a reaction specific to the Wilderness Act. To view any of the nation's federally owned lands as "public," whether designated wilderness or not, is to risk forgetting the process of alienation by which the federal government laid claim to the western lands. More troublesome, suggesting that the Wilderness Act reads Native Americans off western lands also overlooks the important role Native Americans played in shaping the scope of the Wilderness Act and its subsequent implementation. In the late 1950s, Indians successfully lobbied to have potential wilderness areas in federal Indian reservations removed from the Wilderness Act.[67] Since then, some Indian tribes have chosen to manage some portions of their reservation lands as wilderness. For instance, when Pueblo Indians in New Mexico regained Blue Lake, a sacred parcel of land, from the Forest Service in 1970, they chose to continue managing it under the provisions of the Wilderness Act. They viewed the Wilderness Act's provisions as compatible with their cultural priorities, a position the Wilderness Society supported.[68] In Montana, the Salish and Kootenai tribes designated 93,000 acres of land on the Flathead Indian Reservation and adjacent to the Mission Mountains Wilderness as a tribal wilderness area in 1982, following the precepts of the Wilderness Act.[69] And, most importantly, in the 1970s, Native Americans played a crucial role in shaping the specific provisions of the nation's most far-reaching wilderness legislation: the Alaska National Interest Lands Conservation Act.

The last of the critics' charges—and it was on this charge that the political success of the Wilderness Act turned—was that the Wilderness Act stripped Congress of its constitutionally guaranteed oversight of the public lands. One of Aspinall's greatest concerns was that the law would create new powers for the executive branch, giving the president and federal land agencies the power to decide which lands became wilderness, thereby denying such power to Congress.[70] Such concerns were well founded. In early versions of the act, wilderness advocates proposed allowing the executive branch to designate wilderness, creating a National Wilderness Preservation Council to maintain maps and records of the wilderness system. That proposal ran into a storm of opposition, as it encroached on the prerogatives of Congress and the federal land agencies.

Many western politicians, such as Aspinall, Senator Gordon Allott (R-CO), and Senator Joseph O'Mahoney (D-WY), sought to ensure that Congress reserved for itself final say over the dispensation of the public lands. The federal land agencies worried that a new wilderness council would usurp their powers, becoming a new "super agency."

Zahniser abandoned the proposal for a wilderness council after four years of negotiation. The chief sticking point in negotiations then became the question of which branch of government would designate additional wilderness areas in the future. In Zahniser's view, designating wilderness represented the recognition of an "additional value" for already protected lands, which did not require congressional affirmation since the area would remain under the jurisdiction of existing land agencies. He proposed allowing the executive branch to designate wilderness and allowing Congress to veto decisions with which it disagreed. Aspinall refused to yield. In his view, only Congress could ensure that decisions regarding wilderness and the public lands represented the interests of all Americans (and respected the interests of rural westerners, whose representatives dominated the relevant congressional committees). Aspinall got his way. In 1964, wilderness advocates and their champions in the Senate agreed, and the Wilderness Act states that only Congress can designate wilderness. That meant each wilderness proposal—whether a three-thousand-acre addition or a six-million-acre addition—would have to run the same legislative gauntlet: agency reviews in Washington, D.C., hearings and debate in both houses of Congress, and approval of the president. If the initial fight to pass the Wilderness Act was any indication, future wilderness additions would be slow in coming.

In retrospect, the wilderness movement owes a debt of gratitude to its sharpest opponent, Wayne Aspinall. As originally envisioned, Zahniser's Wilderness Act placed its trust in the executive branch and a wilderness council to protect and oversee wilderness; in short, it expected government experts to do much of the work of protecting wilderness. But by demanding that wilderness designation be the responsibility of Congress, Aspinall helped ensure the enduring place of wilderness in American politics and saved wilderness protection from becoming the insular responsibility of the federal government and the executive branch. Pushing wilderness designations down a legislative pathway would be laborious and challenging, but, equally importantly, that pathway created a well-defined and positive role for citizen activism on behalf of wilderness protection. This was what the Wilderness Society described as the "big job ahead" in the mid-1960s.[71] In the decade to come, citizen activism would become the focal point of the Wilderness Society's activities. While wilderness activists and the environmental movement would never fully resonate with social movements of the 1960s or the New Left, in this one way, the wilderness movement began to hitch itself to the rising ideals for a "participatory democracy" that captured the imagination of so many people.

There are many reasons to admire the Wilderness Act. But it is also worth pausing to consider what the law and the wilderness system it established omitted. In 2000, the Forest Service described wilderness as a "cornerstone for protecting biodiversity."[72] While wilderness advocates in the 1960s shared such concerns, such arguments were not at the core of their campaign, and the Wilderness Act makes no mention of endangered species, ecosystems, or ecological values. Nor does the Wilderness Act outline a functional architecture for the wilderness system. While it specifies broad criteria for selecting individual wilderness areas, it provides no criteria for what the larger functional goals for the wilderness system might be.[73] Possible criteria might have included ensuring that every community in the nation was within 200 miles of wilderness; that all ecosystems be represented; or, that wild lands be organized into a system of interconnected networks of habitat. All of those ideas would be broached later, but they received little attention in the 1960s. Some people have come to view wilderness as a challenge to the nation's political system and way of life. In 1983, for instance, one radical wilderness activist argued that the time had come to "throw a monkeywrench into the gears of the political machine and let the broken pieces fall where they may."[74] Although such radicalism would transform American debates over the public lands and environmentalism in the 1980s and 1990s, that was not the case in the 1960s.

What was omitted from the Wilderness Act—an emphasis on the ecological value of wilderness, its functional role in protecting biodiversity, or a radical challenge to American institutions—helps underscore what distinguished the Wilderness Act. In the 1960s, environmentalists described wilderness most clearly as a resource for the American people for now and in the future. Why? One historian suggests that environmentalists make strategic choices: when political expediency requires it, they downplay the intrinsic value of nature or the rights of nature—values that are often assumed to legitimate and motivate environmental ideology.[75] Following that argument, the suggestion is that if one reads between the lines, a more ambitious and biocentric approach to wilderness is evident in the Wilderness Act. But a more straightforward conclusion is that explaining why people have an interest in protecting nature—such as aesthetics, recreation, hunting, and watershed protection—can be a powerful tool for building the political support necessary to protect the environment. It was that approach, which aligned with the politics of the New Frontier and the Great Society and placed great faith in the role of government to meet the nation's common interests, that laid the foundations for a wide range of environmental legislation in the 1960s and early 1970s. Highlighting people's interest in nature should not be viewed as a betrayal of the American environmental tradition; instead, it represents one of its most powerful and successful political strategies.[76]

How Did the Wilderness Act Define Wilderness?

The Wilderness Act gave the idea of wilderness new legal standing, but it did not settle a long-standing and important question: What is wilderness? Instead, it gave that question new consequence. After 1964, how one defined wilderness was no longer a topic only of philosophical or intellectual importance; it had on-the-ground implications for what lands might actually become a part of the wilderness system. Did wilderness include only pristine lands untouched by people, or could it include land with old mines, homesteads, and dams? Could wilderness be near a city or adjacent to a road, or did it have to be remote and isolated? Did wilderness need to be protected primarily for ecological values, such as preserving habitat or endangered species, or could it include areas popular for hiking, horsepacking, and camping? Those were all questions wilderness advocates wrestled with in the campaign for the Wilderness Act, and questions they would revisit in the decades to come. As historian Kevin Marsh has asked, just where do we draw the line that separates what is "wilderness" from what is not? How we answer that question says as much about society, its priorities, and its changing attitudes toward nature as it does about the landscapes we aim to save.[77]

To all of those questions, Zahniser had somewhat surprising answers that embraced a broad conception of what wilderness might be, which many leaders within the wilderness movement shared. Like many who worked to protect the nation's wilderness, Zahniser knew well how little of the nation's wild lands were truly pristine. He knew that Native Americans had altered many ecosystems through fire and hunting. He knew that much of the western landscape had been affected by grazing. He knew that settlers and miners had left behind homesteads, mines, dams, and other legacies of the frontier in seemingly wild areas. And he knew the places that appeared wild in the East often obscured long histories of human use. Zahniser explained that wilderness cannot be

1.1 Howard Zahniser (in white), executive director of the Wilderness Society and chief lobbyist for the Wilderness Act, discusses the proposed wilderness system with Lee Metcalf, a senator from Montana, in the early 1960s. Courtesy the Wilderness Society.

reduced to the physical state of the land—to an essential definition, such as "pristine lands unaffected by people."[78] Instead, he explained, wilderness is a "fancy, a human concept," defined as much by society's values as the state of the land itself.[79] It was that realization that explains his graceful definition of wilderness. "A wilderness, in contrast with those areas where man and his works dominate the landscape, is hereby recognized as an area where the earth and its community of life are *untrammeled* by man, where man himself is a visitor who does not remain."[80]

That definition, little changed from the first draft of the Wilderness Act, is Zahniser's most lasting legacy. It is a descriptive definition, one which includes no specific requirements or provisions such as size, remoteness, or ecological integrity. Its most important stipulation is that most unusual qualifying adjective: "untrammeled." Instead of describing wilderness areas as "untouched" or "pristine," adjectives often used in this context, Zahniser purposefully chose "untrammeled" to describe land that is "not restricted or hampered." In practice, that definition left open the possibility that wilderness areas might have a history of human use—logging, fire, cultivation, or development—but as long as the land had recovered a quality of wildness, it was eligible for wilderness protection. The beauty of Zahniser's language is that it acknowledges the natural world's resilience and adaptability. It offers the opportunity to appreciate what is natural and what is human in wilderness. Zahniser knew that both were important to the "community of life" he celebrated. And while Zahniser never would have been so blunt, the point of his definition was its flexibility: he wanted to ensure that the wilderness system could protect a broad range of lands, both in the East and in the West.

Opponents of wilderness worried that Zahniser's definition was "high-sounding" and "nebulous." They argued that the definition provided insufficient guidance for making decisions about what land should be designated wilderness.[81] In the negotiations that led to the Wilderness Act, Zahniser and his allies met those concerns by agreeing to several more specific criteria regarding which lands qualified as wilderness. First, a wilderness area was to be affected primarily by the forces of nature. Second, a wilderness area was to have "outstanding opportunities" for solitude or primitive recreation. Third, a wilderness area had to be 5,000 acres in size or be of sufficient size for management as wilderness. And fourth, a wilderness area may contain "ecological, geological, or other features of scientific, educational, scenic, or historical value."[82] Opponents hoped that these specific and seemingly practical qualifications would help ensure that the Wilderness Act would be interpreted narrowly. None of these secondary requirements, however, was a mandatory prerequisite for wilderness designation.

In responding to such questions and to other criticisms of the Wilderness Act, wilderness advocates often fell back on their most effective argument: only a small portion of the nation would be designated wilderness. Although they knew far more land might merit wilderness protection (especially in Alaska), time and time again, both in public statements and internal correspondence in the early 1960s, they emphasized the goal of protecting 35 to 55 million acres of land, a little less than 2 percent of all the land in the United States.[83] Their opponents should have been comforted by that goal. Wilderness advocates did not aim to challenge the nation's system of private property rights and they staked no claims to privately owned lands, local or state government land, or Indian reservations. The Wilderness Act applied only to federally owned lands managed by the federal land agencies. When it became law, the National Wilderness Preservation System immediately protected fifty-four wilderness areas totaling 9.1 million acres of land, all of which were in the national forests. The act initiated a set of "ten-year reviews" during which additional lands managed by the Forest Service, the National Park Service, and the Fish and Wildlife Service were to be reviewed by the agencies, the president, and, thanks to Aspinall, Congress as potential additions to the wilderness system. But even these "ten-year reviews" applied only to areas that already enjoyed some special protection. This flexible definition of wilderness and the "ten-year reviews" guaranteed that the Wilderness Act did not mark the end of the debates over wilderness. Instead, it gave them a new beginning.

A Liberal (Democratic) Environmental Agenda

As a political movement, the modern environmental movement started with the burst of legislation during President Lyndon Johnson's Great Society in the mid-1960s. It was a moment of legislative innovation in American history, when a Democratic-led Congress and a Democratic White House aligned behind a far-reaching agenda for social reform. Building on the legacy and optimism of the Kennedy administration's domestic agenda, a growing concern for an array of social issues defined the national political agenda: the Civil Rights Movement, poverty in urban and rural America, and health care for disadvantaged and elderly Americans. Between 1963 and 1965, Congress passed into law some of the most important social and civil rights laws in American history: the Civil Rights Act of 1964, the Voting Rights Act of 1965, the Social Security Act of 1965 (which established the Medicare and Medicaid programs), and the Economic Opportunity Act of 1964 (which supported anti-poverty programs). In a two-year span, President Johnson worked with a Democratic Congress to pass legislation that affected nearly every aspect of American life—legislation that often commanded the support of Republicans too. Such an impressive legacy has made it easy to forget that for President Johnson, the Great Society was not just about social welfare and civil rights; it was also about the environment. As Johnson himself noted in 1964, when he signed the Wilderness Act into law, if Congress had not already distinguished itself as the "education Congress, the health Congress, and the full prosperity Congress, it would be remembered as the conservation Congress."[84] And Johnson would be remembered as the conservation president.

The Johnson administration's environmental record reflected a conviction among liberal intellectuals and Democratic political leaders that the environment was an integral component of a new liberalism. Unlike the 1930s, when the most urgent challenge facing the nation was feeding the hungry, helping farmers, and restoring the economy—which liberal Democrats met under the leadership of Franklin Delano Roosevelt during the New Deal—the challenges were different in the postwar years. A leading Democratic intellectual, Arthur Schlesinger Jr., believed that the nation's newfound prosperity posed a challenge and opportunity for the inheritors of New Deal liberalism. He wondered if "liberalism must for the moment shift its focus from economics and politics"—the earlier concerns of New Deal liberals—"to the general style and quality of our civilization"—new concerns for a new generation of liberals.[85] In that context, as historian Adam Rome has observed, Democratic leaders came to see environmental issues as an important component of the liberal agenda in the mid-1950s that focused on guarding the quality of life for all Americans, not just meeting the basic needs of its citizens.[86] Stewart Udall, secretary of the interior, captured this new outlook in *The Quiet Crisis*, published in 1963. "America today stands poised on a pinnacle of wealth and power," he wrote, "yet we live in a land of vanishing beauty, of increasing ugliness, of shrinking open space, and of an overall environment that is diminished daily by pollution and noise and blight."[87] What liberal intellectuals like Schlesinger, Johnson appointees like Udall, and conservationists like Zahniser shared was the conviction that an active federal government could, and must, take action to protect the environment for the good of all Americans—a conviction that was central not only to the Wilderness Act but also to an emerging environmental movement concerned with air and water pollution, toxic waste, and other threats to human health.

The Democratic Party played a pivotal role in laying the framework for the federal government's proactive role in environmental regulation. In lamenting the deeply partisan tenor of more recent environmental politics, environmentalists and historians often emphasize the bipartisan support for environmental reform in the 1960s and 1970s.[88] The Wilderness Act, like many of the major laws, did enjoy strong support from both Democrats and Republicans. It was approved in the Senate 73 to 12 and 373 to 1 in the House, and Representative John Saylor (R-PA) was one of the legislation's most enthusiastic champions. Still, Democrats consistently took the lead on conservation and environmental issues in the 1960s and 1970s, consistent with the party's liberal platform and concern for quality-of-life issues. With Democrats in control of both chambers of Congress between 1955 and 1980, their power was considerable; even the Republican Nixon administration believed it imperative to make the environment a priority in the early 1970s.[89] That Democratic faith in the role of government, which many Republicans shared, was instrumental in making possible the legislative advances for environmental protection in the 1960s and 1970s.

Johnson signed into law a broad range of legislation to protect the nation's natural resources and environmental health, including the Clean Air Act of 1963, the Water Quality Act of 1965, the Endangered Species Act of 1966, the Land and Water Conservation Fund of 1964, and the Wilderness Act of 1964 — laws that helped lay the framework for the modern environmental regulatory state. All told, Johnson helped enact more than 300 environmental measures, a record that no other president has matched.[90] Some scholars have drawn a clear line between an earlier generation of conservation issues — focused on wilderness, wildlife, and public lands — and an emerging concern for environmental issues such as air pollution, water pollution, and other threats to public health.[91] But to draw the line too sharply between "old" conservation issues and "new" environmental issues is to miss the shared political convictions that made possible the Wilderness Act and other environmental laws during the Great Society. Beginning in the 1960s, environmental activists of all stripes increasingly looked to Congress and the government to address a growing array of "environmental" problems. This was apparent in the case of the Wilderness Act. But each subsequent environmental law for clean air, clean water, and other issues also invested increasing responsibility in the federal government to protect resources considered to be of national importance. Notably, even when the Great Society and the Democratic Party began to founder over the war in Vietnam, social protests, and a weakening economy, the mainstream environmental movement continued to work successfully through government and Congress to achieve its goals. That commitment would be instrumental in bringing about some of the environmental movement's greatest successes and challenges in the decades to come.

Conclusion

President Lyndon Johnson signed the Wilderness Act into law on September 3, 1964, in the Rose Garden. In his brief remarks, he lauded the broad political support for wilderness and the protection of the nation's "scenic" and "spiritual" resources. "In the new conservation of this century," he explained, "our concern is the total relation between man and the world around him. Its object is not only man's material welfare but the dignity of man himself."[92] It was a

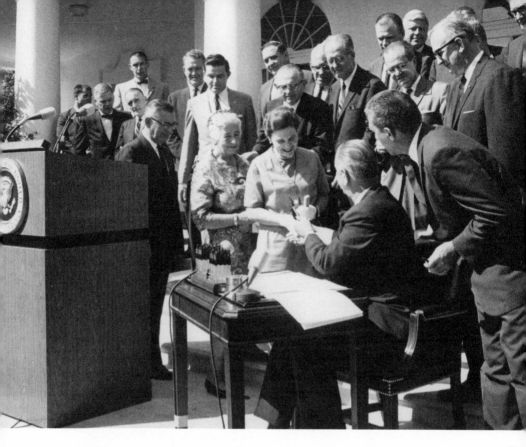

1.2 President Lyndon Johnson signed the Wilderness Act on September 3, 1964. Standing beside him were Margaret (Mardy) Murie on the left and Alice Zahniser on the right, the widows of Olaus Murie and Howard Zahniser. Behind them were key supporters of the legislation. Stewart Udall is leaning over the president's shoulder. John P. Saylor is standing nearest to Udall. Senator Frank Church is standing behind Murie. Notably, Wayne Aspinall, the legislation's most persistent opponent, attended the signing; he is standing behind Zahniser. Photograph by Abbie Rowe. Courtesy National Park Service Historic Photograph Collection, Harpers Ferry Center.

theme that resonated with his vision for a Great Society. As he signed the Wilderness Act into law, the legislation's most ardent supporters arrayed around him: Clinton Anderson, who shepherded the legislation through the Senate; John Saylor, the act's strongest supporter in the House; and Stewart Udall, who as secretary of the interior had done so much to make the public lands a national resource.[93] Frank Church was there, the young liberal senator from Idaho who had been the bill's floor manager. He would be a key ally of wilderness advocates until the election of 1980, when the rising tide of conservatism in the West swept him from office. Standing beside him was Wayne Aspinall, the Wilderness Act's chief opponent, who voted for the final version of the bill.

One person was missing. Howard Zahniser's untimely death the previous May cast a shadow over that September day. His ailing heart had given out amid the travel, stress, and flurry of his final campaign for wilderness. For those closest to the movement, the law's passage was a fitting tribute to the man who had done so much to champion the cause.

In retrospect, the Wilderness Act marked a turning point in American environmental politics—it was among the first of a new generation of environmental laws of national scope that put the government in the business of protecting the environment. The Wilderness Act outlined the architecture for the National Wilderness Preservation System, the most extensive system of protected wild lands in the United States. Unlike many other environmental laws that have been amended by Congress, left unimplemented by federal agencies, or undermined in the courts, the Wilderness Act has never been substantially amended, weakened, or ignored. As one wilderness proponent explained, it is for these reasons that "advocates who are in the trenches turn to [the Wilderness Act] time and time again."[94] If you want to protect the public lands, arguably, there is no more powerful tool than the Wilderness Act.

2 / SPEAKING FOR WILDERNESS

ew ideas have a more storied history in American environmental thought than wilderness. Henry David Thoreau, the ascetic author, naturalist, and thinker, explored the wilds of New England, retreated to Walden Pond, and famously proclaimed, "in wildness is the preservation of the world."[1] John Muir, the popular nature writer, excited the nation's passion for wild lands with books like *My First Summer in the Sierra*. He helped found the Sierra Club in 1892, served as its president until his death, and led a national campaign to protect Yosemite National Park. His cathedral was the soaring peaks of the Sierra Nevada, which he described as the "Range of Light."[2] Aldo Leopold, forester, hunter, philosopher, and writer, first proposed protecting wilderness areas in 1921. His masterpiece, *A Sand County Almanac*, has become a touchstone in environmental thought.[3] Howard Zahniser, the Wilderness Act's champion and executive director of the Wilderness Society, celebrated wilderness as part of the community of life. There are many others, including Mary Austin, Ansel Adams, Edward Abbey, David Brower, and Olaus and Mardy Murie. Each was a formative thinker and activist on behalf of wilderness protection. Another name should be added to this list: Stewart Brandborg. He succeeded Howard Zahniser as the Wilderness Society's executive director, taking the organization's helm in the summer of 1964, just before the Wilderness Act became law.

Brandborg was a bear of a man: tall, handsome, deep voiced, and devilishly charismatic. He could give a busy taxi cab driver reason to care about wilderness and he could hold the attention of a senator on a street corner. His personality was magnetic, drawing activists in, inspiring them, and sending them home with a sense of personal and public purpose. Brandborg himself was evidence of the broad appeal of wilderness, even in the rural West. He grew up in a small logging town south of Missoula, Montana, and his father worked as the forest supervisor of the Bitterroot National Forest. He spent his summers fishing, hiking, and hunting, experiences that would steel him for the fights ahead.[4] Brandborg joined the Wilderness Society's staff as Zahniser's assistant

2.1 Stewart Brandborg, executive director of the Wilderness Society between 1964 and 1976, in Canyonlands National Park. Photograph by Clif Merritt, August 1965. Courtesy the Wilderness Society.

in 1960 and for the next twenty years was a central pillar in the national wilderness advocacy community.[5] Unlike Leopold or Zahniser, who spoke with eloquence and passion about the values of wilderness, such rhetoric was never Brandborg's hallmark. His contribution was an evangelical faith in the role of citizen activists in protecting the nation's wilderness.

In the late 1960s, the Wilderness Society measured success not only by the acres of wilderness saved but also by the number of wilderness activists trained. To meet Wayne Aspinall's requirement that each new wilderness area be approved by Congress, the Wilderness Society re-created itself as a catalyst to a growing citizens' movement for wilderness protection. Thousands of Americans took part in the agency wilderness reviews required by the Wilderness Act in the 1960s and 1970s, surveying potential wilderness areas in the field, attending wilderness advocacy training programs in local communities and in Washington, D.C., and testifying at agency hearings and before congressional committees. This strategy laid the foundation for a coordinated model of wilderness advocacy, in which both the Wilderness Society's leadership and the contributions of citizen activists were essential. For people like Doug Scott, Helen Fenske, Dave Foreman, Bart Koehler, and Bob Hanson—several of whom have made their life's work protecting the public lands—this was the beginning. The new political energy raised many questions about which public lands should be designated wilderness. The Wilderness Society did not take its work as an opportunity to champion a narrow vision of what wilderness might be. Instead, a growing wilderness movement consolidated a more expansive and flexible vision of wilderness within the environmental community, the federal government, and, ultimately, Congress. By 1976, Congress had acted to establish 108 new wilderness areas and, at the behest of citizens, often protected more and a greater variety of land—from swamps to mountains to small islands—than recommended by the federal land agencies.

The Wilderness Society's approach to advancing its agenda between 1964 and the mid-1970s is notable for two reasons: First, the Wilderness Act's requirements invested the federal land agencies and, ultimately, Congress with oversight of wilderness designation. Those procedures might be expected to work to the advantage of western political interests, resource industries, and the agencies, all of which had historically shaped public lands policies to promote economic development and local access to the public lands. Through coordinated and sustained citizen participation, however, the Wilderness Society laid the foundation for a pragmatic approach to the implementation of the Wilderness Act—a task made easier by confusion within the federal land agencies over wilderness policy and the marginal economic value of the forests, parks, and refuges considered for protection in the 1960s. Second, while other social movements stood apart in the late 1960s and early 1970s for their protest activities—the anti-war movement's mass marches, the Black Power Movement, and the confrontations at the 1968 Democratic National Convention— the wilderness movement remained focused on pursuing administrative and legislative action. This approach reflected a faith in the roles both of citizens in government and of the government in American life; this faith was central to environmental reform in the 1960s and early 1970s.

A Citizens' Campaign for Wilderness

For the new director of the Wilderness Society, it was hard not to feel a sense of urgency in the fall of 1964. The Wilderness Act protected 9.1 million acres of wilderness immediately and it required reviews of approximately 53 million acres of additional forests, parks, and refuges over the next ten years.[6] Advocates hoped that much of those lands would gain formal protection as wilderness too, but accomplishing that goal raised new challenges. The campaign for the Wilderness Act had been national, and it focused on enacting a single law, which allowed the Wilderness Society to coordinate a broad coalition in support of one goal. Thanks to Aspinall, implementing the Wilderness Act now required staging more than one hundred local campaigns to pass laws protecting additional wilderness areas nationwide. Brandborg knew the Wilderness Society was poorly prepared for such a decentralized set of campaigns. Like most environmental organizations in the 1960s, the Wilderness Society was small. Its office was located on P Street, two blocks from Rock Creek Park, far from the Capitol. Its professional staff numbered only three: Brandborg, a field director, and the editor of its magazine, *The Living Wilderness*. The Wilderness Society already had strong ties to local and national conservation groups, but Brandborg knew that while some parts of the country, like California and the Pacific Northwest, had well-developed citizen groups, other parts of the country did not. To meet the challenges of the ten-year reviews, the Wilderness Society needed to reposition itself to catalyze local wilderness activities across the country.[7]

In the 1960s, Brandborg chose not to invest the organization's limited resources in economic, scientific, or legal expertise or focus its efforts in Washington, D.C. — strategies that became increasingly important for much of the environmental movement in the 1970s. Instead, he poured the Wilderness Society's resources into supporting existing networks of grassroots activists nationwide and helping build such networks where they did not exist. By 1965, the Wilderness Society's membership had grown to 25,000 (up from 16,000 in 1962), which expanded its budget and supported a growing staff.[8] Clif Merritt, who Zahniser had hired, came on board as the organization's first field director, and Rupert Cutler filled Brandborg's previous position as assistant executive director. Merritt was a lanky resident of Montana, a tireless worker, and a sportsman. He came to the Wilderness Society from the Montana Wildlife Federation, where the most pressing concerns were hunting, fishing, and outdoor recreation — concerns that strengthened his relationship with rural west-

2.2   Clif Merritt, the director of field services for the
Wilderness Society, in Montana, ca. 1970. Courtesy
Clifton R. Merritt Papers, Archives & Special Collections,
Mansfield Library, the University of Montana–Missoula.

erners. Merritt organized the Wilderness Society's first field office, in Denver.[9]
While Merritt focused on the West, Cutler focused on the East. Cutler, whose
background was in journalism, was a determined, professional conservation-
ist who would go on to work for the Carter administration. He had a twinkle
in his eye and a way with people. Cutler oversaw the implementation of the
Wilderness Act in Washington, D.C., and helped organize citizen groups in the
Midwest and East.[10] With this staff, starting in 1964, Brandborg positioned the
Wilderness Society at the head of a growing citizens' movement for wilderness,
which was active and independent, yet cooperative in following the Wilderness
Society's leadership.

The Wilderness Society's membership had grown far beyond what its
founders ever anticipated in the 1930s. A strong direct mail program kept the
Wilderness Society in close communication with a national membership. The
society launched a backcountry travel program under the leadership of its
Denver office; these "Way to the Wilderness" trips formed a part of a growing

boom in outdoor recreation that heightened the popularity of wilderness.[11] But the centerpiece of the Wilderness Society's activities in the late 1960s and early 1970s was its commitment to catalyzing local support by creating new organizations, developing wilderness proposals, and involving citizens in testifying and lobbying. Brandborg believed that success "will hinge on [the Society's] ability to organize and inspire this essential grassroots effort."[12] In his view, the Wilderness Society was better off supporting and facilitating the work of local organizations, rather than establishing its own chapters.[13] Local organizations could speak with more authority about the importance of wilderness than could the Washington-based Wilderness Society. In the winter of 1965, Brandborg, Merritt, and Cutler fanned out across the country to cultivate support. They spread the same message: the Wilderness Act did not mark the end of the campaign for wilderness; it marked a new beginning. These sustained efforts resulted in alliances with existing conservation, hunting, recreation, and wildlife groups, such as Sierra Club chapters, the Mountaineers in Washington state, and the Montana Wilderness Association, as well as the establishment of new wilderness organizations, such as the Colorado Open Space Coordinating Council, the Virginia Wilderness Committee, and the West Virginia Highlands Conservancy — many of which still play an active role in wilderness politics today.

The Institutional Geography of Wilderness

In the 1960s, when Brandborg, Merritt, or Cutler would join interested citizens for organizational meetings in someone's home or office in rural towns near potential wilderness areas, they would explain the Wilderness Act and the upcoming wilderness reviews.[14] At such meetings, one of the documents they were likely to have had was a map of the United States showing the jigsaw puzzle of public lands: the Forest Service oversaw the national forests and grasslands; the National Park Service oversaw the national parks, monuments, and historical sites; the Fish and Wildlife Service oversaw the national wildlife refuges; and the Bureau of Land Management oversaw most of the remaining lands.[15] Although the Forest Service was administered by the Department of Agriculture, the three other land agencies were administered by the Department of the Interior. Like siblings in a family, the federal land agencies often worked together, but rivalries and suspicions divided them too. They competed for land, funds, and prestige important to securing support from Congress and the public. To protect wilderness required understanding these institutions and the public lands they managed.

When the Wilderness Act became law, the first fifty-four wilderness areas were all located in the national forests, which is unsurprising, considering the Forest Service's long history of wilderness protection. Established in 1905, the Forest Service oversees 170 national forests, which include over 193 million acres of land in the East and West (about ten percent of all land in the United States). In 1929, the agency adopted the L-20 regulations, proposed by Aldo Leopold (who worked for the Forest Service for much of his life) to protect "primitive areas" for recreation. In 1939, it adopted the stricter U regulations proposed by Bob Marshall, the agency's chief of recreation and the Wilderness Society's leading founder. The new regulations, which superseded the L-20 regulations, mandated the protection of "wilderness," "wild," and "canoe" areas and reflected the agency's internal commitment to wilderness for some land (usually land with little timber potential). By the 1960s, the agency protected 14 million acres of wild lands under these administrative rules. Some agency employees had a deep institutional pride in the Forest Service's commitment to wilderness and a confidence that it knew best how to choose and protect wilderness areas. It was also the case that when the Wilderness Act became law, it immediately protected the existing wilderness, wild, and canoe areas—giving the Wilderness Act particular urgency at the Forest Service—and it mandated that the remaining primitive areas protected under the L-20 regulations be reviewed for potential wilderness designation.

Although the Forest Service had a long commitment to wilderness protection, more important was its multiple-use approach to managing the forests. In the words of its founder, Gifford Pinchot, the agency aimed to manage the forests for "the greatest good to the greatest number for the longest time."[16] Historically, the Forest Service enjoyed considerable freedom in deciding how to achieve that goal. It prized its scientific expertise, strong management tradition, and congressional support, and it carefully guarded the agency's oversight of the national forests. In 1960, at the agency's behest, Congress passed the Multiple-Use Sustained-Yield Act, which affirmed the agency's discretion in managing the forests for a variety of uses including "outdoor recreation, range, timber, watershed, and wildlife and fish purposes," ensuring "they are utilized in the combination that will best meet the needs of the American people." The Multiple-Use Sustained-Yield Act explicitly affirmed the value of the "establishment and maintenance of areas of wilderness."[17] Although wilderness advocates had fought for that language, they remained deeply concerned about the direction of the Forest Service and its commitment to wilderness. In the 1950s, the agency doubled the timber harvest over the decade, expanded

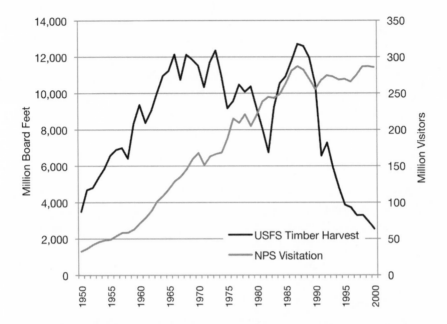

2.3 Demand for timber from the national forests and visitation to the national parks increased dramatically after the 1950s, spurring forward the campaign for the Wilderness Act. National forest timber harvests peaked in the late 1980s, in part due to environmental reforms.

clear-cutting on the national forests, and increased the forest road system by 2,800 miles of new roads each year. And when the choice was between protecting wild lands and logging, the agency chose logging. That became clear when the agency began removing high-value timberland from existing protected areas, as the agency did at the Three Sisters Primitive Area in western Oregon in the mid-1950s.[18] The timber industry and its western political allies seemed to be calling the shots at the Forest Service.[19] For wilderness advocates, that made the Wilderness Act all the more important: it would give the public a stronger say in the Forest Service's management decisions and put Congress in charge of deciding which wild lands were protected as wilderness.[20]

The initial opposition of the National Park Service to the Wilderness Act had been a surprise to the Wilderness Society. Of the federal land agencies, the National Park Service was the one that more closely aligned with the priorities of groups like the Wilderness Society and the Sierra Club. In 1916, Congress created the Park Service to oversee the national parks and monuments, and charged it with a dual mandate: "to conserve the scenery and the natural and historic objects and wildlife therein, and to provide for the enjoyment of the same in such manner and by such means as will leave them unimpaired for future generations."[21] Wilderness advocates worried the agency often emphasized developing the parks, a concern that grew in the 1950s. An American middle class with more money, longer vacations, and more automobiles than ever before seemed to be making a beeline for the parks. Visitation doubled in the 1950s, and parking lots, visitor centers, and accommodations overflowed. In the mid-1950s, the Park Service shifted its efforts away from protecting the parks and toward revitalizing and expanding the park system's infrastructure and facilities. Congress approved a development program, titled Mission 66, in preparation for the agency's fifty-year anniversary in 1966, and allotted one billion dollars to build roads, visitor centers, and other facilities.[22] The Park Service considered the Wilderness Act unnecessary; its director explained that the agency saw "nothing [to] be gained from placing such areas in the National Wilderness Preservation System as provided in the bill."[23] But wilderness advocates worried that what the agency was really doing, as the iconoclastic park ranger and author Edward Abbey put it pointedly, was giving in to the "onslaught of the automobile" and the "indolent masses" who drove them and making the parks into "national parking lots."[24] The Wilderness Act, it was hoped, would guarantee that at least some portions of the parks would be protected as wilderness, safe from the agency's enthusiasm for tourism.

The wild card among the federal land agencies was the Fish and Wildlife Service. Some of the nation's most contested lands are overseen by this agency, notably the Arctic National Wildlife Refuge in northeastern Alaska, an expanse of wild lands nearly the size of South Carolina. The Fish and Wildlife Service's history dates to 1903, when the federal government first created refuges to protect migratory birds and waterfowl. During the New Deal years, hunters offered support to protect the migratory birds and the federal government purchased undervalued lands along migratory flyways on the Atlantic and Pacific coasts and the Mississippi River. In 1940, Congress established the Fish and Wildlife Service to oversee this growing network of refuges.[25] Initially, the agency focused on actively managing the wildlife refuges to restore and manage waterfowl for hunting. After World War II, the agency's responsibilities expanded to address growing national concerns over the loss of endangered species and their habitat. The Fish and Wildlife Service was the only agency that consistently supported the Wilderness Act. The agency's refuges had often been established by presidential or agency actions, not those of Congress. Thus, the Wilderness Act promised to strengthen the refuge system by providing a congressional stamp of approval in the form of designated wilderness areas. One enthusiastic staffer,

Harry Crandell, began working from within the agency to shape its wilderness policies in the mid-1960s. Of the three agencies, the Fish and Wildlife Service was the only one that the Wilderness Society later described as "cooperative," "responsive," and "enthusiastic" about wilderness.[26]

Surprisingly, the Wilderness Act did not apply to the federal land agency with the largest holdings of public lands: the Bureau of Land Management (BLM).[27] Congress established the agency in 1946 to oversee what were often described as "the lands that no one knows."[28] When Congress closed the western public lands to homesteading in 1934, it gave the BLM's predecessor oversight of the remaining public lands—the public domain. These were the wide-open spaces of the American West—sagebrush flats, deserts, and the Arctic tundra that the states, private interests, or other federal land agencies never claimed. The BLM ostensibly managed these lands—totaling more than 470 million acres—for multiple uses, such as timber, grazing, mining, oil, and gas. But, unlike the Forest Service, which had a strong institutional identity and pride, the BLM lacked clear legislative guidance and was perennially underfunded and understaffed. Of the four federal land agencies, the BLM managed its lands most closely in conjunction with local interests. Historically, local grazing boards made decisions regarding access to the range. Local agency offices expedited leasing of the public domain for oil, gas, and mineral exploration. And in the 1960s, the public domain lands were becoming popular for new activities, such as off-road jeep exploration. In the political geography of the American West, the BLM lands would be the toughest sell for wilderness advocates: local communities had a strong role in their management, few people knew about the public domain lands nationally, and these arid expanses were more often viewed as wastelands than valuable wilderness, even in the early 1960s. Instead of picking a fight over the future of the public domain during the campaign for the Wilderness Act, wilderness advocates omitted these lands from the initial campaign for the wilderness system.

The Wilderness Society's leaders emphasized that the Wilderness Act did not redraw the map of the nation's public lands. It did not take land away from the Forest Service and give it to the Park Service, for instance, nor did it create a new agency to oversee the wilderness system. In effect, the Wilderness Act imposed a form of zoning on the public lands, which was compatible with a multiple-use approach to public lands management. At least initially, as historian Kevin Marsh has observed, the Wilderness Act was about halting the loss of existing wilderness rather than protecting new areas or challenging the logging, mining, or grazing industries outright.[29] It required the federal land agencies to review existing lands that might meet the Wilderness Act's requirements and submit recommendations to Congress by 1974. The "ten-year reviews" included the 5.6 million acres of Forest Service lands still protected as "primitive areas" under the 1929 L-20 regulations, all 22 million acres of national parks managed by the Park Service, and 25 million acres of wildlife refuges managed by the Fish and Wildlife Service. Once an area was legislatively added to the wilderness system, the agency was bound by law to protect it as wilderness in perpetuity. That was the opportunity the Wilderness Act presented.

The ten-year reviews would not go as the agencies anticipated. As the reviews got underway, it became clear that the agencies had adopted different and, at times, contradictory wilderness policies that reflected their institutional histories and priorities. The Forest Service, for instance, defined wilderness as the most pristine and untouched wild lands and set a high standard for wilderness under what came to be known as its "purity" policies. The Park Service adopted a more flexible interpretation of the Wilderness Act, but it proposed to exclude buffers and islands of unprotected lands around and within wilderness areas—what wilderness advocates described as "Swiss cheese" wilderness. And the Fish and Wildlife Service adopted what it described as a "creative wilderness philosophy" that contravened the practices of both the Forest Service and the Park Service. The Wilderness Society turned the confusion within the agencies to its advantage by working in close coordination with local wilderness advocates to advance a pragmatic vision for the future of the wilderness system.

The Forest Service and the Purity Policies

The Forest Service moved quickly to formalize its wilderness policies and begin its wilderness reviews. From the agency's perspective, it had been managing wilderness since the 1920s. By moving quickly on the wilderness reviews, the agency hoped to ensure that its wilderness policies, not those of the Park Service or the Fish and Wildlife Service, would become the standard for the new wilderness system. Under the leadership of Richard Costley, the director of recreation, and Bill Worf, a Montana native and ambitious young forester who oversaw the agency's early wilderness reviews, the Forest Service convened a wilderness task force in the fall and winter of 1964 and 1965. The group was charged with determining how the Wilderness Act should be implemented. Worf remembers that despite years of experience with wilderness, the task force found the new law full of paradox and inconsistency. What did Congress mean by "untrammeled" wilderness? How about a minimum size of five thousand acres or whatever was manageable? How could the agency allow visitation without undertaking management activities?[30] The task force found its own way to resolve these tensions: the Wilderness Act should include only the most pristine forest lands in the American West. As Costley explained later, "in the long run, the only practical—and supportable—wilderness management stance which the Forest Service can defend is a 'pure' one."[31]

The Forest Service began the ten-year reviews of thirty-four primitive areas with four areas in the West: the San Rafael and Desolation in California, the Pasayten in Washington, and the Mount Jefferson in Oregon. As would be the case with the Park Service's and the Fish and Wildlife Service's initial wilderness reviews, the Forest Service's reviews followed several steps required by subsection 3(d) of the Wilderness Act: First, local agency personnel reviewed the existing primitive area and assessed its wilderness and other values—such as recreation, wildlife, timber, and minerals. The agency considered whether the existing area merited wilderness protection and, if so, whether changes— either enlargements or reductions of its boundaries—were advisable. Second, the agency developed a proposal, which the public and concerned local, state, and federal officials could comment on at local hearings or in writing. Third, the Forest Service's recommendation—based on its reviews, hearings, and public comments—worked its way through the agency's bureaucracy, from the local office to the regional office to the national office, where it was reviewed before submission to the Department of Agriculture and, ultimately, the White House, which formally sent the president's recommendations to Congress.[32] The Wilderness Society and Sierra Club encouraged citizens to work with agency personnel at every stage of these reviews, submitting comments and letters, participating in local hearings, developing alternative citizen proposals, and lobbying Congress. At times, much to the Forest Service's frustration, it seemed that citizen activists were more knowledgeable about the land at stake than the agency was. As one agency forester griped in 1971, he was tired of hearing "We think it should be wilderness and we know better than you."[33]

The San Rafael proposal offered the first insights into the agency's emerging purity policies. Twelve miles inland from Santa Barbara, California, the San Rafael is located where two coastal mountain chains thrust upwards, framing the scenic California town against the rugged highlands of the San Rafael and the Sierra Madre mountains. From the ridges of these northwest-trending mountains, arid slopes drop down toward the valleys, broken by the occasional sedimentary cliff. In the winter and spring, when the water runs, it spills over the lip of hundred-foot-tall Sisquoc Falls, plummeting toward the Sisquoc River. Most of the year, however, the region is a sere landscape buffeted by dry southern winds. In the southern California summer, extensive patches of tangled brush that blanket the region look like dark shadows across the mountainsides. On the slightly damper northern hillsides, patches of small ponderosa and Jeffrey pines send roots deep for water. Neither the agency nor wilderness advocates expected the proposed San Rafael wilderness to be controversial: it had no minerals, no marketable timber, and minimal grazing lands.[34] The only question was where, exactly, the boundaries of the new wilderness area would be drawn. Since 1932, the agency had protected nearly 75,000 acres of the river's mountainous watershed. In 1968, when Congress designated the San Rafael Wilderness Area, it included nearly twice that amount of land.[35]

Two events in the summer of 1966 shaped the wilderness review at the San Rafael. First, the San Rafael was home to the last of California's wild condors, "feathered pigs" weighing up to twenty-five pounds, with wingspans reaching as much as nine feet.[36] By the 1960s, only forty California condors were left in the United States and biologists considered the San Rafael crucial habitat for the condors that remained. Since 1937, the Forest Service had protected the cliffs along the Sisquoc River where condors roosted. Protecting additional habitat for the condor became a centerpiece of the argument for an expanded San Rafael wilderness area. Fred Eissler, a local teacher and Sierra Club director, noted, "Every indication [is] that expansive wilderness is essential to the survival of the condor."[37] As was the case in many wilderness reviews, identifying wilderness as habitat for an endangered species, such as the grizzly bear or lynx, was an important argument. Second, an airplane crash in June 1966 sparked a wildfire that engulfed 70,000 acres in and around the San Rafael. To bring the fire under control, the Forest Service brought in heavy equipment to clear fire breaks along the grassy balds, known as potreros, that dotted the San Rafael's borders. It was the combination of these two events that sparked controversy. Biologists and wilderness advocates believed that the potreros formed a "historic flyway" for the condors and were an essential part of an expanded wilderness proposal for the San Rafael.[38] The Forest Service refused to include the potreros in its wilderness proposal, in part because they were seen as valuable for fighting fires, but, even more importantly, because they were no longer pristine: many of the potreros had been marred by jeeps and bulldozers, which the agency believed disqualified them as wilderness. In this way, the San Rafael, close to Los Angeles' 6 million residents, partially charred by wildfire,

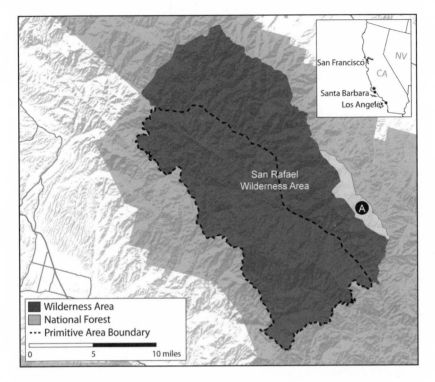

Map 2.1 San Rafael Wilderness Area, Los Padres National Forest, California. The 1968 boundaries of the 143,000-acre San Rafael Wilderness Area marked a significant expansion of the original 75,000-acre primitive area. Congress omitted much of the potreros (A) in the final wilderness, despite active lobbying on the part of wilderness advocates.

and providing habitat for the endangered California condor, was riddled with questions important to the upcoming wilderness reviews.

In 1966, the agency proposed expanding the San Rafael to 142,722 acres, protecting much of the Sisquoc watershed and the condor habitat. To most wilderness advocates, the twofold increase in the size of the San Rafael was a victory. But for the Wilderness Society, the San Rafael promised to set crucial legislative precedents. Testifying before the House Interior Committee, Brandborg and Cutler began to argue for a pragmatic approach to wilderness protection at the San Rafael and nationwide. Their primary concern was the potreros, which the Forest Service excluded from its proposal. The Wilderness Society argued that such lands met Zahniser's standard for "untrammeled" wild lands; even if they had been marred by firefighting in the recent past, they should be included in the expanded wilderness and managed as wild lands since they were important condor habitat.[39] The Forest Service, however, refused to yield. Worf, a member of the agency's wilderness task force, insisted that if the long-term future of the wilderness system was to be properly protected, only pristine lands could be added to it—an argument that was central to the agency's purity policies. In March 1968, Congress designated a 143,000-acre San Rafael Wilderness Area. It added portions of the potreros, but not all, offering no final judgment on the Wilderness Society's debate with the Forest Service. Worf fumed over the Wilderness Society's position. As he saw it, "The Wilderness Society is not concerned with the long-range future of the system, but only in present acreage."[40]

In the years to come, the Forest Service honed its purity policies, arguing that wilderness must be pristine, carefully guarded from over-visitation (even by backpackers), and remote. Some in the agency, like Worf, genuinely believed such policies best protected wilderness. But many in the movement saw the purity policies as a ruse to mask the agency's real agenda: guarding its timber program. Indeed, the agency's purity policies did align neatly with the agency's institutional commitment to logging—protecting a "pristine" wilderness system also meant keeping the wilderness system small. By the late 1960s, the Wilderness Society's new concern was a Forest Service intent on creating a truly "pure" wilderness system.

The National Park Service and "Swiss Cheese" Wilderness

If the Forest Service was the hare in the wilderness reviews, the National Park Service turned out to be the turtle. The Wilderness Act required the Park Service to review all the national parks and monuments, determining which areas within each park deserved formal wilderness protection. The Park Service moved slowly to complete these reviews, and Congress has not yet acted on many of the recommendations, including those for some of our best-known parks, such as Yellowstone, Great Smoky Mountains, and Glacier National Parks. But wilderness advocates succeeded in protecting wilderness in a wide range of other parks and national monuments—including Shenandoah in Virginia, Craters of the Moon in Idaho, and Isle Royale in Michigan—which set important precedents regarding the implementation of the Wilderness Act. The Park Service, much like the Forest Service, resisted the role the Wilderness Act gave Congress and citizens in shaping management of the parks. In its view, the Wilderness Act only complicated the agency's long-term master planning program, which was underway in the mid-1960s. Despite the shared reservations of the Forest Service and Park Service, the two agencies took different approaches to wilderness. The Park Service moved slowly to initiate its wilderness reviews. As its reviews proceeded, it became clear the agency prided itself on its role in cultivating "restored" wilderness. But the agency also riddled its wilderness proposals with buffers and exclusions—what wilderness advocates described with some hyperbole as "Swiss cheese."[41]

It is a wonder that Isle Royale National Park is not a part of Canada. It lies 420 miles north of Chicago, in the northernmost reaches of Lake Superior, and just twelve miles shy of Ontario. The park's glaciated landscape is dominated by a series of narrow island ridges that rise gently from Lake Superior, run for forty-odd miles, and then slip back into the lake. In 1967, the Isle Royale wilderness review offered signs of the National Park Service's approach to implementing the Wilderness Act nationwide. The agency's initial wilderness proposal included 119,612 acres of the park's 134,000 acres.[42] In one respect, that heartened wilderness advocates. In the nineteenth century, portions of the island's forests were logged and small copper mines had been in operation. But the agency saw no obstacles in that history of human use. The authoritarian, cigar-chomping director of the Park Service, George Hartzog, explained that Isle Royale represented the agency's commitment to protecting restored wilderness. "Where other uses have impaired past wilderness values, the national parks are managed to restore their wilderness character."[43] In the view of wilderness advocates, however, the agency's proposal fell short in the details: it included large exclusions and buffers, what the agency described as "wilderness threshold zones." The agency believed such exclusions necessary: they assured the integrity of the protected wilderness areas; they provided less adventuresome visitors with an intermediate recreation experience; and they allowed the agency flexibility in future development in the parks, such as developing tourist facilities at some of the park's bays.[44]

Isle Royale's remote location posed a challenge to wilderness advocates who hoped to use it to establish a precedent for a strong Park Service wilderness program. The agency scheduled local hearings on its initial proposal in the dead of winter in a remote town—Houghton, Michigan, in the Upper Peninsula. One local leader warned the Wilderness Society that the hearing record would be dominated by "those who support every possible tourist-attracting development . . . that will pump visitor dollars into the local economy."[45] That became the inspiration for the "Houghton Safari." When the Park Service refused to hold additional hearings in downstate Michigan, Rupert Cutler at the Wilder-

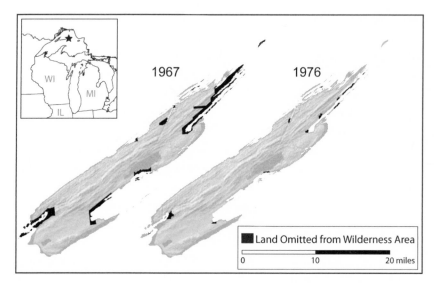

Map 2.2 Isle Royale National Park, Lake Superior, Michigan. In 1967, the National Park Service proposed protecting 119,612 acres of Isle Royale National Park as wilderness, excluding numerous sites, such as harbors, that wilderness advocates worried might eventually be developed for tourism and other services. In 1976, Congress designated a 131,880-acre wilderness with fewer exclusions.

ness Society focused his energies on working with interested citizens in southern Michigan to travel north for the hearing. To make that possible, downstate conservationists and Cutler chartered an airplane from Detroit to Houghton at the cost of $900. Nearly half the cost was covered by the *Detroit News* and the United Auto Workers. (Indeed, labor unions and their leaders played a supporting role in several environmental initiatives as part of the liberal Democratic coalition in the 1960s.) A Douglas DC-3 carrying twenty citizens headed north on the cold, cloudy morning of January 31, 1967.[46] At the hearing—speaking on behalf of the Michigan Natural Areas Council, Michigan United Conservation Clubs, other state organizations, the Sierra Club, and the Wilderness Society— citizens acknowledged the strengths of the agency's proposal: it kept the park roadless, it restricted administrative and visitor developments to a few sites, it included restored wilderness, and it included more than 90 percent of the park as wilderness. But, in their view, the excluded areas formed beachheads for future developments. Gordon Haber, a biology professor, argued: "If this should ever occur, the wilderness character of much more than just the directly affected areas will be destroyed."[47]

The last passenger on the DC-3 that January morning was Doug Scott, a graduate student from the University of Michigan. His testimony on behalf of Isle Royale was his first taste of wilderness politics. The next day he wrote the first of many letters to Cutler and joined the Wilderness Society as a member. In 1968, he persuaded Cutler and Brandborg to hire him as a summer intern in Washington, D.C. When Rupert Cutler left the Wilderness Society in 1969, Scott would join the staff full-time and take up much of his workload.[48] Short, curly-haired, and perpetually animated, Scott had grown up in the Pacific Northwest, where he fell in love with the wilderness. He would emerge as a spirited grassroots organizer, a master draftsman of wilderness legislation, and an indefatigable advocate of wilderness preservation who would play a crucial role in the campaigns for the national forests and Alaska in the late 1970s and in a resurgence of wilderness advocacy in the late 1990s and early 2000s. For the next two years, Scott, Cutler, and the Wilderness Society monitored the agency's progress on Isle Royale. The field hearings established clear support for an enlarged wilderness proposal. Cutler personally acknowledged each of more than one hundred letters local citizens carbon-copied to the Wilderness Society.[49] In 1968, the agency expanded its wilderness proposal to 120,588 acres, reducing the size of two threshold zones.[50] Then, just like the wilderness proposals for the Great Smoky Mountains, Craters of the Moon, and other parks and monuments, the Isle Royale proposal disappeared into the maw of the agency's bureaucratic planning operations. By the time the National Park Service's wilderness reviews finally began to move forward again—in the early 1970s—wilderness advocates would be prepared to leapfrog the agency and take their appeal straight to Congress.[51]

The Fish and Wildlife Service and a "Creative Wilderness Philosophy"

Wilderness in New Jersey? The first wilderness area protected by the Fish and Wildlife Service was located just twenty-seven miles west of Times Square, in Morristown, New Jersey. The Great Swamp, a patch of swamp and forest surrounded by suburban New Jersey, is a shallow depression scoured out by a glacier millennia ago. Most visitors see the thickets of alder, the sugar maple and beech trees, and the open swamp. But careful observers can also see the old homesteads abandoned on the shallow ridges and the occasional split of a drainage channel, a reminder of the government's failed efforts to drain the swamp in the 1930s. Of all the human incursions into the swamp, the easiest to see were a little-used road and power lines that bisected the refuge between Meyersville and Green Village. Protecting this national wildlife refuge did much to expand the framework of the National Wilderness Preservation System and to showcase a citizens' wilderness movement.

The Fish and Wildlife Service chose to review the Great Swamp first in its wilderness program, in part because the forces of development were circling. In 1959, authorities in New York and New Jersey proposed building the metropolitan area's fourth airport on the centrally located flatlands of the Great Swamp, a seemingly undeveloped wasteland. In response, a local housewife, Helen Fenske, initiated a campaign that galvanized the local community, raised $1.5 million, and succeeded in purchasing 2,700 acres of the Great Swamp over the next five years—slowing plans for the airport. In 1964, reflecting the great confidence many citizens had in their government at the time, the land was donated to the Department of the Interior to create the Great Swamp National Wildlife Refuge.[52] That work represented the success of many such middle-class efforts in the 1960s, often led by women, to protect open space and other environmental resources.[53] But protecting the swamp as a refuge did not forestall the airport entirely. In 1966, state authorities again recommended the site for development. For Fenske, her allies, and the Great Swamp, the Wilderness Act seemed propitious—it promised to permanently protect the area from an airport—but could the act apply in the case of the Great Swamp? The wilderness proposed for the refuge was only 2,400 acres, far smaller than most western wilderness areas. The refuge had a road right through it, and the Wilderness Act prohibited roads. And the refuge was in New York City's backyard, where few people thought to look for wilderness.

The Fish and Wildlife Service oversaw many small wildlife refuges like the Great Swamp. It nominated other small refuges for early wilderness review, such as Saint Lazaria off the coast of Alaska, Three Rocks off the coast of Oregon, Monomoy Island off Cape Cod, and Wisconsin Islands in Lake Michigan. Adding these small areas, totaling a few thousand acres, to the 9 million acres of the existing mountainous wilderness system raised new questions about what wilderness could be. The wilderness reviews of the Great Swamp in particular helped affirm a more flexible and expansive approach to wilderness that would increase the scope of wilderness protection throughout the country. At the center of the Fish and Wildlife Service's wilderness reviews was Harry Crandell, the agency's wilderness-friendly planning officer. Crandell was a native of Colorado, where he had been educated before joining the agency in 1955. He was a refuge manager, a wildlife biologist, and then a planner at the agency's Washington office, where he gained a keen understanding of the political bureaucracy and honed his razor-sharp wit.[54] Crandell was passionate about wilderness. When the agency offered to promote him in 1967, just as he got the wilderness reviews underway, he declined, explaining he wanted to see the reviews through. He believed that "this is one of the most important contributions [we] will make this decade."[55] Only an offer from Brandborg to join the Wilderness Society's staff in 1970 as the chief legislative strategist would draw him away.

Working together, the Fish and Wildlife Service, the Wilderness Society, and local conservationists pioneered a "creative wilderness philosophy" in the suburbs of New Jersey. The Wilderness Act stipulates that wilderness areas be 5,000 acres or of a manageable size. In the case of the Great Swamp, the agency judged a 2,400-acre wilderness area on the eastern side of the swamp reasonable. In the agency's view, the Great Swamp may not have been 5,000 acres, but it did meet the Wilderness Act's requirement that the area be manageable as wilderness. The proposal, however, omitted 1,350 acres on the western side of the old Meyersville road that showed more evidence of historical use. But local wilderness advocates challenged that argument in Congress. Since 1967, Fenske and Cutler had been working with local groups to develop a citizens' proposal for the Great Swamp. Fenske went to Washington, D.C., and Cutler traveled to New Jersey to work with citizens. And Cutler emphasized the flexibility inherent in the Wilderness Act. As Fenske later remembered, "Rupert was really the one who led us around, and trained us on how to lobby Congress."[56] At the local and congressional hearings, local activists argued for including not only the eastern swamp, but the western swamp and the road in between. Before Congress, Brandborg and Cutler explained that such areas did not "dilute our wilderness standards." Instead, they were opportunities to "quickly grasp the last dwindling opportunities where we can find them."[57]

The Fish and Wildlife Service embraced this argument in its work on the Great Swamp. Unlike the Forest Service and Park Service, which doggedly defended their interpretation of the Wilderness Act, the Fish and Wildlife Service expanded its recommendation for the Great Swamp to 3,750 acres and included the road. The recommendation pleased many of the sixty-two persons who testified at the local hearings and the 6,655 who sent statements of support. Several themes emerged in that testimony and correspondence. The Great Swamp protected wild lands from the imminent threat of development, offered a psychological refuge from New Jersey's urban growth, provided a laboratory for scientific study (of use to many nearby schools and universities), and protected the Passaic River's watershed. In Congress, hearings before the western-dominated House and Senate committees focused primarily on whether the

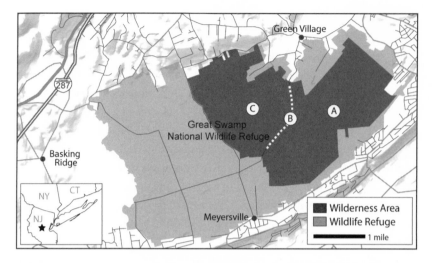

Map 2.3 Great Swamp National Wildlife Refuge, Morristown, NJ. The initial wilderness proposal for the Great Swamp National Wildlife Refuge included only the 2,400-acre unit (A) and excluded the 1,350-acre unit (C) because of the old road (B). The final wilderness area included both units and the road was removed and revegetated.

addition of the swamp would undermine the value of the existing wilderness system. How could a patch of swampland one exit off the highway belong in the same wilderness system as San Rafael or Isle Royale? Congressional critics argued that because of its small size, history, and urban proximity, the Great Swamp fell outside the "wilderness concept as intended and expressed in the Act of September 3, 1964." Furthermore, the proposal used the Wilderness Act as "subterfuge" to stymie development. To critics, like Representatives Aspinall and John Kyl (R-IA), protecting the Great Swamp did "violence to the wilderness concept." Despite their concerns, the Great Swamp had strong local support and faced little opposition.[58]

Congress designated 3,750 acres of the Great Swamp as wilderness in September 1968. With the well-coordinated and strong support among conservationists and government officials at all levels, Congress overrode the legitimate concerns of the congressional committee and reaffirmed the flexible definition of wilderness set forth in the Wilderness Act. In doing so, it endorsed what the Fish and Wildlife Service's director John Gottschalk described as a "creative wilderness philosophy."[59] Far from the spectacular landscapes of the High Sierras and the Rockies, the Great Swamp helped set a broader standard for wilderness. In words that would have pleased Zahniser, Gottschalk explained, "On many refuges . . . areas once used as farms, logged, or drained can, under proper protection, be restored through natural processes, thus benefiting wild creatures and man alike. Even though some of the refuge areas designated today as wilderness may lack the pristine character that our grandfathers knew, they will become the wilderness of tomorrow."[60] So it is today. The Great Swamp remains a unique parcel of wild land, easily accessible from Interstate 287 in northern New Jersey. When it added the refuge to the wilderness system, Congress required the agency to make good on its commitment to restore the area's wilderness character. By 1970, the agency had removed or burned and buried eighteen buildings. The electric company removed the power lines from alongside the old Meyersville road, and trucks removed twenty-five loads of debris and litter.[61] The agency left the area largely to nature. The old road is now an overgrown trail, running through a varied habitat of swamp and woodland that is home to coyotes and foxes.

To Work for Wilderness in the Sixties

What did it mean to be a member of the Wilderness Society in the 1960s? The Wilderness Society invested considerable resources in attracting and cultivating its membership. Most members kept in contact with the Wilderness Society via the mail. Brandborg had gotten his start at the Wilderness Society by developing its direct mail program in the 1950s, and the organization peppered its members with newsletters, alerts, and requests. The most substantial mailing was *The Living Wilderness*, a beautiful quarterly magazine that contained legislative updates, profiles of wilderness areas, and nature writing by writers such as Annie Dillard, a featured columnist. The magazine included articles such as "Status Report on the Wilderness Act Reviews" and "What Is Wilderness?" and editorials titled "Do We Ask Enough?" and "No Room for Apathy." The Wilderness Society's most frequent mailings were detailed alerts intended to keep members posted on the status of wilderness reviews, with summaries of agency and citizen proposals, schedules of hearings, maps, and pleas for involvement. The alerts were usually single spaced and printed on double-sided paper (often legal-size sheets). Being a member of the Wilderness Society meant receiving a regular stream of communications on wilderness legislation and politics, with descriptions of the history, wildlife, recreational opportunities, and nonconforming features of the wild lands at stake. This narrative form of communication stands out: the organization had faith that its members would take the time to grapple with the details of the issues and to play an informed role in the political process; and the Wilderness Society did not trade in an image of wilderness as pristine and unspoiled while pushing for a more flexible and pragmatic approach to wilderness with the land agencies and Congress. In its work, the Wilderness Society actively cultivated a pragmatic approach to wilderness inside and outside of Washington, D.C.

For most of the Wilderness Society's members, paying their dues, reading *The Living Wilderness*, and, perhaps, responding to the Wilderness Society's call for letters would be the limit of their involvement. But for those who wanted to do more, the Wilderness Society offered an open invitation to take part in a training program that connected citizens with the administrative and legislative machinery important to public lands management. To support this coordinated approach to advocacy, which integrated local activism and national leadership, the Wilderness Society's staff grew to a dozen professionals who split their time among lobbying in Washington, D.C., working out of the Washington and Denver offices, and coordinating the growing networks of citizen activists across the country. The Wilderness Society supported local and state wilderness committees in Virginia, West Virginia, New Jersey, Michigan, Colorado, North Dakota, Alabama, Wyoming, and New Mexico, among other states. By 1968, when someone wrote to inquire about how to work for wilderness, they received a booklet, *The Citizen's Guide to the Wilderness Act*, which offered step-by-step instructions on how to organize a wilderness coalition, work with federal land agencies, and approach a congressional delegation. The pamphlet described the implementation of the Wilderness Act as the "Big Job Ahead," justified "Wilderness for Public Purposes," and emphasized "Using the Democratic Process."[62] In Brandborg's words, "[I]nformed people everywhere are our prime resources in this effort. Their energy and enthusiasm, their dedication to a public purpose and a cause goes much farther than any personal or direct benefit, or any remuneration that they themselves might receive."[63]

Considering how many people were drawn into political and social activism across America in the late 1960s, it is worth asking who worked for wilderness. These were pivotal years in American politics, defined by waves of social movements and political activism, each borrowing ideas, strategies, and, at times, leaders and activists from each other—the Civil Rights Movement, the New Left, the anti-war movement, and the women's movement. In some cases, such as French Pete in Oregon, a new generation of youth activism charged wilderness activism.[64] But in most cases, there was little direct crossover between the social movements of the 1960s and wilderness advocacy. Although surveys are not available to answer this question definitively, several points are evident. The wilderness movement was not demographically diverse. It generally attracted whites who were educated and enjoyed the means to invest their weekends exploring the outdoors, to attend meetings on weekday evenings, and to travel to testify and lobby on behalf of wilderness. That is not to suggest that the movement was elitist. There is no indication that wilderness advocates were particularly affluent, that the movement was funded by wealthy patrons, or that it enjoyed any special support from the influential or famous. The individuals who worked for wilderness were diverse in their occupations and backgrounds and included teachers, lawyers, ranchers, students, scientists, housewives, and college professors.[65] Many were women. Some were outdoor enthusiasts, some naturalists and birders, some patriots and westerners; often, they were several of these. Cecil Garland owned a hardware store in Lincoln, Montana. Helen Fenske was a housewife in suburban New Jersey. Doug Scott was a graduate student at the University of Michigan. Like thousands of other Americans in the 1960s and 1970s, each of these individuals committed their personal time to the work of wilderness protection, which to them meant working for a public good.

In many respects, the political engagement that animated the wilderness movement was buoyed by the rising tide of political activism in America. Calls for "participatory democracy" in the student movement and women's movement would have resonated with Brandborg's democratic populism. Some wilderness activists did take part in other protest activities. Historians have often suggested that the protest activities of the 1960s—especially those of the New Left, the anti-war movement, and the women's movement—served as catalysts that helped push a wide range of environmental concerns to the forefront of national attention, a process that culminated with the first Earth Day in 1970. Although the surge of wilderness activism was likely strengthened by the 1960s social movements, in important respects the campaigns for wilderness stand apart. Many of the movements of the Left, which had formed an important part of the coalition that made possible Lyndon Johnson's Great Society in the mid-1960s, had begun to grow frustrated with the Democratic Party, the Johnson administration's involvement in Vietnam, and the American political system.[66] More radical groups began to turn away from liberalism and the political system. Social protest began to spill onto the streets. Race riots shook urban America. Students occupied campus buildings at Columbia and Berkeley. Anti-war protesters burned draft cards and marched on the capitol. The women's movement staged protests at the Miss America pageant. And the Democratic Convention in 1968 degenerated into conflict between anti-war protesters and students and the Chicago police. As one historian argues, amid these protest activities the "glow of liberalism" was "snuffed out during the days of decision as citizens argued over race and war."[67] In place of the Democratic Party's liberal confidence in its agenda for a more inclusive, just, and democratic America, these social movements began to push the Democratic Party onto the fractious terrain of identity politics and special interests.

At least within the wilderness movement, however, a liberal faith in the federal government and the legislative system remained an animating force. Rather than lying down before logging trucks, sitting in protest in trees, or committing acts of eco-sabotage, wilderness advocates worked through the political system. Of course, they would turn to more radical strategies in the future—protest politics would distinguish Earth First! in the 1980s—but in the 1960s and early 1970s, as so many other movements turned away from the political system, wilderness activists focused their efforts on the careful work of the ten-year reviews and cooperated with the federal land agencies (even as they disagreed with them) and Congress to protect wilderness. Such work was often grounded in the particulars of the wilderness areas at stake. Although ecological concerns for wilderness were growing stronger, when the Wilderness Society extolled the meaning of wilderness in the late 1960s, its most frequent argument remained much the same as it had been in the campaign for the Wilderness Act: wilderness remained most valuable for its "human values" and as a legacy to "future generations."[68] As Brandborg reminded Congress, "use is a very important part of the wilderness concept"—for recreation, science, and scenery—"as we see it and the law defines it."[69] At a time when new claims grounded in rights and identity emerged as an organizing force in liberal politics, such appeals to a common public interest remained characteristic of wilderness advocacy. In Brandborg's words, it meant "stimulating widespread involvement of public-spirited private citizens across the country in the work of rounding out the Wilderness System."[70] Working for wilderness was about private citizens working through the political system for a public good.

Historians have often viewed the early efforts toward environmental reform in the 1960s as mere antecedents to the more far-reaching accomplishments of the "environmental decade" of the 1970s. But to understand those later successes requires understanding the liberal confidence that distinguished the emerging environmental movement in the 1960s. A faith in government, a commitment to the political system, and a belief in the public good—all of which were manifest in the wilderness movement—were also characteristic of other efforts toward environmental reform, including efforts to advance some of the "new" environmental issues, such as air and water pollution.[71] This earlier liberal confidence would transcend the burst of social activism in the years before and after the first Earth Day, laying the foundations for the modern environmental regulatory state. This strategy, which invested the government with an ever-larger role in addressing a wide range of environmental issues, made environmental reform characteristic of what conservatives like Ronald Reagan would come to disparage as "big government" in the 1980s. In this faith in government were the seeds of the political backlash to come.

Conclusion

For the Wilderness Society, the success of its campaign for the Wilderness Act was never just about the number of new wilderness areas, their size, or even the diversity of landscapes they protected. At Stewart Brandborg's Wilderness Society, the most important measure of success was the number of citizens it actively involved in the positive work of studying, engaging, and protecting the public lands. "The wilderness advocacy of thousands of men and women, people who know and understand the wilderness review process," trumpeted Brandborg, "has become the foundation of the wilderness preservation movement."[72] The Wilderness Society's membership and budget grew from 24,000 and $229,000 in 1966 to 37,000 and $313,000 in 1968.[73] It held more than a dozen regional leadership-training workshops. And its Denver office, headed by Clif Merritt, in addition to expanding its wilderness trips program, also became an engine behind wilderness organizing in the West, and a seedbed for a new generation of wilderness leaders. In leveraging the Wilderness Society's resources to build a network of local and regional wilderness organizations, Brandborg laid the foundation for a cooperative approach to wilderness advocacy: it was a model that encouraged, supported, and valued the essential role of local citizen activists in advancing the wilderness agenda. But, at the same time, it was a model that strengthened the Wilderness Society's position as a national leader on public lands policy in Washington, D.C., which had been crucial to advancing a more pragmatic and flexible approach to wilderness designation at San Rafael, the Great Swamp, and Isle Royale. This partnership between local groups and national groups was never without its debates and tensions—and, in the 1980s and early 1990s, a burst of more ambitious and independent citizen activism upended this partnership— but it has continued to play an essential role in public lands politics and wilderness preservation to the present day.

3 / THE POPULAR
POLITICS OF WILDERNESS

"I t seems to me that, as matters now stand, the work of the Wilderness Society is bound to fail in the long run." So began a letter from Theodore Kaczynski to the Wilderness Society dated February 1969. At the time, Kaczynski was a young mathematics professor at the University of California at Berkeley, unknown to the nation he would later terrorize. Only in retrospect does Kaczynski's letter offer clues to his later career as one of the nation's best-known domestic terrorists. In fact, many of the questions he posed about wilderness in 1969 resonated with debates that rattled the wilderness movement in the same years that the environmental movement emerged as a popular force in American culture and politics. While the Wilderness Society focused on the immediacy of the Wilderness Act, the ten-year reviews, and the enlargement of the wilderness system, Kaczynski cast his imagination into the future. He warned the Wilderness Society, "I see no reason to suppose that there will be any change in the present trends toward rapidly increasing over-population and over-industrialization, and a technology that grows with uncontrolled and indeed cancerous rapidity."[1]

Foremost among the questions Kaczynski asked, and one that had already begun to divide the wilderness advocacy community, was a concern about the place of recreation in the wilderness system. Wilderness may have been meant for solitude and primitive recreation, but by the late 1960s, a rapidly grow-ing number of backpackers crowded into the nation's wild places. Kaczynski observed, "either the wilderness areas will become so overcrowded that they lose their value, or else public admittance to the areas will have to be severely restricted." Kaczynski also questioned how the popularity of wilderness might threaten its very character. More visitors would require agencies to spend more time managing the wilderness areas. "These conditions," Kaczynski warned, "will make necessary more and more scientific control and manipulation of wilderness areas." Ultimately, "the areas will not really be wild at all, because every aspect of them will be under the control of man." Finally, Kaczynski foreshadowed his own retreat to Montana two years later. He described the tamed, recreational wilderness areas of the future as "artificially maintained museum-pieces with 'do not touch' signs all over them." Then, he wrote with emphasis, "Real wilderness living will be impossible."[2]

It took the Wilderness Society five months to reply to Kaczynski's letter. When Virginia Carney, the Wilderness Society's administrator, did respond, she failed to address the questions Kaczynski posed about the uses and management of wilderness. Instead, she focused on his fear of a future technical-industrial society and she explained that those concerns went beyond the Wilderness Society's agenda. She praised his thoughtful letter and then explained that the Wilderness Society could only "fulfill our primary purpose: the preservation of wilderness."[3] Yet, neither the Wilderness Society nor Theodore Kaczynski would escape the questions he posed. Behind the tensions over recreation, ecology, and wilderness that Kaczynski highlighted were larger questions about the place of wilderness in a world beset by environmental crisis. In the years before and after Earth Day, some wilderness activists saw the intrinsic value of wilderness as the most important argument for protecting wilderness, and they began to press this argument within the Sierra Club and the Wilderness Society. How the mainstream wilderness movement navigated these tensions and consolidated its moderate approach to wilderness was crucial to the wilderness movement's political successes and its limitations since the 1970s.

Kacyznski himself veered away from public wilderness debate. In 1971, he resettled in a rustic cabin in rural Montana and set out to resolve his concerns about modern society in his own violent way. In the 1970s, 1980s, and early 1990s, a string of bombs, one placed onboard a domestic airliner and others mailed to scientists, business executives, and other agents of what Kaczynski called the "industrial-technological system" captured national attention. Three people died, twenty-two were injured, and in time he became known as the "Unabomber." After the publication of his manifesto, "Industrial Society and Its Future," in June 1995, Kaczynski was apprehended and sentenced to four life terms in federal prison.[4]

The Sierra Club and the Wilderness Manifesto

When the Wilderness Act became law, the Sierra Club was busy with other campaigns. In 1965, the threat of dams in the Grand Canyon swept the Sierra Club into a public confrontation with the Bureau of Reclamation that matched the earlier debates over Hetch Hetchy and Echo Park. David Brower, an athletic mountaineer with a shock of white hair, was the organization's charismatic leader. He thrust the Sierra Club into the national spotlight in the 1960s, as it worked for the Wilderness Act, then saved the Grand Canyon, and finished the decade by persuading Congress to create two new national parks—one for the California Redwoods and the other for Washington's North Cascades. These celebrated victories made the Sierra Club the nation's best-known conservation group. But Brower's aggressive leadership split the Sierra Club in two: he gained admiration and incurred wrath for his arrogance and unyielding politics, he lost the club its tax-exempt status for allegedly engaging in political lobbying, and he was a poor manager, often running the club over budget. At the culmination of a bitter internal debate in 1969 over the future of the Sierra Club, Brower was forced to resign.[5] Little did Stewart Brandborg know that he and the Wilderness Society would face a similar crossroads in 1976.

It was left to Michael McCloskey to pick up the pieces at the Sierra Club after Brower's departure. In 1969, to be the executive director of the Sierra Club was an exciting prospect, but filling Brower's shoes posed a formidable challenge. McCloskey did so in his own way. He worked to orchestrate the Sierra Club's growth from a group focused foremost on land preservation to a larger and more professional organization focused on a range of emerging environmental issues, from wilderness protection to air and water pollution and energy policy. McCloskey, a lawyer, would emerge as a methodical strategist, a careful manager, and a critical cog in the environmental movement's legislative achievements of the 1970s and 1980s. But, as McCloskey remembers, the position came with "a cloud of sorts."[6] After Brower's departure, the club's board of directors took steps to reassert the role of the club's members in its governance and conservation activities. At the same time, its membership was growing rapidly and Sierra Club chapters were sprouting nationwide; many of these chapters sought to involve themselves in local and national environmental issues, including wilderness. Although the staff supported such citizen activities, McCloskey never embraced citizen activism with the same fervor as did Brandborg.[7] And, soon, the Sierra Club's leadership found itself again competing with some of its most active members—those on its Wilderness Classification Committee—and in the process bringing to light divisions over the future of wilderness.

Francis Walcott, a Sierra Club volunteer, emerged as a leader of volunteer wilderness activity within the club. Walcott lived in San Francisco and each summer he would take to the mountains, studying potential wilderness areas and making plans for wilderness campaigns. When he returned to San Francisco, he looked like John Muir himself—sporting a long beard and unkempt locks.[8] Passionate, single-minded, and uncompromising, Walcott proved to be an iconoclastic force for wilderness. He served as the chair of the Sierra Club's Wilderness Classification Committee and was the chief author of what became known as the Sierra Club's "Wilderness Manifesto." At a time when the modern world increasingly seemed on the brink of ecological disaster, Walcott and the committee became forceful proponents within the wilderness movement for challenging the "basic philosophy of growth and development to which this country adheres" and adopting wilderness policies that respected the basic value of "maintaining a really undisturbed ecosystem."[9] Such ideas were not new to the wilderness movement. Many in the wilderness movement cared deeply for the intrinsic and ecological values of wilderness. Many believed that access to wilderness had to be carefully managed. And some saw it as a retreat from the nation's commitment to progress and consumerism. Such arguments had been crucial to the Wilderness Society's founding. But as the movement emerged as a popular political movement in the 1960s, more anthropocentric arguments for wilderness came to the fore. The Sierra Club's Wilderness Classification Committee took these more radical ideas important to the wilderness movement and sharpened their ideological edge. The committee argued that the intrinsic value of wilderness was the most pressing priority for wilderness preservation, relegating more anthropocentric concerns, such as its aesthetic value or recreational uses, secondary considerations.

The discussions that led up to the wilderness manifesto took place against the background of an emerging environmental crisis: new concerns about population growth, environmental disasters such as polluted rivers and oil spills, and a United Nations conference ominously entitled "Man and His Environment: A View towards Survival" all captured national news.[10] In this context, the Wilderness Classification Committee advanced several wilderness policy recommendations that divided the club and challenged the moderate political strategies important to the mainstream wilderness movement. First, the committee emphasized that only truly wild areas should be designated as wilderness. This put the committee at odds with the Wilderness Society and its pragmatic strategy for wilderness designation. Second, the committee argued that alternative designations for wild lands—such as backcountry areas or wild areas—should be considered for lower-quality or popular recreation areas, which would leave the wilderness system itself pristine. And, third, the committee suggested that wilderness recreation, such as hiking and backpacking, should be sharply limited, if not eliminated, if it adversely affected the natural processes important to wilderness. Implicit in this argument was the assumption that the intrinsic value of wilderness had to be protected from even its most ardent enthusiasts. Behind these recommendations was a growing conviction that such a principled approach to wilderness protection was necessary to safeguard the natural world from the increasingly destructive forces of modern society. "In light of the current ecological situation," Walcott explained, "it is essential that wilderness management be directed toward the preservation of wilderness for its own sake."[11]

The committee presented the manifesto to the Sierra Club board in February 1970, and the club adopted a watered-down version that December.[12] But the controversy surrounding the manifesto began before and continued beyond the board's deliberations. Ansel Adams, photographer and Sierra Club board member, raised philosophical concerns about the manifesto: "I object to the attitude of some Sierra Club people who feel ALL must be dedicated to 'ecology.'" In his view, it was naive to think that any wild lands, no matter how remote or little used, could truly be isolated from society. Any aspiration to protect pristine wilderness amounted to a "mirage," he explained. "In truth, 'Wilderness' is a state of mind and heart; very little exists now in actuality."[13] Brock Evans, a Sierra Club staffer in the Pacific Northwest, believed the strongest support for wilderness protection came from hikers, backpackers, and other enthusiasts. Shutting them out of the wilderness system would be a political mistake. The immediate task at hand, he argued, was not getting entangled in detailed debates about wilderness management and philosophy, it was adding as much land to the wilderness system as possible—which meant saving it from loggers, miners, and other forces much more destructive than backpackers. Questions of management, such as handling recreation, could be saved for later.[14] And the Wilderness Society viewed the manifesto as placing the Sierra Club in close alliance with the Forest Service and its purity policies— a possibility that threatened the Wilderness Society's pragmatic approach to the Wilderness Act. In its view, if the Forest Service's purity policies succeeded, the result would be a smaller wilderness system in the East and West.[15]

These tensions between the ideological and pragmatic approaches to wilderness emerged clearly over this period. First, in the late 1960s, the timber industry and wilderness advocates began to square off over logging in the national forests. As wilderness advocates began to eye roadless areas beyond the ten-year reviews authorized by the Wilderness Act in 1964, they began to threaten lands that the Forest Service and timber industry valued for logging. As they did so, the agency gave new emphasis to its purity policies—arguing that only by protecting the most pristine lands; limiting hiking, backpacking, and other visitation; and carefully guarding wilderness could the long-term value of the wilderness system be assured. But in the late 1960s, that argument resonated in unanticipated ways within a wilderness movement that itself was conflicted over the purposes of the wilderness system. Second, concerns for the overuse of wilderness stemmed from the growing popularity of wilderness among recreationists. Backpacking was becoming an increasingly popular way to reconnect with nature. But, according to the Forest Service's purity policies, too many visitors could pose a threat to wilderness. In the late 1960s, as more people crowded into wilderness, the ways they traveled began to change. Following new guidebooks, carrying high-tech gear, and setting up temporary camps, backpackers soon began to protect wilderness in a new way: they began to protect it from themselves. This recreational interest in wilderness strengthened the movement's popular appeal and began to ally wilderness advocates with the forces of a modern consumer economy that some environmentalists saw as complicit in the larger environmental crisis.

The Alpine Lakes and a Popular Wilderness

East of Seattle, the Cascade Mountains run from north to south and on a clear day the highest peaks appear above the Puget Sound like distant sentinels. Seattle's proximity to the Cascades, the Olympic Mountains, and volcanic peaks such as Mount Rainer, Mount Saint Helens, and Mount Baker make it a mecca for backcountry recreation. The Alpine Lakes was especially popular among these areas in the 1960s. Flanked by Route 2 on the north and Route 10 (later Interstate 90) on the south, the Alpine Lakes formed a park-like highlands with more than 700 lakes, superb alpine vistas, and easy access from Seattle. But traveling to and from those mountains, hikers and mountaineers vied with logging trucks for space on the back roads. Located so close to the Puget Sound's ports and railroads, the region was a hub of the national timber industry; 35 percent of the state's workforce traced its livelihood to the region's forests. By the 1960s, as the local timber industry, dominated by the likes of Weyerhaeuser and Boise Cascade, exhausted private landholdings, it increasingly looked to the national forests for timber.[16] But in the 1960s, Seattle's urban economy was diversifying, led by Boeing, the University of Washington, the region's growing financial district, and tourism. The citizens who did the most to advance the campaign to protect the Pacific Northwest's wild lands often hailed from these new industries, and they brought with them a new vision for the region's wild lands.

3.1 Brock Evans, who would become the director of the Sierra Club's Pacific Northwest office in 1967, on top of Mount Cleveland, Glacier National Park. Photograph by Fred Koessling, August 1962. Courtesy Brock Evans.

Brock Evans had been enamored with the Alpine Lakes, and the Pacific Northwest in general, since he moved to the region to practice law in the early 1960s. After joining the Mountaineers, a well-established Seattle-based hiking club, Evans soon spent his weekends exploring the nearby mountains with other professionals, such as University of Washington faculty. A Midwesterner by birth, Evans knew little about the nation's public lands, their management, or their history. He remembers being shocked to reach the top of a peak, only to see a scar of clear-cuts unfold before him. Driving home, Evans would give the finger to the logging trucks traveling in the other direction. In 1967, he decided to leave his job as a lawyer and join the Sierra Club as its Pacific Northwest representative. In the 1970s, when the staffs of groups such as the Sierra Club and the Wilderness Society were still small, such a position came with almost overwhelming responsibilities. Evans spent his weekends on what he and his wife called "900-mile drives," exploring a territory that stretched from Montana to Alaska. Everywhere he looked, he saw a timber industry that seemed to be laying flat the region's forests. In the decades to come Evans would prove himself a skilled negotiator and strategist, first for the wilderness movement and then for environmental issues more broadly. And, right from the start, he was worried that the forests around the Alpine Lakes were on the Forest Service's short list for logging.[17]

The Forest Service had protected a portion of the Alpine Lakes as a 256,000-acre "limited area" since 1946.[18] Like many areas the Forest Service protected in the West, the Alpine Lakes was a sliver of high-elevation land. Wilderness advocates referred to such landscapes as "rocks and ice," where little harvestable Douglas fir, cedar, and hemlock—staples of the region's timber industry—grew. The agency believed such highlands made the most economic sense to protect, since they left lower-elevation forests open to logging and they appealed to hikers. Since World War II, the Forest Service had promoted clear-cutting on the national forests, which was economically efficient, but environmentally devastating. In the Pacific Northwest, such harvesting techniques were justified as necessary to promote the regeneration of Douglas-fir trees (which required full sunlight to germinate) and to meet the growing national need for timber.[19] As a result, at Alpine Lakes, as with many of the areas reviewed for wilderness protection in the West, the debate centered on just how much of the cathedral-like, lower-elevation timberlands might be designated as wilderness.

The Alpine Lakes was only one roadless area, among many, that raised new questions about the management of the national forests. By the late 1960s, citizens argued that roadless areas such as the Lincoln Backcountry in Montana, Indian Peaks in Colorado, and the Dolly Sods in West Virginia, all of which were outside the Wilderness Act's ten-year reviews, should be considered for wilderness designation too. Those efforts caught the timber industry's attention. From the start, both wilderness advocates and the Forest Service acknowledged that the wilderness system would eventually include areas outside the ten-year reviews. The question was one of timing. The initial ten-year reviews applied only to areas the agency protected as primitive areas prior to 1964, which were generally areas of little value for timber. The agency argued that the ten-year reviews needed to be completed first before the wilderness reviews expanded.[20] But wilderness advocates worried that a timber-hungry agency was strategically expediting logging in roadless areas in hopes of disqualifying such areas from future wilderness review. Indeed, roadless areas were often land the agency classified as "commercial timberland." Some wilderness advocates argued the priority should not be the areas included in the ten-year reviews, but the more vulnerable roadless areas.[21] That strategy worried the timber industry. The National Forest Products Association began to complain to Congress and the White House about "militant conservation groups" that threatened timber supplies.[22] In 1970, the Western Wood Products Association argued that the national forests were being "managed by popular local vote, public meetings, and opinion polls," not the "professional, objective views" that had been a hallmark of proper forest management.[23] The success of wilderness advocates pursuing wilderness protection for roadless areas, over the objections of the Forest Service and timber industry, made clear the growing power that citizens exerted in public lands debates.[24]

Evans sounded the alarm for the Alpine Lakes in 1967: "The Alpine Lakes are in trouble."[25] Although Evans reported directly to the Sierra Club's national office, he worked closely with the Wilderness Society, and it was the Wilderness Society's approach to wilderness advocacy that inspired his grassroots strategies. Instead of channeling the work of the Alpine Lakes campaign to the Sierra Club's regional chapter, Evans cofounded the Alpine Lakes Protection Society (ALPS), which brought together local lawyers, teachers, and University of Washington faculty and staff to champion wilderness designation.[26] Initially, ALPS proposed protecting a 364,000-acre wilderness area, which would include the mountain highlands and some lower-elevation timberlands, and a surrounding 562,000-acre national recreation area, which would further limit timber harvests.[27] In their view, this strategy would protect the region's lower-elevation forests and its exceptional recreational value and play an important role in the region's growing tourist economy. Although the debate over the Alpine Lakes divided most publicly over the balance between the region's timber industry and its potential for tourism in the mid-1970s, underlying those arguments was a sharp disagreement over the implementation of the Wilderness Act. As David Knibb, an ALPS leader, noted: "The Alpine Lakes contain the necessary ingredients for a major debate on the meaning of wilderness" — "a moderate-sized roadless area and a large number of people who want to go there."[28]

It was in this climate that the Forest Service began to aggressively champion its purity policies. As wilderness advocates prepared their citizens' campaign to protect the Alpine Lakes, the staff of the Snoqualmie National Forest, which oversaw the area, began to voice their own concerns. "Large numbers of people destroy the wilderness by their very presence," the Snoqualmie supervisor L. O. Barrett explained. "Either we block the wilderness against large numbers [of visitors] or we destroy it."[29] The Forest Service worried that the weekend hikers streaming in from around the Puget Sound were compromising the very values the wilderness system was meant to protect. The Snoqualmie office explained, "Our intent is to severely limit this kind of use" within the wilderness system.[30] More and more visitors left the area pockmarked with campsites and laced with trails, diminishing the solitude and wildness the agency believed essential to a high-quality wilderness system. In the late 1960s, the Snoqualmie staff privately considered a 150,000-acre "blue ribbon" wilderness area that would be strictly managed to protect only the most pristine lands, and a secondary "backcountry area" around it which could be managed to accommodate a greater number of backcountry visitors.[31] But for wilderness advocates, the trouble with a "backcountry area" was that it came with no legal protection from logging, mining, and other forms of development, which was precisely the problem that inspired the campaign for the Wilderness Act.[32]

Bill Worf, the Forest Service's national director of wilderness reviews, remained a staunch advocate of the purity policies. He championed the same arguments at the national level that the Snoqualmie National Forest advanced at the local level. Worf worried that the overuse of wilderness would diminish "the very characteristics which made it suitable for wilderness" in the first place. He called this the "unavoidable philosophical conflict in the law."[33] Working out of the agency's Washington recreation office in the late 1960s, Worf became a proponent of alternate land classifications, such as backcountry, intermediate recreation areas, or frontier areas—all of which were meant to provide alternate recreational opportunities while maintaining the purity of the wilderness system itself.[34] To many in the Forest Service, these official wilderness policies aligned neatly with the agency's long-standing institutional priority: meeting the nation's timber needs, a goal which generated much of the agency's political support, financial revenue, and clout in Congress. Worf, however, represented a small and genuine faction within the agency that was committed to upholding the Forest Service's long-standing tradition of wilderness protection that he traced back to Aldo Leopold and Bob Marshall. For Worf, the purity policies were not about timber but about ensuring the long-term viability of a truly exceptional wilderness system.[35] After he retired from the Forest Service in 1989, Worf went on to cofound Wilderness Watch, a small organization that has diligently monitored the wilderness system to those ends ever since.[36]

At the Alpine Lakes it became clear how neatly the agency's purity policies dovetailed with its commitment to the timber industry. At the same time the agency advanced its "blue-ribbon" proposal for a smaller wilderness area, it was making plans for logging roads and timber sales in the forests surrounding the Alpine Lakes Limited Area. For instance, west of Leavenworth, it targeted Icicle Creek and Jack Creek, which the agency had excluded from its wilderness plans, but which had been included by ALPS.[37] As one agency forester in the Pacific Northwest acknowledged, the agency purposefully removed "excellent stands of commercial timber" from proposed wilderness areas.[38] This was often the case nationwide. Thus, for many in the Forest Service, the purity policies not only promised a high-quality wilderness system, they also promised to keep the wilderness system small. In 1972, Richard Costley, the agency's chief of recreation, explained the hazards of abandoning the purity policies. If you allowed wilderness designations to apply to popular recreation areas and areas with a history of human use, the national wilderness system would "mushroom," Costley warned. "You will find yourself with half-baked semi-wilderness all over the National Forest System."[39] What was so convenient about the purity policies was that if they were successfully adopted—giving priority to a wilderness system that was small, pristine, and allowed only limited recreational use—then the wilderness movement's growing popularity also promised to be its own undoing. Too many backpackers pouring into the wilderness became a reason not to protect too much wilderness.

It was for this reason that Brock Evans saw the strategies of the Wilderness Classification Committee as "politically disastrous."[40] Evans argued: "we would be murdered in every debate if we became known as the 'nuts who do not want any people in the wilderness.'"[41] But, to Walcott and the committee, the Sierra Club needed to hold itself to the same standard that it aimed to hold industry. The club opposed logging and mining because they threatened wilderness. In Walcott's view, if backpackers posed a threat to wilderness, then the Sierra Club should supporting limiting their access too. "Otherwise, the damage . . . will be just as severe as if the spoilers and 'developers' had had it all along."[42] At the core of Evans' sense for wilderness politics was an awareness of the growing popularity of wilderness recreation. "I believe that recreation is an important, valid, and fundamental use of our wilderness system," he explained.[43] "Recreation is one of the *named* purposes of the Wilderness Act. In fact, it is the first named purpose—out of alphabetical order. I hope this is made plain again and again and again."[44] Foremost in Evans' mind in the early 1970s was the imminent threat the Forest Service and timber industry posed to roadless areas, especially in the Pacific Northwest. Pointing to roadless areas along the Cascades, he exclaimed, these are the lands "which contain some of the most splendid examples of cathedral-like virgin forests remaining on this continent," and which the Forest Service was making plans to log as quickly as it could.[45] While Evans made that plea in public, in private he warned Walcott and the rest of the Sierra Club's leadership that they must not align themselves with the Forest Service's purity policies. If they did, "few, if any, new areas [will] *ever* [be] added to the Wilderness System."[46]

The internal debates within the wilderness movement never disrupted the coalition led by ALPS, and in the early 1970s the timber industry became increasingly concerned about the growing pressure to protect the Alpine Lakes. In 1971, an official with the Western Wood Products Association warned, "The current ALPS proposal could well be the most revolutionary and damaging to natural resource industries of any withdrawal case in recent years."[47] His specific concern was that the ALPS proposal went beyond legislating wilderness and included a national recreation area in which clear-cuts would be limited to twenty-five acres. As the historian Kevin Marsh has noted, "the particular limits on clear-cuts in the ALPS proposal were not severe enough to frighten [the Western Woods Products Association], but the precedent of setting any limits on their logging operations did scare them."[48] The timber industry began to organize itself and its allies into a coalition aimed at countering the growing influence of ALPS. In October 1973, a newly formed Alpine Lakes Coalition announced that "leading outdoor recreation and resource groups" had formed a coalition to work for a "plan for people" in Washington's Alpine Lakes region.[49] The coalition brought together the timber industry, local loggers, the U.S. Ski Association, and the Trailer Coach Association, to advance an alternative citizen-proposed wilderness plan for the region that it lobbied for at the local, state, and national levels. This organizational strategy, joining together the resource industries and citizens, formed an important precursor to similar efforts in the late 1970s known as the Sagebrush Rebellion.

The conclusion of the Alpine Lakes debate was delayed into the mid-1970s, due to mineral reviews, a national review of roadless areas, and the Forest Service's slow-moving planning process. After the Sierra Club and Wilderness Society resolved their debates over wilderness strategy, they supported ALPS in its campaign to rally local citizens around a more pragmatic approach for an enlarged wilderness area for the Alpine Lakes. In 1975, they lined up behind a proposal for a 575,000-acre wilderness area and a surrounding national recreation area.[50] They faulted the Forest Service, which continued to push a smaller wilderness proposal and an ill-defined surrounding "backcountry area," for its fealty to the timber industry. Specifically, they argued that the agency's wilderness review of the Alpine Lakes overemphasized the economic value of timber, while omitting the economic value of recreational and tourist activities entirely.[51] Wilderness advocates grew confident in their position. In 1973, Evans observed, "Industry will lose any battle with us over Alpine Lakes; there is simply too much favorable publicity on it because of what [ALPS has] done."[52] In 1975, ALPS geared up for what Doug Scott described as a "major citizen

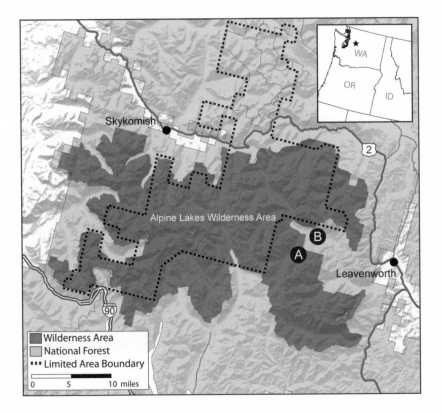

Map 3.1 Alpine Lakes Wilderness Area, Washington. Located east of Seattle, the Alpine Lakes region was a mecca for outdoor recreation. The 393,000-acre wilderness designation in 1976 represented a significant expansion beyond the 256,000-acre 1946 limited area. The most controversial areas were lower-elevation drainages, such as Jack Creek (A) and Icicle Creek (B), which contained harvestable timber.

whammy" in the Pacific Northwest, and Evans worked from his new post at the helm of the Sierra Club's office in Washington, D.C., to oil the legislative gears at the national level.[53] The negotiations moved slowly, but in late 1976, after the timber industry and wilderness advocates struck a deal, Congress designated a 393,000-acre Alpine Lakes Wilderness Area and a surrounding 575,000-acre multiple-use management unit.[54] The final bill dropped the national recreation area and its tighter restrictions on logging, which the timber industry had objected to, but the final wilderness area was far larger than the original 256,000-acre limited area. That success marked the conclusion of one chapter in what had already become a national controversy over the future of the national forest roadless areas.[55]

Debating Wilderness in the Eastern National Forests

When Brock Evans arrived in Washington, D.C., in January 1973 to take the helm at the Sierra Club's national office, Stewart Brandborg met him at the airport. Confusion had beset the wilderness movement in the East, and Brandborg had come to talk. Both men knew that wilderness opportunities in the East were limited. Most of the Appalachian forests had been logged, farmed, and grazed in the previous century and although national forests such as the Jefferson, Pisgah, and Allegheny had begun to recover, little of it remained wild and roadless.[56] The confusion arose as the Forest Service began aggressively pushing its purity policies in the East, claiming that a history of logging and heavy visitation disqualified all eastern lands from wilderness protection. Several eastern Sierra Club chapters and members of its Wilderness Classification Committee were strong supporters of the agency's position. The Wilderness Society worried that with citizen support, the Forest Service might succeed in holding the line on its purity policies in the East. Driving into the city, Brandborg warned Evans that this was not really a debate about wilderness in the East; it was a debate about the future of wilderness in the West. In short, if the agency succeeded in establishing the purity policy, that precedent could limit the future expansion of the wilderness system nationwide.[57]

While the Sierra Club's roots are in the West, the Wilderness Society's are in the East. The Wilderness Society traces its roots to a mythical roadside meeting among a handful of its founders in the shadows of Tennessee's Great Smoky Mountains in 1934.[58] After the Wilderness Act passed, the Wilderness Society's staff fanned out across the nation to lay the framework for a citizens' campaign for the ten-year reviews. Brandborg and Merritt jumped the Mississippi and headed west. Rupert Cutler, however, loaded up his car and began canvassing the East. With the Wilderness Society's encouragement, local conservationists founded the West Virginia Highlands Conservancy in 1967.[59] Like the state itself, however, the conservancy was torn between locals and "outlanders" from Pittsburgh and Washington, D.C. Cutler, echoing Brandborg's philosophy, emphasized that "[o]ur primary concern is seeing that it is West Virginians who lead the campaign to preserve the wilderness areas and wild rivers of West Virginia."[60] In the 1960s, the threat of mountaintop removal coal mining, clear-cut logging, and scenic highways spurred interest in the West Virginia highlands. In the mid-1960s, with the Wilderness Society's encouragement, the conservancy gathered itself to push for wilderness protection for the Dolly Sods, Otter Creek, and Cranberry Glades—three roadless areas in the

Monongahela National Forest. And by 1970, the conservancy was joined by other groups pushing for wilderness in the East, in states such as Alabama, New Hampshire, Tennessee, and Virginia.

John McGuire, associate chief of the Forest Service, jump-started the debate over eastern wilderness in September 1971. Speaking before the Sierra Club's biennial wilderness conference, he addressed a wide range of issues: the agency's purity policies, its commitment to limiting wilderness recreation, its concerns about the roadless areas, and, lastly, the future of eastern wild lands. In the Forest Service's assessment, he announced, no wild lands in the East were eligible for wilderness protection. Instead, the Forest Service would establish an alternate system of eastern "wild areas."[61] The announcement came as a surprise, in part because it went against the precedents Congress had set with the Wilderness Society's support: in 1968 the Great Swamp had been designated in New Jersey, the National Park Service was actively reviewing Shenandoah and Great Smoky Mountains National Parks for wilderness designation, and, most important, the Forest Service already protected eastern wilderness areas. When the Wilderness Act became law, Shining Rock and Linville Gorge in North Carolina and Great Gulf in New Hampshire were among the fifty-four wilderness areas immediately added to the wilderness system. But for the Forest Service, the "wild areas" proposal was about more than wilderness in the East. As one regional forester explained, an alternate eastern "wild areas" system distinguished eastern wild lands from "the true wilderness areas found in the West."[62]

Few areas in the East seemed less likely for wilderness designation than the Dolly Sods in northeastern West Virginia. Unlike the rest of the Allegheny Mountains, which are forested, much of the Sods is open. A quilt of heaths and forest stands unfold across the hills. Despite appearances, glaciers did not sculpt this highland ecology. People did. In the nineteenth century, the Dolly Sods was covered with spruce trees that reached heights of sixty to ninety feet. Between 1879 and 1912, loggers leveled 85 percent of West Virginia's forests, including those at the Dolly Sods. The Forest Service purchased the land in 1916 and added it to the newly established Monongahela National Forest. But fire and cattle kept the saplings of a new forest from taking root and the land was used mainly for grazing. Then, during World War II, the Army included the Allegheny Highlands as part of the West Virginia Maneuver Area. The Dolly Sods was targeted for live artillery and mortar practice. Before turning the Sods back over to the Forest Service, explosive ordnance removal teams grid-searched the Sods and removed any unexploded bombs they could find. After the Army's departure, the Dolly Sods began to recover. Forests began to retake the open fields, the natural and human history became interwoven, and the Sods regained the outward appearance of wilderness. By the late 1950s, the Sods had become popular with backpackers. Unlike most areas in the East, the Sods' open landscape allowed backpackers to leave the trails behind. Yet, according to the Forest Service, the same qualities that made the Sods unique also disqualified it as wilderness. Drawing on arguments familiar from the West, the agency claimed that the Dolly Sods fell short of the Wilderness Act's standards: signs of human use marred the area's wilderness qualities and such small areas required strict management to protect them from overuse, even by backpackers.

As one observer soon put it: "[T]he sound and fury about wilderness has begun again—this time in the East."[63] During 1972, the wilderness community divided into two camps on eastern wilderness and, by extension, the Wilderness Society's pragmatic strategy for a national wilderness system. Following tactics consistent with the Sierra Club's Wilderness Classification Committee's manifesto, the Sierra Club was a cautious champion of the Forest Service's "wild areas" proposal in 1972. Michael McCloskey, along with Peter Borrelli and Jonathan Ela, met privately with the Forest Service in hopes of protecting the eastern national forests. "We all know there is comparatively little real wilderness east of the Mississippi," Borrelli reported. "What about those lands worth preserving that do not strictly qualify as wilderness under the Wilderness Act?"[64] Their collaboration gained legislative momentum when Senators George Aiken (R-VT) and Herman Talmadge (D-GA) introduced the "National Forest Wild Areas Act of 1972," which proposed an alternative system of eastern wild areas.

Within the Sierra Club, three questions shaped the debate over eastern wild lands. First was whether eastern lands with evidence of human history qualified for wilderness designation. Many within the Sierra Club took a narrow view of the potential for wilderness in the East. Francis Walcott, for one, was loathe to "insist on wilderness designation for [lands] which are really not that."[65] Many viewed an alternate system as either a more appropriate or an easier way to secure protection for the eastern national forests, which showed the scars of logging, grazing, and other human activities. Second was how the small, accessible eastern areas could accommodate a growing number of backpackers. The Great Gulf in New Hampshire, for example, was already crowded. Even though the wilderness area was indistinguishable from much of the wild land that surrounded it in the White Mountain National Forest, backpackers were seemingly drawn to it, as if a sign read, "Cross this Line and Your Feet Will Begin to Tingle."[66] Borrelli worried that "man's continuing impact" in the form of backpacking would preclude the recovery of eastern wild lands. He questioned whether "a barbed wire fence" would preserve the Pemigewasset, a roadless area popular with backpackers in New Hampshire.[67] The third question was whether the wild areas system could complement the wilderness system itself. Some Sierra Club staff and board members hoped that the wild areas system would serve as a stepping-stone for recovering wild lands that might later be designated wilderness.

The Wild Areas Act of 1972, which had been crafted with advice from the Sierra Club and the Forest Service, proposed a parallel system of wild areas, with similar protection as the wilderness system. In some respects, the legislation went further than the Wilderness Act, such as banning mining and grazing entirely. But, in other respects, it allowed the agency more discretion, such as installing designated campsites and permitting logging for watershed protection and wildlife habitat improvement. Most troubling for the Wilderness Society, the act explicitly noted that little land east of the Mississippi met the standards set forth in the Wilderness Act. Within the Sierra Club, Borrelli, the club's eastern representative, was the champion of wild areas legislation. In March 1972, he wrote, "at least at the top of the totem, [the Forest Service] is sincerely interested in the creation of a wild lands classification not as a means of getting around the Wilderness Act, but as a means of protecting many lands in the East that need immediate protection."[68] But Borrelli knew that not everyone agreed with his position. He acknowledged that another "camp is arguing that any cooperation with the Forest Service in developing a Wild Lands bill will be the death of the Wilderness Act in the East."[69] To the extent that the Sierra Club shaped and supported this proposal, the club flirted with a narrow conception of wilderness that not only threatened to preclude wilderness in the East, but also extended tacit support for the Forest Service's purity policies in the West.

That was precisely the Wilderness Society's concern. In an emergency 1972 mailer, the Wilderness Society urged conservationists: "Hold your reply to the Forest Service!" The agency's strategy in the East "is a threat to wilderness designation everywhere."[70] The Wilderness Society explained that the wild areas legislation posed several threats: It bolstered the Forest Service's "purity" policies; it called into question the eligibility of the millions of acres of roadless areas in the West; and it threatened to divide the wilderness system and its political support in half—separating the East and the West. In the summer of 1972, Ernest Dickerman, a Wilderness Society staffer and longtime advocate of eastern wilderness protection, championed the Wilderness Society's long-standing vision of a national wilderness system before Congress. He explained that Zahniser, the Wilderness Act's primary draftsman, "took care to frame a definition of wilderness which would include such wild lands, whether found in the East or the West, without geographical distinction."[71] Dickerman knew that few areas, even in the West, met the Forest Service's definition of "pristine" wilderness. The detritus of frontier history—mines, waterworks, cabins—littered existing and potential wilderness areas across the Rockies, the Sierras, and the rest of the West. Conceding the Forest Service's point in the East meant jeopardizing even more potential wilderness areas west of the Mississippi.[72] That was the crux of the issue for the Wilderness Society.

Doug Scott, the Wilderness Society staffer and skilled legislative draftsman who got his start at the Isle Royale wilderness review, gathered eleven citizen proposals for eastern wilderness areas that local wilderness organizations had developed, including the Dolly Sods, and compiled them into an alternate "Eastern Wilderness Areas Act." Senator Henry Jackson (D-WA), a longtime wilderness ally, introduced the legislation to add the eastern areas to the existing wilderness system in May 1972. Protecting these eastern areas—with their small size, heavy recreational pressure, and histories of human use—promised to strengthen the legislative precedents important to the Wilderness Society's pragmatic approach to wilderness. That strategy caught the attention of the timber industry. In the West, a member of the Society of American Foresters commented: "We recognize that any alteration in the Wilderness Act could result in an avalanche of requests to the Forest Service for minute wilderness areas throughout the Nation."[73]

The two competing bills—the wild areas legislation and the wilderness areas legislation—formed the poles of debate over eastern wilderness as Congress convened in January 1973. In preparation, the Wilderness Society worked feverishly to rally support for its pragmatic approach to eastern wilderness. After slow progress in Washington, D.C., in 1972, Scott and Dickerman made an unsurprising move for the Wilderness Society: they pitched their appeal directly to local wilderness supporters from across the East in the hopes of shifting the political balance within the conservation community. Unbeknownst to the Sierra Club's national leadership, Scott and Dickerman invited thirty state wilderness leaders, including volunteer Sierra Club leaders, to Knoxville, Tennessee, for a weekend-long briefing on eastern wilderness in December 1972. Dickerman, who was legendary for his skills as an organizer, explained in the invitation, "this will be a nuts-and-bolts, brass-tacks meeting."[74] Among the thirty volunteer delegates who arrived in Knoxville was Helen McGinnis, a Pittsburgh resident, West Virginia Highlands Conservancy member, Sierra Club member, and proponent of protection for the Dolly Sods. She took detailed notes on the Wilderness Society's presentation. For two days, the Wilderness Society's staff educated, cajoled, and empowered eastern wilderness leaders, explaining to them the pitfalls underlying the wild areas legislation. McGinnis summed up the Wilderness Society's message: "The Forest Service's main tactic is 'divide and conquer.'" The Wilderness Society urged unity about the pragmatic approach to wilderness it had championed since 1964.[75] It found eager allies.

The success of that meeting reflected the organization's growing skill in cultivating citizen support through a network of wilderness advocates nationwide. McCloskey soon received several letters from attendees, urging the Sierra Club to revisit its eastern wilderness policy. Shirley Taylor, from the club's Florida chapter, wrote McCloskey: "I am extremely concerned that the [Sierra Club's strategy] will fragment our big pitch to Congress for wilderness."[76] McGinnis complained that the club's newsletters sounded like Forest Service press releases. With legislative action pending on the two proposals, pressure on both the conservation community and the government built in early 1973. A shift toward consensus on eastern wilderness began to emerge after the Wilderness Society's Knoxville meeting. Brock Evans had arrived in Washington that January and, convinced by Brandborg's argument, he began to lobby within the Sierra Club itself. Late that month, the Sierra Club board met in San Francisco, where an acerbic debate over eastern wilderness spilled over into two days of deliberation. Parties within the Sierra Club most closely allied with the Wilderness Society prevailed, and the Sierra Club formally lined up behind the "Eastern Wilderness Areas Act of 1973."[77] The Forest Service, now faced with a unified wilderness advocacy community and under pressure from the White House to follow a policy consistent with the Department of the Interior, offered conditional support for an Eastern Wilderness Areas Act at congressional hearings in February 1973.[78] The legislation included twenty-eight tracts on eastern national forests—some based on proposals by local citizen organizations (including the Dolly Sods in West Virginia) and some based on the Forest Service's proposals for the wild areas legislation.

When the Forest Service finally offered its support for eastern wilderness, it did so on one condition: It asked Congress to amend the Wilderness Act of 1964 to explicitly limit "restored" wilderness to the East. The Forest Service's opposition to eastern wilderness hinged on a central disagreement over the legislative intent of the Wilderness Act. Richard Costley, the agency's chief of recreation, insisted that marginal lands, such as those in the East, could not be included in the wilderness system because "standards for wilderness classification and the standards for wilderness management must be the same. They cannot be different. They cannot be separated."[79] This was the reasoning the Forest Service first rolled out at the hearings on San Rafael in California in the mid-1960s. The agency believed that a single standard for designation and management was critical to ensuring the future management of the wilderness system. Dickerman and Scott, speaking for the Wilderness Society, took aim at precisely this facet of the Forest Service's argument. They explained: "It is part of the genius of the Wilderness Act that it embodies two quite separate sets of standards." One definition, section 2(c), provides a more permissive standard for designating a wilderness; a second definition, section 4(c), provides strict standards for managing wilderness once designated.[80] They argued that the Forest Service's purity standards and its stand on eastern wilderness conflated section 2(c) and section 4(c) of the act: in their words, the Forest Service had mistaken "the ideal concept of wilderness for the less austere, more practical definition set forth in the Wilderness Act."[81]

That argument was central to the Wilderness Society's pragmatic approach to the Wilderness Act. The organization championed both an expansive concept of which lands were eligible for wilderness protection and careful management of those lands once designated wilderness. In May 1974, after being delayed by the Watergate scandal in Congress, the Senate Agriculture and Interior Committees produced a new bill agreed upon by the two committees. It passed the Senate the same month. That fall, further debate in the House resulted in a slightly reduced bill, with sixteen new wilderness areas and seventeen new wilderness study areas.[82] With Congress preparing to adjourn, the Senate accepted the revised House version, which omitted the Forest Service's proposed amendment. President Gerald Ford signed the so-called "Eastern Wilderness Areas Act" into law on January 3, 1975, protecting sixteen new wilderness areas east of the Mississippi, including 10,215 acres of the Dolly Sods.[83] The timber industry's hopes that the wilderness reviews could be brought to a rapid end had run aground on the growing popularity of wilderness. It would have been dismayed had it known that these initial campaigns for national forest roadless areas would mushroom into much larger national campaigns for roadless areas in the late 1970s and the late 1990s.

"Woodcraft Becomes the Art of Using Gadgets"

"Where did all these damn backpackers come from?" asked a columnist in an early issue of *Backpacker* magazine.[84] In the decade after the Wilderness Act passed, visitation to the wilderness system more than doubled from three to seven million visitor days per year. Near Indian Peaks, a roadless area on the Rocky Mountain Front Range, visitors from Denver and Boulder squeezed their cars and vans into every square foot of the gravel parking lot. On the trail to Long Lake, an average of 250 people hiked in each summer day, leaving behind a trail wide enough for a jeep. After surveying the erosion in the area, one Forest Service researcher asked if it was time to give up and "Let the Bastards have it."[85] At Indian Peaks, Alpine Lakes, and elsewhere, the Forest Service had honed its purity arguments on the threat of recreational overuse in the late 1960s. It is a problem that the Forest Service still faces in the East, the Pacific Northwest, and, especially, the Colorado Front Range, where growing cities like Boulder, Denver, and Colorado Springs crowd up against the Rockies, and climbing the state's fourteeners is a favorite pastime. But today, just as in the 1960s, wilderness advocates often give priority to designating new areas, rather than emphasizing the management of existing areas—in the 1960s it was a strategy meant to cultivate the popularity of the wilderness system, especially with backpackers.

What it meant to visit wilderness began to change in the 1960s and 1970s. Before, a skilled outdoorsman prided himself on his skills with an axe: with it he could chop firewood, build a lean-to, and shelter himself from the elements. In the same years that concerns grew over the overuse of wilderness, the Sierra Club's Outing Committee began to formalize the ways backpackers could minimize the toll they took on wilderness. David Brower foreshadowed the change in the *Sierra Club Wilderness Handbook* in 1971: "There is a deep sense of satisfaction and achievement in the knowledge that one has traveled through an area without leaving perceptible traces." That was backpacking "in harmony with the spirit of wilderness."[86] As the Forest Service focused on its purity policies, arguing for small wilderness areas that could be managed to restrict recreational use, backpackers began to embrace a new wilderness recreation ethic—minimal-impact camping—that promised to protect wilderness from a new threat: themselves.

In the 1970s, a new genre of wilderness manuals such as Harvey Manning's *Backpacking, One Step at a Time* (1972), Paul Petzoldt's *The Wilderness Hand-*

book (1974), and John Hart's *Walking Softly in the Wilderness* (1977) aimed to reeducate wilderness visitors. The new hiking guides replaced sections on old campcraft, such as building lean-tos, trapping, and hunting, with instructions for selecting minimal-impact campsites, slowing trail erosion, and traveling as discreetly as possible. Hart explained the backpacker's new challenge and reward: it is "quite something . . . to know that you might have harmed a place and that you did not."[87] But there was a catch to this new recreation ethic. To go lightly in wilderness meant carrying backpacks filled with the right kind of gear: Portable stoves replaced campfires. Foam pads replaced beds of grass or tree boughs. Nylon tents replaced lean-tos and heavy canvas tents. And clothes made of polypropylene and laminated fabrics, such as Gore-Tex®, became the backpacker's uniform.[88] By the mid-1970s, outfitting backpackers was becoming big business. Major outdoor businesses founded in these years included Sierra Designs (1965), The North Face (1966), Lowe Alpine (1967), Mountain Safety Research (1969), Patagonia (1972), and Marmot (1974).

By the mid-1970s, sophisticated marketing campaigns for outdoor gear were sweeping across the pages of the backpacking magazines and journals. Full-page color ads framed outdoor gear and models against snow-covered mountain peaks, serene lakes, and streamside camps—the iconography of wilderness—advertising a seemingly endless array of outdoor gear. *Backpacker* magazine, founded in 1973, prided itself on a commitment to "spread the new ethic of clean, environmentally aware camping and hiking," but reviews of gear quickly became its best-known feature and manufacturers' advertisements provided a major source of revenue.[89] As the wilderness movement gained steam and wilderness recreation gained popularity, wilderness did not divide so neatly along lines separating corporate interests and idealistic preservationists. In 1975, backpacking retailer Recreational Equipment Incorporated (REI), based in Seattle, Washington, testified in support of the Alpine Lakes wilderness area. Jim Whittaker, general manager, explained that the area was "essential to protect the open space necessary to meet the twenty-five percent annual growth we have in this business."[90] It was the beginning of REI's corporate participation in wilderness politics.

This new wilderness recreation ethic was an important component of the pragmatic and popular approach to wilderness that was at the heart of the Wilderness Society's and, by the early 1970s, the Sierra Club's agenda. Until the late 1960s, both organizations supported caps on wilderness visitation as a necessary tool for protecting the new wilderness system. On some small wildlife refuges and in some national parks, such controls were readily

3.2 In the 1960s and 1970s, The North Face, Patagonia, and Sierra Designs, along with other companies, began manufacturing and selling a wide range of outdoor gear aimed specifically at hikers and backpackers. Synthetic fabrics, such as Gore-Tex®, became an important part of the well-equipped backpacker's uniform. Source: *Backpacker*, August 1977. Courtesy W. L. Gore & Associates.

accepted. But wilderness leaders were concerned that blanket restrictions would weaken enthusiasm for wilderness among outdoor recreationists. Richard Sill, a member of the board of directors of the Sierra Club, warned "if restrictive permits are adopted . . . many of the present supporters of wilderness—particularly the recreationists—will turn against wilderness entirely."[91] In the early 1970s, both organizations clarified their policies in light of the new recreation ethic. Brandborg noted on a draft management policy: "Controls should be as flexible as possible to permit maximum freedom;

dispersal of users should be encouraged; rationing: adopt politically acceptable forms." He emphasized, "carrying capacity should be *increased*" by "training users in wilderness use to reduce impact."[92] All told, as part of a politically viable approach to wilderness, wilderness leaders hoped many more backpackers, if properly educated, could visit wilderness, "before we reach the ecological carrying capacity of intelligent use."[93] In turn, the Sierra Club and Wilderness Society hoped they would file out of the woods ready to champion wilderness.

Wilderness and the "New" Environmentalism

This pragmatic approach made clear some of the answers the Wilderness Society failed to offer in response to Theodore Kaczynski's 1969 letter. Despite the Wilderness Society's cursory response to Kaczynski, the organization was keenly aware of the expanding agenda of environmental issues and increasingly uncertain about how best to position itself amid the changing political and social currents in late-1960s America. In the fall of 1969, the cover of *The Living Wilderness* featured a political cartoon depicting environmental mayhem: forest fires, stream pollution, tankers, atom bombs, and pesticides swirled together in a vortex that led toward unsuspecting people and human deaths.[94] It was a sobering illustration for a magazine—and an organization—that more often focused on concerns for wilderness and wildlife. In private discussions, the Wilderness Society's Governing Council stood back and tried to make sense of wilderness in a new environmental era. As one of its council members asked, what was the place of wilderness in a world now shaped by the "bomb," the "atom," and "space"?[95] Did the Wilderness Society need to actively broaden its constituency, connecting with "trade union and farm groups, women's groups, church groups, and various others"?[96] Had it "been 'fervently' concerned with the preservation of wilderness to the exclusion of all other concerns"?[97] Did the Wilderness Society need to fashion itself as a new "environmental organization"?[98]

These questions gained new urgency in 1970. Environmentalists and historians alike have long pointed to the first Earth Day on April 22, 1970, as the symbolic start of the modern American environmental movement. Earth Day was an exceptional event. Millions of Americans took part in rallies, protests, sit-ins, stream cleanups, hikes, and walks on college campuses, in local communities, at state capitols, and in Washington, D.C. Never before had so many Americans joined together to express their concern about issues such as air and water pollution at home, population growth worldwide, the destructive war in Vietnam, and the future of the American parks, rivers, cities, and wilder-

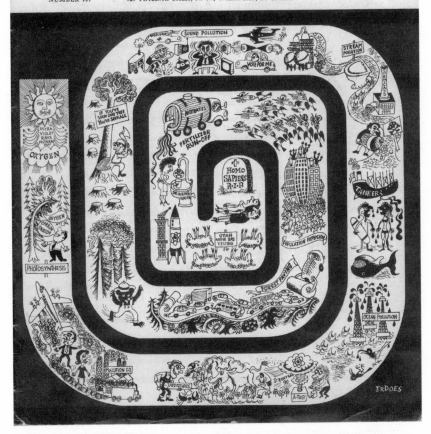

3.3 In the year leading up to Earth Day in 1970, the Wilderness Society's Governing Council engaged in a sustained discussion over the relationship between wilderness and the emerging environmental movement. This cover of *The Living Wilderness*, the Wilderness Society's magazine, captures the scope of the issues discussed. Autumn 1969. Courtesy the Wilderness Society.

ness. So much concern and excitement surrounded Earth Day that even Congress recessed for the day and hundreds of congressional representatives and government officials addressed gatherings from coast to coast. In the words of its student organizers, it was the moment when "a generation dedicated itself to reclaiming the planet."[99] Earth Day was conceived of by Gaylord Nelson, a liberal Democratic senator from Wisconsin; organized by a team of students led by Denis Hayes, a Harvard Law School student; and modeled on the anti-war teach-ins on college campuses. It aimed to harness the social activism and political protest of the 1960s to a new cause: saving the Earth.

Earth Day marked the culmination of a series of high-profile events that thrust environmental concerns onto the front pages of newspapers. In 1968, scientist Paul Ehrlich published *The Population Bomb* and focused attention on the prospect that a rapidly expanding world population could exhaust its resource base. In January 1969, an oil well burst off the coast of California, spilling three million gallons of crude oil into the Pacific Ocean and soiling the coast around Santa Barbara, California. Later that year, the polluted Cuyahoga River caught fire in Cleveland, sending flames five stories into the air. Reports surfaced that the United States was using chemicals to defoliate the tropical forests of Vietnam. And in the fall of 1969 the United Nations convened a conference in San Francisco ominously titled: "Man and His Environment: A View towards Survival." A sense of crisis amplified the concerns for the environment that had been building during the 1960s, and gave new meaning to the work of protecting wilderness. The Wilderness Society reported on these events in *The Living Wilderness*. Doug Scott, still a graduate student at the time, became the organization's liaison to the Earth Day organizational committee.[100] The Wilderness Society provided support to some of the emerging student groups. One of these, ECOS at the University of North Carolina, warned in *The Living Wilderness* that "a crisis exists which endangers the future of America, of mankind, and of life itself." ECOS proposed "a fresh ethical response to the environment; a self-sustaining way of life in which man views himself as part of and dependent upon the natural ecosystem."[101]

A growing popular awareness of the science of ecology also contributed to the changing appreciation for wilderness and the environment. Basic assumptions informed the public's view of how nature worked. Barry Commoner, the "Paul Revere of Ecology," boiled these assumptions down to four "laws of ecology": 1) everything is connected to everything else; 2) everything must go somewhere; 3) nature knows best; and 4) there is no such thing as a free lunch. Taken together, the four laws affirmed one general premise: a rapidly growing, technologically sophisticated, modern society threatened to disrupt the harmonious, interconnected, and cyclical processes that governed the natural world.[102] As Rachel Carson suggested in *Silent Spring*, nature had always been a dynamic and changing web of life. But where before those changes took place over millennia, now it seemed that the rapid pace of modernity threatened to tear the fabric of life apart in a matter of years.[103] As one ecologist explained in *The Living Wilderness*, "we, too, are a part of the total systems of living and non-living things, and . . . a thorough knowledge of the functioning of our house, or environment, is fundamental to our survival."[104] This holism ran like a powerful current through the rhetoric on Earth Day, as speakers emphasized the need to protect the "whole society," the "whole earth," and the "total environment."[105] In the late 1960s, when political concerns often centered on the individual, identity, and political rights, this preoccupation with "holism" in environmentalism ran counter to political trends.

On Earth Day, as never before, it seemed a new environmental movement was poised to emerge as a social movement with broad ambitions to reform American political, economic, and cultural life. Self-proclaimed "environmental vigilantes" dumped oil in the reflecting pool at Standard Oil of California's corporate offices. Activists in Indiana blocked offending sewage pipes with concrete. The counterculture, back-to-the-land movements, and recycling initiatives all advanced critiques of the modern consumer economy. And speakers across the nation drew on the charged rhetoric of the 1960s, challenging the "ecological catastrophe" in Vietnam, questioning "corporate irresponsibility," and weaving together a decade of concerns—"racial injustice, war, urban blight and environmental rape have a common denominator in our exploitative economic system."[106] Drawing on the radical critiques of liberalism and the government that coursed through other social movements in the late 1960s, many activists claimed a revolution based on the platform of ecology was an imperative. One college professor argued in his Earth Day speech that a politically effective ecological movement "will be radical in nature, because the solutions of the problem require revolutionary changes in social, economic, and political institutions." Even politicians spoke of the need for "fundamental changes in [the nation's] economic habits, social values, and national priorities."[107] And some argued that the revolution had to be centered on the individual: "Each person must become ecologically responsible—not only as a consumer of the planet's resources, but as a procreator of its most prolific species."[108]

What did it mean to protect wilderness in light of the modern environmental crisis? In late 1969 and early 1970, the Wilderness Society's Governing Council actively set about trying to revise the organization's mission statement, which it had always published on the back cover of *The Living Wilderness*. Some on the council argued that the Wilderness Society needed to cultivate a broader membership, seek outside funding, and reposition the organization to address a wide range of issues, including population growth, pollution, and "the well-being of mankind in general."[109] Several council members, while sympathetic to such concerns, noted that they were unsure of what it meant to be an "environmental organization" and what productive policy position the Wilderness Society could take on issues such as "population."[110] Notably, no one argued that wilderness was the most pressing problem facing society or that it was a cure-all for larger problems. But many on the council emphasized that the Wilderness Society might be most effective if it maintained its focus on wilderness, where there was still much work to be done.[111] In the end, there was no clear resolution. Instead of revising the mission statement, the council removed the statement from its magazine altogether.

What never merited serious discussion within the Wilderness Society was whether wilderness should be refashioned as a radical challenge to the political system, the economy, or American culture and life. In these years, the Wilderness Society made many small decisions that helped keep the organization on a more moderate and pragmatic political path. Although many at the Wilderness Society saw wilderness as important to protecting endangered species, wildlife habitat, and, as Mardy Murie argued in 1970, a way to recognize the "rights of nature," the organization never took any formal stand on the intrinsic value of wilderness or made the "rights of nature" a centerpiece of its mission or its policies.[112] Although many at the Wilderness Society knew that recreational overuse could pose a threat to wilderness, the Wilderness Society actively supported programs and policies that fostered the popularity of wilderness and cultivated the support of backpackers.[113] The Wilderness Society even began to sell patches, mugs, and other hiking-related memorabilia to its members. And although some at the Wilderness Society sympathized with the radical protests of the late 1960s and supported Earth Day activities, no one ever broached the possibility of abandoning Brandborg's commitment to legislative activism in favor of more radical strategies. This faith in the value of wilderness for nature and for people and the workings of the political system were deeply rooted at the Wilderness Society. Despite the turmoil of the late 1960s and early 1970s, that faith would transcend the social ambitions of Earth Day and define the Wilderness Society's work into the 1970s.

Conclusion

The debates over wilderness in these years reveal the beginnings of more radical ideas important to wilderness and American environmental politics. The philosophy that underlaid the Sierra Club's Wilderness Classification Committee and the urgency with which some activists pushed for wilderness as a bulwark against the ills of the modern world tapped into powerful currents of discontent in the late 1960s and early 1970s. They drew on the apocalyptic strains of modern environmental thought that ran through works such as Rachel Carson's *Silent Spring*, Paul Ehrlich's *The Population Bomb*, and Barry Commoner's *The Closing Circle* and gained popular attention on Earth Day. But in the view of the wilderness movement's leadership, the future of the wilderness system depended foremost on cultivating a broad base of popular support for wilderness and maintaining their ability to build political coalitions and advance legislation in Congress. Challenging the recreational use of wild lands, the consumer economy, or the nation's commitment to progress by aligning wilderness activism more closely with the radicalism of the 1960s and 1970s all threatened, rather than bolstered, that mainstream strategy. Wilderness, for the Wilderness Society, the Sierra Club, and a growing portion of the wilderness community, was a pragmatic tool for protecting the nation's federal lands, not an ideological challenge to the American way of life. In the face of "over-population," "over-industrialization," and cancerous technology, all of which troubled Kaczynski, the wilderness movement began to position itself in an uncomfortable alliance with the forces of consumerism that Kaczynski and others, of saner minds and methods, worried might ultimately destroy it.[114] The radical concerns for wilderness that first emerged around Earth Day in 1970 did not disappear, however. Instead, different people with similar concerns would reshape wilderness politics in the early 1980s under another banner: Earth First!.

4 / NEW ENVIRONMENTAL TOOLS FOR AN OLD CONSERVATION ISSUE

I n the fall of 1971, Michael McCloskey took the podium at the Sierra Club's Twelfth Biennial Wilderness Conference. It was the first time the prestigious gathering had been held east of the Mississippi. For three days, hundreds of professional conservationists, government employees, congressional staffers, and citizen activists convened in the fancy halls of the Washington Hilton Hotel, not far from Capitol Hill. The theme of the conference was "Action for Wilderness," but McCloskey, the Sierra Club's executive director, had come to ask, "Is the Wilderness Act working?"[1] His answer was no. Despite the swell of citizen activism across the nation, the booming interest in wilderness recreation, and a growing environmental movement, McCloskey described the wilderness movement as at a "crossroads." He warned: "the movement to save America's surviving wilderness is in decline at the very moment that enthusiasm for the environment has reached an all-time high."[2]

The most immediate problem was the slow progress expanding the wilderness system. In 1971, seven years into the ten-year reviews, Congress had added only 33 of 179 potential areas to the wilderness system. Together, they amounted to 1.4 million acres, a small fraction of the 53 million acres scheduled for review. In public, McCloskey blamed the "agonizingly slow pace" of the ten-year reviews on the long process of reviews, hearings, and legislative action Congress required for each area.[3] But, in private, McCloskey faulted Stewart Brandborg's citizen-oriented and pragmatic strategy for the Wilderness Act.[4] Where Brandborg saw each new wilderness area, such as San Rafael, Isle Royale, and Great Swamp, as setting important precedents for an expansive wilderness system, McCloskey saw nit-picking over minor boundaries that slowed the review process. Where Brandborg saw a citizens' movement that empowered individuals, McCloskey saw a tediously slow and inefficient process that would "exhaust" the wilderness movement's "energies."[5] And where Brandborg saw an increasingly pragmatic and coherent approach to wilderness

designation, McCloskey saw a movement increasingly devoid of "any momentum and unity of focus."[6]

Behind those specific concerns, McCloskey had grander visions for the
future of wilderness. By 1971, the future of the "roadless areas" had taken
center stage in discussions of wilderness politics. Initially, when wilderness
advocates discussed roadless areas, they referred specifically to places like
the Alpine Lakes and the Dolly Sods, which were outside the scope of the
Forest Service's ten-year reviews. But events in the early 1970s thrust a much
broader set of roadless areas to the forefront of wilderness politics. Wilderness advocates began to work actively to expand the wilderness reviews
beyond the initial ten-year reviews to include all eligible public lands managed by the federal land agencies: the vast expanses of Alaska, from its coastal
rainforests to the steppes of the Arctic coastal plain; the national forest land
that remained roadless and undeveloped nationwide; and the public domain
overseen by the Bureau of Land Management (BLM), which stretched from
the mountainous deserts of California to the canyon country of Utah to the
sagebrush country of eastern Oregon. The wilderness movement had deferred
efforts to protect these lands in the 1960s for fear of antagonizing western
politicians and the resource industries. Many advocates hoped to press their
political advantage in the wake of Earth Day.

McCloskey was unsure how well that strategy would work. As he put it in
1971, "in the context of the new environmental movement"—one preoccupied
with pollution, population, and pesticides—"wilderness preservation appears
to many as parochial and old-fashioned."[7] McCloskey was a careful observer of
the changing landscape of American environmental politics in the afterglow
of the inaugural Earth Day. He sensed that the surge of popular interest and
environmental legislation had changed both the issues and the strategies at the
heart of American environmentalism. McCloskey saw the wilderness movement as a whole, and the Sierra Club in particular, poised between a past rooted
in the conservation movement and a future hitched to the rising star of American environmentalism. He questioned if "the new environmental enthusiasts
would rally to another major campaign to save America's wilderness."[8] But
Stewart Brandborg read the events surrounding Earth Day differently. In the
early 1970s, Brandborg saw the emerging environmental movement as a catalyst for the Wilderness Society's citizen campaigns for wilderness. He remained
steadfast in his focus on citizen activism and wilderness protection.

Neither McCloskey nor Brandborg could anticipate fully the opportunities or challenges of these years. In light of the new environmental movement,

4.1 Mike McCloskey, executive director of the Sierra Club, speaking with Frances Gendlin, editor of the club's magazine. Photograph by Tim Thompson, ca. 1975. Courtesy Sierra Club Library.

McCloskey firmly believed that the wilderness movement needed to "regroup and devise new strategy" if it was to successfully advance its campaigns.[9] In addition to education and citizen lobbying, he called for more professional strategies—such as more efficient legislative packages and legal suits—that could both protect more wilderness and allow time for addressing other environmental issues. The Sierra Club began to aggressively take advantage of the new laws and legal strategies important to the emerging environmental movement to expand the wilderness reviews beyond the initial ten-year reviews to include other roadless areas. The Wilderness Society began to adopt new strategies too, particularly in the coming campaign for Alaska, but for Stewart Brandborg, the most important strategy for wilderness advocacy was an approach that joined citizen activists and the Wilderness Society in a cooperative effort. As the ten-year reviews came to a close in the early 1970s, he redoubled the Wilderness Society's commitment to making citizen activism a centerpiece in efforts to consolidate a broad set of legislative precedents for the future of the wilderness system. Working in parallel, these two leaders and their organizations would lay the groundwork in the mid-1970s for the wilderness movement's successes into the 1980s and 1990s. As these changing currents of environmental politics gave the Sierra Club an increasingly central role in the wilderness movement, however, they would ultimately plunge the Wilderness Society and Stewart Brandborg into crisis.

New Tools for an Old Issue

On January 1, 1970, President Richard Nixon signed the National Environmental Policy Act (NEPA), kicking off what became known as the "environmental decade."[10] That little-known law was the first of a burst of legislative activity that expanded the federal government's responsibility for environmental protection. Never before had Congress acted with such speed or commitment to address environmental concerns. Between 1969 and 1973, Congress emerged as a driving engine behind environmental reform, led by Senators Henry Jackson (D-WA) and Edmund Muskie (D-ME). In its first term, the Nixon administration also moved quickly to make the environment a key component of its domestic agenda. It was a unique moment in the political history of American environmentalism. A Democratic Congress and a Republican White House competed for leadership to advance the most far-reaching and comprehensive legislation to address environmental reform.[11]

Building on the earlier environmental initiatives of the Great Society, Congress enacted what have become the basic laws important to the nation's federal environmental regulatory system. The National Environmental Policy Act (1969) promised new consideration for environmental issues in federal decision-making; a revised Clean Air Act (1970) set tighter standards for utility and auto emissions; a revised Clean Water Act (1973) aimed to bring a new measure of health to the nation's rivers, bays, and estuaries; and the Endangered Species Act (1973) charged the federal government with protecting species from extinction. Most important, the government gained new powers of enforcement. In July 1970, President Nixon established the Environmental Protection Agency to oversee and coordinate much of this activity. Of all the environmental laws, NEPA became the linchpin in the new environmental regulatory framework. Congress described NEPA not as a response to an earlier generation of conservation issues, but as a response to new issues such as "population growth, high-density urbanization, industrial expansion, resource exploitation, and new and expanding technological advances."[12]

No one saw NEPA as a Trojan horse that would carry environmental concerns into a central place in the federal government's activities. In the Nixon

White House, the legislation seemed most significant because it required the creation of a three-person Council of Environmental Quality to advise the president. Newspapers reported on the new law as if it were yet another anti-pollution measure, much like those of the Great Society. In Congress, the popular legislation faced little opposition from industry or other stakeholders; it was an easy "yes" vote. Few observers paid attention to Section 102. It turned out to be the Trojan horse. Before NEPA, the federal government had few obligations to consider the environmental ramifications of road-building, power plant siting, dam construction, or other such activities. The National Environmental Policy Act changed that. Section 102 required a detailed environmental impact statement for any activity undertaken, permitted, or funded by the federal government that had significant environmental consequences. To meet NEPA's procedural requirements, the agency had to undertake an interdisciplinary analysis, document the potential environmental consequences, consider alternatives, undertake consultation with local and state governments and federal agencies, and engage the public in the process through hearings and comment periods.[13] It was an unprecedented tool for citizens to monitor and affect the federal government's activities.

The National Environmental Policy Act was part of a revolution in environmental law. Before the mid-1960s, most environmental lawsuits rested on common law or international treaties (such as those to protect wildlife). The problem with common-law suits was that the plaintiff had to be directly affected by the nuisance, whether it was pollution, logging, or a new road. That meant that concerned citizens or environmental groups in Washington, D.C., had no standing to sue the government for building a road in a western national forest, unless they happened to own property nearby. The National Environmental Policy Act was one of many laws that gave environmentalists new standing in the federal courts. Plaintiffs could challenge the government for failure to observe, implement, or follow new environmental laws, such as NEPA. That opened up what would become an increasingly important pathway for policy reform and intervention—judicial appeal—and the courts played by a very different set of rules than did Congress. Appeals turned on legal expertise, the quality of the argument and evidence, and the rulings of a judge or a panel of judges, not constituent mobilization, interest-group lobbying, or, in theory, political considerations, as was the case in Congress.[14]

If anyone could claim to be the architect of the new legal strategies, it was a suite of new environmental organizations, led by the Environmental Defense Fund and its scientists, the Natural Resources Defense Council (NRDC) and its lawyers, and the Sierra Club Legal Defense Fund (now Earthjustice), a spin-off of the Sierra Club, which McCloskey was instrumental in creating. In the early 1970s, these groups used NEPA to challenge a range of government activities, including siting nuclear power plants, auctioning oil and gas leases, and permitting pesticide application programs. Issues that once had been matters of energy policy, civil engineering, and agricultural policy were now "environmental" issues too. *Science* magazine described the resulting legal victories as "stunning."[15] By the mid-1970s, these legal strategies raised concerns about an environmental movement that might be too effective. It began to seem that way inside the Nixon White House. As one advisor noted privately, "our batting average" against the NEPA lawsuits "has been dismal." One of those lawsuits was described as the "kingpin"—the suit against the Trans-Alaska Pipeline.[16]

Wilderness advocates harnessed NEPA to protect the future of the public lands in the early 1970s. The most pressing concern was the roadless areas. Since the mid-1960s, wilderness advocates had successfully pursued protection for some roadless areas, such as the Alpine Lakes and the Dolly Sods, on a case-by-case basis. But in the 1960s, those efforts moved slowly through the agencies and Congress, reflecting the inefficient strategy McCloskey believed was exhausting the wilderness movement. In the early 1970s, wilderness advocates turned to Congress and the courts to secure three new public land reviews that became a focal point of American environmental politics in the late 1970s and 1980s: the national interest lands in Alaska, the national forest roadless areas, and the BLM public domain. But unlike the initial set of ten-year reviews, which included only public lands that already enjoyed protection as primitive areas, parks, or refuges, these roadless areas included a much larger set of lands, many of which the states and industry eyed for logging, energy exploration, and other activities. As the promise of wilderness swelled in the 1970s, the wilderness movement would begin to run up against the growing opposition of the timber, mining, and grazing interests and their allies in the rural West.

The Trans-Alaska Pipeline and the Future of Alaska

The vast landscape of the Alaskan wilderness dwarfs anything in the lower forty-eight. All told, the state measures three times the size of California. Where Alaska hugs the northern Pacific Ocean, its lowlands and islands are a coastal habitat rich in wildlife and forests. The center of the state is dominated by the Alaska Range, where the nation's highest peak, Mount McKinley, rises, its glacier-clad shoulders towering above the flatlands of central Alaska.

Three hundred miles to the north, the Brooks Range runs like a crown from east to west across Alaska's northern brow. Between these ranges is a wide-open landscape of tundra, broad river basins, foothills, and interior plains. These wild lands gave birth to some of the wilderness movement's greatest ambitions. Alaska occupied a central place in the lore of the wilderness movement: it had been explored by John Muir and Bob Marshall and by Mardy and Olaus Murie, pioneering wildlife biologists and leaders at the Wilderness Society who urged protection for the Arctic National Wildlife Range. But for most Americans, Alaska remained a mystery. What made Alaska exceptional also posed new challenges for the wilderness movement. Its remoteness meant that it was little known, and the best hope for the future of Alaska's public lands was to make it an issue of national importance.

In June 1968, the public announcement of oil under Alaska's northern coast put the nation's forty-ninth state on the nation's front pages. Petroleum engineers had struck oil on the remote expanse of the North Slope near Prudhoe Bay the previous February. Within months, engineers realized that the new oil field matched Alaska's vast scale. At an estimated 9.6 billion barrels, it was the largest oil field yet discovered in North America.[17] In 1969, a consortium of petroleum companies began making plans for a pipeline to link the northern oil fields at Prudhoe Bay with the southerly port of Valdez. They planned for a forty-eight–inch diameter pipeline that would snake its way across the Arctic tundra, over the Brooks, Alaska, and Chugach ranges, and down to Valdez's ice-free port—789 miles from well to tanker.[18] The project's trim geometry evoked a century of civil engineering accomplishments in American history: the trans-continental railroads, the grand dams of the American West, and the streamlined federal interstate highway system. Boosters expected the federal government to give its stamp of approval to this project as well. But along with the oil, long-standing questions about the future of Alaska, the indigenous people who lived there, and the state's wild lands welled up too.

The discovery of oil telescoped a process of land selection that had taken a century in the lower forty-eight into a decade in Alaska.[19] The state did not gain statehood until 1959, and 97 percent of its land was still managed by the federal government. Nineteen percent of its population was native Indians, Inupiat, or Aleut. And, in the 1960s, ownership of Alaska's lands remained a complicated issue. The state of Alaska had rights to select 103.5 million acres of federal land; it gained those rights in its statehood act. In 1971, Alaska's Natives gained the right to claim 44 million acres of land in the Alaska Native Claims Settlement Act of 1971 (ANCSA), along with a one-billion-dollar settlement. Envi-

ronmentalists successfully lobbied Congress to protect up to 80 million acres
of land in the "national interest"; that provision was also part of ANCSA and
the "national interest" lands were to be managed by the National Park Service,
Fish and Wildlife Service, and Forest Service.[20] Sorting out who got what land,
however, became a tortuous process that would play out between 1973 and 1980.
For the state government, it was about oil, resources, and economic growth. For
some Natives, it was about the same; for others, it was about access to land for
hunting, fishing, and their subsistence way of life. For wilderness advocates, it
was the best chance to protect the unparalleled scenic and ecological values of
Alaska's wild lands.[21]

Alaska was a high priority on Nixon's domestic agenda in 1970. The outgoing Johnson administration had put a land freeze in place on Alaska's public
lands, pending resolution of Native claims. As a result of the surge of popular
concern for the environment surrounding Earth Day, the White House realized
that environmentalists had a seat at the table in discussions over Alaska's future.
One Nixon advisor warned if they did not, "we have [political] troubles we cannot live with, at least south of Alaska."[22] But while Nixon saw environmental
protection as good politics, he would not allow it to interfere with the nation's
commitment to economic growth and energy development—a position that
grew stronger as the world petroleum market grew more volatile in the early
1970s. He supported the environmentalists' proposal for protecting "national
interest" lands only insofar as that support would help settle the questions
about land ownership in Alaska, lift the land freeze, and pave the way for the
pipeline. Rogers Morton, chair of the Republican National Committee, emphasized the pipeline's political importance in a private briefing with the president.
"Great economic power and big money" hung in the balance in Alaska, Morton
explained. Supporting the pipeline now meant "control[ling] the political balance [in Alaska] for a long time in the future because of the tremendous money
that will flow through their state government."[23] In 1970 the Nixon administration made every effort to expedite the pipeline, first appointing Alaska governor
Walter Hickel secretary of the interior and, later, appointing Morton secretary
of the interior, in which capacity they oversaw the pipeline proposal.

"How on earth could we ever stand up against all the might and power of
the oil industries, which literally run the world?" asked Brock Evans in 1969.[24]
In 1970, just as the petroleum industry prepared to start construction on the
pipeline, wilderness advocates used new legal tools to answer Evans' question.
Following on efforts by Alaskan Natives, who feared the pipeline right-of-way
threatened their villages, the Wilderness Society, Friends of the Earth, and the

Environmental Defense Fund filed suit in federal court in March 1970, arguing the Trans-Alaska Pipeline project violated the Mineral Leasing Act of 1920 and NEPA.[25] A federal judge issued an injunction on twenty miles of the route in response to the Native suit in April 1970. Two weeks later, the same judge ruled that national wilderness groups did have legal standing to sue, that the entire project violated the Mineral Leasing Act (the requested right-of-way for the pipeline was twice as wide as allowed by the 1920 law), and that the Department of the Interior had to meet NEPA's requirements for an "environmental impact statement" (the department's initial eight-page statement was ruled insufficient) before permitting the pipeline.[26] This was the lawsuit the Nixon administration described as the "kingpin" of NEPA lawsuits.[27] To wilderness advocates, it exemplified the new leverage the legal pathway provided in shaping public policy.

The National Environmental Policy Act forced an exacting review of the pipeline's potential environmental effects. Between 1971 and 1973, the Department of the Interior released detailed assessments of the potential problems and mitigation strategies for the 800-mile pipeline: safety valves, earthquake engineering, and revegetation plans aimed to reduce the pipeline's impact on the Arctic environment; elevating the pipeline was intended to stop the hot-oil pipeline from melting the Arctic permafrost, but at the risk of impeding wildlife migration; and safety precautions and clean-up plans would protect Prince William Sound at Valdez from oil spills. Public hearings in Anchorage and Washington, D.C., drew hundreds of concerned citizens. In December 1971, a federal appeals court ruled that NEPA also required consideration of alternatives. The most viable alternative was routing the pipeline through Canada toward the Midwest—a possibility many environmentalists preferred. This route, although longer, had the advantages of being an all-land route that avoided the risk of oil spills from oceangoing oil tankers and of supplying petroleum directly to the populous Midwest.[28] The Department of the Interior, however, never fully considered that alternative. The state of Alaska feared a Canadian route would diminish its financial gains from the project. The petroleum industry worried involving Canada would introduce additional delays. By 1972, the Department of the Interior had produced a nine-volume environmental impact statement in hopes of satisfying NEPA. Even the environmentalists' strongest ally in the Nixon White House complained about the "fantastically detailed" environmental impact statement necessary to get through the "minefield of environmentalists' lawsuits."[29] Yet, neither the environmental nor the scientific community considered the statement sufficient.[30]

4.2 The Trans-Alaska Pipeline approaching the South Fork of the Koyukuk River, Alaska. Photograph by Steve McCutcheon, ca. 1975. Courtesy Alyeska Pipeline Corporation and Anchorage Museum at Rasmuson Center.

In 1973, international events overtook the domestic debate on the pipeline and short-circuited wilderness advocates' legal strategy. A year earlier, the court had ruled in favor of the Department of the Interior on both granting the right-of-way under the Mineral Leasing Act and the sufficiency of the environmental impact statement. But the first decision was overturned on appeal in February 1973 and, most importantly, the federal appeals court refused to rule on the adequacy of the environmental impact statement. For the pipeline to proceed, it would need congressional legislation exempting it from both laws. A falling stock market, the Watergate scandal, and concerns over an impending oil shortage weakened the economy that spring. Facing an economic downturn, Congress grasped at projects already in the wings to strengthen the economy. The pipeline topped the list. On July 17, 1973, the Senate narrowly voted

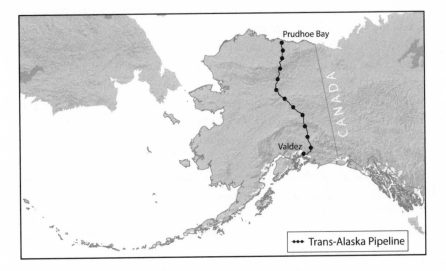

Map 4.1 The Trans-Alaska Pipeline transports oil 800 miles from Prudhoe Bay on the North Slope to the ice-free port of Valdez on the Prince William Sound, where the oil is loaded onto tankers. Operations began in 1977.

to exempt the pipeline from NEPA's requirements. That fall, the Yom Kippur War between Israel and Egypt broke out in the Middle East. When the United States supported Israel, the Organization of Petroleum Exporting Countries embargoed petroleum exports to the United States. By the end of 1973, the price of oil had jumped from three to over eleven dollars per barrel. That November, the pipeline received its final legislative approval and President Nixon billed it a part of a new "Project Independence" that would ensure the United States' energy independence.[31] The Trans-Alaska Pipeline was a go. Contractors began construction on the pipeline in 1974 and completed it three years later. Since then, it has carried approximately one-fifth of domestic petroleum production, and, in 2001, it provided one in every twenty barrels of crude oil consumed in the United States.

The Trans-Alaska Pipeline debate had important consequences for the future of the wilderness movement. The Wilderness Society funded much of the environmental movement's opposition to the pipeline, both legal and otherwise. That commitment strained the organization's finances, and contributed significantly to growing financial problems that would undermine Brandborg's leadership and the Wilderness Society's work on the Wilderness Act. Growing tensions between Brandborg and his staff would erupt in crisis in the summer of 1975. Despite those challenges, wilderness advocates had succeeded in questioning, challenging, and improving—although not stopping—the Trans-Alaska Pipeline. One of their greatest fears, an oil spill in Prince William Sound, would come to pass on March 24, 1989, when the Exxon *Valdez* ran aground, spilling 257,000 barrels of oil into the sound. Finally, the environmentalists had been able to use their new political and legal clout to secure the "national interest" provision in the Alaska Native Claims Settlement Act of 1971, which required Congress to allocate up to 80 million acres of Alaska's public lands to the federal land agencies by 1978. By the time the pipeline was approved, that provision had already become a vehicle for the first of three major public land reviews that would occupy the environmental movement in the 1970s.[32] Yet even as the pipeline debate set the stage for more expansive wilderness designations, it highlighted a new challenge: it would not be the last time wilderness politics were pinched off by energy debates.

The National Forests and the Future of the "Roadless Areas"

When the Wilderness Act of 1964 became law, it posed little threat to the timber industry. The new wilderness system protected largely the high-elevation areas of "rocks and ice" that had little valuable timber. That began to change in the early 1970s. Initially, the Wilderness Act's ten-year reviews included only land the Forest Service protected as "primitive areas." Those lands totaled 5.6 million acres, or about 3 percent of the national forests. Beyond those areas, however, was a wide expanse of roadless areas, like Alpine Lakes, Dolly Sods, and other areas in the East and the West that were also wild lands potentially deserving protection. In the 1960s, no one knew just how much of the national forests actually met the criteria of the Wilderness Act, including the Forest Service. And, unlike the barren "rocks and ice" the Forest Service willingly recommended as wilderness, the roadless areas included a greater diversity of lands, such as lower-elevation forests and potential timber lands.

What seemed impossible in the early 1960s—reviewing all of the national forests for wilderness designation—began to seem possible amid the enthusiasm surrounding Earth Day. But doing so posed a more direct challenge to the timber industry. Nearly half of the land wilderness advocates viewed as roadless areas, the Forest Service classified as "commercial forest land."[33] Since the 1950s, the Forest Service had accelerated commercial logging on the national forests. In the 1970s, the agency classified 48 percent of the national forests as "commercial forest land," 5 percent more than in 1945. These policies were

popular with the agency, industry, and local communities: government foresters saw their operating budgets, staff, and bureaucratic power increase as
timber sales brought money into the agency, the timber industry reaped the
benefits of an inexpensive timber supply, and local communities enjoyed high
employment, tax revenues, and a 25 percent share of all proceeds from federal
timber sales (to support local schools and rural roads). Of course, Congress did
charge the Forest Service with managing the national forests for "multiple-use
sustained-yield" purposes. But, as one historian noted, "any ambitious young
forester could see that in the Forest Service, timber was where careers were to
be made."[34]

The future of the national forest roadless areas commanded the attention
of the Nixon administration and the Forest Service in the late 1960s and early
1970s. In 1968, western legislators and the timber industry urged the Nixon
administration to push for a Timber Supply Act in Congress that would guarantee that national forests were primarily for logging.[35] That legislation failed as
concerns over the management of the national forests deepened. Local wilderness advocates urged Congress to protect some roadless areas, such as Alpine
Lakes and the Dolly Sods. Elsewhere in the West, advocates began questioning
the value of timber sales in roadless areas in Montana, Colorado, and Oregon.
And new questions began to emerge about the ecological consequences of
clear-cutting on the national forests.[36] As Brock Evans explained in 1973, the
issue was no longer just wilderness, it was "pushing for good land management
. . . everywhere in the national forests."[37] As public concern over the Forest Service's logging policies and the roadless areas grew, the Nixon administration,
under pressure from the Wilderness Society and Sierra Club and well aware
of the environmental movement's growing political power, considered issuing a presidential executive order that would halt logging in all national forest
roadless areas to allow time for the agency and Congress to review those areas
as potential wilderness.[38] After flirting with the proposal in 1971, however, the
Nixon White House declined to issue the order. An advisor noted the decision
was political; it reflected the "President's concern on overplaying the environment."[39] It also reflected the Forest Service's success arguing that such an executive order, which encroached on the agency's administrative autonomy, was
unnecessary; the agency already had such a "roadless review" in the works.

The Forest Service accelerated its planning for the roadless areas in the
early 1970s. Since 1967, the agency's wilderness team had acknowledged that
some roadless areas outside the original ten-year reviews deserved consideration as wilderness. But the agency decided such reviews would have to wait

until 1974, when the ten-year reviews were completed. (Wilderness advocates, increasingly suspicious of the agency, believed such delays were meant to give the agency's "timber beasts" a chance to open up the best of those lands for logging in the interim.)[40] In 1971, the agency announced it would undertake its own internal review of all national forest roadless areas: the Roadless Area Review and Evaluation (RARE). It was the first time the agency had systematically documented the extent of undeveloped land remaining on the national forests. In its assessment, 1,449 roadless areas encompassing 56 million acres in the national forests deserved review to determine their potential economic and wilderness values.[41] To facilitate a system-wide evaluation, the agency developed a quantitative "wilderness quality" index to assess each roadless area. The index reflected the agency's "purity policies" and gave the highest values to large, pristine, and remote roadless areas little used for backcountry recreation. The agency also assessed the type, value, and accessibility of timber and other natural resources.[42] The review was a massive undertaking. Nevertheless, the Forest Service anticipated completing it (including field surveys, public hearings, and final recommendations) in less than two years.

Wilderness advocates viewed RARE as a rushed and superficial effort geared more toward expediting wilderness reviews than actually protecting wilderness. Although Michael McCloskey appreciated the expedited pace of RARE because it addressed some of his concerns about the slow progress of the ten-year reviews, he complained to the Forest Service in February 1972 about the "mammoth number" of decisions being made on the roadless areas. Neither "substantial analysis" nor "meaningful public participation" was possible, he noted.[43] Wilderness advocates asked for an extension to allow the agency and citizens two full summers to review the potential roadless areas. The agency refused to adjust its schedule. That spring, the Forest Service's preliminary recommendations included much less land than the Sierra Club, Wilderness Society, and their local allies anticipated. Consistent with its institutional history and approach to wilderness, the agency followed the purity policies, omitted all areas in the East, and arbitrarily split roadless areas into smaller units. Public hearings on RARE drew attention from both supporters and opponents of wilderness designation. Wilderness advocates criticized the unrealistic timeframe and the limited wilderness recommendations. The timber companies urged their employees to testify against expanded wilderness. Boise Cascade ran advertisements in Idaho newspapers reading: "You bet we have an economic interest. You do too. So does your whole town."[44]

As the Forest Service spun into high gear—the agency worked furiously to analyze the hearing records and submit a final recommendation to the agency's Washington office by June 1972—the Sierra Club Legal Defense Fund turned to the courts. The Sierra Club had pursued legal strategies on the national forests in the 1960s, but NEPA provided it with new leverage. The Sierra Club filed suit in San Francisco federal court that June, arguing that the Forest Service neither possessed adequate information for the review nor allowed sufficient time for public input. On those grounds, it argued that RARE failed to meet NEPA's standards for an environmental impact statement.[45] In August, the court issued a preliminary injunction, which halted timber sales in roadless areas, pending a full hearing in November.[46] Where citizens' wilderness proposals for the Alpine Lakes or the Dolly Sods involved individual roadless areas, the Sierra Club's lawsuit stopped logging on all roadless areas nationwide. These events ushered in a new era of uncertainty for the timber industry. An Oregon congressman explained the implications of these delays for the timber companies and local communities in his district that relied on the national forests. "We are in a crisis now," he emphasized, "and we are rapidly bobsledding toward catastrophe."[47]

The Sierra Club Legal Defense Fund's lawsuit marked a crucial turning point for the future of wilderness in the national forests. The immediate recommendations that emerged from RARE, released in January 1973, were of little consequence. The agency recommended 274 wilderness study areas totaling 12.3 million acres, which fell far short of wilderness advocates' expectations.[48] More significant, the agency—worried that a trial would be lengthy, would slow down timber harvests, and would be unsuccessful—settled with the Sierra Club out of court. The settlement agreement blocked roadless area timber sales in 1973 (with a few exceptions). Most importantly, the agency agreed to comply with NEPA's requirements for all future management activities in all roadless areas. That meant the agency could undertake no new logging, road-building, or other development activities until it completed an environmental review of each roadless area. That victory set the stage for the second new wilderness review—that of the national forest roadless areas—which would shape the future of the wilderness movement most immediately during the Carter administration in the late 1970s, but again during the Clinton administration in the late 1990s.[49]

The Bureau of Land Management and the Future of the Public Domain

The fluted canyons, endless deserts, and wide-open sagebrush flats, hemmed in only by the mountains, give the American West its awesome dimensions.

Much of this land is overseen by the BLM. In the 1970s that agency oversaw more public land than the other three federal land agencies combined, yet the public domain was omitted from the Wilderness Act. Unlike the Forest Service, for instance, the BLM had no tradition of wilderness protection. Of all the agencies, it was most oriented toward resource production. Nor did such lands fit with most people's conception of wilderness. As one Nevada wilderness advocate noted, most people viewed such lands as "monotonous," "bleak," and "godforsaken."[50] And most problematic was the political geography of the BLM lands. The BLM had long been dominated by local interests, such as miners and cattlemen, rural communities, and their allies in Congress, which had carefully and successfully guarded their "home rule" over the public domain. For much of its history, the debate over the public domain had not been how to manage it, but whether the land should be given to the states. The BLM oversaw a substantial proportion of land in Nevada (69 percent), Utah (41 percent), Wyoming (28 percent), and Oregon (25 percent), and many officials and citizens believed the states should manage those lands.[51] In the campaign for the Wilderness Act, wilderness leaders knew better than to include the public domain in the Wilderness Act's ten-year reviews; such a move would have only exacerbated western opposition. But in the 1960s and 1970s, as concern for wilderness and the environment began to mount, so too did questions about the future of the BLM and the public domain.

The BLM had long been the stepchild among the federal land agencies: it was the most poorly funded and staffed relative to the expanse of land it was responsible for overseeing. It had no clear congressional mandate. Instead, it was saddled with thousands of contradictory laws and regulations regarding the public domain which had accumulated since the mid-nineteenth century. Congress gave attention to the future of the agency and the public domain in the early 1970s, beginning with the 1970 report, *One Third of the Nation's Land*, from the Public Land Law Review Commission. The review, which had been chaired by Wayne Aspinall (D-CO), the longtime wilderness opponent and ally to resource industries, was clearest on one point: it recommended a limited multiple-use mandate for the BLM that emphasized zoning the public domain for specific uses, such as grazing, mining, logging, and other forms of development, based foremost on economic productivity. That proposal, however, made little headway in Congress in the early 1970s. It ran counter to the wishes of the agency, the Department of the Interior, and the environmental community. As negotiations proceeded, discussions turned toward the possibility of establishing a multiple-use sustained-yield mandate for the BLM, modeled on that of the Forest Service. But the challenge was how to set the agency on that course, considering how deeply embedded it was in a thicket of public land laws that had served ranching and mining interests for so long.[52]

Congress passed the Federal Land Policy and Management Act (FLPMA) in 1976.[53] The new law established that the public domain, some 174 million acres in the lower forty-eight, would remain under the stewardship of the BLM, which was given the authority to manage it for multiple uses and values. Many provisions of the law facilitated the agency's new mission. The agency was required to produce and maintain a comprehensive inventory of the public domain and associated resources, with special attention to "areas of ecological concern." The agency was required to undertake a systematic planning process for the public domain—modeled on environmental impact statements—that included public input, interdisciplinary analysis, and intergovernmental consultation. Although the law repealed nearly 2,000 old statutes that generally facilitated disposal of the public domain, it did not wipe the slate clean: thousands of old laws remained on the books, including major laws such as the Mining Law of 1872, the Mineral Leasing Act of 1920, and the Taylor Grazing Act, which underpinned mining and grazing activities on the public domain. The law did little to fundamentally reform grazing management, despite the fact that much of the agency's range was overgrazed, and instead called for further studies that would precipitate new debates in the late 1970s and 1980s. The law strengthened the agency's oversight over mining marginally, but it omitted any provisions for charging mining companies royalties for the minerals they took from the public lands. And the law did not entirely stop the disposal of the public lands: under the planning program, the secretary of the interior could sell parcels of the public domain to state and local governments or private interests, after appropriate reviews, if such sales were in the national interest. As the historian James Skillen observes, the law "reflected rather than resolved the complexity of public lands management."[54]

Wilderness advocates also succeeded in staking their claim to the public domain in FLPMA. Since the 1960s, interest in protecting the public domain had been growing among wilderness advocates. National wilderness leaders, such as Stewart Brandborg, spoke privately of the potential for BLM wilderness even as the Wilderness Act became law. New citizen groups began to lay the groundwork for such a campaign. For instance, the Nevada Outdoor Recreation Association independently catalogued the wilderness potential of BLM lands under the direction of its energetic leader, Charles Watson.[55] As discussion got underway regarding FLPMA, the Wilderness Society and Sierra Club formed the Public Lands

Conservation Coalition to urge the federal government to revise existing mining and grazing laws, retain oversight of the public domain, and undertake a wilderness review of all BLM lands.[56] During public hearings on the lands legislation in 1974, the Public Lands Conservation Coalition organized a strong turnout in support of a wilderness review that would pay dividends during the legislative debates to come. When FLPMA became law, it required the BLM to undertake a comprehensive wilderness review of the public domain. Of 57 million acres of roadless areas, the agency selected 24 million acres for intensive review in 1980. Those reviews were to be completed on a state-by-state basis by 1991. Importantly, FLPMA specifically provided that these potential wilderness areas, so-called "wilderness study areas," would generally be managed to keep them suitable for wilderness designation until Congress acted on formal wilderness proposals. Of the three new wilderness reviews, however, the unfavorable political geography of the public domain would make it the most challenging for wilderness advocates.

The Future of the Roadless Areas and American Environmental Politics

At the heart of each of these new public land reviews—for Alaska's public lands, the national forest roadless areas, and the BLM public domain—were two principles: first, that the public had a say in the future of the public lands and, second, that the federal government must consider alternate uses for the public lands (such as wilderness designation) any time it considered opening a parcel of land for logging, oil and gas exploration, or other forms of development. Using the tools important to the environmental movement—NEPA, legal suits, and growing political clout—wilderness advocates succeeded in achieving what the Wilderness Act of 1964 did not: wilderness reviews of almost all federally owned public lands in the nation. In 1964, the wilderness system measured 9.1 million acres and required wilderness reviews of 53 million acres of public land. In 1976, the wilderness system had only grown modestly—to approximately 15 million acres—but its potential scope had expanded dramatically to include roughly 197 million acres of public lands. In this way, the wilderness movement harnessed the tools of the "new" environmental movement and used them to advance long-standing concerns for an "old" conservation issue.

It is worth noting, however, what wilderness advocates did *not* aim to accomplish: a systematic overhaul of public lands management. Even in the case of the BLM, where the conversation about public lands management was most far-reaching, there was little effort to fundamentally change the role of logging, mining, and other development activities on the public lands. Rather

Table 4.1 Although the area of wilderness managed by the Forest Service, National Park Service, Fish and Wildlife Service, and Bureau of Land Management grew modestly between 1964 and 1976, the area of land to be reviewed for wilderness designation expanded dramatically during the same time period, setting the stage for the major wilderness reviews since the 1970s.

| | Wilderness Areas (millions of acres) | | | | | Wilderness Reviews (millions of acres) | | | | |
	FS	NPS	FWS	BLM	TOTAL	FS	NPS	FWS	BLM	TOTAL
1964	9.1	0.0	0.0	N/A	9.1	6.0	22.0	25.0	0.0	53.0
1976	12.9	1.3	0.8	0.0	15.0	60.0	80.0*		57.0	197.0

* The national interest provision of the Alaska lands act led to wilderness reviews of approximately 80 million acres most of which would be overseen by the NPS and FWS.

than challenging the multiple-use framework for public lands management, in the 1970s wilderness advocates more often worked within it. They emphasized that wilderness was an important multiple-use category for public lands management; it provided recreation, wildlife, and watershed protection, for instance. And protecting discrete wilderness areas bolstered the multiple-use framework, since it allocated some land for wilderness protection, but allowed logging, mining, and other activities on unprotected lands. In the early 1970s, more systematic challenges to the multiple-use management framework were emerging—as concerns about clear-cut logging, endangered species protection, and grazing mounted—but those efforts would not transform the debates over wilderness until the 1980s.

Advancing these wilderness reviews would pose new challenges for the movement. Unlike the ten-year reviews, which focused on areas the federal government already protected and wilderness advocates already knew, much of the land at stake in Alaska, the national forests, and in the public domain was unfamiliar to wilderness enthusiasts. Protecting such lands required new strategies and arguments, which began to shift the balance in the wilderness movement away from local groups and toward professional advocates at the Sierra Club and the Wilderness Society in Washington, D.C. Wilderness advocates marshaled new media strategies to place the campaign for Alaska at the center of the nation's environmental attention. They drew increasingly on scientific arguments for identifying and protecting ecosystems and endangered species to justify the value of protecting wild lands. And wilderness advocates drew on resource and economic analyses to criticize existing management policies. In advancing these campaigns, what began to dwindle were sweeping claims on behalf of the public interest, appeals to patriotism, and an emphasis on the historic value of wilderness, which had characterized the outreach of Zahniser, Udall, and an earlier generation of wilderness champions. Starting in the 1970s, professional and technical strategies characteristic of the modern environmental movement as a whole would become increasingly important to wilderness advocacy.

Pragmatic Wilderness and the End of the Ten-Year Reviews

When Michael McCloskey criticized the slow pace of the ten-year reviews at the Sierra Club's Biennial Wilderness Conference, few would have disagreed with his assessment. But it soon became clear that not everyone in the wilderness community or even at the Sierra Club agreed with his prescription to "regroup and devise new strategy."[57] The wilderness conference itself emerged as a source of discontent for those who saw a different promise in wilderness. The next month, the club's Wilderness Classification Study Committee suggested that the conference had been a "crashing failure." In a sharp letter to the club's president, the committee emphasized that despite the conference's theme, "Action for Wilderness," it had done nothing to encourage "*effective* rather than merely *concerned* conservationists." They faulted the conference's expensive venue, that it was a privilege to attend, and that it failed to involve the club's broad membership. "We favor [a] more localized and personalized method for actually *involving* people."[58] In their view, the conference was more of an effort to stake out a symbolic new place for a professional and powerful Sierra Club in the heart of the nation's capital than an inspiring effort to link local groups and national groups to advance wilderness legislation. Such concerns marked new divisions over the best ways to organize on behalf of environmental reform.

Even as the Sierra Club volunteers criticized McCloskey, their statements offered tacit support for the Wilderness Society's model of wilderness advocacy. As McCloskey began to push the Sierra Club and the wilderness movement onto the terrain of litigation and technical expertise in the mid-1970s, the Wilderness Society deepened its commitment to strengthening and expanding the wilderness movement's partnership with citizen advocates. Like McCloskey, the Wilderness Society's staff was concerned about the logjam of ten-year reviews in 1971. But that fall, as the reviews began to regain momentum, the Wilderness Society focused its efforts on strengthening its citizen training programs and working through Congress to bring the ten-year reviews to a close. To realize the full potential of the future wilderness reviews, the Wilderness Society still believed it imperative that Congress set generous legislative precedents for the Wilderness Act, ones free of arbitrary restrictions such as the Forest Service's purity policies or the National Park Service's development-oriented "Swiss cheese" approach to wilderness designation. Since the early reviews at San Rafael, Isle Royale, and Great Swamp, wilderness advocates had succeeded in setting some legislative precedents in Congress. In the mid-1970s, the Wilderness Society and its allies consolidated those earlier successes into key legislative precedents for a pragmatic and flexible future for the Wilderness Act.

In some respects, the Wilderness Society's emphasis on grassroots organizing was born of necessity. If the Wilderness Society's membership had continued to grow as rapidly as it had before Earth Day, the Wilderness Society might have accomplished its goals: expanding its staff of field consultants to twenty-four and supporting wilderness activities in fourteen states, covering the rapidly growing costs of the Alaska campaign and litigation, and expanding its program of citizen training seminars to prepare for the end of the ten-year reviews.[59] But as a 1972 article in *Science* noted, "activist environmental organizations have fallen into the doldrums" as the economy slowed, the glow of Earth Day faded, and membership growth leveled off.[60] The Wilderness Society depended on small member donations and the organization, especially Brandborg, remained wary of seeking support from large donors or a growing number of philanthropic foundations, even though such sources of support were crucial to many of the new environmental organizations (and would be to the Wilderness Society in the future). In 1972, the Wilderness Society faced a budget deficit. It was the beginning of a cycle of expanding programs and tightening budgets that began to undermine the Wilderness Society and Brandborg's leadership.

The uptick in the ten-year reviews in the early 1970s was, in part, a result of the Nixon administration's concerns. Immediately after McCloskey's conference address, the Nixon White House began to put pressure on the federal land agencies to expedite the wilderness reviews. Two Nixon staffers—John Whitaker and Russell Train—were crucial allies to the environmental community on a wide range of issues, including wilderness.[61] Between 1970 and 1972, the White House browbeat the directors of the federal land agencies, urging them to get the wilderness reviews back on schedule.[62] While Whitaker and Train were genuine allies to the wilderness movement, others in the Nixon White House saw other reasons to resolve the ten-year reviews as quickly as possible.

The Nixon administration was well aware that the federal land agencies had taken contradictory approaches to the wilderness reviews. With so many differences in wilderness policy, it was impossible to know "How much is enough?" That was the concern that many within industry were beginning to express, and they had the ear of some Nixon staffers. Those questions gained new urgency as wilderness advocates challenged the Alaskan pipeline and threw the future of logging in roadless areas into uncertainty. During the summer of 1972, the Nixon administration acknowledged that "strategically, the executive branch must put its house in order" with respect to wilderness policy.[63]

As the ten-year reviews began to move forward in Congress, the wilderness review process that had begun with field studies and local hearings across the nation began to converge in Washington, D.C. This pattern of legislative activity was matched by a coordinated model of environmental advocacy, which depended on the activism of local groups but looked to national groups for leadership. In the early 1970s, Brandborg's vision of a citizens' wilderness movement reached its culmination, as activists nationwide were increasingly linked with the legislative process in the nation's capital. The campaigns for Eagles Nest in Colorado and Isle Royale in Michigan demonstrate how Brandborg and his colleagues at the Wilderness Society catalyzed a citizens' movement that was at once independent and cooperative.

Eagles Nest, Isle Royale, and the Close of the Ten-Year Reviews

When the Wilderness Society established its first field office in Denver, Colorado, in 1965, Clif Merritt chose office space adjacent to the newly formed Colorado Open Space Coordinating Council (COSCC). That decision only strengthened existing ties between the two organizations. The Wilderness Society provided the COSCC with seed money in 1964, co-sponsored five citizen wilderness workshops across the state in 1965, and became the COSCC's partner in the campaign to protect high mountain areas of Colorado, such as Sangre de Cristo, the San Juans, and Flat Tops.[64] Eagles Nest was one of the most contentious primitive areas the Forest Service evaluated during the ten-year reviews. Its mountain highlands rise up like a rampart east of Vail. Early season storms usually cap the rock-ribbed peaks with snow by early fall. Framed against the blue sky, Eagles Nest evokes the majesty of the Rocky Mountains. The original primitive area encompassed approximately 80,000 acres of the Gore Range and a host of small mountain lakes—largely "rocks and ice." As the ten-year reviews began, Colorado wilderness advocates, led by the COSCC, initially proposed a 110,000-acre

Eagles Nest wilderness area, which would include the original primitive area and additional lower-elevation forests.[65]

Progress toward wilderness protection for Eagles Nest was slow in the 1960s. A proposed route for Interstate 70 would cut through the southern portion of the primitive area. The Denver Water Board eyed Eagles Nest as a prime source of water to be channeled to the Front Range. And the Forest Service's plans for a timber sale in Meadow Creek led to local protest and a precedent-setting lawsuit on roadless lands adjacent to existing primitive areas.[66] In each instance, the COSCC worked actively at the local level to advocate expansive wilderness protection for Eagles Nest. Working in conjunction with the Wilderness Society, the organization issued joint alerts, made coordinated statements at hearings, and ran educational workshops to involve interested citizens. For the Forest Service's Colorado offices, the COSCC proved to be a nettlesome watchdog. In the 1960s, the COSCC members surveyed both the primitive areas included in the ten-year reviews and additional roadless areas, gathering information on wilderness qualities and potential conflicts while developing recommendations for more than thirty potential Colorado wilderness areas.[67] The COSCC, like advocates across the country, had begun to accumulate more specific knowledge about potential wilderness areas than even the Forest Service's full-time staff possessed.[68]

By the early 1970s, the Eagles Nest proposal had weathered the possibility of the interstate highway, but growing urban demand for water remained a threat. A proposed twenty-three-mile tunnel promised to channel water from Eagles Nest, beneath the Rocky Mountains, and into the Front Range's suburban spigots. COSCC's homegrown support for Eagles Nest proved crucial in blocking the Denver Water Board's and Forest Service's efforts to limit the size of the wilderness. In 1972, the COSCC squared off with the Forest Service over the agency's 87,750-acre wilderness recommendation. That proposal marked a modest increase over the original primitive area; but since 1970, COSCC, the Wilderness Society, and other citizen groups had expanded their proposal to 125,000 acres. Clif Merritt, who during his tenure at the Wilderness Society often championed the value of wilderness as wildlife habitat, argued early on that protecting the lower-elevation forests was essential to Eagles Nest's future. Mountain wilderness should not just be "barren peaks and beautiful natural lakes," he said. It should "encompass a liberal cross-section of the natural landscapes—from the foothills and narrow valleys to the highest rocky ramparts . . . such a wilderness area transcends the great number of life zones and, accordingly, ensures a great variety and abundance of plant and animal

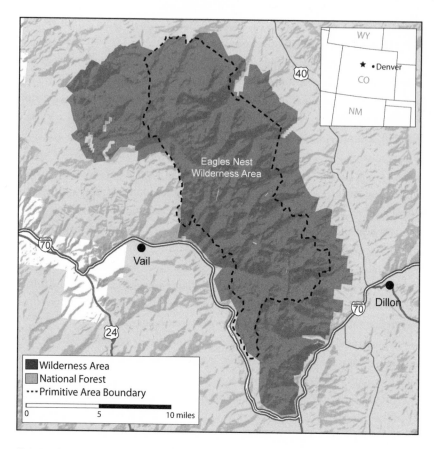

Map 4.2 Eagles Nest Wilderness Area, Colorado. Wilderness advocates succeeded in expanding on the original 80,000-acre primitive area, which was largely rocks and ice, to protect a 133,910-acre wilderness in 1976 by including ecologically valuable lower-elevation forests. It was a significant victory over the Forest Service and the Denver Water Board, which had hoped to divert water from those lands for urban use in Denver. The two western inholdings were acquired by the Forest Service in 1989.

forms."[69] What the COSCC was unable to accomplish with the Forest Service in Colorado, the Wilderness Society would help it win in Congress.

The same strategy would prove crucial to reforming the National Park Service's restrictive wilderness policies. In April 1971, under pressure from the Nixon White House, the agency released wilderness recommendations for Isle Royale, Shenandoah, Kings Canyon, North Cascades, and several other parks and monuments. After bottling up the proposals for more than two years, the agency finally proceeded with the ten-year reviews. But as the proposals reached Congress, it became clear that the agency had further reduced its wilderness recommendations. The Park Service had carved out additional non-wilderness enclaves within the proposed wilderness areas to accommodate potential development, as became apparent in its revised 1971 Isle Royale wilderness proposal. The Park Service proposed a 120,588-acre wilderness area—short of the wilderness advocates' proposal to protect 132,700 acres. These exclusions, which were located near the harbors and bays, appeared to be beachheads for future tourist services.[70]

Bob Hanson, chair of the newly formed Northern Michigan Wilderness Coalition (NMWC), described the new proposal as a "desecration."[71] But unlike four years before, when downstate conservationists traveled en masse to Houghton, Michigan, to testify for Isle Royale, Hanson spoke on behalf of new local interest. For the Wilderness Society, fostering such local activism had been its key goal for the past three years. In 1971, as the Isle Royale proposal went to Congress, the Wilderness Society demonstrated its maturing organizational and political strategies. In the spring, the Wilderness Society invited Hanson to the capital to participate in a weeklong training seminar on wilderness advocacy leadership. Afterwards, Art Wright, a longtime Wilderness Society affiliate and field organizer, spent a week in the Upper Peninsula working with local activists. And in May, the new organization and the Wilderness Society co-sponsored a wilderness workshop in Marquette, Michigan. Doug Scott, still a Wilderness Society organizer at the time, remarked, "I was immensely impressed by the caliber of local leadership developing."[72] That strategy reflected a commitment to a coordinated approach to wilderness advocacy that joined together local activism and national leadership in support of a common goal.

Hanson and the NMWC and Scott and the Wilderness Society formed a dynamic team pushing for an expanded Isle Royale proposal in the Upper Peninsula and in Washington, D.C. Knowing that the Park Service would not budge on its existing proposal, Hanson and Scott prepared an alternative citizens' proposal. While Hanson and the NMWC gathered support among local governments and conservation groups in Michigan, Scott kept in close touch with congressional representatives in Washington, D.C. As with the COSCC and Eagles Nest, the Wilderness Society coordinated the NMWC's activities in Congress, and it played an increasingly familiar political card: when faced with a weak agency proposal, the Wilderness Society and its allies turned to Congress to support an independent citizens' proposal instead. In 1972, Congress entertained the National Park Service's "Swiss cheese" proposal for Isle Royale and a larger citizens' wilderness proposal. As often was the case in the early 1970s, Congress sided with the wilderness advocates.

The COSCC and the NMWC were two of dozens of local organizations that the Wilderness Society cultivated during the ten-year reviews. Other groups included the Alpine Lakes Protection Society, Lincoln Backcountry Association, Montana Wilderness Association, North Jersey Conservation Foundation, West Virginia Highlands Conservancy, and local Sierra Club chapters. This strategy formed but a part of a broader surge of organizing activity around environmental issues in the 1960s and 1970s. What distinguished the work for wilderness, however, was that the ten-year reviews allowed local organizations to work independently on local wilderness areas while actively contributing to and cooperating in a national movement. The Wilderness Society coached the organizations, guiding them through the long process necessary to advance a wilderness proposal to Congress, and, in doing so, ensured that the local proposals aligned with the Wilderness Society's pragmatic wilderness strategy. Even as the changing environmental movement bestowed wilderness advocates with powerful legislative and legal tools, the Wilderness Society remained most committed to citizen engagement. One by one, these local organizations began to fly the same flag for wilderness. By the mid-1970s, the fact that so many organizations were flying the same colors formed a powerful argument for a generous and pragmatic approach to wilderness designation in Congress.

The Wilderness Society's Washington Training Seminars

The Washington training seminars became the centerpiece of the Wilderness Society's citizens' campaign, as the ten-year reviews shifted out of the field and into the halls of Congress. Starting in the late 1960s, hundreds of activists took part in such seminars. As Brandborg remembers, he looked for the "people who would bring unity rather than the one-man band."[73] Brock Evans, who worked for the Sierra Club at the time and had been a strong supporter of citizen-oriented campaigns in the Pacific Northwest, remembers, "It was a brilliant stroke on the part of the Wilderness Society."[74] The seminars usually lasted one week, with the respectable Washington Hotel serving as home base. Each day participants left the hotel and circulated through the capital, learning about the workings of Congress and the executive branch. Instructional sessions were held in government buildings, such as the Department of Agriculture, the Department of the Interior, the Old Executive Office Building, New Senate Office Building, and the Rayburn House, as well as in the nearby Cosmos Club.[75]

Wilderness advocates came to Washington, D.C., with expertise in the physical geography important to their wilderness proposals; they left the Washington seminar with an understanding of the political and institutional geography of the nation's capital. The Wilderness Society's staff, which included Brandborg, Scott, and Ernie Dickerman, a veteran Wilderness Society organizer, ran informal training sessions. Executive agency representatives such as George Hartzog, director of the Park Service, and Robert Cahn, a member of the White House's Council on Environmental Quality, hosted sessions to answer questions and offer advice about the executive agencies. Congressional representatives including John Dingell (D-MI), Morris Udall (D-AZ), and John Saylor (R-PA) explained the workings of Congress. And at dinners, participants met the staff from other organizations such as the National Wildlife Federation, National Audubon Society, Sierra Club, Friends of the Earth, and Environmental Action. Participants also attended sessions on working with the press, organizing and leadership, and lobbying. This preparation culminated with lobbying trips on Capitol Hill. On one day, an experienced Wilderness Society staffer would lead a group to a friendly congressional representative's office for a mock lobbying call, and the next day, participants would lobby their own representatives and senators.[76] "We would send them home with smoke blowing out of both ears," remembers Brandborg. Participants would have a "new confidence to work with the government."[77]

The Washington training seminars formed a crucible for a new generation of wilderness leaders. Bob Hanson, from Michigan, and Helen Fenske, from New Jersey, who played important roles in the campaigns for Isle Royale and Great Swamp, respectively, both participated in the trainings, as did many other leaders who were instrumental in the ten-year reviews. The program also helped train the Wilderness Society's growing cadre of field-based organizers, who formed a new generation of future wilderness leaders that would spearhead campaigns for the national forests, Alaska, and the BLM public domain in the 1970s and 1980s. Those leaders included Dave Foreman and Bart Koehler, two of the Wilderness Society's most active organizers in the West in the 1970s and cofounders of Earth First!, an organization that would change wilderness politics in the 1980s. [78] In the early 1970s, the Wilderness Society's emphasis on citizen organizing reflected Brandborg's faith in participatory democracy. He still believed that the "people's will can be directly translated into action" through legislation and was "confident that the people want firmly protected wilderness."[79] This approach demanded and encouraged the active engagement of citizens, while strengthening the Wilderness Society's leadership and clout in Congress.

Pragmatic Precedents for Wilderness

The Wilderness Society's success guiding the implementation of the Wilderness Act is notable in the context of environmental politics. Many of the ambitious environmental laws passed in the 1970s were subsequently scaled back by the agencies, industry, or later administrations. That was not the case with the Wilderness Act. This difference is explained partly by what was at stake; although the stakes on the public lands were considerable, they were not as high or complex as the regulatory consequences of other new laws such as the Clean Air, Clean Water, or Toxic Substances Control acts. Equally important was the coordinated and sustained role citizens played in overseeing the implementation of the Wilderness Act. The significance of this strategy was clearest in the early 1970s. Despite the efforts of the Park Service and, especially, the Forest Service to shape the implementation of the Wilderness Act, the Wilderness Society made citizens the dominant force in Congress's approach to the act through legislative campaigns for areas such as Eagles Nest, Isle Royale, Alpine Lakes, and the Eastern Wilderness Areas Act. In the mid-1970s, spurred forward by strong citizen interest, Congress resolved key differences over wilderness designation that the federal land agencies could not.

Congress singled out the National Park Service's policies first. In May 1972, at a Senate hearing on Isle Royale, Senator Frank Church questioned the agency's wilderness policies. Church specifically praised the agency's approach to restored wilderness, especially at Isle Royale, but he pointed out the idiosyncrasies in the agency's approach to buffer areas, enclaves, and other issues such as grazing. He noted the agency was not at liberty to interpret the Wilderness Act as it deemed appropriate; it was to implement the law as consistent with the intent of Congress and the people of the United States. "I do not—and I think this Committee does not—want to see the promise of a truly diverse National Wilderness Preservation System cut short by unnecessarily restrictive policies," he warned. He encouraged the agency to finish the ten-year reviews of the parks in a "positive, constructive, flexible manner."[80] Of all three federal land agencies, the Park Service had moved the slowest. That public rebuke represented one part of a careful campaign to affect the Park Service's policies. As

Church delivered his critique, Doug Scott sat tired, yet pleased, in the back of the hearing room. He had been up late the night before drafting Church's comments.[81] Within weeks, the agency received over two hundred letters from local organizations and citizens affirming Church's position. And the Wilderness Society and Sierra Club lobbied the agency and the Department of the Interior too. Bowing to the pressure, the National Park Service revised its wilderness standards in late 1972. "Under these [new] guidelines," an Interior staffer explained, "many of the areas previously excluded will be recommended for wilderness designation."[82]

As the Park Service revised its remaining wilderness proposals, the NMWC kept a close eye on the revisions for Isle Royale, and when the new proposal excluded land to protect a "solitude area," the coalition chided the Department of the Interior: "We thought those concepts and old arguments had been laid to rest by Senator Church."[83] By 1974, the agency had increased its wilderness recommendation from 120,588 acres to 131,932 acres (only 768 acres short of the citizens' proposal). As the proposal was finalized, Doug Scott reminded the congressional staff: "This Isle Royale thing has been a long and uphill effort and we must recognize the persistence of key conservation leaders in Northern Michigan."[84] Congress acted on a major set of national park wilderness proposals in 1976. Following one of McCloskey's prescriptions, it lumped thirteen proposals into a single omnibus bill that protected over one million acres of land. When it passed in 1976, it reflected the agency's revised wilderness policies, brought the total number of Park Service wilderness areas to seventeen, and protected 131,880 acres of Isle Royale. It also marked the successful close of similar citizen campaigns for Shenandoah, Badlands, and Mesa Verde national parks. In the years to come, the Park Service would gain vast tracts of wilderness in the review of Alaska's "national interest" lands. But, to this day, many national parks, including some of the best known, such as Yellowstone and the Great Smoky Mountains, are still without formal wilderness designations.[85]

The Forest Service's purity policies also suffered a series of setbacks in the mid-1970s. In 1972, Congress added the first national forest roadless area, the Scapegoat Wilderness in Montana, to the wilderness system. In 1973, the Wilderness Society and its allies forced the agency to acquiesce to protecting eastern wilderness areas.[86] And, as the ten-year reviews proceeded, citizen activists had succeeded in protecting wilderness areas that exceeded the agency's original recommendations at places such as San Rafael in California, Weminuche in Colorado, and Eagles Nest in Colorado. Eagles Nest was one of the last primitive areas to be added to the wilderness system. When the proposal arrived in

Congress, the agency still recommended an 87,750-acre wilderness. Behind the scenes, the Denver Water Board and local timber industry lobbied fervently to omit low-elevation lands. Despite the formidable power of the timber and water industries, which often determined public lands policies in the West, the campaign orchestrated by the Colorado Open Space Coalition and the Wilderness Society pushed through a 133,910-acre Eagles Nest wilderness in 1976. As the *Rocky Mountain News* noted, conservationists "scored a major victory over the Denver Water Board" and brought to a halt a $222 million water diversion project.[87]

These achievements eroded the legislative foundation for the Forest Service's purity policies. In 1971, one of the agency's staffers noted the constant citizen protest over the purity policies. Dick Joy asked, "Are we truly listening to their message?" He suggested that the Forest Service be "less defensive" and do "more listening" to "concerned citizens at the grassroots level."[88] But the agency never followed that suggestion—indeed, the Forest Service often guarded its administrative autonomy and expertise from public oversight. But, precedent by precedent, Congress dismantled the purity policies and legislated into reality the Wilderness Society's vision of a wilderness system that included not only high-mountain wilderness, but more low-elevation forests, recovering cutover lands, small wilderness areas, and popular hiking areas. The agency itself would not abandon the purity policies until 1977, when Rupert Cutler, a former Wilderness Society staffer, joined the Department of Agriculture during the Carter administration. Yet, even today, vestiges of the purity policies remain in the Forest Service's wilderness activities.

By the mid-1970s, wilderness advocates had secured a position of strength in Congress, and the logjam of wilderness legislation that had troubled McCloskey mostly gave way. Through that opening poured a raft of wilderness legislation: Eagles Nest and other primitive areas; many of the small Fish and Wildlife refuges; the omnibus Park Service wilderness legislation, including Isle Royale; and roadless areas, such as Alpine Lakes and Dolly Sods. Between 1974 and 1976, the wilderness system expanded by more than 70 areas and 3 million acres. The wilderness system would include not only iconic mountain wilderness areas—such as the High Sierras or the Rocky Mountains—but small islands, restored wild lands, and popular recreation areas too. But it was only a start. All told, by 1976, the National Wilderness Preservation System included 15 million acres, a 65 percent increase since the Wilderness Act had become law, but still less than one percent of all the land in the United States. In the years to come, the wilderness movement's focus shifted toward the upcoming campaigns for Alaska, the national forest roadless areas, and the BLM public domain. As a result of the new wilderness reviews, the wilderness system would measure more than 100 million acres of land, much of which would be in Alaska, by 1994.

The Wilderness Society's Crossroads

Even as the Wilderness Society's efforts to build a national wilderness movement and advance its legislative agenda began to yield new successes in the mid-1970s, the organization itself was on the verge of collapse. Since the early 1970s, the Wilderness Society had struggled to support a growing array of campaigns—challenging the Trans-Alaska Pipeline, overseeing the ten-year reviews, and working on the new roadless area reviews. The financial problems that began in 1972 were undermining the organization by 1974. And with little forward-looking financial planning for its one-million-dollar budget, many on the Wilderness Society's staff grew worried as Brandborg acted with greater autonomy to keep the organization afloat. Facing a growing deficit, Brandborg began to borrow money from the Denver office's wilderness trip budget; he also tapped into the organization's endowment and spent lifetime membership funds.[89] To make ends meet, Brandborg began cutting staff and programs. He laid off thirteen of twenty-five employees immediately.[90] Most of those were the field consultants who operated on a shoestring budget and had worked closely with Clif Merritt to foster a strong network of grassroots activists in the West. By 1974, their numbers had been reduced from fourteen to five. Brandborg also canceled local and regional wilderness training programs and the Denver office's independent fundraising activities.[91] These decisions were largely made in secret in Washington, D.C., and handed down by Brandborg and his assistant, Virginia Carney. The drastic reduction in staff opened up a chasm of mistrust between the Wilderness Society's Washington office and Denver office, and especially between Brandborg and his staff.[92]

In 1974, the Wilderness Society's staff and advisors considered alternate sources of funding. The Denver office, still under Clif Merritt's direction, was most aggressive in pursuing grants from foundations. Merritt had hoped to secure up to $60,000 from foundations in 1974, following the model of other environmental groups such as the NRDC and the Environmental Defense Fund.[93] The Wilderness Society also hired a consultant to explore holding fundraising dinners across the country. But several of the Governing Council, and Brandborg in particular, expressed concerns about relying on foundations or large donors. Brandborg reminded his colleagues that the organization needed "to be sensitive to offers of contributions from donors who might seek to weaken wilderness policies and programs . . . because of their personal interests."[94] Faced with crisis, Brandborg never enthusiastically explored such alternatives. Instead he reached into his familiar stock of ideas. In a memo to the Governing Council, he wrote it was time to reemphasize a "brave new program aimed at developing a large core of well-trained citizen leaders in a hurry."[95] Brandborg saw Operation Grass Roots as a replacement for the Wilderness Society's diminished network of field organizers that could involve thousands of citizens.[96] Brandborg would hold fast to that idea until he was fired. In his mind, the Wilderness Society was meant to be "a catalyst, trainer, and organizer, providing guidance and direction to volunteer teams which can bring to realization the society's wilderness preservation goals."[97] That vision only became more ironic as Brandborg's own leadership crisis deepened.

In June 1975, after another series of staff reductions, the problems that had accumulated in the previous eighteen months at the Wilderness Society spilled over in a few days. A half-dozen of the Washington, D.C., staff resigned immediately. Others submitted a petition to the Governing Council urging Brandborg's removal.[98] It was a bitter and personal confrontation. The letters of resignation charged Brandborg with poor management, misrepresentation, and dishonesty. An administrative assistant wrote, "I can only hope that . . . the integrity of those who have chosen to remain here can override the Nixonian attitude that permeates your office."[99] On one letter, the Wilderness Society's stationery was altered to read "The Brandborg Society."[100] The Governing Council, which had been slow to address the organization's growing problems, convened an emergency meeting in July. Clif Merritt was appointed temporary director, pending an outside review. The successes that year rested more and more on the ongoing efforts of local wilderness advocates and the work of the Sierra Club. When the consultants completed their review of the Wilderness Society in December, they returned a damning indictment of Brandborg's leadership and management practices. In retrospect, the report appears to have reflected more the personal animosity that pervaded the Wilderness Society than the organization's performance under Brandborg's guidance. To this day, many leaders within the wilderness movement question Brandborg's dismissal. But Brandborg had proven to be an impenetrable administrator who, despite his evangelical belief in citizen organizing, had undermined his own leadership of the Wilderness Society. The report noted the changing environmental movement, the waning public support, and the organization's internal management problems and stated, "the Society is at a crossroads of development requiring

the careful reflection and unemotional action of its governing body, the Council."[101] The council voted to fire Brandborg on January 10, 1976.

Conclusion

For the Wilderness Society and the wilderness movement, Brandborg's departure emerged as a crossroads. During his tenure, the Wilderness Society had
been pivotal in shaping the Wilderness Act's implementation. After Brandborg's ouster, the new focal point for the wilderness movement would be the
upcoming reviews of Alaska, the national forests, and the public domain, all
of which posed new challenges and opportunities. After several years of internal turmoil, the Wilderness Society reemerged in the late 1970s as an expert-
driven, foundation-funded professional environmental organization which
would reclaim leadership of public lands policy. In place of Brandborg's evangelical focus on citizen activism in the field, the Wilderness Society emphasized
hard-nosed economic and scientific analysis centered in Washington, D.C.
While the citizen-oriented approach to wilderness advocacy would not disappear, the Wilderness Society's new strategies reflected changes in the ways that
citizens interacted with environmental groups, the government, and the public lands. Historians, however, have given little attention to Brandborg's ouster
or the changing scope and strategies of the wilderness movement. To scholars
and environmentalists alike, it seemed that the Wilderness Society and the wilderness movement were secondary to an emerging environmental movement
focused on a new generation of environmental issues. As one historian argues,
the Wilderness Society collapsed not so much from its internal problems, but
because of external factors: it was "unable to make a clear transition to the new
era of mainstream environmentalism."[102] The ways in which wilderness advocates navigated this changing landscape of environmental politics, however,
suggests the complex place of wilderness in the environmental movement and
of the environmental movement in American politics.

Historians have often drawn three lessons from the events surrounding
Earth Day and the rise of the environmental movement in the early 1970s.
First, Earth Day is seen as a turning point for the issues important to American environmentalism. In place of the earlier concerns for the public lands,
wilderness, and wildlife—the issues of the conservation movement, which
dominated national discussion of the environment into the 1960s—emerged
a new generation of environmental issues focused on air and water pollution,
nuclear fallout, toxic waste, population growth, and other threats to human

and environmental health in the 1970s.[103] Second, Earth Day revealed the extent to which the modern environmental movement was rooted in the social and political ferment of the Sixties protest movements—giving new emphasis to challenging the status quo, embracing militancy, and pushing for social and cultural change. No longer was environmentalism just about political reform, it was poised to emerge as a far-reaching social movement.[104] And, third, the environmental movement commanded newfound popular and political support that transcended the nation and its political parties. The rapid progress on environmental regulation demonstrated the importance of bipartisan political support for environmental reform.[105] But the debates over the public lands that preceded and followed these years offer reasons to consider these three lessons carefully.

Judging by the surge of legislative accomplishments, new environmental groups, and issues that now occupy a central place in American environmentalism, it is evident that the new environmental movement broadened the issues at the forefront of American environmental concern. But to assume that the rise of these new issues made debates over the public lands secondary is to overlook the dynamic role earlier conservation issues continued to play in environmental politics. Neither the wilderness movement nor the Wilderness Society was left behind by the new environmental movement. In the early 1970s, wilderness advocates actively adopted new tools, especially NEPA, litigation, and public comment periods, and used them to advance an old conservation cause: protecting wilderness. As wilderness advocates did so, they expanded the federal government's role in protecting the public lands, which set the stage for a political backlash against big government in the late 1970s and early 1980s. What is important to recognize is that the divisions that emerged in modern American environmental politics—radical activists against mainstream environmentalists, rural Westerners against urban environmentalists, and Democrats versus Republicans—were not just in reaction to a new generation of environmental issues, but were often publicly and forcefully in response to new debates over conservation issues, including wilderness.

The far-reaching social ambitions for environmentalism that characterized Earth Day were evident not only in the rhetoric of its activists, but also in its early legislative accomplishments. Some of the key environmental laws passed in the early 1970s—NEPA, the amended Clean Air and Water Acts, and the Endangered Species Act—mark a degree of legislative ambition unmatched in later environmental policy initiatives: large-scale environmental planning, eliminating pollution, and restoring species (goals which were scaled back in implementation or by subsequent legislation). It is quite remarkable, nevertheless, that the social protest which characterized Earth Day, which often raised questions about the role of government in environmental reform, could be channeled so effectively into political gains in Congress. It is a paradox with which historians have not fully wrestled. One way to explain this paradox is to emphasize the exceptional nature of the politics surrounding Earth Day: the mass outpouring of popular concern for the environment made possible such far-reaching policies. An alternative explanation is that the political achievements for environmental reform in the 1970s owe as much to Lyndon Johnson's Great Society, a liberal faith in the role of government in protecting the public interest (despite some rhetoric to the contrary), and those earlier political precedents as they do to the social politics of the early 1970s. This was the case with the wilderness movement's gains in these years: it built on earlier legislative precedents to strengthen the federal government's role in public lands protection. At its heart, both before and long after Earth Day, the mainstream American environmental movement continued to invest its faith in the federal government as the necessary and most effective vehicle for protecting the environment.

The debates over the public lands also raise questions about the bipartisan roots of environmental reform. On the highest-profile environmental issues in these years, Republicans provided crucial support in Congress: NEPA passed by voice vote in the Senate and 372 to 15 in the House; the Clean Air Act passed 73 to 0 in the Senate and 374 to 1 in the House and the Clean Water Act passed 74 to 0 in the Senate and 366 to 11 in the House (and Congress subsequently acted to override a Nixon veto). Such strong political support, transcending party and region, suggests the powerful appeal of environmental reform. But those votes, while crucial, should not be allowed to obscure a broader trend. As the Nixon administration's tenuous commitment to public lands protection—evident in its frustration with NEPA, its concern about the new roadless reviews, and its support for the timber industry—all suggest, for many Republicans, votes for the environment were often secondary to concerns about government regulation, industry, and economic growth. Despite variations based on geography (for instance, Northeast Republicans were strong environmental supporters; Southern Democrats generally were not) and individual exceptions (such as Republican John Saylor's outstanding work for wilderness in the House), Democrats were more often the driving force in advancing environmental legislation and supporting such reform in Congress. For instance, in the Senate, Democrats supported the League of Conservation Voters' agenda 53 percent of the time between 1970 and 1972; Republicans supported the agenda

28 percent of the time.[106] Studies by political scientists indicate the persistence of partisan cleavage in environmental politics in these years, too.[107] All of this suggests that the strong support for environmental reform in the early 1970s, rather than representing an era of straightforward bipartisan support for conservation and environmental reform, formed a part of an emerging transition in American politics as a whole.

Events of the mid-1970s marked a crossroads for the place of environmental reform in American politics. In the years to come, debates over the public lands would be caught up in a broad transformation of American politics as the liberal politics of the Great Society of the 1960s began to wane and modern conservatism began to gain political strength. Although historians suggest that the Democratic Party's liberal agenda crested with Johnson's Great Society and died in the social turmoil of the late 1960s and early 1970s, the sustained legislative action for the public lands, and environmental reform more broadly, in the 1970s reflected the continuing ability of the Democratic Party to command broad support for a liberal environmental agenda, even amongst Republicans, which emphasized the public interest in environmental protection and invested increased powers in the federal government. But as both the Democratic Party and the Republican Party began to reposition themselves as the economy weakened, concerns over taxes grew, and concerns for property rights and free enterprise increased, maintaining such strong support in Congress would become difficult. In the late 1970s and 1980s, debates over wilderness and the public lands would help consolidate the Republican Party's growing political power in the West and in small but essential ways contribute to the rise of modern conservatism nationwide. One thing was certain: in the years to come, no one could describe wilderness as "a motherhood and apple pie" issue anymore.[108]

PART TWO

THE POLARIZATION OF AMERICAN ENVIRONMENTAL POLITICS, 1977–1994

5 / ALASKA

"THE LAST CHANCE TO DO IT RIGHT THE FIRST TIME"

N ews of Stewart Brandborg's departure from the Wilderness Society spread quickly through the ranks of the wilderness community in the winter of 1976. Within weeks, the Wilderness Society's Governing Council began to receive letters from activists across the country. Many expressed their outrage: "What a strange way to reward a leader!"[1] "You have, no doubt, brought joy to the hearts of the exploiters."[2] They praised Brandborg's leadership, his "bold and imaginative" training sessions, and his ability to "weld, enthuse, and train workers from all environmental organizations."[3] But the problems that had been mounting at the Wilderness Society had not gone entirely unnoticed. Other members remarked that the Wilderness Society's administration was sloppy, tensions with the field staff were growing, and the organization was losing its momentum.[4] One longtime associate summed up the Wilderness Society's ordeal as one that demanded the council's "judgment and courage." Despite Brandborg's unfailing commitment, "the job had, perhaps, outgrown him."[5] In the aftermath of Brandborg's departure it would take the Wilderness Society four years to right itself. Three executive directors would come and go. Membership would drop to two-thirds of what it had been in the mid-1970s. The society's budget would remain in the red. Yet, at the moment of the Wilderness Society's crisis, the wilderness movement itself faced its greatest opportunities.

In the spring of 1976, Chuck Clusen, the Sierra Club's chief public lands lobbyist, sent a confidential letter to Michael McCloskey, the club's executive director. He noted that Brandborg's departure and the staff turnover had crippled the Wilderness Society's legislative program. If the wilderness movement was to advance, Clusen noted, the Sierra Club would have to make "additional extra efforts during the period of the Society's lapse."[6] Clusen, like many others in Washington, D.C., realized that the legislative and legal advances for wilderness protection in the mid-1970s had set the stage for three major wilderness reviews: Alaska's "national interest" lands, the national forest "roadless areas," and the Bureau of Land Management (BLM) lands. In the 1960s, wilderness advocates had hoped to protect 35 to 55 million acres of wilderness. The new wilderness reviews encompassed nearly 200 million acres of land, from the arid expanses of southwestern deserts to the wilds of Alaska. Of these reviews, Alaska was most pressing: its December 1978 deadline for congressional action was less than two years away. The campaign for Alaska became a focal point of American environmental politics in the late 1970s. With the Sierra Club in the lead, the environmental community organized under the banner of the Alaska Coalition—which emerged as a well-oiled advocacy machine, spanning dozens of national organizations and 1,500 local and national affiliates; its cogs and gears linked the nation's environmental constituency with a professional lobbying campaign in Washington, D.C. This tight coordination meshed the old and the new in environmental advocacy: it encouraged the citizen involvement that had been important to Stewart Brandborg's vision of the wilderness movement. Its national scope, professional coordination, and financial resources marked the increasing sophistication of the mainstream environmental movement. That synergy would sustain the Alaska Coalition and its campaign through its denouement in 1980.

Environmentalists and historians alike have heralded the Alaska campaign in the late 1970s as a highpoint for wilderness protection. The historian Roderick Nash described it as the "greatest single instance of wilderness preservation in world history."[7] But that viewpoint obscures the pivotal role of the Alaska campaign in American environmental politics. When the campaign began in the mid-1970s, wilderness advocates enjoyed strong support from the Carter administration and Democratic allies in Congress. Buoyed by such a favorable political moment, wilderness advocates advanced ambitious plans for Alaska, emphasizing the unparalleled opportunity to develop scientifically informed conservation plans for the nation's wildest lands. Such ambitions ran up against the changing landscape of American environmental politics, however. As the future of Alaska drew the nation's attention in the late 1970s, the campaign itself opened up deep divisions over the place of local, state, and national interests in public lands protection and governance. Native Alaskans, such as the Eskimo and Inupiat, affected both the protection and the development of Alaska's public lands in ways that reflected their divided interests. As the Alaska Coalition consolidated in Washington, D.C., it faced growing opposition among grassroots wilderness advocates, both in Alaska and nationwide. And some Alaskans, such as hunters and resource industry employees, many of whom resented the federal government's expanding role in land management and environmental protection, succeeded in allying with the natural resource industries and the state of Alaska to challenge the Alaska Coalition. The growing frustration with the role of the federal government in Alaska and the national campaign for Alaska's public lands formed new currents in a rising tide of conservatism that would sweep Ronald Reagan and the Republicans into office in 1981. Ultimately, the future of Alaska was determined as much by the changing landscape of American politics as by the exceptional landscape of the nation's forty-ninth state.

A National Campaign for Alaska

Being a mapmaker in Alaska would have been a very busy job in the 1970s. In 1970, 97 percent of Alaska's land was still overseen by the federal government.[8] By 1981, much of that land would be parceled out to the state, Alaska's Natives, and the federal land agencies. Of that, what would be protected as wilderness? Several agreements structured lands selections in Alaska in these years. The state of Alaska aimed to complete its selection of the 103.5 million acres it had been granted under its 1959 statehood act. Alaska's Natives began to organize their villages and newly formed Native corporations to select 44 million acres to support their subsistence way of life and meet their economic needs as granted to them in the Alaska Native Claims Settlement Act of 1971 (ANCSA). And, most important to wilderness advocates, the federal government began reviews to protect 80 million acres of Alaska's lands in the "national interest" as national parks, wildlife refuges, forests, and wilderness. Alaska's lands were expansive—366 million acres all told. But with construction of the Trans-Alaska Pipeline underway, it was clear that Alaska was on the verge of transformation, a realization that only heightened competing claims over its lands.

Resolving the future of Alaska's national-interest lands was a two-step process. Initially, the secretary of the interior made preliminary withdrawals from Alaska's public lands based on the recommendations of a federal Alaska Planning Group (dominated by the National Park Service and Fish and Wildlife Service). Those withdrawals, which sparked considerable study and jockeying among the federal land agencies, wilderness advocates, and the state of Alaska (which unsuccessfully tried to preempt the federal selections), were announced initially in 1972 and finalized in 1973. The final withdrawals temporarily allocated 32.6 million acres to national parks, 31.6 million acres to wildlife refuges, and 18.8 million acres to national forests, for a total of 83 million acres, and additional lands to the state and Natives.[9] For the environmental community, most disappointing were the new national forests, which would be managed on a multiple-use basis. But to make those initial withdrawals permanent, Congress needed to pass legislation confirming that those withdrawals met the "national interest." Under section 17(d)(2) of ANCSA, which authorized the national-interest withdrawals, the 83 million acres of selected lands were generally protected from some Native and all state land selection, pending congressional approval (which would make them permanent) or December 1978 (when the temporary withdrawals expired). But any congressional legislation for the Alaskan national-interest lands was a nonstarter in Congress in the mid-1970s. Disorganization within the environmental community, continuing confusion over the withdrawals, and concerns about the economy stymied legislative action.

With construction of the Trans-Alaska Pipeline underway, the threats to Alaska seemed to mount by the day. National and Alaskan conservation organizations gathered together to launch a coordinated Alaska campaign in 1975 and 1976. At an initial meeting in 1975, the Alaska Conservation Society, Wilderness Society, Sierra Club, National Audubon Society, and other Alaskan groups agreed to push a single bill that protected more than 100 million acres of land and included extensive wilderness designations. In May 1976, a second meeting was held to further develop the proposal and to give more specific attention to issues such as Native subsistence practices (which most wilderness advocates supported) and wilderness in southeast Alaska's national forests.

Both meetings were marked by important divisions between Alaska's interested citizens, Alaskan Natives, and the national wilderness organizations. Although the cooperation of Alaskans, Natives, and national wilderness leaders would always be fragile, Celia Hunter would play a crucial role in holding the coalition together. Hunter was a longtime leader of the Alaska Conservation Society, an early champion of the Arctic National Wildlife Range, a member of the Wilderness Society's Governing Council, and its executive director from 1976 to 1978 (making her the first female leader of a national environmental organization). Hunter knew that the campaign for Alaska was going to be won in the lower forty-eight and, ultimately, in Congress. Harry Crandell, chief of the Wilderness Society's legislative program under Brandborg, put that point to her sharply in 1976. "The 'little old lady in tennis shoes' in Rhode Island and elsewhere will get the job done in Alaska—not Alaskans," he wrote.[10] For the Alaska Coalition, making Alaska's public lands a national issue would be a political imperative.

The campaign for Alaska opened in a moment of political opportunity.

5.1 Celia Hunter (center), a longtime leader of the Alaska Conservation Society and executive director of the Wilderness Society from 1976 to 1978, reviewing proposals at an Alaska Coalition conference in 1978. Courtesy the Wilderness Society.

Jimmy Carter was elected president in November 1976 on a platform that invoked his down-to-earth sensibilities, the need to revive the economy, and the importance of addressing the nation's persistent energy and environmental issues. At the urging of national environmental leaders, who met with Carter after his election, he made Alaska a top environmental priority and filled posts with environmentally minded individuals. Rupert Cutler, who had worked for Brandborg at the Wilderness Society, became assistant secretary of agriculture. Cecil Andrus, who had been an ally to wilderness advocates as governor of Idaho, became the new secretary of the interior. Down the Washington Mall, reshuffling in the House of Representatives also favored the Alaska Coalition. Representative Morris Udall (D-AZ) became chair of the House Interior Committee, which oversaw parks and wilderness issues—an outcome that pleased six-foot-five-inch Udall so much, he lifted five-foot-five-inch Chuck Clusen off his feet in a bear hug when they next met.[11] With the Alaska Coalition's support, Udall created a new subcommittee to oversee Alaska's public lands, with the key goal of making Representative John Seiberling (D-OH) its chair. Udall and Seiberling formed a powerful and enthusiastic pair of legislative allies for the Alaska Coalition. Behind that alliance was the work of the Interior Commit-

5.2 Arizona Representative Mo Udall, who championed H.R. 39, the Alaska Coalition's proposal for Alaska public lands, spoke to the coalition at a 1978 workshop. Courtesy the Wilderness Society.

tee's newest staffer, Harry Crandell. Crandell brought the same enthusiasm that had distinguished his work at the Fish and Wildlife Service and the Wilderness Society to his newest post in the inner workings of Congress. With Democrats controlling the White House and Congress and with key political allies in the Carter administration and the House, the Alaska Coalition had set the stage for an ambitious campaign for an Alaska lands act.[12] But in the November 1976 elections, there was also a clue to the political challenges that lay ahead. In 1977, for the first time since World War II, the twelve western states sent more Republicans (thirteen) than Democrats (eleven) to the Senate. The Republicans' capture of four western Senate seats marked the party's growing political strength, which would change the balance of political power nationwide and transform the endgame for Alaskan wilderness in 1980.[13]

Behind the national campaign for Alaska was a growing conviction within the wilderness leadership that Alaska presented a unique opportunity to put scientific concerns for public lands protection first. Unlike the lower forty-eight, where roads, homes, and cities—and the property rights and competing interests they represented—constrained conservation efforts, wilderness advocates often described Alaska as a blank slate. "Nowhere else in the United States will we have the opportunity to protect whole ecosystems intact," explained the coalition.[14] That became its refrain, as the coalition emphasized the opportunity to establish ecologically reasoned parks, refuges, and wilderness areas to protect critical habitats, entire watersheds, and migratory wildlife. The concept of the ecosystem dated to the 1930s, but a broad concern for the protection of ecosystems was the work of Eugene Odum, who in the 1950s and 1960s popularized the ecosystem as the basic unit of ecological study.[15] He described ecosystems as functional units that included organisms, the environment, and the ecological processes that structured the natural world. Odum, and many environmentalists, invested ecosystems with intrinsic qualities: they were self-regulating systems, they followed orderly successional patterns over time, and, as they matured, they became more complex and, ultimately, more stable. If left undisturbed, ecosystems eventually achieved a climax state, best represented by an old-growth forest, a trophically rich lake, or a diverse meadow.[16]

By the early 1970s, wilderness advocates had made these lessons from ecology a centerpiece of their arguments for protecting wilderness areas.[17] This strategy reflected a subtle shift in the language of science within the wilderness community. Wilderness advocates had emphasized the scientific value of wilderness protection in the campaign for the Wilderness Act; but when they did so, the emphasis was often on the "uses" of wilderness for scientific study in the early 1960s—as an educational resource, a scientific laboratory, or a benchmark for measuring ecological change—rather than the intrinsic value of wilderness. Despite the growing importance of these scientific arguments for wilderness protection in the 1970s, the wilderness movement did not actively partner with academic ecologists. There was no Paul Ehrlich, E. O. Wilson, or other leading ecologist of the wilderness movement in the 1970s. Even as the ecosystem concept gained a prominent place in wilderness advocacy, many academic ecologists began to question the holistic and teleological reasoning that underlaid it; they began to shift their work to focus on simpler systems, individual populations, and mathematical modeling—ideas important to the theory of island biogeography, which would play an important role in the wilderness debates in the late 1980s.[18] In this respect, the popular scientific ideas important to wilderness advocacy were a step behind the work of leading ecologists.

Yet, the popular concern for protecting complete ecosystems and the imperatives of wilderness politics formed a powerful symmetry in the early 1970s. Wilderness designation promised to protect undisturbed ecosystems, and ecosystem theory justified expansive wilderness designations. Wilderness advocates drew on that argument to justify their efforts to move the Alaska legislation forward quickly. When the Department of the Interior made its initial survey of Alaska public lands in the early 1970s and temporarily withdrew the 83 million acres of potential national-interest lands, many of the proposed conservation units omitted land that the federal land agencies deemed to be "areas of ecological concern." As the historian Gary Williss notes, much of the subsequent debate over Alaska's public lands centered on expanding the final conservation units to encompass these "areas of ecological significance."[19] But to achieve that goal, the final legislation for Alaska needed to become law before the national-interest lands were re-opened to land selections by the state and Natives on December 10, 1978. If that deadline passed without legislative action, such selections could create a patchwork of land ownership that would compromise any efforts to achieve comprehensive ecosystem protection in Alaska.[20]

Representative Udall introduced the coalition's proposal, House Resolution 39, on the first day of the 95th Congress in 1977. The legislation had been drafted by Clusen to reflect the coalition's greatest ambitions; it included expansive boundaries for every potential park, refuge, and wilderness area the coalition hoped to protect in Alaska—64 million acres of national parks, 46 million acres of wildlife refuges, and 145 million acres of new wilderness areas (including most of the existing parks and refuges and 5 million acres of national forest lands). The wilderness proposal amounted to nearly half the land in Alaska and would have increased by more than tenfold the size of the wilderness system nationwide. Even though the coalition knew the proposal was an ambitious starting point for negotiations, it hoped to win big in Congress.[21] To draw attention to the proposal, the coalition urged Representative Seiberling (and his staffer Crandell), to whose subcommittee the legislation was referred, to immediately hold public hearings. Seiberling, a Democrat from Akron, Ohio, had a passion for the outdoors. He cut his teeth on public lands protection at Cuyahoga National Recreation Area in Cleveland's backyard. And from the late 1970s until his retirement in 1987, he was a driving force in Congress for wilderness preservation in the national parks and national forests.[22] That record of accomplishment started with Alaska. Seiberling took to the idea of hearings. Instead of holding hearings just in Alaska and Washington, D.C., as might be expected, the Alaska subcommittee worked with the Alaska Coalition in the spring of 1977 to hold five daylong public hearings across the lower forty-eight to establish the national importance of the legislation, as well as ten hearings in Alaska.[23] In Washington, D.C., Atlanta, Chicago, Denver, and Seattle, the coalition urged: "Everyone should testify!"[24] In the subsequent testimony, Alaska emerged as a land of superlatives—"unspoiled," "priceless and irreplaceable," and "unique." And, at least in the lower forty-eight, many citizens echoed the two main themes that came to define the Alaska Coalition's campaign: the historical significance of the Alaskan wilderness and the opportunity to protect complete ecosystems.[25]

Alaska and its landscape occupied a symbolic place in American history. As the Alaska Coalition argued, "Alaska was the last chance to do it right the first time."[26] Describing Alaska as the nation's last wilderness not only wrote it into the nation's mythical narrative, it also re-created Alaska as a site of national renewal at the time of the nation's 1976 bicentennial. As the scholar Susan Kollin argues, the ways Americans have imagined Alaska says as much about America's national identity as it says about Alaska as a "natural" entity.[27] Many citizens justified their support for the Alaska Coalition's proposal by emphasizing its ecological values: it was an opportunity to preserve a "fragile and delicate" landscape, "complete ecosystems," and endangered species.[28] Unlike wilderness campaigns in the lower forty-eight, where the most enthusiastic advocates could speak of their personal knowledge and appreciation for the wild lands at stake, relatively few people had visited Alaska in the 1970s. But by drawing on scientific arguments, citizens could speak with enthusiasm about setting aside parks, refuges, and wilderness areas that would protect migrating wildlife populations and intact ecosystems. Together, these two themes formed the cornerstone of the Alaska Coalition's national campaign for Alaska; it drew on the historical and the ecological, taking elementary concepts from both and projecting them onto Alaska's iconic landscape. The Alaska Coalition mobilized thousands of citizens, from school children to outdoor clubs, to support the campaign for Alaska with testimony, telephone calls, outdoor gear raffles, bake sales, slideshows, and visits to Washington, D.C.[29] More than two thousand people testified during the 1977 hearings. What was remarkable about the campaign was the moral conviction with which citizens in the lower forty-eight voiced their visions for the future of the forty-ninth state. It was a campaign that hinged on the fundamental premise of the wilderness movement: these were public lands of national importance.

At an early meeting of the Alaska Coalition, one participant from Alaska warned that the national organizations should not take a "monolithic view" of Alaska's public lands. That strategy may work for "political purposes" in the lower forty-eight, but it would not work "here in Alaska."[30] During the early hearings, opposition to H.R. 39 had been slight. That changed when the hearings reached Alaska. In smaller towns in Alaska, such as Ketchikan, opponents turned out in force. Loggers raised concerns about the threat wilderness posed to logging on the Tongass National Forest. Boosters raised concerns about oil and gas development. Landowners raised concerns about access to private lands inside new conservation areas. Although some Natives praised the extensive land protections, others raised concerns about the slow progress of land selections under ANCSA and the implications of park and wilderness management for subsistence activities. In larger towns, such as Juneau, Fairbanks, and Anchorage, testimony regarding H.R. 39 split evenly between opponents and proponents of the legislation. Support among Alaskans emerged from the growing environmental community in Alaska, much of which was affiliated with the Alaska Conservation Association. These differences between the hearings in the lower forty-eight and Alaska foreshadowed the deliberations to come. In the lower forty-eight, the national-interest legislation folded a vastly diverse set of landscapes, resource issues, and political interests into one all-encompassing piece of legislation, around which the Alaska Coalition could build national support. While that strategy would give the Alaska Coalition's campaign its strength, the final legislation would turn as much on the particular issues raised in the Alaska hearings, as on the celebration of Alaska's wild lands that characterized the hearings in the lower forty-eight.[31]

The Peculiarities of Alaska

Behind the blitz of national enthusiasm for Alaska lay a land and a wilderness campaign deeply shaped by Alaska's peculiarities. In the fall of 1977, Seiberling and his staff drafted a revised version of H.R. 39 that proposed 45 million acres of national parks, 53 million acres of wildlife refuges, and 6 million acres of new national forests and designated 84 million acres of wilderness areas.[32] The proposal suggested establishing or expanding forty-five conservation units, including areas as different as Mount McKinley, Gates of the Arctic, Yukon Flats, Admiralty Island, and the Arctic National Wildlife Range. Brief sketches of two of the landscapes at stake in Alaska—the Arctic Range in the far north and Admiralty Island in the southeast—illustrate the similarities and differences that not only shaped the campaign for Alaska but also shaped local, state, and national interests over the future of the public lands. Native and non-Native Alaskans, local and national conservationists, resource industries, and the state of Alaska all contested the future of Alaska's public lands. In the same way that extending the wilderness system to include popular backcountry areas in the West or rejuvenated wild lands in the East had tested the wilderness movement's pragmatism in the lower forty-eight, so too would addressing questions about subsistence use, sport hunting, and non-conforming uses on Alaska's wild lands.

The Brooks Range rises to its greatest heights in northeastern Alaska, where it towers over wide river basins and a sprawling coastal plain that borders the Arctic Ocean. In 1960, President Eisenhower's secretary of the interior, Fred Seaton, designated 8.9 million acres of the region as the Arctic National Wildlife Range (ANWR).[33] The refuge rises gently from the Beaufort Sea, follows the rivers of the coastal plain upstream into the foothills, and then rises precipitously to the sharp peaks of the Romanzof and Davidson mountains of the Brooks Range. The refuge is year-round habitat for polar bears, grizzly bears, moose, wolves, lynx, and marten. Although it appears to be a bleak landscape of snow and ice in the winter, come summer the range hosts a busy assembly of bird life and migratory mammals. It is habitat for at least 163 species of birds — a raucous and social gathering of avian life distinguished by the dazzling aerials of Arctic terns, the threatening pirouettes of jaegers, the clouds of gulls, and foraging flocks of ducks. Birds migrate from all reaches of the Americas to nest in the coastal plain's maze of lakes, lagoons, and estuaries. It is home to forty-four species of mammals, most notably the Porcupine caribou herd — 60,000 to 165,000 strong — that migrates from its southern range in the boreal forests south of the Brooks Range to the Arctic coastal plain to calve each year.[34] In 1959, the Fish and Wildlife Service described the refuge as "biologically irreplaceable."[35]

The Alaska Coalition's plans for ANWR, like its plans for Alaska as a whole, were grand. H.R. 39 proposed doubling the size of the refuge and designating the entire area as wilderness. It gave permanent protection to the critical nesting and calving habitat along the Arctic coastal plain and protected the caribou herd's migratory paths in the United States (the herd ranges into Canada as well). Those plans, however, were met with controversy in Alaska. Like so much of Alaska's public lands, the interests of Alaskan Natives, sport hunters, other citizens, the state, and extractive industries formed a complex terrain that would shape the future of ANWR. Of these interests, the most powerful were the state of Alaska and the petroleum industry. Geography and geology made the region's coastal plain an exceptionally promising prospect for energy exploration. The geological structure of the sedimentary basin underlying the coastal plain suggested the potential for an oil field on par with the major finds at Prudhoe Bay to the west. Equally important, the coastal plain was located in proximity to the northern terminus of the Trans-Alaska Pipeline. If the refuge could be opened for petroleum exploration, then it would be comparatively easy to get the oil to market.[36]

Immediate opposition to expanding ANWR in the mid-1970s did not come from petroleum companies alone. It also came from Natives, who had a vital stake in the future of the refuge. One hundred and twenty Athapascan Indians lived in Arctic Village south of the Brooks Range, and 150 Inupiat Eskimos lived in Kaktovik on the Arctic coastline. Although the residents of rural Alaska were slowly being drawn into the orbit of commercial America, many Native and rural Alaskans subsisted on the land in the 1970s, as they still do today. The well-being of residents of both villages depended on their ability to harvest blueberries, salmonberries, and huckleberries, to fish for salmon, grayling, and whitefish, and to hunt moose, sheep, and bear (the Inupiat hunted sea mammals, too). For both the Athapascans and the Inupiat, however, it was the herds of caribou that gave rhythm to their year. When the Porcupine caribou migrated, each village killed up to 400 per year, drying and freezing the meat to last the winter. All told, each Athapascan and Inupiat consumed an average of 500 and 350 pounds of food, respectively, taken from the land each year. The Natives in Arctic Village and Kaktovik, along with other rural Alaskans, no longer relied solely on traditional methods to maintain their subsistence way of life: snowmobiles, airplanes, and high-powered rifles had become important tools of the hunt.[37]

For that reason, the Athapascans and Inupiat, like many Natives across Alaska, worried that protecting the national-interest lands meant pushing them off the land. In the lower forty-eight, Native Americans had been forced onto reservations and seen their traditional ways of life destroyed. Often, that process was followed by the protection of the land as national forests and national parks.[38] In contrast, ANCSA gave Alaska's Natives an unprecedented degree of autonomy. Each Native village had the right to select a portion of the 44 million acres of land granted to Alaska's Natives under the provisions of ANCSA. For most Native communities, however, 23,040 acres of village lands was insufficient. To meet subsistence needs in the Arctic, they needed to range over vast areas of land to forage, hunt, and trap, including lands the Department of the Interior had withdrawn for the "national interest." As one Native mayor asked, if H.R. 39 became law, "Can we continue to hunt for our food? Can we use our snowmachines in such a park? If not how will we eat and how will we travel?"[39]

Initially, many Alaskan Natives, including those who lived in Arctic Village and Kaktovik, opposed the Alaska Coalition and H.R. 39. They believed the proposal to expand the refuge and designate it a wilderness area would limit hunting and gathering and ban the vehicles important to their way of life.[40] For philosophical and political reasons, however, the Alaska Coalition's leadership supported Native subsistence claims; not only did it consider such uses appropriate and necessary, it also knew Native support would be crucial to the campaign for H.R. 39. In the mid-1970s, the coalition's leadership at the state and national level actively worked to accommodate the concerns of Alaska's Native villages. Such an alliance was not easy. Many Native villages and corporations aimed to exercise their rights under ANCSA to select lands rich in timber and minerals. But, as one Sierra Club staffer emphasized, for the Alaska Coalition and those Natives concerned foremost with subsistence, there was a fundamental "commonality between the protection for large and complete ecosystems which support the biological situations upon which subsistence depends."[41] When the Alaska Coalition drafted H.R. 39 in 1977, it included provisions guaranteeing Native Alaskans and other rural Alaskans the right to continue their subsistence activities on the national-interest lands, if their family had traditionally used those lands for such purposes. In practice, that would mean subsistence users could hunt in national parks, use motorized vehicles in wilderness areas, and supply their camps using snowmobiles, boats, and other vehicles.[42]

The Alaska Coalition's willingness to support subsistence uses won the support of some local Native groups, and in 1978, the Native villages living nearest to ANWR reversed their position on H.R. 39. The city council of Kaktovik wrote Congress that it supported the plan "to expand the Arctic National Wildlife Range [and] to place it in Wilderness *with* strong provisions for continued subsistence uses of renewable resources and to include the continued use of motorized vehicles such as snow-machines and outboard motors." It also warned, however, that "if subsistence uses as outlined in this bill are not included, we cannot support the designation of Wilderness."[43] In particular, the Natives emphasized the importance of protecting the migration routes of the caribou and the caribou's calving grounds on the coastal plain from the threat of petroleum development—precisely the arguments wilderness advocates made. During the debates over Alaska's public lands, the Alaska Federation of Natives—a statewide alliance that included both those more committed to development and those concerned with subsistence—remained neutral on Alaska's land legislation overall, but negotiated actively for strong subsistence language. For the Alaska Coalition, ensuring the support, or at least neutrality, of Native groups would be crucial to debates over Alaska's public lands, particularly as the opposition of the state, industry, and their allies grew in the years to come.[44]

One thousand miles to the southeast, a coastal habitat of rainforests replaces the gaunt beauty of northern Alaska. Admiralty Island is a rolling landscape of forested valleys and bald peaks that runs for one hundred miles north to south along Chatham Strait. Each year the island receives an average of more than four feet of rain. Its forests of spruce and hemlock are home to a dense population of grizzly bears and bald eagles—an average of one bear per square mile and two eagle aeries every three miles of shoreline, giving it as many grizzlies as in all of the Rocky Mountains and more eagles than in all the lower forty-eight. The island had long been home to the Tlingit people, many of whom lived in the small village of Angoon, on the island's western side. During the twentieth century, some Tlingit left the island to pursue opportunities in nearby cities, such as Sitka, Ketchikan, and Juneau, where there was work in the canneries and lumber mills. And outsiders—loggers, miners, sport hunters, fisherman, environmentalists, and those who worked for the Forest Service—began to explore Admiralty Island for their own purposes. These competing interests would shape the future of Admiralty Island or, as the Tlingit referred to it, the "Fortress of the Bears."

For two millennia, Tlingit living on Admiralty had subsisted on the bounty of the sea and forest and had defended the island's shores. In the nineteenth century, as waves of Russians and other Euroamericans swept through southeast Alaska, Angoon had sheltered native Tlingit culture. The local economy and the island changed as whaling operations, fox farms, salmon canneries, and small mining operations came and went, and many Tlingit engaged in the cash economy, selling fish, producing crafts and goods for sale, and serving tourists. But for most of the 400 Tlingit who still lived in Angoon in the 1970s, subsistence activities remained the foundation of their community. The seasonal gathering of herring eggs, shellfish, and seaweed, hunting Sitka deer, and fishing of salmon and halibut bound Angoon to Admiralty Island and the waters and forests around it.[45]

Although the Tlingit viewed Admiralty Island as their home, it and much of southeast Alaska had been part of the 16.7-million-acre Tongass National Forest since 1907. With the support of boosters in Alaska, the Forest Service had aggressively opened the region's forests to economic development after World War II. The turning point for the Tongass National Forest had come in the 1950s, when the Forest Service negotiated two fifty-year contracts that guaranteed a steady supply of timber to companies that built new paper mills in the region; but meeting the terms of those contracts would require logging much of the old-growth timber in the forest. By 1960, two new pulp mills in Ketchikan and Sitka became the hubs for the region's economy. As the mills went into operation, the Forest Service accelerated logging on the Tongass. Clear-cuts pierced the low-elevation valleys of islands such as Baranof, Chichagof, and Revillagigedo.[46] In 1965, the Forest Service took steps to finalize a third fifty-year contract for one million acres of timberland, including half of Admiralty Island.[47]

Southeastern Alaska was a difficult place to be an environmentalist. The Forest Service was especially determined to log the Tongass, and it enjoyed the strong support of the state, the timber industry, and local communities, including some Natives aligned with Sealaska, the Native regional corporation, and urban Native corporations, such as Shee Atika and Goldbelt. Since the late 1960s, a small group of environmentalists and concerned fisherman had partnered with state and national environmental groups to protect the Tongass. In 1970, the Sierra Club sued the Forest Service over its third fifty-year timber contract; although the suit failed, it was the beginning of a series of delays that would be crucial to protecting Admiralty Island. In 1975, wilderness advocates identified forty-five areas in the forest that they believed deserved long-term protection. The Southeast Alaska Conservation Council (SEACC) reorganized itself in 1976, in anticipation of advancing a positive campaign for these areas. But local conservationists soon noted an "uncanny relationship" between the areas they had suggested deserved wilderness protection and those that were scheduled for logging.[48] By September 1976, the Forest Service had initiated logging on six such areas and scheduled logging on fourteen others. For that reason, local conservationists saw the Alaska Coalition's campaign for the national-interest lands as a prime opportunity to advance their campaign for the Tongass. Although the national-interest withdrawals authorized under ANCSA applied only to unreserved public lands, not the Tongass, SEACC urged the Alaska Coalition to add wilderness designations for the Tongass to H.R. 39. "National enthusiasm [for Alaska] may never again be duplicated. It would be unfortunate if [the] Southeast lost out."[49]

Advancing the "national interest" in the future of Admiralty Island, however, meant navigating the complex interests of the Tlingit Natives. When ANCSA became law, it gave the Tlingit and all Alaska Natives a right to the lands they had traditionally used to support their way of life. But, as was important in this case, the statute also recognized the interests of Natives who had moved to nearby cities, such as the Tlingit living in Juneau and Sitka. To meet the

needs of both groups, the law recognized two different types of Native interests. First, it allowed village corporations, such as Kootznoowoo in Angoon,
to select 23,040 acres of nearby lands important to their subsistence activities.
Second, it allowed newly formed urban Native corporations, such as Gold Belt
in Juneau and Shee Atika in Sitka (which represented Natives who had lost
their traditional rights to the land), to select 23,040 acres of land within fifty
miles of each city. The village and urban Native corporations approached those
land selections in very different ways. While the Angoon Tlingit selected land
near the village because it would be useful for subsistence, the two urban corporations staked claims to the most valuable stands of Sitka spruce and western hemlock, which were located in Admiralty Island's western valleys. With
unemployment hovering around 20 percent in the region, they aimed to create
jobs and generate revenue by logging the island.[50]

The Angoon Tlingit countered this new threat by allying themselves with
the national campaign for Alaska. In 1975, national leaders of the Sierra Club
took a canoe trip to Angoon, laying the foundation for this partnership. One
elder remembered, "we were accused of going to bed with the Sierra Club. The
Sierra Club had been trying to protect Admiralty Island for fifty years. It just
happened that we were advocating the same thing."[51] In 1977, in correspondence with John Seiberling, who was sympathetic to Native land claims, and
the Alaska Coalition, the Angoon Tlingit advanced their own proposal for the
future of Admiralty Island. In hopes of blocking the urban corporations' land
claims, they urged legislation to bar all extractive industries, allow only subsistence activities and sport hunting, and shift administrative oversight of the
island to the National Park Service. As an Angoon representative explained,
"We are trying in a very unique way to save our culture, and a way of life, by
putting the island that we depend on for our sustenance into a protective status
for the use and enjoyment of all Americans." That strategy also offered a sharp
rejoinder to the Native corporations: "The [urban Natives] chose to live in the
city and enjoy the comforts of urban life while they propose to rape the land of
their ancestors, over our objections, for their own economic well being."[52] By
1978, H.R. 39 included 4.4 million acres of wilderness on the Tongass National
Forest, including all of Admiralty Island with the exception of Angoon and
surrounding villages' lands.

Hitching the future of southeast Alaska to the campaign for the national-
interest lands would prove to be a fateful decision for the Angoon Tlingit,
SEACC, and the Alaska Coalition. The expansive proposals for wilderness protection, especially those on Admiralty Island, met with sharp opposition from

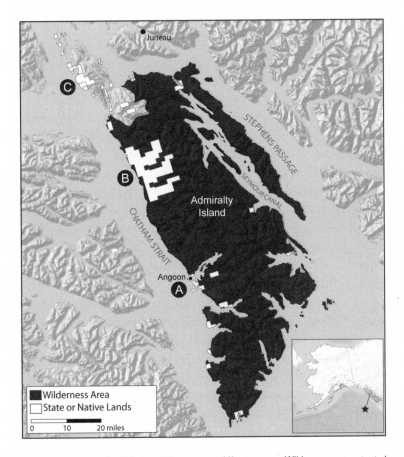

Map 5.1 Admiralty Island National Monument and Kootznoowoo Wilderness, as protected by the Alaska National Interest Lands Conservation Act. Note the Angoon village land claims (A), the Shee Atika land claims, since clear-cut (B), and the state lands at Greens Creek Mine (C). Almost all of the land shown on the map is in the Tongass National Forest; the map shows only state and native land claims and wilderness on Admiralty Island.

both the urban Native corporations and the region's timber industry and their employees. One-tenth of the timber on the Tongass National Forest grew on Admiralty Island. The local timber industry described H.R. 39 as anything but "a fair, livable, or workable plan." One Sitka resident explained: "When you lock up land, you lock up hope." The owners of the Ketchikan pulp mill boiled it down to terms everyone could understand: "Lost: Two Billion Payroll Dollars!"[53] And behind the scenes, the state of Alaska actively worked to exclude rich mineral lands on the northern end of Admiralty Island, at Greens Creek, which was a promising gold and silver mine site. In the final negotiations toward the Alaska legislation, national priorities for the future of Alaska would force difficult choices over the future of the Tongass National Forest and Admiralty Island. But, in the mid-1970s, few foresaw the challenges to come.

These complex local interests important to ANWR and Admiralty Island often disappeared amid the national campaign for Alaska. Unlike earlier wilderness campaigns, in which the Wilderness Society involved citizen activists in the particulars of wilderness proposals, H.R. 39 encompassed so many proposals and so much land that such particulars were often subsumed in a simple debate over which of Alaska's resources would be protected and which would be developed. But the local cultural, political, and economic complexities at ANWR and Admiralty Island suggested two lessons important to the future of the Alaska campaign. First, Alaska's Natives played an active role in advancing their cultural and economic interests in the future of Alaska's public lands. As the historian Theodore Catton has noted, some Natives carefully cultivated their image as a people of nature to secure protection for their subsistence activities and the lands they depended on.[54] This was the strategy of the Gwich'in, Inupiat, and Tlingit at ANWR and Admiralty Island. Accommodating the Natives' interests did not come without some misgivings on the Alaska Coalition's part. One Sierra Club leader argued that permitting subsistence in parks and wilderness areas with snowmobiles and motorboats was "radically different" from "ancient, simple ways." He called on the Alaska Coalition to have the "courage" to "fight for the voiceless wildlife—an international treasure not only for the Eskimos and natives, but all the people of all cultures in all lands."[55] But such a viewpoint was in the minority. The Alaska Coalition, like Seiberling, supported Native land claims and subsistence rights. And the Alaska Coalition knew well that if it was to successfully counter other Native groups, such as the urban Tlingit in Juneau and Sitka, who were "hell-bent" on developing their lands, cultivating the support of Natives, such as the Gwich'in, Inupiat, and Angoon Tlingit, was crucial.[56]

Those efforts, however, strained an already weakened relationship between the wilderness community and sportsmen in Alaska and nationwide. This is the second lesson. While the coalition proved willing to allow non-conforming planes, boats, and snowmobiles for subsistence uses in the national-interest lands, including wilderness areas, it resisted such exemptions for sport hunters. For the coalition, it was a strategic choice: honoring the traditional and preexisting subsistence activities was a moral imperative and a position it deemed compatible with its larger goal of protecting Alaska's wildlife and intact ecosystems; but permitting sport hunting — an established tradition in Alaska — in new national parks and allowing vehicles for such purposes in wilderness areas was unthinkable. Many local conservation groups, including the Alaska Center for the Environment, argued the distinction was arbitrary: there is "no rational, nor fair basis for defining such a difference."[57] The national magazine *Outdoor Life* reported that "many Alaska citizens, as well as most sportsmen, are violently opposed to H.R. 39."[58] Sporting groups, such as the National Wildlife Federation and the Izaak Walton League, urged the Alaska Coalition to move more land into national preserve status, which allowed sport hunting, and to eliminate wilderness designations that would hinder access.

Fostering a pragmatic approach to Alaska's national-interest lands that joined the interests of Alaska's citizens, the Natives, and the national groups remained a constant challenge for the Alaska Coalition, even as the legislative campaign for Alaska gained momentum in Washington, D.C. In late 1977, when Congress began to take up the national-interest legislation and the campaign shifted from Alaska to Washington, D.C., so too did the power in the Alaska Coalition. In many respects, the coalition followed the advice Harry Crandell had offered in 1976: "Alaska is going to be won in Congress by a national campaign, simply stated, and aggressive action. If people in Alaska are still worrying about boundaries, what areas are going to be called, hunting in the park system units, etc., and these same people are calling the shots, then you can kiss Alaska's [public lands] good-bye."[59] The Alaska Coalition linked the interests of many of Alaska's conservationists and the enthusiasm of wilderness activists across the lower forty-eight into a seemingly unified campaign for the future of Alaska's wild lands. But even as the coalition succeeded in capturing the nation's imagination with descriptions of Alaska as the "last great wilderness," such sweeping rhetoric only masked the underlying complexities important to Alaska's past and future.

The Alaska Coalition and the Deadline

The Alaska Coalition set its lobbying machinery in motion in the spring of 1978. As the coalition prepared for a national campaign that was larger in scope than any of the previous wilderness campaigns (even for the Wilderness Act), it championed the iconographic power of Alaska in the American environmental imagination. The coalition emphasized the fragility of the Alaskan wilds, the threat of development, and the importance of protecting complete ecosystems. Its first national campaign flyer asked "Last Frontier or Lasting Frontier?" The

detritus of industry—four oil drums, a rusting bulldozer, and assorted litter—
was framed against the backdrop of an Alaskan peak. The coalition warned
that the "pro-exploitation army is focusing everything they've got on [their]
anti-conservation campaign."[60] It was that strategy that often obscured the local
concerns and complexities important at ANWR and Admiralty Island. But for
the Alaska Coalition, the driving goal was to secure congressional legislation
that expanded on the 1973 national-interest land withdrawals before the withdrawals expired on December 10, 1978.

In 1978, the Alaska Coalition organized its national office, which drew
most heavily from the ranks of the Sierra Club, into a well-funded hub of a
campaign that meshed the activities of thousands of activists nationwide with
a carefully staged lobbying effort in Washington, D.C. Chuck Clusen, the Sierra
Club's chief public lands lobbyist, took the helm of the Alaska Coalition. Clusen was a native of Wisconsin, an Eagle Scout, and an admirer of Aldo Leopold (Clusen and his family celebrated Leopold's birthday every year with a
cake). In the mid-1960s, when Clusen was an undergraduate at the University
of Michigan, Doug Scott was a graduate instructor in one of his classes. Clusen
remembers Scott filling their section with news of wilderness organizing. It was
the beginning of an enduring friendship. Clusen and Scott roomed together in
Michigan and then in Washington, D.C. As Clusen moved up the ranks of the
Sierra Club, Scott moved up the ranks of the Wilderness Society. In the spring
of 1978, Clusen tapped Scott (who had joined the Sierra Club staff in 1973) as
the Alaska Coalition's chief lobbyist. Clusen, patient and sensitive to internal
politics, maintained the coalition's internal harmony. Scott, an experienced and
effective lobbyist, coordinated the coalition's activities in Congress.[61]

The Alaska Coalition's campaign marked the changing strategies of the
American environmental movement. In the 1970s, the national environmental
movement began to consolidate in Washington, D.C., as organizations became
more professional, better funded, and engaged in government activities.[62] The
Alaska Coalition marked an important shift in the structure of wilderness advocacy. It still viewed widespread and active citizen involvement as an imperative and made a tremendous commitment to grassroots outreach (including
more than a dozen grassroots coordinators, daily briefings for citizen leaders,
and an active role for citizens in lobbying campaigns). But when faced with a
campaign of national scope and great legislative complexity, the coalition consolidated organizational responsibilities, strategic planning, and training with
its staff in Washington, D.C., which then orchestrated the activities of groups
and citizens across the nation. Where Brandborg's Wilderness Society focused

5.3 Chuck Clusen, who worked for the Sierra Club in the 1970s and the Wilderness Society in the 1980s, served as chair of the Alaska Coalition. Courtesy the Wilderness Society.

on empowering its activists, the Alaska Coalition saw its local allies and volunteers as essential, but subordinate, cogs in its lobbying machine. In short, the coordinated model of wilderness advocacy in which local and national groups were essential remained, but the power in that relationship increasingly shifted toward Washington, D.C. This became a point of friction, especially with Alaskan leaders who were often pushed to the side in the national campaign.

Running the Alaska Coalition's campaign required a good deal of money. Between 1977 and 1980, the coalition campaign was supported by several million dollars in funds; securing such large sums of money required the coalition and its member organizations to expand their fund-raising activities.[63] Wealthy individuals, foundations, and the outdoor recreation industry all helped to bankroll the coalition's activities. Larry Rockefeller, scion of the Rockefeller family and an active environmentalist, was an instrumental fundraiser.[64] Some of this support came through a group of wealthy donors, Americans for Alaska. Also important were alliances with the outdoor recreation industry. Recreational Equipment Incorporated (REI), for instance, provided free mailings for the coalition to its customers and tens of thousands of dollars in support.[65] Unlike the early 1970s, when the majority of the Wilderness Society's funding came from small donors, the wilderness community could count on its own set of influential financial patrons for the Alaska Campaign.

Three strategies structured the Alaska Coalition's campaign: citizen activism, publicity, and professional lobbying. National mailings, such as the "Last

Frontier or Lasting Frontier?" flyer, were frequent. The mailings encouraged involvement: citizens wrote letters, met with congressmen, and made last-minute telephone calls as the Alaska legislation moved in Congress. The coalition also relied on a network of several hundred Alaska coordinators, which included volunteer citizens and professional environmentalists across the country. These coordinators received regular Alaska status reports to help them coordinate local activities, such as letter-writing parties and fundraisers. In Washington, D.C., a phone bank staffed by 140 volunteers handled "phone blitzes" that targeted key congressional districts during the legislative campaign.[66] And, as the campaign gained steam, the coalition set up a twenty-four-hour hotline to keep citizens and campaign staff informed of up-to-the-minute developments. This carefully orchestrated network of grassroots communication allowed the Alaska Coalition to call forth bursts of activity when and where they were needed. Its largest mailing and telegram bills topped $100,000 each.[67] This was political organizing and outreach of the highest order.

The synergy in the Alaska Coalition campaign came from the coordination of these national activities with congressional lobbying. The coalition matched up twenty core lobbyists, mainly staffers drawn from national member organizations, with congressional representatives. Doug Scott explained, "Our objective must be to make this lobbying campaign a professional, tightly coordinated operation." The lobbyists represented the wilderness movement's accumulated expertise: some were veterans of Brandborg's citizen training programs who had become full-time advocates, and others were veteran lobbyists from other organizations. Together, they navigated the political terrain of Congress with confidence. Lobbyists visited their assigned representatives in a "pre-planned, coordinated, and sequential basis." As the campaign developed, "barnstormers" handled emergency lobbying calls; "captains" headed up special details, such as overseeing congressional committees; and "droppers" filled in the gaps.[68] By mid-May, with H.R. 39 on the floor of the House, the Alaska Coalition had set its grassroots citizen campaign and its professional lobbying machinery in full motion.

"The objective is *not* to win," wrote Doug Scott. "The objective is to win BIG."[69] As the Alaska Coalition knew, the entire Alaska congressional delegation and many western representatives were opposed to H.R. 39. They objected to such large land withdrawals, the potential impact on the state's economic development, and the limits on access to public lands for hunting and recreation. In the House, the numbers were against Alaska's lone representative, Don Young (R). But in the Senate, Alaska's two senators, Mike Gravel (D) and Ted

Stevens (R), wielded more power. If the full Senate was to override the concerns of Alaska's senators, the Alaska Coalition knew an overwhelming vote in the House was crucial: it would demonstrate the national support for Alaska and give the Alaska Coalition bargaining chips in the Senate. On May 19, 1978, following the leadership of Representatives Seiberling and Udall and the considerable legwork of the Alaska Coalition, the House came through after intense negotiations: it voted 277 to 31 to protect 27.1 million acres of national parks, 15.6 million acres of national preserves (compromise park areas which permit sport hunting), and 76.8 million acres of new wildlife refuges. It also designated 65.5 million acres of wilderness on new and existing conservation units across Alaska. Notably, the revised legislation proposed doubling the size of the Arctic Range, designated much of ANWR and Admiralty Island as wilderness areas, barred state land selections within the conservation areas, and gave subsistence uses priority.[70] The legislation had been scaled back as expected, but in the eyes of the Alaska Coalition, it remained grand.

The high hopes for the national-interest lands ran aground in the Senate. In January 1978, Senator Lee Metcalf (D-MT), who the Alaska Coalition's leaders expected to champion the bill, passed away suddenly. The lack of a strong Senate champion would dog the coalition's campaign from start to finish. Signs of trouble emerged quickly. In 1978, the Alaska legislation was substantially weakened when it came up for review in the Senate Energy and Natural Resources Committee. The coalition reported that under Senator Henry Jackson's (D-WA) leadership the Senate energy committee "gutted" the bill, reducing the size of the national parks and wildlife refuges from 119 to 93 million acres and wilderness designations from 66 to 38 million acres, and it prioritized goals important to the state of Alaska and industry. In the case of ANWR, it dropped wilderness protection, divided the range among three agencies, and mandated an eight-year oil and gas survey of the coastal plain. In the case of Admiralty Island, it allocated it to a type of "special management area" that the coalition described as "deferred cut." The changes were unacceptable to the coalition, which remained confident that the full Senate would pass much stronger legislation. In the fall of 1978, fully aware of the approaching December deadline, the coalition played its only card: it withdrew support for the weak committee bill, and instead focused on encouraging the full Senate to amend the legislation on the Senate floor.[71] With the clock ticking toward the end of the session, the coalition, its allies in the Senate and House, and the Carter administration tried to get the bill in front of the Senate. Serious negotiations between the Alaska Coalition and its congressional allies and Alaska's congressional delegation proved fruitless, and efforts to pass stopgap legislation to extend the deadline by a year were blocked. In the final days of the 95th Congress, Senator Gravel played his trump card: he filibustered the Senate and single-handedly shut down any Senate action on the Alaska legislation.[72]

When Congress adjourned in October 1978, it did so without taking any action on Alaska. "We had the votes," the Alaska Coalition reported. "Only one person stood between all our efforts and the passage of a strong Alaska lands bill—Mike Gravel."[73] Gravel would have put it another way: he had used the prerogatives of the Senate to guard Alaska's interests. Although Senator Stevens criticized Gravel's action, he did not support the final Senate bill either.[74] And, in the long run, it was Senator Stevens that most concerned the Alaska Coalition; where Gravel was prone to grandstanding, Stevens was better positioned to work behind closed doors to advance the state of Alaska's goals. Congress's failure to act left the national-interest lands in a state of limbo. On December 10, 1978, the Department of the Interior's temporary withdrawals of the 83 million acres of national-interest lands would expire. In the worst-case scenario, that would allow the state of Alaska and Native corporations to proceed with land selections inside the proposed conservation units—for instance, allowing the state to claim rights to ANWR's coastal plain or Sealaska to claim rights to Admiralty Island's timber.

Congress's indecision led to a political opportunity for President Carter. In November 1978, Clusen wrote to the White House that the "President would be viewed as a dynamic, decisive and strong leader" if he took executive action where Congress had failed.[75] The Carter administration was at a low point. A weak economy had done much to sap the public's enthusiasm for the president, and environmentalists had grown especially frustrated. Although the administration billed itself as pro-environment, it had overseen the weakening of the Endangered Species Act, failed to strengthen the Environmental Protection Agency, and had produced no decisive environmental victories.[76] Clusen, aware of Carter's tenuous political position, argued that presidential action for Alaska would strengthen Carter's credentials: "President Carter clearly could go down in the history book as the greatest conservation President rivaled by none."[77] Most important to Clusen and the Alaska Coalition was the advantage that permanent administrative protection for Alaska would convey: it would give the coalition the upper hand in future congressional deliberations.[78]

In December 1978, in a series of sweeping designations, the Carter administration did in less than two weeks what Congress had been unable to accomplish since 1973: it conveyed permanent protection for much of the national-interest lands in Alaska. The primary tool for those efforts was the Antiquities Act of 1906. That little-known law allowed the president to withdraw from the public domain at "his discretion . . . historic landmarks, historic and prehistoric structures, and other objects of historic or scientific interest which are situated upon lands owned or controlled by the Government of the United States to be national monuments."[79] Every president, Republican and Democrat alike, had used the Antiquities Act to protect national monuments (some of which later became parks), including the Grand Canyon (1908), Dinosaur (1915), Bryce Canyon (1923), Arches (1929), and Joshua Tree (1944). But since World War II, national monument withdrawals generally had been small. Carter broke with that pattern. He declared 56 million acres of Alaska's national-interest lands, most of which were proposed parks, as national monuments. He also called on Secretary of the Interior Andrus to temporarily withdraw an additional 40 million acres as refuges, which included the additions to the Arctic Range.[80] Although Carter's actions did not protect all the areas the Alaska Coalition wanted to protect and, most troublesome, did not designate any wilderness (only Congress could do that), the burden now fell on the "exploiters" to undo the designations—which was the Alaska Coalition's goal.[81]

This turn of events in the campaign for Alaska offers two lessons, one old and one new. The old lesson is one that wilderness advocates would struggle with often in the years to come: Congress rarely overrides a state's congressional delegation on matters of importance to the state. And, as was made clear by Gravel's filibuster, states can defend their interests in the Senate. This had rarely been a problem for wilderness advocates in the 1960s and early 1970s, because they successfully built local support, engaged in pragmatic negotiations with their opponents, and secured allies in the congressional delegations for wilderness protection—an easier task in those years when faith in the work of the federal government remained strong, Democrats held a commanding majority in Congress, and the scope of wilderness designations remained modest. But as wilderness advocates' ambitions expanded in the 1970s and 1980s and included more challenging political territory, such as Alaska, and intermountain states, such as Idaho, Utah, and Nevada, cultivating such support would prove increasingly difficult. In the late 1970s, the growing opposition to the Alaska campaign represented only one current of increasing opposition to the federal government's tightening regulations over the public lands nationwide—protests that soon became part of the Sagebrush Rebellion.

The Carter administration's actions represented a high point for the Alaska

Coalition. The coalition's cogs and gears linked environmentalists from across the nation with the growing ranks of professional environmental lobbyists in Washington, D.C. Although that pressure failed to win the Senate, it did prompt quick action in the White House. One lobbyist for the opposition described it this way: "In a nutshell we were outgunned. Never before [had] such a small group of well-financed, wild-eyed extremists had the power the Alaska Coalition has . . . today."[82] That response suggests the second lesson. Although the wilderness movement had long invested its faith in the federal government and the democratic workings of Congress, its appeal to the Carter administration moved the Alaska campaign forward on an alternative policy pathway that allowed for no public input and mandated no consultation with the state, industry, other stakeholders, or with Alaska's congressional delegation.[83] It was a strategy wilderness advocates would turn to more often in the decades to come. To many Americans—such as hunters, loggers, miners, and the companies they worked for—that strategy and the subsequent administrative withdrawals marked the work of a national environmental community, a federal government, and a White House that were running roughshod over the democratic workings of Congress. In the late 1970s, the landscape of American environmental politics was changing. In doing so, it generated powerful tremors of discontent—among both wilderness advocates and a growing opposition.

"The Big Federal Land Grab"

The *Conservative Digest* summed up the Carter administration's actions in December 1978 as the "big federal land grab."[84] In Alaska, citizens marched in the streets and called for the forty-ninth state to secede from the union. As they saw it, the federal government had staked a permanent claim to one-third of the state over the protests of their state government and congressional delegation. Picket signs read "State Rights!" and "Alaskans Can Manage Alaskan Lands."[85] Many Alaskans argued that the president's actions violated the Alaska Statehood Act. A protest song asked, "Where is the statehood promised long ago? Where did our rights and freedoms go?"[86] Three groups formed the vanguard of the opposition: Citizens for the Management of Alaska Lands (CMAL), the REAL Alaska Coalition, and the state of Alaska itself; they could count on strong support from other groups, such as the AFL-CIO, the Teamsters, and the National Rifle Association.[87] CMAL represented the timber and mining industries. One lobbyist explained that CMAL's "battle cry" was "(M Squared)" for "Members and Money."[88] Small in size, CMAL membership included the Alaska

Building Contractors Union, Kenworth Trucks, the Operating Engineers Union, and Alaska Loggers, each contributing from $4,500 to $120,000. The REAL Alaska Coalition represented the state's sport hunters, off-road vehicle users, and outdoor guides. It called for opening more of the national-interest lands to hunting and limiting wilderness designations to allow easier access, and it criticized the preferential treatment given to Native subsistence users.[89] Of the three, the best-funded and most effective opponent of the Alaska lands legislation was the state of Alaska itself. Between 1978 and 1980, the state legislature appropriated $5.7 million to fund lobbying activities, media efforts, and legal action aimed at guarding what it saw as Alaska's interests and its prerogatives for economic development.[90]

Access to the national-interest lands—for sport hunting and economic development—galvanized the opposition, especially after Carter's executive withdrawals. Access had been a concern from the start of the debate; as one Alaskan staffer noted, "sport hunters may well be the group most adversely affected by H.R. 39."[91] In the mid-1970s, the Alaska Coalition and the House of Representatives shifted more and more land from national park to national preserve status to meet the concerns of hunters and the state of Alaska. But those modest gains for the opposition had disappeared when Carter used the Antiquities Act. Most of the new national monuments barred sport hunting and oil and gas exploration, which meant the executive withdrawals were even more restrictive than if H.R. 39 had become law. As the Alaska Coalition quickly realized, sport hunters had good reason to seek legislative changes to override the Carter administration's actions.[92] That fall, the REAL Alaska Coalition coordinated the "Great Monument Trespass." On opening day of the Dall sheep and caribou hunting season, the coalition urged Alaska's hunters to disregard the new national monument designations. Local newspapers reported dozens of hunters flying, four-wheeling, and boating into national monuments such as Gates of the Arctic and Wrangell-Saint Elias, which had long been favorite places to hunt Dall sheep.[93] It was an act of civil disobedience aimed at a federal government that many citizens believed had overstepped its bounds. In Washington, D.C., the National Rifle Association backed the REAL Alaska Coalition, describing the "anti-gun, anti-hunting" Carter administration as trying to "ramrod" the Alaska legislation through Congress.[94]

For the state of Alaska and allied industries, the two biggest prizes in the land debates were ANWR's coastal plain and the Tongass National Forest. In the early 1970s, geologists estimated ANWR might yield six to twenty billion barrels of oil. As the price of oil climbed in the late 1970s and the Middle East remained unstable, the Alaska Coalition noted, "the 'energy crisis' has given the oil companies, miners, and developers a scare tactic they will surely use."[95] Already, in its second year of operation, the Trans-Alaska Pipeline was delivering a tenth of domestic production; a major find in ANWR might boost domestic output significantly.[96] The continued volatility of the world's petroleum markets and economic inflation offered good reason to consider developing the nation's domestic energy sources. Such developments on federal land reduced oil imports, generated profits and jobs in the domestic petroleum industry, and yielded taxes and royalties for the federal government and the individual states. And, after 1977, when Alaska took steps to create a system for disbursing a quarter of the royalties from oil and gas drilled in the state directly to residents in an annual dividend check (which amounted to $1,000 in 1982, $990.30 in 1995, and $3,269 in 2008), each Alaskan had a direct interest in the future of ANWR, too.[97]

For those who worked in the timber and mining industries in southeast Alaska, the concern was not ANWR, but the sweeping national monument designations on the Tongass National Forest. President Carter had withdrawn 4 million acres of land from the 16.7-million-acre forest, expanding Glacier Bay National Monument and establishing Misty Fiords and Admiralty Island National Monuments, which sharply cut into the timber base and mining opportunities in the region. On Admiralty Island, the new national monument encompassed the entire island, with the exception of its northernmost peninsula, where new mining sites were being explored. In proclaiming the national monument, Carter's language might have been that of the Alaska Coalition's. He emphasized the cultural tradition of the Tlingit, the historical significance of the island's abandoned villages, canneries, and mines, and specifically emphasized that the designation "serve[d] the scientific purpose of preserving intact this unique coastal island ecosystem."[98] Activities such as hunting were allowed to continue in the monument, but mineral exploration and logging were barred. The designation at Admiralty spurred the opposition of the state, industry, and urban Tlingit in Juneau and Sitka. During the final negotiations on the Alaska legislation, the future of Admiralty Island and the Tongass would become key bargaining chips.

For the Alaska Coalition, one course of action would have been to celebrate the Carter administration's executive withdrawals and conclude its campaign. The November 1978 mid-term elections had resulted in a more conservative House and Senate and the economy had begun to slow. The Alaska Coalition knew that Alaska and its allies would press for legislative redress in the new Congress—the state of Alaska had allocated $2.5 million for lobbying and Exxon and the National Rifle Association had also assigned their national lobbyists to the issue.[99] But the Alaska Coalition had its own reasons for continuing the campaign for congressional legislation: despite the strength of Carter's actions, only Congress could designate wilderness. Thus, when the 96th Congress convened in January 1979, so too did the Alaska Coalition and its opponents. Representative Udall introduced an expanded version of H.R. 39, which included few of the compromises with which it had passed the House in May 1978, and began to pilot the legislation through the House Interior Committee, which he chaired. That March, the opponents demonstrated their growing power. By a single vote, the House Interior Committee blocked Udall's bill and reported out a different Alaska lands bill. The Huckaby substitute halved the acreage designated as national parks, shifted much of that land into national preserves open to sport hunting, opened up additional lands for resource production, and reduced wilderness designations to 50 million acres. Two changes in the legislation suggested its overall implications for Alaska: it mandated oil exploration in ANWR's coastal plain and it allocated half of Admiralty Island for logging.[100] "The level of opposition to a strong bill is *much* higher this year than last," reported a surprised Alaska Coalition. "The mining, oil and gas, timber, and fur industries are out in force, as is labor, the National Rifle Association, and the State of Alaska. This is going to be a hard fight."[101]

That spring, the Alaska Coalition put its lobbying operation back into gear with national mailings, telegrams, and telephone campaigns, and a coordinated lobbying effort in Congress. It succeeded in doing what it had failed to do in the Senate in 1978: it overrode the committee's bill and orchestrated a 268 to 157 vote in the House for a Udall-sponsored version of H.R. 39, which would protect ANWR and Admiralty Island, designate 67.4 million acres of wilderness, and include more national preserves in place of national parks.[102] Important to that victory was the support of the National Wildlife Federation, which represented sport hunters nationally. In February 1979, the Alaska Coalition struck a deal to expand the national preserves, which allowed hunting and maintained the ecological integrity of the conservation units (since most of the new preserves were still designated as wilderness areas).[103] The Alaska Coalition was quick to celebrate the victory in the House. In a confidential memo, it suggested that the vote in the House demonstrated the "political clout of wilderness conservationists (and our broad public support)" which would have "significant

Table 5.1 Selected proposals for Alaska lands legislation (1977–1980)

	A	B	C	D	E	F
YEAR	1972	1977	1978	1978	1979	1980
PROPOSAL	D(2)	HR39	HR39	CARTER	HR39	FINAL
National Park Service (total)	32.6	64.1	42.7	44.9	44.0	43.6
Parks and monuments	27.9	51.5	27.1	44.9	27.0	24.6
Preserves	4.7	12.6	15.6	—	17.0	19.0
Wilderness	—	64.1	41.69	—	34.1	32.4
Fish and Wildlife Service (total)	31.6	46.4	76.8	55.8	79.5	53.7
Wilderness	—	46.4	19.9	—	27.5	18.9
Forest Service (total)	18.8	0.0	2.7	3.3	2.7	3.4
Wilderness	—	5.4	3.9	—	5.9	5.4
TOTAL WILDERNESS	—	145.0*	65.5	—	67.4	56.6

NOTE: Areas are in millions of acres.
COLUMN A: Original d(2) withdrawals made by the Nixon administration on 12/17/72.
COLUMN B: H.R. 39 as introduced in the House on 1/4/77.
COLUMN C: H.R. 39 as it passed the House on 5/19/78.
COLUMN D: Carter administration's executive withdrawals in Nov. and Dec. 1978.
COLUMN E: H.R. 39 as it passed the House on 5/16/79.
COLUMN F: The Alaska lands act as it was signed into law on 12/2/80.
* Includes wilderness designations on existing parks and refuges.

'carry-over' impacts" for other wilderness campaigns in the lower forty-eight for the national forests and BLM public domain.[104]

The House victory would have carryover effects, but not the effects the Alaska Coalition or the wilderness leadership anticipated. The close of the Alaska public lands debate once again hinged on action in the Senate. It would be fifteen months before the Senate would take up the legislation and during that time, a powerful political backlash against both the environmental community and the federal government began to stir. The delay was in part a product of the Senate's arcane parliamentary procedures, which invested senators with considerable power to slow or block legislation. Ted Stevens, Alaska's senior senator, had joined the Energy and Natural Resources Committee, giving him a role in shaping the legislation before it even reached the Senate floor.

The Alaska Coalition worried that Stevens and the state aimed to weaken the "national-interest" legislation in committee, delay full Senate consideration of any legislation to the last moment, and turn the Senate debate into an "energy" fight.[105] The coalition was right to worry. The state of Alaska, Stevens, and their allies saw good reason to keep delaying the legislation in an increasingly conservative political climate. It was from this uneasy position that the Alaska Coalition launched its final campaign for the legislation that became the Alaska National Interest Lands Conservation Act of 1980.

The Alaska National Interest Lands Conservation Act of 1980

Harry Crandell knew that the Alaska Coalition had problems other than the changing political climate and the state of Alaska. Since Crandell left the Wilderness Society in 1975 and joined the staff of the House Interior Committee, no one had done more behind the scenes to advance the Alaska Coalition's campaign. And from his vantage, he could see the coalition's mounting internal problems. Crandell worried about its inexperience in mounting a Senate campaign. For all its strengths in the House, Crandell noted that with the exception of Doug Scott, "none of the folks representing the Coalition have been involved in a major Senate campaign." He also knew that the economic downturn in the late 1970s had begun to sap the Alaska Coalition's resources. Its core lobbying staff was reduced during the 1979 delays in the Senate. "My concern here," he said, "is that the 'push' behind the [Alaska Coalition's] position has slacked off for nearly six months and it might be difficult to get up a full head of steam."[106] Most troubling, however, was the wear and tear within the coalition itself. Two years of sustained campaigning and lobbying had begun to wear down the cogs and gears that made the coalition so effective. In January 1980, the coalition's newsletter acknowledged that even as the opposition gained strength, there was a "slackening of grassroots conservationists' work on Alaska." Not only did activists seem to be tiring of the Alaska issue, but other wilderness reviews for the national forests in the lower forty-eight had begun to attract attention. As the Alaska campaign entered its final year, it seemed the coalition's carefully synchronized lobbying machine had begun to slip. "PERSISTENCE" urged the Alaska Coalition's newsletter.[107]

The ten-year anniversary of Earth Day in April 1980 only heightened these concerns. The national media took the milestone as an opportunity to gauge the broader environmental movement's strength. One newsmagazine asked if "the environmental movement is . . . going the way of previous grassroots political movements in American history" and another suggested it was the "end of an era."[108] Within the Alaska Coalition, frustration was growing over the changing role of citizens in the wilderness movement. "What the Club seems to expect from the grassroots," one Sierra Club leader complained, "is the assurance that there is this bunch of people, out there, who will respond with a torrent of mailgrams when requested." We must be "ready to salivate when the bell rings."[109] That was only one of dozens of such comments regarding the lack of citizen involvement and leadership training in the Alaska campaign. Such complaints within the Alaska Coalition marked new frustrations with an increasingly professional and centralized wilderness movement. Brock Evans noted that there was a "strong feeling, among those who had recently been to the field, that the movement as a whole is losing touch with its grassroots."[110] Doug Scott acknowledged that the Sierra Club was rethinking how "to truly *involve* Club volunteer leaders . . . in planning, preparing, and implementing our legislative and non-legislative campaigns."[111] But actively engaging citizens in national campaigns, rather than just counting on them for donations and telephone calls, was a problem national environmental organizations would increasingly struggle with in the 1980s. The Alaska Coalition had mounted a sustained campaign for three years. It was a remarkable achievement—in its scope, complexity, and duration—for the American environmental movement. But the coalition struggled to maintain that commitment for a fourth year.

In October 1979, the Senate Energy Committee finally reported out a sharply reduced Alaska lands bill that followed the outline of the Huckaby substitute and was much weaker than the Carter administration's existing protection, the bill that had passed the House, or the Alaska Coalition's proposals. But the full Senate moved slowly to take up the legislation. In February 1980, Carter's secretary of the interior, Cecil Andrus, tried to spur action by making permanent the 40 million acres of temporary withdrawals his office had made in December 1978. But the Senate floor debate on Alaska remained delayed until late summer 1980, at least, raising the prospect of another stalemate amid the fall elections. In the spring of 1980, the state of Alaska had poured its tax dollars into an ambitious lobbying campaign, national media blitz, and a 2.3-million-piece mailer explaining the state's position to citizens nationwide— it spent over $2 million before May.[112] Yet, when the full Senate finally took up the legislation, it quickly became evident that the Alaska Coalition still commanded strong support. The coalition had recruited newly elected Senator Paul Tsongas (D-MA), a former House representative and member of the Interior Alaska Subcommittee, to shepherd the legislation through the Senate Energy

Committee and to champion it on the Senate floor. Behind the scenes, Alan Cranston, a veteran Democratic senator from California, played a crucial role rounding up support.[113] That summer the Alaska Coalition's first three amendments to significantly strengthen the weak Senate bill passed the full Senate by two-to-one margins.[114] But just as the political momentum built for the Alaska Coalition, Senator Stevens made his move: he delayed additional votes on the remaining amendments, stalled debate with parliamentary tactics, and forced further negotiations off the Senate floor.[115]

It was behind the scenes that the fragility of the Alaska Coalition became apparent. It had a long list of goals for improving the Senate bill: restoring full protection to key conservation units, such as ANWR; expanding the wilderness designations, which had been sharply reduced; and eliminating provisions that favored the petroleum industry, such as oil exploration in ANWR, and the logging industry, such as large government subsidies and mandated timber goals for logging on the Tongass National Forest. Was no legislation better than a weak compromise bill? That was the question the Alaska Coalition faced, as negotiations between Stevens, the Carter administration, and the Alaska Coalition's allies began. It was a trying time for the coalition. Clusen warned against rushing into a deal, "so we can strengthen our [congressional] champions and get 'ball control.'"[116] As concern grew over the coalition's negotiating position, internal divisions began to deepen. Some groups, such as the National Parks Conservation Association, strongly supported the bill, since it dramatically expanded the park system.[117] But to other conservationists, it seemed better to have no bill, which would leave the Carter administration's executive withdrawals in place. Especially concerned were wilderness advocates from southeast Alaska who hoped to protect 40 percent of the Tongass National Forest as wilderness.[118] But the Senate Energy Committee's version of the Alaska legislation authorized a $40 million federal subsidy to fund an annual timber harvest of 450 million board feet.[119] Logging at that level threatened to devastate areas of the forest left unprotected. In the final negotiations, SEACC protested vehemently to the Alaska Coalition: "It is unconscionable for any of us to accept, let alone support, the sections on the Southeast." SEACC urged the Alaska Coalition to withdraw support for the Alaska lands legislation, sink the bill, and wait until the next year.[120] Other wilderness advocates—who voiced concerns about a range of issues, from petroleum exploration in ANWR to the amount of preserves open to sport hunting—agreed. As one insider noted tersely, "Coalition together publicly; divided internally."[121]

But the Alaska Coalition's national leadership and, more importantly, its allies in Congress and the Carter administration remained committed to passing a law. After four years of campaigning and negotiating, anything else would have been viewed as a failure. Three weeks of closed-door negotiations produced a bill that the Senate would finally move on. The Tsongas-Jackson substitute replaced the weak legislation produced by the Senate Energy Committee and moved to the floor. The bill staked out a middle ground—it required exploratory oil and gas surveys in ANWR, supported the timber industry on the Tongass, gave the state other key land claims in the conservation units, shifted more land from parks to preserves, and designated 56 million acres of wilderness. On August 19, 1980, four years after the congressional campaign began, the Senate finally voted 78–14 for an Alaska lands bill. It was substantially weaker than H.R. 39 as passed by the House and, in some respects, the executive protection afforded by the Carter administration. For the Alaska Coalition, the Senate bill was meant to be the next-to-last stop in its campaign: the coalition expected to strengthen the bill—substantially, it hoped—in a House-Senate conference, where the differences between the two versions of the legislation would be ironed out. At the top of the list would be eliminating mandatory petroleum exploration in ANWR and logging subsidies on the Tongass, neither of which were in H.R. 39. But the coalition failed to achieve either goal.

The November 1980 national election marked a turning point in American environmental politics. The Alaska Coalition spent the early fall working feverishly with its allies to advance their goals with Senator Stevens in the House-Senate conference. A formidable negotiator, Stevens refused to budge on any of the state's priorities for economic development, despite some concessions by the Alaska Coalition.[122] By late September, Scott and Clusen complained, "we have sweetened the kitty for nothing but Stevens' interest in further talks."[123] In the fall of 1980, national attention was fixed on the upcoming elections. The weak economy, frustration with the federal government, and the Iranian hostage crisis all made Carter the underdog in the presidential race against former California governor Ronald Reagan.[124] Although environmental issues never figured prominently in the race, Reagan's criticisms of the growth of the federal government and its cumbersome regulations resonated with the anti-environmental sentiment that charged the Alaska debate and was important to congressional races across the American West. In Washington, D.C., it was clear that no immediate resolution of the Alaska legislation was forthcoming. In October, with the elections less than a month away, Senator Stevens returned to Alaska to wait out the results. That November, Reagan was elected president and, more importantly for the Alaska campaign, he carried the Senate for the Republicans for the first time since 1955. The window of political opportunity the Carter administration had thrown open in 1976 had closed. The Alaska Coalition interpreted the new Republican administration and its three-seat majority in the Senate as defeat. When Congress reconvened for the lame-duck session in mid-November, the Alaska Coalition and its allies in the House accepted the Senate version of the legislation without further negotiations. On December 2, 1980, President Carter signed the Alaska National Interest Lands Conservation Act (ANILCA), which protected 100.7 million acres of Alaska's public lands as national parks, refuges, preserves, and forests, designated 56.4 million acres as wilderness, and facilitated land transfers to the state and Native interests.[125]

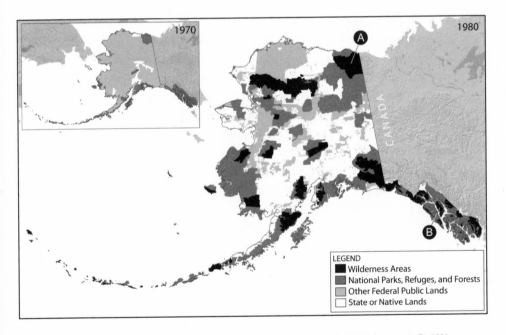

Map 5.2 In 1970, 97 percent of the land in Alaska was managed by the federal government. By 1981, much of the land had been allocated as a result of the Alaska Native Claims Settlement Act of 1971 and the Alaska National Interest Lands Conservation Act of 1980. State and Native interests claimed 103.5 million acres and 44 million acres of land, respectively. Congress protected 100.7 million acres as national parks, preserves, monuments, wildlife refuges, and forests; it designated 56.4 million acres as wilderness. The Arctic National Wildlife Refuge (A) and Admiralty Island National Monument (B) are marked.

Conclusion

"Carter Signs Alaska Bill" shouted the Alaska Coalition's congratulatory news-letter. "Over 100 million acres of pristine wildlands teeming with wildlife pre-served for future generations. Feel proud that you made it happen."[126] That final cheer for the grassroots and the emphasis on Alaska as a "pristine" wil-derness brought the Alaska Coalition's campaign to a close at the same time those claims veiled the many complexities from which the final legislation had been wrought. In many respects, ANILCA marked a crowning achievement for the nation's wilderness community—it doubled the size of the national park and wildlife refuge systems and expanded the size of the wilderness system threefold. Much of the land the Carter administration had protected through executive action in 1978 gained congressional protection too. The law expanded existing national parks, such as Mount McKinley National Park (renamed Denali), and created new ones, such as Gates of the Arctic and Wrangell-Saint Elias National Parks and Preserves. It expanded wildlife refuges, such as ANWR, and protected new ones, such as Yukon Flats and Noatak National Wildlife Ref-uges. And it protected more than half of those lands as designated wilderness areas. It was an extraordinary accomplishment for wilderness advocates and their allies. Despite these successes, not all of their supporters viewed the final law as a product of successful compromise. Four years later, Harry Crandell wrote in a blaze of lasting frustration: "The fact remains that the State of Alaska, the Alaska natives, industry, and most of all, the Alaska [congressional] delega-tion (especially Ted Stevens) whipped our asses in the Senate and what became the final product signed by Jimmy Carter."[127]

The Arctic National Wildlife Range reflected the strengths and weaknesses of the Alaska lands act. Congress expanded the renamed Arctic National Wild-life Refuge (ANWR) from 8.9 to 19 million acres (an area close to that of the state of South Carolina). The expansion had been an important goal for wil-derness advocates: the additions encompassed winter habitat for caribou in the Yukon Flats to the south and important habitat areas to the west, near the Trans-Alaska Pipeline. Congress designated 8 million acres of the original ref-uge as wilderness. But the final legislation also included numerous compro-mises that belied any assertions of ANWR as a "pristine" wilderness. Natives and the state had claimed some inholdings in the refuge. Most obvious, the refuge and wilderness designations permitted the continued use of motorized vehicles, such as airplanes and snowmobiles, for subsistence activities, as was the case in much of Alaska's newly protected lands.

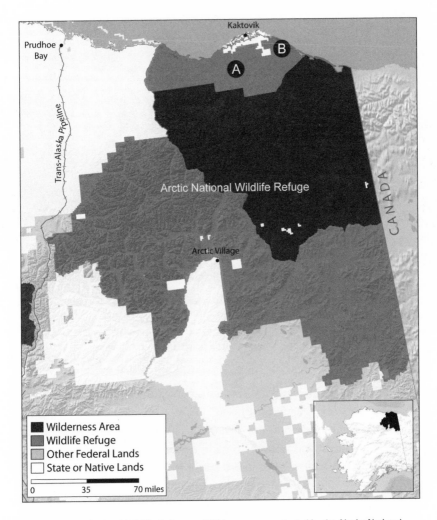

Map 5.3 Arctic National Wildlife Refuge and Wilderness, as protected by the Alaska National Interest Lands Conservation Act. Note the contested Arctic coastal plain (A) and Arctic Slope Regional Corporation's inholdings south of Kaktovik (B).

The final legislative compromise also set the stage for the longest-running wilderness debate in American history: the future of ANWR's coastal plain. Geological assessments, released in 1980, further suggested that ANWR's 1.5-million-acre coastal plain was a potentially valuable source of petroleum: government geologists estimated there was a 5 percent chance of a 17-billion-barrel oil field and a 95 percent chance of a 160-million-barrel oil field.[128] But the Alaska

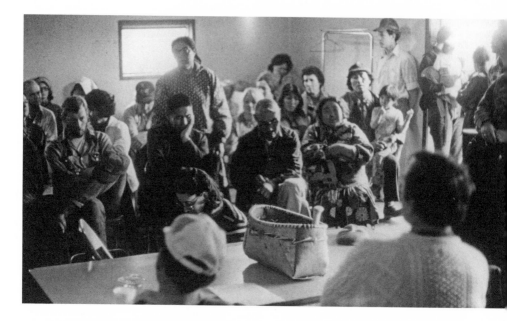

5.4 A meeting of Tlingit Natives in Angoon, Alaska, regarding the Alaska National Interest Lands Conservation Act, ca. 1981. Courtesy Conservation Collection, Denver Public Library.

Coalition continued to emphasize that the coastal plain was the most ecologically important area of ANWR—it hosted many of the migratory birds in the spring and summer and it was the calving site for the Porcupine caribou herd. The Alaska Coalition and Natives—both in Arctic Village and Kaktovik—had argued fervently for protecting the coastal plain as wilderness. Congress deferred any decision regarding the coastal plain, instead mandating seismic surveys for oil and gas, to be completed in 1985. In a surprising turn of events, the Inupiat Eskimos in Kaktovik and the Arctic Slope Regional Corporation stood to gain mineral rights inside ANWR through a land exchange in 1983.[129] That land swap became the template for a series of proposed deals to give Native corporations a vested interest in opening up ANWR for energy development. Congress amended ANILCA to prohibit such exchanges in 1988. But the first deal, orchestrated by the Reagan administration, stood: the Arctic Slope Regional Corporation and Kaktovik Inupiat Corporation gained ownership of 92,000 acres of land on the coastal plain. In the mid-1980s, the Kaktovik Inupiat shifted their official position from wilderness designation to energy exploration in ANWR, deepening the split within the Native community. The proposed land swaps, the completion of oil exploration in the late 1980s, the Exxon *Valdez* oil spill in 1989, and the Persian

5.5 A photograph of the Alaska Coalition's leadership at its celebration of the Alaska National Interest Lands Conservation Act in December 1980. Courtesy Conservation Collection, Denver Public Library.

Gulf War in 1991 would again thrust ANWR to the forefront of American environmental politics in the late 1980s and early 1990s.[130]

The consequences of the Alaska lands act for the Tongass National Forest can be read on an aerial map. Admiralty Island remained a national monument under ANILCA and all but 10 percent of the island gained a wilderness designation. Shee Atika's Native claims to 23,000 acres of rich timberlands on the west coast of the island were upheld and 100,000 acres of the northern panhandle of the island were omitted to allow for mineral development. The Angoon Tlingit retained subsistence rights to the island, but the Natives' and Alaska Coalition's hopes for full protection of the island's habitat and wildlife were lost. Today, the lands managed by Shee Atika stand out like scars on an aerial map. Shee Atika, the urban Native corporation based in Sitka, clear-cut the land. But Admiralty Island fared better than the rest of the Tongass. The most troublesome provision of the act was the subsidy the state of Alaska and the timber industry wrested in exchange for 5.4 million acres of wilderness designations. The law retained the annual timber harvest of 450 million board feet and the forty million dollar annual federal subsidy to support road construction and other timber activities, which aimed to stabilize the region's sagging economy. Only in

1990, after another sustained campaign, did Congress pass the Tongass Timber Reform Act, which somewhat improved management of the forest, eliminated the guaranteed subsidy, and designated an additional 300,000 acres of wilderness. Despite those successes, the Tongass remains one of the most controversial forests in the nation.[131]

In retrospect, the Alaska lands act was an extraordinary victory for wilderness advocates that protected a tremendous amount of land, but the price of such expansive land-use legislation was a host of compromises and exceptions, such as those in ANWR and on the Tongass, that undermined the Alaska Coalition's larger goal of protecting ecologically reasoned conservation units. Exceptions for subsistence use allowed the operation of motorized vehicles, including airplanes and snowmobiles, in national parks and wilderness areas in Alaska and owners of private inholdings in national forests and public domain lands (even in the lower forty-eight) gained new rights for vehicular access.[132] Critical ecological areas were omitted, as in the case of the Arctic refuge wilderness, or shifted into preserve status that allowed sport hunting. Resource industries forced major compromises, as in the case of logging on the Tongass. As with other wilderness legislation, politics—not science—determined the final boundaries of ANWR, Admiralty Island, and other conservation units across Alaska. The final wilderness designations and regulations in Alaska are some of the most permissive in the nation, including an array of exceptions to meet the concerns of Natives and state interests. These compromises reflected a logical extension of the pragmatic approach to wilderness designation that the Wilderness Society worked so hard to forge in the 1970s. If either the Forest Service's purity policies or the Sierra Club's wilderness manifesto had been honored, such exacting requirements for wilderness would have likely resulted in more modest wilderness designations in Alaska.[133] As subsistence activities and vehicular and other non-conforming uses have all increased since 1980, the ultimate price of those compromises remains a continuing point of frustration within the wilderness movement. That is the mixed legacy of ANILCA.[134]

The Alaska debate both shaped and reflected a shift in American environmental politics in the late 1970s. The Alaska Coalition succeeded in giving Alaska's landscape national significance, overcoming the objections of the entire Alaska congressional delegation. But the state of Alaska and its allies' successes in shaping the final legislation reflected the growing power of an opposition, rooted in local communities, state government, and industry, in contesting just what was in the "national interest." In part, this was a reaction to the growing ambitions of the wilderness community, which eyed a larger portion of the public lands for wilderness and other forms of protection. In part, this represented the conservative Right's growing success in mobilizing citizens and other interests frustrated with the federal government. Sport hunters and motorized recreationists argued that wilderness threatened their freedom to hunt, recreate, and enjoy the outdoors in ways that many rural Americans valued. The resource industries continued to challenge wilderness as a lockup of important economic resources. Such arguments had had currency in earlier wilderness debates, but starting in the late 1970s a new populism charged the environmental opposition, aligning the interests of industry, hunters, off-road vehicle enthusiasts, and rural Americans across the nation against the role of the federal government in public lands protection. In the 1980s, wilderness occupied an increasingly contentious place not only in the debates over the nation's public lands, but also in those over the place of government in American life.

6 / NATIONAL FORESTS

THE POLARIZATION OF ENVIRONMENTAL POLITICS

W hen Dave Foreman woke up on the morning of May 30, 1989, three law enforcement officials surrounded his bed, their .357 Magnums drawn. He thought they were there to kill him. They arrested him and charged him with conspiring to sabotage power plants, including the power lines that carry electricity from the nation's largest nuclear power station west of Phoenix, Arizona.[1] Since the mid-1980s, the Federal Bureau of Investigation (FBI) had been following the activities of a radical environmental organization—Earth First!—that gained national attention with a series of publicity stunts in the early 1980s and then became involved in more secretive strategies of monkeywrenching and eco-sabotage in the mid-1980s. Ever since he quit his post with the Wilderness Society, Foreman had been Earth First!'s most visible leader. As he later put it, "it was time for a new joker in the deck: a militant, uncompromising group unafraid to say what needed to be said or to back it up with stronger actions than the established organizations were willing to take."[2] Earth First! aimed to be a radical organization for the protection of nature; but, as Foreman's comment suggests, it also marked a sharp reaction to the changing culture of mainstream environmentalism.

Foreman got his start in wilderness politics as an organizer for the Wilderness Society. He had grown up a military brat, attended the University of New Mexico, and campaigned for Barry Goldwater in 1964. In 1972, Foreman attended a local organizing meeting sponsored by the New Mexico Wilderness Study Committee and the Wilderness Society. That year, he oversaw the citizens' proposal for the Gila National Forest in New Mexico during the Forest Service's first roadless area review. In January 1973, the Wilderness Society invited him to its Wilderness Training Workshop in Washington, D.C. The following month, the Wilderness Society hired him as its representative for New Mexico and made him a part of Clif Merritt's growing team of field organizers based out of the Denver office. Even in 1973, $300 a month did not go far. But, as Foreman remembers, "it beat shoeing horses" and he got to "work full-time on wilderness preservation."

Foreman was like a lot of the wilderness leaders who worked their way up the staff at the Wilderness Society in the 1960s. He was an Eagle Scout, he fell in love with wilderness on a trip in Glacier Peak Wilderness Area in 1962, and he was committed to a citizen-oriented and moderate approach to wilderness advocacy. Few people knew that Foreman had been affiliated with Black Mesa Defense, an eco-anarchist group active around Earth Day in 1970.[3]

Foreman exemplified the mainstream political work for wilderness that anchored the Wilderness Society's legislative successes in the 1970s. For Foreman, that meant running local citizen-training workshops in New Mexico and Arizona. "You are the wilderness movement," Foreman championed to local leaders.[4] It meant wearing a coat and tie (and his cowboy boots) to meetings with the Forest Service and congressional delegations. It meant supporting the Sierra Club and Wilderness Society's national campaigns for Alaska and the national forest roadless areas. "Keep up the good work," Foreman wrote to his colleagues in 1977, "and let me know how I can help (but don't try to work me to death—I'm nearly there already)."[5] After Brandborg's ouster, Foreman was soon tapped to move to Washington, D.C., to coordinate the Wilderness Society's field program. In that capacity, he played an important role coordinating the wilderness movement's strategy on the Forest Service's second review of national forest roadless areas (RARE II) that began in 1977. It was a turning point for Foreman. After the Carter administration disappointed wilderness advocates by recommending only one-quarter of the roadless areas for wilderness protection in 1979, Foreman decided it was time to get out of town. His job may have been in Washington, D.C., but his heart was still in the West.[6]

The West that Foreman returned to and the Wilderness Society he left behind at the start of 1979 had begun to change in ways Foreman did not fully anticipate. Back in New Mexico, on a six-month sabbatical from the Wilderness Society, he found the West edgier than when he had left a few years before. Many ranchers, loggers, and other rural westerners viewed the expansive new wilderness reviews on the national forests and the public domain as an attack on their way of life, a waste of the government's time and taxpayer money, and the work of urban environmentalists. Even if Foreman was a local, he was guilty by association. One local rancher commented to the *New York Times*, "Dave Foreman is lucky to be alive."[7] That same month, four men accosted Foreman and threatened his life.[8] Not only was being moderate not saving wilderness in Washington, D.C., Foreman realized, it was doing little to meet the concerns of these westerners, who had begun to organize under the banner of the Sagebrush Rebellion in the late 1970s. That summer, Foreman rejoined the Wilderness Society as its New Mexico field representative. But while he had been away, the Wilderness Society's new executive director, William Turnage, had begun to restructure the organization's strategies and goals. Turnage was unlike any of the Wilderness Society's previous leaders: he was an Ivy League graduate, a businessman, and he was determined to return the Wilderness Society to the forefront of wilderness politics as a professional and well-funded lobby in Washington, D.C. That did not make sense to Foreman. Out West, westerners were putting bumper stickers reading "REPEAL THE WILDERNESS ACT" on their cars and threatening Foreman's life, and the Wilderness Society planned to respond with well-educated lobbyists and foundation-funded analyses?

Foreman chose a different path. In the spring of 1980, Foreman, Howie Wolke, and Mike Roselle headed off on a road trip to climb Pinacate Peak in Mexico. Three guys. The wide-open highway of southern New Mexico. They left Albuquerque full of frustration with the mainstream wilderness movement and the federal government and the shortcomings of RARE II and the Alaska lands act. By the time they returned, legend has it, they had hatched plans for Earth First!.[9] That summer, the loose-knit group began to take shape. Foreman quit his post with the Wilderness Society. Wolke left Friends of the Earth. Bart Koehler, the Wilderness Society's former Wyoming representative, came on board. And so too did Susan Morgan, who had been on the Wilderness Society's Denver staff. Roselle, a former anti-war activist, was there too. It was a mixed crew spilling over with ideas, enthusiasm, and, it seems, a lot of cheap beer. They shared several commitments: In place of moderation, Earth First! would take principled stands that put nature first. In place of legislation, Earth First! would encourage direct action. In place of professionalism, Earth First! would be adaptable, resourceful, and organic. And they agreed "that in any decision, consideration for the health of the Earth must come first."[10] The best known of Earth First!'s activists was Foreman—the former Eagle Scout, registered Republican, and wilderness lobbyist. For Foreman, founding Earth First! was the decision that set him on that long trip toward a Phoenix jail cell. Before he got there, he and those with whom he founded Earth First! would deepen the radical currents of American environmentalism.

The origins and significance of Earth First! to American environmental politics rest in three interrelated episodes in public lands debates in the late 1970s and early 1980s: the Forest Service's second review of the national forest roadless areas, the growing opposition to wilderness in the rural West, and the restructuring of the Wilderness Society. Although the Wilderness Society had succeeded in rallying popular political support around a moderate and

pragmatic program of expansion in the 1960s and 1970s, such consensus collapsed in these years. Earth First! marked but one reaction to the changing
landscape of American environmental politics. Local wilderness advocates,
with whom the Wilderness Society had worked so closely, began to question
the strategies and priorities of the mainstream wilderness movement. Rural
westerners began to actively challenge the role of the federal government in
the management of the nation's public lands. And Earth First! began to explore
more ambitious, biocentric visions of wilderness and radical strategies to protect the nation's wild lands. Although each of these was a different reaction
to the changes in wilderness politics, each was rooted in similar frustrations
with an increasingly professional and bureaucratic approach to environmental decision-making centered in Washington, D.C. In these ways, debates over
the public lands would help drive the polarization of American environmental
politics — generating new radicalism and partisanship that, in turn, would profoundly shape debates over the public lands.

RARE II and Environmental Decision-Making

The Forest Service's Roadless Area Review and Evaluation II (RARE II) was the
work of Rupert Cutler. Cutler had played a key role in the early implementation of the Wilderness Act, when he served as the Wilderness Society's assistant
executive director under Brandborg. But in 1969, Cutler, sensing the volatility
of Brandborg's leadership, left to pursue graduate studies at Michigan States
University's Department of Resource Development.[11] That academic trajectory
carried Cutler away from the wilderness movement and into the mechanics of
environmental regulation. After he completed his doctorate, Cutler stayed on
to teach at Michigan State and began educating a new generation of environmental decision-makers. In 1975, Cutler even resigned his post on the Sierra
Club's wilderness committee. "In all candor," he wrote, "I'm no longer a 'wilderness expert.' My backpack and boots are dusty."[12] But in the fall of 1976, Jimmy
Carter's election brought Cutler back to Washington, D.C. Cutler was one of a
handful of environmentalists tapped for a post in the Carter administration.
His appointment as assistant secretary of agriculture, with oversight of the Forest Service, catapulted a former leader at the Wilderness Society into a top government forestry position. This was why Foreman looked to Carter as "a great
friend of wilderness."[13] And it was why the incoming Carter administration
troubled timber industry officials. Before Cutler's appointment, industry representatives arranged a private meeting with Cutler and the new Secretary of

6.1 Doug Scott (left), Rupert Cutler (center), and Tom Barlow (right), August 1980. Cutler served as assistant secretary of agriculture during the Carter administration. Scott was the Sierra Club's chief wilderness advocate and legislative strategist in the early 1980s. Barlow spearheaded the NRDC's studies of below-cost timber sales in the national forests in the late 1970s.

Agriculture, Robert Bergland, outside Chicago. Industry representatives questioned Cutler's background, while urging him to resolve the confusion over the future of the national forests.[14] It was with this double burden that Cutler arrived in Washington, D.C. Cutler was independent-minded and determined to be beholden neither to the timber industry that questioned his appointment, nor to the wilderness advocates with whom he had once worked.

A cloud of frustration hung over the national forests in the 1970s. Questions about the roadless areas, timber sales, environmental reviews, and lawsuits increasingly occupied the Forest Service's staff and consumed its operations. As historian Paul Hirt observes, the agency fell victim to a "conspiracy of optimism." In trying to meet so many competing demands on the national forests, it often seemed to meet none.[15] Behind the Forest Service's difficulties were the requirements that new environmental regulations placed on the agency. Between 1960 and 1976, Congress passed four laws, each of which restricted the agency's long-standing administrative autonomy: the Multiple-Use Sustained-Yield Act (1960), the Wilderness Act (1964), the Forest and Rangeland Renewable Resources Planning Act (1974), and the National Forest Management Act (1976).[16] The last two laws aimed to place the Forest Service on a firm foundation of forest planning, which would include public involvement, resource assessments, and goal-setting every ten to fifteen years. Such formal planning was meant to protect the agency from a growing number of lawsuits and appeals that slowed down management of the national forests. Most troublesome were the 1972 settlement with Sierra Club, in which the agency agreed to conduct environmental reviews of all roadless areas, and a 1974 lawsuit that challenged the agency's clear-cutting practices on the Monongahela National Forest in West Virginia and called into question the agency's timber policies nationwide.[17] With the agency's new planning program, however, it seemed that bureaucracy had come to the backwoods.[18] By 1976, the agency warned that it would take a decade to clear its planning backlog. Increasingly, working for the Forest Service would mean less time in the forest and more time at a desk.

For wilderness advocates in the early 1970s, the most pressing question was the future of the national forest roadless areas. (This would change in the mid-1980s, as broader concerns about forest management, below-cost logging, and biodiversity protection came to the forefront.) Since 1972, the Forest Service had been undertaking reviews of the roadless areas to meet its settlement agreement with the Sierra Club. But those reviews had proceeded slowly. In 1976, the agency had completed only 25 percent of the necessary reviews. Even when the reviews were completed, wilderness advocates pursued two strategies that raised further uncertainty. Citizens filed administrative appeals with the agency regarding forest plans, timber sales, and other management decisions. If those appeals failed, they often turned to the courts. The Wilderness Society pursued this strategy most aggressively out of its Denver office under the leadership of Tim Mahoney.[19] In 1977, it forced the Forest Service to remove all roadless areas from its timber plans for the Rocky Mountain region.[20] The Wilderness Society considered pursuing a national lawsuit on the same grounds before the Forest Service announced RARE II.[21] The second strategy was to continue working through Congress to designate new wilderness areas. In 1976, Doug Scott and Chuck Clusen spearheaded a national campaign for the Endangered American Wilderness Act. The compromise legislation included seventeen roadless areas that added up to 1.3 million acres of vulnerable national forest roadless areas across the West. Scott described that campaign as a model for future national campaigns. In 1977, Dave Foreman praised the legislation, saying it was "one of the best ideas to come out of the conservation movement in a long time," and he volunteered to rally the "troops in New Mexico, West Texas, and Arizona to gear up for the fight."[22] Only later, after founding Earth First!, would Foreman dismiss the strategy as the "beginning of a strategy of weakness."[23]

For the timber industry, the slow progress reviewing the roadless areas,

6.2 Dave Foreman (left), still with the Wilderness Society at the time, and Doug Scott, of the Sierra Club. In 1980, Foreman helped launch Earth First! and became a sharp critic of the pragmatic strategies that Scott and the Sierra Club pursued. Photo ca. 1978. Courtesy the Wilderness Society.

the endless appeals and lawsuits, and new wilderness proposals all raised uncertainties over its access to the national forests. Those concerns formed the substance of the timber industry's secret Chicago meeting with Cutler and Bergland in January 1977. From the industry's perspective, the Forest Service's failure to expedite the roadless reviews threatened the nation's timber supply. When the agency did complete a review, it seemed wilderness advocates quickly filed appeals, disrupting planned sales. And while the lands were tied up in planning and appeals, wilderness advocates pursued new wilderness bills in Congress. The Endangered Wilderness bill was a case in point, the industry argued. It sacrificed 500,000 acres of commercial forestland, more than 4,000 direct and indirect jobs, and forty million dollars in annual timber sales—just for wilderness.[24] In truth, the amount of timber offered for sale in the national forests remained relatively constant between 1972 and 1976, as did the price of timber.[25] But these concerns over the future of the timber supply and protection of the roadless areas spilled over at congressional hearings on the legislation in May 1977. At the hearings, Cutler faced withering criticism of the agency. Only three months into his new job, Cutler reached for a program that the timber industry and the Society of American Foresters had been pushing for behind closed doors since the Chicago meeting.[26] He announced that the Forest Service would launch a second comprehensive review of the national forest roadless areas to replace the failed RARE I and meet the Forest Service's legal obligation to conduct environmental reviews of all roadless areas.[27] The press christened the program as "RARE II" the next day.[28]

RARE II reflected an increasingly technical approach to environmental decision-making that had become institutionalized since the National Environmental Policy Act (NEPA) became law in 1970. RARE II promised a systematic review of the national forest roadless areas that would prevent future lawsuits and end piecemeal wilderness legislation. Under Cutler's leadership, the agency pitched RARE II as a rational, comprehensive, and apolitical review of the nation's remaining 2,916 roadless areas that encompassed 62 million acres of land (one-third of the national forests). RARE II aimed to improve on RARE I in three ways. First, following Cutler's specific instructions, RARE II abandoned the agency's purity policies—which had been a major point of critique of RARE I.[29] Second, RARE II gave new attention to roadless areas in the eastern national forests and western grasslands. Third, and most important, RARE II was based on a new foundation of technical analysis. To quantify the wilderness and economic value of each roadless area, the Forest Service developed the Wilderness Attribute Rating System (WARS), the Development Opportunity Rating System (DORS), and the Economic Impact Analysis (EIA). WARS incorporated numerical estimates of a broad array of wilderness qualities included in the Wilderness Act—such as natural integrity, apparent naturalness, solitude, and primitive recreation opportunities—to rate each roadless area on a twenty-four-point scale.[30] It gave secondary attention to ecosystem representation, mapping potential roadless areas using the Kuchler-Bailey ecosystem classification system.[31] DORS provided a cost-benefit analysis for each roadless area based on local data detailing natural resources, economic value, and development costs. And the EIA estimated how the overall allocation of roadless areas would impact the local, regional, and national economy.[32] If successful, RARE II would satisfy the agency's legal obligation under the 1972 settlement with the Sierra Club and lift the cloud of uncertainty that hung over the national forests.

It was an ambitious undertaking, but the Forest Service completed RARE II on time. In April 1979, the Carter administration announced its recommendations based on the agency's final environmental impact statement. For the 62 million acres of roadless areas, it recommended 15.4 million acres for wilderness and 36 million acres for non-wilderness; it left 10.6 million acres undecided and in "further planning."[33] If RARE II had achieved its goal, those recommendations would have provided a framework to resolve wilderness debates on the national forests through congressional legislation. But RARE II satisfied few that were party to the process. Wilderness advocates were dissatisfied with the methodology and results. They questioned the speed of the review, the quality of the agency's quantitative assessments, how it tallied public comments, and the range of alternatives considered. In their view, WARS and DORS were unintelligible "black boxes" which used "suspect data, out-of-date resource evaluations, and misinterpreted public input results" to make faulty recommendations.[34] The state of California, where the agency left the most land in a "further planning" category, filed suit on grounds that RARE II did not meet NEPA's requirements for environmental review. In 1979 the courts sided with California, deeming RARE II insufficient—but that decision was quickly appealed, throwing the future of the roadless areas and RARE II into legal limbo.[35] And the timber industry and its allies continued to emphasize the importance of ending the uncertainty over the roadless areas and expediting logging on the national forests. The price of timber tripled between 1976 and 1979, giving their claims new urgency.[36]

No one could foresee how important RARE II would be to the future of the wilderness movement. In retrospect, the structure of the wilderness movement and its particular role in environmental politics make sense only in light of the dramatic changes that affected both wilderness advocates and their opponents in these years. In many respects, RARE II represented a high point of liberal faith in the role of the federal government and citizens to advance protection for the public lands. For Cutler, it marked an opportunity to put eight years of academic training in natural resource policy into action on a national scale. For the Forest Service, it marked an opportunity to demonstrate its growing managerial and analytical capabilities and to resolve the uncertainty over the roadless areas. And, for the mainstream wilderness movement, it offered a chance to build on its growing organizational strengths, harnessing the enthusiasm and energy of citizens, and, more importantly, its expanding resources in technical analysis and political lobbying to secure protection for the national forests. Instead of resolving questions over the national forests, however, RARE II collapsed into a high-profile stalemate. The reactions that stalemate inspired— among local citizens and resource industries—represented common reactions to the failure not just of the Forest Service or the wilderness movement, but of a liberal political formula that invested its faith in the federal government, which had been central to the wilderness movement and American environmentalism since the 1960s.

Stirrings of a Sagebrush Rebellion

The start of RARE II caught the wilderness movement off guard. In the late 1970s, environmentalists focused their attention on the future of Alaska's wild lands; but in the rural West, it was RARE II that commanded local headlines in cities like Dubois, Idaho, and Las Cruces, New Mexico. The stirrings of organized opposition that wilderness advocates had seen before—in the campaign for Alpine Lakes, the Eastern Wilderness Areas Act, and the Endangered American Wilderness Act—emerged with new force and coordination. For many rural communities, RARE II was not just about the national forests, but about public lands that they considered to be extensions of their backyards and important to their local economies. The Southern Oregon Resource Alliance warned its members that "Uncle Sam Wants Your Job! Your Taxes! And Your Recreation Lands!" It urged westerners to get involved. "RARE II is a threat. Fight the Great Federal Land Grab."[37] A New Mexico jeep club urged people to "Act now! Join the grassroots rebellion against 'over-government.'" It positioned its citizen-campaign as a protest against RARE II and the Wilderness Act, which it described as the work of a "small group of extreme environmentalists" and "Big Brother" in Washington, D.C. Members received a bright-red bumper sticker with bold black lettering that shouted "REPEAL THE WILDERNESS ACT."[38] In the late 1970s, the Southern Oregon Resource Alliance and the Las Cruces Jeep Club were part of a growing, loose-knit alliance that challenged the federal government's jurisdiction over the federal lands and the environmentalists' proposals for public lands reform. Rooted in the rural West, angry over a slowing economy, and frustrated with public lands regulations, this opposition to RARE II formed part of a growing conservative outcry that in 1979 became known as the Sagebrush Rebellion.[39]

The Forest Service began RARE II with 227 public meetings to develop a preliminary inventory of the national forest roadless areas and to establish basic priorities for evaluating them. While the wilderness movement was focused on Alaska, the timber industry, its employees, and local allies packed these early hearings in many western communities. Several hearings started after protest parades headed by logging trucks, tractor trailers, and pick-up trucks thundered down rural main streets with their horns blaring on their way to the hearing. Protesters carried signs reading: "[We] need more timber sales—not wilderness," "Stop the Sierra Club," and "We can't make a living by hiking."[40] In Bonners Ferry, Idaho, in the heart of timber country, the hearing drew so many people that it had to be moved to the high school football stadium. The crowd numbered over one thousand people.[41] This was unlike anything wilderness advocates had witnessed before. As such activism was meant to demonstrate, and westerners emphasized in their testimony, it was not just the industry that opposed wilderness, but also local citizens who argued that wilderness designations would lock up natural resources, weaken rural communities, cater to environmentalists, and waste taxpayer money. As one Nevada congressman noted, the "entire federal decision-making pendulum" had swung toward policies that aimed to "exclude, restrict, or limit use" of natural resources in western states.[42] The protest also included elements of a tax revolt, as rural westerners complained vigorously about the use of tax revenues to support inefficient federal environmental reviews and subsequent legal suits. "If they can't get it right in two tries, I don't want them taking money out of my pocket to do it again," complained one Montanan. "I pay too many taxes as it is."[43] Most important, the Sagebrush Rebellion emphasized states' rights: many westerners viewed these lands as properly belonging to the states, not the federal government. Some western states, congressional representatives, and citizens began to argue that the best way to solve the problem was to give the public lands to the states, a proposal that would gain traction in the debates over the Bureau of Land Management public domain.[44] Graffiti on one national forest sign summed up such frustrations: "RARE II is a rip-off!"

If RARE II had been a vote, wilderness advocates would have lost.[45] The opposition overwhelmed advocates at early stages of the review, arguing for prioritizing economic development and local interests. Public response was dominated by citizens who favored management for multiple-use purposes (62 percent of comments) over protection (7 percent of comments).[46] Although wilderness advocates criticized how such public input was tallied, the Forest Service gave priority to economic development in its analysis. The agency ranked six general objectives based on initial public feedback. The top three objectives gave priority to meeting the agency's long-term planning goals for increasing timber harvests, supporting local economies, and prioritizing national issues such as energy independence, housing starts, and inflation.[47] The fourth, fifth, and sixth objectives reflected the concerns of wilderness advocates to protect high-quality roadless areas and diversify the wilderness system.[48] Even as opponents protested RARE II, they had begun to borrow organizing strategies from wilderness advocates. The Western Timber Association, for instance, coordinated over ninety on-the-ground surveys of roadless areas in California through its local affiliates, which ranked the areas' importance for timber, wilderness values, and ecological values.[49] The energy industry undertook a systematic review of the roadless areas, highlighting those they considered most valuable prospects for oil, gas, and other minerals.[50] And in 1978, the opposition organized a symposium to consider RARE II. It included big hitters, such as the timber lobby and petroleum companies, and representatives of ranchers, hunters, and off-road vehicle enthusiasts concerned about access to the public lands. The symposium's goal was to foster grassroots political support and develop "simple" themes that appealed to "the perspective of middle America."[51]

The timber industry knew that their efforts were working. In private memos, industry lobbyists described the progress on RARE II as "extremely favorable to industry's multiple-use position."[52] In part, this was because of the opposition's coordinated protest against RARE II. In part, it was because behind the scenes, the Carter administration was courting the timber industry's support for a reorganization of the executive branch—a failed plan that would have moved the Forest Service from the Department of Agriculture to the Department of the Interior. In public, however, the timber industry never acknowledged that RARE II was going in their favor.[53] When the draft and then final recommendations were released, the timber industry and other natural resource industries criticized the program for allocating too much land to wilderness, leaving too much land in further planning, and, when it failed to quickly resolve the roadless areas debate, as an example of government mismanagement. But for industry and its allies, their concern was not just how many roadless areas were designated wilderness, but that the endless environmental reviews and legal suits over the national forests be brought to a close. One lobbyist outlined the timber industry's strategy for an "end-game" to RARE II: it could accept the agency's wilderness recommendations, but, most pressing, "this should be the end of wilderness expansion on the National Forests."[54] Starting in 1979, the industry's goal was new legislation formally barring further wilderness designations on the national forests—in effect, an anti–Wilderness Act that would resolve the uncertainty surrounding forest management. Such legislation had never seemed necessary or possible when wilderness reviews remained modest and posed little threat to economic development; but as the scope of the reviews expanded and frustration with "big government" grew, especially in the West, reining in wilderness protection gained urgency.

The Sagebrush Rebellion in the West formed one current in a rising tide of conservatism nationwide in the 1970s. Concerns over the expansion of federal power, inefficiencies of government bureaucracy, and disregard for local and state concerns were also at play in discussions of other issues, such as education policy, desegregation, and reproductive rights. In 1981, the Repub-

licans gained a majority in the Senate for the first time since 1955. That majority rested, in part, on their strong showing in the West and a new generation
of ideologically conservative westerners, such as Orrin Hatch of Utah, Samuel
Hayakawa of California, and Steven Symms of Idaho, all of whom opposed a
large federal government, emphasized local autonomy and states' rights, and
made the public lands important to their agendas. In the pivotal November
1980 elections, the Senate race in Idaho was particularly symbolic for wilderness politics. Symms, a representative in the House, leading supporter of the
Sagebrush Rebellion, and ally to the timber industry, defeated Frank Church,
a longtime leader of the liberal Democrats and one of the nation's foremost
political champions of federal wilderness protection since the 1960s. On the
campaign trail, Symms emphasized public lands issues, arguing that Idahoans
knew how to manage their lands better than "the people on the banks of the
Potomac."[55] Symms and Ronald Reagan campaigned together in Idaho, with a
shared commitment to returning the government to "the conservative, free-
enterprise, God-fearing people" that made America strong.[56] In the late 1970s,
across much of the West, citizens voted for candidates like Symms and against
candidates like Church. It was a sea change in western and national politics that
helped Republicans consolidate their power in Congress and posed new challenges for wilderness advocates.

"Soft–Release" Language and the State-by-State Compromises

In August 1977, Doug Scott noted, "It is clear that opposition to RARE II is building up."[57] He did not seem to realize that by then the opposition had largely swept
the summer hearings.[58] That fall the wilderness leadership began to reckon with
the challenges RARE II posed: it overlapped directly with the Alaska campaign,
it required national coordination, it dramatically raised the short-term stakes
for the national forest roadless areas, and it superseded citizen-initiated wilderness campaigns across the nation. Tim Mahoney, the Wilderness Society's chief
strategist, remembers, "The last thing we needed was [to make it] a short-term
crap shoot."[59] For RARE II, the wilderness leadership deployed the same tools
they relied on during the Endangered Wilderness and Alaska campaigns. The
Sierra Club and Wilderness Society joined their efforts under the leadership
of what became known as the "Gang of Four"—Doug Scott, Tim Mahoney,
John Hooper, and John McComb. These experienced strategists orchestrated
a national campaign, on par with the campaign for Alaska. Initially, RARE II's
national scope, review of all roadless areas, and extensive program of public

involvement seemed well-suited to the wilderness movement's coordinated strategy of the 1960s and 1970s, which depended equally on the work of local and national groups in championing wilderness proposals. It was just this type of work that Dave Foreman organized in New Mexico in 1977 and oversaw from his post at the Wilderness Society in 1978. Noting how the wilderness advocates had been "beaten last summer" by their opponents, Foreman laid out a strategy for RARE II: "we want to appear reasonable, we want to encourage consensus where wilderness values will not be excessive sacrifices, we want to minimize polarization and chaos . . . and we want to know what we are talking about."[60] Where the Sagebrush Rebellion seemed to attract attention because of its protests and extremism, Foreman emphasized that wilderness advocates' best strategy was to play by the rules, work through the review process, and advance well-informed and moderate proposals.

Such a large-scale review required the Forest Service to automate the review of its national public comment system. The agency received more than 250,000 responses to the draft environmental impact statement. To quantify and analyze so many comments, the agency assembled a team of data analysts in Salt Lake City to systematically code public responses based on three characteristics: the format of the feedback (personal letter, signed petition, pre-printed card, etc.), the specificity of the recommendation (general statement, detailed argument for a particular area, management suggestion, etc.), and the content of the comments offered. Like the data from WARS and DORS, these data were entered onto computer cards and transmitted to the agency's data processing center in Fort Collins, Colorado, the analytical hub of RARE II. RARE II reduced the review of the roadless areas to a blizzard of quantitative data.[61] This automated methodology helped usher in a changed language of wilderness advocacy. The personal testimonies, recreational enthusiasm, and aesthetic concerns that had been so important to the spirited advocacy of local citizens disappeared amid the abstract language of technical natural resource assessment. Arguing to protect a wilderness area meant engaging in a complex calculus that weighed that area against the WARS, DORS, and overall EIA for dozens or hundreds of other wilderness areas. One of the wilderness movement's biggest frustrations with RARE II was that it gave too much weight to mass-produced form letters, such as those Sagebrush Rebels sent in, and too little attention to the site-specific recommendations local wilderness advocates more often submitted. It became clear to the Wilderness Society that if it was to successfully engage in such large-scale technical reviews, it needed its own economists, scientists, and lawyers.

In Colorado, Oregon, New Hampshire, and dozens of other states, the existing networks of local wilderness advocacy groups ramped up their efforts with "adopt-a-roadless area" programs, letter-writing campaigns, and citizen training seminars in 1978.[62] What the Western Timber Association did on ninety areas in California, wilderness advocates did for hundreds of roadless areas nationwide, making detailed studies and recommendations for their future. The product of these efforts was "Alternative W"—a comprehensive citizen proposal that offered an alternative to the agency's RARE II proposals. The agency's draft environmental impact statement considered ten alternatives, most of which were skewed towards development: nine of the alternatives allocated less than 36 percent of the roadless areas to wilderness; the tenth alternative proposed designating all roadless areas as wilderness. Wilderness advocates knew that the all-wilderness alternative was impractical; in the 1970s, neither in public nor in private did they broach the possibility of protecting all roadless areas as wilderness. Instead, they focused their efforts on a strategy consistent with the moderate tack Foreman described. The citizens' Alternative W recommended protecting 63 percent of the roadless areas as wilderness. And that was why wilderness advocates found the Carter administration's final recommendation, which allocated 25 percent of the roadless areas for wilderness protection, so disappointing.[63] They had made a reasonable proposal, they believed, but that did them little good in a review justified by WARS, DORS, and an EIS.

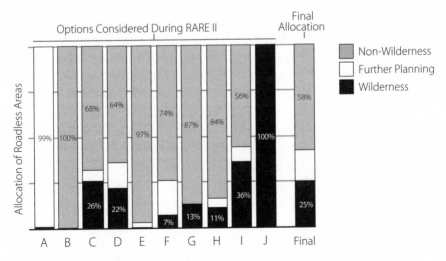

6.3 During the Roadless Area Review and Evaluation II, the Forest Service considered ten alternatives (labeled A to J), which were skewed toward non-wilderness (with the exception of alternative J). The Carter administration announced the final allocation in April 1979.

6.4 Representative John Seiberling of Ohio on a field trip to inspect potential wilderness areas in Colorado with members of the Colorado Open Space Coalition, ca. 1979. Seiberling made numerous such trips in the 1970s and 1980s. Courtesy Conservation Collection, Denver Public Library.

In mid-1979, the Gang of Four considered two strategies for addressing the shortcomings in RARE II—one legal and one legislative. If they pursued judicial appeal, they could file a national lawsuit on the same grounds as the state of California had and challenge RARE II's sufficiency under NEPA. Foresters, economists, and other experts employed by and working with the Wilderness Society and the Sierra Club had assembled detailed briefs questioning the methodology that underlaid RARE II. Considering that California had already won such a lawsuit, it seemed likely that a national suit would succeed, too; if it did, it would leave the future of the roadless areas as uncertain as it had been before RARE II began. But the Gang of Four feared that such a lawsuit "could easily lead to backlash in Congress."[64] In the worst case, it might even lead Congress to pass legislation ratifying the non-wilderness recommendations in RARE II. Indeed, Representative Tom Foley (D-WA), from a rural and resource-dependent district in eastern Washington, introduced such national release legislation in 1979.[65] Instead of going to court and risking a political backlash that might jumpstart such anti-wilderness legislation, the Gang of Four focused foremost on a legislative strategy. In 1979 and 1980, the Gang of Four counted on John Seiberling in the House to promote a legislative process that could lead to negotiations with the timber industry, Forest Service, and state congressional delegations in an effort to resolve the stalemate on a state-by-state basis. For such a legislative strategy to succeed, however, it became apparent that three issues had to be addressed: first, the allocation of the roadless areas had to be agreed upon; second, the legislation had to affirm that RARE II was sufficient to meet NEPA's requirements (thus negating future lawsuits); and third, the future of the roadless areas not designated wilderness had to be resolved. This last issue became the sticking point.[66]

When the Gang of Four started pushing wilderness bills through the House's Subcommittee on Public Lands, which Seiberling chaired, the timber industry and its allies made a clever move. Instead of opposing the new wilderness bills outright, they countered with a proposal that would meet their most pressing concern—resolving the uncertainty that clouded the future of the national forests. Their proposal was this: any legislation that designated wilderness based on RARE II should also legislatively release non-wilderness areas for multiple-use management. In effect, they were demanding a quid pro quo: if you protect some areas as wilderness, you have to release the remaining areas for potential development. The industry's proposal seemed eminently reasonable. But, in fact, it represented a major shift in how wilderness legislation was negotiated. Before, wilderness legislation did only one thing: it added new areas to the wilderness system—which allowed wilderness advocates to focus all of their energies on the positive goal of expanding wilderness. If the timber industry's proposal succeeded, suddenly wilderness legislation would do two things: it would add areas to the wilderness system and it would explicitly open areas for multiple-use management. That could put wilderness advocates on the defensive. Andy Wiessner, a key staffer on the House Interior Committee and ally to the wilderness movement, was party to the negotiations and warned that if the release strategy succeeded, it would "be a sign of weakness in the wilderness fortress, and once opened, will greatly expand."[67] The Gang of Four did everything it could to resist this type of wilderness legislation in 1979 and 1980, and in doing so it succeeded in wresting one crucial compromise.[68] With the help of Seiberling, wilderness advocates blocked "hard-release" language for non-wilderness areas—a strategy that would have barred future wilderness reviews of those areas forever. Instead, they substituted "soft-release" language, which opened the areas for potential development in the short term but, importantly, allowed for future wilderness reviews of those areas during the next cycle of forest plans under the National Forest Management Act (anticipated to take place in ten to fifteen years).[69]

Why were the modest gains in this compromise so important to the Gang of Four? In short, Congress had never passed legislation that specifically prohibited future wilderness reviews. The soft-release language kept the door to future reviews propped open, however slightly, where the hard-release language would have slammed it shut. But making this strategy work in Congress required careful coordination within the wilderness community. The Gang of Four worried that any break in the ranks could jeopardize the soft-release compromise. One concern was that a local or state group might file suit against the Forest Service over RARE II. Wilderness advocates in Oregon, where the RARE II recommendation was particularly disappointing, threatened as much in 1979 and 1980. Al Sample, one of the Wilderness Society's forest specialists, later explained, "if any of our uncontrolled grassrooters file suit [the Forest Service and timber industry become] the beleaguered victim of obstructionist greenies."[70] Another concern was that local wilderness groups might engage in independent negotiations over the controversial release language—some leaders in the East, for example, had no problems with hard release, but such independent negotiations could set problematic precedents for western timber states where the stakes were higher.[71] Finally, if local leaders were too ambitious in their goals for wilderness designations, they might undermine the soft-release compromise. To secure soft release over hard release in Colorado, the Gang of Four urged local groups to accept much less wilderness than they would have otherwise.[72] The Colorado bill contained only 70 percent of the wilderness acreage the Forest Service had recommended in RARE II (and far less than Alternative W for Colorado). For the Gang of Four, preserving the soft-release compromise was more important than securing wilderness designation for particular areas or addressing the priorities of local advocates. This episode reflected a reconfiguration of wilderness advocacy; to manage the intricate legislative strategy, national groups increasingly commanded local activists to ensure policy success. It was this dynamic that troubled Dave Foreman. Something was wrong, he said, when those in Washington "were plotting how to keep the grassroots in line."[73]

In 1979 and 1980, the Gang of Four oiled the gears of legislative compromise with strong citizen support and succeeded in moving two statewide bills with soft-release language for Colorado and New Mexico as well as a separate bill for Idaho in Congress. The Colorado bill protected 1.5 million acres as wilderness and 500,000 acres of wilderness study areas, and released 4 million acres for potential development. The New Mexico bill protected 600,000 acres as wilderness and 100,000 acres of wilderness study areas, and released 1.5 million acres for potential development. And the Idaho legislation, championed by Frank Church, protected 2.2 million acres in central Idaho and included no release language.[74] But efforts to pass statewide legislation following the Colorado template for Oregon, West Virginia, Florida, and, most importantly, California in the 96th Congress failed. Reagan's election to the White House and Republican gains in the Senate in November 1980 changed the political equation for the roadless areas, just as it had for Alaska.[75] Negotiations toward soft-release state bills fell apart after the election; western senators notified the Gang of Four that they wished to renegotiate the release language. Mahoney warned that western senators were preparing to "give us a decisive defeat" in the next Congress.[76]

At the start of the 97th Congress, the Republicans stacked the Senate committees most directly responsible for the national forests in their favor—James McClure, the senior senator from Idaho, staunch supporter of industry, and ally to the Sagebrush Rebellion, became the chair of the Senate Energy and Natural Resources Committee. Reagan appointed John B. Crowell, a former timber company lawyer, as assistant secretary of agriculture in place of Cutler. The timber industry and its allies were quick to press their advantage. In March 1981, Senator Hayakawa introduced the RARE II Act of 1981. The bill's cosponsors read like a roster of conservative Republicans sympathetic to the Sagebrush Rebellion, including Senators Hatch, Symms, McClure, and Alan Simpson (R-WY). Mahoney described it as "the most radical timber industry initiative thus far."[77] The legislation proposed releasing roadless areas recommended for non-wilderness and further planning in RARE II immediately and releasing areas proposed for wilderness by 1985, if they had not yet been designated wilderness (and any such designations seemed unlikely, considering the new Senate). In short, the legislation aimed to do precisely what the timber industry hoped: close out the wilderness reviews quickly with "national release legislation."

The new Republican majority in the Senate marked a watershed for wilderness politics, just as it did for American politics. Most obviously, the changed balance of political power in the White House and Senate gave the environmental opposition an unprecedented opportunity to set the political agenda. When historians consider the surge of environmental opposition in the early 1980s, however, they often focus on the Reagan administration and its appointees, such as Secretary of the Interior James Watt, who came to symbolize its anti-environmental agenda, but that risks overlooking how important the changed Senate was for environmental reform.[78] The new Republican majority in the Senate, which was made possible, partly, by anger over the expanding role of the federal government in the West, the support of western industry and its allies, and the Sagebrush Rebellion, most immediately short-circuited wilderness advocates' ambitions for both the Alaska legislation and the soft-release RARE II bills. Starting in 1981, wilderness advocates found themselves on the defensive. By then, however, the mainstream wilderness movement, especially the Wilderness Society, had already begun to reorganize itself to meet such challenges. The lesson the Wilderness Society drew from RARE II was the importance of cultivating its own expertise and professionalism. In RARE II and the legislative negotiations important to the subsequent wilderness bills, those strategies, more so than earlier strategies of citizen organizing, seemed necessary to address the legal, scientific, and economic complexities on which the future of the national forests hinged. Starting in 1979, the Wilderness Society undertook a dramatic program of internal reform aimed at meeting that challenge.

Reinventing the Wilderness Society

Two visions were at stake at the Wilderness Society in 1979. One vision was represented by Dave Foreman, who had worked his way up the Wilderness Society's ranks from his position as New Mexico field representative. He had put in his time shouldering a backpack and surveying wilderness in the field, maintained a firm faith in citizen activism, and was known to pop a can of beer in the office. For Foreman and his cohort, the Wilderness Society was a welcome refuge from the beltway scene in Washington, D.C. It set aside pretensions and worked diligently to achieve its goal: protecting wilderness. The hub of this "anti-D.C." sentiment at the Wilderness Society was the Buckaroo Bunkhouse. Foreman, Debbie Sease, and Tim Mahoney, all underpaid Wilderness Society staffers transferred from the West after Brandborg's departure, rented out an old, uninsulated farmhouse just across the Potomac from the Lincoln Memorial in Rosslyn, Virginia. They formed the heart of the Wilderness Society's conservation staff under the leadership of Celia Hunter, an experienced wilderness champion from Alaska and longtime member of the Governing Council. The Buckaroo Bunkhouse occupies a mythical place in the history of the wilderness movement. Foreman was the director of the Wilderness Society's field program at the time, and as representatives came in from Montana, Idaho, or New Mexico to Washington, D.C., they often boarded at the bunkhouse, which meant a constant flow of overnight guests linking the Wilderness Society's conservation staff with its field program and volunteer allies in the West. During the day, Foreman, Mahoney, Sease, and their colleagues coordinated the Wilderness Society's conservation work on Alaska and RARE II from the offices at

1901 Pennsylvania Ave. Come evening, the bunkhouse was known for its singing, hard drinking, poker games, and late-night parties.[79]

The other vision of the Wilderness Society was embodied by William
Turnage, who had been hired as the Wilderness Society's new executive director in the fall of 1978. Often dressed in a suit, wearing thick-rimmed glasses,
and bearing an earnest disposition, Turnage brought a determined and forward-looking presence to the Wilderness Society. Turnage's vision for the new
Wilderness Society was one of "more responsibility and less stridency, more
professionalism and less emotionalism, more dialogue and less diatribe."[80] Turnage himself embodied many of the changes he sought to cultivate at the Wilderness Society. A graduate of Yale, Oxford, and the Yale School of Forestry,
Turnage claimed impressive academic credentials. When Turnage arrived at
the Wilderness Society, he brought with him an extensive network of personal
connections, both from his days at Yale and his previous position as the photographer Ansel Adams' publicist and business manager. In the latter position,
Turnage had become involved in debates over Yosemite National Park, which
formed the springboard for his involvement in the Wilderness Society. Where
most of the Wilderness Society's leadership worked their way up by organizing the grassroots and shouldering a backpack in the field, Turnage found his
way to the Wilderness Society toting a shiny briefcase. He was a very different
leader than his predecessors, most notably Stewart Brandborg. In the office, he
kept a fancy fountain pen on his desk. In the field, the Wilderness Society's field

6.5 William Turnage, executive director of the Wilderness Society from 1979 to 1985,
testifying at a hearing with Ron Tipton in 1980. Turnage restructured the organization
as a professional environmental lobby. Courtesy the Wilderness Society.

representatives soon learned, he carried mineral water in a canteen. After Turnage arrived at the Wilderness Society, it was the rowdy culture of the Buckaroo Bunkhouse and its seat-of-the-pants approach to wilderness advocacy that seemed increasingly out of place.

The Wilderness Society had struggled to regain its footing ever since it stumbled in 1975. After Brandborg's ouster, the organization had rebuilt and expanded its field staff and citizen advocacy program, and George Davis and Celia Hunter provided crucial leadership. Clif Merrit in Denver and Dave Foreman in Washington, D.C., coordinated almost a dozen field representatives nationwide, making it one of the best developed and most experienced field programs in the country. But in these years, the society's effectiveness ebbed as it struggled to rebuild its legislative staff and its finances deteriorated. By 1979, the Wilderness Society was losing eight thousand members a year. Income had dropped by one-third since 1976, the annual deficit had climbed to $200,000, and the organization's endowment was exhausted.[81] The Sierra Club increasingly took the lead in the wilderness movement, spearheading the campaigns for Alaska and RARE II in the late 1970s and early 1980s. The more technical approach to federal decision-making, exemplified by RARE II, and the growing environmental opposition further challenged the Wilderness Society's focus on citizen activism. To Turnage, the attitude and style of the Buckaroo Bunkhouse was not going to get the job done. If the Wilderness Society was founded in 1935 as an elite and idealistic interest group, repositioned at the forefront of a popular and mainstream wilderness movement in the 1960s, then, in the late 1970s, the Wilderness Society undertook its third major reorganization. Under Turnage's leadership, the Wilderness Society rebuilt itself as a professional environmental lobby.

New strategies for the Wilderness Society had been circulating before Turnage arrived—the possibility of emphasizing technical expertise, expanding fundraising efforts, and exploring support from foundations had all been broached, even during Brandborg's tenure. Turnage arrived not just with a briefcase full of new ideas, but also with the mandate and the ambition to organize these ideas into a coherent strategy. The Governing Council looked to Turnage to bring stability to the Wilderness Society, and his first hires helped set the organization's new direction. In the fall of 1978, Turnage convinced Chuck Clusen to leave the Sierra Club and join the Wilderness Society as its senior conservation director.[82] Equally important, Turnage hired new directors of development and finance. Sarah Muyskens left Yale University's office of development to revamp the Wilderness Society's membership program and fundraising efforts. Phil Steele, a top graduate of Stanford Business School, was responsible for restructuring finances and planning.[83] This new management team cultivated a professionalism that distinguishes the organization to the present day.

Turnage and Muyskens moved aggressively to shore up the Wilderness Society's finances. Membership dropped by nearly half between 1979 and mid-1981, bottoming out at 35,000 members.[84] Yet, during the same period, the Wilderness Society's annual budget nearly doubled to four million dollars.[85] Behind these changes was a new fundraising strategy. It was Turnage's goal to balance the budget in equal parts between unpredictable membership donations and sources of "soft" money from wealthy donors, corporations, and foundations.[86] The newly structured Governing Council was meant to include one-third conservationists, one-third policy experts, and, for the first time, one-third individuals who could either "provide funds" or "access to funds."[87] In May 1979, the Wilderness Society held its first private fundraising party in New York City. Afterward, Turnage touted it as the event that "launched the new and more professional administration of the Wilderness Society."[88] This strategy opened up new sources of foundation funds. The largest initial grant came from the Richard King Mellon Foundation for an Economic Policy Department (comprised of two economists, a forester, and an ecologist), which played a crucial role in latter debates over RARE II and the public domain. Turnage billed the unit as a pioneering program to enhance the wilderness movement's "factual base, our economic and scientific research capacity, and our professional competence." Most important, he explained, it would focus on "a more mature and collaborative" approach that would link government, industry, and conservationists in productive dialogue.[89] The Mellon Foundation funded the program with a $620,000 contribution over three years (which came in the form of stock in Gulf Oil).[90] That donation stamped what Muyskens described as "the Good Housekeeping Seal of Approval" on the Wilderness Society—and marked the beginning of a series of foundation grants that expanded the organization's budget and capabilities in the early 1980s.[91]

The changing direction of the Wilderness Society was not lost on Foreman or his cohort at the Buckaroo Bunkhouse. From the start, Turnage had made it clear that the field program needed to be revamped. But as Chuck Clusen soon realized, "The buckaroos didn't believe in the high-powered professionals, and Turnage didn't believe in the grassroots."[92] Clusen, who had worked with most of those buckaroos since he got his start in wilderness politics in the early 1970s, found himself caught between two visions of the Wilderness Society.

Turnage and Clusen met with the field staff several times in late 1978 and 1979. They were uneasy meetings. Where the field staff was used to cheap motels or tents, Turnage booked them in hotels. Where the field staff focused on working with citizens, Turnage expected them to undertake fundraising and cultivate influential locals. Where the field staff took pride in their informality and commitment, Turnage expected a new measure of decorum and professionalism. As relations reached a low point, Turnage and the field representatives met in the California Sierra in the summer of 1979. The meeting ended with plans for a brief overnight trip into the proposed Granite Chief wilderness. En route to the trailhead, they stopped at a grocery store for supplies. What they bought was telling. Foreman bought a steak. Turnage bought SpaghettiOs and mineral water. By the time they got to camp that night, it was too late for a fire. And, as Susan Zakin recounts in her book *Coyotes and Towndogs*, Foreman "ripped the raw steak out of its cellophane package and tore into it with his teeth, horrifying everyone except Jim Eaton." Eaton, the California field representative, Foreman's friend, and a buckaroo, joined in. Then "they both did a caveman jig, grunting and hopping around in front of Bill Turnage."[93] Soon, Foreman would make a career of such showmanship. By the end of the trip, Turnage seemed to have made up his mind: the field representatives had to go.

In Turnage's view, the society's field program of the mid-1970s had been given "slightly mythological and historic proportions."[94] He was not alone in that assessment. In the federal land agencies, the young staff at the Wilderness Society was regarded as inexperienced and ineffective.[95] The Sierra Club doubted the society's capabilities.[96] As Ted Swem, the Wilderness Society's president, jotted in his notes, "TWS way down line—most of people green" and "Impression—organization dead in the water."[97] In time, Foreman, Sease, Mahoney, and many of the buckaroos in the field would emerge as key leaders. But none made their careers at the Wilderness Society. Turnage began by closing the Denver office, effectively forcing Clif Merritt, who had been a mentor to a whole generation of field representatives and wilderness activists, from a job he had held since Zahniser hired him in 1964. In 1979 and early 1980, Clusen remembers that Turnage was determined to turn over the staff. And he did, firing all but two of the field representatives. As news of the firings spread through the wilderness community, it was greeted with bitterness. That winter, Bernard Shanks, a member of the Governing Council and a staunch defender of the grassroots program, reported that "the hostility to the Wilderness Society among our best friends is a sad and serious problem."[98] Even as he dismantled the field program, Turnage promised to rebuild it in the future;

but in place of informal, localized grassroots organizers, he envisioned a well-funded, full-time, office-based team of regional representatives who focused on local issues, public relations, and fundraising. "My concern is to stabilize and professionalize the field program," he explained.[99] In private he admitted that local citizen involvement in the Wilderness Society interested him the least.[100]

Looking backward in 1983, Turnage took pride that almost the entire Wilderness Society staff had been hired since he took over. "Best of all," he wrote, "the place is rife with Yale forestry people!"[101] Drawing on the new foundation funds, he and Clusen focused on rebuilding the organization's capabilities. The new Economic Policy Department was one such program: the technical reports, policy recommendations, and press releases that accompanied its studies provided clear evidence of the Wilderness Society's new direction. A smaller grant was secured from Ted and Jenny Stanley for a forest management oversight program. Such grants funded technical analyses that became a staple of the Wilderness Society's efforts to fend off the Reagan administration in the early 1980s. As the Wilderness Society moved away from a focus on citizen outreach and advocacy, it placed new emphasis on hiring well-educated lawyers and lobbyists who, while not necessarily versed in public lands issues, could be trained quickly and would strengthen the society's image as a high-powered environmental lobby. New staffers, such as regional representative Peter Kirby, forest-issues lobbyist Peter Coppelman, and forester Al Sample, became key players in the Wilderness Society's policy work. The Wilderness Society also hired prominent beltway figures forced out after the November 1980 elections. Former Wisconsin Senator Gaylord Nelson and Carter's former Secretary of the Interior Cecil Andrus joined the Wilderness Society as special consultants in 1980 and helped raise the organization's profile. Behind these new strategies was Turnage's conviction that it was time to embrace a "more mature and collaborative approach" toward public lands protection—the type of strategy that proved important to compromise legislation like the soft-release RARE II bills.

The Wilderness Society's new approach to wilderness advocacy raised concerns among its longtime supporters. Chuck Stoddard, a member of the Governing Council, worried that "money changers have taken over the temple." He thought that Turnage believed that "$$$$" was all it took to win the fight. In 1980, Stoddard declined another term on the council in protest of a new Wilderness Society corporate-giving program.[102] George Marshall, brother of Wilderness Society founder Bob Marshall, warned against permitting "the smell of money to undermine and destroy us as an effective conservation organization."[103] And Harry Crandell, from his post on the staff of the House Interior Committee, cautioned that the society risked losing its "wilderness fighter" image.[104] There was good reason for those long affiliated with the Wilderness Society to be concerned about the scope and pace of change. In November 1979, Turnage, Clusen, and the senior staff revealed to the Governing Council that they had engaged in confidential discussions with the larger and wealthier Natural Resources Defense Council about a potential merger. Clusen stressed the organizations' complementary strengths: "the NRDC was strong on legal activities, scientific expertise, and energy problems; TWS was strong on legislative lobbying and public lands matters; NRDC was new; TWS had tradition and long-term membership."[105] The Governing Council quashed the idea immediately, warning that "to merge would be to sell out the Wilderness Society's philosophy and unique mission."[106] The Governing Council had hired Turnage with a mandate to rebuild the Wilderness Society. He pursued that goal enthusiastically. And although the council halted the merger with the NRDC, that did not stop Turnage from remaking the Wilderness Society in its image. Indeed, in the 1980s, the Wilderness Society would take up a broader agenda for public lands reform, including addressing below-cost logging and grazing on the public lands, which NRDC began exploring in the mid-1970s.

Under Turnage's leadership, the Wilderness Society caught up with the changes that had swept through the mainstream environmental movement in the 1970s. It joined the ranks of professional environmental lobbies, which the NRDC, Environmental Defense Fund, and, in many respects, the Sierra Club, had already joined in the early 1970s. As its budget reached four million dollars, the Wilderness Society formalized its internal planning, accounting, and communications procedures: a five-year planning program structured long-term goals and internal quarterly reports and public annual reports documented the Wilderness Society's standing for members and foundations alike. These practices marked a change from the early 1970s, when more than two-thirds of the one-million-dollar budget came from membership contributions, planning was largely ad-hoc, and the Wilderness Society's conservation program focused on education, citizen activism, and legislative change. With this new organizational structure came a different approach to wilderness advocacy. At Brandborg's Wilderness Society, political power came through involving citizens, developing relationships with local communities and congressional representatives, and addressing the concerns of critics and opponents. At Turnage's Wilderness Society, political power came through foundation funds, analytical expertise, and professional lobbying capabilities. The new Wilderness Society marked a shift away from a politics of persuasion, rooted in personal communication and dialogue, to a politics of proof, driven by empirical studies, economic and scientific analysis, press releases and white papers. Swem, the Wilderness Society's president, described Brandborg's tenure as "the good old days." But, he noted, "I wouldn't trade the Society of today for the Society of those recent years."[107]

This broad transition in mainstream environmentalism—toward increasingly professional, Washington, D.C.-based, and foundation-funded organizations—has been central to our understanding of the modern American environmental movement, but the Wilderness Society's reinvention challenges the argument that a transition from first- to second-generation environmental issues drove the change. It was not so much a transition from place-based, public lands conservation issues of the 1950s and 1960s to the more abstract pollution, energy, and environmental-health issues of the 1960s and 1970s that drove the restructuring of the mainstream American environmental movement. Rather it was an iterative process of organizational transformation, the availability of new funding sources, a stronger opposition, and changes in federal environmental decision-making, all of which formed important components in a feedback loop that encouraged the consolidation and professionalization of environmental advocacy starting in the 1960s. For instance, professional lobbies played a key role in establishing the importance of laws such as NEPA in the early 1970s, and as the regulatory provisions of NEPA gave new weight to scientific and social analysis, those provisions, in turn, encouraged more professional strategies within environmental groups. This transformation was important for even the oldest of conservation issues— wilderness. By 1984, the Wilderness Society, drawing on such strategies, became the fourth-largest environmental organization in the nation. Yet even as the Wilderness Society regained its footing, it struggled to maintain its leadership of the wilderness community as a whole.

Could foundation grants, economic analysis, and slick publications and press releases save more wilderness? That was the question Foreman was asking in New Mexico in 1980. If the Wilderness Society, Sierra Club, and the Gang of Four's strategy on the statewide RARE II bills was any indication, the answer was no. The 1980 soft-release state bills may have protected 2 million acres of wilderness in New Mexico and Colorado, but what galled Foreman was what the "wilderness" bills gave away: the two laws released 6 million acres of roadless areas for potential development. Of course, it was soft release, which meant it would be reviewed again in the mid-1990s during the next round of forest plans, but when timber prices were three times what they had been in 1976, it seemed likely that the "Freddies"—as the Forest Service came to be known in the 1980s—were determined to log those roadless areas as quickly as they could. If Turnage's strategy, emphasizing dialogue, cooperation, and compromise, meant giving industry three acres of wild lands for every one acre of wilderness saved, then Foreman had had enough. In the spring of 1980, Turnage had yet to fire Foreman. Instead, Foreman quit. And when he did, the groundwork for Earth First! was already in place.[108]

Earth First!

The date: March 21, 1981. The occasion: the vernal equinox and the rebirth of nature. The scene: the 583-foot tall, gracefully arched, concrete plug of a dam on the Colorado River, better known as Glen Canyon Dam, which to many environmentalists represented the most misguided of the federal government's attempts to harness the West's natural resources. The plan: Earth First!'s stage debut. In 1976, the iconoclastic western author Edward Abbey published *The Monkey Wrench Gang*, a raucous novel about a small group of freedom-loving, adventure-seeking, environmentally minded (more or less) activists who set out to sabotage the industrial machinery that was tearing apart the American Southwest. Their grandest dream was to destroy the Glen Canyon Dam, and that became Earth First!'s symbolic start. That cold Saturday morning, five Earth First!ers, including Foreman, Wolke, and Koehler, headed straight for the top of the dam, where they hopped the fence and ran for the dam's midpoint, all while lugging an enormous black bundle. There, nearly two football fields above the Colorado River, they unfurled a 300-foot-long sheet of black plastic, trimmed to look like a splintering crack, down the face of the dam. "Earth First!" they shouted. And so did Edward Abbey, who they had invited, along with a small group of supporters and, most importantly, the press.[109] Photos of the "cracked" dam appeared in newspapers across the West, *Outside* magazine published a story that captured the attention of the yuppie-outdoor set, and the Associated Press newswire carried the story under the headline: "Group Vows to Dismantle Glen Canyon Dam."[110] Civil disobedience never drew much attention among wilderness advocates in the years around Earth Day in 1970, but that was about to change.

By the time of the stunt at Glen Canyon Dam, Earth First! could claim three hundred members, its own journal, and a vision. The previous year, it had held its first Round River Rendezvous outside Dubois, Wyoming, just east of the Washaki Wilderness. The invitation read: "WHY: To reinvigorate, enthuse,

6.6 Dave Foreman (left) and Ed Abbey (holding sign) at Earth First!'s protest of the Glen Canyon Dam in 1981. Photograph by Dawson Henderson. Courtesy Dawson Henderson and Dave Foreman.

inspire wilderness activists in the West; to bring passion, humor, joy and fervency of purpose back into the cause; to forge friendships, cooperation, and alliances throughout the West; to get drunk together, spark a few romances, and howl at the moon" and "who: Wilderness warriors, shamans, and chiefs from around the West and a few honorary westerners from Washington, D.C. A few of the grey-hairs of the tribe to pass on the torch."[111] Earth First! was meant to be the antithesis of the new Wilderness Society.[112] In the early 1980s, across the West, there was a growing frustration with the national wilderness leadership and new concerns about the anti-environmental machinations of the Reagan administration. After Glen Canyon, Earth First!'s ranks began to expand. That fall, Earth First! took its show on the road. Foreman and Koehler, along with a few others, traveled the country in their beat-up Volkswagen bus, telling stories, singing songs, and raising hell from Lander, Wyoming, to

6.7 Earth First! grabbed the media's attention when it unfurled a 300-foot sheet of black plastic that symbolically split open Glen Canyon Dam in 1981. Photographs by Dawson Henderson. Courtesy Dawson Henderson and Dave Foreman.

Staunton, Virginia, to New Haven, Connecticut.[113] The road show's pitch came to be known as "The Speech." It was all Foreman. He kept the audience riveted with a talk, a plea, and a challenge that ranged from Aldo Leopold to James Watt and had people doubled over in laughter, hell-raising mad, and quietly pensive. His message: sometimes you have to put your body on the line.[114]

In the early 1980s, while the Wilderness Society and the Sierra Club dickered over release language and fended off the Reagan administration in Washington, D.C., Earth First! began to do what Foreman promised and more. From the start, its founders emphasized that Earth First! did not "operate from a basis of political pragmatism." As the organization's name suggested, "wilderness, natural diversity, is not something that can be compromised in the political arena."[115] Earth First! may have seized national attention from atop Glen Canyon Dam, but no issue fired the organization's early activities more than the fate of the national forest roadless areas. Earth First! advanced a range of protest techniques for the sake of protecting wilderness. Some strategies were familiar: In 1983, Earth First! championed the aggressive use of litigation to derail the RARE II process. Back in Washington, D.C., what Earth First! described as the "moderate wilderness clique" was still warning wilderness groups away from legal action—for fear of political backlash. Earth First! saw that as the movement's best bet: if such a suit succeeded nationally, it would throw the future of the national roadless areas into confusion, delaying action until a friendlier administration and Congress took office.[116] If that did not work, Earth First! encouraged its allies to appeal timber sales in roadless areas. An issue of the *Earth First! Journal* even included fill-in-the-blank forms. "Stop those 'dozers with a little piece of paper. It is up to you."[117] Earth First! was not opposed to working through the system when it thought it would make a difference.

But few remember Earth First! for those strategies. Instead, Earth First! electrified wilderness politics with its protest activities. Drawing on the strategies of the Civil Rights Movement, the anti-war movement, and the women's movement, Earth First! made the principled individual the physical guardian of wilderness: blockades, tree-sitting, and sit-ins opened up a whole new physical dimension of wilderness protest. According to Earth First! the real grassroots were no longer backpackers surveying wilderness areas, holding save-the-wilderness hikes, or testifying in Congress; they were radicals willing to place their bodies on the line.[118] The seedbed for these strategies was the Siskiyou Mountains along the Oregon-California state line just inland from the Pacific coast. Located at an ecological and geological crossroads, the Siskiyou protected steelhead and salmon runs, spotted owls, wolverines, otters, mountain lions, and bears and included large tracts of unlogged coniferous forest. The Wilderness Act added the existing 78,850-acre Kalmiopsis Wilderness Area to the new National Wilderness Preservation System in 1964. And in 1978, the Endangered American Wilderness Act expanded it to 170,850 acres. But much of that land was still the highlands, which meant several hundred thousand acres of ecologically rich forest land surrounded the existing wilderness in unprotected roadless areas. Since the early 1970s, the Oregon Wilderness Coalition had been fighting to save as much of the Siskiyou as possible. No group had been more incensed by the Gang of Four's maneuverings in Washington, D.C., than local wilderness advocates in Oregon. Lead by Jim Monteith, a wildlife biologist, the Oregon Wilderness Coalition had watched as its hopes to protect a 325,000-acre Northern Kalmiopsis wilderness were negotiated away first during the Endangered American Wilderness Act, then during the Gang of Four's failed efforts to secure a soft-release RARE II bill for Oregon, and finally effectively blocked when the Sierra Club and Wilderness Society questioned Oregon wilderness advocates' plans to file a California-style suit against RARE II.[119]

When Foreman and Earth First! arrived in southern Oregon in the summer of 1983, they made quick friends among local wilderness advocates. The Forest Service's most immediate plan for the Kalmiopsis was a six-mile road along the northern boundary of the existing wilderness to the top of Bald Mountain. It was a strategic move: the road would separate the existing wilderness area from the roadless old-growth forest to the north and it would undermine future wilderness proposals. As Susan Zakin notes, there was nothing particularly special about Bald Mountain, but "when bureaucratic hubris so blatantly imposed its badly tailored laws on nature" the mountain, its ecological diversity, and its future became a leading cause for Earth First![120] Road construction was scheduled to begin in late April. But when the bulldozer came rumbling up the road grade, four Earth First! activists stood in its way. It piled up dirt on their feet. They climbed atop the pile of dirt. The bulldozer turned back, and Les Moore, the construction chief, called the sheriff. For Earth First!, the "Oregon blockade" showed that the organization was more than "empty rhetoric."[121] Roselle, the Earth First! leader who orchestrated the initial standoff, wrote that with the blockade of Bald Mountain, "so too, began the nonviolent struggle to save all wilderness."[122] In the next four months, Earth First! orchestrated seven blockades on Bald Mountain in which forty-four people were arrested. The arrest that is best remembered was Foreman's. In May, the stakes at the blockade had been rising, until in an iconic moment Foreman stood alone in front of Moore and a truck full of construction workers. Moore decided to call Foreman's bluff. He nudged Foreman with his truck, and Foreman stood his ground. Moore accelerated slowly, and Foreman began walking, then running backwards, gripping the hood for balance. When Foreman lost his footing, he caught the truck's front bumper, and held on for his life, as it dragged him up the forest road until Moore finally stopped. Moore erupted from the truck, "You dirty communist bastard! Why don't you go back to Russia!" To which Foreman, bruised, scared, but alive, replied, "But, Les, I'm a registered Republican." It was Foreman that the sheriff arrested, not Moore.[123]

These events marked the beginning of the confrontations between radical environmentalists and the Forest Service and timber industry in the Pacific Northwest. In August 1984, Earth First! activists, along with several other Oregon citizen groups, staged a takeover of the regional Forest Service headquar-

6.8 Earth First! protested Getty Oil's oil exploration in the Gros Ventre mountains outside Jackson, Wyoming. A sustained campaign that included pulling survey stakes, sabotaging exploration equipment, and staging protests, such as this one, contributed to opposition to oil exploration. The area was added to the wilderness system by the Wyoming Wilderness Act of 1984. Photograph by Peter Dustrud, July 1982. Courtesy Peter Dustrud and Dave Foreman.

ters. In 1985, Earth First!ers ascended into the canopy of the Cathedral Forest in Oregon, camped out on platforms 200 feet above the ground, and delayed timber harvests for six months.[124] During those years, while most Earth First!ers remained focused on civil disobedience, some began to explore more shadowy forms of ecotage. In 1985, Foreman published *Ecodefense: A Field Guide to Monkeywrenching*, a handbook for wreaking havoc with the apparatus of industry.[125] The book laid out in exacting detail the philosophy and strategies important to successful and secretive industrial sabotage. One stand of spiked trees, one disabled bulldozer, or one sabotaged road at a time, monkeywrenching could help save wilderness, and the Earth, from an "overconsumptive technological human society."[126] "What is eco-defense?" Edward Abbey asked in the book's foreword. "Eco-defense means fighting back. Eco-defense means sabotage. Eco-defense is risky but sporting; unauthorized but fun; illegal but ethically imperative."[127] Such activities did take place sporadically across the West in the mid-1980s. It was meant to be a nonviolent enterprise aimed at, in

Foreman's words, "hitting exploiters where it hurts—in the pocketbook."[128] At least in theory, Foreman justified monkeywrenching as an economic strategy, meant to increase the cost of exploiting the public lands. Monkeywrenchers, not surprisingly, kept to themselves. But substantive references in the national press include pulling survey stakes in Wyoming, disabling bulldozers in Utah, sabotaging airstrips in Idaho, and spiking trees in Oregon, Washington, and Kentucky.[129] In 1986, an Oregon timber worker was seriously injured when a saw blade shattered upon cutting into a spiked tree.[130] Such activities drew the attention of the FBI, whose undercover agents infiltrated Earth First! and began building the case in which Foreman became ensnared after the bust outside the Central Arizona Project in 1989.

Although it was these public protest activities and more shadowy forms of ecotage that captured headlines in the mid-1980s, Earth First! did more than popularize civil disobedience among environmental activists in the United States. The organization was also brazen in its willingness to explore and test the boundaries of environmental thought. The *Earth First! Journal*, tabloid-size and loosely edited, formed a rich arena for environmental debate beneath the symbolic upraised fist that crowned its masthead. Earth First! broached divisive questions about nature, population growth, technology, and the future. The questions about modern society that Theodore Kaczynski raised in his 1969 letter to the Wilderness Society or the vision of an ecological wilderness that the Sierra Club's Wilderness Classification Subcommittee advanced in its early drafts of the Wilderness Manifesto in 1970, both of which had been dismissed at the time, would have generated open discussion within the ranks of Earth First! in the 1980s. In the pages of the journal, the organization's followers downplayed the importance of aesthetic, recreational, and utilitarian arguments for wilderness, and instead argued for wilderness because "wilderness is"—it is "the real world, the flow of life, the process of evolution, the repository of three-and-a-half billion years of shared travel."[131] This rhetoric—which was transformed into action in Oregon, Wyoming, and elsewhere—gained its philosophical convictions from a new stream of thought called Deep Ecology. As became apparent in the late 1980s, Deep Ecology, the new discipline of conservation biology, and Earth First! helped give new importance to the ecological primacy of wilderness in American environmental thought and politics.[132] That intellectual influence, as much as its brand of radical activism, would prove instrumental to the future of the wilderness movement. In 1983, Earth First! set forth its vision for the wilderness system. It measured 716 million acres, protected large-scale ecosystems nationwide, and was meant not just to protect wilderness but also to restore wild lands. It explicitly put the "ecosystem" before human recreation, safety, and convenience.[133] While such ideas drew little attention in comparison to monkeywrenching, these plans marked the beginning of large-scale, biocentric proposals that would transform the aims of wilderness advocates in the late 1980s and 1990s.

"The Wilderness Destruction Acts"

In the early 1980s, action on the roadless areas seemed to be on the ground in the West, not in the halls of Congress. Despite Senator McClure and his (generally) Republican allies' high hopes to pass national release legislation opening up most of the roadless areas to development, the 97th Congress had been a stalemate; such legislation would never get through the Democratic House. The gears of legislative compromise only began to turn again late in 1982, when the timber industry's appeal of the California suit against RARE II (in which the Ninth Circuit Court of Appeals found RARE II insufficient) was rejected.[134] If the appeal had been successful, the agency could have begun releasing the roadless areas. Instead the decision left the future of the roadless areas in a state of limbo. To the Gang of Four, the best strategy was not to pursue a new agency review, executive action, or additional legal suits (which seemed very likely to succeed based on the California precedent); it was to work through Congress. Already, the timber industry and its Republican allies in the Senate hoped the failed appeal would make clear the urgent need for national release legislation, which could end the uncertainty over the national forests. But wilderness advocates managed to flank the timber industry's stronghold in the Senate. In the early 1980s, they continued to work through the House Interior Committee, where they could count on the strong support of Seiberling and his staffers Crandell and Andy Wiessner. Their hope was that if the House started passing compromise state bills following the 1980 soft-release model for big timber states such as California and Oregon (states where the timber industry was eager to resolve the stalemate over the roadless areas), then the timber industry's allies in the Senate would be forced to adopt the state-by-state approach and give up on sweeping national release legislation.[135]

It worked. That March, the House started sending soft-release state RARE II bills to the Senate—California and Oregon first, West Virginia and Florida next, then Wisconsin, Vermont, New Hampshire, and North Carolina. As the soft-release RARE II bills started to pile up in the Senate Energy and Natural Resources Committee, the state-by-state strategy gained momentum and appeared to offer the quickest way to resolve the impasse over RARE II. After delaying for a year, McClure finally agreed to consider the House bills in the spring of 1984 on one condition: that the Gang of Four renegotiate the release language. The timber industry counted on McClure to secure hard release— which prohibited future wilderness reviews—in place of the soft release that had been agreed to in 1980. Since the Senate had passed a hard-release RARE II bill for Wyoming, whose congressional delegation was especially opposed to soft release, such negotiations were necessary. In April, various versions of release language were shuttled back and forth between Seiberling and the House Interior Committee and McClure and the Senate Energy and Natural Resources Committee. The tedious negotiations hinged on a half-dozen sentences, clauses, and words that spelled out precisely how the roadless areas that were released would be managed. But facing so many House-passed bills and the strong support of state congressional delegations to move those bills forward, McClure and Representative Dick Cheney (R-WY) succeeded in wresting only minor technical clarifications in the release language. The soft-release model prevailed, which meant that new state bills would designate some wilderness immediately, delay future wilderness reviews until the next round of forest planning in ten to fifteen years (as scheduled under the National Forest Management Act), and allow potential development of the remaining roadless areas in the interim.[136]

"We have reached an extraordinary confluence of events," Bill Turnage reported to the Wilderness Society's Governing Council. He described the agreement as an unprecedented opportunity to advance wilderness for the national forests. "We are going 'to the wall' (*and beyond!*) . . . the next six months."[137] The agreement over the release language opened the possibility for a raft of wilderness bills in the 98th Congress to finally close out the debates over the national forest roadless areas. In 1984, the Wilderness Society and Sierra Club, captained by Clusen and Scott, launched "Wilderness '84." With a $100,000 grant from Recreational Equipment Incorporated (REI), they brought together forty local wilderness activists and staffers from Wilderness Society and Sierra Club offices to lay the groundwork for the biggest grassroots push for wilderness since the Alaska campaign in 1980.[138] As this campaign gained momentum, however, it soon brought to light the changed dynamics of citizen wilderness advocacy. For the local activists who formed the backbone of the wilderness movement in the 1960s and 1970s, the secretive negotiations in Washington, D.C., over the release language made clear their diminished role in the hierarchy of wilderness advocacy. Despite the renewed push for citizen activism, the Wilderness Society and Sierra Club had reduced their focus on grassroots training and citizen involvement sharply in the early 1980s. And as the final stages of the roadless areas campaign began, the weakened relationship between the grassroots and the national leadership, the sheer number of wilderness areas at stake, and the increasingly contentious arena of environmental politics undermined the active cooperation that had once been the hallmark of local, state, and national wilderness advocacy.

Oregon had become notorious for intergroup quarrels among the state Sierra Club chapter, the Oregon Wilderness Coalition, the Oregon Natural Resources Council (ONRC), and the national wilderness leadership.[139] After the 1983 standoff at Bald Mountain, Earth First! and the ONRC received enough donations to allow them to challenge the new road in court and then, breaking ranks with the national wilderness movement, file a California-style lawsuit against RARE II, with Earth First! as the lead plaintiff.[140] The first lawsuit resulted in an injunction against the road; the second lawsuit got hung up on technicalities. But those lawsuits were overtaken by negotiations in Congress toward a soft-release state bill for Oregon. While those negotiations proceeded, Oregon activists watched as negotiations in Washington, D.C., further reduced the acreage of proposed wilderness areas from 1.9 to 1.2 to .85 million acres between 1982 and 1984 — the final bill did not even include any expansions for the Kalmiopsis.[141] The problem in New Hampshire was the opposite. In New Hampshire, the Wilderness Society split with local wilderness activists representing the Appalachian Mountain Club and the Society for the Preservation of New Hampshire Forests over whether enough land was proposed for wilderness protection in the White Mountain National Forest. The local consensus bill recommended less wilderness than the Wilderness Society proposed. The organization risked "alienating the strongest supporters of Wilderness in New Hampshire," the society's regional representative warned, if the Wilderness Society proceeded with its proposal.[142] In an internal memo, Turnage responded: the local proposal "is *terrible* and we should oppose it flat-out! No bill until we get a decent bill — or [the local activists] will *never* give us what we want."[143] That comment was an example of the tensions that had arisen between the reinvented Wilderness Society and local activists. As many longtime wilderness activists noted, the Wilderness Society's respect for and ability to work with local activists had diminished significantly. The Wilderness Society acknowledged as much in its own long-term plans.[144]

The state-by-state strategy for the roadless areas commanded a sustained, national campaign for wilderness in 1984. Despite the tensions in the wilderness movement—between the mainstream and radicals, and national leaders and local activists—the letter-writing campaigns, constituency pressure, and congressional visits generated by the citizen campaign played a crucial role in securing political support for compromise RARE II legislation. Wilderness advocates succeeded in pushing eighteen state RARE II bills through Congress. As a result, Ronald Reagan signed into law more national forest wilderness legislation than any other president. The compromise laws designated 6.6 million acres of new national forest wilderness and released 14 million acres of roadless areas for potential development. In Oregon, the legislation protected 850,000 acres and released 2 million acres. In New Hampshire, the final legislation followed the New Hampshire consensus bill, not the Wilderness Society's proposal, and protected 77,000 acres and released 188,000 acres.

In general, the final legislation did improve on the Forest Service's recommendations from RARE II, protecting approximately 30 percent more wilderness than the agency had recommended.[145] Some of these areas were old primitive areas that had never been acted upon during the ten-year reviews. But most places were unprotected roadless areas, now designated wilderness. There were reasons to be concerned about these new bills. Although they did designate new wilderness, some included exceptions and special provisions that had been tacked on in negotiations. The soft-release language was the most prominent example. New language acknowledging grazing and water rights appeared in several bills. More troublesome were efforts to add language permitting bicycles and snowmobiles, which failed. Nor did the burst of legislation in 1984 carry the debates over the roadless areas to their conclusion. Additional compromise RARE II bills passed for Kentucky, Tennessee, Nebraska, Georgia, Texas, and Michigan between 1985 and 1987. And other states, such as Idaho and Montana, where pressure to stick with hard release was particularly high and debates over the allocation of the roadless areas remained divided, never produced compromise legislation that succeeded in becoming law. Instead, legislation for those two states became entangled in a debate over the future of the Greater Yellowstone Ecosystem in the 1980s and 1990s.

What the Wilderness Society described as the culmination of "Wilderness '84," Earth First! dismissed as the "Wilderness Destruction Acts of 1984."[146] In Foreman's words, the compromise state-by-state wilderness legislation exemplified a "strategy of weakness" that had begun with the Endangered American Wilderness Act in 1978—in which wilderness advocates entered into negotiations with moderate proposals that were further reduced in the face of strong opposition. Nor did such compromise legislation fully address the ecological concerns important to Earth First!. In 1983, Earth First! urged the mainstream wilderness groups to "kill all further wilderness bills" and wait for a more favorable Congress after the 1984 elections.[147] When that failed, Earth First! plotted out its own strategies: pursuing further legal action challenging RARE II, undertaking protest activities, and challenging the compromise legislation. Its goal, Earth First! explained, was "to radically alter the nature and management of the national forest system. We envision management based not upon the nebulous and destructive principle of multiple abuse, but on the biocentric philosophy centered around the maintenance and enhancement of natural, biological diversity."[148] As Earth First! noted, the final legislation released two acres for every acre it protected. Earth First! criticized the grassroots strategy with its "fat grant" from REI, the mainstream groups' failure to take a more principled stand on behalf of wilderness, and the resulting legislation.[149] Such critiques would begin to take root in the years to come.

Hopes to advance ecologically reasoned wilderness areas went largely unrealized with RARE II. During the initial review, protecting representative ecosystems had been an important topic of discussion among wilderness advocates and the agency. But, as had been the case with Alaska, the scope and final boundaries of the RARE II bills more reflected a process of political negotiation, shaped by wilderness advocates, the timber and other industries, and congressional stakeholders, than any overarching vision of an ecologically reasoned wilderness system (one that protected endangered species, unique ecosystems, or functional wildlife reserves). More recent research on the distribution of nature reserves in the lower forty-eight states confirms the trends apparent in the RARE II legislation. Nature reserves, such as wilderness areas, tend to be located at higher elevations (59 percent lie at elevations above 8,000 feet) and in areas of low soil productivity (63 percent are classified in the two lowest classes of soil productivity), which limits their role in protecting biodiversity on the public lands.[150] But the concerns Earth First! raised in the early 1980s would become driving concerns for the entire wilderness movement by the early 1990s. A new concern for the ecological value of the national forests, the agency's forest management plans, and the economics of the agency's management practices all would draw the sustained attention of the wilderness community in the years to come. RARE II had made clear just how extensive the remaining wild lands on the national forests were, and the inventory would form an important foundation for future wilderness advocacy. Not until the Clinton administration entered office, however, would the prospect of large-scale protection for the national forests arise again. When it did, wilderness advocates would entertain even more ambitious goals: ending all logging on the national forests and protecting all of the remaining roadless areas.

Conclusion

Debates over the national forest roadless areas contributed to the polarization of American environmental politics in the late 1970s and early 1980s. The institutionalization of the federal government's responsibility for public lands management—represented best by the Forest Service's RARE II—and the transformation of the mainstream wilderness movement—represented best by the Wilderness Society's reinvention as a professional environmental lobby—helped spark radical sentiments both in support of and in opposition to wilderness under the banner of Earth First! and the Sagebrush Rebellion. Historians have often viewed these movements as two distinct reactions to the evolving debates over the public lands. Earth First! saw the federal government and the mainstream wilderness movement as representative of a bureaucratic system that placed the political process before the fundamental imperative to save nature. In its view, it was time to "throw a monkey wrench into the gears of the political machine and let the broken pieces fall where they may."[151] The Sagebrush Rebellion joined western citizens, states, and industry in response to "over-government," "Big Brother," and "extreme environmentalists," all based in Washington, D.C. Wilderness, rather than symbolizing a national heritage, challenged the sovereignty of the western states and local interests in economic development. Although the aims of these two loose-knit movements were diametrically opposed, they shared common frustrations with the failures of the federal government, the bureaucracy of environmental decision-making, and the mainstream environmental movement—precisely the institutions which wilderness advocates had done so much to strengthen and expand in the 1960s and 1970s. Although the frustration that drove Earth First! and the Sagebrush Rebellion stemmed from public lands debates, their ideological positions for and against wilderness and their strategies of protest were important contributions to American environmental politics. In this way, the changing debates over the public lands helped reshape American environmental politics more broadly.

The partisan boundaries of environmental politics emerged with clarity in a 1982 Republican Study Committee special report ominously titled "The Specter of Environmentalism." The report warned of environmentalists' expanding agenda. Groups like the Sierra Club, the National Audubon Society, and the Wilderness Society were "intent on promoting environmental interests to the detriment of energy development and economic prosperity." Research indicated that environmentalists were "overwhelmingly Democrats and predominantly liberal." It noted that a new school of thought in environmentalism, Deep Ecology, promoted a "liberal, almost counter-cultural view of the world." With an expanding membership, more sophisticated political lobbying, and a new interest in the electoral process, the environmental movement posed a growing threat to the nation's economy and development. All of this, the report argued, distanced environmentalism from its roots in the conservation movement of the early twentieth century, with its focus on stewardship and the wise use of natural resources. The report marked a new strategy for the Republicans. For the first time, the party specifically targeted environmental reform as representative of government bureaucracy and inefficiencies, and saw political advantage in challenging it both in the Reagan administration and in Congress. But the "Specter of Environmentalism" took that strategy one step further. If Reagan's popularity in the West, the Sagebrush Rebellion, and the objections of industry first aligned on resistance to an overbearing federal government and infractions against states' rights, then this report freighted those concerns with new cultural baggage. It described environmentalism as an issue in the culture wars of the 1980s; environmentalism was the issue of radicals, extremists, and the counterculture. Environmentalism, like so many other social issues that the Republican Party distanced itself from in the 1980s, was cast as another legacy of the permissive and radical social movements of the 1960s.[152]

The "Specter of Environmentalism" invented its own history of American environmentalism, which overlooked the movement's more moderate and popular roots in the 1960s. But in the years to come, the debates over the public lands often tended toward these new extremes. In the late 1980s and early 1990s, the Sagebrush Rebellion, the resource industries, and their conservative political allies continued to refine their anti-environmental strategies, which reemerged under the banner of the Wise Use Movement. In place of the reactionary agenda of the Sagebrush Rebellion, which emphasized states' rights, Wise Use advanced itself as a positive social movement to protect the rights and interests of Americans nationwide. And Earth First!, always loosely organized, suffered its own internal difficulties in the late 1980s, as the organization split over environmental and social concerns. During these years, the FBI finally caught up to Foreman, arresting him at his home on charges of conspiring to sabotage nuclear power plants. In August 1991, Foreman pleaded guilty to one felony count of conspiracy with terms that kept him out of jail. The most important stipulation was that he sever his ties with Earth First!.[153] In the early 1990s, Foreman helped start a new organization, the Wildlands Project, which drew on the moral convictions of Earth First! and the growing scientific concerns for biodiversity protection to advance a new agenda for the public lands. The "Specter of Environmentalism" warned that environmentalism was not just about the environment; it was about "an entire outlook of broad political and social affairs." In the case of the public lands, that claim is better understood as a harbinger of what was to come, than as a reflection on the past.[154]

7 / THE PUBLIC DOMAIN

ENVIRONMENTAL POLITICS AND THE RISE OF THE NEW RIGHT

I n November 1980, just after Ronald Reagan's landslide election, Senator Ted Stevens from Alaska took the podium at a convention in Salt Lake City, Utah. With the incoming Reagan administration and the newly elected Republican majority in the Senate, Stevens had come to talk of change. He spoke before the League for the Advancement of States' Equal Rights (LASER), which included state and local government officials, industry representatives, and citizens who made their living in the natural resource industries—many of whom considered themselves to be "Sagebrush Rebels." Stevens's driving concern was the expansion of environmental regulations during the Carter administration. The 1970s had witnessed an explosion in federal environmental programs—such as wilderness reviews, the Alaska lands debate, and endangered species regulations—which disproportionately affected public lands in the West. Some opponents described it as a "War on the West." Stevens was there to pump up expectations for the new Reagan administration. Anticipating the incoming administration and Congress, he crowed, "The overwhelming change represents, to my point of view, that the emerging philosophy is one of Western thought: less government, wise use of lands, and movement towards the private sectors."[1] Stevens's boast about the ascendancy of "Western thought" was not an idle claim.

In retrospect, the West has played an important supporting role in the consolidation of Republican political power in national politics. Before the mid-1970s, the West was reliable country for the Democrats. In 1964, when the Wilderness Act became law, the West sent seventeen Democrats and seven Republicans to the Senate.[2] But the Democrats' western stronghold in the Senate began to slip in the late 1960s. The turning point came in 1977, when western Republicans first outnumbered Democrats thirteen to eleven. Between 1977 and 2009, the West consistently sent more Republicans to the Senate, peaking in 1982 with nineteen western Republicans (and five western Democrats). Republicans controlled the Senate in nine of fourteen sessions of Congress between

1981 and 2009. Often, the South is viewed as the region driving the rise of the Republican Party in the postwar era. But the Republican West helped provide the necessary margin to make Republicans the majority party in the Senate during several crucial periods in modern American political history: the start of the Reagan administration, the Republicans' "Contract with America" in the mid-1990s, and the start of George W. Bush's administration. The West's turn toward the political right did more than mirror the rise of Republican power nationwide; it helped make it possible.[3]

Why did the West play such an important role in the consolidation of Republican power in the postwar era? As Senator Stevens's remarks suggest, one way to approach this question is to consider the debates over the public lands. In these years, the mainstream wilderness movement pursued the third major wilderness review initiated in the 1970s, for the deserts, canyons, and sagebrush flats overseen by the Bureau of Land Management (BLM). But unlike earlier campaigns for the forests and parks, it was often rural westerners—loggers, ranchers, and off-road vehicle enthusiasts—who knew these wild lands best and organized most effectively to determine their management. The activities of the opposition did not represent a simple response to the threat of wilderness protection, however. The opposition—represented most popularly by the Sagebrush Rebellion and the Wise Use Movement—evolved in ways that shaped and reflected broader shifts in conservative politics, as opponents of environmental reform gravitated toward a political strategy grounded in rights-based claims to property and liberty characteristic of conservatives nationwide. Equally important, however, was the way in which environmental groups like the Wilderness Society responded to this changing opposition. Although wilderness advocates responded confidently to the Sagebrush Rebellion in the early 1980s, casting it as the work of narrow special interests, that was not the case with the Wise Use Movement in the early 1990s, which described itself as a social movement of rural westerners. The evolution of this political relationship between wilderness advocates and their opponents—defined by competing claims over individual rights, the public good, and the role of government in managing the public lands—has been important, not just to environmental politics and the American West, but to the rise of modern conservatism in American politics.[4]

The Sagebrush Rebellion and States' Rights

From the perspective of many rural westerners, the Carter years had been a disaster. Carter had never been popular in the West; he had not carried a single western state in the 1976 election. During his administration, Carter had strengthened the federal land agencies' responsibilities and stewardship programs on the public lands in Alaska, on the national forests, and on the BLM public domain. By the late 1970s, the West was a political tinderbox, and nowhere was the tinder drier than on the lands managed by the BLM. In 1980, the agency oversaw 174 million acres of land in the lower forty-eight. In some states, the agency controlled significant portions of land, such as in Nevada (69 percent), Utah (41 percent), and Oregon (25 percent).⁵ Of all of the federal land agencies, the BLM had the weakest congressional mandate. Since 1946, when Congress gave the BLM formal oversight of the unclaimed public domain, the agency had loosely managed the lands by following a byzantine set of land laws and policies. The ranchers, loggers, miners, and off-road vehicle users who used the public domain were accustomed to playing by a set of rules that generally favored their interests: almost all of the public domain was open to mining exploration, leases for mineral development were easy to come by, grazing was locally regulated and inexpensive, and recreational activities, such as off-road vehicle use, was little regulated. Scholars described the BLM as a "captured agency" beholden to ranchers and miners and the "step-child" among the federal land agencies. Environmentalists dismissed the BLM as the "Bureau of Livestock and Mining." These institutional roots did much to shape the agency's approach to wilderness.⁶

The rules began to change quickly in the mid-1970s, however. First, the agency faced a series of National Environmental Policy Act (NEPA) lawsuits that successfully challenged its planning processes for programs such as the Trans-Alaska Pipeline, oil drilling on the Outer Continental Shelf, coal mining, and grazing. Regarding the latter issue, the Natural Resources Defense Council filed a suit challenging the BLM's grazing program under NEPA in 1974. As a result, the agency was required to file 144 comprehensive environmental impact statements assessing each grazing district by 1988, rather than producing a single national review of its grazing program. The subsequent analyses increased knowledge of the (generally poor) condition of the western range, slowed down the process of renewing leases, and raised questions about the future of grazing on the public lands.⁷ Second, Congress passed the Federal Land Policy and Management Act (FLPMA) in 1976. That law affirmed and extended the power of the BLM over the public domain: it explicitly stated that the public domain would be permanently overseen by the federal government (not given away to states or other interests, except under special circumstances), that it would be managed by the BLM in the public interest for multiple-use purposes (similarly to the national forests), and that the agency would undertake a wilderness review. FLPMA was signed into law by Gerald Ford, but it was left to the Carter administration to implement it. Under the leadership of Secretary of the Interior Cecil Andrus, the Carter administration launched the BLM wilderness review of the public domain in the lower forty-eight, broached the possibility of raising the historically low grazing fees, and considered reducing the number of cattle and sheep grazed on the public lands.[8] The Carter administration and the BLM hoped that a better-funded and more proactive agency could balance grazing, mining, and other activities, while also protecting the public domain for recreation, wildlife, and wilderness. But, as a more recent observer put it, the basic assumption seemed to be: "Building bureaucracy [at the BLM] was good for the land."[9]

No specific policy decision that resulted from FLPMA explains the start of the Sagebrush Rebellion.[10] In fact, those party to the Sagebrush Rebellion—who had long been adept at advancing their interests in the public domain with the BLM and Congress—continued to do so, even as the Carter administration attempted to advance far-reaching reforms. In the case of the wilderness reviews, the agency's first step was to determine which lands deserved detailed study for their wilderness potential. Rural westerners made a strong showing at BLM wilderness hearings in 1977 and 1978. As one Sierra Club staffer noted, a handful of wilderness activists were outnumbered by nearly one hundred "anti-wilderness folk" at hearings in Wyoming.[11] The same was true in Utah, Colorado, and other states.[12] In the fall of 1979, the BLM selected 57 million acres out of 174 million acres for initial wilderness consideration—the agency omitted the public domain in Alaska, due to the ongoing deliberations over the Alaska legislation.[13] In 1978, Congress passed the Public Rangelands Improvement Act (PRIA), addressing the question of grazing fees, which had been left unresolved in FLPMA. PRIA increased the BLM's funding for range management, allocating $345 million over twenty years, but it did little to change grazing fees. The Carter administration hoped to raise grazing fees on the public lands to "fair market value" to match fees on comparable private lands. Instead, PRIA adopted a formula that was favorable to ranchers; changes in the grazing fee were determined annually, based on forage costs and beef prices, and changes in the fee in any year were limited to 25 percent—at least through 1985, when the formula expired.[14] In the case of grazing, ranchers and their allies enjoyed much success at minimizing the consequences of reform at the BLM, if not turning it to their advantage.[15]

Thus, when the Sagebrush Rebellion surged onto the national political scene in the summer of 1979, it emerged more out of a growing anger over the increasing bureaucracy of public lands policy than it did in reaction to any specific event. In 1978 and 1979, a number of programs suggested the government's expanding reach. The Carter administration withdrew 96 million acres of national-interest lands in Alaska in December 1978 in response to Congress's failure to pass an Alaska lands bill, the administration announced the controversial results of the Roadless Area Review and Evaluation II (RARE II) in January 1979, and the administration selected 5.5 million acres of the public domain in the California desert for wilderness study in March 1979. The administration also announced other new initiatives in the spring of 1979, including regulations for off-road vehicle use in the public domain, changes in grazing management that diminished local input and threatened to reduce grazing activity, and new plans for deployment of mobile nuclear warheads on public lands in Nevada and Utah. That summer, Nevadans began wearing buttons that read "Welcome to the West. Property: U.S. Govt."[16] In the face of such a rapid expansion of federal power, the Sagebrush Rebels decided that the quickest way to cut through the ever-expanding list of regulations was to end the federal government's oversight altogether. It was time to return the West's federal lands to their rightful owners: the western states. It was an old idea in western politics. Westerners had tried to lay claim to the federal lands for the western states in the 1920s and 1940s, but such efforts had been blocked in both the courts and Congress.[17] But in the late 1970s the Sagebrush Rebels once again raised the banner of states' rights.[18]

All of the frustrations over the public lands that had been building in the 1970s—the Alaskans marching in the streets with signs reading "States' Rights" and "Alaska Can Manage Alaska," the jeep enthusiasts in New Mexico warning of "over-government" and "creeping wilderness," the loggers caravanning to forest hearings, toting signs reading "RARE II is a Rip-Off," and the ranchers and miners frustrated with the BLM—finally captured national attention with the Sagebrush Rebellion.[19] Nevada acted first. In July 1979, the state legislature passed a resolution laying claim to the public domain within its borders. Next, in August 1979, Senator Orrin Hatch (R-UT) introduced legislation in Congress to transfer all public domain and national forest land in the West to the states. As the *Los Angeles Times* reported, "the 'Sagebrush Revolt' is on" and "federal land is the prize."[20] By the next summer, Wyoming, Utah, New Mexico, Montana, Colorado, and California were all entertaining similar resolutions. Alaska even toyed with seceding from the union but focused on Sagebrush legislation instead.[21] In November 1980, the Sagebrush Rebels coordinated a congressional hearing on Sagebrush legislation in conjunction with the LASER conference in Salt Lake City. Senator Hatch explained that it was "fundamentally wrong for Uncle Sam to own, control, and regulate one-third of America." The western states had "rights to vast amounts of land within their boundaries" that were being denied by the federal government.[22] One rancher echoed that argument, explaining that "agencies like the BLM and the Forest Service are in violation of the Constitution."[23] Among Sagebrush Rebels, the presumption was that a state like Nevada should oversee its own land, because it could better manage it to meet local interests and promote economic development. On the campaign trail in 1980, Ronald Reagan proclaimed himself a Sagebrush Rebel: he emphasized the importance of developing the public lands for national security, energy independence, and economic growth and he promised to reduce the size of the federal government. Such political rhetoric played well, especially in the West.[24]

In many respects, the Sagebrush Rebellion seemed to align neatly with the surge of modern conservatism in the 1970s that came to be known as the New Right and helped propel Reagan into office. Just as conservatives had begun to mobilize over social issues such as education reform, right-to-life, and neighborhood integration—all of which marked growing grassroots activism on the political Right—the Sagebrush Rebellion marked a significant uptick in conservative citizen involvement in public lands politics.[25] Behind this citizen activism were the institutional structures of the New Right. In the case of the Sagebrush Rebellion, the Mountain States Legal Foundation, wealthy conservative donors (such as Joseph Coors), industry groups (such as the National Cattlemen's Association), and companies (such as Louisiana Pacific and Boise Cascade) all provided varying degrees of logistical, financial, and political support. But, in important respects, the politics of the Sagebrush Rebellion were not entirely congruent with the New Right. The new conservatism drew on a growing sense of positive rights and "middle-class entitlement," more than a reactionary politics rooted in states' rights, to challenge the growth and power of the federal government. Starting as early as the 1960s in the South, for instance, conservative citizens adopted a new language that privileged their own positive rights–based claims to individual liberty and property—the "right" to choose their neighbors and their children's classmates, and to remain free from what they saw as dangerous encroachments by the federal government.[26] In contrast, the Sagebrush Rebellion's rights-based claims were often crowded out by an emphasis on states' rights, both in the movement's political rhetoric and in its agenda at the national level. At the time, the Sagebrush Rebellion often sounded more like an older version of conservatism, which focused on states' rights, than it did the changing politics of the New Right that propelled Ronald Reagan into office.

The importance of these differences in conservative politics was not readily apparent during the Republican successes in the 1980 election, however. With Reagan's sweeping victory over Carter, it seemed that the Sagebrush Rebellion was poised to realize its greatest ambitions. The *Rocky Mountain News* reported that what may have looked like a "hare-brained cowboy scheme" before had now "come of age" with a Republican administration and Senate majority.[27] After the election, Reagan telegrammed the Sagebrush Rebels who had convened at the LASER conference. "I renew my pledge to work toward a 'Sagebrush Solution,'" Reagan promised. "My administration will work to ensure that states have an equitable share of public lands and their natural resources."[28] Expectations for the Reagan administration only quickened after Reagan selected his nominee for secretary of the interior. To oversee the public lands, Reagan chose James Watt, a Denver-based lawyer, a supporter of the Sagebrush Rebellion, and the head of the Mountain States Legal Foundation—the think tank that had supported the Sagebrush Rebellion, was funded by the mining industry, and worked to protect the "American way of life" from "extremists," "narrow special interests," and a "bureaucracy which is out of control."[29] To many rural westerners, Watt seemed to be one of their own.[30] He would do much to advance the interests of the Sagebrush Rebels on every front but one: he never supported a wholesale return of the public lands to the states.

James Watt, the Reagan Administration, and the Public Lands

James Watt brought a blustery presence to the Department of the Interior: he was forthright, outspoken, and confident. No one, one newspaper editor wrote, could sustain an hour of "bellicosity, hectoring, hair-splitting, self-righteousness and Messianic fervor" quite like Watt.[31] He was a political cartoonist's dream: a tall and lanky figure, with sharp features and a big grin, a balding head, and large eyeglasses. But what made Watt so important to the Reagan administration and environmental politics were his convictions. A proud conservative, an evangelical Christian, and a small-"c" conservationist committed to managing the public lands for their use, Watt came to the Department of the Interior determined to reshape public lands policy. In an early speech, he made the following key points: The Reagan administration represented a "change" that would end "fifty years of bad government." The problem with government management was straightforward—"We're tired of paralysis by analysis." He promised to "err on the side of public use versus preservation." And he made no apologies for having "a bias for private enterprise."[32] Watt criticized "old-time liberals" who placed their faith in government. He prided himself on being a conservative who placed his faith in people and emphasized managing resources for economic development.[33]

Wilderness groups stridently opposed Watt's nomination from the start; the Wilderness Society and Sierra Club argued that his industry ties disqualified him from service.[34] But it was for such reasons that Watt seemed so closely aligned to the Sagebrush Rebellion and its goals for the future of the West. Conservatives such as Joseph Coors, who helped fund the Mountain States Legal Foundation, described Watt and the Reagan administration as a "turning point for America."[35] An executive at the petroleum company Amoco responded to Watt's nomination with one word: "HALLELUJAH!"[36] Although Watt was only one member of a team of high-level Reagan appointees charged with reforming the federal government's environmental bureaucracy, he became the public face of the administration's environmental agenda.[37] He was clear about his allegiances. In his words, he was prepared to oppose "the tremendous alliance" of "very liberal" and "environmentalist" groups that sought shelter in the Democratic Party.[38]

7.1 James Watt, Ronald Reagan's first secretary of the interior, promised to roll back environmental reforms when he took office. Lander, Wyoming, 1982. Source: James G. Watt Collection, Box 32, American Heritage Center, University of Wyoming.

7.2 Environmental groups sharply opposed James Watt's nomination as secretary of the interior, as suggested by this political cartoon. 1981. Courtesy Steve Greenberg.

Watt wasted no time in changing the direction of the Department of the Interior, adopting policies that reduced the power of the federal government, promoted economic development on the public lands, and expedited decision-making. He attempted to weaken regulations on strip-mining, open offshore coastal zones to energy exploration, narrow the scope of wilderness reviews, and return oversight of grazing to local grazing boards.[39] One issue stands out for the threat it posed to the wilderness system: starting in 1981, Watt attempted to prop open the wilderness system for mineral, oil, and gas exploration. It was not an unreasonable proposal. When the Wilderness Act became law, section 4(d)(3) of the legislation permitted mineral, oil, and gas exploration in wilderness areas through December 31, 1983.[40] This had been a key concession wrested by Wayne Aspinall in the negotiations that produced the Wilderness Act.[41] Despite that compromise, the land agencies had not offered leases in wilderness areas, nor had the energy industry pushed for them; conducting such explorations in wilderness areas was difficult and such development promised to be controversial. Starting in 1981, however, Watt put the administration's support squarely behind extending the 1983 deadline for mineral exploration for another twenty years. With energy prices more than double what they had been in the early 1970s, continued instability in the Middle East, and the possibility of new energy reserves in the northern Rockies, Watt emphasized that domestic energy production, including that from wilderness areas, promised to strengthen America's energy independence and its economy.[42] As had been the case in the mid-1970s during the debate over the Trans-Alaska Pipeline and would be the case again in the early 1990s during the Persian Gulf War, the future of wilderness was pushed onto the unforgiving terrain of energy debates.

Despite the common ground between Watt and the Sagebrush Rebellion, Watt did not simply advance the Sagebrush Rebellion's agenda within the Reagan administration, however. In public, Watt actively catered to the concerns of many westerners. Indeed, many of the regulatory and legislative initiatives that Watt advanced—promoting energy exploration, economic development, and mineral development, and reducing wilderness reviews—helped defuse the anger that inspired the Sagebrush Rebellion. But the Reagan administration never fully embraced the claims of states' rights or a large-scale transfer of the public lands to the states. In 1981 and 1982, Watt did expedite the transfer of small tracts of federal land to the western states under a "good neighbor policy."[43] But Watt, like Reagan, was more likely to emphasize the importance of reducing the federal bureaucracy, protecting individual liberties, and promoting free enterprise than to explicitly argue for states' rights. And in 1982, the Reagan administration considered selling off large portions of the public lands to private interests in order to strengthen free enterprise and raise funds to pay down the federal debt.[44] But that proposal not only deepened public opposition to the administration's public lands policies, it also raised concerns among Sagebrush Rebels. If the lands became private, ranchers, loggers, and other users might have to pay higher rates to access the lands, if their access did not disappear altogether. Ultimately, neither the Reagan administration's privatization scheme nor the proposed legislation at the state or federal level to transfer federal lands to the states was ever implemented. Instead, in the early 1980s, the Sagebrush Rebellion contented itself, at least temporarily, with the policy direction set by Watt and the Reagan administration's reforms, which promised to expedite development, respect western interests, and promote "good neighbor" relations between states and the federal government in the West.

At the same time that Watt emerged as the wilderness movement's chief antagonist, he also unwittingly emerged as its greatest ally. In 1979, wilderness advocates began to plot a response to the growing threat of the Sagebrush Rebellion. Instead of acknowledging the legitimate frustrations of rural westerners or the problems with government oversight, the wilderness leadership instead portrayed the Sagebrush Rebellion as a "land raid by big commodity interests," an "assault on balanced multiple use," and the work of big corporations with an economic stake in the future of the public lands. The Sagebrush Rebellion, in other words, was the work of special interests, not grassroots citizens.[45] Wilderness advocates did not want to be in the business of attacking the little guy—local ranchers, miners, or small-scale loggers—and after 1981, they did not have to be. As Doug Scott at the Sierra Club explained, Watt provided a "unifying thread through many of our otherwise segmented and defensive political efforts."[46] Instead of focusing on the particulars of interim management of BLM wilderness study areas, mining under the Wilderness Act, or grazing allocations, and how such policies might affect rural westerners, wilderness advocates could instead focus attention on Watt, the Reagan administration, and its allegiances to industry. National environmental groups consistently emphasized the conflict between Watt's responsibilities as a public official and the private economic interests he often seemed to champion. With the Sierra Club in the lead, environmentalists gathered one million signatures for a petition supporting their "What's Wrong? Watt's Wrong!" campaign to oust the secretary.[47] The media focused attention on Watt and the administration's pro-development public lands policies. The strategy worked. Between 1979 and 1983, membership jumped from 48,000 to 100,000 at the Wilderness Society and from 181,000 to 346,000 at the Sierra Club; their budgets grew proportionately.[48] Editorial pages denounced Watt and ran hundreds of political cartoons challenging his positions. In 1980, newspapers across the country had asked if the environmental movement was fading into insignificance.[49] But in 1982, *Fortune* magazine described the resurgent environmental movement as a "super-lobby" on par with the National Rifle Association or the right-to-life movement.[50]

Few railed against Watt harder or more aggressively than William Turnage and the Wilderness Society, which honed its more professional strategies challenging Watt. In 1981, in an analytical tour de force, the Wilderness Society published the "Watt Book," a two-volume compendium which detailed Watt's connections to industry, highlighted the pro-development policies he promoted, and raised questions about the legality of the administration's public lands agenda.[51] Gaylord Nelson, the Wilderness Society's new chairman and the former Democratic senator from Wisconsin (who had lost his seat in the watershed 1980 elections), captured the critique: "The administration, spearheaded by Watt and prodded into action by the industries that have backed both, intends to do nothing less than plunder the last wild places we have left in America."[52] A centerpiece of the Wilderness Society's counter-campaign was the Economic Policy Department's analysis of Watt's plans to extend mineral and energy exploration in the wilderness system. The department found that existing and potential wilderness areas held only 2 percent of oil reserves and 1.6 percent of gas reserves nationwide, a fraction of what was necessary to affect domestic production.[53] To establish its credibility, the Wilderness Society submitted the report for peer review by government and industry experts and the American Petroleum Institute—a strategy consistent with Turnage's vision of a professional Wilderness Society.[54] Indeed, the Wilderness Society claimed the report generated over 400 newspaper editorials across the country.[55] In February 1982, Watt warned President Reagan in a confidential memo that he and the administration were going to be on the losing side of the issue.[56] A surge of public opposition and wavering among Republicans in the run-up to the midterm elections in 1982 weakened Watt's efforts. In 1982 and 1983, the House and Senate acted decisively to end the threat of oil and gas leasing in wilderness areas—initially rejecting Watt's efforts to extend such exploration for twenty years and then blocking another legislative initiative that proposed reviewing the entire wilderness system in 2000.[57]

By 1983, it was clear that the efforts of wilderness advocates, sustained public outcry, and aggressive litigation had done much to blunt the Reagan administration's most problematic public lands policies. Watt was forced to resign his post in December 1983, in part because of his own political missteps—his inappropriate comments regarding Native Americans, Jews, and African Americans drew opprobrium—but also as a result of sustained public opposition.[58] As one of his colleagues lamented, Watt's "crusade" at the Department of the Interior had come to an end.[59] In retrospect, it is evident that although the Sagebrush Rebellion commanded national headlines, it remained a regional issue, rather than an issue of importance to conservatives nationwide. Anti-environmentalism, focused primarily on laying claim to the public lands for the states, never resonated with the New Right nationally. This was an important weakness of the Sagebrush Rebellion's strategy. With attention focused foremost on the claims to states' rights and the interests of industry rather than on the concerns and complaints of western citizens, the Sagebrush Rebellion and its allies in the Reagan administration were effectively dismissed as proponents of special interests. The wilderness community successfully sidestepped the populist concerns of the Sagebrush Rebellion by attacking Watt, the Reagan administration, and their ties to industry. That strategy helped limit conservative efforts to roll back federal environmental regulations in the 1980s and laid the groundwork for strategic successes, such as the burst of state-by-state national forest wilderness bills that Reagan signed into law in 1984. This failed political formula would distinguish the Sagebrush Rebellion from a later, more nuanced, and, in some respects, more effective anti-environmental campaign—the Wise Use Movement—which, in the late 1980s, adopted the evolving strategies of the New Right to mount a new challenge to the wilderness movement nationwide.

Wilderness and the Public Domain: "The Land No One Knows"

The campaign for the public domain has been the wilderness movement's Achilles heel. It was the last of the three major wilderness reviews that had been initiated in the 1970s—and, in many respects, the opportunity it presented and its scope were similar to those for Alaska and the national forests. But it posed unique challenges: Unlike the national forests, which often commanded strong local support, the public domain generated little enthusiasm. As a Sierra Club task force warned in 1979: "We are in terrible shape demographically—in general the states with the greatest BLM roadless acreage have the least population, including the least population of active conservationists." The public domain was located in more remote and, often, politically conservative regions of the West. "In many cases, wilderness opponents know the land better than we do— they have been grazing it, mining it, and logging it for years, whereas we are just now finding it."[60] Unlike Alaska, which few people knew firsthand, but which commanded national support, the public domain had no such national profile. From the fluted canyons of Utah to the expanses of the Mojave Desert, these were the lands most Americans did not know. It was for these reasons that few in the wilderness community gave much attention to the public domain before the mid-1970s. In deference to western political opposition, these lands went unmentioned in the Wilderness Act. But interest in and concern for the western badlands had been growing since the late 1960s. Books like Edward Abbey's *Desert Solitaire* cultivated an appreciation for the stark beauty of the western deserts and canyonlands.[61] Scientists began to highlight the ecological diversity of the deserts and the threats that grazing, off-road vehicles, and development posed.[62] And as the region's cities, like Las Vegas, Phoenix, and Tuscon, began to grow, so too did interest in protecting the surrounding landscape.

When the BLM wilderness review began under the Carter administration in 1978, the Buckaroo Bunkhouse was still in full swing in Washington, D.C. One of its confederates, Debbie Sease, a native New Mexican, part Cherokee Indian, and entrepreneur (she started her own wilderness guiding company in

7.3 Debbie Sease, August 1977. Sease played a
key role in the early BLM campaigns as a staffer at
the Wilderness Society. After being fired from the
Wilderness Society in 1979, she would eventually rise
to the position of national campaign director for the
Sierra Club. Courtesy Debbie Sease.

the early 1970s), had come to Washington, D.C., with Dave Foreman, whom
she met at the University of New Mexico and married in 1973. When Foreman
returned west and joined Earth First!, however, Sease stayed put in Washington.[63] A strategic mind, a clear sense for legislative politics, and a love of the
western badlands put Sease at the forefront of the national campaign for BLM
wilderness. Indeed, in a world of environmental politics often dominated by
men (especially at the upper levels), Sease steadily rose up the ranks of the Sierra
Club, becoming its legislative director in the early 1990s. But all of that was in
the future; in the late 1970s, Sease, still new to Washington, worked to keep the
Wilderness Society abreast of the BLM's wilderness review. The agency's review
followed two primary tracks, as outlined in FLPMA. First, the agency was
required to undertake a comprehensive wilderness review of all roadless areas
in the public domain (much as the Forest Service, National Park Service, and
Fish and Wildlife Service had done). That fifteen-year process, which included

evaluating roadless areas, soliciting public feedback, and issuing final recommendations, was to be completed in three stages, with a final recommendation in 1991. Second, the BLM was required to undertake an accelerated review of the California Desert Conservation Area, where planning had already started. This second review was part of the expedited California Desert Plan—a comprehensive, multiple-use plan that included wilderness recommendations for California's southern desert, to be completed before October 1980.

No one knew better than Sease how poorly the early stages of the BLM wilderness review had gone. During the Carter administration, the BLM did take steps to strengthen its oversight of the public lands—enough to help spark the Sagebrush Rebellion—but it showed little enthusiasm for extensive wilderness designations that would restrict its management prerogatives. In the early stages of its wilderness review, the agency revived a number of problematic policies that limited the scope of its wilderness inventory: it adopted some aspects of the Forest Service's discredited "purity" policies, employed a broad definition of what constituted a "road" (which would limit wilderness designations), and raised questions about whether the federal government could claim water rights in wilderness areas.[64] Mustering an effective citizen campaign to affect both the early inventory and these management regulations proved difficult in the late 1970s, when much of the wilderness movement's attention, enthusiasm, and resources were focused on Alaska and RARE II. In 1979, the BLM received only 5,000 letters from wilderness supporters regarding its initial inventory and 500 letters regarding its interim management plans. (By comparison, the Forest Service received more than 250,000 comments regarding RARE II that year.) "This lack of support," Sease noted, "has not gone unnoticed by the BLM."[65] At the height of the inventory, in 1979, Turnage cut Sease's position as he turned over the staff of the Wilderness Society, with no immediate plans for replacing her.[66] A hostile agency and weak public support help explain why the agency further narrowed its wilderness review to 24 of 174 million acres in November 1980.[67]

Although the scope of the agency's wilderness reviews was disappointing, the Department of the Interior did affirm its commitment to protecting the 24 million acres of potential wilderness areas from most conflicting activities until Congress could consider wilderness legislation. Section 603(c) of FLPMA required that the "Secretary shall continue to manage such lands according to his authority under this Act and other applicable law in a manner so as not to impair the suitability of such areas for preservation as wilderness, subject, however, to the continuation of existing mining and grazing uses and mineral leasing in the manner and degree in which the same was being conducted on the date of approval of this Act."[68] The interim management guidelines were not as strong as wilderness advocates had hoped: the regulations stated that any newly permitted activities must be temporary and easily reversible such that activities did not preclude wilderness designation; existing activities, such as preexisting rights associated with grazing and mining, were grandfathered in; and exceptions were made for emergencies, such as wildfire and public health.[69] The interim management standards would become an ongoing source of controversy during the BLM wilderness review. Wilderness advocates were often frustrated because the agency permitted grandfathered activities to continue at levels that degraded potential wilderness areas. And opponents were disappointed because, as the congressional debates over the Bureau of Land Management wilderness reviews stretched out into the twenty-first century, the agency continued to manage potential wilderness areas for non-impairment. That gave wilderness advocates little incentive to support legislation that did not significantly expand upon the existing wilderness study areas.[70]

The wilderness movement's successes for the public domain during the Reagan administration were largely defensive. James Watt specifically targeted the BLM's wilderness review, since it was known within the administration that it was the wilderness community's weakest front. In 1981, Watt prohibited any wilderness review of remaining BLM lands in Alaska—which had been omitted from the initial FLPMA wilderness inventory due to the Alaska lands act deliberations in the late 1970s.[71] In February 1982, the agency adopted new policies that waived the need for individual environmental studies of each potential wilderness area in favor of statewide reviews.[72] Several months later, in December, the agency began dropping areas from the wilderness review. The BLM removed all areas under 5,000 acres in size first: 158 areas totaling 340,526 acres were gone. All lands held in "split estate," where the federal government owned the surface rights to the land but the subsurface rights were owned by the state or private interests, would be eliminated; that meant 106 areas totaling 464,975 acres were gone and there were questions about the wilderness reviews for the remaining 3.6 million acres of wild lands of which they were a part. Then the agency announced it would reconsider all potential wilderness areas that were contiguous with existing wilderness areas (on grounds that the areas might have been selected because of their proximity to existing wilderness areas, not because they deserved wilderness consideration on their merits): that put 5.1 million additional acres at risk.[73] All told, that meant questions had been raised about one-third of the land the BLM had selected for wilderness review under the Carter administration. In the mid-1980s, the courts answered most of them. The Sierra Club challenged Watt's actions in court, and in 1985 most of the areas were reinstated; the state-by-state approach to the BLM wilderness reviews and the prohibition on reviewing the remaining 92 million acres of public domain in Alaska stood, however.[74]

For the reinvented Wilderness Society, the BLM wilderness review seemed primed for the organization's professional strategies in the early 1980s. Although there were few local wilderness advocates involved in the public domain, Turnage hoped that the Wilderness Society's technical resources and expertise would give it a unique position in the campaign. Terry Sopher, who had overseen the BLM's wilderness reviews during the Carter administration, had joined the Wilderness Society as its director of BLM affairs in 1981, filling the position left open when Sease was fired in 1979. In the mid-1980s, William Turnage requested that Sopher develop a "serious plan" for a multi-year, large-scale campaign for the public domain that would culminate in the late 1980s, when the agency began releasing its state-by-state wilderness recommendations. Reflecting the strategy that had transformed the Wilderness Society, Turnage emphasized: "tone it down, avoid gimmickry, and develop a slow, step-by-step long-term education program aimed at KEY OPINION LEADERS (not the general public)."[75] In the mid-1980s, the Wilderness Society adopted an ambitious campaign for the public domain—at least on paper. It included plans for three new well-funded and professionally staffed regional offices in the West; a new BLM analysis unit in the Resource Policy and Economics division to provide economic and scientific analysis; and a sustained media campaign aimed at print, radio, and television that would cultivate a positive image of the public domain.[76] But launching that program had to wait until the campaign for the national forest roadless areas came to a close in 1984. By the time the Wilderness Society committed resources to the campaign for the public domain, it found itself playing catch-up to local wilderness advocates who had been working on the issue since the late 1970s, and the Sierra Club, which under Sease's leadership had an active public domain agenda. A closer examination of the campaigns for public domain wilderness in two states, Utah and California, suggests why wilderness advocates struggled to realize the promise of wilderness on the public domain.

The news on wilderness in Utah was often grim. While there was much support for wilderness protection in northern Utah, centered around Salt Lake City, the opposition to wilderness designation and federal control of the public lands more generally was strong in rural southern and western Utah, where much of the 22 million acres of public domain was concentrated. And it was rural Utah that the BLM listened to. In the first round of the wilderness inventory, the agency selected 2.6 million acres as wilderness study areas meriting interim protection and full review. The scope of the agency's review in Utah seemed especially capricious. In Mancos Mesa, the agency halved the wilderness recommendation due to illegal uranium exploration. In Fish Creek Canyon, the agency omitted areas identified for intensive cattle management. At Fifty Mile Mountain, Wahweap, and Burning Hills, the agency opted against wilderness due to the potential for coal mining.[77] In short, the agency often sided with the interests of ranchers, miners, and industry, and reduced wilderness recommendations. Often, these decisions were made with minimal on-the-ground study. In the early 1980s, the Sierra Club and other groups worked through an appeals process and succeeded in forcing the agency to expand the wilderness study areas to include a total of 88 units encompassing 3.2 million acres.[78] Even with the additions, the scope of the agency's wilderness study fell short of wilderness advocates' hopes for the future of Utah's canyonlands, deserts, and slick rock country. In the mid-1980s, Utah became a hotbed of citizen activism for public domain wilderness. The Southern Utah Wilderness Alliance (SUWA), which has emerged as the driving force behind public lands advocacy in Utah, was organized in 1983. The Wilderness Society opened a new regional office in Utah in 1985. And that same year, the newly formed Utah Wilderness Coalition, which joined local and national wilderness advocacy groups, organized nine citizen-organizing workshops around the state.[79] The product of those efforts was a field-researched citizens' proposal that recommended protection for 141 units of Utah's public domain totaling just over 5 million acres of wild lands.[80] It included most of the areas recommended by the BLM, plus additional areas such as the Wah Wahs, Dog-Water Creek, Ragged Mountain, Moonshine Draw, and Harmony Flat.

The question for wilderness advocates was whether to wait for the BLM's final wilderness recommendations for Utah, drawn from the 3.2 million acres of wilderness study areas, or to appeal directly to Congress in hopes that a citizens' proposal could spark national support for strong Utah wilderness legislation. In 1989, Representative Wayne Owens (D-UT), who represented Salt Lake City and its growing suburbs, introduced the Utah Wilderness Act of 1989, which proposed protecting 5.1 million acres.[81] But the same day, Representative James Hansen (R-UT) introduced legislation that proposed protecting 1.4 million acres. Support for the competing bills split along party lines, with Utah's lone Democrat supporting expansive legislation, and the four Republicans supporting limited legislation.[82] Then the George H. W. Bush White House threatened a veto of any big Utah wilderness bill.[83] When the BLM released its final recommendation for Utah in 1991, the agency recommended 1.9 million acres for wilderness protection.[84] But that did nothing to move negotiations forward.

What made the BLM wilderness review in Utah different from almost every wilderness review which had preceded it—dating back to the Wilderness Act of 1964—was that neither side saw any reason to engage in negotiations toward a compromise. Publicly, Senator Jake Garn (R-UT), who supported the Hansen bill, described Owens's legislation as "so excessive it's not worth consideration."[85] In turn, local wilderness advocates allied with SUWA wrote off discussions with the local and county governments, rural citizens, and resource industries. SUWA considered "rational discourse" impossible, and instead aimed to invest its energies in working elsewhere "in Utah and the nation" to secure protection for Utah wilderness.[86] As wilderness advocates knew well, without a legislative proposal that substantially improved upon the initial wilderness inventory, the existing 3.2 million acres of wilderness study areas enjoyed some protection under the agency's interim management guidelines. To overcome local opposition and to improve on the existing inventory, wilderness advocates in Utah came to believe that their best bet was to make Utah's wild lands a national issue. But that strategy had worked only once before—for Alaska.[87]

The campaign for the public domain in California enjoyed broader public support. The California desert encompasses much of the lower third of the state. This is not a desert of sand dunes and broad vistas; it is a desert of sharp mountain ranges and broad, dry, dusty valleys. Lying near Los Angeles, San Diego, and Las Vegas, three of the fastest growing urban areas in the country, the California desert commanded public attention—from both wilderness supporters and opponents. The region had a long history of grazing and mining. Much of the desert had been crisscrossed with roads, utility lines, and water canals. And it was especially popular for driving dune buggies and off-road vehicles. As the growing threat of off-road vehicles, mining, and suburban development (especially along the region's eastern edges near Palm Springs) became apparent, local activists, drawn from the Sierra Club's Angeles and San Gorgonio chapters, formed a deep well of support for what became a fifteen-year campaign to protect the desert.[88] Starting in the 1970s, these local activists watchdogged the agency's management of the desert and its planning process for the California Desert Conservation Area. Unlike the rest of its reviews, the BLM was to complete its plans for California by October 1980. The resulting California Desert Plan classified the public domain into areas for intensive

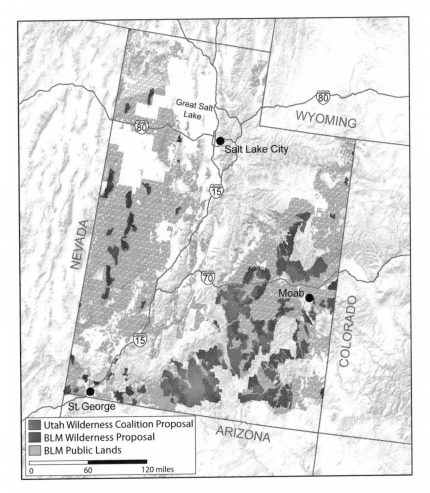

Map 7.1   The Utah Wilderness Coalition proposed 5.1 million acres of wilderness on BLM lands in 1989, including the 1.9 million acres of wilderness study areas the agency recommended for wilderness protection. The BLM manages approximately 41 percent (22 million acres) of the land in Utah.

resource development, mixed-resource development, recreational use, and conservation (including specific areas to protect wildlife, and cultural and scenic resources). The final plan, approved under the Carter administration, left most of the desert open for development and other activities, and proposed designating 2 million acres (of 12 million) as wilderness.[89]

The Reagan administration weakened even these modest recommendations for the California desert. Most notably, Watt's Department of the Interior delayed sending the wilderness recommendations to Congress, instead calling for further mineral studies.[90] In response, local wilderness advocates shifted their attention toward a citizens' wilderness proposal that would give priority to protecting the desert's ecological resources. Starting in the early 1980s, local Sierra Club members such as Jim Dodson, Judy Anderson, and Peter Burk formed the nucleus of a committed contingent of volunteers who publicized the need to protect the desert, developed detailed maps and descriptions of potential wilderness areas, and championed turning more of the California desert over to the National Park Service. The legislative window for California desert legislation opened in 1984, after the California national forest bill became law. It was here that the work of local advocates, the Sierra Club, and the Wilderness Society meshed most successfully for the public domain. In 1986, these groups jointly formulated a legislative proposal for the future of California's desert. Senator Alan Cranston (D-CA), who had emerged as a strong and enthusiastic ally to wilderness advocates on the Alaska campaign and the national forests, would be instrumental in efforts to protect the California desert. He introduced the California Desert Protection Act in Congress in February 1986. The legislation proposed a dramatic restructuring of land management. It would designate 4 million acres of wilderness areas on the public domain. It would expand the existing Death Valley National Monument from 2.1 to 3.3 million acres, increase the existing Joshua Tree National Monument from 550,000 to 800,000 acres, and create a new 1.5-million-acre national park in the Mojave desert, designating much of all three units as wilderness areas. All told, the act proposed 8 million acres of wilderness designations—four times the agency's 1980 recommendation.

Starting in 1986, the Wilderness Society's new California regional office began to work actively on the citizens' campaign already underway in California. Patricia Schifferle, the regional director, and Nobby Riedy, a staffer, worked in conjunction with local activists and the Sierra Club to advance the legislation. In 1986, the Wilderness Society kicked off its participation in the campaign with the publication of *Failure in the Desert*, a report enumerating the shortcomings of the BLM's management in the region since FLPMA became law in 1976, and justifying expansive wilderness legislation.[91] The Wilderness Society's Resource and Economic Policy Unit conducted studies of mineralization in the California desert, which became the basis of the wilderness community's efforts to remove mineral-rich areas and existing mines from the citizens' proposal.[92] And the Wilderness Society helped lay the groundwork for congressional hearings in Washington, D.C. In 1987, the California office coordinated a high-profile list of witnesses on behalf of the legislation, orchestrated a celebrity and press tour of the desert, and scored front-page coverage in the *Los Angeles Times* and supporting editorials in the San Francisco newspapers. The Wilderness Society viewed these strategies—rather than building local citizen support—as its key contributions to the California desert campaign.[93] But, as Schifferle noted, it was one thing to produce reports criticizing the management of the public lands. It was quite another to advance positive legislation. And in her view, the Wilderness Society risked mistaking "a series of reports on a shelf or a series of press clippings" for "accomplishing our goal of protecting the public lands."[94] Privately, she warned that it was the opposition that was doing the most to engage citizens in the future of the California desert.

"Do you know what wilderness is?" asked the Pro-Desert Coalition. "Betcha don't." Local ranchers, miners, hunters, and off-road vehicle enthusiasts formed the Pro-Desert Coalition in the mid-1980s to challenge what they described as the environmentalists' bid to "lock up" the region.[95] The proposal's vast scope, the restrictions it imposed on uses of the desert, and especially its inclusion of the eastern Mojave—which was popular for off-road vehicles, was important to local ranchers, contained some mineral resources, and was favored by hunters—all angered the opposition. The BLM viewed the legislation as an unnecessary challenge to its decade-old planning process for the California desert and resisted efforts to transfer land to the Park Service. The military objected on grounds that the proposal might limit access to airspace for low-level desert training flights. Hunters opposed wilderness designations that would limit opportunities to hunt deer and upland game and restrict wildlife management. The Pro-Desert Coalition warned that the legislation would place "severe restrictions" on the military, undermine the region's $200 million mining industry, and take away the "homes and livelihood" of desert ranchers and miners. If the proposal passed, it warned, it would "virtually deny the desert to the very people who use it most."[96] Senator Pete Wilson (R-CA) emerged as the proposal's most formidable congressional opponent. And, as one Wilderness Society staffer noted, Wilson seemed to have bought into the opposition's message. "He looks at four-wheel driving as a way to keep the family together and keep the kids off drugs."[97] The legislation had several false starts in the late 1980s and early 1990s. With Senator Cranston's consistent support, wilderness advocates tried to advance the legislation several times in Congress, but in each instance it was "stonewalled," first by Wilson and then by his successor John Seymour (R-CA).[98] Wilderness advocates made their strongest run in 1992, as Cranston's final term drew to a close. The legislation passed the House, but failed in the Senate under the threat of a Bush veto.

The legislative fates of Utah and California were not unique in the late 1980s and early 1990s—Congress passed less wilderness legislation in these years. There were many reasons for this. Few wilderness bills were in the congressional hopper, legislation for the public domain provoked new opposition, and the wilderness movement was less prepared to advance its agenda. In addition, the political climate in Washington, D.C., remained unfriendly. Although George H. W. Bush had proclaimed himself the "environmental president" in 1988 and emphasized consensus politics, he was a weak ally to the wilderness movement. He appointed Manuel Lujan, who had served as a representative from New Mexico in the House of Representatives since 1969, as the secretary of the interior. Although Lujan was generally viewed as a moderate Republican, in 1982 he had sponsored some of Watt's most aggressive efforts to open the public lands for development and, as secretary of the interior, he proved more interested in developing than protecting public lands. In the early 1990s, the Bush administration pushed for a comprehensive energy bill, which included opening up the Arctic National Wildlife Refuge (ANWR) for oil development (that effort failed), slowed efforts to protect the spotted owl as an endangered species, and did little to advance efforts to protect new wilderness areas. In 1991 and 1992, the BLM finally released its wilderness recommendations, which had been in the works since 1977. All told, the agency recommended wilderness protection for 9.7 of the 23 million acres of the public domain still under review.[99] And in states where Congress was considering more expansive wilderness proposals, such as California and Utah, the Bush administration threatened vetoes. Midway through the Bush administration, the Wilderness Society released its assessment of Bush's record. "It's a discouraging document, especially for someone who pledged to be a leader in protecting the environment."[100] The Bush administration's weak record on the environment would play to Bill Clinton's advantage in the 1992 election.

Within the wilderness movement, there were real concerns about whether groups like the Wilderness Society could advance a positive legislative agenda in Congress. During the 1980s, much of their energy had been channeled into alternative policy pathways, such as the appropriations process, administrative rulemaking, and judicial and administration appeals, which diminished their ability to advance positive a legislative agenda in Congress. Harry Crandell, a former Wilderness Society employee and staffer on the House Interior Committee, warned the Governing Council that as the "modus operandi of the Society" had changed "from an activist outfit to another conservation foundation type organization," it had lost its ability to effectively lobby Congress.[101] Ernie

Dickerman privately commented that the organization had become "one more cozy, private, Washington bureaucracy" which had forgotten how to build a political campaign.[102] Such criticisms were clearly informed by some nostalgia for Brandborg's Wilderness Society, with its emphasis on a cooperative model that made local and national wilderness organizations partners in advancing wilderness legislation. To many observers, that model seemed in disrepair by the late 1980s. And such concerns emerged from within the Wilderness Society's current staff, too. It was this concern that Schifferle raised in the California campaign. Other staffers saw citizen organizing increasingly being driven by their opponents, not their allies, across the West. Yet, in the 1980s, many staffers at the Wilderness Society saw the organization trapped in a zero-sum game: resources that went to cultivating citizen support took resources away from D.C.-based programs.[103] And since the late 1970s, the Wilderness Society had made a name for itself as a professional environmental lobby with a focus on the public lands. Some at the Wilderness Society considered its weak outreach program an underappreciated strength. As one staffer argued, because the Wilderness Society lacked a high degree of member involvement, it could "change in quantum leaps" as necessary.[104] In the early 1990s, such a quantum leap would seem increasingly necessary.

Wise Use and the New Right

In June 1988, the Wilderness Impact Research Foundation held its inaugural wilderness conference in Las Vegas, Nevada. This was not a revival for the wilderness movement's faithful, however. It was a conference for the wilderness movement's opponents. "We have come a long way since 1964 when the Wilderness Act was passed," noted James S. Burling, one of the conference organizers. "At that time no one, not even in their wildest imaginations, dreamed that so many millions of acres of the public lands would be set aside for wilderness."[105] Although wilderness was a spark behind the emerging Wise Use movement in the late 1980s, a decade of economic restructuring helped stoke its broader anti-environmental agenda. In the boom and bust cycle of the natural resource industries, the 1980s had generally been a bust. By 1992, employment in the western natural resource industries had diminished dramatically from a peak in the early 1980s: agricultural jobs were down by 17 percent since 1983, lumber and wood products jobs were down by 26 percent since 1978, and mining and smelting jobs were down by 44 percent since 1981.[106] Despite the promise of the Reagan and Bush administrations, it was a decade full of frustration and disappointment for many westerners who invested their hopes, ambitions, and often, their identities in working the lands of the American West. Although the West's changing economy may have rested on broader structural shifts, such as increased competition from abroad in logging and mining and decreased labor needs in resource industries, for many westerners, the most visible antagonists were the environmentalists with their lawsuits, wilderness proposals, and other challenges to resource development. One t-shirt advertising the recipe for "logger's stew" captured such frustrations; the ingredients included four spotted owls, three peregrine falcons, and "two well-beaten environmentalists."[107]

Starting in the late 1980s, rural westerners began to do something wilderness activists had done very well in the 1960s and 1970s: organize into a national coalition. By the early 1990s, a familiar sight at weekend markets, county fairs, and rodeos was a recreational vehicle or a pick-up truck proudly displaying a banner which read "People for the West! Fighting to keep America strong by keeping public lands open." Beneath the banner, local citizens stood by a card table handing out literature that urged westerners to defend the public lands, local industry, and their way of life.[108] People for the West! argued that the best way to challenge environmental regulations was through "an informed and intelligent public" and it urged westerners to "get involved in the political process."[109] Involvement was easy: membership was five dollars, an annual conference trained local citizen leaders, and a state gained a seat on the governing board of People for the West! when members organized ten local chapters.[110] The organization openly acknowledged that its funding came from the mining industry (more than 100 mining companies nationwide), but it emphasized that its purpose was fostering a grassroots campaign.[111] By the end of the decade, People for the West! claimed more than 100 chapters and 30,000 members.[112] It aimed to help each of these members "make a difference in the real world."[113] People for the West!, both in its organizing strategies and its political message, reflected one strand of environmental opposition in the West—the Wise Use Movement—which served as an organizational umbrella for local organizations nationwide. Wise Use marked the resurgence of populist activism against public lands reform in the late 1980s and 1990s, drawing together many of the constituencies of the Sagebrush Rebellion in an effort to blunt a wide range of environmental initiatives such as efforts to curb logging in the Pacific Northwest, reform management of the Greater Yellowstone Ecosystem, and pass wilderness legislation for the public domain, including that for Utah and the California desert.

7.4 The Wise Use Movement engaged western citizens in protests against federal environmental policies such as those that would limit logging on the national forests. Photograph by Rick Swart, 1994. Courtesy *Wallowa County Chieftain* and *High Country News*.

7.5 The Wise Use Movement spearheaded opposition to public lands reform in the late 1980s and early 1990s. It was funded by industry, but it billed itself as a grassroots movement and committed resources to involving and training local citizens, as reflected in this 1994 advertisement. Courtesy Conservation Collection, Denver Public Library.

The movement's manifesto was Alan Gottlieb's *The Wise Use Agenda: The Citizen's Policy Guide to Environmental Resource Issues* (1989), published by Ron Arnold, founder of a small western think tank, Center for the Defense of Free Enterprise, a former member of the Sierra Club, and a self-proclaimed environmental maverick. Arnold emphasized that Wise Use was representative "of a new balance, of a middle way, between extreme environmentalism and extreme industrialism." The manifesto outlined a twenty-five-point platform for reforming the nation's environmental policies. Many items on the Wise Use agenda posed a direct challenge to the wilderness movement: opening ANWR for petroleum development, reducing the scope of wilderness reviews, and reforming the Wilderness Act itself.[114] Just as the Wilderness Act guaranteed wilderness protection, Wise Use advocated legislation to create a National Mining System, National Timber Harvest System, and National Rangeland Grazing System that would protect those industries and their employees.[115]

The Wise Use Movement's leaders deliberately billed the movement as something other than an "anti-environmental" one. Instead, they staked a new claim to the ideological middle ground of American environmentalism. Wise Use elbowed aside two decades of environmental reform—what it described as the work of "single-minded preservationists" and the product of a "fanatic anti-people ideology"—to make room for a new positive vision of environmentalism that protected "ecology and economy."[116] In truth, the Wise Use Movement denied the reality of a long list of environmental problems that the scientific community largely agreed on: from the ozone hole to the threatened spotted owl. Instead of such extreme positions, with their negative implications for the nation's industries, Alan Gottlieb, president of the Center for Defense of Free Enterprise, explained that Wise Use offered a "straight-forward" agenda: "We can do it right. We can live in productive harmony with nature." Where the Sagebrush Rebellion had often opposed efforts to protect the public lands and other environmental reforms outright, the Wise Use Movement aimed to be "the environmentalism of the 21st century."[117]

Wise Use reflected the increasingly well-oiled gears of citizen organizing on the political right.[118] During the 1980s, the political right reformulated and consolidated the networks of political activism that first propelled Reagan into office. The New Right, Moral Majority, and Sagebrush Rebellion became building blocks for conservative political activism. Behind these movements was a shared set of strategies that increasingly welded citizen activists, corporate interests, like-minded foundations, and political institutions in Washington, D.C., into distinct and powerful networks of conservative political influence.[119]

Many of the local organizations affiliated with Wise Use described themselves as community-based grassroots groups that aimed to protect the rural way of life important to the West. One group explained that it embraced a "grassroots 'bottom up' philosophy," that left the "control and project work in the communities."[120] Where the Sagebrush Rebellion generally worked at the state level, the geographical center of Wise Use was the local community.[121] One of the most enthusiastic champions of these citizen-oriented efforts was Chuck Cushman, a property rights activist and founder of the National Inholders Association. Cushman was the Stewart Brandborg of Wise Use. His office was armed with nine fax machines to communicate with 1,800 groups and 8,000 key individuals nationwide. As Cushman explained, the goal was to serve as a hub for the growing Wise Use Movement by "provid[ing] information, guidance, and leadership to other organizations."[122] Indeed, through the leadership of regional organizations, including the Alliance for America, Multiple Use and Inholders Association, the Center for the Defense of Free Enterprise, the BlueRibbon Coalition, the Mountain States Legal Foundation, and the Western States Public Lands Coalition, Wise Use succeeded in drawing national political and media attention to its concerns.[123]

What most distinguished the Wise Use movement from the Sagebrush Rebellion was its emphasis on defending the basic constitutional rights of Americans. Although such concerns had been present in the Sagebrush Rebellion, they were pervasive in the Wise Use Movement. Dick Carver, a Nevada resident and Wise Use leader, explained, "we get called Sagebrush Rebels, but we're as far from the Sagebrush Rebellion as you can get."[124] Carver carried a copy of the Constitution in his breast pocket. Wise Use advocates argued that they had a right to hunt and bear arms on public lands. "Hunting, fishing, and trapping are among our oldest rights."[125] Off-road vehicle enthusiasts who enjoyed snowmobiles and four-wheel-drive vehicles claimed a right to access the public lands for their enjoyment.[126] And, most often, the Wise Use movement emphasized the threats to property rights, including real estate, grazing permits, timber contracts, and water rights. "Private property rights, guaranteed to each of us by the Constitution, are being jeopardized by laws intended to protect the environment."[127] Wayne Hage, another Nevada rancher and Wise Use leader, noted that it was this emphasis on rights that addressed a central shortcoming of the Sagebrush Rebellion. "I was right in the middle of the Sagebrush Rebellion," he explained. "So many mistakes were made. The answer isn't shifting from federal to state control, substituting one sovereign for another." Instead, it was defending the basic rights of individual citizens.[128] In the com-

7.6 Dick Carver, photographed here in January 1995 at the Win Back the West rally in Alturas, California, was a leader of the Wise Use Movement. Carver and other Wise Use activists argued that federal public lands policies infringed on individual rights guaranteed by the U.S. Constitution, a copy of which Carver carried in his breast pocket. Courtesy Jon Christensen and *High Country News.*

ing debates over the public domain, the right to access private inholdings and the right to graze cattle on the public lands would be especially contentious. In these ways, Wise Use cast itself foremost as a social movement, centered on western citizens and their individual rights, rather than the concerns of western industry or state government. The Sagebrush Rebellion had tried some of these tactics, too. But in the early 1990s, Wise Use succeeded in shifting the debates away from the vested interests of the natural resource industries (and their employees) to a much broader constituency. Wise Use was, at least rhetorically, about people and communities, not special interests. That strategy helped align Wise Use with the consolidation of the New Right nationally.[129]

The Wilderness Society struggled with its response to Wise Use. To some observers, the Wise Use Movement was just the Sagebrush Rebellion sporting a new cowboy hat. Tom Watkins, the editor of the Wilderness Society's magazine and a respected historian, wrote that there is nothing "new about the movement, save for its glaze of sophistication and professionalism."[130] One Wilderness Society staffer urged the organization to pursue an aggressive campaign to expose Wise Use for what it was: "an organized, slick public relations campaign to advance an environmentally destructive agenda, NOT a real grassroots movement."[131] But many on the field staff feared that an aggressive strategy that ignored the broad appeal of the Wise Use movement in the West would only deepen the wilderness movement's political difficulties. Publicly, the Wilderness Society responded to Wise Use by comparing it to the Sagebrush Rebellion. "[T]he last time we saw a posse like this it was the early 1980s and Ronald Reagan's Interior Secretary, James Watt, was riding at its head."[132] But, privately, Wise Use provoked uncertainty and introspection among wilderness advocates. At the Wilderness Society, its leaders worried that the organization was being "out-gunned" in the local media, "over-powered" at government hearings, and, most troubling, that it was losing "hearts and minds" in the rural West.[133] The organization's professional strategies may have strengthened its credibility in Washington, D.C., but they had narrowed its political constituency in the West. Such uncertainty undermined the wilderness movement's efforts to protect wilderness in the public domain.

California, Utah, and the Political Seesaw in the 1990s

Prospects for wilderness legislation brightened in 1992 with Bill Clinton's election to the White House. The Clinton administration raised high hopes in an environmental community that had actively supported the Democratic ticket in the campaign and seeded the administration with friendly appointees, such as Secretary of the Interior Bruce Babbitt and Assistant Secretary George Frampton. But as wilderness advocates in California and Utah knew well, prospects for wilderness depended upon each state's congressional delegations more than on national politics. That meant good news for California and bad news for Utah. In 1992, the election of two Democratic senators from California—Dianne Feinstein and Barbara Boxer, both of whom pledged their support for the California Desert Protection Act—opened a new window of political opportunity for the California desert. With the advent of an environmentally proactive administration in the White House and the support of both California senators, the California legislation seemed poised for rapid enactment in the 103rd Congress. But in 1992, Utah's Representative Owens, who had been wilderness advocates' only legislative ally in the congressional delegation, lost his bid for a Senate seat. With his exit from Congress, Utah wilderness advocates lost the support of a native of southern Utah, a Mormon, and an ardent defender of wilderness—indeed, Owens joined the board of directors of SUWA in the mid-1990s.[134] The wilderness campaigns for California and Utah became playing cards amid the increasingly polarized debates over public lands reform and environmental policy in the early 1990s.

The California Desert Protection Act was the most ambitious wilderness bill since the Alaska campaign. Starting in 1993, the Wilderness Society and Sierra Club leadership worked closely with Senator Feinstein to advance the 7-million-acre wilderness proposal in the 103rd Congress. Supporters billed the California desert as a wonderland of unique scenery, endangered species, and fragile desert ecology. Opponents did not object to protecting the California desert. "But we must do so in a realistic way," explained one congressional representative. "A way in which the desert can be properly maintained and managed in order to assure various uses in the years to come."[135] Opponents sided with the BLM and proposed protecting just over 2 million acres as wilderness — a plan which left more of the region open for off-road vehicles and mining, and allowed for more liberal management of grazing and other activities. Otherwise, as one Wise Use proponent argued, "The 'real' environmentalists, the ones who live it and practice it, are going to be the losers."[136] In the case of California, mainstream wilderness advocates approached the campaign with a willingness to negotiate. As the Wilderness Society's leadership acknowledged in private, "minor accommodations for mining, off-road vehicle, and military interests" were necessary.[137] Feinstein made those accommodations a centerpiece of her efforts. She struck deals to allow grazing in the new national parks, to explicitly permit low-level military flights above wilderness areas, to exclude additional mines and potential mining sites from protected areas, and to accommodate some access for motorized recreation in the desert. Compromise politics moved the legislation out of the Senate, where it passed by a vote of 69 to 29 in March 1994.

But the Wise Use Movement's stronghold was in the House of Representatives. Five congressional representatives from districts including the California desert formed a stubborn bloc of opposition that forced further compromises. The National Rifle Association and the Wise Use Movement made the right to hunt a major issue in the proposed Mojave National Park. To avoid permitting guns and hunting in a national park, the House instead downgraded the park to a national preserve (which permitted hunting). The House also took steps to ensure the legislation did not encroach on private property rights. The California Cattlemen's Association, for instance, emphasized that its members held "private property" rights in the form of water rights and grazing permits. Rob Blair, a local rancher, warned that the legislation would "deprive me of my home, my way of life, and not only my heritage, but my children's inheritance."[138] Those were concerns the House responded to. It included provisions which affirmed that neither park nor wilderness designations would limit

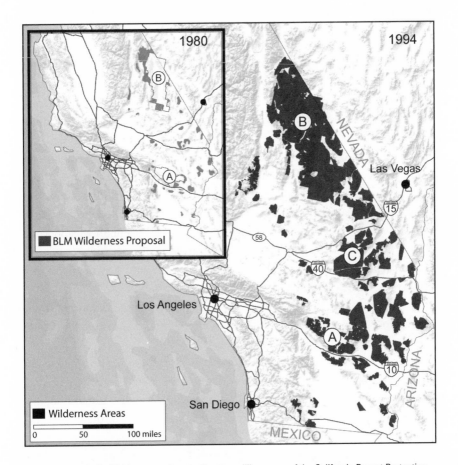

Map 7.2 In 1980, the BLM proposed protecting two million acres of the California Desert Protection Area as wilderness (inset). In 1994, the California Desert Protection Act protected 7 million acres of wilderness on BLM and National Park Service lands, upgraded Joshua Tree National Monument (A) and Death Valley National Monument (B) to national parks, and created the Mojave National Preserve (C). (The 1994 map shows wilderness areas designated within Joshua Tree in 1976.)

access to private lands, affirmed that the legislation would not restrict development of private property, and gave priority to acquiring property owned by ranchers (if they so desired). The House passed its version of the desert legislation in July 1994 on a vote of 298 to 128.[139]

The California Desert Protection Act and 7 million acres of new wilderness seemed assured in the summer of 1994. The *San Francisco Chronicle* called the House legislation an "incomplete victory," but with negotiations scheduled to iron out the differences between the Senate and House versions of the legislation, it described it as "sure-fire."[140] But any expectations for a speedy conference between the House and Senate collapsed as the agenda of the Democratic Party and the Clinton administration fell into disarray. At its start, the Clinton administration advanced a broad range of reforms for logging, grazing, and mining policies on the public domain. For that reason, one representative from the California desert described the desert act as another part of the Clinton administration's "War on the West." And as anger with the Clinton administration began to build over numerous issues—such as health care nationally and public lands regionally—Republicans sensed the potential for a major victory in the 1994 mid-term elections. In the 103rd Congress, Democrats controlled both the House and Senate. But as the elections approached, Republicans began to slow the workings of Congress, halting dozens of bills in anticipation of a major post-election realignment. The desert act became a playing card in these national political stratagems. In the fall of 1994, Senator Feinstein was in a tight race for reelection with Michael Huffington, a Republican opposed to the desert legislation.[141] Republicans hoped that by derailing the California desert legislation, they could disrupt Feinstein's reelection bid and strengthen their chances for gaining a majority in the Senate.[142]

Their strategy failed. The California Desert Protection Act became law just before the November 1994 elections. The *San Francisco Chronicle* described Feinstein's success with admiration. "It is only a little less than astonishing that Feinstein, a Democrat, succeeded in winning final passage of the biggest wilderness measure in the history of the continental United States despite fierce opposition by Republicans, who had already laid waste to virtually the entire Democratic agenda."[143] At the end of the 103rd Congress, little of the Clinton administration's agenda had became law, whether for environmental or other issues. Republicans, led by the conservative senator and Wise Use ally Malcolm Wallop (R-WY), had hoped to make this true of the California legislation too. Wallop worked to delay action on the bill into October, in hopes that Feinstein's allies and Senate Democrats would abandon the bill in their rush to get back to the campaign trail. Instead, Democrats rallied to support the legislation and, by extension, Feinstein's reelection bid. Their success was made possible by the support of fourteen Republican senators. Feinstein and the wilderness advocates accepted the changes adopted in the House, which attracted the necessary support in the Senate, and led to the final legislation protecting 7 million acres of the California desert as wilderness.[144] Explaining his support for the legislation, Senator Robert Bennett (R-UT) praised Feinstein for "show[ing] a willingness to solve problems rather than trumpet the issue."[145] But that comment, from the junior senator from Utah, seemed as much a criticism of wilderness politics in Utah as praise for Feinstein.

The road to wilderness protection for the public domain in Utah was rocky and without end. In the early 1990s, wilderness debates in Utah were more often defined by antagonism and, at times, violence than productive dialogue: Activists were accused of slaughtering cattle grazing in potential wilderness areas near Escalante Canyon, protesters burned wilderness advocates in effigy near Moab, and shots were fired at hikers in the backcountry.[146] In the mid-1990s, two proposals remained at the forefront of the Utah wilderness debate. Without Owens's support, wilderness advocates had turned to allies outside Utah for leadership. In 1995, Maurice Hinchey (D-NY) introduced a 5.7-million-acre bill for Utah, bearing the new title "America's Red Rock Wilderness Act" to signify its national significance. Any hopes of advancing that legislation disappeared with the new Republican majority in the 104th Congress, however. Instead, the engine behind Utah wilderness discussions in the mid-1990s was the congressional delegation's proposal.[147] Starting in 1994, the Utah delegation, in cooperation with state governor Michael Leavitt (R) and Utah counties, set in motion a process to develop a Utah wilderness bill from the ground up. It called on the counties to hold meetings to discuss potential wilderness areas; those meetings informed the governor's recommendation; and that recommendation was then fashioned into a bill by the Utah congressional delegation with the leadership of Representative Jim Hansen. Despite strong support in Salt Lake City and moderate support in some rural areas for wilderness protection, Hansen proposed designating only 1.8 of the 3.2 million acres of wilderness study areas as wilderness (out of Utah's 22 million acres of federal public domain).[148] But that proposal would be swept up by partisan wrangling over public lands legislation in the 104th Congress.[149]

In the 1990s, California proved to be the exception and Utah the rule in wilderness politics on the public domain. There was to be no burst of legislative action for the public domain, as there had been for the national forest roadless areas in the mid-1980s. From the start, wilderness advocates knew the public domain posed challenges: the lands were little known, overseen by an unfriendly agency, and traditionally managed in close conjunction with local and state interests. The West's turn to the political right and the Republicans' growing power nationally compounded those challenges. The political stars for wilderness in the public domain aligned above only two states in the 1990s: Arizona and California. In 1990, under the leadership of Morris Udall, Congress designated 1.1 million acres of public domain wilderness in Arizona. And in

1994, Arizona and California together accounted for 5 million of the 5.2 million acres of designated BLM wilderness. Between 1995 and 1999, however, Congress designated only 66,000 acres of additional wilderness nationwide. In response, wilderness advocates began to look for other ways to achieve their goals. Some decided to appeal to the White House to take action where Congress seemed stalled; that strategy would lead to a flurry of controversial national monument designations, including a 1.8-million-acre monument in the heart of Utah's canyon country. Some began to lay the framework for an alternative, less controversial system of land protection for the BLM lands—the National Conservation Landscape System. In both cases, the shift in strategies away from wilderness and congressional action and toward other policy pathways was not unique to efforts to protect the public domain. Instead, it pointed toward a new era in environmental politics that defined the 1990s and early 2000s.[150] Some wilderness advocates, however, remained committed to building local support for wilderness in Nevada, Idaho, Utah, and other western states. Their efforts would not pay off until the early 2000s.[151]

Conclusion

In the 1970s, Michael McCloskey had wondered if Americans would rally to another campaign to save the nation's wilderness. The three major wilderness reviews—for Alaska, the national forest roadless areas, and the public domain—offered the answer. In each case, wilderness advocates had turned those reviews into legislative victories—the Alaska National Interest Lands Conservation Act, the burst of national forest wilderness designations in the mid-1980s, and the California Desert Protection Act in 1994—that expanded the wilderness system to 100 million acres. That meant one out of twenty acres of land in the United States was protected from all forms of development in perpetuity. Even if half of that land was in Alaska, it was still a stunning accomplishment. While those victories brought some closure to the wilderness reviews, they did not bring these stories to an end. In each case, the reviews set in motion debates that would carry on into the twenty-first century: the fate of ANWR's coastal plain, the national forest roadless areas in the northern Rockies, and wilderness designation on much of the public domain all remained important issues of debate. But McCloskey's key point had been that the environmental movement's new concerns would draw attention away from wilderness. On that point he was right, even in the case of the public lands. By the late 1980s, environmentalists increasingly pushed other concerns to the forefront of public lands politics, such as endangered species protection, eco-system management, and the broader ecological consequences and economics of logging, grazing, and other industries. In 1992, even the Wilderness Society's staff ranked new wilderness designations a second-tier priority.[152] For that reason, the uneven close of these three wilderness reviews marks a waypoint in American environmental politics: it concluded an era when wilderness was at the forefront of national public lands debates and marked the beginning of new era dominated by a broader agenda for public lands reform.

Before turning to this new era in public lands debates and environmental politics, it is worth remembering the strategies and commitments that defined the 1970s and 1980s for the wilderness movement. First, wilderness occupied a central place in national debates over the public lands. Although wilderness was hardly the exclusive focus of public lands politics, even efforts to advance environmental reform using other policy pathways—such as the courts, administrative rulemaking, and executive action—were often done to lay the groundwork for congressional action on wilderness. Second, wilderness advocates gave new emphasis to the role of science in guiding the protection and management of the public lands. This was most apparent in the campaigns for Alaska and the national forest roadless areas, where wilderness advocates organized campaigns to protect complete ecosystems. But in each case, efforts to advance scientifically informed proposals in Congress, where proposals competed with the interests of the agencies, industry, and local communities, meant political concerns, more than scientific priorities, determined the final boundaries of wilderness areas. Starting in the late 1980s, wilderness advocates would advance their scientific claims in other policy arenas, such as the courts and agencies, with more success. Third, a cooperative model of wilderness advocacy linked local activists with the national groups. Unlike in the Brandborg years, however, when this relationship empowered local groups, in the 1980s local activists were increasingly cast in a supporting role to increasingly professional and powerful national groups, such as the Wilderness Society and Sierra Club. In the 1990s, wilderness advocacy would nearly collapse before reemerging in a more distributed model of environmental advocacy, which yielded new tensions and, eventually, cooperation. Fourth, opponents of wilderness and public lands reforms emerged as creative and effective players in environmental politics between the late 1970s and early 1990s, both drawing on and contributing to broader shifts important to the New Right. Rural westerners organized themselves in opposition to environmental reform, drawing on the support of industry and conservative foundations, to challenge envi-

ronmental protection under the leadership of the Sagebrush Rebellion and the
Wise Use Movement. This mobilization of western citizens played a supporting role in the Republican Party's national political strategy that would build
toward its successes in the mid-1990s and early 2000s.

Taken together, these changes drove the polarization of American environmental politics along several axes in the 1980s and the 1990s—tensions grew
between grassroots and national groups over strategies for public lands protection, radical approaches in support of and opposition to environmental reform
contributed to environmental debate, and a deepening partisanship divided
Democrats and Republicans on environmental reform. These changes combined to make public lands debates an increasingly contentious, even hostile,
arena of environmental politics. It is worth remembering that these changes
emerged not just in response to debates over new environmental issues, such
as air pollution or toxic waste disposal, but in response to the changed debates
over old issues, especially wilderness.

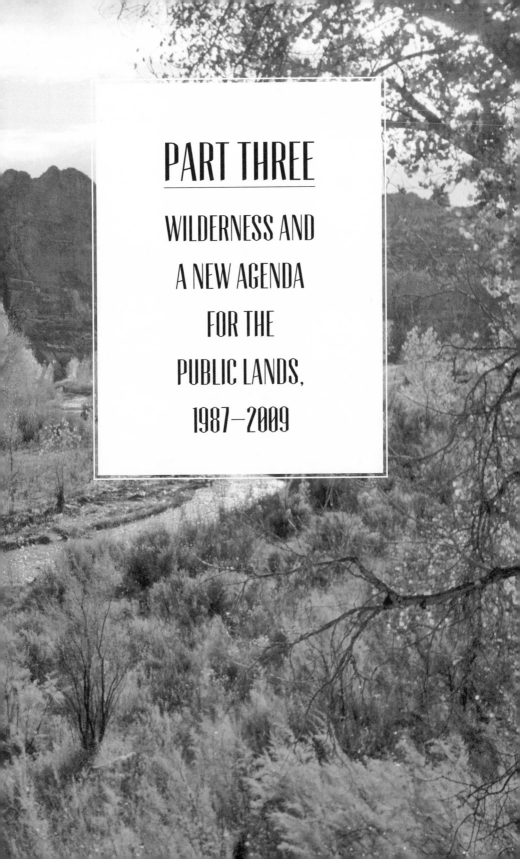

PART THREE

WILDERNESS AND
A NEW AGENDA
FOR THE
PUBLIC LANDS,
1987–2009

8 / FROM WILDERNESS
TO PUBLIC LANDS REFORM

T he Wilderness Society kicked off the silver anniversary of the Wilderness
Act with a gala celebration at Union Station in Washington, D.C., on February 28, 1989. There was much to celebrate. Since 1964, the wilderness
system had grown more than tenfold, from 9.1 million acres to 92.3 million acres of public land. The wilderness system included areas from the Great
Swamp in New Jersey to entire watersheds and mountain ranges in Alaska. It
was an accomplishment that would have astounded Howard Zahniser. Looking
forward, George Frampton, the Wilderness Society's president, called for doubling the wilderness system's size to include "whole ecosystems" nationwide.[1]
But even as Frampton highlighted the importance of wilderness, the Wilderness
Society's agenda was broadening.

For twenty-five years, wilderness advocates had followed a tacit set of
rules in pursuing legislative action to expand the wilderness system. They
emphasized the importance of citizen involvement in administrative and congressional action. They engaged in negotiation and compromise on the size of
wilderness areas, they usually moved such legislation on a state-by-state basis
(which gave local and state interests an important role in political negotiations), and they accommodated specific management exceptions to address
the concerns of other stakeholders on issues such as grazing, release language,
and water rights. This approach to wilderness advocacy succeeded, in large
part, because it avoided a systemic challenge to the interests of resource industries, western communities, and their allies, or to the multiple-use framework
that guided public lands management for the national forests and public
domain. In short, wilderness advocates had spent twenty-five years asking for
a slice — granted, a larger and larger slice — of wilderness from the public lands
pie, but in doing so, they had granted loggers, ranchers, and miners their share
of the pie, too.

Beginning in the 1980s, environmentalists began to focus on the basic
recipes that guided resource activities on the public lands. This shift had been

in the making since the late 1960s. Even as environmentalists pursued wilderness designations, they engaged in early campaigns that challenged logging and grazing practices. New laws such as the National Environmental Policy Act, the National Forest Management Act (NFMA), and the Endangered Species Act (ESA) gave environmentalists new leverage in public lands policy. And early legal suits, especially those pioneered by the Natural Resources Defense Council (NRDC) over grazing and timber policies, set important precedents for a broader public lands reform campaign. In the mid-1980s, public lands advocates began to actively draw on the provisions of these laws and, equally important, on new lessons from natural resource economics and conservation biology, to push long-standing concerns about resource management to the forefront of public lands politics: Why did the Forest Service keep selling federal timber when it lost money on most timber sales? Why did the Bureau of Land Management lease out grazing lands at below-market rates? Why were such money-losing activities permitted when they wreaked havoc on the ecological values of the public lands? How many and how large should protected areas be to protect the nation's biodiversity?[2]

These questions opened up a new era in public lands debates in the mid-1980s. Such questions effected two changes that wilderness advocacy did not. First, these questions challenged the multiple-use framework that stabilized public lands politics. In practice, multiple-use management resulted in the zoning of public lands to separate conflicting activities—some land was protected as wilderness, while other land was clear-cut, mined, or intensively developed for recreation and tourism—rather than managing each acre of land for multiple uses. Wilderness protection worked within the multiple-use framework more than it challenged it. Second, focusing on such management issues posed a systemic challenge to the resource development activities on the public lands. Wilderness reviews had generated much uncertainty regarding land management, but those disputes were usually resolved through negotiations that protected some wilderness and left other land open for resource development. But economic and scientific analyses highlighting the shortcomings of existing forest, grazing, and land management policies had the potential to fundamentally restructure and, in some cases, end such activities on the public lands. The work of the Wilderness Society on three issues—logging and grazing reform, protection of the spotted owl, and energy policy and wilderness protection—highlights the society's role in opening up a new era of public lands reform.

Economics, Conservation Biology, and Public Lands Reform

Broadly speaking, the Wilderness Act of 1964 had been crafted such that it posed little threat to the future of the nation's economy or to that of the West's natural resource industries.[3] It explicitly allowed the continuation of grazing in perpetuity and mining through 1983. The scope of the initial ten-year reviews avoided posing any direct challenge to valuable public lands. Starting in the 1980s, however, the Wilderness Society joined two analytical strategies—one grounded in resource economics, another in conservation biology—to advance a broader agenda for public lands reform. These efforts began with the Wilderness Society's reinvention as an environmental lobby under William Turnage's leadership. That transformation had taken full effect by the late 1980s. In 1987, the organization had 105 staffers, ten offices, 220,000 members, and a $9.4 million budget.[4] George Frampton, a well-respected lawyer, became president in 1986 and continued to lead the Wilderness Society on the same course as had Turnage, expanding its ranks of staff lawyers, economists, and scientists. In Frampton's opinion, a commitment to rigorous policy analysis made the Wilderness Society "the organization with the most credibility on public lands and wilderness issues . . . on the Hill."[5]

8.1 George Frampton, president of the Wilderness Society from 1986 to 1993, was a prosecuting attorney during the Watergate scandal in 1973 and became involved in public lands issues in the 1980s. Courtesy Conservation Collection, Denver Public Library.

Concern about the economics of public lands management was not new in the 1980s. Marion Clawson, a resource economist who had grown up on a Nevada ranch and trained as an agricultural economist, pioneered this line of analysis in the postwar era. He brought to public lands policy a rural westerner's belief in resource development and an economist's emphasis on efficiency. Working with Resources for the Future, a think tank based in Washington, D.C., Clawson focused attention on the economics of public lands management, especially national forest management. His work addressed a range of issues: the inefficiencies of congressional oversight and budgeting, the increased cost of forest management due to administrative and legal appeals, and the overhead necessary to involve the public in policy making. He also documented the Forest Service's failure to fully account for the costs and benefits of public lands management, including clean water, wilderness, and recreation. If the public lands were to be managed efficiently, he thought, the inputs and outputs had to be reduced to economic terms.[6] Although Clawson was not a wilderness advocate, he argued that for groups like the Wilderness Society and Sierra Club, "an approach based upon the economics . . . will do more to help these interests attain what they want from the national forests than will exclusively emotional appeals."[7]

If Clawson's goal was to get people to rethink the economics of public lands management, he succeeded. It is unlikely that he anticipated that the Wilderness Society would carry his campaign forward with particular enthusiasm. But the Wilderness Society's agenda hinged on the work of its economists and policy analysts in the 1980s. In 1981, Turnage had secured a grant to create an Economic Policy Department from the Richard King Mellon Foundation. That unit had been instrumental in fending off the Reagan administration's anti-environmental campaigns. In 1985, the Wilderness Society expanded the department into a new Resource Planning and Economics Department (RP&E) with the specific purpose of monitoring the new national forest planning process.[8] From the start, there had been concern that the Wilderness Society's new direction would take the organization away from its core focus on wilderness. In 1981, George Marshall, brother of Robert Marshall, had noted that the Mellon Foundation's initial grant for the Economic Policy Department addressed "'resource economics, management, and forestry,' but not a word about wilderness."[9] Marshall's concerns were well placed. As the RP&E emerged as the most dynamic and productive engine within the Wilderness Society, the organization issued dozens of technical analyses, such as *America's Vanishing Rain Forest: A Report on Federal Timber Management in Southeast Alaska* (1986),

Below-Cost Sales: Proceedings of a Conference on the Economics of National Forest Timber Sales (1987), and *National Forests: Policies for the Future* (1988).[10] None focused specifically on wilderness protection.

Such studies raised one overarching question: Why did the federal government lose money on many of the extractive activities on the public lands? The government frequently spent more taxpayer funds to administer logging, grazing, and mining programs than it recouped in receipts from timber sales, fees from ranchers, or land sales to mining companies. Such policies may have made sense in the nineteenth or early twentieth centuries, when they encouraged settlement and development, expanded the western economy, and integrated the West into the nation. And loggers, miners, and ranchers argued that such policies remained appropriate even in the 1980s. Doing business on the public lands was often more expensive, because the land was of lower quality and difficult to access, and such activities also supported rural communities. The federal land agencies also argued that below-cost activities were reasonable because such activities provided additional public benefits, such as new roads, reforestation, and wildlife habitat management. And both westerners and the agencies were quick to note that other activities, such as hiking and camping on the public lands, were often administered free of charge to users. Starting in the 1980s, however, wilderness advocates began to make below-cost activities a centerpiece of their campaigns, arguing that such policies amounted to public subsidies for private interests that cost the federal government and taxpayers money and encouraged the degradation of the public lands.

Although scientists contributed to these studies, there was no scientific counterpart to the RP&E at the Wilderness Society. It might seem logical that scientists would have occupied such an office; many of the Wilderness Society's leaders, including Robert Marshall, Aldo Leopold, Olaus Murie, and Stewart Brandborg, had been trained scientists, but as Donald Worster has argued in his classic history of ecology, *Nature's Economy*, just as the modern environmental movement flowered in the 1970s, a new generation of ecologists retreated from the immediacy of environmental politics.[11] This was true in the case of wilderness advocacy. Academic ecologists worried that overt engagement in politics and policy would undermine the integrity of their scientific research.[12] Also, the direction of ecological research was raising conceptual questions about wilderness protection. Wilderness advocates continued to emphasize the importance of protecting "complete" and "climax" ecosystems, which rested on assumptions about an ordered, balanced, and predictable natural world. But ecologists increasingly focused on population ecology, disturbance theory, chaos theory, and paleoecology, all of which emphasized the dynamics (and often unpredictability) of ecological systems. For these reasons, academic scientists played little role in shaping the outcome of the major public lands reviews of the 1970s and 1980s.

The disjuncture between academic ecology and wilderness advocacy began to close in the early 1980s. Michael Soulé, an outspoken, forward-thinking, and charismatic population geneticist, issued a call to arms to the scientific community in 1980. "Never in the 500 million years of terrestrial evolution has this mantle we call the biosphere been under such savage attack."[13] Since the mid-1960s, a growing body of research had pointed toward an accelerating global extinction crisis. Soulé noted that while other scientists, such as those in wildlife management and forestry, had remained engaged in public policy, "the large majority of their academic colleagues thought the subject was beneath their dignity."[14] Academic scientists, Soulé said, no longer had the luxury of standing on the sidelines. He proposed a new interdisciplinary, "mission-oriented" field of science—conservation biology—to bring science to bear on policy issues.[15] In September 1986, conservation biologists raised a warning flag for the world to see at the National Forum on Biodiversity in Washington, D.C.[16] In 1987, the newly founded Society for Conservation Biology launched *Conservation Biology*, a journal that became a forum for both pure and applied studies of conservation science and policy. By the early 1990s, conservation biologists emerged as a new source of scientific and moral authority in public lands debates.[17]

The Wilderness Society worked to incorporate conservation biology into its advocacy. In 1986, the Wilderness Society published *Conserving Biological Diversity in Our National Forests* in cooperation with the Ecological Society of America.[18] The 115-page report served as a primer on ecology, conservation biology, and citizen involvement in federal forest planning. That spring, the Wilderness Society devoted its magazine, *Wilderness*, to biodiversity on the public lands and began to commit more of its in-house resources to scientific research and advocacy.[19] In 1986, it hired David Wilcove, recently graduated from Princeton University, as its first staff ecologist. Wilcove, whose doctoral research focused on the ecological consequences of habitat fragmentation in forests, soon became known as "Dr. Science" at the Wilderness Society. When he left in 1991, Mark Shaffer, who pioneered theory on endangered species protection as a graduate student at Duke University and at the Fish and Wildlife Service, took his place. In 1990, Frampton claimed that "concern for biological diversity is inseparable from everything we do" at the Wilderness Society.[20]

Conservation biology transformed the conceptual landscape of public lands politics in the 1980s. In the 1960s and 1970s, wilderness advocates often considered wilderness areas discrete and self-sustaining samples of climax eco-systems. Conservation biology recast wilderness areas as functional units in larger networks of habitat protection, defined by dynamic ecological communities, immigration, and extinction. None of these ideas was wholly new, but conservation biologists drew on contemporary research and a commitment to public outreach to advance these concerns with new success in the late 1980s and early 1990s.[21] The lessons of conservation biology, however, did not always align neatly with the priorities of wilderness advocates. In the early 1980s, debates over protecting numerous small areas versus fewer large areas divided ecologists.[22] In the early 1990s, new concern for sustainable development siphoned attention away from protecting wilderness areas.[23] And questions arose about when active intervention in natural systems—such as reintroducing species, thinning forests, and introducing fire—was necessary to protect habitat and species.[24] For these reasons, despite Frampton's emphasis on biodiversity protection, the Wilderness Society would struggle with how to integrate the scientific imperatives of conservation biology into the organization's policy goals and political strategies.

The lessons of resource economics and conservation biology gave wilderness advocates new leverage to advance long-standing concerns in public lands debates and environmental policy, as is evident in three case studies: below-cost logging and grazing, the spotted owl and Ancient Forests in the Pacific Northwest, and the Arctic National Wildlife Refuge (ANWR). These strategies, however, played different roles in public policy. Economics was grounded in a reductionist approach to public lands policy, which measured value in dollars and cents. That strategy played well with federal agencies and Congress, particularly as budget constraints became more important to public policy in the 1980s, and wilderness advocates gave new attention to the congressional budgeting process as a venue for policy reform. This strategy was crucial in opening up policy debates over below-cost logging and grazing. In contrast, the emerging field of conservation biology was rooted in an ethical commitment to the value of biodiversity and, often, a holistic approach to ecological science; those values challenged, rather than aligned with, existing approaches to decision-making in the federal land agencies and Congress. For that reason, conservation biology proved most decisive in securing court rulings which blocked logging on the Ancient Forests in the Pacific Northwest to protect a threatened species: the spotted owl. Most often at the Wilderness Society, these strategies for public lands reform proceeded separately from its wilderness advocacy. In the case of ANWR, however, the Wilderness Society's efforts to foster a broader environmental agenda and its wilderness work intersected directly.

The Below-Cost Argument: Logging and Grazing

The spectacle of destruction left after clear-cutting a patch of forest had long served as a call to action for environmentalists. The same could not be said of grazing. Its consequences were so slow and ubiquitous that few realized how cattle had transformed the western landscape. But in the 1980s, the Wilderness Society helped move both below-cost logging and grazing to the forefront of public lands debates. How the Wilderness Society addressed these two issues suggests the challenges it faced in navigating among the new lessons of conservation biology, the imperatives of public lands reform, and its long-standing political commitments, especially to ranchers.

The burst of national forest wilderness legislation in the mid-1980s had captured national attention, but even as President Reagan signed those laws, the implementation of the NFMA raised new questions about the national forests. Which parts of the forests should be logged? Where should new roads and trails be built? How should biological diversity be protected? How would each national forest balance resource needs, ecological values, and public preferences? Since the 1950s, the Forest Service had been reacting to competing demands on the national forests—advanced by industry, environmentalists, ranchers, and Congress—because it had no systematic process for answering such questions. The NFMA aimed to fix that problem.[25] The legislation required the Forest Service to develop long-term plans that incorporated public input to guide multiple-use management on each of the nation's 155 national forests (a planning process that was to be repeated every ten to fifteen years). In response to nascent concerns about the economics of logging, Congress required the agency to apply economic analysis to its timber program. The legislation also required the agency to protect the diversity of plant and animal communities. That last provision would give conservation biologists a new say in forest policy. The NFMA was signed into law in 1976, but implementation was slow: developing the necessary administrative rules to implement the legislation had been delayed by the roadless area review in the late 1970s. The first round of forest plans was finalized between 1982 and 1992.[26]

The forest plans created a new opportunity for citizen involvement. But, as one Sierra Club volunteer noted, the technical plans often required a "year of study and a Ph.D. in computer science."[27] Bruce Hamilton, a senior Sierra Club leader, emphasized that the club "need[ed] to keep participation simple and demystify the planning process."[28] In the mid-1980s, with the Sierra Club and the National Audubon Society in the lead, citizen groups engaged in the forest planning process and scrutinized proposed timber and grazing quotas, recreation plans, roadless area protection, and wilderness proposals. The National Trails Coalition, a new umbrella organization for forest advocacy funded by Recreational Equipment Incorporated (REI), supported such local efforts.[29] In the early 1980s, the Seattle-based retailer saw an opportunity to take "the lead [in advocacy] in a way no other outdoor business is doing."[30] But unlike a wilderness campaign, which culminated with congressional legislation and a tangible accomplishment, there was no "up or down vote" on forest plans to reward activists.[31]

By 1985, more than 100 plans were underway.[32] Most of them, however, wound up tangled in administrative and judicial appeals over issues such as proposed logging levels, management of specific areas, or species protection—all of which contributed to growing frustration with the Forest Service. But it was in these appeals that the Wilderness Society's professional expertise proved most effective. In 1983, the Wilderness Society appealed the national forest plans for four forests in Colorado on grounds that they were unviable. Based on its assessment, the proposed timber sales would cost the agency more to administer than private timber companies would pay for the timber.[33] In a 1984 op-ed in the *Wall Street Journal*, the Wilderness Society argued that over the previous decade, including both good and bad years, the Forest Service had spent two billion dollars more to administer timber sales than it earned back in revenue. In 1982, a bad year for timber prices, 97 of 155 national forests lost money on timber sales.[34] Those figures did not even begin to take into account intangible losses such as diminished water quality, wilderness protection, or scenery.[35]

The Wilderness Society and its allies called on the government to reform its basic approach to logging practices by phasing out below-cost timber sales and helping rural communities that depended on such sales to restructure their economies. But such arguments fell on deaf ears at the Forest Service. From the start, the agency had prioritized timber production in its forest plans, and these appeals did not cause it to waiver. The agency argued that such below-cost sales were appropriate, since they provided ancillary benefits, such as new forest roads and improved wildlife habitat. It questioned the Wilderness Society's analysis. Federal timber sales presented a complex accounting problem: sales were completed one year, but harvested in later years; major expenses, such as new roads, were capitalized over multiple years; and non-market goods, such as wilderness and watershed protection, were not factored in. And the agency was quick to point out that it was not just federal timber sales that lost money. So too did programs wilderness advocates cared about, such as the agency's recreation program. But the Wilderness Society knew the recreation program was small potatoes relative to the timber program. Such below-cost sales should be the exception, it argued, not the rule, in national forest management.[36]

The Wilderness Society did not expect to win its argument with the Forest Service. Instead, it looked to Congress. In 1983, Congress requested that the General Accounting Office review the agency's timber program. Its findings were largely consistent with those of groups such as the NRDC and Wilderness Society.[37] In 1984, Congress demanded that the Forest Service develop more precise accounting procedures for its timber program—a process that delayed reforms into the 1990s.[38] In the interim, wilderness advocates remained engaged in forest plans nationwide—pushing to reduce logging and to increase support for protected areas and trails. And nationally, wilderness advocates secured several victories. In 1986, the Forest Service was required to separately allocate for trails in its annual budget (before the agency had funded trails at its own discretion out of the annual transportation budget).[39] In 1990, the Tongass Timber Reform Act designated 300,000 acres of wilderness and eliminated the most egregious provisions of the Alaska National Interest Lands Conservation Act, such as the forty-million-dollar annual subsidy for timber harvest in Alaska, but did little to slow the pace of logging.[40] Despite these victories, below-cost logging nationally remained unaddressed.

In the 1980s, when environmental reform increasingly divided Democrats and Republicans, the below-cost reform campaigns appeared unique in their potential to build bipartisan consensus. While wilderness advocates counted on Democratic support, they hoped that below-cost arguments would also draw support from conservative Republicans and the Reagan administration. Indeed, in the 1980s, fiscal responsibility, reducing "big government," and promoting free-market economic policies were a centerpiece of the conservative political agenda. The Reagan administration supported deregulating industries, such as air travel, banking, trucking, and telecommunications, and it had called for dismantling the nation's network of social welfare programs. Wilderness advocates saw an opportunity to harness that agenda to environmental reform. As the *Washington Post* editorialized, "[W]hen so many other forms of federal support are in jeopardy, there is no excuse exempting [public lands subsidies]."⁴¹ Indeed, it seemed such deregulation was imperative after Congress passed the Gramm-Rudman-Hollings Act in 1985, which aimed to eliminate the nation's deficit. But the below-cost argument held little sway within the Reagan administration or with western congressmen. How they negotiated the contradiction between their public lands policies and their fiscal conservatism is especially clear in the case of grazing reform.

Cattle and sheep were the omnipresent and unrelenting agents of ecological change on the nation's western public lands in the nineteenth and twentieth centuries. The interaction of cattle, which graze selectively, and plants, which exhibit varying degrees of resiliency, transformed much of the western landscape: grazing reduced species diversity, encouraged invasive species, and undermined basic ecological processes, such as nutrient cycling and ecological succession. Over time, grazing could alter entire ecosystems: grasslands gave way to creosote bush, sagebrush gave way to cheat grass, and perennial streams eroded into gullies. And grazing was widespread. During the twentieth century, 165 million acres of public domain lands and 103 million acres of national forest lands were leased for grazing. Research by range managers, scientists, and the federal government indicated that much of the land was overgrazed. But the problem, as Thomas Fleischner explained in 1994, was that "the destruction caused by livestock grazing is so pervasive and has existed for so long that it frequently goes unnoticed."⁴²

The real reason wilderness advocates had avoided picking a fight over grazing was the political power of ranchers, who have long played an outsized role in public land debates in the West. Western ranching on federal lands was trivial to the nation's beef industry: only 2 percent of cattle producers held leases on the public lands.⁴³ Some ranchers were small operators, for whom the leases were essential to their ranching operations. They often counted on public pasture, paid extra for ranches that included government leases, and considered their grazing leases a right, not a privilege granted by the federal government. For this reason, the small family rancher was often at the heart of debates over grazing.⁴⁴ But many ranchers did not fit that profile. The biggest and most powerful ranchers were wealthy interests, like the Mormon Church, Metropolitan Life Insurance Company, and J. R. Simplot, the Idaho potato magnate. It was these politically well-connected and entrenched interests, not family ranchers, who controlled the majority of grazing leases. But, as Bernard DeVoto remarked in 1947, the myth of the independent West "has always made the small Western operator a handy tool of the big one."⁴⁵

A deadline put grazing back on the political agenda in 1985. Grazing fees had last been a point of public debate in the mid-1970s, in the wake of FLPMA. In 1978, Congress passed the Public Rangelands Improvement Act (PRIA), which set grazing fees at a low rate that was pegged to the market price of beef, at least until the policy was set to expire in 1985.[46] To outsiders, it looked like a sweet deal for ranchers. Under the PRIA formula, grazing fees had fluctuated between a high of $2.36 per animal per month (AUM) in 1980 to a low of $1.35 per AUM in 1985.[47] Ranchers, however, argued the PRIA formula was no giveaway: access to public lands was often difficult, ranchers had to pay for improvements such as fences and watering holes, and they had to deal with the federal bureaucracy. But as the expiration of the PRIA formula approached, pressure to raise grazing fees grew.[48] Indeed, a government study indicated that ranchers paid one-fifth of market rates to run their livestock on public lands, the revenue from grazing permits was insufficient to cover federal costs, and most federal grazing lands were overgrazed.[49]

Congress had until December 31, 1985, to adopt a new grazing fee policy. Initially, it appeared that fiscal conservatives and environmentalists might join together to reform federal grazing practices. The Office of Management and Budget took the lead, appealing to a basic principle: "This administration is committed to the philosophy that those who benefit from a specific federal service should pay the costs of providing that service where charges can reasonably be applied."[50] The Wilderness Society saw environmental benefits in raising grazing fees. It would have the effect of "remov[ing] cattle and sheep from the more marginally productive lands" and raising revenue for the management of federal grazing.[51] In 1985, Congress entertained legislation to double or triple grazing fees. But neither Democrats nor Republicans proved capable of advancing the proposal against the overwhelming opposition of western Republicans. As Senator Alan Simpson (R-WY) put it, enacting those proposals would raise fifteen million dollars a year, which was hardly "enough money to wad a shotgun."[52] The issue stalled in congressional gridlock in 1985, leaving the question of grazing fees open.

Western Republicans turned to an alternative policy pathway to advance their agenda: executive action. After congressional legislation stalled, twenty-eight senators and forty representatives called on the president to resolve the debate. Republicans avoided the issue of fiscal responsibility in making their case and appealed to another Republican political formula grounded in family values and community stability. Senator Simpson warned that higher grazing fees would force many hardworking but embattled ranching families to default on their mortgages.[53] Senator Jake Garn (R-UT) went even further, predicting that raising grazing fees would "destroy the family rancher's way of life and the spirit or even the existence of some western communities."[54] In late 1985, the Reagan administration considered its options, which included doing nothing, freezing rates for a year to allow for congressional action, or issuing a presidential executive order to retain the PRIA formula.[55] As Reagan deliberated, western senators leaned on the administration. Simpson reminded the president that "it was Western Senators who carried the water [for the party] and we would sure appreciate his help on this one."[56] In February 1986, Reagan sided with western ranchers and signed an executive order that extended the PRIA formula indefinitely.

The Wilderness Society never organized around grazing reform with the same conviction as it did around below-cost logging. Its opportunity came in the late 1980s, with the return of a Democratic majority in the Senate. Two legislative proposals were on the table. First, local wilderness advocates in Oregon proposed a wilderness bill for the public domain which phased out all grazing over ten years. It was the first wilderness proposal to challenge the grazing covenant included in the Wilderness Act.[57] Second, a group of Democrats, led by Representative Mike Synar (D-OK), moved grazing fees onto another policy pathway: the congressional budgeting process.[58] Internally, the Wilderness Society acknowledged the importance of grazing as an issue and in 1988 it began a full-scale investigation of its economic and ecological consequences.[59] But the Wise Use Movement was growing in the West, and the society's western staff saw an anti-grazing campaign as a political mistake. Three regional directors warned that if the Wilderness Society allowed "our enemies to claim that our real goal is the destruction of the livestock industry, we will pay dearly in Congress."[60] The Wilderness Society never followed through on the grazing study, never became a leader on the grazing issues, and withdrew support for any wilderness legislation that did not allow the continuation of grazing—a position the organization maintains today.

These campaigns to reform below-cost logging and grazing pointed toward important changes in public lands politics. In both cases, economics raised new policy questions that aligned with the emerging concerns of conservation biology. And, in both cases, Congress proved unable to effect reform. Instead, both below-cost logging and grazing reform highlighted the growing importance of alternative policy strategies.[61] In the case of logging and grazing fees, reform hinged on the arcane arena of the congressional budgeting process, which allowed for little discussion and debate over the merits of reform. And the most decisive action on grazing reform was President Reagan's executive order on grazing fees, which was still in effect in 2011. In both cases, wilderness advocates had raised key questions about the economic and ecological consequences of public lands policies. While the Wilderness Society and other national groups proved hesitant to follow those arguments to their logical conclusions—fearing the backlash a sustained campaign against logging or grazing might provoke—a new generation of public lands advocates, carrying less political baggage, would have no such hesitations.

The Spotted Owl, the Ancient Forests, and Conservation Biology

The below-cost argument against logging gave public lands advocates a powerful tool to pry open the timber industry's grip on the national forests, except in one crucial case—the Pacific Northwest. By the Forest Service's measure, the region's timber program was an engine of economic growth, returning nearly four dollars to the federal treasury for every dollar spent in 1985. Those timber operations contributed to the employment of 126,100 people, accounted for more than one-quarter of Oregon and Washington's economic activity, and supported local school and road budgets (one-quarter of federal timber receipts went to the counties in which the logging took place to make up for lost tax revenues).[62] In short, in the Pacific Northwest logging on the national forests was good business for the Forest Service, communities, industry, and workers. Following that logic, the timber industry had cleared more than 85 percent of the region's old-growth forest by the mid-1980s.[63]

Wilderness advocates had already staked a claim to the public lands pie in the Pacific Northwest. Between 1964 and 1984, 5 million acres of wilderness had been protected in Oregon and Washington, and the hardest fought contests were over lower-elevation forests. Wilderness advocates won some important victories, such as protecting the Salmon-Huckleberry Wilderness in Oregon and the Salmo-Priest Wilderness in Washington, both of which included cathedral-like forests of old-growth firs and hemlocks, 175 to 850 years old, that stood as tall as 200 feet. But the timber industry, the Forest Service, and their allies in Congress had fought doggedly to exclude commercially valuable forests from new wilderness areas. The high stakes in the Pacific Northwest made public lands debates especially divisive. In the 1960s and 1970s, environmentalists had rallied to save specific areas, such as French Pete in Oregon. In the late 1970s and early 1980s, mainstream and more radical wilderness advocates split over RARE II in Oregon. And in the early 1980s, activists from Earth First! began organizing road blocks and conducting tree-sits in Oregon and

Washington. Despite this array of legislative, legal, and extralegal activities aimed at protecting the region's old-growth forests, none had succeeded in shaking the timber industry's or the federal land agencies' hold on the national forests. Two chains of events in the 1980s, one scientific and one administrative, finally put the timber industry on the defensive and threatened to fundamentally change the scope and scale of logging in the Pacific Northwest.

The spotted owl showcased the new role for conservation biology in public lands management. Conservation biologists, inside and outside of government, studied the species' life history, range, habitat needs, and population dynamics and played an active role in determining agency policy. This first chain of events, which was driven by scientific research and conservation biologists' new commitment to advocacy, began with scientists such as Eric Forsman, an Oregon native and Forest Service employee. The second chain of events followed the Forest Service's new administrative rules under the NFMA. In 1982, the agency finalized procedures for logging, recreation, wilderness protection, and forest planning. And, most important for the spotted owl, the agency spelled out its responsibility for protecting "viable populations of existing native and desired non-native vertebrate species" in the national forests. Taken together, the scientific concern for the spotted owl and new rules for protecting species gave wilderness advocates leverage in the debates over logging in the Pacific Northwest which would have implications for forest management nationwide.[64]

Eric Forsman's interest in the spotted owl started at home. In 1970, Forsman adopted a sickly owlet he discovered in the Oregon Coast Range. The owl, which earned the nickname "Fat Broad" because of her tendency to overeat, became his backyard boarder, research subject, and family member. Over the next decade, Forsman earned his masters and doctorate degrees from Oregon State University for his research on the spotted owl in Oregon. In the field, he used radio telemetry to observe the home range size, foraging patterns, and roosting behavior of spotted owls. He collected thousands of pellets to document the owls' diet and searched the forest to learn their nesting patterns. At home, he recorded his observations of Fat Broad's molts, vocalizations, and other behaviors. In the early 1970s, Forsman alerted state and federal officials and environmental organizations to the threat to the spotted owl.[65] Forsman played a crucial role in helping to develop plans to protect the owl in the late 1970s, 1980s, and 1990s. Fat Broad played her own role in owl politics too, often accompanying Forsman to visit classrooms and meetings and posing for photo opportunities.[66]

Spotted owls were few: three to five thousand nested in the forests of west-

8.2 Eric Forsman, a Forest Service biologist, with Fat Broad, the spotted owl he adopted in 1970 and cared for until 2002. Courtesy Eric Forsman.

ern Washington, Oregon, and northern California. They are small: spotted owls weigh about a pound and a half, have wingspans of forty inches, and are dark brown with light spots. And they are inconspicuous: like most owls, spotted owls are nocturnal, fly quietly, and nest out of sight in tree cavities. Forsman's research played an important role in raising concern about the owl's dependence on large patches of old-growth forests. His telemetry work indicated that spotted owls had large home ranges (2,270 to 8,040 acres) and foraged and roosted primarily in old-growth forests (92 and 97 percent of the time, respectively). His observations suggested that the owl depended on the old-growth because of the greater availability of prey (such as flying squirrels, voles, and mice), the cover forests provided from predators (namely, great horned owls), and the availability of preferred nesting sites (especially cavities in old-growth Douglas-fir trees).[67] Even if the spotted owl was easy to miss in the forest, it was hard to miss the debate about the spotted owl in the late 1980s. As one bumper sticker instructed, "Save a logger—kill a spotted owl."[68]

The Forest Service took the initiative on owl protection. Following early action by the states of Oregon and Washington to give special consideration to the owl in the late 1970s, the agency accorded the owl special status as an indicator species for old-growth forests. The agency's draft regional forest plan in 1981 gave special attention to the owl, and in the early 1980s the agency began to pursue and support research on the owl and its habitat needs. In 1984, the agency hosted a research symposium. The following year, the agency published an edited volume summarizing owl research. An agency scientist explained, "The accumulated information shows that spotted owls need old-growth forests to maintain healthy populations."[69] Questions remained: What constituted a viable population of spotted owls? How would invasive species, such as barred owls, interact with the spotted owl? Just how much old-growth habitat was necessary to protect the owl? The debate was never about whether the owl was at risk or if it depended on old growth—those facts were established from the start. The debate was over who had the authority to decide how to balance the needs of the owl with the region's timber industry: Congress, the federal land agencies, the industry, or scientists?

The Wilderness Society was part of a loose coalition that saw the owl as a central component of a broader campaign to save the Pacific Northwest's old-growth forests. The question was how to accomplish that goal. Few had invested more in answering that question than Brock Evans, the feisty lawyer who had been the Sierra Club's Pacific Northwest staffer in the late 1960s and early 1970s. Evans, now at the National Audubon Society, described the future of the region's timber industry this way: In twenty years, all Pacific Northwest forest would be second-growth timber. The question was whether the timber industry would fell the last remaining old-growth timber in the near term, or, preferably, make the transition to harvesting second-growth sooner and leave the remaining old-growth standing. Evans did not think the future of the region's forests would turn on the fate of the owl or the "learned papers of scientists." This was the "time to mount the last offensive to save our old growth forests," he said, "all of them we can."[70] That meant a political campaign that rallied citizens to protect big trees (rather than owls), drew public attention with adopt-a-forest campaigns and slide shows, and advanced a new legislative goal—an Ancient Forest Preserve System.[71] Evans and his allies envisioned a citizen-oriented legislative campaign modeled on the Wilderness Act that looked to Congress, not the Forest Service, for action. In the late 1980s, the National Audubon Society, Wilderness Society, and local environmental groups laid the framework for what became the Ancient Forest Alliance.[72]

While national groups looked to Congress, the Forest Service continued to take its own steps to protect the owl. Indeed, the agency had to meet its obligations under the NFMA to protect a minimum population of at-risk species and their necessary habitat. What did that mean in the case of the spotted owl? In 1984, the agency proposed protecting 375 owl pairs in Oregon and California by setting aside 550 1,000-acre old-growth forest habitat areas. Environmentalists responded to those plans by appealing the decision to the Forest Service, arguing the plans did not incorporate recent science or comply with applicable environmental laws.[73] To resolve the appeal and subsequent debate, the Forest Service undertook a supplementary environmental impact process, an advisory panel of scientists co-sponsored by the National Audubon Society studied the issue in 1987, and an interagency scientific panel initiated by Congress produced its own report in 1990.[74] The government committee, under the leadership of Jack Ward Thomas, a member of the Society for Conservation Biology and a well-respected agency forester, outlined a plan to protect fewer, but larger, blocks of habitat (193 areas averaging 40,000 acres each), each of which would support more owls (twenty pairs, where possible), be clustered to facilitate dispersal between reserves, and limit clear-cut logging in surrounding forests.[75] In 1984 the Forest Service proposed setting aside approximately 500,000 acres of old-growth forest to support the owls; in 1990, drawing on the lessons of conservation biology, that proposal had swelled to protect more than 7 of the remaining 8.9 million acres of old-growth forest.[76]

The campaign to protect the owl and the forests began to gain momentum in the late 1980s, and it moved most quickly on administrative and judicial pathways. Declining numbers of spotted owls, the Forest Service's unwillingness to limit timber sales in old-growth forest, and the requirements of key environmental laws, including the NFMA, NEPA, and ESA, created several opportunities to challenge federal policy in court. In 1987, the Sierra Club Legal Defense Fund filed suit against the Bureau of Land Management (which managed one million acres of old-growth forest in Oregon) for offering timber sales without complying with NEPA's requirements for environmental reviews, particularly with respect to the spotted owl. In January 1987, a small Boston-based organization petitioned the federal government to list the spotted owl as an endangered species.[77] That petition failed, but the Sierra Club Legal Defense Fund followed up on behalf of twenty-eight other environmental groups with a more comprehensive petition in November 1987. That petition was rejected, and subsequently appealed. Lastly, the Sierra Club Legal Defense Fund sued the Forest Service in early 1989 for failure to follow through on its obligations under the NFMA to protect the owl (which the agency argued would be unnecessary if the government instead protected the owl as an endangered species).[78] The fate of the owl and the Ancient Forests turned on these legal strategies.

The Wilderness Society and its allies saw this strategy as politically problematic. It was no secret the Forest Service's approach to species management was vulnerable to legal challenge.[79] It was also evident that the owl provided a useful proxy for protecting the Ancient Forests. Andy Stahl, who crafted the legal strategy for the Sierra Club Legal Defense Fund, described the owl as "the perfect species to use as a surrogate" for protecting the old-growth forests.[80] But the national groups viewed the legal strategy as a political gamble that risked pitting the fate of the owls against the fate of the region's workers. Brock Evans argued that the trick in the Pacific Northwest was going to be "preserving options for old growth protection" while not "precipitating a false jobs crisis that leads to congressional override."[81] The concerns were the same at the Wilderness Society. Its strategists estimated that if the courts halted timber sales in all old-growth forests, 5,000 workers in Oregon and Washington would immediately be thrown onto the unemployment rolls. They knew how this would play in the media: two workers unemployed for each owl saved.[82] For that reason, the Ancient Forest Alliance continued to push for a legislative compromise in the late 1980s.

But the action was in the courts. Instead of an open, deliberative legislative process to protect the spotted owl, the three legal strategies formed a complex and closed policy arena in which the region's timber sales hinged on judicial decisions. And in the late 1980s and early 1990s, despite numerous delays, appeals, and countersuits, one by one, each decision went in favor of the environmentalists and the owl. In November 1988, a federal court agreed that the government had been "arbitrary and capricious" in its decision not to list the spotted owl under the ESA; in June 1990, the government formally listed the owl as a threatened species, which required the government to protect the spotted owl and the habitat it depended upon, and develop a restoration plan. In March 1989, a federal court agreed that the Forest Service had demonstrated a "remarkable series of violations" of the NFMA and issued a temporary injunction on timber sales in and around spotted owl habitat. And in June 1992, after lengthy appeals and congressional intervention, a federal court issued an injunction against timber sales in spotted owl habitat on Bureau of Land Management (BLM) lands on grounds that the agency had not complied with NEPA's requirements for environmental reviews. Taken together, these judicial decisions required the government to develop coherent plans to protect the owl before timber sales on federal lands in the region could continue.[83] Most immediately, it meant that as of the spring of 1992, all new old-growth timber sales on federal lands were shut down. Between 1988 and 1992, the timber harvest from federal lands in the Pacific Northwest dropped by 30 percent and the volume of new timber sales dropped by more than 80 percent.[84]

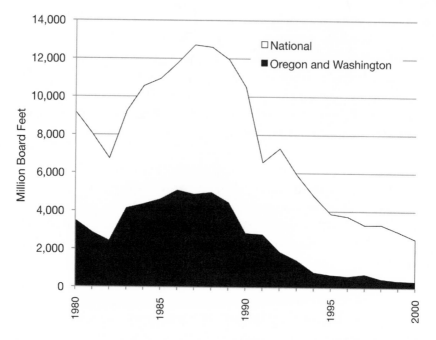

8.3 Timber harvests from national forests in the Pacific Northwest constituted a significant share of national forest timber harvests until the 1990s, when the debates over the spotted owl and Ancient Forests led to reductions in logging.

The decision sparked a swift and angry response among rural western-ers. After the temporary injunction in 1989, logging trucks roared through the streets of downtown Seattle. Logging families handed out Douglas fir seedlings to passersby in the street.[85] Jeannette Basl, a Wise Use leader, explained that the issue was not just endangered species, it was "endangered people."[86] The Oregon Lands Coalition's rallying cry became "Put People Back into the Envi-ronmental Equation."[87] From their perspective, the "Endangered Species Act . . . focused only on biological matters and gives no consideration to the impact of listing on human activity."[88] The timber industry warned that 160,000 jobs were at stake.[89] This caught the attention of both the Bush White House and regional politicians: in their view, federal forest policy had become arbitrary, unpredict-able, and mired in environmental bureaucracy. The Bush administration tried to delay the decision to list the owl as threatened in 1989 and took executive action to exempt some timber sales from the requirements of the ESA.[90] Con-gress entertained numerous bills to develop a legislative resolution in the late 1980s and early 1990s, none of which gained momentum. Instead, its only sub-

8.4 Pro-logging demonstrators in Grants Pass, Oregon, May 15, 1989. Photograph by David J. Cross. Courtesy of *High Country News* and David J. Cross.

stantive intervention came in October 1989, when Congress responded to the March 1989 injunction with a one-year temporary agreement that authorized new timber sales, put potential spotted owl habitat areas off-limits to logging, authorized the interagency scientific task force and, most troubling to environmentalists, blocked appeals and legal suits of the newly authorized sales. That temporary solution did prop up timber sales, but the temporary law itself was challenged in court, only deepening the crisis in the Pacific Northwest.[91]

The spotted owl debates marked a crucial turning point in public lands politics. A decade before, who would have guessed environmentalists would nearly shut down the Pacific Northwest timber industry? This was not the work of national groups and their legislative strategies or Earth First!ers and their sit-ins and protests. Instead, it was the work of lawyers, judges, and conservation biologists.[92] The interests of a non-human species—the spotted owl—and a scientific rationale for protecting it that was grounded in conservation biology formed the fulcrum for far-reaching changes in federal forestry policy. The lessons and engagement of conservation biologists proved crucial in the judicial proceedings. First, drawing on population ecology, scientists emphasized that the owls could not be thought of as one large population; instead, the most applicable theory described the owl as a metapopulation of numerous subpopulations linked together by migration and interbreeding over time and space. Mark Shaffer, who worked for the Wilderness Society in the early 1990s, pioneered such research.[93] Second, drawing on island biogeography theory and forest structure, conservation biologists focused new attention on the importance of protecting large reserves. The smaller a reserve, the greater the percentage of the reserve is exposed to changes in vegetation, climate, and community structure at the edges, which diminishes the interior habitat on which a species depends. David Wilcove, the Wilderness Society's chief scientist in the mid-1980s, had pioneered this research and served on the 1989 interagency scientific task force. The spotted owl debate left Wilcove "more convinced than ever that conservation biology is something novel, useful, and exciting."[94]

The Wilderness Society never succeeded in leading the environmental movement's strategy on the spotted owl and the Ancient Forests. If the Wilderness Society had succeeded, the policy discussion regarding the future of the Pacific Northwest's forests would not have been so narrowly focused on the fate of the owl. Since 1987, the Wilderness Society had tried to foster a wider debate about the structural issues driving the regional timber industry's decline: mechanization and exports were reducing employment in the wood products industry, more logs were being exported to Asia rather than being processed at mills in Oregon and Washington, and the timber industry had clear-cut most of its private lands, which was intensifying demand on the public lands.[95] The timber industry's problem was not the spotted owl. The Wilderness Society invested considerable analytical and outreach work in crafting policy solutions such as raising taxes on exported logs, instituting tax credits for domestic mill expansion, and providing government funds to retrain workers. These proposals formed an important part of the legislative proposals to protect the Ancient Forests and restructure the region's economy in the late 1980s and early 1990s. Jeff Olson, a Wilderness Society analyst, argued that "careful planning for sustainable economic development" could create a "win-win scenario that protects old growth and jobs."[96]

But those broader concerns were often eclipsed by a legal strategy that turned most sharply on the status of the spotted owl, the technicalities of the NFMA, and the research of conservation biologists. When the spotted owl was listed as threatened, Larry Tuttle, the Wilderness Society's regional director, said he felt as if he were "in a boxing match, arms tied to my sides." Once again, the debate collapsed into "cute birds vs. sobbing millworkers' children [and] elitist environmentalists vs. vacant school buildings."[97] What was in the public interest? Arguably, protecting the owl and the forests and restructuring the region's economy was in the public interest. But that was not what brought the future of the region's forests to the forefront of public debate. It was the lawyers and scientists who had advanced a much narrower argument in defense of the owl—not with the Forest Service, or Congress, or the public, but with federal judges. And that suggested there was much more work to be done before the debate over the spotted owl and the Ancient Forests could be resolved.[98]

Wilderness, the Arctic National Wildlife Refuge, and Energy

The Wilderness Society's expanding agenda for public lands and environmental reform was the centerpiece of the organization's efforts in the mid-1980s. But those efforts often proceeded separately from its wilderness campaigns. This was true within the organization. Its policy agenda on forestry and grazing was spearheaded by its office in Washington, D.C., which housed the organization's leadership, the RP&E, its scientific team, and its media offices. More specific wilderness campaigns were coordinated by the society's regional offices, such as those in the northern Rockies and California. This was true outside the organization. The most active arenas of the policy agenda were often administrative rulemaking and appeals, congressional budgeting, and the courts, while Congress remained the most important arena for wilderness protection. But in some cases, the organization's efforts to advance a broader agenda for environmental reform and its specific work on wilderness intersected. This was the case with the debate over the economics of domestic energy production, energy efficiency, and the future of ANWR's coastal plain in the late 1980s and early 1990s.[99]

The Reagan administration had made opening up ANWR's coastal plain for petroleum exploration a priority since James Watt's tenure in the Department of the Interior. When the Alaska lands act became law in 1980, it designated 8 million acres of ANWR as wilderness. Despite the urging of environmentalists and Alaska Natives, Congress left the fate of the 1.5-million-acre coastal plain undecided, pending further study. Two events were important to future debates over the refuge. In 1983, the Reagan administration arranged a land swap between the Inupiat village of Kaktovik and the Arctic Slope Regional Corporation, giving the Native-run corporation rights to 92,000 acres of land inside the refuge on the Arctic coastal plain. If Congress opened the refuge to drilling, the Inupiat stood to profit from leasing their land. That move split the Natives who had generally supported wilderness designation for the refuge in 1980.[100] In 1987, the Department of the Interior released a comprehensive report on the coastal plain that emphasized a one-in-five chance of a 3.2-billion-barrel oil field, the need for a small production infrastructure covering 6,000 acres of land, and the area's ecological value.[101] Drawing on the infrastructure and strategies developed at Prudhoe Bay, the Reagan administration, the petroleum industry, and the state of Alaska claimed that oil exploration in the refuge need not force a choice between developing energy resources and protecting the environment. "I think we can do both," said Secretary of the Interior Donald Hodel. Amid sharp debate, Congress appeared poised to open the region to petroleum exploration in 1989.[102]

But that proposal ran aground with the Exxon *Valdez*. On March 24, 1989, the *Valdez* was loaded with 1.26 million barrels of North Slope crude oil, which had been pumped from Prudhoe Bay through the Trans-Alaska Pipeline to Valdez. As the 980-foot tanker headed south through Prince William Sound and toward the open waters of the Gulf of Alaska, it began maneuvers to avoid icebergs that had calved from the Columbia Glacier to the north. The ship never returned to the designated shipping lane. Instead, it breached its hull in the shallows of Bligh Reef. At the time, the captain, who had been drinking before leaving port, was in his quarters. Within hours, 257,000 barrels of crude oil (enough oil to fill 125 Olympic-sized swimming pools) spilled into the clear waters of the sound.[103] Within a week, the oil had fouled 1,100 miles of shoreline, disrupting the region's marine ecosystem and the lives of the Alaskans who depended on the sound for their livelihood.[104] It was the worst oil spill in American waters, prior to the explosion of the *Deepwater Horizon* oil rig in the Gulf of Mexico in April 2010.

The reprieve for ANWR did not last long. In August 1990, Saddam Hussein's Iraqi military forces invaded neighboring Kuwait, and U.S. and allied forces commenced the Persian Gulf War in January 1991. Petroleum production in the Middle East was disrupted, and the price of oil jumped from seventeen dollars a barrel to forty dollars between July and October 1990.[105] In February 1991, the Bush administration responded with a national energy strategy that promoted domestic energy production and diversification. President Bush promised that "never again will this nation's energy well-being be swayed by events in a single foreign country." The strategy focused on new fuel sources for vehicles (such as ethanol and natural gas) and alternative energy sources (such as solar and nuclear). Bush called on Congress to pass a domestic energy policy that would "maintain an uncompromising commitment to energy security and environmental protection."[106] There was one non-negotiable point: the Bush administration promised to veto any legislation that did not open ANWR for petroleum exploration.[107]

The Wilderness Society positioned ANWR as a vehicle for organizing a campaign to reform national energy policy. This was a new strategy for the Wilderness Society. In the late 1960s and early 1970s, the organization had purposefully chosen to limit its agenda to wilderness and public lands issues. But in the mid-1980s, even before the Exxon *Valdez* ran aground or the Persian Gulf War began, the Wilderness Society actively engaged in a broader environmental campaign. In February 1987, Frampton argued that "only a balanced energy policy for the 1990s, emphasizing energy conservation and development of alternative sources" can lead to energy independence. "Destruction of our remaining wilderness cannot."[108] In 1990, the Wilderness Society pursued foundation support for policy research focused on energy efficiency in buildings, vehicles, and power plants. Frampton publicly argued for enacting a carbon tax, raising the price of gasoline, improving auto efficiency, creating incentives for energy conservation, and regulating greenhouse gas emissions.[109] In 1991, the Wilderness Society's public affairs director summed up the organization's goal. It was to shift the argument over the refuge "out of the Arctic 'battlefield'" and into "a broader energy policy arena."[110] Within the environmental community, the hope was to join energy security and environmental reform to redefine the debate over energy—it was a strategy the nation's environmental community rallied around in the early 1990s.[111]

The energy debates never moved past two specific issues in 1990 and 1991, however: raising fuel efficiency standards for automobiles and drilling in ANWR. Environmentalists yoked these two issues together in 1989, emphasizing that improving automobile fuel efficiency would save far more oil than the refuge could ever produce.[112] In 1990, legislation to raise fuel efficiency standards by 40 percent over ten years nearly passed with the support of environmental groups and the leadership of Senator Richard Bryan (D-NV).[113] The policy would have dramatically changed the American automobile industry, requiring cars to get forty miles per gallon by 2001. The Sierra Club described the proposal as the "cornerstone" of a "safe national energy policy."[114] But concerns about the impact on Detroit automakers and the idea that Americans would be forced to drive small cars combined to sink the proposal in 1991. The Bush administration threatened a veto, and Republicans filibustered. The next spring, after the Persian Gulf War, Senator Bennett Johnston (D-LA), chair of the Senate Energy and Natural Resources Committee, tried to strike a deal on new energy legislation. He proposed opening the refuge for drilling and raising fuel efficiency standards as part of a comprehensive energy package that included incentives for energy conservation, nuclear energy, and more. The proposal fell apart in committee. When the legislation went to the full Senate, it included provisions to open the refuge but omitted mandatory fuel efficiency standards. Johnston pushed for a deal. "To just say no to any compromise on ANWR is to say no to a national energy policy and yes to reliance on the Middle East for the lifeblood of our economy."[115]

Neither the Wilderness Society nor its allies were willing to make ANWR a bargaining chip in national energy policy. The refuge was the only remaining stretch of the Arctic coastal plain protected from drilling. The coastal plain was an extraordinary assemblage of resident animals, such as musk oxen, grizzly bears, and Dall sheep, and migratory animals, including polar bears, Arctic terns, and the Porcupine caribou herd. Many Natives, especially the Gwich'in Indians living on the south side of the refuge, wanted the region protected and opposed any development that threatened the seasonal migration and calving of the caribou. Sarah James, a Gwich'in Indian, acknowledged that the issue split between oil and wilderness in the lower forty-eight states. But for the Gwich'in living on the edge of the refuge, she explained, it was a "question of survival." She argued that "any sound national energy policy must work on energy gains that will last forever," not a "temporary fix of fossil fuels" that would destroy another Native culture.[116] Scientific estimates indicated that the refuge could produce 3.2 billion barrels of oil over twenty-five years. Bill Horn, a congressional staffer and longtime champion of Alaskan development, described it as "by far the most outstanding frontier oil and gas area left in the United States." But opening the region for energy development meant threatening the nation's most exceptional wild landscapes for what would amount to less than 3 percent of the nation's annual petroleum needs.[117]

The energy industry pegged the environmental community as reactionary obstructionists with only one concern: safeguarding ANWR. A Mobil advertisement featured a Wyoming politician complaining, "Against ANWR, against nuclear, and against hydro. . . . Theirs is not an energy policy. Theirs is not a national security policy. It is the essence of no policy at all."[118] But that was an unfair indictment. As Frampton explained internally to his staff, with or

8.5 Sarah James, a Gwich'in Indian leader, protesting plans to open the coastal plain of ANWR to energy exploration, ca. 1989. Courtesy Conservation Collection, Denver Public Library.

without ANWR, the Johnston bill was "bad energy policy, bad for consumers and bad for the environment as well."[119] The legislation limited citizen review of nuclear power plant siting, weakened existing air and water quality laws, and expanded energy production in sensitive environmental areas. What was missing from the legislation were policies that would redirect American energy policy, explained Frampton, such as "investments in energy efficiency, conservation, and alternative sources."[120] The legislation did include provisions for new fuel efficiency standards and energy efficiency measures, but the provisions were voluntary. Indeed, the bill did far more to promote the fossil fuel industries than it did to put the United States on a path toward a more sustainable energy policy. In November 1991, a filibuster by Senate Democrats brought the Johnston energy bill to a halt. Senator Paul Wellstone (D-MN), who led the filibuster, described it as a "special-interest bill" with "something . . . for every oil company."[121]

Senate Democrats picked up the remaining pieces of the energy bill in 1992, hoping to capitalize on the waning momentum of the Persian Gulf crisis, and struck a deal on a final energy bill in October, just before the federal elections. The final law still included provisions considered favorable to energy interests, such as deregulating the electric utility industry, expanding natural gas production, and providing one billion dollars in tax relief for independent oil and gas producers. It also streamlined the permitting for hydroelectric dams and nuclear power plants. But many of the changes addressed environmental concerns. The bill included modest incentives for renewable energy technology, new standards and incentives for building efficiency (which were mandatory for federal buildings), support for alternative fuels for vehicles (such as ethanol), and support for energy- and climate-related research.[122] The best-known program to emerge from the bill was the federal government's Energy Star labeling system. But to move the legislation through Congress, Senate Democrats dropped drilling in ANWR and increases in auto efficiency standards.

The Arctic National Wildlife Refuge had become a powerful—and problematic—symbol in American environmental politics. To proponents of drilling, the refuge had come to represent a commitment to domestic energy production and national security. In 1995 and 2005, Republican-led Congresses nearly opened ANWR's coastal plain. The most sustained attempt came in 2005, under President George W. Bush's leadership. Likewise, auto efficiency standards represented the nation's best—but most controversial—strategy for addressing petroleum consumption. During the 1990s and early 2000s, fuel efficiency standards remained unchanged, as a booming market for low-efficiency vans, pick-up trucks, and sport-utility vehicles propped up American automakers. The most significant changes in fuel efficiency standards came in 2005, when Congress first raised fuel efficiency standards to 35 miles per gallon, and in 2009, when the Obama administration accelerated the timetable for implementation to 2016.[123] For the Wilderness Society and its allies, it became clear how difficult it was to use ANWR as a vehicle to advance a broader agenda for energy reform. In the early 1990s, some critics faulted national groups for putting wilderness protection, and ANWR in particular, before a broader commitment to environmental reform.[124] While that may have appeared to be the case to some observers, it was not the case behind the scenes. The Wilderness Society's failed strategy had been organized around a broader campaign for energy reform, not just the protection of ANWR as wilderness.

Conclusion

The Wilderness Society played a crucial role in opening up a new era of public lands reform in the 1980s and early 1990s, drawing on new strategies grounded in natural resource economics, conservation biology, and existing environmental laws to raise the possibility of far-reaching public lands reform, such as ending below-cost logging and grazing and fundamentally reshaping the timber harvest to protect endangered species. This turn in public lands politics runs counter to some assumptions about the trajectory of American environmentalism. Critics often describe the mainstream American environmental movement as on the retreat in the 1980s and 1990s: growing political opposition put environmentalists on the defensive, the new professionalism of environmental advocacy blunted the environmental agenda, and attention shifted from expanding environmental protection to maintaining existing laws. As a result, critics argue the American environmental movement retreated from more ambitious positions in the 1960s and 1970s—such as calling for an end to all pollution, addressing population growth, and effecting corporate reform—and moved toward more pragmatic and moderate strategies in the 1980s and 1990s.[125] But that generalization does little to explain the trajectory of public lands advocacy, which became more ambitious, more contested, and more volatile in the 1990s. Instead of retreating from earlier ambitions, these strategies marked an expansion of the goals for public lands reform.

Despite the sophistication of these new policy agendas, they prompted little decisive action in Congress. This is not surprising, considering the broader shifts in American politics in the 1980s and 1990s. Congress's success in achieving policy reform had generally been on the decline since the 1960s across all policy issues, not just environmental ones, and it reached a low point in the late 1980s and early 1990s.[126] What explains the gridlock? The commonsense answer is divided government: between 1980 and 1993, neither the Democrats nor the Republicans controlled the House, Senate, and White House simultaneously. But that had not been a prerequisite for environmental reform in the 1970s, when Nixon was president and Democrats controlled Congress. Nor would a Democratic Clinton administration and Democratic Congress end the gridlock starting in 1993. Scholars have offered other explanations for gridlock. Some have pointed to changes internal to Congress, such as a new emphasis on budgetary concerns, more frequent use of filibusters, and weakening party discipline.[127] Others have attributed the problem to a proliferation of interest groups. A growing number of interest groups, each with its own agenda, and each effectively involved in the policy process, made reform inefficient. One observer described this phenomenon as "demosclerosis." Too many interest groups "begin to choke the system that bred them, to undermine confidence in politics, even to erode political stability."[128] And, in the case of environmental policy, the tendency toward gridlock increasingly pushed environmental reform onto alternative policy pathways, such as congressional appropriations, judicial review, and executive action and administrative rulemaking.[129] Each of these arguments helps to explain the gridlock and policy action that would define this era of public lands politics in the 1990s.

But it is worth remembering that the most important explanation for legislative gridlock in the case of public lands reform may also be the most straightforward: advocates' hopes for public lands reform were far more ambitious and less coordinated starting in the late 1980s than they had been in the 1960s and 1970s. For the first time in American history, public lands advocates seemed poised to upend the existing state of regulatory affairs on the nation's public lands and usher in a new era that put concerns for biodiversity, wild lands, and ecosystem processes before economic development. As the Wilderness Society's president, Jon Roush, announced before Congress in 1994, the time had come for Congress to put the Forest Service on a new course that made "protection of biological diversity and maintenance of natural ecosystem function . . . the fundamental goals for national forest management."[130] Such goals unsettled the arena of public lands politics: it challenged the multiple-use framework, it posed a more direct threat to the resource industries and their political allies, and it demanded more ambitious and difficult political action in Congress. It was one thing to ask for a slice of the public lands pie, but another to ask to change the recipe for public lands management nationwide. This shift helped precipitate a new era of instability and gridlock in public lands politics in the 1990s which posed new challenges for the federal land agencies, the resource industries, and, most immediately, the Wilderness Society itself.

9 / THE NEW PROPHETS OF WILDERNESS

n the late 1980s and early 1990s, a proliferation of local and regional organizations charged public lands advocacy with new energy. The Arizona-based Wildlands Project promised to join grassroots environmental activists and conservation biologists behind science-based proposals for wilderness and the public lands. In the mid-1990s, it proposed protecting and restoring not 10, not 25, but 50 percent of the land in the United States as wilderness. The Montana-based Alliance for the Wild Rockies harnessed that strategy to a new vision for the Greater Yellowstone Ecosystem. In the 1980s, it first proposed protecting 15 million acres of interconnected wilderness areas, parks, and private and public lands in Montana, Idaho, and Wyoming to protect the region's biodiversity, more than five times as much land as national wilderness groups suggested. And the Oregon-based Native Forest Council rallied activists around an ambitious goal: ending all logging on federal lands nationwide. In place of endless scientific study and weak regulatory enforcement, the Native Forest Council argued that the virtue of "zero cut" was its simplicity; it required no interpretation, no studies, and no complex regulatory oversight.[1] Its "sole purpose [was] saving the last of America's priceless virgin forests."[2] Each of these organizations had different strategies, but they shared one conviction: they had no use for the leadership of the Wilderness Society, the Sierra Club, or other national organizations. As Mat Jacobson, an emerging leader for forest reform, argued, "The nationals are fading. They have had their day. This is ours."[3] Dave Foreman, Earth First! cofounder, described these new strategies and organizations as the beginnings of a "New Conservation Movement."[4]

When we remember the environmental politics of the 1990s, it is often the challenges from the political Right that appear to have been most pressing. But the Wilderness Society's leadership knew that it faced challenges from across the political spectrum. Christopher Elliman, the chair of the Wilderness Society's Governing Council, noted privately, "It seems ironic that just as we approach an apogee of intellectual leadership in natural resource and

public lands issues, the [Wilderness Society] is faced with so many immediate questions about its future message, finances, and leadership."[5] Since 1986, the Wilderness Society had consolidated its technical expertise, expanded its cadre of economic, scientific, and policy analysts, and maintained its leadership role on public lands policy. In these ways, the Wilderness Society had helped open a new era of public lands reform that raised broad questions about resource extraction, biodiversity and ecosystem protection, and long-range planning for the public lands. But in the early 1990s, the consequences of those strategies were unclear. Much of its legislative agenda was trapped in congressional gridlock. And the Wilderness Society faced a cacophony of critiques from environmental justice advocates, supporters of the Wise Use Movement, and more ambitious advocates for public lands protection.

Political scientists have noted two dominant trends in the structure of modern environmental advocacy: first, the steady growth in the number of environmental organizations since the 1960s, and, second, the crucial role of well-staffed and well-funded national groups that provide the resources, stability, and resilience necessary for the environmental movement to participate in the policy process.[6] Neither of these trends, however, accounts for the surge of local environmental advocacy in the late 1980s and early 1990s or its significance. Political scientists have often assumed that the well-established national organizations have been the dominant force in environmental advocacy. But that argument, while still relevant in the 1990s and today, better explains the structure of the environmental movement in the 1970s and 1980s, which concentrated power in the national groups, than it does environmental advocacy in the 1990s and 2000s, in which the initiative was increasingly distributed among local groups, ad hoc coalitions, national environmental groups, and foundations. In the early 1990s, the Wilderness Society found itself trying to work with, catch up to, and rein in the New Conservation Movement and its ambitions for the future of the public lands.

The Political Authority of the Mainstream Environmental Movement

Jon Roush was hired as the Wilderness Society's new president in October 1993. His charge was clear: to restore the organization's confidence in its mission. The Governing Council noted frankly, "The internal reality at the Wilderness Society is that there is fuzziness about what we do: a congruence of mission and image is badly needed."[7] The Wilderness Society's expanding public lands agenda in the 1980s had pulled the organization in multiple directions. By the early 1990s, with a staff of 125, an office in Washington, D.C. and ten regional offices, it was a large organization with a number of productive, but under-coordinated, programs. The economic recession in the early 1990s hit the organization hard: between 1990 and 1995 its membership dropped by 30 percent to 250,000 and its budget by 15 percent to fifteen million dollars. Roush brought a wealth of experience in environmental advocacy, from his work at the Nature Conservancy and in environmental consulting, to the Wilderness Society. During the early 1990s, he led the Wilderness Society through a sustained period of self-study and reorganization.

Groups such as the Wilderness Society were once confident and successful in speaking for the public interest. Consider Howard Zahniser's rhetoric in the early 1960s. "We are advocating a program for the people of the United States of America," wrote Zahniser. "We are asking the *whole* people to espouse something that we, in our conviction of the public interest, have come to regard so highly that we will put great effort into it." And Zahniser emphasized it was the breadth of public support that was most important. "When the wilderness law is enacted it will be the whole nation who will be for it."[8] Zahniser was not alone in making such claims on behalf of wilderness, nor were such claims limited to public lands issues.[9] Such confidence in the value of environmental regulation for all Americans was characteristic of much of the advocacy and legislation important to the origins of the modern environmental regulatory state, including the Wilderness Act, clean air and water legislation, and the Endangered Species Act.

That formula of reform liberalism, which emphasized the role of an active government and involved citizens in protecting the public interest, had faced sharp challenges from the political Left and Right. But in the 1970s and early 1980s those challenges served to strengthen the national environmental groups' political confidence. National environmental leaders responded with confidence both to conservative efforts to roll back environmental reform and to radical efforts to revolutionize public lands protection. Remember how effectively the Wilderness Society responded to the Reagan administration and the Sagebrush Rebellion and how little success Earth First! had in affecting the strategies of the national environmental groups in the early 1980s. This was not the case a decade later. When Jacobson said the nationals "have had their day" or Foreman implied the nationals represented the "old" conservation movement, those arguments struck a chord, but not solely because of shrinking budgets or new ambitions. Such statements marked a broader set of political challenges to the authority of the national environmental groups that stemmed from the prolif-eration of local advocacy groups organized around alternative approaches to and agendas for public lands reform in the late 1980s and early 1990s.

The Wise Use Movement represented one such challenge that put the Wil-derness Society on the defensive. As one staffer warned, "We need to be very careful not to attack the little guys. These folks have legitimate concerns, and if we don't honestly understand that, or if we have no sympathy for them, then we really are the elitist snobs they say we are."[10] Like the Sagebrush Rebellion, the Wise Use Movement aimed to loosen environmental regulations on the public lands, increase the autonomy of communities and states, and promote the interests of the natural resource industries. Unlike the Sagebrush Rebel-lion, which most effectively allied itself with the interests of western states and industry, the Wise Use Movement worked to organize itself as a social move-ment that defended the rights of westerners and forged a new approach to envi-ronmentalism. Instead of emphasizing states' claims to overseeing public lands within their borders or the importance of logging to the timber industry, Wise Use emphasized the rights of homeowners to develop their property, the rights of ranchers to graze cattle on public lands, and a new approach to environmen-talism that better integrated human concerns into environmental protection. Wise Use described environmental regulations as infringements on the rights of individuals and the interests of local communities. That strategy unsettled national groups in ways the Sagebrush Rebels never did. Had the Wilderness Society lost touch with local citizen groups in the West? Was Wise Use winning on its policy agenda? Was the Wilderness Society losing the battle in the media and the public eye?[11]

Environmental justice advocates also challenged the Wilderness Society's claims to speak for the public interest. Despite the gains of the modern envi-ronmental movement since the 1970s, such as policies to curb air and water pollution and hazardous waste, environmental justice advocates highlighted the failure of those policies to address the most pressing concerns of minor-ity and disadvantaged communities, such as Native Americans or African Americans. Studies showed that many such communities faced disproportion-ate exposure to pollutants, hazardous waste, and other environmental threats. In 1991, the first National People of Color Environmental Leadership Sum-mit released a statement of seventeen principles of environmental justice. The overarching theme was that each individual had a right to a safe and healthy environment, to self-determination, and to participate in the environmental regulatory process. In advancing these claims, environmental justice advocates faulted not only the government and industry, but, more specifically, the main-stream environmental groups. In their view, groups like the Sierra Club had failed to engage minorities in environmental concerns and gave little attention to the issues that concerned them most. In short, the national environmental groups had not succeeded in representing the broad public interest. Instead, in the words of scholar Giovanna Di Chiro, they remained most concerned with a "mainly white, middle-class, and uncritically 'preservationist' political culture" that prioritized "wildland preservation and endangered species protection," and did little to address issues of environmental injustice.[12]

Clearly, the Wise Use Movement, the environmental justice movement, and the New Conservation Movement all aimed to move environmental poli-tics in very different directions in the early 1990s. Wise Use advocates wished to weaken the environmental regulatory state. The environmental justice move-ment aimed to restructure regulations to ensure environmental protection for all, with particular attention to safeguarding minority and disadvantaged com-munities. And the New Conservation Movement aimed to shift the balance of public lands management decisively toward protecting biodiversity. But in two crucial ways, these divergent responses to environmentalism aligned to challenge the political authority of the national environmental groups. First, and most obvious, each directly challenged the priorities, strategies, and orga-nization of national groups like the Wilderness Society. Second, each move-ment gave new attention to a narrower set of rights-based political arguments that advanced the interests of specific constituencies more than they appealed broadly to the public interest. Wise Use appealed to property and constitutional rights, environmental justice appealed to individual rights, and the New Con-servation Movement gave specific attention to the rights of nature. Such spe-cific rights-based claims undermined the broad and sweeping claims on behalf of the public interest that characterized an earlier era of American environ-mentalism. While the early 1990s may have marked the "apogee of intellectual leadership" for the Wilderness Society, it marked a low point for its political capabilities, within both the public lands and the environmental community more broadly. In these ways, the new conservation movement—represented by groups such as the Wildlands Project, Alliance for the Wild Rockies, and the Native Forest Council—heightened the challenges the national environmental movement already faced.

Earth First! to the Wildlands Project

The transition from Earth First! to the Wildlands Project highlights the changing relationship between more radical local groups and more moderate national groups in these years. Dave Foreman, cofounder of both Earth First! in 1980 and the Wildlands Project in 1991, explained that the Wildlands Project aimed to marry "conservation biology" with a renewed commitment to grassroots conservation activism.[13] To many observers, the Wildlands Project appeared to simply be Earth First! minus the monkeywrenching, but it was more complex. Three overlapping circles of thought and activism that gathered energy within Earth First! in the late 1980s informed the rise of the Wildlands Project: the biocentric philosophy of Deep Ecology, conservation biology's commitment to political outreach, and the changing configuration of radical and national environmental activism. Each of these three influences could be considered independently—indeed, conservation biology had its own internal logic rooted in the sciences—but it was the intersection of these circles of thought that became so powerful. The most dynamic arena of wilderness thought and activism in the late 1980s and early 1990s emerged from growing alliances that joined activist scientists, local citizen groups, and more radical environmentalists behind expansive, biocentric proposals for wilderness protection. Earth First! had begun to make those connections in the 1980s; the Wildlands Project completed that circuit in the early 1990s. The result electrified public lands advocacy.

Earth First! is often remembered for making real Edward Abbey's fictional *The Monkey Wrench Gang* (1975). Although the group's extralegal activities—tree spiking, blockades, and office sit-ins—captured the most attention, it is worth remembering that Earth First! also formed an active arena of intellectual exchange and debate regarding the goals and strategies for environmental reform. The philosophical roots that inspired Earth First! and informed the Wildlands Project can be traced back to Arne Naess, a Norwegian philosopher and environmental activist. Naess argued that the environmental movement could be divided into two separate currents: "a shallow, but presently rather powerful movement, and a deep, but less influential movement, compete for our attention." Naess argued the mainstream movement, with its pragmatic and reform-oriented agenda, exemplified "shallow ecology." Naess contrasted such forms of "shallow ecology," which focused on protecting human health and the interests of the privileged, with a "deep ecology" that plumbed the fundamental relationship between humans and the natural world.[14]

The connection between Earth First! and Deep Ecology was not obvious, at first. In Naess's view, Deep Ecology represented a holistic outlook that emphasized biospherical egalitarianism and an appreciation for natural and human diversity. He encouraged socioeconomic equality, fighting pollution and resource depletion, respecting the complexity inherent in human relations, and promoting local autonomy and decentralization.[15] In fact, he gave no particular attention to wilderness or wild lands at all. While Earth First! may have claimed Edward Abbey for inspiration, Deep Ecology most profoundly shaped its structure and priorities: Earth First's embrace of a biocentric worldview, its decentralized organizational structure, and its strong critique of the national environmental groups all reflected tenets of Deep Ecology.[16] In Foreman's words, "Our philosophy, our worldview, our *religion* must be one of Deep Ecology. Biocentrism."[17]

Even as Earth First! borrowed from Deep Ecology in the early 1980s, the organization turned the philosophy to its own ends—wilderness. In 1983, Earth First! set forth its vision for the future of wilderness in the United States. Foreman, Bart Koehler, and Howie Wolke, all cofounders or leaders of Earth First!, were of an ambitious mindset. In the lower forty-eight, their largest proposed reserves—to protect the Great Basin, the Great Plains, and central Idaho—measured in the millions of acres (larger than most states back East). As they explained, "these would not be puny and truncated wild areas now protected as parks and wilderness areas."[18] They proposed protecting 716 million acres of land, 37 percent of the continental United States. They acknowledged their proposal might seem "impractical and outrageous" in the context of the "bizarre utilitarian philosophy that separates one species (*Homo sapiens*) from its place in the biosphere." The proposal was far-fetched. But, in many respects, it was a blueprint for the work of the Wildlands Project in the early 1990s.

To translate that broad vision into more specific regional plans, Earth First!ers began to draw on the science of conservation biology in the mid-1980s. Reed Noss, an Ohio native with long-standing interests in the outdoors and nature conservation, emerged as a crucial go-between. By day, Noss was a graduate student in the Department of Wildlife and Range Sciences at the University of Florida, working on his Ph.D., which he received in 1988. In 1983, Noss published a paper that focused attention on nature reserves as components in regional networks of interconnected habitat that would be more than the sum of its parts. This "regional landscape approach" to conservation drew on the theories of conservation biology, focused on large-scale conservation planning, and aimed to protect endangered species by preserving large

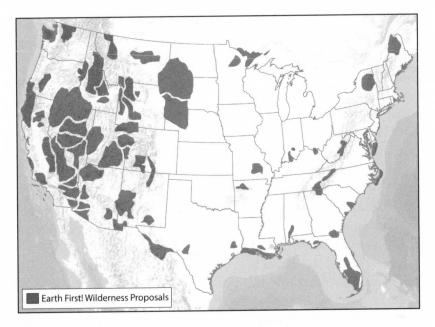

Map 9.1 In 1983, Earth First! outlined a proposal for 716 million acres of wilderness areas in the continental United States. Although that proposal was not taken seriously at the time, such far-reaching plans were central to the work of the Wildlands Project in the early 1990s. Map adapted from "Earth First! Wilderness Preservation System," *Earth First! Journal*, June 1983.

wild areas—themes which would emerge as central to his scientific research and policy activism.[19] By night, Noss was an active member of Earth First! in Florida and a contributor to the *Earth First! Journal*. Locally, Noss helped coordinate Earth First! activities in the mid-1980s, including protests, sit-ins, and other actions aimed at protecting habitat from development. Nationally, Noss became the leading scientific contributor to the journal, writing articles, reviewing conservation proposals, and emerging as a de facto consulting scientist to Foreman and David Johns, the editors. In Noss's view, it was time for activists to focus on the big picture and to adopt a "warlike mentality." That meant acknowledging that conservation biology is "more value laden than any" other science, explained Noss. "It has to be."[20]

Noss was not alone in drawing new connections between ethical values and conservation biology. Even as conservation biology emerged as a new field of interdisciplinary study, with all the trappings of academic respectability, in the mid-1980s—including a peer-reviewed journal, a professional society, and scientific sponsors at institutions ranging from Harvard and Stanford to the Universities of Florida and Oregon—some of the most active conservation biologists saw their work as aligned with the ethical concerns of Deep Ecology. Michael Soulé, president of the newly founded Society for Conservation Biology, suggested a basic set of values informed conservation biologists' outreach in the mid-1980s: "diversity of organisms is good," "ecological complexity is good," "evolution is good," and "biotic diversity has intrinsic value." Soulé singled out the last claim for special attention: "Species have value in themselves, a value neither conferred nor revocable but springing from a long evolutionary heritage and potential or even more from the mere fact of its existence." Soulé explicitly described conservation biology's ethical framework as an "ecosophy"—a term Naess invented to describe Deep Ecology in 1973.[21] It was an association Naess welcomed. Naess praised conservation biology for finally returning academic ecologists to the public arena in 1990.[22]

Conservation biology began to reorient Earth First!'s vision for wilderness protection starting in the mid-1980s. Foreman described wilderness as the "arena for evolution" and emphasized that it "must be large enough so natural forces can have free rein." To explain how to do that, Foreman and other contributors to Earth First! increasingly drew on concepts such as keystone species, biogeography theory, and minimum viable population studies to describe and justify wilderness proposals that prioritized conserving biological diversity, included habitat corridors between reserves to facilitate migration and genetic exchange, and protected large areas to guard against habitat fragmentation.[23] Islands, core areas, corridors, and networks became watchwords in a new vision of wilderness protection that flourished within Earth First!. The *Earth First! Journal* published a series of large-scale regional proposals for wild lands protection: 17 million acres in California deserts, 11 million acres in the Greater Yellowstone Ecosystem, and 19 million acres in the Southwest. Each proposal called for ending hunting and grazing and creating "human exclosure areas" that prohibited all human presence.[24] In place of the state-by-state approach to wilderness protection that had dominated the Forest Service and Bureau of Land Management (BLM) wilderness reviews and the work of the national groups, Earth First! aimed to follow ecological boundaries that put scientific imperatives before political convenience.

In the late 1980s, Earth First! formed a dynamic arena for reconceptualizing the scope and goals of wilderness protection nationwide. But even as those ideas gained new energy, the organization itself had begun to splinter. Since the mid-1980s, Earth First! had grown. By 1987, more than 10,000 people subscribed to the *Earth First! Journal*. Some Earth First!ers explored ambitious plans for wilderness protection. Others focused on monkeywrenching and direct action. Some factions retreated into eco-anarchism, social ecology, and misanthropy. A dark undercurrent of anti-humanism had begun to well up in Earth First!, coming into public view in the mid-1980s and staining its already controversial reputation. The *Utne Reader* republished an article from the *Earth First! Journal* that argued AIDS was a natural solution to a growing world population problem.[25] In the end, however, those ethical trespasses did not precipitate Earth First!'s internal collapse. Sometime in the mid-1980s, the Federal Bureau of Investigation's anti-terrorism division began the undercover investigation of Earth First! that culminated in the arrest of several Earth First!ers in Arizona, including Foreman. By the time Foreman extricated himself from legal accusations, by entering a plea bargain, he had become a stranger to a changing Earth First!. Out of the fragmentation of Earth First! emerged a new organization focused on a biocentric vision of wilderness grounded in conservation biology. In 1991, Foreman and a handful of Earth First! veterans, and Noss and an activist-oriented group of conservation biologists joined together to form the Wildlands Project.

This transition from Earth First! to the Wildlands Project marked an important waypoint in the relationship between radicalism and public lands politics. In the mid-1980s, despite Earth First!'s ambitions to transform broader debates over the public lands, its ties to monkeywrenching and undercurrents of misanthropy had overshadowed its rationales and goals for public lands protection. Foreman was publicly known for describing famine in Africa as nature's efforts to restore balance to the human population.[26] In comparison, the Wildlands Project and its allies focused foremost on the science of conservation biology and actively distanced their work from the controversial moral and political claims which tainted Earth First!. Nor had Earth First! ever become a vehicle for mobilizing a broader array of citizens or citizen groups in public lands activism. As a result, while Earth First! drew considerable media attention, it remained a marginal player in debates over public lands policies. For instance, Earth First!'s 1983 proposal to protect more than one-third of the United States as wilderness drew little attention. In comparison, the Wildlands Project more effectively positioned itself as an alternative to the national groups for citizen activism. While national leaders could dismiss Earth First! "as more fun, games, and potential backlash," neither the Wilderness Society nor the Sierra Club exhibited such assurance in response to the Wildlands Project or the New Conservation Movement in the early 1990s.[27]

The Wildlands Project and the New Conservation Movement

The Wildlands Project was meant to be a response to an immediate and catastrophic problem: Earth faced the biggest extinction crisis in four billion years;
one-third of species were at risk of extinction in the next thirty years; and over-
population and overconsumption were driving habitat destruction worldwide.
And while much attention had been focused on the fate of tropical forests, the
future of ecosystems in the United States was crucial too. But beneath these
material problems, Dave Foreman explained that the real problem was the idea
"that human beings are separate from and superior to the natural world." To
address both the biodiversity crisis and this cultural problem, Foreman, the
Wildlands Project, and the New Conservation Movement focused foremost on
protecting and restoring wild lands. "On a practical level, this means that conservationists must no longer look on National Parks, Wilderness Areas, and
other protective classifications as natural museums, outdoor gymnasiums, [or]
scenic art galleries." Instead, he argued, "We must rethink the role of Wilderness Areas and Parks, and consciously design them so they maintain and help
restore biological diversity." Groups from the Wilderness Society to the Society
for Conservation Biology had begun to reorient their arguments for wild lands
protection to emphasize biodiversity.[28]

When the Wildlands Project was founded in 1991, its goals evoked Earth
First!'s beginnings, even as it moved in a different direction. Its financial support came from Doug Tompkins, founder of Esprit Clothing and The North
Face, through the Foundation for Deep Ecology.[29] The Wildlands Project was
small: two years later, only 2,500 people subscribed to its journal. Its cofounders included leading conservationists, such as Reed Noss and Michael Soulé,
and veteran leaders of Earth First!, such as David Johns and Howie Wolke. Two
strategies were central to the Wildlands Project. First, as it positioned itself to
engage in public policy, instead of allying with national groups, it aimed to
build a "new conservation movement." And, second, the Wildlands Project also
represented the changing understanding of the role of wilderness in protecting
biodiversity and ecosystems: it gave new emphasis to wild lands restoration,
regional-scale wild lands planning, and scientific and ethical arguments (rather
than more pragmatic arguments) for wilderness.

The Wildlands Project was both a response and catalyst to a flourishing of
local public lands advocacy that began in the late 1980s and gained momentum
in the early 1990s. The ranks of the New Conservation Movement included
groups formed in the mid-1980s to engage in the local forest plans mandated

by the National Forest Management Act, other local groups that spun off from Earth First!, and, in a few cases, groups that dated back to the Wilderness Society's grassroots outreach in the 1960s and 1970s.[30] All shared dissatisfaction with the moderate strategies and centralization of national environmental groups, particularly the Wilderness Society and Sierra Club. Most were concerned with advancing large-scale wild lands protection, basic reforms of public lands management, or, in many cases, both. The ranks of the New Conservation Movement included organizations such as Alliance for the Wild Rockies, Native Forest Council, and Oregon Natural Resources Council. These groups became sources of instability in public lands politics, advancing more ambitious policy goals, pursuing independent policy strategies, and often challenging, rather than cooperating with, national environmental groups. As Jim Eaton, a one-time Wilderness Society regional director, argued, "If [the national organizations] will not join the New Conservationists, they should get out of the way."[31]

The melding of science, grassroots outreach, and wild lands protection that defined the New Conservation Movement was apparent in *Wild Earth*, the Wildlands Project's affiliated periodical. Unlike the *Earth First! Journal*, which looked like a tattered news rag, *Wild Earth* was a beautiful publication with elegant hand-drawn illustrations printed on recycled paper. Its pages included a range of articles, some of which touched on immigration, population, and Deep Ecology. But from the start, Foreman made it clear that *Wild Earth* was most important as a venue for the "principles, ideas, and wisdom of the growing science of conservation biology."[32] Contributors included Soulé and Noss and other luminaries, such as E. O. Wilson and Paul Ehrlich. Noss simultaneously served as science editor at both activist-oriented *Wild Earth* and the academic journal *Conservation Biology*. *Wild Earth* featured long scientific articles on topics such as forest ecology, population dynamics, and wild lands reserve protection. In the 1990s, it emerged as the most prominent activist-oriented and science-centric forum for rethinking wild lands protection and conservation biology. "Good science such as conservation biology within the context of a profound respect for life and natural processes is a powerful force for wilderness," argued one longtime wilderness activist. "When transformed into activism it wins converts and puts exploiters on the defensive. It's tough to oppose good science."[33]

The Wildlands Project's mission was to "protect and restore the ecological richness and native biodiversity of North America." It emphasized the need to protect large areas of wild land that represented a variety of ecosystems, protected species, and were large enough to support ecological processes (includ-

9.1 After his arrest for monkeywrenching activities associated with Earth First!, Dave Foreman helped found the Wildlands Project, which advanced large-scale, science-based proposals for public lands protection. Foreman at the Wildlands Project Vision Mapping Northeast Meeting, Sagamore, Vermont, 1993. Courtesy Dave Foreman.

ing succession and disturbance). It emphasized the importance of protecting viable populations of species. Protecting umbrella species such as lynx or grizzly bears, with their expansive habitat needs, could protect 90 percent of the rest of biodiversity in a region. It emphasized that protecting key species and habitat required more than just protecting existing wild lands; it also meant restoring land to a wild and untrammeled state. And the Wildlands Project emphasized the importance of establishing networks of wild lands that included strictly managed core reserves, carefully managed buffer areas, and the necessary corridors to ensure functional connectivity. In short, the Wildlands Project drew on science to advance proposals "to protect wild habitat, biodiversity, ecological integrity, ecological services, and evolutionary processes—that is, vast interconnected areas of true wilderness."[34] A sizable body of theory and research affirmed these convictions.[35]

These ideas were not unique to the Wildlands Project: such concerns had made inroads at other environmental organizations, such as the Wilderness Society and the Nature Conservancy, in the 1980s. Nor were these ideas all new: ecological concerns for wild lands protection dated back to the earliest advocacy of the Ecological Society of American in the 1930s, had long figured in efforts to protect low- and mid-elevation forest lands, and had been central to campaigns such as that for Alaska's public lands. But no organization moved as aggressively to draw on new research in conservation biology to advance an overarching vision for public lands protection as did the Wildlands Project. These ambitions were most apparent in 1993, when Noss, Soulé, and Foreman made a joint presentation to a packed audience at the Society for Conservation Biology's annual conference in Tempe, Arizona. They outlined a proposal for protecting more than 50 percent of the lower forty-eight in core wilderness areas and interconnecting corridors. It was an audacious proposal. In many respects, it was even more far-reaching and ambitious than Earth First!'s 1983 proposal for the future of the National Wilderness Preservation System. But unlike Earth First!'s agenda, which had limited impact outside Earth First!'s loose-knit community, the Wildlands Project's debut at the Society for Conservation Biology drew new attention (and controversy) among conservation biologists, national environmental groups, and even *Science* magazine. *Science* described the proposal as "the most ambitious proposal for land management since the Louisiana Purchase of 1803." The proposal promised to protect the nation's biodiversity in all of its richness and complexity. But, as *Science* noted, "It may be too much to ask of the people who already live there."[36] It was. But that expansive vision played a crucial role in drawing the boundary between the New Conservation Movement and the national groups. It did so most publicly in the northern Rockies.

Thinking Big in the Northern Rockies: The Northern Rockies Ecosystem Protection Act

The northern Rockies occupy an outsized place in the lore of American environmental history. The nation's first national park at Yellowstone had protected the geysers, hot springs, canyons, and mountains since 1872. South of Yellowstone, the Grand Tetons rise like spectacular granite pyramids above the basin of Jackson Hole. And three hundred miles to the north, the ice-carved peaks, basins, and lakes of Glacier National Park crown northwest Montana. Around and between these national parks lay an expanse of public lands—the Madison, Wind River, and Flathead mountain ranges and the watersheds of the Green, Selway, and Yellowstone rivers—home to grizzly and black bears, elk, bison, lynx, and mountain lions. It was this region that environmentalists had begun describing as the Greater Yellowstone Ecosystem in the 1970s.[37] In practice, however, the region was managed piecemeal: oversight was split among three states (Wyoming, Idaho, and Montana), the four federal land agencies, five national forests, and three national parks. And in many places the consequences of such disjointed management could be seen on the ground: clear-cut national forest land bordered Yellowstone's western boundary; bison, elk, and other animals that strayed from the national park in search of winter forage were often shot; and development, such as energy and mineral extraction, vacation homes, and additional logging, were planned in proximity to park borders.

If ecological imperatives could be put before administrative boundaries and politics, then Yellowstone was the place. The beginnings of regional approaches to wild lands protection can be traced to the northern Rockies. Research on the region's wildlife, particularly the grizzly bear, bison, and elk, emphasized that their habitat needs required not just the resources of Yellowstone National Park, but those of surrounding national forests too.[38] In most cases, animals needed to migrate to lower elevations in search of wintertime forage. Research showed that none of the national parks were sufficiently large to protect viable populations of native wildlife. And as the parks grew more isolated and fragmented due to human settlement, land development, and resource development, even the biggest parks, like Yellowstone, were at risk of what scientist William Newmark described as a "faunal collapse."[39] Two issues focused attention on the need for regional coordination in the Greater Yellowstone Ecosystem. In 1987, the Fish and Wildlife Service released preliminary plans to reintroduce the locally extinct gray wolf. That proposal sparked debate over the wolf's extensive habitat needs, state versus federal jurisdictions, and the threat the wolf posed to private property (particularly livestock). In 1988, summertime lightning strikes and human carelessness set Yellowstone's forests ablaze and within ten weeks wildfires had burned 793,000 acres, nearly one-third of the park, crossing into and out of the neighboring national forests. Those events helped spur the work of the Greater Yellowstone Coalition's efforts to promote a regional approach to public lands management in the northern Rockies.[40]

Although both the Wilderness Society's and Sierra Club's staff shared such concerns, neither organization was ready to act on a new regional vision in the late 1980s. Much was at stake in the northern Rockies: 12.7 of 37.4 million acres of the national forests in the states had been classified as roadless areas in 1979, not to mention additional BLM public domain land. But the Wilderness Society and Sierra Club had made the state-by-state approach to wilderness legislation the cornerstone of their strategy. Since RARE II, congressional delegations,

9.2 Smoke billows above Mirror Plateau in Yellowstone National Park in July 1988. Fires burned one-third of Yellowstone National Park that summer, crossing in and out of neighboring national forests. Photograph by Jim Peaco. Courtesy Yellowstone National Park.

state governments, and many stakeholders viewed that approach—with its provisions for compromise on acreage, its soft-release language, and its respect for state boundaries—as the most expeditious strategy for determining the future of wilderness for the roadless areas. But such wilderness legislation for Montana and Idaho had moved forward at a glacial pace. Negotiations traversed familiar territory such as detailed negotiations over release language, water rights, and off-road vehicle corridors, which masked broader concerns over the future of the resource industries, the role of local interests in public lands management, and the power of the federal government.[41] Wise Use was a strong presence in the northern Rockies. It helped elect Republican Conrad Burns as a senator from Montana in 1988, the same year President Reagan vetoed a bill that would have protected 1.4 million acres of new wilderness in the state.[42] Local and state opposition also limited efforts to move wilderness legislation forward for either Montana or Idaho in the early 1990s, despite the active leadership and lobbying of the Wilderness Society and the Sierra Club.[43]

The opposition to such proposals did not come only from Wise Use allies. It also came from the New Conservation Movement. Mike Bader, founder of the Alliance for the Wild Rockies, described the RARE II strategy as an "unmitigated ecological disaster."[44] Even as the national groups moved forward with their proposals, the New Conservation Movement, led by the Alliance for the Wild Rockies and supported nationally by the Wildlands Project, launched its vision for the Northern Rockies Ecosystem Protection Act (NREPA). Dave Foreman hailed the proposal as a "window on today's sea change in conservation policy, theory, and strategy." Foreman described it as "the first wilderness proposal based on island biogeography and conservation biology to be introduced in Congress." It proposed protecting more than 13 million acres of public land in Idaho, Montana, and Wyoming. It included "core ecosystem reserve areas," which were protected as wilderness, and additional "biological connecting corridors" that together formed a functional "ecological reserve system" and could sustain the region's ecosystems, processes, and species. Marking the confluence of science and activism characteristic of the New Conservation Movement, fifty conservation biologists, including Soulé, Noss, and others, such as the pioneering grizzly bear research scientists Frank and John Craighead, wrote a letter to Congress supporting the proposal.[45]

The political fortunes of NREPA reflected the growing tensions between local and national groups. The Alliance for the Wild Rockies moved quickly to line up congressional sponsors in 1990 willing to introduce or cosponsor the legislation in Congress. But that strategy ran afoul of the national groups. In 1990, the Sierra Club and the Wilderness Society worried NREPA might undermine a compromise Montana wilderness bill that was already moving through Congress. They used their influence in Washington, D.C., to block the introduction of NREPA. The move infuriated local activists.[46] "It seems the Sierra Club's paid lobbyists," fumed one NREPA proponent, "will go to any length to ensure that we get no new wilderness unless we ask their permission first."[47] Foreman described it as the "nastiest catfight within the conservation community in recent memory."[48] For the national groups, this was a new problem. Before the 1990s, national groups had served as clearinghouses coordinating wilderness strategy nationwide—such leadership generated tensions, but it had almost always been respected. The rise of the new conservation movement challenged that hierarchy.

A series of events in the fall of 1991 gave new impetus to a regional strategy for the future of the northern Rockies. The Forest Service reaffirmed its commitment to timber production in the region when it fired the regional forester for failing to make the annual timber quota.[49] The National Park Service and Forest Service concluded a joint planning program for the region with scaled-back plans that disappointed many environmentalists. (A result that many credited to Wise Use activists.) And the mining industry pushed for a new gold mine just outside the boundaries of Yellowstone National Park. More than ever, the jigsaw puzzle of administrative oversight threatened the future of the northern Rockies. In May 1992, forty-nine local, regional, and national wilderness leaders met at Redfish Lake Lodge in Idaho to discuss strategy. The meeting included three generations of wilderness leaders: Stewart Brandborg and Clif Merritt, Montana residents and Wilderness Society leaders in the 1960s and 1970s; Bart Koehler, Mike Roselle, and Howie Wolke, cofounders of Earth First!; and Mike Scott and Debbie Sease, rising leaders of the Wilderness Society and Sierra Club. Out of that meeting came a plan to balance the prerogatives of the national organizations with the new enthusiasm and initiative at the local level. One theme stood out: "*avoid in-fighting* (particularly in the public eye)."[50]

The Redfish meeting resulted in a cooperative, but uneasy, framework for national groups and local activists. A regional steering committee would coordinate strategy between local and national wilderness advocates and the wilderness community would pursue a "double-barreled approach" that included state-by-state legislation and "big picture" bills like NREPA. In the 1990s, the national groups pursued several state wilderness bills aggressively, but with little success, as the political tide turned increasingly conservative nationwide. And local advocates focused their energies on NREPA. In 1993, Bart Koehler, the Earth First! cofounder and a longtime wilderness leader, predicted "it will take at least ten years to pass some version of a big picture bill in the Senate."[51] The Northern Rockies Ecosystem Protection Act was first introduced in the House in the 103rd Congress in 1992 with five cosponsors; support peaked in the 108th Congress in 2004 with 185 cosponsors; and the bill remained under consideration in the 111th Congress in 2010. A supportive *New York Times* editorial noted the legislation's long history in July 2009 and suggested it was worth "holding out for a truly wild wilderness bill in the hope that someday politics will catch up with [the bill's sponsors'] farsighted idealism." Notably, none of those cosponsors was from Idaho, Montana, or Wyoming—the states most affected by the legislation. For that reason, as the *New York Times* admitted, the bill "could be waiting a while."[52]

"Zero Cut": The New Conservation Movement and Forest Reform

The New Conservation Movement was redefining the structure of wilderness advocacy in the early 1990s. What was the New Conservation Movement's problem with the national groups? Most obviously, it was that the national groups put political considerations—historic compromises, political access, and pragmatism—before the imperative of protecting the environment. This seemed to be the case with NREPA. But those concerns came bundled with other frustrations that stemmed from earlier tensions between local and national groups. Margaret Hays Young, who would become a forceful proponent of national forest reform, complained that the nationals purported to "'represent' our interests in Washington, D.C. Like elected politicians, our big-time environmental politicians decide what is best for all of us." In her view, the national groups were out of touch with what their memberships really desired.[53] Another activist complained of how the national groups treated local organizations. "The nationals presume to organize—i.e., manipulate—in the only way they know how: from an assumption of superiority" which was a product of their "insider's world of power and politics."[54] These were tensions the Wilderness Society and other national groups were aware of in the early 1990s. The society's Governing Council warned its staff that it had to be "cautious in assuming 'We're from Washington and we're here to help you' attitudes; these attitudes rightly infuriate local activists."[55] But forging a new model of advocacy that valued the work of local and national groups proved difficult. The growing tensions were especially sharp in the case of forest reform.

Forest reform became an increasingly active and disjointed arena of policy debate in the late 1980s and early 1990s, as advocacy groups sprouted beneath the canopy of the New Conservation Movement. In the Midwest, Andy Mahler founded Heartwood to protect the heartland's hardwood forests. Mahler admitted it was "more idea than organization." But the idea was this: the central hardwood forests of the upper Mississippi and Ohio rivers were resilient. How could they be restored? Heartwood's goal was to "broaden the terms of the debate to question the very legitimacy of logging." It was time to "leave the public forests alone."[56] In Texas, Ned Fritz founded Federal Forest Reform, which aimed to prohibit clear-cutting and force a shift to selective logging and the protection of biodiversity. And in Oregon, Tim Hermach founded the Native Forest Council, which aimed to protect the nation's "virgin, old-growth" forests, specifically those in the Pacific Northwest.[57] It was Hermach's group that would gain the most momentum. Its publication *Forest Voice*, Hermach's leadership, and the Native Forest Council's publicity strategy helped propel the Native Forest Council to the forefront of forest reform debates.

In the late 1980s and early 1990s, below-cost timber sales, the spotted owl controversy, the persistence of clear-cutting, concerns about the limitations of wilderness designations, and the national forest planning process all broadened the scope of the forest reform agenda in different and oftentimes conflicting directions. In general, environmentalists aimed to reduce logging on the forests and give new attention to protecting ecological values. But the national groups and the New Conservation Movement were of different opinions about how to achieve that goal. Should the focus be on eliminating below-cost timber sales? (But that strategy did little to protect old-growth forests in the Pacific Northwest.) Should the focus be on transitioning from clear-cut logging to selective logging? (But that strategy could require more roads and intensive forest management.) Should the focus be on protecting the remaining roadless areas in the national forests? (But that overlooked new scientific research that emphasized the importance of protecting a variety of habitats and the growing threat of catastrophic wild fire.) Hermach acknowledged the importance of all the proposals for forest reform—eliminating below-cost sales, using selective logging, ending clear-cuts, and protecting endangered species. "[W]e would like to do all of these things and more," argued Hermach, "but individually, they are only steps along the contested road to Zero Cut."[58]

"Zero cut" was not the Native Forest Council's initial strategy. Hermach founded the group out of frustration with the Sierra Club's cautious approach to forestry policy. He was tired of the club's "willingness to compromise away the forests at any cost."[59] Initially, Hermach focused on legislation to protect the nation's remaining 4 to 5 percent of "virgin, old-growth" forests. "[T]hese are the original, untouched forests that existed when the first settlers arrived in North America."[60] While that argument ignored both a lesson of conservation biology—which emphasized the importance of protecting a range of habitats (not just old-growth)—and environmental history—which demonstrated that no landscapes were untouched by humans—the Native Forest Council's most careful arguments focused on the economics of federal forestry policy. Hermach often emphasized that "[a]s taxpayers we subsidize the timber industry with over two billion dollars a year."[61] In the early 1990s, his frustration mounted with each bureaucratic turn in the debates over the spotted owl and the Ancient Forests. And in 1993, the Native Forest Council took up Mahler's idea for forest reform—an end to all logging on the public lands—and began to work to move "zero cut" to the forefront of forestry debates.

Never before had forest advocates taken such an unyielding stand on timber policy. The position drew support from many groups allied with the New

Conservation Movement. To advance this strategy, the council emphasized economic arguments in hopes of appealing to fiscal conservatives and the public more generally. Hermach argued that without the public subsidies for logging on public lands, the free market would result in better-managed private timberlands and fewer exports of raw timber products to Asia. He claimed that private timberlands alone could meet the nation's domestic wood products needs. The Native Forest Council also linked domestic forest reform to rising concerns for global environmental issues. Since the mid-1980s, the Amazonian rain forests, biodiversity, and global warming had become front-page news. Hermach leveraged these concerns into an argument for domestic forest policy reform. Why was the United States lecturing Brazil on preserving the rain forest, when the United States had felled 95 percent of its native forests (Brazil had felled only 20 percent), and the United States was logging its forests at twice the rate of Brazil? Writing in a *New York Times* op-ed, Hermach concluded "Let's stop logging on public lands and put our forest policies in line with our rhetoric."[62]

"Zero cut" was not so different than the more extreme arguments Earth First! made in the mid-1980s for ending resource activities on the public lands. But where Earth First!ers put their bodies on the line, the Native Forest Council pursued a different set of strategies which ultimately made it a more disruptive force in policy discussions. The Native Forest Council focused on generating national media attention. It worked with LightHawk, a nonprofit organization founded in 1979 to serve as the air wing for environmentalists, helping advocates survey and photograph the public lands. The product was a series of graphic depictions of the consequences of federal timber policy.[63] The Native Forest Council described current forestry policy as a "slaughter" and "holocaust" and the work of "butchers." And, at the same time, it appealed to the public interest, describing national forests as a "birthright" and children's inheritance.[64] These photographs and arguments began to gain public attention, including coverage in the *New York Times*, *Atlantic Monthly*, and *Forbes* magazine. The Native Forest Council also became the champion of a National Forest Protection and Restoration Act, which included proposals to change the economics of forest management, provide alternative economic support to timber-dependent rural communities, end road-building on the national forests, and ban logging.[65] And, starting in 1992, the Native Forest Council actively worked to upend the Sierra Club's timber policy by working through the club's annual election process, with hopes of making "zero cut" the Sierra Club's official forestry policy. These efforts formed a sharp wedge that began to split the New Conservation Movement from the national groups in the early 1990s.

The Pew Charitable Trusts
and a National Campaign for Forest Reform

The start of the Clinton administration in 1993 opened up the possibility for a new direction on environmental policy, including forest policy. George Frampton, president of the Wilderness Society, described it as a "new era of stewardship for our natural resources and environmental assets."[66] And, behind the scenes, national groups worked to shape the administration's agenda by recommending policy priorities and administration nominees. Save America's Forests, the D.C.-based umbrella group for the New Conservation Movement's forest reform efforts, did not enjoy such access, but it also held high hopes for the Clinton administration. Its goals were complete protection for native forest ecosystems nationwide, a shift from timber production to ecosystem restoration, and integrated bioregional proposals to "recreate ecosystems, ecological corridors, and evolutionary preserves, such as the Ancient Forest Protection Act and NREPA."[67] The last time the environmental community's hopes for environmental reform had risen so high was during the Carter administration in the late 1970s.

The Philadelphia-based Pew Charitable Trusts emerged as the driving force behind efforts to consolidate a national forest reform campaign in the 1990s. The source of the multi-billion-dollar trust was the petroleum industry. Between 1989 and 1994, Pew funding for the environment expanded threefold from $6.8 to $20.5 million. Pew's interest in environmental issues ramped up at a propitious moment, when individual donations to many national groups had slumped. Foundation support for the environmental movement, either locally or nationally, mainstream or radical, was not new. The Ford Foundation supported the creation of the Natural Resources Defense Council in 1970, the Richard King Mellon Foundation provided seed funds for the Wilderness Society's Economic Policy Department in 1981, and the Foundation for Deep Ecology bankrolled the Wildlands Project in 1991. But Pew's role in the environmental community was different.

Pew took an increasingly active role in shaping the agendas and strategies of environmental groups in the early 1990s. The *Boston Globe* described Joshua Reichert, who oversaw Pew's environmental program, as a "kingmaker." When Reichert was funding an average grant of $310,000, his "ideas [had] a way of becoming reality." Pew often directed its biggest grants to coalitions, which it described as a "new model for collaborative work among local, state, regional, and national environmental organizations."[68] And Pew's commitment to public lands reform was not token, nor was it passing.[69] Since the late 1980s, Pew had emerged as a crucial player in public lands advocacy; it continued this commitment into the twenty-first century, funding major initiatives such as the Western Ancient Forests Campaign, the American Forest Protection Campaign, Heritage Forests Campaign, and the Campaign for America's Wilderness.[70]

Why the surge in support from the Pew Trusts? Notably, the primary concern was not that the environmental movement lacked technical or professional expertise—which had been the concern in the early 1980s.[71] Instead, as Philip Shabecoff explains in *Earth Rising*, many funders worried that the environmental movement had lost its ability to mobilize citizens, was failing to form effective coalitions, and was not taking advantage of new communications strategies.[72] These concerns informed a wide array of foundation-funded environmental programs in the mid-1990s. The Pew Trusts, for instance, funded large-scale initiatives, such as Environmental Strategies, which aimed to coordinate the policy efforts of the national environmental movement. And it funded specific programs, such as those focused on climate change, pollution, ocean conservation, and forest protection. In the early 1990s, Reichert began discussing a new commitment to build a national forest reform campaign. Pew made it clear from the start that it did not wish to take a piecemeal approach, disbursing funds to the already numerous forest advocacy organizations. Instead, under the leadership of Reichert and Tom Wathen, Pew began laying the groundwork for a multi-million-dollar grant to support a two- to four-year campaign to weld a disjointed advocacy community into a coalition for the national forests. It was no easy task. As one cynical observer noted, the Pew Trusts are "dangling a foundation-size forest-grant in front of a yelping pack of activists. But before it drops the bait, it wants to make sure that the yelping pack can sit up and roll over—if not on command—at least in unison."[73]

The Pew Trusts set in motion a collaborative approach to building a national forest advocacy coalition. In 1993 and 1994, four meetings were held to bring together the full spectrum of forest reform organizations—from Tim Hermach of the Native Forest Council to Brock Evans of the National Audubon Society—to hammer out a campaign proposal for Pew and other major foundations by May 1994. A few broad points of agreement emerged in the spring of 1994: a unified campaign was desirable, local and grassroots activity should be a priority, a national public education campaign was important, and legislative action was the best vehicle for reform. But any specific policy or strategy proposals split the group, and the divisions only grew deeper as the May 1994 proposal deadline approached. Which was more practicable—a national approach banning all commercial or clear-cut logging, or a regional approach adapted to each region's forest and economy? Zero-cutters pushed hard to eliminate all logging. What balance should there be between the national groups and grassroots organizations? The initial tilt of the coalition gave more representation to grassroots organizations. And how should funds be allocated between national initiatives, such as a public education campaign and policy development and lobbying in Washington, D.C.? And which organizations would be responsible for what? To resolve these differences, the Pew Trusts assembled an interim board of directors made up of five representatives from the national groups and eleven representatives from grassroots groups (many of which fell beneath the umbrella of the New Conservation Movement) to forge a proposal under the leadership of Andy Mahler at Heartwood. The initial proposal was for a $10.8-million, three-year grant for an American Forests Protection Campaign. But the Pew Trusts declined to fund it: the final proposal lacked specificity regarding goals and responsibilities, the overall scope was too broad, the budget was too large, and it lacked a clear commitment of support from either national or local groups. Or, to put it another way, despite Pew's encouragement, there was no working coalition united behind a clear set of goals.[74]

Much of the friction in the forest reform community's efforts was the product of a standoff between the zero-cut contingent and more moderate groups. As one participant recounted, the meetings often followed a predictable pattern: One activist would "demand an end to clearcutting and the substitution of selective logging on all Federally owned forests." Another activist (usually Tim Hermach) would retort, "'No selection logging! No logging on federal forests! Zero Cut!'" And then "Pandemonium. Shouting. Debate. Drinking. Repeat."[75] In the spring of 1994, the most outspoken advocates of zero cut reacted furiously to the proposal to the Pew Trusts because it included no explicit language barring clear-cutting. Chad Hanson, who was affiliated with the Native Forest Council, described it as a "vehicle for further rampant clearcutting, even of native forests, on my public forests." He verbally abused other activists who stood up for alternatives. "Do not offend me or anyone else with the 'political realities' argument. What has been done to our forests is a holocaust of a magnitude humankind has never before seen. It is the deepest, darkest moral crime ever perpetrated by our species." Such hyperbole is telling. Who was to blame? Hanson assigned blame foremost to weak-kneed environmentalists beholden to "political realities."[76] Ned Fritz, who founded Federal Forest Reform and remained the most active grassroots proponent of a selective-cut policy, countered "It is time that we consider the zero cut issue resolved and get on with the campaign."[77] Efforts to stitch the community together proved painful. The only general points of agreement seemed to be building grassroots infrastructure and initiating a massive public education campaign, both of which left aside the specific "policy differences which seem to drive us so crazy." In the summer of 1994, the forest reform community assembled a one-year planning grant to "define, organize, and plan and secure funding for a comprehensive, effective, and democratic American Forest Protection Campaign Plan" and to secure the support of a "critical majority" of local and national groups working on forest reform.[78]

One key issue received very little attention among forest reform advocates in the early 1990s: the issue of local forest conditions and, especially, forest health. Since the Yellowstone fires burned through the park and surrounding national forests in 1988, concerns that the public lands were increasingly prone to large-scale wildfire had been growing. Since the early twentieth century, the Forest Service and other federal land agencies had followed a "no-fire" policy. That meant all fires, both human and natural, were extinguished as quickly as possible (instead of being allowed to burn, as would have been the case prior to federal management). The result was that many forests had an accumulation of downed trees, underbrush, and other fuel which could sustain unusually large wildfires. This was old news within the federal land agencies; the Forest Service had been actively concerned about managing fuel loads since the late 1970s. But after Yellowstone, the issue drew public attention. Intense fire years in 1988, 1990, and 1994 amplified such concerns. Several overlapping strategies emerged for managing fire, including prescribed burning, selective logging and thinning, and ecosystem management—all aimed at reducing fuel loads. The question of fire management did arise within the forest advocacy community. As one advocate explained, some conservation biologists have "conclude[d] that Zero Cut may not be the proper solution across the landscape, and that logging in selected cases is necessary to improve forest health."[79] But such arguments were never a centerpiece of policy discussions, either among the New Conservation Movement or the national groups. But it was an issue that would not disappear. In the mid-1990s, forest advocates would be outflanked by their opponents. Supporters of logging in the Forest Service, Congress, and industry would seize on the forest health argument as a mandate for an expedited logging program— what soon became known as the "salvage rider" in the 104th Congress.

There was no breakthrough on forest reform in the mid-1990s. Despite the Pew Trusts' efforts to forge a working coalition, a new wariness clouded the relationship between forest advocates and the Pew Trusts. The leaders of the interim forest board remained optimistic about the "unprecedented opportunity for the forest protection movement, despite some rancor and conflict." Moving forward, the cochair of the interim planning board, Phil Berck, signaled a shift in organizational strategies that many others supported. It was time to "de-link" the work of forest planning from any single foundation. And "the Campaign should embrace a diversity of organizations (diverse in terms of official policy, organizational structure, pay scale, memberships, past blunders, and victories, etc.) Every group has a role."[80] But that approach seemed like a formula for more of the same—the disagreement, inaction, and confusion that had undermined forest reform efforts since the late 1980s. The Pew Trusts took a different approach, one that it had explored in the early 1990s. When Pew began to pick up the pieces of the failed Save America's Forest Campaign, it came away with new priorities. Pew's leadership increasingly "pushe[d] environmentalists to be practical, even if that mean[t] bruising egos or accepting compromises that purists detest."[81] There would be even less tolerance for activists pushing uncompromising positions such as "zero cut" in the future. And in place of the deliberative approach to coalition-building that paralyzed forest advocates in the early 1990s, Pew began to put its organizational muscle behind a more centralized approach run by a "professional campaign manager."[82] That strategy shifted initiative away from the national groups and toward the Pew Trusts. These priorities would take shape during the next major forest campaign: the push for new protection for the national forest roadless areas in the late 1990s, which would be spearheaded by the Pew-funded Heritage Forests Campaign.

Playing Catch-Up
to the New Conservation Movement

Something odd happened in the early 1990s: the Wilderness Society and Sierra Club staffers found themselves increasingly out of the loop. New publications like *Wild Earth* and *Forest Voice*, fax machines, and e-mail put local conservationists in better touch with one another, but not necessarily with national groups. Local activists were gaining places on national steering committees, such as the Pew Trusts forest campaign. They published their own op-eds in national publications like the *New York Times*. And they were going straight to Congress, seeking support for national legislation. It was this changed dynamic that added urgency to the Wilderness Society's institutional crisis in the early 1990s. "Many grassroots groups are springing up where we have traditionally done our best work," noted the Governing Council. Consider the questions the organization entertained in 1993: "What is the role of the grassroots in the future success of the Wilderness Society? What was it we provided to these upstart groups? Why are they so effective?" The Wilderness Society hazarded some answers: grassroots groups could concentrate their resources, they had close ties to the land they wished to protect, and they had energy and sparked innovation. Despite their small size and minimal funding, groups like the Wildlands Project and the Native Forest Council leveraged their arguments, strategies, and enthusiasm to affect the public lands advocacy agenda to a far greater degree than their organizational footprint would suggest. It was clear to the Wilderness Society that new technology had leveled the organizational playing field. All of which suggested to the Wilderness Society that "we need to rethink the role of our federal offices."[83]

Both the Wilderness Society and Sierra Club scrambled to maintain their leadership on public lands reform in these years. As Craig Gehrke, the Wilderness Society's Idaho office director, argued in 1992, the organization had to broaden its approach to wild lands protection. "Otherwise, we'll deal ourselves out of the discussions."[84] The Wilderness Society developed a new framework, the American Lifelands Trust, to reinvigorate its wild lands protection efforts. The program's architect was Mark Shaffer, a Wilderness Society staffer and a conservation biologist. Its goal was to "assemble and maintain a network of public and private lands across the nation that will provide the habitat variety, stability, and continuity essential to maintaining our native biodiversity over the long term."[85] The program aimed to include public, private, wild, and restored lands and to put scientific goals first. Darrell Knuffke, a long-term Wilderness Society strategist, explained that achieving these goals would mean doubling the size of the wilderness system. "[W]e will describe our wilderness proposals differently, map them differently, advocate for them differently," explained Knuffke. "We will draw [boundaries] more and more to include critical pieces of the natural whole and we will use science to defend them."[86] The Sierra Club moved in a similar direction. The Sierra Club's new Critical Ecoregions Program made it a priority to "protect and restore" regional ecosystems across North America. Bruce Hamilton, the Sierra Club's lead strategist, who once dismissed Earth First! and its ecological vision for wilderness as "more fun, games, and potential backlash," described the new program as the work of a new generation of "wildlands advocates, as passionate as the old-timers but much more scientifically savvy."[87]

Forest reform advocates challenged the Sierra Club even more directly. The Sierra Club's bylaws required annual elections, which usually were limited to electing the organization's board of directors, but sometimes included votes on other matters. In 1993, allies of the New Conservation Movement proposed a referendum on the club's logging policy that called for an immediate halt to logging in all sensitive areas, such as old-growth forests, and a phaseout of logging on all public lands. But the measure was opposed by the club's staff and its board of directors, which viewed the proposal as politically unwise and a constraint on the club's efforts on forest policy. When the ballot went to members in 1994, the proposed "zero-cut" referendum was summarized confusingly. When it failed, many supporters of the referendum blamed the outcome on the maneuverings of the club's staff. In 1994, David Orr and Chad Hanson, two activists allied with the Native Forest Council, launched a new campaign. Instead of leaving it to the club's staff to summarize their proposal for the ballot, they cleverly proposed a one-sentence measure: "The Sierra Club support[s] protecting all federal publicly owned lands in the United States and advocate[s] an end to all commercial logging on these lands." In 1995, Orr and Hanson visited Sierra Club chapters nationwide to drum up support for the proposal. The measure won by a margin of two to one. By popular vote, "zero cut" became the Sierra Club's official policy position.[88]

These developments captured a far-reaching, but uncertain, transformation of the public lands agenda. This was not Howard Zahniser's moderate and pragmatic wilderness movement of the 1960s. By the mid-1990s, an expanded scope and ambition for public lands protection—both in the national groups and the New Conservation Movement—had gained new traction. The groundwork for this transformation emerged from within the mainstream groups: the attention to conservation biology and economic analysis had loosened public lands politics from the moorings of a multiple-use framework in the 1980s. But it was the outreach of conservation biologists, the enthusiasm of the citizens who signed on with the New Conservation Movement, and the changing support of the Pew Trusts and other foundations which shifted public lands debates toward a new framework in which biodiversity, ecosystem processes, and wild lands protection were foremost. For scientist-activists, like Reed Noss, who argued that "wilderness recovery . . . is the most important task of our generation," these changes marked initial, but promising, steps in the right direction.[89] But not all observers were so sure. As one scholar observed, these visions for wild lands protection were built on a flawed premise. In the words of Ramachandra Guha, the error was "to equate environmental protection with the protection of wilderness."[90]

The Great New Wilderness Debate

There is one more challenge to public lands advocacy we should consider in the early 1990s: the great new wilderness debate. In 1989, Guha, an Indian scholar, questioned the American fascination with wilderness in an essay titled, "Radical American Environmentalism and Wilderness Preservation: A Third World Critique." Guha warned of the radical wilderness movement's connections to Deep Ecology, the inherent problems of wilderness as a consumer ideal, and the implications of wilderness protection for the developing world. Until the late 1980s, to the extent that scholars gave any attention to wilderness debates and the public lands, most followed the model of Roderick Nash's *Wilderness and the American Mind*, which singled out the importance of wilderness protection in American history and held it up as a model for international conservation.[91] It was that patriotic celebration of American wilderness that Guha took as the starting point for his critique. Many scholars followed in his footsteps, bringing the tools and priorities of new fields of scholarly inquiry to bear on wilderness: attention to Native American studies, the legacies of imperialism, and postmodern cultural studies established a new critical framework within which to reexamine the historical, philosophical, and social implications of wilderness protection.

Consider a few of the most important questions that began to swirl around wilderness in the early 1990s: Did wilderness—pristine, untouched, and unpeopled nature—exist? Many scientists said no. "[S]cientific findings indicate that virtually every part of the globe, from the boreal forests to the humid tropics, has been inhabited, modified, or managed throughout our human past."[92] Some geographers said no, too. William Denevan argued that to idealize the pristine was to fall for the myth of 1492—that North America had been unchanged prior to Christopher Columbus's arrival.[93] Did the American wilderness ideal perpetuate an artificial divide between humans and nature? The philosopher Baird Callicott was one among many who argued this was so. It was the Wilderness Act which described wilderness as a place "where man himself is a visitor who does not remain." In his view, that definition obscured the social consequences of protecting wild lands and limited visions of sustainable approaches that integrated the interests of humans and the environment.[94] Was the wilderness ideal ethnocentric? Critics argued this was true for several reasons. In many cases, wild lands now protected as wilderness had once been homelands for Native Americans, indigenous peoples, and rural communities who were pushed off the land to create an idealized "wilderness." Environmental justice advocates, for instance, argued that wilderness distracted from issues more important to minority and rural communities. Did the wilderness ideal blind Americans to the ecological consequences of their day-to-day activities as consumers? Guha pointed out that wilderness advocacy did little to force American consumers to confront the ecological consequences of their resource-intensive lifestyles. "For most Americans," he wrote, "it is perfectly consistent to drive a thousand miles to spend a holiday in a national park."[95]

What began as a discussion among academics in the late 1980s went public in the mid-1990s. In a provocative essay titled "The Trouble with Wilderness" in the *New York Times Magazine*, historian William Cronon traced the roots of America's fascination with wilderness to two wellsprings: wilderness as remnant of the American frontier and wilderness as emblematic of the sublime.[96] His argument linked formative environmental thinkers, such as Henry David Thoreau and John Muir, with more recent wilderness advocates, such as Dave Foreman and the New Conservation Movement, in a shared veneration of wilderness. Wilderness, he argued, overlooked the historical claims and roles of Native Americans on the public lands, often put a concern for wild nature before the interests of rural communities, and limited the ways Americans often thought about the relationship between society and nature. In Cronon's words, this "wilderness dualism tends to cast any use as *ab*-use, and thereby denies us a middle ground in which responsible use and non-use might attain some kind of balanced, sustainable relationship."[97] One crucial distinction separated Guha's earlier critique and Cronon's essay. When Guha initiated the debate in 1989, his article was a narrow assessment of radical environmentalism, its shortcomings, and its implications for the developing world. In 1995, Cronon criticized wilderness on those familiar grounds, yet he framed his critique as a challenge to the basic assumptions of American environmentalism. Wilderness, he wrote, was "the unexamined foundation on which so many of the quasi-religious values of modern environmentalism rest."[98]

The debate tapped into powerful cultural assumptions and biases that underlay the American wilderness ideal, but to the extent the wilderness debate was framed as a critique of a transcendent American wilderness ideal, it risked simplifying the complexities of wilderness thought and politics. In many respects, the great new wilderness debate was a response not just to a timeless wilderness ideal, but to specific changes in American environmental politics.

The wilderness debate was not borne of the public lands politics of the 1960s and 1970s. In those decades, as wilderness advocates at the Wilderness Society, Sierra Club, and regional organizations helped implement the Wilderness Act, their commitment to pragmatism and compromise offered little traction for such critiques. They emphasized the variety of values important to wilderness (historic, recreational, aesthetic, and scientific), worked to protect land profoundly shaped by human history in the East, and pursued compromises with Indians, Inupiat, and other subsistence users in Alaska. Instead, the wilderness debate makes more sense in the context of the early 1990s: it was informed by the science of conservation biology (which often emphasized the crucial role of wild lands in protecting biodiversity), it captured some of the concerns raised by the Wise Use and environmental justice movements regarding the disregard for the interests of human communities, and it was very much a reaction to the expanded agenda for public lands protection precipitated by the New Conservation Movement.

Conclusion

The balance of power within the public lands advocacy community changed in the early 1990s. Before, if you wanted to get the scoop on the current issues and strategies important to public lands advocacy, your first stop was clear: the national offices of the Wilderness Society or the Sierra Club. In the early 1990s, however, visiting the national groups alone was insufficient. For a full picture of public lands advocacy a visit to the offices of the Wildlands Project in Arizona, the Native Forest Council in Oregon, or the Pew Charitable Trusts in Philadelphia was just as important. Those organizations emerged as new sources of initiative and instability in public lands politics.

Political scientists have rightly looked to the national interest groups as the driving engine in American environmental politics. Groups such as the Wilderness Society and Sierra Club have gained power through their consistent presence in environmental politics, their large staffs, budgets, and memberships, and their accumulation of policy expertise. As the political scientist Christopher Bosso has noted, "there is no doubt that environmental advocacy at the national level in the United States is dominated by a loosely knit community of established organizations."[99] Such analyses have not overlooked the important role of local and grassroots organizations in environmental politics. Nor have they overlooked the adaptability and flexibility of national groups. But in the case of the New Conservation Movement, its original policy proposals and its independence from the national groups, as well as the direct communication among local interest groups and between local groups, foundations, and Congress, all point toward a crucial restructuring in environmental advocacy. In place of the hierarchical structure of advocacy, that made grassroots groups secondary to national groups in the 1970s and 1980s, there developed a more distributed model of advocacy in the 1980s and 1990s, in which the initiative in public lands reform emerged as often from grassroots groups as national groups. This distributed model of advocacy emerged as an important source of instability in public lands politics: It challenged the leadership of groups such as the Wilderness Society and the Sierra Club, contributed to ambitious and far-reaching policy goals for public lands reform, and exacerbated the polarization and volatility of public lands politics.

The New Conservation Movement, however, struggled to effect reform, either through Congress or the federal land agencies. Despite their creativity, no groups affiliated with the New Conservation Movement could match the Wilderness Society's expertise in science, economics, and policy, or its knowledge of and ability to engage the full array of pathways important to policy reform. Linking the ambitions of the New Conservation Movement with the strengths of the national groups proved challenging. Beginning in the mid-1990s, however, the Wilderness Society, the Pew Charitable Trusts, other national groups, and allies in the New Conservation Movement began to lay new foundations for some surprising successes in the late 1990s and early 2000s. The political challenges of the 104th Congress, when Congress swung decisively toward the Republicans, would complicate such efforts, but these new initiatives would yield important administrative actions, such as the Clinton-era national forest roadless rule in the late 1990s, and legislative actions, including a burst of new wilderness designations for unlikely states, such as Nevada, Idaho, and Utah, at the start of the twenty-first century.

10 / THE PATHS TO PUBLIC LANDS REFORM

B ill Clinton's 1992 election to the White House raised high hopes in the environmental community. To many, it seemed the stage had been set for a return to the heyday of environmental politics in the 1960s and 1970s, when a coordinated environmental movement, a friendly Congress, and a proactive White House worked together to advance an active agenda for environmental reform. But those expectations faltered in 1994 when Republicans captured the House and Senate for the 104th Congress, only to be revived during Clinton's second term, and dashed again by George W. Bush's election to the White House in 2000. Consider how quickly events turned: In August 1993, Clinton's new secretary of the interior proposed raising grazing fees on the public lands from $1.86 to $5 per animal unit month (AUM) as part of an environmentally minded overhaul of grazing policy; two years later most reforms had been blocked and grazing fees dropped to $1.61 per AUM. In the meantime, angry westerners hung environmentalists in effigy and vandalized Forest Service and Bureau of Land Management (BLM) offices. In July 1994, President Clinton protected 75 percent of the Ancient Forests important to the spotted owl from logging; the next year, Republicans passed legislation—a salvage logging rider—that temporarily opened some of the same forests to expedited logging with limited environmental reviews and appeals. That led more than a thousand people to march in the streets of Seattle in protest. In 1994, Congress rejected a Republican proposal to protect 1.8 million acres of wilderness across Utah; two years later, President Clinton took executive action to protect that much federal land in a single national monument in southern Utah. Utahns came to the signing dressed as if for a funeral wake. And, in January 2001, President Clinton protected 58.5 million acres of national forest roadless areas in response to the public support of more than one million Americans; but within months, newly elected President Bush took the first steps to undo that protection, signaling the first of many challenges to public lands protection.

What explains this seesaw of environmental politics? Political scientists

Christopher Klyza and David Sousa point to one crucial factor underlying the dynamics of environmental policy in the 1990s and 2000s. As congressional gridlock intensified, they argue it "channeled tremendous political energies down other policymaking pathways, creating considerable instability in policy as policymakers and interest groups have pursued their agendas—sometimes momentous policy shifts—in other venues."[1] Despite pursuing very different policy goals, the Clinton administration, Republican leaders in Congress, and the Bush administration shared a willingness and an ability to circumvent the traditional legislative process to pursue alternative policy pathways, such as executive action, administrative rulemaking, and congressional appropriations. Such strategies were not new, but what had been a trend in the 1980s became a defining characteristic of environmental politics in the 1990s and 2000, especially in the case of the public lands. Equally important was the increasingly contested and expansive agenda for public lands reform that had emerged since the mid-1980s. The most active proposals were not incremental policy changes, but more ambitious reforms of grazing, logging, and wild lands protection policies that directly challenged the western communities and industries dependent on the public lands. A disjointed network of interest groups struggled to effect legislative reform in Congress: the rifts between national groups like the Wilderness Society and the New Conservation Movement had political consequences, especially in the early 1990s, as they divided over strategy for public lands reform.

The Clinton-era roadless rule exemplified these changes. It represented the fruition of efforts to protect the national forests that dated back to the Wilderness Act and before. But the strategies central to the roadless rule campaign suggest that instead of being the last great wilderness campaign of the twentieth century, it was the first national campaign of a new era of public lands reform. The core rationale for the roadless rule was the fiscal unsustainability of existing forestry policies and the ecological importance of roadless areas. Instead of pushing this agenda through Congress, a strategy that had proven politically impossible since the late 1980s, public lands advocates looked to the Forest Service to advance this policy nationally through an administrative rulemaking process. Although the Clinton administration and the Forest Service have been credited most publicly for the roadless rule, a coalition of public lands groups and allies, bringing together local and national environmental organizations under the umbrella of the Heritage Forests Campaign, played a decisive role. For the first time since the Alaska campaign of the late 1970s, public lands advocates joined together in support of a national campaign, one that was distinguished by a new role for grassroots groups, relied on new communications strategies made possible by the Internet, and largely depended upon the oversight and financial support of a single foundation—the Pew Charitable Trusts. The close cooperation between the Clinton administration, the Heritage Forests Campaign, and the public lands advocacy community yielded a robust administrative rule to protect all remaining national forest roadless areas, a rule that faced eight years of sustained legal and administrative challenges during the Bush administration.

The Clinton Administration and a New Agenda for the Public Lands

The environmental community had invested much in Clinton's election: the national groups had provided policy analysis for the presidential debates, given ample advice during the transition period, and suggested and vetted potential presidential appointees.[2] In the beginning, that hard work promised to pay off. Clinton appointed Bruce Babbitt as secretary of the interior. Babbitt had a vision for the future of the public lands and the American West that electrified the environmental community. He was an Arizona native and son of a prominent ranching family. He had worked for the Forest Service in high school, and he prided himself on being an outdoorsman. He had an undergraduate degree in geology from Notre Dame and a law degree from Harvard Law School. As governor of Arizona, he had brokered deals that brought together ranchers and environmentalists. He had also served as president of the League of Conservation Voters, a leading environmental organization in Washington, D.C. To national environmental leaders, Babbitt was one of their own, and he embraced the association. Babbitt took Aldo Leopold's *A Sand County Almanac* as his touchstone and he emphasized the importance of adopting its values: it was time for Americans to rethink their relationship to the land, viewing it not just as property, but as a community of which they were a member. He and the Clinton administration, Babbitt said, were "set on creating a new American land ethic."[3]

Babbitt may have explained his aspirations in moral terms, but what justified his agenda for the public lands was an effort to join the concerns advanced by resource economics and conservation science with new public lands policy. Since the mid-1980s, economic analysis and scientific research had reshaped environmentalists' goals for public lands reform. Those aspirations seemed primed for realization at the start of the Clinton administration. Instead of subsidizing the private use of public resources, such as timber and grazing land,

Babbitt promised the administration would adopt new policies grounded in economic efficiency that would require loggers, miners, and ranchers to pay their fair share for use of the public lands.[4] Instead of setting aside individual national parks or wilderness areas, Babbitt emphasized that it was crucial to think on a larger scale about the threat to wild lands, endangered species, and biodiversity. "Ecosystems do not recognize political and bureaucratic boundaries," Babbitt explained to Congress.[5] Joining Babbitt at the Department of the Interior were two of the Wilderness Society's own: George Frampton, the Wilderness Society's president, was appointed assistant secretary of the interior for fish, wildlife, and parks, and Jim Baca, a member of the Governing Council, was appointed director of the BLM. As the *Washington Post* observed, favorable appointments and strong allies in Congress had "set toes tapping in anticipation at groups such as the Wilderness Society and Sierra Club, and worry beads jiggling at groups that represent the miners, cattlemen, irrigators, and the wood products industry."[6]

The Clinton administration bet that the future of the West was going to lean toward the politics of cities like Seattle, Washington, and Jackson, Wyoming, not timber towns like Forks, Washington, or mining towns like Butte, Montana. And they bet big. Clinton had won the West in the 1992 election, carrying seven of twelve western states.[7] The Clinton administration saw that success as a harbinger of change. In the early 1990s, economists, journalists, and politicians began to describe the rise of the "New West." If the "Old West" was dominated by rural residents, who depended on the natural resource industries, and harbored suspicions of the federal government, then the New West was dominated by urbanites who lived in booming cities like Denver, Seattle, and Las Vegas, worked in technology, health care, and finance, and prized the West for its landscape and recreational opportunities. Statistics suggested a broad demographic and economic transition was underway in the West. The number of people employed in the natural resource industries and their importance to the West's economy was eclipsed by rapid economic growth in technology, services, and the defense industry. While such a straightforward dichotomy did not hold up to careful scrutiny, as a broad idea it had merit, and the potential for the New West gained popularity in environmental circles and the Clinton administration.[8] Babbitt was a self-described "big believer in the New West . . . theory."[9]

But there were other changes that would complicate environmentalists' expectations for public lands reform and the Clinton administration's agenda in the 1990s. Much of the population growth in the West was in urban areas and in counties that were located closest to the national parks and wilderness areas. Some of this development was concentrated in the wildland-urban interface, which grew in size by 61 percent between 1970 and 2000; more troubling, the number of homes in this zone grew by 68 percent in the 1990s alone. Half of the land in the wildland-urban interface was dominated by forests prone to high-severity fires.[10] Severe fire seasons in 1993 and 1994 drew public attention to the growing threat wildfire posed for western communities and pushed fire-fighting and fire-mitigation to the forefront of public lands debates. And across much of the country, one of the fastest growing uses of the public lands in the 1990s was for off-highway vehicles such as dirt bikes, all-terrain vehicles, and snowmobiles. Between the mid-1990s and 2000, the number of off-road vehicle drivers increased by 32 percent and sales doubled to one million vehicles per year.[11] Since 1987, the Idaho-based BlueRibbon Coalition had emerged as a national umbrella organization coordinating riders and dealerships in support of keeping public lands open for off-road vehicles. And, although Clinton had succeeded in winning several western states, the region remained home turf for the Republican Party. In 1994, fifteen of the region's twenty-four senators were Republicans.

In the spring of 1993, Babbitt and the Clinton administration set forth a vision for the West that was as dramatic and far-reaching as anything the Reagan administration had proposed in the early 1980s; only this time, it was oriented toward joining economic and ecological imperatives toward public lands reform. Two policy initiatives dominated the administration's public lands agenda at the start of the Clinton administration: Babbitt pursued grazing and mining reform through the congressional budgeting process and the White House convened a "timber summit" to resolve the debate over the spotted owl in the Pacific Northwest.

When the Clinton administration swept into Washington, D.C., budget reform topped its domestic priorities in the 103rd Congress. In March 1993, Clinton outlined a plan that included tax increases for the wealthy and for corporations, cuts in government spending, and an economic stimulus package. The proposal had implications for every major government program, including defense, social security, Medicare, and the public lands.[12] The Clinton administration chose the budget as a vehicle to advance fiscally minded reforms to public lands policy, in hopes of appealing both to environmentalists and conservatives concerned with government spending. The target was below-cost activities on the public lands: under the General Mining Act of 1872, mining companies could still purchase public lands for as little as $2.50 per acre and extract gold, silver, and other minerals without paying a royalty to the government. Ranchers still paid the federal government a fraction of what they paid private landholders to run cattle and sheep on the western range. And loggers still enjoyed below-cost access to the national forests. The Clinton budget addressed the first two issues head-on: it proposed charging a 12.5 percent royalty on mineral extraction and raising grazing fees from $1.86 to $5.00 per AUM.[13] In the case of the public lands, Babbitt explained, it was time for miners, timber companies, ranchers, and water users to "pay their fair share" for the public's resources. His goal was to bring "old and true economic values to a new and urgent cause: the imperative to live more lightly and productively on the land—our land."[14] The Wilderness Society predicted that the new administration's proposals would "pull the plug on the bath of red ink that has soaked the taxpayers and devastated our natural legacy."[15]

The budget debate offered Clinton a quick lesson in the curious politics of the West and the fractious politics of the Democratic Party. Some in Congress warned the administration that the budget process was ill suited to debating such extensive public lands reforms. That said, the budget process had become an important strategy for advancing environmental policy.[16] Budget bills are the equivalent of the legislative express: Congress passes them annually to appropriate funds for government activities and, most important to environmental policy, changes in funding levels or legislative riders can be included. With billions of dollars of federal funding at stake, Congress and the White House are often reluctant to derail a spending bill to block specific funding changes or riders. This was the most immediate problem for Babbitt's proposed fee increases on the public lands. The projected savings from public lands reform accounted for only $2 billion of the $500 billion in Clinton's budgetary savings. As Clinton maneuvered carefully to advance his budget package through Congress, near uniform Republican opposition forced him to aggressively cultivate the support of Democrats. When the budget passed by razor-thin margins in August 1993, it did nothing to change public lands management. One of the very first political deals Clinton struck to protect the budget bill was on public lands reform. Western Democrats, such as Representative Tom Foley (D-WA) and Senator Ben Nighthorse Campbell (D-CO), who objected to raising fees for grazing and mining, put regional concerns before their party affiliation on public lands issues.[17]

Facing gridlock in Congress on public lands reform, Babbitt turned to administrative rulemaking—a strategy that would become central to the Clinton administration's environmental policy agenda during its second term—

and initiated a process to change the rules that guided how the Department of the Interior administered existing law, including the Federal Land Policy and Management Act (FLPMA) and the Public Rangelands Improvement Act (PRIA). "[T]he question is not if these changes will occur," explained Babbitt, "but how they will occur."[18] In August 1993, he released Rangeland Reform '94, an administrative proposal that would raise grazing fees from $1.86 to $4.28 per AUM over three years and overhaul management and oversight of grazing on public lands. The proposal challenged ranchers' inexpensive and locally regulated access to the public range in numerous ways, such as linking future grazing leases to their "stewardship record."[19] Western opposition was immediate and fierce. People for the West! described Babbitt as an "environmental zealot" who aimed to "destroy our rights."[20] In Congress, western Republicans and Democrats maneuvered to block the proposal. Senator Alan Simpson (R-WY) complained that the proposal put the interests of environmentalists before the "generations of westerners who have preserved, protected, and improved western rangelands." That September, western senators joined together under the leadership of moderate Democrat Harry Reid (D-NV) and conservative Republican Malcolm Wallop (R-WY) to cut funds for any administrative rule-making that changed fees or range management for one year through the budget process. In October, Reid tried to cobble together a compromise package, which raised grazing fees to $3.45 and included fewer management reforms, to satisfy fiscal conservatives and environmentalists and to address the concerns of westerners.[21] But Simpson and his colleagues were in no mood to be "steamrolled," as Simpson put it.[22] Forty Republicans and five Democrats filibustered the Senate, forcing Reid to withdraw the compromise. There would be no grazing reform in the 103rd Congress.[23]

The Clinton administration had more success in breaking the gridlock over the Ancient Forests. On April 2, 1993, President Clinton hosted the Pacific Northwest Forest Conference in Portland, Oregon. It was a remarkable display of administrative initiative. Warning that the outcome of the conference "cannot possibly make everyone happy," Clinton appealed for common ground. Loggers knew and loved the Pacific Northwest, he said, and he emphasized that most environmentalists were working people who knew the importance of jobs. After six years of congressional inaction and judicial litigation, he positioned his administration to take action on an issue for which "there are no simple or easy answers."[24] Nearly one-third of the president's cabinet participated in the daylong summit, listening to and asking questions of local loggers, environmentalists, scientists, and agency employees. Two weeks later, the

White House convened three interagency working groups on ecosystem management, labor and community assistance, and agency coordination, and gave them sixty days to develop a set of options to meet the requirements of federal law and produce the greatest economic and social values from the forests. The Wilderness Society's interim president, Karin Sheldon, praised the conference as a breakthrough.[25] The driving force behind the administration's subsequent recommendations was the Forest Ecosystem Management Assessment Team—which brought together ecology, biology, economics, and sociology specialists from inside and outside of government—to take an "ecosystem approach to forest management" that protected biological diversity, maintained sustainable timber harvests, and stabilized rural communities. This shift in emphasis, from protecting a single species to protecting the biological diversity of the entire ecosystem, met the concerns the courts raised in the spotted owl litigation and the concerns of environmental advocates.[26] In the words of Jerry Franklin, a university scientist and team member, the plan marked an important step "toward recognition of the value of biodiversity and ecosystem management" within the federal government.[27]

The Forest Team presented the administration with ten options, and "option nine" became the basis for the Pacific Northwest Forest Plan. It marked a sharp reorientation of forest management. It projected a reduction in federal timber sales in the region by 73 percent from 1980s levels and withdrew 18.8 of 24.5 million acres of forest land from traditional multiple-use management.[28] The broad outlines of the plan—which drew on earlier proposals by the Forest Service, environmental groups, and scientists—included a system of reserves to protect owl habitat, restricted multiple-use management of the remaining forest lands, and protected riparian zones. Yet, option nine also permitted some thinning and salvage logging activities in old-growth reserves and was projected to maintain a slightly higher level of timber harvest than most other options. The plan allocated 1.5 million acres to "adaptive management areas," usually located near distressed timber towns. In those areas, the federal government would set the forest goals, but local communities could develop strategies to meet them. The hope, in the words of government planners, was that those who lived closest to the forests would "work together to develop innovative management approaches."[29] The administration took additional steps to decouple the financial future of rural counties and timber sales. Historically, rural counties received a 25 percent share of annual federal timber receipts in the county to support local schools and roads. Starting in 1994, the revenue-sharing program was reformulated based on average timber harvests between 1986 and 1990—

before the spotted owl crisis. The administration also pledged $1.2 billion over five years to promote a regional economic transition, including programs such as the "adaptive management areas," local economic diversification, and worker retraining. Lastly, working with the Pacific Northwest congressional delegation, Clinton signed into law a ban on the export of raw logs from federal forest land, which aimed to slow the export of lumber-processing jobs from the region. Despite the timber industry's efforts to derail the plan in the courts and ongoing legal suits by environmentalists, the federal courts accepted the Northwest Forest Plan as sufficient for meeting the Forest Service's and BLM's obligations under the National Forest Management Act (NFMA), National Environmental Policy Act (NEPA), Endangered Species Act (ESA), and other laws in December 1994. That decision eased, but did not eliminate, five years of uncertainty that had begun with the court injunctions blocking timber sales in 1989.[30]

Such accomplishments were rare for the Clinton administration in the 103rd Congress. Environmentalists had expected White House leadership on a wide range of legislative initiatives, including energy policy, existing environmental legislation (such as the ESA and Superfund hazardous waste remediation), and the public lands. But much of the agenda ran into congressional gridlock. The 103rd Congress, the League of Conservation Voters concluded, had not passed "any significant environmental legislation," and the environmental community sharply criticized the administration for retreating on its broader commitment to public lands reform.[31] On grazing reform, the Wilderness Society lamented that, "in the end, the political support of western governors and their livestock ranchers . . . won the day."[32] The Northwest Forest Plan was judged a hollow victory, and the Wilderness Society described the final provision for stewardship logging and the ill-defined plans for "adaptive management areas" as "serious flaws."[33] The Native Forest Council and its allies broke with the national groups and filed suit against the Clinton forest plan, describing it as "a clever package of abused science and public-relations jargon like 'ecosystem-management.'"[34]

Despite those shortcomings, the administration's emphasis on ecosystem management signaled a shift in multiple-use management. As Bruce Babbitt explained in testimony before Congress, "Ecosystem management is the most effective and efficient natural resource management strategy, and we must organize our biological information on that basis."[35] Although George H. W. Bush's administration had publicly embraced ecosystem management, it fell to the Clinton administration to reorient the agencies' management priorities.[36] While the administration's legislative initiatives were stymied in Congress, the president's appointees embraced this new direction. For the first time, the federal land agencies were being led by agency scientists who had worked their way up the ranks—not foresters or ranchers. Jack Ward Thomas, a research biologist, was promoted to chief of the Forest Service and made it clear that he hoped to reorient the agency. Explaining the challenges of ecosystem management, he said, "Unless we implement management strategies that truly conserve biodiversity and maintain aesthetic values, while producing needed commodities, we have changed only labels, not actual management."[37] And Michael Dombeck, a fisheries biologist, was named director of the BLM. He described ecosystem management as a chance to manage not for single species or commodities, but for "ecological systems as a whole."[38] When the opportunity for reform arose again during Clinton's second term, such leadership would be pivotal.

The most obvious causes of the Clinton administration's failed agenda were the deepening partisan and geographic divisions that hampered efforts to advance public lands reform in the early 1990s. Even in a Democratic Congress, the Clinton administration discovered it had little room to maneuver. Despite making strong arguments grounded in economics and science, the administration ran up against entrenched interests—the grazing and mining industries which were powerful defenders of long-standing laws and a partisan Congress in which filibusters and appropriations riders undermined and complicated legislative reform.[39] Important too was the ineffective mobilization within the environmental community. Despite the high hopes for the Clinton presidency, national environmental groups had not been able to rally national attention to the administration's environmental agenda or even to unite advocates of public lands reform behind common goals. Faced with opportunity, they divided over strategy. These were failures both the administration and environmentalists would learn from in the years to come. For the administration and environmentalists, the success with the Northwest Forest Plan demonstrated the potential for administrative initiatives that ran around, rather than through, Congress, especially if those initiatives enjoyed strong citizen support.

The Republican Revolution and the Public Lands: Appropriations and the Salvage Rider

The mid-term elections in 1994 made it clear that the Clinton administration's hopes for the New West had been a political miscalculation. Republicans, Wise

Use activists, and their allies saw the Clinton administration's failed public lands agenda as an opportunity to parlay their political efforts into an electoral force for the Republican Party. As the mid-term elections approached in 1994, People for the West!, the strongest arm of the Wise Use Movement, launched a get-out-the-vote operation in the West. "The House of Representatives has been beating the daylights out of us on everything from mining and ranching to timber and recreation—and all 435 House members face reelection this year." Although action in the House of Representatives had hardly been as coordinated or effective as People for the West! implied, it urged its members to "VOTE FOR PUBLIC LANDS ACCESS, JOBS, RURAL COMMUNITIES, AND A RESOURCEFUL AMERICA—don't accept anything less." Most important, "Vote in 1994."[40]

On the campaign trail that fall, westerners played up the Clinton administration's "War on the West." Ron Arnold, a Wise Use leader, described Babbitt "as the perfect Darth Vader."[41] Veteran Republican senators such as Slade Gorton (R-WA) and Conrad Burns (R-MT) and new candidates for the House such as Helen Chenoweth in Idaho and Cy Jamison in Montana echoed those themes on public lands issues. Burns emphasized that the real issue was not grazing fees or mining royalties, but "a bureaucrat in Washington, D.C., who wants to run your ranch, your farm, your business."[42] Gorton described the final Northwest Forest Plan as a travesty that would "extinguish" the region's timber towns. Candidates targeted the administration's proposed grazing, mining, and water reforms, Secretary of the Interior Babbitt, and the administration's close ties to the environmental community as a threat to western property rights, jobs, and independence. And the Republican Party rallied around the "Contract with America" nationally, which promised to get "Washington off our backs," roll back "bureaucratic red tape," and promote small business entrepreneurship— "the heart and soul of our economy."[43] In the West, not all Wise Use candidates won their campaigns—Gorton, Burns, and Chenoweth did, but Jamison lost. But such voter anger and Wise Use activism played an important role at a pivotal moment in American political history; with strong support in the West, the Republican Party gained majorities in the Senate (52–48) and, for the first time since 1955, the House (230–204).

Republicans started the 104th Congress with a disciplined campaign to advance the Contract with America in the House. The broad legislative agenda included welfare reform, middle-class tax cuts, a line-item veto, and restrictions on unfunded mandates.[44] Although the contract itself included few specific provisions regarding the environment or the public lands, efforts at reforming federal regulatory procedures and reducing the size of the federal government threatened sharp new limits on environmental regulations and Republicans were quick to introduce additional legislation to roll back key environmental laws and sell off public lands. The Wilderness Society warned that the "extremists in Congress are preparing to wage war on the environment."[45] And, as its strategists noted, the 104th Congress's agenda for the public lands was an extension of the Wise Use Movement. In the first one hundred days of the 104th Congress, House Republicans passed nine of ten planks of the contract in an impressive display of party unity. Republicans crowed: "The new Republican Congress—making Washington work, for a change."[46]

The most direct legislative attack on the wilderness system came in Utah. Since the late 1980s, the future of Utah's 22.5-million-acre share of the nation's public domain remained uncertain. Seeing an opportunity to break the stalemate, Representative Jim Hansen (R-UT) and Senator Orrin Hatch (R-UT) proposed a bill protecting 1.8 million acres of the state's red rock canyon country as wilderness—about two-thirds the land the BLM had identified as potential wilderness in its initial study (2.6 million acres) and one-third of the land the Southern Utah Wilderness Alliance (SUWA) and its allies proposed (5.7 million acres). Hansen argued the proposal protected "the most pristine of all" Utah's wild lands.[47] But to observers, it was clear that the bill's real aim was to expedite development, such as coal mining on the Kaiparowits Plateau. Ken Rait, with SUWA, likened giving Utah's politicians control of wilderness legislation to putting "Dracula in charge of the blood bank."[48]

If the proposal's only fault had been its limited wilderness designations, it may have become law. But the legislation also included a long list of provisions that ran counter to the broad intent of the Wilderness Act. The bill included numerous special exceptions, such as language allowing roads, water projects, pipelines, and temporary communications towers, and release language that permanently opened all remaining public domain lands in Utah for potential development. Such provisions were not unprecedented, but the number of exceptions in the Utah bill was.[49] With the strong support of the wilderness community—especially the Wilderness Society and SUWA—Democrats moved to block the bill in Congress and the White House threatened a veto. Democrats warned that the bill would "not only be a disaster for wild public lands affected by the bill, but also for the National Wilderness Preservation System."[50] When the Utah delegation could not move the bill in the House, Senator Hatch attached the legislation as a rider to a popular parks bill in the Senate. The strategy failed. Senate Democrats, led by Bill Bradley (D-NJ), filibustered the parks bill, and Republicans fell short of the sixty votes necessary to overturn it. "You wouldn't sell your family's heirlooms in order to pave your driveway," Bradley commented to the press. Nor would the Senate sacrifice Utah's wild lands to secure a parks bill.[51] The tools of gridlock delivered wilderness advocates a crucial defensive victory, led by SUWA, that left the future of Utah's wild lands in limbo.

If the Republicans had advanced the rest of their environmental agenda through the usual legislative process, then it is likely the outcome would have been the same as for the Utah legislation: filibusters, delay, and defeat. So they turned to an alternative policy pathway: the fast-moving congressional appropriations process. This was not a new move—the Reagan and Clinton administrations had done the same—but Republicans made this a centerpiece of their strategy in the 104th Congress. Consider these examples: In a major budget reconciliation bill, aimed at balancing the budget, Republicans tried opening the Arctic National Wildlife Refuge's (ANWR) coastal plain by allocating $1.3 billion in projected revenues from oil drilling in the refuge. The same bill included a rider reforming the 1872 mining law. Instead of restricting mining and increasing royalties, as the Clinton administration proposed in 1993, western senators included language that expedited mining claims and instituted new, but minimal, royalties on mineral extraction. In an appropriations bill for the Department of the Interior and related agencies, Republicans prohibited the National Park Service from spending any funds to manage the newly protected Mojave National Preserve in the California desert, mandated higher levels of logging on the Tongass National Forest in Alaska, and placed a moratorium on listing additional species and designating critical habitat under the ESA.[52] These proposals, attached to key spending bills, moved through Congress over Democrats' strident objections. Clinton vetoed both the reconciliation and Interior appropriations bill, however, resulting in a series of government shutdowns that lasted into January 1996.[53] All told, Republicans attached more than fifty riders to seven budget bills.[54] With the strong support of the environmental community, the Clinton White House forced Republicans to abandon most such provisions through vetoes and subsequent negotiations. But one anti-environmental rider did slip through in 1995: salvage logging in the national forests.

The fastest moving budget bill in the 104th Congress was a rescissions bill that included emergency spending for hurricane relief on the Gulf Coast and assistance funds in response to the 1995 Oklahoma City bombing. Senators Slade Gorton and Mark O. Hatfield (R-OR) hitched a timber program to that bill. The "Emergency Salvage Timber Sale Program," described as a temporary forest health program, marked a strategic change in efforts to expand logging in the national forests. Instead of trying to increase timber sales of healthy forests, the timber industry and its allies targeted trees already killed by fire, disease, and drought. Who could object to harvesting dead trees, especially if they heightened the threat of wildfire on the national forests? Environmentalists did. They argued that these harvests removed standing timber that played an important ecological role in the forests, required additional roads in already disturbed watersheds, and generally yielded low-quality wood, which meant it was necessary to log additional live trees to make the practice profitable. Gorton argued back: "These radical environmental organizations literally don't want any harvest at all under any circumstances, even of trees that are dead and turning into kindling for forest fires."[55] Although the salvage rider proposed ways to improve forest health, several unrelated provisions suggested that its real intent was to expedite logging, including in the Pacific Northwest, where the Pacific Northwest Forest Plan was tied up in appeals and litigation.

The salvage rider was included in a House rescissions bill in March. To the surprise of wilderness advocates, it withstood a challenge on the Senate floor in May and was poised for congressional approval. Internally, environmental leaders acknowledged that their efforts had been "frighteningly poor," especially in the House.[56] In the Senate, environmentalists' efforts were hampered by internal divisions, which undermined their lobbying strategies: national groups knew there were not enough votes to block the rider, so they focused on minimizing the damage; allies of the New Conservation Movement, including the Native Forest Council, tried to sink the rider. There were three key problems with the bill: first, it streamlined the regulatory process the Forest Service and BLM followed to comply with existing environmental laws such as NEPA; second, it limited citizens' ability to seek administrative appeals and judicial review of timber sales; and third, it was permissive in its definition of "salvage logging," which could be interpreted to include any forest land.[57] Opponents described it as "logging without laws."[58] But its supporters argued that the legislation was necessary, considering the ongoing administrative appeals, judicial reviews, and legislative debate that contributed to gridlock on the national forests. On May 25, 1995, Congress passed the rescission bill and sent it to the White House.[59] President Clinton vetoed the bill, concluding that "it is not appropriate to use this legislation to overturn environmental laws . . . in an effort to increase timber salvage."[60]

With $16.4 billion in funding at stake, both the House and Senate voted to override the president's veto. The revised bill included minor compromises on the salvage logging provision, most notably shortening the emergency period by nine months. But the final legislation pushed aside two decades' worth of regulatory protection for the national forests. Efforts to weaken the rider were immediate: Democrats introduced legislation to reverse or amend the rider in 1995 and inserted language in the budget to de-fund it in 1996. Neither strategy succeeded. The White House issued several memoranda ordering the secretaries of agriculture and the interior to strictly limit application of the rider to emergency situations, and wilderness advocates filed suit, questioning the constitutionality of the rider's limits on appeals. Those legal actions slowed, but did not overturn, the rider. By December 31, 1996, the program had increased federal timber sales by 35 percent to 4.6 billion board feet and resulted in some 650 million additional board feet of timber sales in the Pacific Northwest.[61] It was a sharp blow to Clinton's environmental record.

The fast-moving salvage rider had outpaced the Wilderness Society in the spring of 1995. Privately, the society's strategists described the proposal as a throwback to the Reagan era, "a complete abandonment of the doctrine of ecosystem management," and "old-time special interest politics at its worst."[62] After Clinton vetoed the initial bill, at the environmental community's behest, they thanked "President Clinton for standing tall!"[63] But after he signed the final legislation, Debbie Sease, the Sierra Club's lead Washington lobbyist, scolded: "Your decision . . . to cut a deal and sign the bill, even though it would still devastate our forests, wildlife, and the environment is a betrayal of your covenant with the American public."[64] On the day that Clinton signed the revised legislation into law, twenty-one of the nation's environmental leaders—including those from the Wilderness Society, Sierra Club, and Natural Resources Defense Council (NRDC)—gathered across from the White House to give him a chainsaw salute.[65]

The 104th Congress had put public lands advocates on the defensive on seemingly every front, from Alaska to Utah, from grazing to logging. In the early 1980s, fending off the Reagan administration had been a boon for environmental groups, raising their public profiles, expanding their memberships, and increasing their clout; the same was not true in the mid-1990s. Membership at the Sierra Club, the Wilderness Society, and the National Audubon Society, all stalwart defenders of the public lands, declined in the early 1990s. The organizations that grew, such as NRDC and the Environmental Defense Fund, had broader agendas or different strategies.

The forces of change in public lands politics that had been building since the early 1990s converged powerfully in 1994 and 1995. The Wilderness Society was at the center of the storm. At the beginning of the 104th Congress, the organization's leadership remained focused on a strategic visioning process that had been underway since 1993: Would the organization broaden its focus to other environmental issues? Would it expand its concern for biodiversity protection beyond the public lands? Would it take more aggressive policy positions? That planning process was overtaken by more immediate challenges. In February 1995, pundits such as Alexander Cockburn and Jeffrey St. Clair at *The Nation* ramped up their criticisms of national environmental groups, taking special aim at the Wilderness Society, its flawed leadership, and its "fealty to the Clinton administration."[66] In April, the Wilderness Society's new president, Jon Roush, became entangled in a public dispute over logging practices on his ranch in Montana.[67] In August, historian William Cronon published an article in the *New York Times Magazine* titled "The Trouble with Wilderness," which questioned the environmental movement's focus on wilderness protection.[68] And the New Conservation Movement's aggressive activism continued to undermine the national groups' political authority—as it had in the case of the salvage rider.[69] Since the summer of 1994, the Wilderness Society's membership and revenues had been declining. As Republicans maneuvered to advance their agenda in Congress, the organization was forced to lay off staff and reduce its office space in Washington, D.C. In the mid-1990s, the Wilderness Society remained one of the nation's leading environmental groups—with a fifteen-million-dollar budget, 275,000 members, and sixty years of experience—but no one had a steady hand on the rudder and these were not calm seas.

The 104th Congress could have been a disaster for environmental laws and regulations. It was not. The Republican Party's discipline in the House did not extend to the Senate—which proved slow or unwilling to take up much of the Contract with America—nor did it apply evenly in the case of environmental reform. The Republicans' most visible efforts to reform existing environmental laws—including the Clean Water Act, the ESA, the Superfund hazardous waste law, and the privatization of federal lands—stalled because of near uniform opposition from Democrats, veto threats from the president, and uncertain support from moderate Republicans.[70] By the summer of 1995, it was evident that the Republicans did not command the necessary support to mount a direct challenge to environmental laws and regulations. As the *New York Times* editorialized, the Republicans' most effective offensive on the "laws and regulations that protect America's natural resources has been a masterpiece of legislative subterfuge." Instead of posing a direct challenge, the party had "seductively" repackaged its agenda "as 'deregulation,' 'property rights,' and 'balancing the budget.'"[71]

By the start of 1996, the Republican leadership had decided that the party's tactics on the environment were a political loser with the public. In the case of public lands, one party strategist noted, what galvanized the party's conservative base in the rural West did not play with "our growing Republican majority—especially suburban women and young people."[72] The polls said as much. Voters consistently indicated, usually by overwhelming margins, that they trusted Democrats to protect the environment. Senator Lincoln Chafee, a moderate Republican from Rhode Island, warned that the party had handed the issue to the Democrats on a "silver platter."[73] Looking toward the 1996 congressional elections, Republicans tried to refashion their environmental agenda, emphasizing their goals of "updating environmental legislation" to make it more efficient, protecting a "safe and healthy environment," and replacing "command-and-control micromanagement by federal bureaucrats" with local, "common-sense," and cooperative efforts.[74] Despite several legislative successes ahead of the 1996 elections, including laws to strengthen drinking water standards and restructure regulation of pesticides in food, as well as national park legislation, the 104th Congress had strengthened the Republican Party's reputation for opposing environmental reform—a reputation George W. Bush would consolidate four years later.

Clinton's Administrative Agenda for the Public Lands

On September 18, 1996, President Clinton established the 1.7-million-acre Grand Staircase-Escalante National Monument in southern Utah.[75] Even wilderness advocates were surprised. After the 1994 legislative debate, the Utah wild lands had seemingly been pushed onto an administrative sidetrack. Secretary Babbitt had directed the BLM to reinventory the disputed canyonlands, focusing on areas proposed in the 5.7-million-acre America's Red Rock Wilderness Act (a reinventory that would result in 2.6 million acres of new wilderness inventory areas in 1999).[76] Behind the scenes, SUWA and its allies were lobbying key administrative officials, including Katie McGinty, chair of the Council on Environmental Quality, John Leshey, solicitor in the Department of the Interior, and George Frampton, the assistant secretary in the Department of the Interior. Facing reelection in the fall, Clinton needed to shore up his environmental credentials. A special team in the Department of the Interior had worked overtime to produce options for a Grand Staircase-Escalante announcement that year, but first Earth Day and then the Fourth of July passed without any action. Babbitt was unenthusiastic about the Utah monument, believing a surprise announcement would only deepen the opposition he and his department faced in the West.[77] Nevertheless, forty-eight days before the 1996 elections, motivated foremost by political considerations, Clinton used his authority under the Antiquities Act of 1906 to set aside a vast tract of spectacular canyonlands that was also coveted by energy interests for its coal reserves. He made the announcement a safe distance away, at the Grand Canyon. "Our parents and grandparents saved Grand Canyon for us," he said. "Today, we will save the grand Escalante Canyons and the Kaiparowits Plateaus of Utah for our children."[78] It was an easy political move for Clinton, who had no chance of winning Utah and was able to strengthen his environmental credentials by taking action where Congress had failed to.[79] For wilderness advocates, especially SUWA, it was a sweet victory. The new national monument was twice the size of the existing wilderness study areas and nearly five times larger than the agency's recommendations for wilderness protection in the region.[80] The monument prioritized ecosystem management, without revoking existing rights or uses. To many locals, the surprise announcement and expansive designation

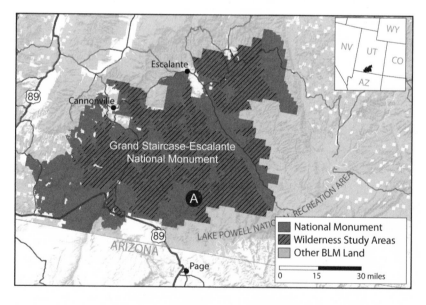

Map 10.1 Grand Staircase-Escalante National Monument, Utah. On September 18, 1996, President Clinton established the 1.7-million-acre Grand Staircase-Escalante National Monument, which included 877,000 of wilderness study areas (only WSAs located within the monument are shown on the map). It also prevented mining for an estimated 11.4 billion tons of recoverable coal on Kaiparowits Plateau (A).

ran roughshod over their interests. Utahns described it as a violation of their rights, an act of imperialism, and evidence of the administration's "War on the West." Visitors to nearby Kanab, Utah, would soon be able to buy "Clinton-burgers: 100 percent chicken."[81]

With Republicans in control of the House and Senate in the mid-1990s, environmental reform seemed most likely to move through the White House, not Congress. Congressional action had been the touchstone for public lands protection since the Wilderness Act of 1964, but since the mid-1980s efforts to designate new wilderness areas and reform public lands management had often led to disappointment. Now, faced with an unsympathetic Congress, the Clinton administration and the nation's environmental leadership began to give new attention to the Antiquities Act and administrative rulemaking. The Antiquities Act offered a powerful, but closed, path to public lands protection, since the president could exercise his powers without any oversight (except in Wyoming and Alaska, which had passed laws limiting the extent of such withdrawals). But after Clinton's surprise announcement for the Grand Staircase-Escalante, Secretary Babbitt made it clear that any future monument withdrawals would involve local consultations. In contrast, administrative rulemaking offered a more open venue for public lands reform since it required public notice, public comments, and environmental impact statements. Notably, however, it did not require congressional approval. Using these two strategies, the administration and its environmental allies took crucial steps toward grazing and mining reform, protection of Utah's public lands, and, most far-reaching, protection of the national forest roadless areas.

The path for administrative rulemaking on grazing reform was rocky from start to finish. After Babbitt's proposed grazing rules ran into a bloc of western opposition in the Senate at the end of the 103rd Congress, the BLM picked up the remaining pieces and took the final steps in 1994 and 1995. The new rules proposed significant changes in who had a say in western grazing and how it was managed. Most importantly, the rule replaced local grazing boards, which were dominated by ranchers, with multi-constituency boards, which included scientists, environmentalists, ranchers, and local and state officials. The rule also established a process for assessing and maintaining the health of rangelands, although on a state-by-state basis, rather than nationally. Whether the new rules would go into effect remained a persistent question for both the administration and western ranchers in 1995. Babbitt had agreed to delay the new rules for six months to allow the 104th Congress time to consider new grazing legislation. Initially, it appeared that Republican senators from the West, led by Pete Domenici (R-NM), would pass congressional legislation overriding the administration's new rules. But that proposal failed along with much of the Republican anti-environmental agenda in 1995. In deference to the concerns of westerners, Babbitt withdrew the proposed increases in grazing fees in 1995, leaving in force the rancher-friendly grazing fee formula that Reagan had made permanent in 1986. Ironically, not only did grazing fees not increase to $3.96, as Babbitt had proposed in 1994, or even to the compromise $3.45, as Senate Democrats proposed in 1993; instead they dropped from $1.98 to $1.61 per AUM to reflect lower beef prices.[82] It was, the NRDC charged, "worse than doing nothing."[83] Despite sharp disappointment in the environmental community, the administration's new rules went into effect in August 1995.[84] That September, Babbitt traveled to Colorado to celebrate. He described it as a "momentous day. We are beginning a new chapter on range issues in the West."[85] In truth, it was a modest victory in a campaign that cost the Clinton administration much political capital among both its friends and its detractors in the West.[86]

When Congress failed to act on mining reform, Babbitt and the Clinton administration again turned to administrative rulemaking. The mining industry still enjoyed preferential access to the nation's public lands: it acquired public lands for as little as $2.50 an acre, paid the government nothing for the minerals it extracted, and faced few environmental regulations. Despite strong support for mining reform from many Democrats and moderate Republicans, western senators remained unyielding allies to the mining industry throughout the 1990s. Starting in 1994, Congress included a rider in the Department of the Interior's annual appropriations bill curtailing land sales under the General Mining Act of 1872; but that rider did nothing to establish royalties on mineral extraction or tighten environmental safeguards on mines. In response, Babbitt initiated a new rulemaking process in 1997 to change how the BLM regulated hard rock mining under FLPMA. The existing "3809" regulations had been adopted under James Watt in 1981. Environmentalists viewed those rules as a Reagan-era giveaway, outdated by new chemical-intensive technology (such as cyanide leaching) and insufficient in the requirements they imposed to ensure the cleanup of exhausted and abandoned mines. The Clinton administration's proposed rule explicitly stated that the BLM could block mines that threatened the public interest, established stronger guidelines for environmental remediation, and expanded mining companies' financial obligations to guarantee there would be clean-up funds when the mines were closed. Concern over the existing 3809 regulations was not uniform, however. The National Academy of Sciences reviewed the regulations and concluded the problem was not the existing regulations, but how the regulations were being enforced. The academy called for more site-specific regulation.[87] From the start, the mining industry and its congressional allies were dead set against the BLM's proposed rules, and the academy's conclusion only hardened their opposition. The Northwest Mining Association described the proposed rules as "back door mining law reform" that gave bureaucrats at the BLM, not Congress, the power to determine mining policy.[88] Between 1997 and 2000, the mining industry and its allies in the Senate delayed new rules by withholding funds for rulemaking during the appropriations process and tried to make the academy's recommendations binding. But in November 2000, the agency succeeded in finalizing the 3809 regulations, which went into effect on the final day of Clinton's administration. The Mineral Policy Center, which had long championed such reforms, described the regulations as a "huge victory."[89]

The unlikely star of Clinton's turn toward administrative action was the Forest Service and its new chief, Michael Dombeck. The five-foot five-inch fisheries biologist was known to be quiet, modest, and even-keeled. When he was appointed, one environmental leader lamented, "There goes any chance of reform at that agency."[90] But Dombeck would turn out to be a crucial ally to the environmental community. Starting in 1996, he reshuffled top management at the Forest Service, pushing timber barons out and bringing in a new generation of scientists. Chris Wood, a conservationist with a keen sense for public relations, became his assistant. And Dombeck initiated a scientific review of the agency's forest planning process, which pleased environmentalists. Starting in 1997, the Forest Service began to take steps toward what would become an administrative rulemaking process to protect roadless areas in the national forests. Wilderness advocates had been working to protect roadless areas one wilderness area at a time in the 1960s and 1970s, as part of statewide packages in the 1980s, and in regional conservation networks since the early 1990s. But those efforts had been slow, especially as they became more ambitious. For instance, the Northern Rockies Ecosystem Protection Act had gone nowhere since its introduction in 1991. Working together, the environmental community and the Forest Service returned the 58.5 million acres of national forest roadless areas to the national spotlight.[91]

Wilderness advocates had been pursuing a multipronged approach to protecting roadless areas since the mid-1980s: reducing timber sales through the forest planning process and administrative appeals, lobbying Congress to address below-cost timber sales, and working through the congressional appropriations process to reduce the Forest Service's funding for road building. These strategies were spearheaded by the national groups, especially the Wilderness Society, which had been calling for an end to below-cost logging since the mid-1980s. But what wilderness advocates had not done until the early 1990s was publicly advocate for an end to all road building and the protection of all road-less areas in the national forests.[92] This proposal first emerged out of the New Conservation Movement in the early 1990s, when the Save America's Forests coalition made it a plank in its platform.[93] In 1994, when Jon Roush, the Wilderness Society's president, called on Congress to reform the Forest Service's mission to protect biodiversity and ecosystems, he made a similar proposal.[94] These efforts slowly pried open the window of opportunity in the mid-1990s. Then, in 1996 and 1997, Congress came within a few votes of cutting funding for road building in the national forests in the House and Senate.[95] That put Dombeck on notice. He knew the roadless issue was pressing: the agency could not maintain its existing road system (in 1997, it faced an $8.4 billion backlog of road repairs); Dombeck believed roadless areas provided important values to the public, such as ecosystem services and opportunities for outdoor recreation; and the agency's roadless policies had become an unending source of controversy, frustrating the public and sapping agency morale. In his view, the agency needed to reclaim the initiative on forest management.[96]

In the fall of 1997, wilderness advocates discussed how best to press their opportunity. Should the White House issue an executive order to protect the roadless areas? Should the agency undertake a new study of roadless areas under the guidance of an independent scientific panel? Should the administration make new wilderness recommendations to Congress? Ken Rait, who had moved from Utah to Oregon and from canyonland issues to forest issues in 1997, had been a key strategist in the timber roads appropriations campaign that summer. He quickly became a leading proponent of abandoning that congressional strategy in order to focus the movement's collective energy on the Clinton White House. It was a strategy that had worked for him once before, when the Clinton administration took action to protect the Grand Staircase-Escalante in Utah. Rait saw several strategic advantages in an administrative campaign: It moved the initiative out of a partisan Congress into an increasingly friendly administrative arena. It addressed roadless protection separately from the legislative issue of wilderness designation, which Rait described as a political "albatross." And, most importantly, a campaign focused on the White House could make the roadless areas a national issue.[97]

On November 14, when Clinton signed the Interior appropriations bill, he acknowledged the special value of roadless areas and announced that the

Forest Service "is developing a scientifically based policy for managing road-less areas in our national forests."[98] That December and January, wilderness leaders met privately with administration officials on the issue, conservation biologists signaled their support for a "science-based policy for roadless areas" in a public letter, and wilderness groups encouraged their members to telephone, fax, and write the White House.[99] Nothing happened. Instead, Dombeck and the Forest Service focused on addressing the agency's roads problem. It was a logical position for the agency to take; it was roads, not roadless areas, that had been the focal point of debate over the appropriations process in Congress. Starting in January 1998, the agency initiated a rulemaking process to develop a new agency-wide transportation policy. During that time, the agency ordered a temporary eighteen-month moratorium on new roads. But this was not the sweeping policy wilderness advocates hoped for: it focused solely on roads, it exempted fifteen million acres of national forest with recently completed forest plans from the moratorium (including much of Alaska and the Pacific Northwest), and it specifically noted that the new transportation policy was not meant to protect roadless areas. Instead, the agency explained that roadless area protection was best handled through existing forest planning processes authorized by the NFMA.[100] That did not mean the agency was unconcerned with protecting roadless areas in 1998. As Chief Dombeck explained, a science-based roads policy would "limit, if not eliminate, costly new road construction in sensitive areas that can cause erosion, imperil rare species, or fragment habitat."[101] But it was evident that, for the Forest Service, the most politically viable and defensible policy strategy put roads first and roadless areas second in 1997 and 1998. "The Forest Service was missing the point," Rait remembers thinking.[102]

The campaign for the roadless rule exemplified public lands advocates' changing organizational structure and political strategies. In October 1998, the Pew Charitable Trusts funded the Heritage Forests Campaign through the National Audubon Society to spearhead a campaign for roadless area protection. Pew would invest more than three million dollars in the campaign over the next two years. It hired Rait to lead the campaign. With Rait's credentials as a scrappy organizer who got his start with SUWA, and a tight-knit group of established leaders from the Wilderness Society (Mike Francis), National Audubon Society (Dan Beard), NRDC (Niel Lawrence), and Earthjustice (Marty Hayden), the campaign was positioned to work both locally and nationally, bridging the divides that often split the wilderness advocacy community. In some respects, the campaign was traditional—harking back to the

Alaska Coalition's campaign in the late 1970s. For instance, the campaign kept hundreds of local and regional partner organizations updated via e-mail and conference calls, counting on those groups to drum up citizen participation. But the campaign also relied on new communication strategies, including a sustained media campaign to reach a mass audience and an Internet strategy that would eventually reach more than a million interested citizens. Unlike the Alaska Coalition, the campaign eschewed the existing bureaucracy of the wilderness movement. Instead of partnering with national and local groups, which would have meant a large steering committee, its tight-knit leadership outsourced responsibilities to specific environmental groups and consulting firms. Contracts were drawn up to compensate environmental groups for the staff time they committed to the campaign: NRDC and Earthjustice for legal

10.1 Ken Rait, the chair of the Heritage Forests Campaign, in The Brothers Wilderness in Olympic National Forest, Washington. Photograph by Eric Rait, 2000. Courtesy Ken Rait.

expertise; the Wilderness Society for administrative lobbying, policy work, and media outreach; and the U.S. Public Interest Research Group (PIRG) for citizen organizing and outreach. Independent technology consultants handled Internet outreach. And advertising firms designed the print, radio, and television campaigns. While this ad hoc campaign model overlapped with the existing wilderness movement, it ensured that the hub of the campaign was Rait, his inner circle of advisors, and the Pew Charitable Trusts. Paradoxically, the campaign would concentrate organizational responsibility even as it engaged an unprecedented number of wilderness groups and citizens nationwide in a positive campaign to protect the nation's public lands.[103]

"Protect Heritage Forests TODAY!" was the Heritage Forests Campaign's response to the Forest Service's new transportation policy review. "Our Heritage Forests belong to you, to me, and to all Americans." The Forest Service's moratorium was "a really good idea, but it's not nearly enough" and "unless we act now, our Heritage Forests will be gone forever."[104] Concerned citizens were directed to forward the e-mail to friends and visit a website to send a fax to the White House. The Heritage Forests Campaign crafted a political message meant to galvanize people across the nation, not just environmentalists, and to create a political opportunity for the Clinton administration. Since the late 1980s, the national wilderness community had been hammering away at forestry policy with economic arguments, emphasizing timber subsidies, scientific research, and ecosystem and biodiversity protection. While the campaign's policy goals were grounded in such arguments, the campaign made an emotional appeal that underscored the unique value of roadless areas and the unprecedented opportunity to protect them. Immediately after the February 1999 moratorium, campaign allies began laying the groundwork to expand that moratorium into a public referendum on the roadless areas.

While the Heritage Forests Campaign set in motion a public campaign with e-mail, advertising, street-tabling, and door-to-door canvassing, it also strengthened its working relationship with the Clinton administration. That spring, the campaign pursued meetings with Dombeck, Vice President Gore, and the White House's new chief of staff John Podesta. The meeting that counted most was with Podesta. Dombeck and his able assistant, Chris Wood, were sympathetic to the campaign but were not prepared to initiate administrative protection for roadless areas. Gore was distracted by his presidential campaign and did not figure as a key player in initiating or advancing the roadless rule. The driving force behind the roadless rule was the synergy between the

Heritage Forests Campaign, the Clinton White House, the staff of the Council on Environmental Quality, and, eventually, the Forest Service. In July and August, in meetings and communications with Podesta, the campaign spelled out a procedure and timeframe. What were the goals? An administrative rule protecting all roadless areas of 1,000 acres or more, addressing all management issues (not just roads), and having the new policy in place before Clinton left office. It was Clinton's "unique chance to achieve a lasting lands legacy" on the scale of Theodore Roosevelt's actions at the start of the twentieth century. To begin, they determined, "Chief Dombeck needs the President's direction in order to move the Forest Service bureaucracy" to undertake a roadless rulemaking process. The campaign urged the administration to make such an announcement shortly after Labor Day.[105]

On October 13, 1999, a sunny fall day in Virginia, the president's helicopter touched down in a field near Reddish Knob in the George Washington National Forest. Surrounded by the folds of the Blue Ridge Mountains, Clinton emphasized Roosevelt's historic legacy and looked forward to creating a new lands legacy. "In weighing the future of these lands," he said, "we are presented with a unique historic opportunity." He directed the Forest Service "to develop, and propose for public comments, regulations to provide appropriate long-term protection for most or all of these currently inventoried 'roadless' areas,

10.2 At Reddish Knob in the George Washington National Forest, President Clinton announced that the Forest Service would undertake a review of all remaining national forest roadless areas, October 13, 1999. Courtesy William J. Clinton Presidential Library.

and to determine whether such protection is warranted for any smaller 'road-less' areas not yet inventoried."[106] The next day, in a letter to the Forest Service, Dombeck described the initiative as a response to strong public concern for roadless areas, the accumulated evidence of the social and ecological value of roadless areas, and the continued political, judicial, and legislative debate over forest management. Most importantly, he emphasized, the process would be public. "All we are proposing is to begin an open and public dialogue with the American people."[107] Neither Clinton nor Dombeck said as much, but it was clear from the start what the most divisive issues in the rulemaking process would be: Would the rule be comprehensive, or would it exempt some national forests, such as the timber-rich Tongass in Alaska? Would the rule apply to all roadless areas greater than 1,000 acres, or only those of at least 5,000 acres in size? And would the rule address only road building, or would it also prohibit logging, mining, and off-road vehicles?

The agency released a notice of intent to prepare an environmental impact statement on October 19. The proposal quickly became a political lightning rod. During the initial scoping period, the agency received 517,000 public comments and held 187 public meetings. After hearings in one western town, a Forest Service regional forester warned Dombeck, "I have never experienced such public disbelief and animosity directed toward any policy proposal as this one." The policy, he cautioned, "mocks every speech and public statement regarding collaboration you have made since becoming Chief."[108] A quarter of the regional foresters were of a similar mind.[109] Dombeck did not let such concerns go unaddressed. Was such a proposal a land grab for only a few Americans? Dombeck argued no. "In 1997, 860 million national forest visitors took advantage" of recreational opportunities in the national forests. Was such a centralized rulemaking process undemocratic? In Dombeck's view, if the American people and the Forest Service did not resolve this issue, then industry, interest groups, lawyers, and the courts would—just as they had for the previous three decades. "These are the people's lands, and their voices will be heard," he promised.[110] The administrative rulemaking process became a powerful vehicle for public engagement, on which the Heritage Forests Campaign proved well positioned to capitalize.

The campaign set a goal of securing one million comments on the draft environmental impact statement that January. Polling showed surprisingly strong support for the proposal: 76 percent of all voters, 62 percent of Republicans, and 72 percent of westerners supported protection for roadless areas. Follow-up surveys targeting western states were encouraging too. Even in Idaho and Montana, hotbeds for the opposition, 64 and 59 percent of voters supported the plan. The campaign ran a newspaper advertisement, emphasizing "A majority of every major demographic group supports full protection. Men and women. Democrats and Republicans. Hikers and hunters. City dwellers, suburbanites, and rural Americans."[111] On May 10, 2000, the agency released a draft environmental impact statement which recommended ending road construction on 43 million acres of roadless areas, protecting all areas larger than 5,000 acres, and leaving specific management issues (such as helicopter logging, off-road vehicle use, and mining) to local forest plans. But the proposal satisfied no one: Opponents saw it as an intrusion of the federal government and environmentalists into local forest management. The Heritage Forests Campaign saw it as falling short of the "president's historic declaration."[112] And scientists and environmentalists considered it an imperative that all roadless areas 1,000 acres or larger be protected.

That summer the Heritage Forests Campaign swung into high gear. The agency's public comment period lasted until July 17, during which time the agency hosted more than 400 public meetings around the country. The Heritage Forests Campaign sent e-mail reminders to the 1.5 million people on its e-mail lists notifying them of nearby hearings and ran newspaper, television, and radio advertisements before hearings. One advertisement described the rulemaking process as if it was a blockbuster movie. "Two thumbs up! The critics are raving about Bill Clinton's Heritage Forests."[113] The U.S. Public Interest Research Group organized canvassers who set up street tables to draw public attention and went door-to-door to encourage citizen participation. The campaign was so successful that PIRG had difficulty keeping its canvassers stocked with postcards.[114] To generate additional written comments, the campaign sent out 3.3 million mailers that included postcard responses that it preceded and followed with telephone calls from a commercial phonebank. Opponents made their voices heard too, although not with the same coordination or resources. Hearings drew organized protests in many western states. In Missoula, Montana, more than 2,000 loggers and off-road vehicle enthusiasts arrived at the public hearing with a pine coffin that read, "R.I.P Clinton-Gore Roadless Initiative."[115] Despite the organizational strength of the Wise Use Movement in the early 1990s, it did little to coordinate opposition to the roadless rule in the late 1990s.[116] The agency received 1.6 million comments, 95 percent of which supported the rule.[117]

Piloting the roadless rule and environmental impact statement through two rounds of public scrutiny and subsequent revisions in fifteen months marked an extraordinary coordination of public and agency activity. The agency undertook a systematic review of public comments, as is standard procedure for all environmental impact studies. Notably, the agency did not reduce public comments to a vote-counting exercise. The purpose of the rulemaking process, the agency explained, was to create a forum for considering all viewpoints and a mechanism for conveying that information to the appropriate decision-maker.[118] In particular, the analysis noted that opponents viewed the rulemaking process as unfair: they complained of being disenfranchised, of an overreaching of federal oversight, and of a rulemaking process that was driven by "big money" environmentalists.[119] The agency's review of public comments also gave specific attention to the ecological value of roadless areas, which often drew on up-to-date research of conservation biologists: habitat fragmentation, connectivity of roadless areas, and species' viability were all considered both on a species-by-species and a landscape basis. It described inventoried roadless areas and wilderness areas as "biological strongholds" of unique value in protecting native species, biodiversity, and ecosystem health. Lastly, the analysis gave careful consideration both to timber production from the national forests and forest products consumption nationally. It noted that the restrictions in federal timber sales in the United States in the 1990s, particularly for softwoods, had resulted in increased pressure on private timberlands in the United States and boreal forests in Canada. In short, the "effect of a shift to ecological sustainability on United States public lands has been to shift the burden and impacts of that consumption to ecosystems somewhere else."[120] But, it also noted, inventoried roadless areas played a small role in meeting national timber demand. Ending commercial logging in roadless areas would reduce the national timber harvest by one-third of one percent. Figures were similar for mineral and energy resources.[121]

There was one crucial flaw with the roadless rulemaking process: it took too long. Under the Administrative Procedure Act, any major administrative rule was vulnerable to reversal by the president or Congress within sixty days of being published in the *Federal Register*. If Al Gore had become president after the 2001 election, that would not have been an issue. But while the nation remained riveted by the post-election maneuverings between November and December 2000 that sent George W. Bush to the White House, the roadless rule faced procedural hurdles. On November 13, Chief Dombeck detailed the agency's preferred alternative for the roadless rule: 58.5 million acres of roadless areas would be protected, including 49.2 million acres immediately and 9.3 million acres in the Tongass National Forest starting in 2004. The plan also prohibited all roads (except in cases of public safety or resource protection), ended all logging (except for "stewardship" logging to protect ecosystem health) in inventoried roadless areas of at least 5,000 acres in size, and promised twenty million dollars to help timber industry employees in affected communities.[122] Only one hurdle remained: a decision by the secretary of agriculture and the Clinton White House.

The Heritage Forests Campaign counted on the White House to strengthen the final rule. "Our highest priority for improvements are restricting some of the spurious 'stewardship' activities and strengthening the protection for the Tongass," Rait explained in a conference call with wilderness leaders and forest activists nationwide.[123] The Heritage Forests Campaign coordinated one last mailing of postcards and e-mails and launched a final series of radio and television advertisements. Then it waited. On January 5, President Clinton announced the final roadless rule. The final rule replaced the broad "stewardship" language with specific requirements allowing logging of small-diameter trees to reduce wildfire potential and to improve habitat for endangered and threatened species. It also applied to the Tongass National Forest when the rule went into effect (not in 2004), a significant improvement. But it also allowed for new roads to reach existing mineral leases. The rule was published on January 12, eight days before President George W. Bush was inaugurated, and was scheduled to take effect on March 13, 2001.

The outcome of the Clinton administration's efforts at public lands reform was both extraordinary and vulnerable. The final roadless rule conveyed a new level of protection to 58.5 million acres of national forest roadless areas nationwide. It was also the highest-profile in a series of administrative rules, including new rules to guide forest planning and the forest transportation system, that collectively required the Forest Service to manage the forests more sustainably, to give more attention to biodiversity protection and ecosystem processes, to promote collaborative decision-making, and to better integrate science into policy. In addition, the BLM's new 3809 mining regulations were scheduled to take effect on January 20, 2001. And in President Clinton's final year, Babbitt, who was secretary of the interior during the entire Clinton administration, succeeded in making the Antiquities Act a centerpiece of the president's public lands protection legacy. Clinton exercised his authority under the Antiquities Act of 1906 to establish nineteen new national monuments and expand three more to protect areas such as Giant Sequoia in California, Canyons of the Ancients in Colorado, Cascade-Siskiyou in Oregon, Vermilion Cliffs in Arizona, Carrizo Plain in California, and the Sonoran Desert in Arizona.[124] The actions incensed opponents of public lands protection in the West, especially Republicans who had tried to revoke the Antiquities Act or amend it to include public input, require environmental impact statements, and otherwise limit the president's discretion. All told, in Clinton's final years, the administration had protected 6 million acres as national monuments and 58.5 million acres of national forest through the roadless rule, initiated tighter rules on logging, grazing, and mining, and overseen important shifts in the staff and priorities of the federal land agencies.

The Wilderness Society's president, Bill Meadows, praised Clinton's "legacy of protection for our wild forests."[125] The *New York Times* described the roadless rule as the "capstone in the president's efforts to protect the public lands from development."[126] But opponents in the West decried the new rule. Many observers, especially westerners, conservatives, and allies of the resource industries, complained that the new national monuments and the administrative rules had been pushed through in the very last moments of an administration that had never given their concerns a fair hearing. Representative Jim Hansen (R-UT)

described the roadless rule as an "administrative fiat."[127] Despite the controversy, political scientists have viewed the roadless rule as a model for how a
seemingly broken federal bureaucracy can work to advance the public interest
by empowering the president to effectively advance a policy agenda in the face
of congressional gridlock. Such analyses highlight the Clinton administration,
the Forest Service and its leadership, and especially Dombeck. But the turn
toward administrative rulemaking for the national forests was not the product of administrative initiative and the new importance of alternative policy
pathways alone. Equally important was the success with which a reorganized
wilderness movement had expanded the agenda for public lands reform and
the new organizational strategies that had restructured national environmental advocacy (best represented by the Heritage Forests Campaign). Thus, the
roadless rule was not only a significant administrative accomplishment, but, in
important respects, it marked the first national environmental campaign in a
new era of public lands advocacy.[128]

The Bush Administration and Failed Efforts at Public Lands Reform

With the start of George W. Bush's administration in 2001, public lands policy
turned on larger events.[129] On the campaign trail, Bush had been explicit about
his opposition to the Clinton administration's environmental policies. "I don't
believe in command and control [environmental policy] out of Washington,
D.C.," he explained in a presidential debate. He pointed specifically to the roadless rulemaking process, describing it as a Washington, D.C.-based policy that
was being advanced over the concerns of local communities. "That's not the
way I would have done it," he said, "I certainly would have consulted with governors and elected officials before I would have acted unilaterally."[130] President
Bush, Vice President Dick Cheney, and the administration's appointees sharply
reversed the priorities for the public lands. While Clinton had looked to environmental groups for his appointees, Bush looked to the energy and resource
industries. Gale Norton, Colorado's attorney general, who had worked with
James Watt both at the Mountain States Legal Foundation and in the Reagan
administration during the 1980s, replaced Bruce Babbitt as secretary of the
interior. Steven Griles, a coal industry leader, was appointed her deputy, a position in which he became a strong proponent for expanding energy production
on the public lands. James Connaughton, an attorney with strong ties to the
energy sector, replaced George Frampton as chair of the Council on Environmental Quality. Mark Rey, former timber industry lobbyist and vice president

of the American Forest and Paper Association, was appointed undersecretary of agriculture with oversight of the Forest Service. Kathleen Clarke, the director of Utah's Department of Natural Resources, who had a track record of favoring energy development, was appointed director of the BLM. The response from the environmental community was alarm. Norton's nomination was the "scariest" in twenty years, exclaimed Brock Evans. "Bush is calling for a war on the environment."[131]

The administration's earliest actions pointed to the challenges to come: Bush took steps that immediately delayed the Clinton roadless rule (and all other unimplemented administrative rules) pending further review, targeted the new national monuments for energy exploration, and announced a comprehensive energy plan that would expand production on the public lands. And like his father before him, the new president's energy plan specifically targeted ANWR's coastal plain. To many environmentalists, the administration's public lands policies seemed to have been lifted straight from the Reagan era. It appeared that way to James Watt, President Reagan's first secretary of the interior, too. "Everything Cheney's saying, everything the president's saying," remarked Watt, is what "we were saying twenty years ago, precisely."[132] The policy goals may have been similar, but the Bush administration did mark an important shift in strategy from the Reagan era. In the early 1980s, when Reagan and Watt challenged environmental protection, the president had promised to end the "lockup" of the public lands and to "roll back" environmental regulations as part of a broader anti-federal agenda. That more overt anti-environmental agenda, with Secretary Watt in the vanguard, was an easy target for the environmental movement. Media campaigns, petition drives, and strong public support had galvanized the environmental community, thwarting much of Reagan's anti-environmental agenda. But the Bush administration and its allies had learned two lessons from environmental politics in the 1980s and 1990s: demonizing environmental regulations outright was a political loser and moving quietly on alternative policy pathways was the most effective way to affect environmental reform.

The Bush administration learned the first lesson from the Wise Use Movement, which positioned itself as the champion of a new approach to "environmentalism." Even as Bush challenged the nation's basic environmental laws, opened the public lands to resource development, and avoided new concerns such as global warming, he offered a relentlessly positive environmental message. The president celebrated the nation's commitment to environmental protection: reducing air and water pollution, regulating hazardous waste sites, and supporting the national park system. Looking forward, he promised, "my administration will adopt a new spirit of respect and cooperation, because in the end, that is the better way to protect the environment we all share— a new environmentalism for the twenty-first century."[133] Bush promised that "Wise regulation and American innovation will make this country the world's leader in energy efficiency and conservation in the twenty-first century."[134] He emphasized that his wildfire policy would empower local communities, reduce bureaucratic red tape, and result in "less bickering, less politics, and more sound, common-sense policy."[135] And while there were plenty of experts on environmental issues in Washington, D.C., his policies on endangered species protection would give new respect and attention to the local "folks that are actually protecting the environment."[136] In 2002, a Republican pollster reported that the environment remained one of the most problematic issues

10.3 To many observers, the election of George W. Bush and his appointment of Gale Norton as secretary of the interior heralded a return to the days of Ronald Reagan's Secretary of the Interior James Watt, as this 2001 political cartoon by Steve Greenberg suggests. But the Bush administration had learned from the Republican Party's earlier failures. His agenda resembled the Reagan administration's, but it was disguised by more environmentally friendly rhetoric. Courtesy Steve Greenberg.

for Republicans, but that by emphasizing "common-sense" policies, claiming "a commitment to 'preserving and protecting' the environment," and pledging to do better than their predecessors, Republicans could make a "conservative, free market approach to the environment" a political winner.[137] The emphasis on stewardship, local initiatives, a smaller federal bureaucracy, and a balance of economic growth and environmental protection harked back to the Wise Use Movement.

The Bush administration learned another lesson from the Reagan era and the 104th Congress: even with Republican control of Congress, it could achieve its goals more effectively by pursuing administrative action on alternative policy pathways, such as administrative rulemaking and judicial action. Thus, the policy initiatives the Bush administration did choose to push in Congress were calculated (not always correctly) to draw public support. The first was the administration's energy plan, spearheaded by Vice President Cheney, which emphasized the importance of conservation and energy efficiency and called for the expansion and diversification of domestic energy production. The plan gave the most attention to expanding natural gas and petroleum production and restarting the expansion of the nation's nuclear power industry. The key arguments rested on the importance of meeting growing national energy demand, holding down prices, and securing national energy independence. Bush argued that ANWR could provide enough oil to replace what the United States imported from Iraq in 2000.[138]

Bush's energy plan, which had been developed with no input from the environmental community, faced strong opposition immediately. When Senator Jim Jeffords (VT) left the Republican Party to become an independent in the spring of 2001, Senate leadership returned to the Democrats, signaling new challenges for the Bush administration's agenda. Even after the terrorist attacks on September 11, 2001, the Bush administration and conservative Republicans struggled to advance the administration's energy policy. Disagreements over opening up ANWR, increases in fuel efficiency requirements for automobiles, deregulation in the energy industry, and support for nuclear power dominated congressional debate between 2001 and 2005. Congress passed a scaled-down energy plan in 2005 that omitted the most controversial issues, including automobile efficiency and ANWR.[139] A separate effort in 2005 to open ANWR through the congressional appropriations process was blocked, just barely, by moderate Republicans and Democrats with strong support from the environmental community.[140] The Bush administration miscalculated the breadth of public support for energy development, especially in ANWR.

The administration was more successful in advancing its forestry policies. Intense wildfire seasons in the West in 1999, 2000, and 2002 captured national attention with images of devastated forests, evacuees, and the charred remains of homes, along with reports of high firefighting costs and dead firefighters. Promoting "healthy forests" became a centerpiece of Bush's forest policy. In the face of catastrophic wildfire due to historical fire suppression, suburban growth, and drought conditions, the administration argued active management, such as selective logging and prescribed burns, was imperative.[141] During the Clinton administration, the Forest Service and Department of the Interior cooperated on a National Fire Plan that aimed to expand firefighting capabilities and pre-emptive forest treatment.[142] The Bush administration expedited and expanded those programs, arguing that lack of funding, bureaucratic inefficiencies, and lawsuits had delayed forest treatment. Supporters argued that zealous environmentalists had shut down logging on the national forests through wilderness designations and administrative and legal appeals, actions that contributed to the wildfires of the late 1990s and early 2000s.[143] When the 107th Congress failed to pass forest reform legislation, the administration announced administrative reforms in August 2002: it exempted small-scale fuel reduction activities (of fewer than 1,000 acres) and prescribed burns (of fewer than 4,500 acres) from environmental review, and it limited the administrative appeals process for such emergency actions.[144]

The Wilderness Society and the environmental community agreed with the Bush administration on the importance of reforming forest policy to protect homes, vulnerable communities, and forest health, but they saw a threefold threat in the Bush administration's Healthy Forests Initiative. First, it misrepresented the obstacles to wildfire mitigation. Contrary to the Bush administration's assertions, only 1 percent of fire reduction programs had been appealed (and none litigated). Second, it prioritized forest thinning activities on federal lands, even though other strategies could more effectively protect vulnerable communities. The Wilderness Society emphasized that the most effective way to protect exposed homes was to fireproof them and clear fuels in their immediate vicinity. But the administration's proposals allocated 94 percent of funding to the federal lands, even though they accounted for only 15 percent of the land immediately adjacent to vulnerable communities.[145] In the summer of 2003, the NRDC argued that the "hidden purpose of the bill is to allow timber companies to evade environmental laws and circumvent public input in order to cut down large, fire-resistant trees on millions of acres of public forestlands."[146] Third, the Wilderness Society and NRDC warned that the initiative aimed to roll back existing environmental regulations, such as the requirements for environmental review under NEPA, and it limited opportunities for public comment.

Congress passed the Healthy Forests Restoration Act with strong bipartisan support the following year.[147] When President Bush signed it in December 2003, the law expanded the scope of the forest treatment program (it targeted 20 million acres) and prioritized protection for "at-risk communities" and municipal watersheds. Environmentalists succeeded in making specific improvements to the law with the help of Senate Democrats: it required that 50 percent of funds be spent in areas within a mile and a half of at-risk communities, put wilderness areas and wilderness study areas off limits, required limited reviews under NEPA, and allowed for court appeals and injunctions in some instances. The legislation marked the Bush administration's greatest success in joining its environmental policy agenda to its strategy to reframe public debate and effect environmental reform. But the program brought little immediate relief: the 2004, 2007, and 2008 fire seasons were exceptionally intense. During those years, only 11 percent of fuel treatments occurred in the wildland-urban interface, and 62 percent occurred more than six miles from vulnerable communities, often with no demonstrable fire mitigation goals. Those results raised questions about the subsequent implementation of the Healthy Forests Restoration Act.[148]

While legislative debates over energy policy and wildfire management moved slowly through Congress during Bush's first term, administrative action came quickly. In the 1990s, the Clinton administration had exercised its administrative authority to align the federal land agencies with the environmental community's goals, culminating with a burst of administrative initiatives at the end of its second term. In the early 2000s, the Bush administration moved aggressively to reverse those gains. An observer at *High Country News* explained the mindset of Bush's allies succinctly: "It's payback time."[149] The administration made energy development the top priority for the BLM: the agency expedited permit applications, streamlined environmental reviews, and relaxed its inspection and oversight work. Between 1999 and 2004, the number of oil and gas permits processed annually tripled to 6,399; 97 percent of those permits were issued in Colorado, Montana, New Mexico, Utah, and Wyoming.[150] The immediate consequences were local—toxic waste, contaminated water supplies, and industrial development—and regional—fragmented wildlife habitat and disrupted migratory corridors.

Most vulnerable were Clinton's administrative reforms such as the mining rule, the scientifically informed forest planning rule, the grazing rule, and the roadless rule. In October 2001, the Department of the Interior reversed much of the Clinton mining rule, notably the provision allowing the secretary of the interior to veto environmentally damaging mines, but it retained Clinton's bonding requirements meant to ensure adequate funds to guarantee cleanup of mines.[151] In December 2002, the Department of Agriculture proposed a new set of forest planning rules based on the 2000 Clinton-era rules. Instead of giving priority to ecological sustainability, as Clinton had intended, the new rule called for balancing ecological, social, and economic sustainability. In lieu of the requirement to protect viable populations of vertebrate species (on which the spotted owl debates turned), Bush made the requirement non-mandatory. And regional foresters were given more flexibility in complying with NEPA, handling forest plan appeals, and making management decisions. To environmentalists, the new rule reversed the commitment to science and ecological protection that had been ascendant in the 1990s.[152] And in December 2003, the Bush administration took the first steps toward amending the grazing rules that Secretary Babbitt had pushed through in 1995. The newly proposed rules addressed ranchers' concerns, giving them part ownership of range improvements such as fences or wells, spacing out any reductions in grazing over five years, relaxing requirements for public comment on grazing decisions, and limiting the ability of the agency to declare rangeland "unhealthy."[153]

Of all the Clinton initiatives, the roadless rule became entangled in the most protracted legal debate during the Bush years.[154] From the start, some western states and the timber industry mounted a sustained legal challenge against the Clinton-era rule, arguing that it circumvented forest planning procedures (in violation of NFMA), designated wilderness (a privilege the Wilderness Act reserved for Congress), and failed to sufficiently involve the public (in violation of NEPA and the Administrative Procedure Act). Such claims led to an injunction by an Idaho district court in May 2001, two days before the rule was to go into effect. By 2003, additional legal suits and appeals resulted in a series of contradictory court rulings. The Ninth Circuit Court of Appeals overturned the Idaho district court decision in 2002 and affirmed the legality of the rule, but a Wyoming district court in the tenth circuit decided it was illegal on grounds it violated the Wilderness Act in 2003. In response, the Bush administration mounted a weak legal defense of the rule and chose, instead, to initiate a new regulatory process for the roadless areas that appeared to render both suits moot.

To reform the rule nationally, the Bush administration undertook a new rulemaking process in 2004 that led to a revised rule requiring that states peti-

10.4 Jonah Natural Gas Field, south of Pinedale, Wyoming, 2006. Drilling for natural gas expanded significantly on public lands in the intermountain West during the Bush administration, with consequences for both air quality and wildlife habitat. Photograph by Bruce Gordon. Courtesy Ecoflight, Aspen, Colorado.

tion the Forest Service to protect roadless areas on a state-by-state basis in 2005. In response, the Tenth Circuit Court of Appeals set aside the Wyoming court's decision that invalidated the Clinton-era rule on grounds that it was no longer relevant.[155] But the new Bush roadless rule was also quickly challenged in court. In August 2005, the states of California, Oregon, and New Mexico filed suit in the ninth circuit, which had upheld the Clinton-era rule in 2002, on grounds that the Bush administration had failed to complete an environmental impact statement for the new rule. Even as the Heritage Forests Campaign launched an initiative to support strong state petitions, twenty environmental groups joined that suit in October 2005. They rightly worried that some states would pursue lesser levels of protection.[156] Idaho, which successfully completed a petition under the Bush rule in 2008, weakened protection on 5.3 of the 9.3 million acres of roadless areas in the state to allow for temporary roads in special cases, and effectively opened .4 million acres for potential development.[157]

The Bush administration's efforts to reform public lands policy—including the new grazing, forest planning, and roadless rules—were largely ruled illegal. Courts threw out most of the new Bush-era rules, with the exceptions of the administration's mining reforms and the Idaho roadless rule. The new grazing rules and the forest planning rules were deemed illegal in 2007 and 2009 respectively on grounds that the agency failed to meet NEPA's requirements for environmental review and the ESA's requirements for consultation with the Fish and Wildlife Service. The story was similar in the case of the roadless rule. In September 2006, a California federal district court determined that the Bush administration's new state petition rule was illegal on grounds that the agency conducted neither additional environmental analysis as required by NEPA nor the interagency consultation required by the ESA. The decision invalidated the 2005 state petition rule and reinstated the 2001 Clinton-era roadless rule. Opponents immediately looked to the Wyoming federal district court, which had ruled the Clinton-era rule illegal in 2003, for relief. A new suit in the same court resulted in the same decision in August 2008 and an injunction against the implementation of the Clinton-era rule.[158] That decision directly contradicted the September 2006 decision in the California federal district court. In August 2009, the Ninth Circuit Court of Appeals upheld the California court's decision reinstating the roadless rule, but limited the scope of its decision to the states in the ninth circuit. In October 2011, the Tenth Circuit Court of Appeals reversed the Wyoming district court's decision, effectively reinstating the Clinton-era roadless rule (with the exception of Idaho). Thus, the Clinton roadless rule largely survived the persistent challenges of western states, the timber industry, and the Bush administration. The durability of the roadless rule depended on the legal skill with which the rulemaking process was originally crafted under the Clinton administration and on an exceptional legal defense mounted by lawyers at Earthjustice led by Jim Angell.[159]

Bush's public lands agenda never succeeded in rallying a populist Sagebrush Rebellion or Wise Use Movement. The administration did have strong allies on public lands issues, such as conservative Republicans Jim Hansen of Utah and Larry Craig of Idaho. And some Bush policies did play well in the West, such as those emphasizing local decision-making, fighting wildfire, and support for off-road vehicle use, and there was national support for energy development. But from the start, it was clear the Bush administration could not count on the support of moderate Republicans. Senator John Warner (R-VA) sponsored legislation in the Senate to legislatively enact the roadless rule during Bush's first term. Moderate Republicans sunk the administration's best opportunity to open ANWR to petroleum exploration in 2005 as part of a filibuster-proof rescissions package. And a renewed Republicans for Environmental Protection refused to endorse Bush during his reelection campaign. Most significantly, the Bush administration's emphasis on energy development, especially in the Mountain West, alienated some of the Republican Party's key allies in the region: rural residents often protested the accompanying air and water pollution, ranchers resisted encroachments on grazing lands, and the "hook and rod" constituency of hunters and anglers viewed energy development as a threat to wildlife habitat. Research demonstrated that the expansion of drilling in states such as Colorado, Montana, Wyoming, and Utah was especially problematic for key game species, such as mule deer, elk, and antelope.[160] National groups like Trout Unlimited and the Theodore Roosevelt Conservation Partnership and local groups such as the Great Falls Bowhunters Association and the Custer Rod and Gun Club—many of which had been actively courted by the broader environmental community and national foundations— became important players in public lands policy, often aligning with environmental groups in opposition to the Bush administration and the Republican Party's priorities.[161] Those shifting allegiances reflected broader changes in a region that was no longer safe turf for the Republican Party.

Conclusion

What was the legacy of the Bush administration's agenda for the public lands? Some analysts have highlighted the Bush administration's effectiveness in achieving its goals not only for the public lands but for environmental policy more broadly.[162] The Bush administration worked to change the rules governing the implementation of the Clean Air Act to give priority to market-based regulations, the Clean Water Act to redefine protected wetlands, and the ESA to relax requirements for scientific consultation. In most cases, the Bush administration took steps that undermined the existing environmental regulatory state, including advances made during the Clinton administration. But, in retrospect, it is clear those efforts proved generally unsuccessful. As the political scientists Klyza and Sousa explain, despite the Bush administration's anti-environmental policy agenda, the enduring power of the existing environmental regulatory state, the effective mobilization of interest groups, and widespread but shallow public support for environmental reform all combined to continue to push American environmental policy in "directions favored by environmentalists."[163] In light of the series of judicial rebukes that struck down most of the Bush administration's administrative initiatives both on public lands issues, such as grazing and the roadless rule, and other issues, such as the regulatory requirements of the Clean Air Act and the ESA, this analysis has merit.[164] Although the Bush administration succeeded in weakening the Clinton administration's legacy, it failed to effect any fundamental reforms in the environmental regulatory state. Klyza and Sousa describe this "slow and even halting" trajectory of American environmental policy toward environmental goals as "green drift."[165] They offer that metaphor not to diminish the underlying volatility of environmental politics, but to highlight the dominant trend in environmental policy since the 1990s.

The story of public lands politics and policy offers two reasons to think carefully about the implications of that metaphor, however. First, it diminishes the very real and significant anti-environmental eddies that run counter to "green drift." While the Bush administration did not succeed in accomplishing its regulatory reform goals for the public lands, in many instances it did succeed in fundamentally changing the western landscape and institutional priorities. In the first decade of the twenty-first century, the West witnessed a tremendous expansion in public lands energy development, particularly in Colorado, Wyoming, Utah, and Montana, which was accompanied by sprawling infrastructure, polluted groundwater, and diminished wildlife populations. It also effected an important shift in the priorities of the BLM away from grazing and toward energy development. Second, although "green drift" is not meant to diminish the significance of partisan politics, its tacit optimism runs that risk. Therefore we should be specific: such anti-environmental eddies have been created most often and proved most significant due to the goals of Republican administrations. History reminds us that Nixon championed the Trans-Alaska Pipeline, Reagan and Watt teamed up to push for domestic energy production in Alaska and the West, and George H. W. Bush and George W. Bush made ANWR the centerpiece of their energy policies. Although Democrats have promoted domestic energy production, Republican administrations have taken the lead on putting short-term concerns for energy development first. In short, laws may not have been changed during George W. Bush's administration, but the nation's public lands were changed and changed for the worse. And, as the chants of "Drill, Baby, Drill!" during the summer of 2008 reminded us, such policies have a powerful populist appeal. "Green drift" is not assured.

There are reasons to hold out guarded optimism regarding the direction of environmental reform, however. Again, focusing specifically on the public lands yields an important point. "Green drift" has not been a passive process determined by underlying structural forces—which is the metaphor's implication. To accept that implication is to miss a crucial development since the early 1990s. The national environmental movement, represented by interest groups, such as the Wilderness Society, and national coalitions, such as the Heritage Forests Campaign, has played an essential role in environmental politics. This point may seem surprising, considering the sustained critique of mainstream American environmentalism.[166] But this point is not predicated on hopes for a green revolution, but rather Klyza and Sousa's prediction of a slow, halting "green drift." And to the extent there is such a "green drift," it is in large measure a product of how successfully interest groups have not just "mobilized," but demonstrated their resiliency, adaptability, and creativity in both defending the existing environmental regulatory state and advancing new environmental goals across a wide range of pathways to environmental reform since the 1990s.[167] In short, the synergy of the Heritage Forests Campaign, the efforts to cultivate a broader constituency, and a new commitment to building coalitions of grassroots organizations reflect important strategic shifts. These changes have been especially evident in the case of public lands advocacy. The end product is a more politically capable movement for public lands protection than was present in the early 1990s, despite the unfavorable political climate in the intervening years. The "green drift" of the 1990s and early 2000s, in the case of the public lands, was the work of environmental advocates who actively piloted the environmental regulatory state through an ever-contested landscape of American environmental politics.

EPILOGUE

REBUILDING THE WILDERNESS MOVEMENT

rnie Dickerman lived on a modest farm at the base of Elliot's Knob near Buffalo Gap in western Virginia, not too far from Ramsey's Draft Wilderness in the George Washington National Forest. Dickerman was a stalwart in the wilderness movement: dogged, focused on citizen activism, respected by friend and foe alike, and resolute in his commitment to wilderness. He had gotten his start in wilderness politics in Knoxville, Tennessee, in the 1930s, where he was a member of the Smoky Mountains Hiking Club and came to know the Wilderness Society's founders, including Harvey Broome, Bob Marshall, and Benton MacKaye. There, he emerged as a champion for wilderness in the Great Smoky Mountains National Park. When he moved to Washington, D.C., in 1966 to join the Wilderness Society's staff, he became a linchpin in citizen wilderness advocacy, especially for Virginia and Alaska. And after he retired from the Wilderness Society in 1976, just as the organization began its turn toward professionalism, he moved to the farm at Buffalo Gap where he kept busy—churning out wilderness correspondence on his 1940s Royal Portable typewriter, reading the *Wall Street Journal* (to keep tabs on the opposition, he said), coordinating grassroots wilderness advocacy in Virginia, and counseling wilderness leaders nationwide. In 1986, the Sierra Club described him as the "granddad of the Eastern wilderness." He was that and more. Dickerman had been a mentor to a generation of wilderness advocates and a leader and supporter of every major wilderness campaign from the Wilderness Act of 1964 to the California Desert Protection Act of 1994.

It was for that reason that the events of July 31, 1998, caught many of those in the wilderness community by surprise. At the end of a beautiful summer day on his farm, Dickerman took the short walk from his home to a nearby cherry tree, removed his shirt, carefully hung it on a branch, and shot himself. He was eighty-seven years old. In his words, "I'm the captain of my ship / And the master of my fate, In the wilds of this wild country." Inside the cabin, all was in order. Dickerman had left a prepared announcement of his death:

E.1 Ernie Dickerman (holding microphone), who was renowned for his skills as an organizer and lobbyist, at the start of the "Save-Our-Smokies-Wilderness Hike" at Clingmans Dome parking area in Great Smoky Mountains National Park, October 23, 1966. Photograph by Bill Russell. Courtesy Liane Russell.

E.2 Ernie Dickerman retired to a small farm in the George Washington National Forest in Virginia, which became an important hub of wilderness advocacy in the 1980s and 1990s. This picture was taken in April 1998, shortly before Dickerman's death that September. Photograph by Shireen Parsons. Courtesy Shireen Parsons, Gerhild Dickerman, and Bob Dickerman.

"On (date) Ernest M. 'Ernie' Dickerman, a lifelong bachelor, died at age 87 by his own hand as he had long planned, on the little old farm in the Alleghany Mountains where he had lived since retiring in 1976. 'Quit while you are ahead' is sound philosophy, both in poker and in life. For over sixty years, as an amateur or as a professional, he was an active conservationist, especially in wilderness preservation." Dickerman requested that the announcement be sent to his friends in the wilderness movement around the country; the mailing labels were pre-printed. "Reasonably early mailing of the announcements will be appreciated." His papers, at least the most pressing ones, were sorted into stacks, each marked with the name of the activist who would find them most useful. In the months before his death, Dickerman had made the rounds of his friends and colleagues, saying what in retrospect were clearly his final goodbyes. In sending out the announcement, his nephew, Bob Dickerman, eased the news with a letter. In it, he reported: "While Ernie's physical frailties were becoming increasingly apparent, there was never *any* diminishment of his intellect, humor, articulateness, memory or counsel—nor of his love of a good environmental fight (with, of course, an eventual win/win outcome). He remained Ernie to the very end."[1]

Turning Points in Wilderness and Environmental Politics

Dickerman's passing is a fitting place to bring this book to a close. Not only had he witnessed the key turning points in the history of wilderness advocacy since the 1960s, he had also shaped them. He had opinions—often quite strong—about them. And, in retrospect, his death came at and, in fact, influenced a new beginning.

Dickerman's approach to wilderness was representative of the work of the Wilderness Society and the national environmental movement in the 1960s and 1970s. In 1962, when he testified on behalf of the Wilderness Act, he described wilderness as "among the great heritages of our Nation" that "shaped our destiny . . . and forged the character of our people." He highlighted its scientific value as a source of knowledge "concerning the laws of nature." Its value, he emphasized, needed to be "preserved for ourselves and future generations."[2] Dickerman's emphasis on the uses of wilderness for science and recreation and his appeal to the national interest were characteristic of wilderness advocacy during the years of the Great Society. After the Wilderness Act became law, Dickerman was at the forefront of efforts to make the law a vehicle for citizen involvement in public lands decision-making nationwide. Who owns the public lands? Not the loggers, the oil industry, or the government, he replied. It was "the people."[3]

In 1966, Dickerman quit his job in Knoxville to move to Washington, D.C., to work for the Wilderness Society. No one had offered him a job. Instead, Dickerman just showed up for work. After Dickerman turned up at the society's offices day after day, Stewart Brandborg put him on the payroll. Between the late 1960s and mid-1970s, as a staffer, Dickerman supported local groups in the East, coordinated wilderness training sessions in Washington, D.C., and shepherded citizen wilderness proposals from ideas to law.[4] He was a dogged advocate for a pragmatic approach to wilderness. He warned Congress in 1973 of the hazards in "mistaking the ideal concept of wilderness for the less austere, more practical definition set forth in the Wilderness Act."[5] These strategies worked for Dickerman, the Wilderness Society's staff, and its allies.

In 1976, when the Wilderness Society fired Stewart Brandborg, its executive director and chief proponent of citizen activism, Dickerman left too. Those events marked a crucial turning point for the Wilderness Society and helped set the stage for its transformation into a professional environmental lobby that depended on foundation funds, poured its resources into scientific and technical expertise, relaxed its commitment to citizen outreach, and began to push wilderness aside as it focused on a broader and more far-reaching agenda for public lands reform. The Wilderness Society followed the trajectory of the national environmental movement toward professionalism and consolidation in Washington, D.C. Dickerman could see the advantages in such strategies. Apart from eastern wild lands, his other passion was Alaska, especially the Arctic National Wildlife Refuge (ANWR). And it was the strategies of this new, more professional environmental movement that proved important to protecting Alaska's public lands.

Starting in the 1970s, wilderness advocates used tools such as the National Environmental Policy Act to expand their agenda for public lands protection. Its requirements for environmental review and public involvement gave wilderness advocates new leverage in public lands policy decisions. But Dickerman lamented the Wilderness Society's withdrawal into professionalism and its growing distance from citizen groups. In the late 1970s and early 1980s, the wilderness movement faced separate challenges from radical environmental groups such as Earth First! and from rural citizens who joined together under the banner of the Sagebrush Rebellion. In the past, an active program of citizen outreach had done much to address, even defuse, such challenges, but in

1987, Dickerman described the Wilderness Society as "one more cozy, private Washington bureaucracy, happily spinning its wheels, free from the dust and sweat of citizen contact, self-satisfied with its frequent, erudite publications." The organization had new strengths, but they had come "at the expense of grassroots motivating."[6]

The Wilderness Society did not heed Dickerman's criticism. In 1986, its new president, George Frampton, argued that the Wilderness Society remained committed to the grassroots while it vastly expanded its other capabilities. "The Wilderness Society is stronger today, has more contacts at the grassroots, and more clout on Capitol Hill than at any time in its history," he said.[7] But in the late 1980s and early 1990s, the Wilderness Society faced an increasingly complex federal environmental policy system and growing public opposition. It redoubled its commitment to pursuing new strategies grounded in natural resource economics, conservation biology, and policy expertise. Those strategies helped move other important issues to the forefront of public lands debates: protecting endangered species such as the spotted owl, ending below-cost timber sales, and reforming grazing practices on the public lands. Often, those strategies moved along non-legislative pathways, such as administrative rulemaking and litigation, rather than through Congress. While citizen involvement was important to many of these campaigns, the active partnerships that joined local and national groups weakened. The most active citizen involvement often seemed to come from the opposition, as rural communities, natural resource industries, and their conservative allies came together under the banner of the Wise Use Movement. In the 1980s and 1990s, the political climate for public lands reform grew increasingly unfriendly, as conservative Republicans and allies of the resource industries gained power first in Congress and then in the White House. It was these changes that put public lands reform on a political seesaw in which the prospects for reform rose with opportunities such as the Clinton-era roadless rule and fell with challenges such as the Republican salvage rider.

The 1990s were full of disappointment and frustration for wilderness advocates. At the start of the decade, a burst of energy around the New Conservation Movement and the Wildlands Project raised expectations for wilderness designation. In the early 1990s, the Wilderness Society and the Sierra Club began charting out expansive regional visions for public lands protection. But a more ambitious generation of wilderness advocates proved unable to oil the legislative gears of Congress. Despite some successes in the early 1990s, notably the California Desert Protection Act of 1994, Congress designated fewer than

100,000 acres of new wilderness areas between 1995 and 1999. Instead, wilderness advocates spent much of the decade trying to hold the line against efforts to roll back wilderness and public lands protection advanced by a Republican-led Congress. They weathered a storm of criticism in the 1990s. Resource industries, conservative politicians, and allies of the Wise Use Movement continued to criticize wilderness as a lockup. Environmental justice advocates raised concerns about the disconnect between wilderness campaigns and local, pressing urban issues.[8] Scholars and some activists began to describe wilderness as a distraction from other environmental issues.[9] Even as legislative efforts to protect wilderness seemingly ground to a halt and such critiques mounted, new and old generations of wilderness advocates worked together to lay the foundations for a resurgent wilderness movement. It would take more than a decade for the significance of their efforts to become apparent.

Rebuilding the Wilderness Movement

Brian O'Donnell learned of Ernie Dickerman's death as he came off a week-long rafting trip on the Green River in Utah. He had seen Dickerman only a few months before at the first Wilderness Mentoring Conference at Rex Ranch in southern Arizona. That conference marked a new beginning for wilderness advocacy. At the start of the conference, Tim Mahoney, a veteran wilderness lobbyist, explained, "we've skipped a generation of people who moved [wilderness] bills." The conference, organized by a handful of young wilderness leaders with the support of several foundations, aimed to introduce a rising generation of wilderness activists to mentors who had shepherded big legislation for the national forests, Alaska, and California through Congress. The starting point for the conference was not philosophical questions about wilderness and its place in environmental advocacy—questions that had preoccupied critics during the "great new wilderness debate" in the 1990s. Its starting point was politics. As Mahoney emphasized, this was about "pragmatism and realism" and how to get "the votes." The conference brought together leaders such as Doug Scott, Tim Mahoney, Debbie Sease, and Bart Koehler, who echoed that viewpoint. But O'Donnell remembers that it was Ernie Dickerman who stole the show. At the start of the conference, everyone wondered who the elderly guy in the corner with the plaid shirt and stiff baseball cap was. By the end, Dickerman had captured the imagination of a new generation of wilderness advocates: his emphasis on pragmatism, his belief that all stakeholders be engaged, and his respect for the opposition all resonated. "Respect, honesty, and cour-

E.3 Brian O'Donnell and Melyssa Watson cofounded the Wilderness Support Center with Bart Koehler and helped strengthen citizen wilderness advocacy in the late 1990s and 2000s. Teklanika River, Denali National Park. Photograph by Kevin Mack, June 2000. Courtesy Melyssa Watson.

tesy will carry you far in lobbying," explained Dickerman. "Lobbying succeeds through trust."[10] When O'Donnell returned to the office from his trip on the Green River, he found Dickerman's self-penned obituary in the mail. Dickerman's preparations brought a chuckle, but his death made evident a realization O'Donnell had come to that spring: "I guess it is up to us now."[11]

O'Donnell has a strong presence: he has light-brown hair and blue eyes, a tall frame, and broad shoulders. It is easy to imagine him matching Dickerman step for step on a wilderness trail, but he came to wilderness advocacy on a different path. He was born in New Jersey, but spent much of his youth living in Egypt. Vacations in the country south of Cairo sparked his passion for open desert and the relics of human history. After attending college in Florida, he followed his girlfriend, Melyssa Watson, to Washington, D.C. Once there, O'Donnell worked his way up the ladder of public lands advocacy. He volunteered for the Sierra Club at the tail end of the campaign for the California Desert Protection Act and worked on a failed Democratic representative's campaign in Washington state in the fall of 1994. Good timing and his promise thrust him into the executive director position of the Alaska Wilderness League in the mid-1990s, where he spent four exhausting years fending off a parade of conservative efforts to roll back environmental protection for the state's wilderness areas and the Tongass National Forest and to open up ANWR's coastal plain to energy exploration. During those years, Watson worked for a women's rights lobby during the day but spent her evenings and weekends volunteering for wilderness groups and her vacations out West with O'Donnell. Soon her future would be in wilderness advocacy too. O'Donnell made his reputation early by cultivating moderate Republicans to help protect Alaska's public lands—a strategy that played a crucial role in defusing the threats of the 104th Congress and, later, George W. Bush's administration. Those experiences led O'Donnell to three realizations: he did not want to spend his life fighting defensive campaigns that had beaten him and his colleagues down in the 104th Congress; wilderness campaigns that tried to rally national support to overcome local opposition, as was the case for Alaska and Utah, were often uphill battles; and he and Watson wanted to get out of Washington, D.C.—to protect wild lands, you needed to know them.[12]

In the summer of 1998, O'Donnell kept pushing a plan he, Watson, and several friends had hatched the previous year. It had gained momentum at the Wilderness Mentoring Conference, and now seemed more urgent than ever: a Wilderness Support Center. The strongest wilderness campaigns in the 1990s were focused on Utah and Alaska, states whose congressional delegations were hostile to wilderness. Many other states, such as New Mexico, Montana, and Nevada, still had exceptional unprotected wild lands (many of which were Bureau of Land Management public domain lands) and they had neutral, even friendly, congressional delegations. But there was a problem. "There were a lot of groups out there passionate about protecting a wild place," remembers O'Donnell, "but they did not know where to start." The Wilderness Support Center would be a "tag team," as Watson envisioned it, which "could be an extra pair of hands for events, fundraising, organizing, and inventory work."

The center would teach wilderness advocates how to do what they had been so good at in the 1960s and 1970s: building wilderness campaigns, generating grassroots support, negotiating with opponents, and moving wilderness legislation. The Wilderness Mentoring Conference was a first step in this direction; the Wilderness Support Center would sustain the effort. In the fall of 1998, the now-married O'Donnell and Watson set up shop on Main Avenue in Durango, Colorado. As O'Donnell remembers, their goal was not to create an organization, but to help rekindle a movement. But they knew no one was going to trust a couple of twenty-somethings to advance this agenda. To strengthen their credibility, they partnered with Bart Koehler, who had gotten his start in grassroots organizing with the Wilderness Society in the early 1970s, had helped organize Earth First! in the early 1980s, and had led the Southeast

Alaska Conservation Council since the early 1990s (where he worked closely with O'Donnell and the Alaska Wilderness League). Koehler had been enthusiastic about the project since first learning of it at the Wilderness Mentoring Conference. In 1998, they received start-up funds for the Wilderness Support Center from several foundations, but to make a go of it they needed long-term support. That led them into what, at the time, was a seemingly unlikely partnership with the Wilderness Society.[13]

O'Donnell was leery of the Wilderness Society. In 1996, it had run roughshod over the Alaska Wilderness League when it tried to convince President Clinton to designate ANWR's coastal plain as a national monument. The Alaska Wilderness League learned of the unsuccessful proposal only after it broke in the news media. O'Donnell thought of the Wilderness Society as the "country club" of wilderness advocacy. But the Wilderness Society had begun to change. In 1996, Bill Meadows replaced Jon Roush as president. No one expected much from Meadows. As *High Country News* reported, "All anyone knew about Meadows was that 'III' followed his name and he had raised ninety-two million dollars for the Sierra Club."[14] Meadows's professional career had been in fundraising—in higher education initially, then the Sierra Club's centennial campaign in the early 1990s. What few appreciated was that he had gotten his start in environmental activism as a volunteer with the Sierra Club in Tennessee in the early 1970s. When Meadows arrived at the Wilderness Society, at the end of the 104th Congress, it was evident that the organization lacked focus, had diminished lobbying ability in Congress, and had poor working ties to other organizations. The organization's strength was in its technical capabilities and policy staff. Meadows realized that it needed to match those strengths with better outreach and political organizing.

Meadows has an easy way with people. His presence is warm and open and he speaks with a soft Southern accent. In the decade after he took the helm of the Wilderness Society, he became a leading figure in the wilderness movement. With the support of Bert Fingerhut, a charismatic, energetic, wealthy financier who became the chair of the Wilderness Society's Governing Council in 1997 and had long-standing ties to the Southern Utah Wilderness Alliance (SUWA), Meadows reached out to local groups. When he traveled to regional offices, he met not only with his local staff, but also with other local groups working on public lands campaigns. He took part in the Idaho Conservation League's annual gathering of grassroots groups, and in the fall of 1998, he saw the proposal for a Wilderness Support Center as an opportunity for the Wilderness Society and a larger wilderness movement.[15]

E.4 Bill Meadows, president of the Wilderness Society from 1996 to 2012, has strengthened the organization's commitment to citizen wilderness advocacy. Courtesy the Wilderness Society.

No one appreciated the symbolism of the Wilderness Society partnering with the Wilderness Support Center more than Bart Koehler. Koehler started in wilderness politics working with Doug Scott, Ernie Dickerman, Clif Merritt, and Stewart Brandborg at the Wilderness Society in the early 1970s. He attended one of the first wilderness-training seminars the Wilderness Society ran in Washington, D.C., in 1973, and he became a crack organizer in the West. But Koehler's career with the Wilderness Society ended in 1979 when Bill Turnage closed down the Buckaroo Bunkhouse, which was the center of its grassroots operation, and restructured the organization as a professional environmental lobby. For Koehler, the prospect of teaming up with the Wilderness Society to establish the Wilderness Support Center offered a chance to return the organization to its roots. It was a sentiment that Dickerman would have appreciated. Despite Meadows and Fingerhut's enthusiasm for the proposal, support for the Wilderness Support Center within the Wilderness Society was not automatic. Many on the Governing Council saw a new program as a potential drain on an organization that had struggled financially since the early 1990s. Many staff members argued it was an unnecessary duplication of work they thought they were doing, or could do, in their regional offices. In fact, the Wilderness Society's regional office in New England was doing just this kind of work to build support for a new wilderness bill. But Meadows and Fingerhut were convinced that if the Wilderness Society was going to rebuild its grassroots capability, it had to reorganize—not just add staff to existing regional offices. The prospect of significant and long-term support from the Pew Charitable Trusts ensured that the center would not become a fiscal drain on the organization. And, in the spring of 1999, the Wilderness Support Center became an arm of the Wilderness Society.[16]

It was bad timing. The late 1990s and early 2000s, at the end of the Clinton administration and the start of George W. Bush's administration, were an inauspicious moment for rebuilding the local roots of the wilderness movement. Anti-environmental initiatives in Congress peaked during the 104th Congress but did not disappear in the 105th and 106th Congresses. The Utah congressional delegation attempted to pass legislation that would "sunset" the BLM wilderness study areas after ten years of congressional inaction. Environmentalists fended off Senator Ted Stevens's attempt to open up Alaskan wilderness areas to helicopter landings by changing a single word, "airplane," to "aircraft" in the Department of Transportation appropriations bill. Republicans tried to scrap funding for rulemaking activities, such as the Clinton administration's mining regulations. Such maneuvering, none of which ultimately succeeded, kept environmentalists on the defensive. In contrast, the most significant advances for public lands protection at the end of the Clinton administration followed administrative pathways that ran around, not through, Congress. The most prominent such initiative was the administrative rule to protect 58.5 million acres of national forest roadless areas, which was orchestrated by the Clinton administration, the Forest Service, and the Heritage Forests Campaign. The Clinton administration's other key environmental initiative was a flurry of national monument designations, spearheaded by Secretary of the Interior Bruce Babbitt, which proceeded with strong support from the environmental community. But the Wilderness Support Center played little role in the administrative campaigns in the late 1990s. It seemed to have hitched its cart to the wrong horse.

Although the roadless rule and the national monuments captured the headlines in 2000 and 2001, five wilderness bills did move through Congress. After a five-year dry spell, during which Congress designated only four small wilderness areas, these bills helped demonstrate that wilderness remained a viable legislative vehicle. The Wilderness Support Center threw its efforts behind the largest bill, which protected ten new wilderness areas in Nevada's Black Rock Desert. Nevada was a most unlikely place for wilderness: it was the redoubt of the Sagebrush Rebellion and the Wise Use Movement, and the state aggressively opposed reforms of public lands mining and grazing policies. As recently as 1995, *Time* magazine had featured Nevada's Wise Use Movement on its cover with the headline "Don't Tread on Me."[17] Many wilderness leaders in Washington saw the Wilderness Support Center's Nevada campaign as quixotic, but the center's staff saw potential: the state had 4.3 million acres of wilderness study areas, a congressional delegation open to discussions, and an established, but not crowded, wilderness advocacy community, creating an opportunity for the Wilderness Support Center to get involved.

The Wilderness Support Center played an important supporting role in the creation of the Nevada Wilderness Project and the larger Nevada Wilderness Coalition, which included the existing Friends of Nevada Wilderness, in 1999. They worked with Senator Richard Bryan (D-NV) to move legislation to protect the Black Rock Desert. But their real contribution was building sufficient political support in urban areas, such as Las Vegas and Reno, to allow Senator Harry Reid (D-NV) maneuvering room to support the legislation. By early 2000, the Wilderness Support Center was working full-time on the Nevada legislation, organizing for town hall meetings, drumming up letters to the editor, coordinating on legislative strategy, and providing lobbying support in Washington, D.C.[18] In the end, the bill moved as a rider on an appropriations act. Representative Jim Gibbons (R-NV), sixteen of seventeen Nevada counties, and many Nevadans, especially hunters, opposed the legislation. Despite those shortcomings, the legislation pointed toward a new strategy for wilderness: it broke with the omnibus state-by-state model that had been prevalent since the 1980s, it protected a significant amount of land (757,000 acres), and it rebuilt political momentum around wilderness legislation, especially in Nevada.[19]

The conservative turn in national politics in the early 2000s forced wilderness advocates back on the defensive. Rhetorically, the Bush administration's approach to public lands protection highlighted a commitment to conservation through "communication," "consultation," and "cooperation."[20] An important priority during the Bush years was shifting public lands policy decisions back to the local level, a trend that the agencies, western congressional representatives, and wilderness advocates—especially those at the Wilderness Support Center—positioned themselves to take advantage of. But the Bush administration moved most quickly to put issues such as energy development and wildfire management at the forefront of its agenda. The administration made opening up ANWR a centerpiece of national energy policy, promoting energy independence and linking oil revenues from the refuge with federal financing for alternative energy development—a goal that failed only in 2005, when moderate Republicans refused to support opening the refuge through a filibuster-proof budget bill.[21] The administration worked to reverse the Clinton-era protection for national forest roadless areas by giving states a new say in roadless area management. It also advocated a reorientation of forest management to give priority to wildfire mitigation, timber harvesting, and other local concerns. In the most direct challenge to wilderness protection on the public domain, the administration settled a lawsuit with the state of Utah that invalidated all wilderness inventory areas established by the BLM since 1991, when George H. W. Bush's administration recommended 1.9 million acres of the Utah public domain for wilderness protection, and it restricted the agency's ability to create new wilderness study areas or manage other lands for future wilderness protection.[22] This decision meant that the 2.6 million acres of potential wilderness in Utah identified during the Clinton administration could not be elevated to wilderness study area status or managed under non-impairment standards pending congressional action. The administration signaled that the policy applied agency-wide. "Only Congress can create a wilderness area," Secretary of the Interior Gale Norton argued. "We are making that clear by settling the lawsuit."[23] From start to finish, the Bush administration demonstrated little enthusiasm for wilderness or public lands protection.

This is when the wilderness movement's changing strategy began to pay dividends. Mike Matz, the executive director of the Campaign for America's Wilderness, described the goal this way: to make wilderness legislation "politically inevitable." Starting in 2001, the Wilderness Support Center had a new ally.[24] The Pew Trusts reorganized its wilderness program as the Campaign for America's Wilderness in 2001. Matz, the former executive director at SUWA, Ken Rait, the leader of the Heritage Forests Campaign, and Doug Scott, who spearheaded the lobbying campaign for the Alaska lands act, emerged as its key leaders. Three priorities linked the Wilderness Support Center and the Campaign for America's Wilderness: first, they aimed to empower local organizations to take the lead on wilderness advocacy—a strategy even more important given the Bush administration's emphasis on local planning; second, they advanced campaigns that consistently reached out to a wide range of stakeholders, including hunters, ranchers, anglers, local and rural residents, and Democrats and Republicans; and, third, they emphasized incremental, pragmatic, and politically feasible wilderness legislation that would break the grid-lock on wilderness in Congress. To implement these priorities, the two groups provided financial support to local groups, jointly organized the biannual Wilderness Mentoring Conference for rising leaders, hosted a biannual Wilderness Week in Washington, D.C., for activists, and, most importantly, supported local groups by offering counsel on organizing, working with the media, engaging the agencies, lobbying Congress, and assembling a wilderness proposal. The two organizations were complementary, too: the Wilderness Support Center worked with groups from the very start, while the Campaign for America's Wilderness tended to serve as "finisher"; the Campaign had a larger public pro-file, while the Wilderness Support Center worked behind the scenes. Together, Matz explained, they could build a "better movement, foster camaraderie, and give people a sense of being a part of something bigger." [25]

By the time George W. Bush left office, he had signed into law thirteen bills protecting 2.2 million acres of new wilderness, in large part due to the swell of wilderness organizing nationwide. The most significant accomplishments were in Nevada, which was home to 1.7 of the 2.2 million acres of new wilderness areas. But the Nevada law also exemplified a changing model of wilderness legislation. Starting in the late 1990s, Nevada's congressional delegation began moving land-use legislation for federal lands in Nevada on a county-by-county basis. In fast-growing Nevada, where cities like Las Vegas were pressing up against surrounding federal lands, the prime motive was expediting land sales and exchanges, utility right-of-ways, and other federal land-use issues that were limiting suburban growth.[26] Reid made it clear that if wilderness advocates were willing to negotiate, such land-use legislation could include wilderness designations too. But Nevada wilderness groups initially declined to come to the negotiating table, not wanting wilderness to be the caboose on develop-ment-oriented legislation.

As county-level land-use planning gained momentum in Nevada in the early 2000s, however, the Nevada Wilderness Coalition, with the support of the Wilderness Support Center, decided to come to the negotiating table. If land-use disposal was going to take place, it was better to be at the table than not, and in the best-case scenario, such legislation might yield significant wil-derness protection.[27] The Nevada Wilderness Coalition actively worked to broaden the base of support for wilderness in Nevada, in hopes of establishing a strong record of local support during the land-use deliberations. By 2005, one organizer for the Nevada Wilderness Project could boast that its member-ship included a waitress in Mesquite, a homebuilder in Reno, and a bartender in Vegas. "These locals are the fabric of the Nevada Wilderness Project," he said, "and deliver its successes."²⁸ And wilderness advocates worked with other stakeholders involved in the negotiations, including ranchers, hunters, off-road vehicle enthusiasts, and county commissioners who had often been hostile to wilderness. Instead of dismissing their concerns, wilderness advocates demonstrated a willingness to make accommodations on grazing, hunting, water rights, and, most controversial, land disposal. As Friends of Nevada Wilderness explained: "As much as we believe in wilderness, we believe in American Democracy more."²⁹

The Lincoln County Conservation, Recreation, and Development Act of 2004 exemplified the challenges and opportunities of this process for wilderness advocates. Lincoln County, in southern Nevada, is the size of Massachusetts, but home to only 4,165 people and no stoplights. Most importantly, the federal government owned 98 percent of the land.³⁰ In 2001, Nevada's senators initiated land-use planning in Lincoln County, following the model underway in Las Vegas and Clark County: they appointed a collaborative team that included representatives from county government, local agencies and universities, environmentalists, and other stakeholders and undertook a series of public hearings. Wilderness advocates from across the state began working Lincoln County, reaching out to individuals one at a time. Allies were few in a county that had long been opposed to wilderness. As O'Donnell explained, "whether ranchers or hunters, they had long, emotional, relationships with the land."³¹ With the assistance of the Wilderness Support Center, local advocates worked to accommodate hunters' concerns about vehicular access and developers' worries about land sales and water rights. The Nevada congressional delegation drew on these discussions to forge what Senator Reid described as a "comprehensive plan that balances the needs for infrastructure development, recreation opportunities, and conservation of our natural resources and public lands."³²

The final Lincoln County bill became law with broad public support and bipartisan political support. It designated fourteen wilderness areas protecting 768,294 acres. The law released 245,516 acres of wilderness study areas for potential development and protected less than a third of the land wilderness advocates had identified as potential wilderness.³³ More troublesome, the wilderness designations came packaged with a long list of provisions that ran counter to wilderness advocates' goals. Several wilderness areas included long cherry stems along roads. Grazing was allowed in perpetuity (as usual). Permanent wildlife water development projects were permitted if they encouraged "healthy, viable, and more naturally distributed wildlife populations." Motor-

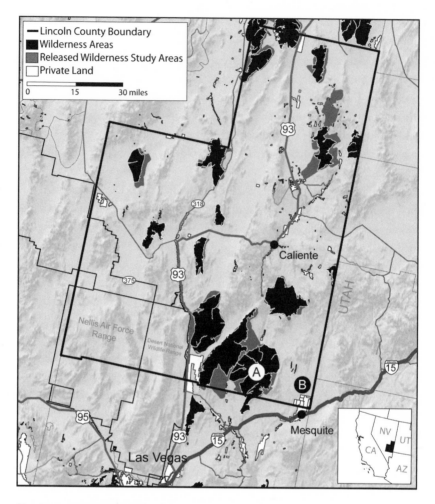

Map E.1 The Lincoln County Conservation, Recreation, and Development Act designated 14 wilderness areas protecting 768,294 acres in Nevada, but it included provisions that wilderness advocates opposed. For instance, it included long cherry stems for roads in some wilderness areas, such as Mormon Mountains Wilderness (A), and it authorized the immediate sale of 13,328 acres of public land north of Mesquite without environmental review or public participation (B).

ized vehicles were permitted in wilderness areas in some instances for managing wildlife, including maintaining such water projects. The law denied federal water rights.[34] It authorized utility corridors for pipelines to move groundwater from White Pine and Lincoln counties south to the Las Vegas area in an effort to reduce that city's dependency on the Colorado River. And, most troubling, the law opened up to 103,328 acres of federal lands for auction (homebuilders eyeing new suburbs bid up the first 13,328 acres of land, located north of Mesquite, Nevada, for $47.5 million in 2005).[35]

When the wilderness community celebrated Wilderness Week in September 2004, the wilderness leadership highlighted the success in Nevada. The Wilderness Society awarded Senator Reid its Ansel Adams Award for leadership. It touted Nevada as a model for other states. For Bill Meadows and the Wilderness Support Center staff at Wilderness Week, the emphasis on local organizing, the partnership between local and national groups facilitated by the Wilderness Support Center, the engagement with the opposition, and the give-and-take of the negotiations were essential to wilderness advocacy, and had often been lacking in the 1990s. What they did not focus on during Wilderness Week were the downsides of the legislation, but the concerns were manifold.

Nowhere did the Nevada bills break with precedent more clearly than in the case of land-use disposal. Since the Federal Land Policy and Management Act (FLPMA) became law in 1976, the overarching federal policy had been to retain the public domain in the national interest. FLPMA did authorize land disposal in special circumstances, but only after a public planning process, a NEPA environmental review, and congressional approval for large sales. The Nevada land-use bills exempted numerous land sales, including up to 103,328 acres in Lincoln County, from those provisions.[36] Historically, proceeds from federal land sales went to the federal treasury to be used for the public interest. In 1998, the Southern Nevada Public Lands Management Act first broke with that model; it reserved proceeds from land sales in Clark County for Nevada: 5 percent for the state's general education program, 10 percent for local infrastructure projects, and the balance for funding administrative oversight (including environmental reviews), acquisition of conservation lands (such as inholdings within wilderness areas), and other projects (such as an off-road vehicle trail).[37] These were not trivial amounts of money; the balance of the Southern Nevada account grew to $1.3 billion by 2006 as a result of high-value land sales around Las Vegas.[38] Other Nevada land-use bills, including Lincoln County, followed that disbursement model. Even as the Wilderness Society trumpeted success in Nevada, difficult questions were being raised about whether Senator Reid's strategy in Nevada would become the model for resolving the stalemate over public domain and wilderness across the intermountain West.

That question topped the Wilderness Society's agenda when its Governing Council convened its annual meeting at Grand Teton National Park in September 2006. "No issue has become more discussed within the wilderness community than the new family of public lands/wilderness legislation," Meadows acknowledged.[39] The spark behind that discussion was Senator Robert Bennett's (R-UT) newly introduced Washington County Growth and Conservation Act of 2006. The bill packaged a minimalist set of wilderness designations centered around Zion Canyon National Park in southwestern Utah with the least desirable provisions of the Nevada land-use bills—including land disposal, exemptions from FLPMA, and local control of the proceeds.[40] Bert Fingerhut, a council member, and SUWA (on whose board Fingerhut also served) raised the warning flag for the Wilderness Society.[41] They worried that wilderness legislation risked becoming a vehicle for land-use planning that circumvented environmental laws, limited public participation, and hastened suburban sprawl. As one concerned council member put it, the new Utah bill was "an extreme demonstration of how far this approach will go if we do not stop it."[42] Public concern was mounting too. "It is the worst sort of Congressional earmarking," editorialized the New York Times. "It gives true wilderness bills a reputation they do not deserve."[43]

The Wilderness Society remained committed to engaging in negotiations. Over the next year, Bill Meadows and the Wilderness Society worked with Senator Bennett and his staff, and the negotiations resulted in an improved Washington County bill in 2008. Although the bill still protected only a modest amount of wilderness, it no longer exempted land disposal from FLPMA's requirements for public participation and environmental review. In testimony, Meadows criticized the land disposal provisions, but supported the overall bill. He described it as a "breakthrough in [the] long polarized debate in Utah over land protection."[44] But the opposition of SUWA and the Sierra Club sunk the legislation in 2008. The bill still followed the Nevada model for redirecting the proceeds from federal land sales to the state and county for a variety of uses, including public safety and transportation projects.[45] As the Sierra Club noted, "Local governments should not develop a dependence on selling off public lands to fund local projects."[46]

Despite the shortcomings of the Nevada legislation and concerns about the Utah legislation, the fact that Congress was designating wilderness again, and substantial amounts of it, helped oil the gears of legislative action nationwide. Between 2002 and 2008, locally supported wilderness proposals began to gain momentum in states from Washington and California to Vermont and New Hampshire. By 2008, the Senate's legislative hopper was filling up with bills that enjoyed strong local support and had already passed in the House of Representatives. Senate Majority Leader Harry Reid and Senator Jeff Bingaman (D-NM) bundled more than a dozen wilderness bills and additional public lands legislation into the proposed Omnibus Public Land Management Act of 2008. The bill demonstrated the renewed political strength of the wilderness movement and its willingness to engage in negotiations to address the concerns of ranchers, outfitters, land managers, and others. The Omnibus Public Land Management Act proposed 517,025 acres of wilderness in the Owyhee canyonlands in southwestern Idaho, but it included permissive language regarding grazing activities and wildlife management and denied federal water rights. The bill proposed 39,105 acres of wilderness in Virginia, but it included specific language to meet the concerns of mountain bikers, who wanted access to a newly designated scenic area and lands adjacent to a wilderness area. The bill proposed adding 13,700 acres of wilderness to the Copper Salmon Wilderness in Oregon, and it specifically noted that the designation would not "diminish the right of any Indian tribe" and made provisions for access for the Coquille Indian Tribe for historical and cultural activities.[47] All told, it was an omnibus public lands bill of national scope. But the legislation did omit more controversial legislation, such as the proposal for Utah's Washington County, on account of the disagreement over federal land sales. Before the omnibus bill moved in the Senate, however, the chants of "Drill, Baby, Drill!" at the Republican National Convention and the collapse of the financial system that September combined to thwart progress in the 110th Congress.

The political stars for wilderness began to align during the federal elections in November 2008. Barack Obama carried six of twelve western states, including New Mexico, Colorado, and Nevada, in a decisive victory over westerner John McCain (R-AZ). For the first time since 1976, Democrats held a majority (fourteen) of the West's twenty-four senatorial seats. It was the culmination of a trend that had begun in 2000, as a growing cohort of Democrats had made inroads in the West, focusing on economic development, local autonomy, and regional concerns, including conservation, hunting, and fishing. Arizona Governor Janet Napolitano, Colorado Senator Ken Salazar, and Montana Senator Jon Tester were emblematic of this new generation of Democrats.[48] No longer could Republicans consider the Mountain West "home turf." In January 2009, the Obama administration swept into Washington, D.C., with broad public support and Democratic majorities in the House and Senate. The administration was on the defensive from the start, trying to shore up the national economy amid a growing international financial crisis. But even as the administration poured its efforts into a fiscal stimulus package and began to lay the groundwork for health-care reform, new financial regulations, and energy and climate policy, the Omnibus Public Land Management Act of 2009 was among the first bills to move in the 111th Congress. Notably, the 2009 legislation included Washington County, Utah. As it became clear that the Nevada land-use bill's special provisions were no longer tenable, Senator Bennett signed onto a bill that accomplished much of what wilderness advocates hoped, handled land disposals in accordance with FLPMA's regulatory provisions, and placed funds from such land sales in a special account which was to be used to acquire inholdings or lands adjacent to the new protected areas in Washington County—not to fund administrative activities, transportation or public safety projects, or other unrelated local projects.[49] That success and the bill as a whole marked a hard-won victory for wilderness advocates. Its national scope, bipartisan political support, and significant wilderness designations made it, in Meadows's view, the "most important public lands conservation measure since the Alaska lands act."[50]

When President Obama signed the Omnibus Public Land Management Act on March 30, 2009, he described the law as having "the backing of Americans from every walk of life and corner of this country. Ranchers and fishermen, small business owners, environmentalists, conservative Republicans and liberal Democrats on the local, state, and federal levels."[51] Ray Ring, a writer for *High Country News*, described it as a "ghost from the golden age of the environmental movement, the 1970s, when Republicans and Democrats worked together to pass major environmental laws."[52] The victory was gratifying for the Wilderness Support Center, along with the entire Wilderness Society, the Campaign for America's Wilderness, and their local allies, with whom they had worked to build the necessary political support. The victory was especially sweet for SUWA, which had spearheaded efforts to block the Nevada model for land-use disposal in the Washington County legislation. The Omnibus Public Land Management Act secured permanent protection for 2 million acres of wilderness from California to West Virginia, including controversial areas, such as the Owyhee canyonlands in Idaho and Washington County in Utah, and more straightforward areas, such as those in Rocky Mountain National Park in Colorado. But, even more importantly, in its national breadth and its degree of popular support, the act demonstrated the success of a strategy that wilderness advocates had cultivated since the late 1990s. Area by area, bill by bill, and person by person they had rebuilt the political momentum around wilderness legislation as a viable component of the public lands agenda. Their success was a fitting tribute to Ernie Dickerman. This was his kind of organizing. And the final legislation included the Virginia Ridge and Valley Act, which designated six new wilderness areas and expanded six existing wilderness areas in Virginia.

E.5 President Obama signed the Omnibus Public Land Management Act of 2009 into law on March 30, 2009. It protected 2 million acres of wilderness across the nation. Courtesy the White House Photo Office.

The Wilderness Movement's Lessons

The Omnibus Public Land Management Act of 2009 brought the size of the National Wilderness Preservation System to 757 areas protecting 109.5 million acres of federal lands in perpetuity. It was a remarkable accomplishment. Since 1964, when the Wilderness Act became law, Congress had expanded the wilderness system in fits and starts, making progress in the West and the East and in periods of Democratic and Republican leadership, to protect mountains and deserts, canyons and coasts, old-growth forests and islands, and tundra and marsh nationwide—all at the behest of citizens. The majority of designated wilderness, 57.4 million acres, is in Alaska, but there are wilderness areas in forty-three other states and Puerto Rico too. Measured by the expectations of the champions of the Wilderness Act, the wilderness system has been a tremendous success, protecting more than twice as much land as they had hoped for. But for more recent activists, such as those associated with the Wildlands Project and the New Conservation Movement, the progress has been incre-

mental and insufficient to protect the nation's biodiversity. And in the context of a broader environmental agenda, the wilderness system seems like a
small victory in comparison with global issues such as climate change and basic
human health issues like access to fresh water. In one crucial respect, however, the wilderness movement has been a clear success: its political endurance.
How has the wilderness movement maintained its momentum as a vehicle for
engaging citizens and local, regional, and national interest groups in a common
project to protect the public lands? The history of the wilderness movement
offers a handful of lessons to carry forward on how to organize citizens, interest
groups, and their allies in the work of environmental protection.

*Wilderness protection has provided an immediate, tangible, and positive goal
for environmental advocates.* Drawing new lines on a map has been a powerful
goal for public lands advocates. Creating a wilderness area protects a discrete
place. You can locate a wilderness area on a map, you can drive to an overlook
and look out at protected peaks and valleys, you can hike into it, and you can
share it. Place is a powerful tool for environmental advocates.[53] But a wilderness area is more than a single place. The genius of the wilderness system is that
each new area is a singular victory, but each of those victories also taps into and
contributes to a longer history of wilderness protection, a broader community
of wilderness advocates, and the wilderness system as a whole. Working for
wilderness invites, if not demands, enthusiasm, passion, and commitment. In
the realm of environmental policy where the key issues turn on technical and
scientific criteria, wilderness, more than other issues, values passionate individuals who can bring essential and valuable knowledge of place to the table.
For these reasons, the Wilderness Act created a durable goal that has proven
politically relevant across generations and places.

*A politically pragmatic approach to reform is necessary to oil the legislative
machinery in Washington, D.C.* If there is one group that has never fallen for
the myth of pristine wilderness, it is those who have worked hardest to protect
the public lands. Few wilderness advocates, either in the 1960s or today, are
beholden to the idea that wilderness is pristine. Looking to the past, they know
that even the nation's wildest lands often include remnants of old dams and
mines, abandoned homesteads, and the scars of overgrazing. Looking to the
future, they well know that a changing climate will have far-reaching consequences for the nation's wilderness system. A pragmatic approach to wilderness
protection has been important for two reasons: First, it has meant wilderness
advocates have adopted a broad notion of what types of wild lands qualify as
wilderness. In the early 1970s, Ernie Dickerman was one of many who empha-

sized that the Wilderness Act advanced not a philosophical and pure definition for wilderness, but a practical working definition that could accommodate a wide range of wild lands in the West and the East, including those with a history of human use. Second, that pragmatic approach has allowed wilderness advocates the necessary flexibility to engage other stakeholders in the give-and-take of negotiations. More often than not, since the 1960s, this commitment to pragmatism has kept wilderness advocates at the negotiating table, engaging with ranchers, hunters, Native Americans, industry, off-road vehicle drivers, and others—engagement that has proven crucial in moving wilderness legislation through Congress.

This strategy has been cause for debate. Some advocates see the wilderness legislation of the 2000s as a dangerous break with earlier wilderness legislation. Consider the special management provisions regarding grazing, man-made watering holes, and wildlife management included in the Omnibus Public Land Management Act of 2009. Such provisions were not new, but the number of such provisions was troublesome. George Nickas warned that while such special provisions met the concerns of stakeholders, such exceptions were "cheapening the very meaning of wilderness." Nickas is the executive director of a small, but important, organization, Wilderness Watch, which has watchdogged the implementation of wilderness legislation and the integrity of the wilderness system nationwide since 1989. In his view, each special provision was a new crack in the wilderness system that could weaken it in ways that might not become apparent for years.[54] Or consider the give-and-take that underlays the Nevada wilderness bills: Some observers argue that packaging wilderness legislation with legislation that sold off public lands and created new utility corridors was unwise. Two public lands advocates, Janine Blaeloch and Katie Fite, argue that after all of the rhetoric about consensus and collaboration is stripped away, there was nothing visionary or inspirational about the new wilderness legislation—it was simply "quid-pro-quo" wilderness, where protection hinged on development.[55]

Skeptics of the pragmatic turn in the 2000s wilderness legislation were right: the wilderness movement had taken more rigid and principled stands in the past. But arguing for eliminating grazing in new wilderness areas outright or for uncompromising large-scale wilderness designations rarely yielded legislative gains for public lands protection. Instead, such strategies often encouraged political opposition by ignoring the concerns of local communities and resource users. The dominant and more successful tradition in wilderness advocacy since the 1960s has been a pragmatic approach concerned with building local political support, advancing an inclusive definition of which lands qualify for wilderness protection, and perpetuating a politically sustainable approach to wild lands protection. That is why the Wilderness Act's architects, such as Howard Zahniser, were willing to make specific accommodations for grazing, mining, motorboats, and, in one instance, a road to move the Wilderness Act through Congress.[56] That is why every major wilderness bill since has included similar compromises and exceptions: the Alaska National Interest Lands Conservation Act made exceptions for subsistence activities; the national forest wilderness bills included release language that opened up roadless areas for potential development; and the California Desert Protection Act allowed military overflights and authorized land swaps for private landowners. Special provisions can undermine the wilderness system in ways we cannot foresee, but to criticize the commitment to negotiation and compromise as an abandonment of a more pure or principled wilderness tradition is to overlook more than four decades of wilderness politics. The engagement with local stakeholders and the political pragmatism of the 2000s did not abandon the values embodied by the Wilderness Act; instead, it marked a return to it.

How to balance the imperatives of the political process with the long-term stewardship of the wilderness system was precisely the issue that occupied the Wilderness Society, as it engaged in a "vigorous discussion" over the implications of the Nevada wilderness bills for future wilderness legislation at its Governing Council meeting at Grand Teton National Park in 2006.[57] In the aftermath of that debate, the Wilderness Society decided to codify its pragmatic approach to wilderness legislation: it established a clearly defined process by which the organization vetted wilderness proposals and, to guide that process, it adopted a set of overarching "wilderness principles." The challenge was to "evaluate each campaign for land protection on its own merits while recognizing its implications for the public domain as a whole." Four principles guided that balancing act:

> Provide the best possible protection for public land, especially in places with high wilderness value;
>
> Avoid harmful precedents that might undermine the wilderness system and other public lands;
>
> Hold federal agencies to the highest standards of stewardship and accountability; and
>
> Respect the cultural, social, and economic needs of local communities while working to conserve the land on which those communities ultimately depend.[58]

By those standards, the wilderness community had gone too far in the case of the Lincoln County Conservation, Recreation, and Development Act: the final legislation weakened protection on public lands that were released from wilderness study status and it loosened existing regulatory procedures that protected the public interest more broadly (it exempted federal land sales from public review and environmental impact statements, as required by NEPA — both of which risked becoming problematic precedents). And, in light of those principles, it is easy to understand why the organization celebrated the Omnibus Public Land Management Act of 2009. After sustained negotiations with a wide range of stakeholders, it helped produce a final bill which avoided the most troublesome aspects of the Nevada legislation, and set no new precedents.

The engine driving wilderness and public lands advocacy has been the alliances linking local and national organizations to a common cause. The work of the Wilderness Support Center, the Wilderness Society, and the Campaign for America's Wilderness marked a return to the Wilderness Society's vision under the leadership of Stewart Brandborg in the 1960s and 1970s. These organizations succeeded by catalyzing local groups and matching local efforts with support in Washington, D.C. They have provided seed funds, leadership training, and political counseling during the legislative process. The resurgence of this strategy since the late 1990s has not been an easy or automatic return to the past. In the 1960s and 1970s, when communication was more difficult, the resources of local groups more limited, and access to Congress more challenging, the Wilderness Society served as a gatekeeper coordinating local wilderness groups' efforts in Congress. But the world of political advocacy has changed greatly since the 1960s. Efforts, such as the Pew Trust's work to build a coalition around forest reform in the early 1990s, failed due to mistrust and a lack of a common goal. Indeed, the early 1990s marked a high point in tensions between local and national groups. To make the relationship between local and national groups work today, when communication is instantaneous, the capital costs of organizing have decreased, and Congress is more accessible, national wilderness groups have successfully repositioned themselves as essential resources in distributed networks of political advocacy. Instead of promoting themselves as leaders, national staffers describe local organizations as their "partners" and "peers" in the shared work of wilderness protection.

Acknowledging the importance of such partnerships raises an important point about environmental advocacy. Scholars have emphasized the leadership of national organizations: well-developed national groups specialize in specific policy niches and ensure access to the policy arena. These qualities, they argue, have been essential to American environmental policymaking.[59] But more often, national groups have been subject to criticism for being disconnected from local issues and constituencies, eager to put political access first, and unsuccessful in effecting fundamental policy change.[60] One sympathetic critic, William Shutkin, gathered many of these concerns together and warned that national groups were sapping the environmental movement of its democratic strengths. "With its direct mail machinery, centralized structure, and top-down decision-making, mainstream-professional environmentalism has cultivated a largely passive constituency and in the process has stripped itself of the ability to activate and inspire robust political participation and civic engagement." Shutkin, like other observers, has argued that cultivating such engagement and reinvigorating American environmental politics requires rebuilding grassroots organizations.[61] The product of this discourse need not be, but often has been, a false choice that dismisses national groups while making spirited calls for grassroots advocacy. To make such a choice is to overlook what may be most effective: not the grassroots or the national groups alone, but the relationship between them and their shared ability to mobilize people in environmental politics at all levels.

It is this lesson that wilderness advocates knew well in the 1960s and 1970s, often forgot in the 1980s and early 1990s, and have relearned in the twenty-first century. When the partnerships between local and national organizations were weakest, wilderness advocates paid the political price. Frustrations over that relationship played an important role in precipitating radical efforts, such as Earth First!, and the ambitious scientific efforts of the New Conservation Movement. In both cases, those movements emerged in reaction to a national movement seemingly beholden to compromise and the political process. And, in the late 1980s and early 1990s, the diminished commitment to working with local groups meant that the Wise Use Movement's charges that wilderness advocates were outsiders, elitist, and unconcerned with the issues important to rural and local communities resonated more strongly than they had in the past. Local involvement has not always been necessary to advance policy reform; important accomplishments have hinged on the Wilderness Society's and it allies' technical expertise, policy strategies, and access in Washington, D.C.—remember Grand Staircase-Escalante National Monument. But, at its best, when the wilderness movement has proven most effective as a positive political force, it has measured success not just in terms of new wilderness areas or policy reforms, but in terms of the number of people and breadth of local groups meaningfully engaged in the political work of designating wilderness and managing the public lands. Often those two metrics have gone hand in hand.[62]

Public land reforms proceed on different policy pathways, each demanding specific organizational strategies. The Wilderness Society cheered the quick action on the Omnibus Public Land Management Act at the start of the 111th Congress. But even as it did so, it pursued other pathways to policy reform just as energetically, such as appeals regarding oil and gas leasing on the public lands, administrative rules for implementing the Endangered Species Act, and litigation defending the Clinton-era roadless rule. In January 2009, one of Ken Salazar's first actions as secretary of the interior was to halt oil and gas leases near several national parks in Utah on grounds that they needed additional environmental review.[63] In July, the Obama administration withdrew support for Bush-era forest plans that would have doubled logging in old-growth forests on Bureau of Land Management (BLM) land in Oregon. And, the next month, the Obama administration filed an appeal in federal court that defended the Clinton-era administrative rule protecting the national forest roadless areas. As the political scientists Christopher Klyza and David Sousa have argued, the growth of the federal environmental state and congressional gridlock since the early 1990s often combined to push policy reforms, often key policy reforms, onto alternative policy pathways such as congressional appropriations, administrative rulemaking, and the courts.[64] At the start of the Obama administration, environmental groups were well prepared to facilitate policy reform, especially along these administrative pathways. A "Conservation Playbook" for the incoming Obama administration outlined "high-impact recommendations" which could be implemented through administrative action quickly by rescinding executive orders and initiating new agency rulemaking procedures. Many of the new administration's actions followed this playbook.[65]

These successes were a product of the wilderness and public lands advocacy community's capacity to work across a range of policy pathways. Most important, it had learned to hone its resources and strategies to exercise leverage most effectively on different pathways. This has been especially clear in the case of the Clinton-era roadless rule. The Heritage Forests Campaign proved adept at organizing public involvement in the administrative rulemaking process that led to the roadless rule: it emphasized Internet organizing, citizen involvement, support from scientists and economists nationwide, large-scale media campaigns, and public polling. When the roadless rule was forced onto the judicial pathway by legal suits starting in 2001, Earthjustice spearheaded the environmental community's legal strategy, intervening on behalf of national groups like the Heritage Forests Campaign and the Wilderness Society. Since the 1970s, the Sierra Club Legal Defense Fund, renamed Earthjustice, has specialized in the legal, policy, and technical work necessary to win suits in the courts. It mounted a sustained and successful defense of the roadless rule.[66] And starting in the late 1990s, the Wilderness Support Center and the Campaign for America's Wilderness emerged as key players in facilitating local-level legislative initiatives with grassroots groups to build a legislative strategy in Congress to protect roadless areas as wilderness. The complexity of the federal environmental regulatory state demands a robust, resourceful, and well-coordinated environmental advocacy community at the local, regional, and national levels, able to organize deliberately to address challenges and seize opportunities on multiple policy pathways. Various organizations have essential roles to play in environmental advocacy.

A limited and specific role for science has facilitated wilderness advocacy and public lands policy. Politicized debates over scientific findings often serve to undermine efforts to advance environmental policy. As the historian Stephen Bocking has observed, "advocates on all sides of [an environmental] controversy can evade responsibility for their value choices, hiding instead behind the protective veil of science."[67] Although the Wilderness Act of 1964 makes only passing reference to the scientific values of wild lands, scientific concerns have played a crucial role in public lands policy since the 1960s. Many of the Wilderness Act's champions were scientists who described wilderness areas as representative samples of climax ecosystems, important habitat for wildlife and, most often, essential laboratories for scientific research. Since the late 1980s, wilderness areas have more frequently been conceptualized as dynamic units of larger networks of habitat necessary to sustain biodiversity, including endangered species and migratory animals. Like many arenas of environmental policy, a growing scientific knowledge base has transformed understandings of the threats, values, and management strategies important to the public lands. Advocacy organizations such as the Wilderness Society and the federal land agencies such as the Forest Service have invested in such research, hiring scientific staff and partnering with university scientists. In the case of the public lands policy, the research, theory, and outreach of conservation biologists have been most important. Like other areas of scientific inquiry, conservation biology generates much debate, uncertainty, and, at times, controversy; but wilderness advocacy and public lands debates have rarely become trapped in debates over "sound science."

While science has played an essential role in identifying potential wilderness areas and shaping public lands policy, public lands politics have rarely turned solely or even primarily on scientific considerations; other concerns, such as economics, aesthetics, political values, and moral beliefs have played an equally important role. In the case of wilderness politics, this strategy has an obvious shortcoming: scientific imperatives have rarely determined the boundaries of the nation's wilderness areas. At times, wilderness advocates have tried to put scientific concerns foremost. This was the case with the original Northern Rockies Ecosystem Protection Act in the early 1990s, which outlined a large-scale plan for protecting biodiversity and ecosystem health in the northern Rockies. But such far-reaching plans ran into political roadblocks in Congress.[68] During the campaign for the roadless rule, environmentalists mounted a sustained campaign to protect all roadless areas over 1,000 acres in size, as consistent with the recommendations of conservation biologists, not the 5,000-acre limit the Clinton administration adopted. At times, wilderness advocates have deliberately put political concerns before scientific considerations. In the 1990s, for instance, the Wilderness Society dropped grazing as a priority legislative issue because it was deemed politically unworkable, despite a growing body of scientific research on the ill consequences of grazing for ecosystem health.[69]

These examples suggest the complex role that science plays in public lands debates. Most importantly, public lands advocates have learned that science functions differently in different policy arenas. In the legislative arena, the imperatives of political negotiations resulted in incremental and pragmatic advances toward scientifically informed goals. In the administrative arena, when steered by a sympathetic administration, the autonomy of agency scientists and decision-makers led toward more far-reaching and scientifically informed policies; this was the case with many of the administrative rules for forests, grazing, and mining during the Clinton administration. Finally, science can be an especially potent tool in the courts, trumping other concerns and values. Indeed, the court decisions that sharply reduced logging on federally owned Ancient Forests in the Pacific Northwest rested on the research and testimony of conservation biologists.[70] What lobbying could not accomplish in Congress, lawyers, scientists, and judges accomplished in the courts.[71] The point here is that scientific knowledge has been crucial in transforming political debates over public lands and how they are managed. At its best, the wilderness movement has configured the relationship between science and policy in different ways to advance its agenda in different policy arenas.

Bipartisan support is important to environmental reform, but Democratic leadership has been essential. In surveying the partisan state of environmental politics today, scholars and environmentalists often emphasize the bipartisan support for environmental reform in the 1960s and 1970s. The historian William Cronon made this argument most publicly in an op-ed in the *New York Times*. Addressing the incoming Bush administration in 2001, Cronon emphasized the Republican Party's concern for the environment, dating back to Theodore Roosevelt, and highlighted the Reagan administration's anti-environmental policies. "Until the 1980s," he argued, "Republicans could claim with considerable justification that their party's environmental record was no less distinguished than that of the Democrats."[72] It is true that major legislation, such as the Wilderness Act (1964), the Clean Air and Water amendments (1970 and 1972), the Endangered Species Act (1973), and the Superfund legislation (1980), all enjoyed such strong support, but the political science literature makes clear that partisanship also played an important role in environmental policy in the 1960s and 1970s. Analysis of voting patterns in Congress in the 1960s and 1970s reveals consistent partisan division on a broad range of conservation and environmental issues and highlights the leadership role Democrats exercised on such initiatives. Such partisanship has only deepened in recent decades: Republicans voted for the environmental reform agenda 27 percent of the time in 1973, 19 percent of the time in 1994, and 10 percent of the time in 2004. In contrast, Democrats voted for the same agenda 56 percent, 68 percent, and 86 percent of the time, respectively.[73]

Emphasizing the role of partisanship in environmental politics is not meant to suggest that environmental concerns map neatly onto party politics. As historians have shown, that relationship is complex and is often affected as much by regional politics or personal priorities as by party affiliation. Many politicians have broken with their parties on environmental issues for such reasons. Examples include the leadership of Republicans John Saylor (PA) for public lands protection in the 1960s and 1970s, John Chafee (RI) for clean air and water legislation in the 1980s and 1990s, and John McCain (AZ) on climate change legislation or John Warner (VA) in support of the roadless rule. Moderate Republicans have also been a crucial swing vote in national environmental politics. And prominent Democrats have slowed efforts to advance environmental reform. Consider Wayne Aspinall (CO), who opposed the Wilderness Act, Thomas Foley (WA), who was a powerful ally to the timber industry, and John Dingell (MI), who defended the automobile industry from increased fuel efficiency standards. In each case, those Democrats put regional concerns before party interests. And in the 2000s, Republicans such as Senators Bennett (UT), Mike Crapo (ID), and John Ensign (NV) took the lead on advancing land-use legislation, including wilderness protection. Their efforts demonstrate the importance of political opportunism. In each case, their support came with significant accommodations for land disposal, utility rights of way, and other policies favoring development in their states.

Considering American environmental politics in its historical context—in this case, examining changes in political strategy, interest group politics, and the shifts in national politics relevant to debates over the public lands in the West—reveals the important role that partisan differences and political opportunism have played in environmental politics. Not surprisingly, wilderness advocates emphasize their commitment to and success in building bipartisan support for public lands legislation. As Mike Matz at the Campaign for America's Wilderness explained, they are "emphatic" about working with Democrats and Republicans alike.[74] Legislation such as the Omnibus Public Land Management Act enjoyed such support. But underlying the claims of bipartisanship are important party and regional drivers shaping public lands policy. Leadership on public lands reform more recently, as has been the case historically, has most often come from Democrats. In 2009, the efforts of Democratic Senators Harry Reid (NV) and Jeff Bingaman (NM) and Representative Nick Rahall (WV) were instrumental in moving the omnibus act through the House and Senate. And the importance of party has been most apparent in the White House, where environmentally minded public lands policy has generally risen during Democratic administrations and fallen under Republican leadership. Democrats' willingness to entrust responsibility for the public good in the federal government has made the party a crucial ally to public lands advocates.

Conclusion

The map of the National Wilderness Preservation System is the legacy of nearly five decades of wilderness advocacy. From the shifting sands of Passage Key in Florida to the mountain highlands of the La Garita Wilderness in Colorado to the vast expanses of the Wrangell-St. Elias in Alaska, one out of every twenty acres in the United States has been set aside in perpetuity as wilderness. Those areas are meant to be, as the Wilderness Act proclaimed, "an enduring resource" for the American people.[75] One observer recently suggested that the Wilderness Society should make plans to disband: its work was nearly done. "They shouldn't feel bad if they achieve their mission and just close down. They should celebrate."[76] But for those who have worked hardest to protect wilderness, that map does not represent 757 wilderness areas that are now isolated and effectively insulated from future challenges and threats. Instead, it affirms something John Muir learned over a century ago: "When we try to pick out anything by itself, we find it hitched to everything else in the universe."[77] The health of the nation's wildest landscapes depends on the health of the larger landscapes in which they are embedded. Protecting wilderness means protecting the surrounding public lands, on which the water, wildlife, and aesthetics of wilderness depend. Protecting wilderness means cultivating a rural landscape and economy in which people can work the land sustainably. Protecting wilderness means engaging in other environmental issues, such as climate change, which will transform even the wildest of places. And, finally, protecting wilderness means fostering a healthy political landscape—the future of wilderness depends on a vibrant and engaged polity too.

Most critiques of wilderness begin and end with the Wilderness Act. Specifically, they highlight the definition of wilderness: "A wilderness, in contrast with those areas where man and his own works dominate the landscape, is hereby recognized as an area where the earth and its community of life are untrammeled by man, where man himself is a visitor who does not remain." Critics argue that such a wilderness ideal, which draws a sharp line between humans and nature, perpetuates a romantic conceptualization of wild nature that is, at best, naive, and has little to offer in the face of the most pressing modern environmental dilemmas.[78] But the problem with such readings of the Wilderness Act is that they often stop at that definition. The Wilderness Act did more than set forth a definition; it also established a political process. That process has been the engine that has powered a sustained political effort to designate additional wilderness and protect the public lands. As many observers agree, although they rarely look to wilderness advocacy as a model, it is such political engagement that modern American environmentalism needs more of, not less. Instead of a retreat from pressing realities, wilderness advocacy has been an ongoing exercise in citizen organizing, policy negotiations, and judicial and administrative maneuvers. Wilderness means more than pristine wild lands, backpacking adventures, or a stronghold for biodiversity; wilderness also means engaging citizens—both for and against wild lands protections—in a sustained discussion toward the common interest. All of that is the promise of wilderness.

NOTES

Introduction

1   Department of the Interior agencies oversee 442.3 million acres of public land. (The National Park Service, Fish and Wildlife Service, and Bureau of Land Management oversee 84.4, 96, and 261.9 million acres, respectively.) The Forest Service, in the Department of Agriculture, oversees 193 million acres of public land.

2   The best compilations of literature on recent debates over wilderness are J. Baird Callicott and Michael P. Nelson, eds., *The Great New Wilderness Debate* (1998); and J. Baird Callicott and Michael P. Nelson, eds., *The Wilderness Debate Rages On: Continuing the Great New Wilderness Debate* (2008).

3   *Wilderness Act*, Public Law 88-577, 88th Cong., 2nd sess. (September 3, 1964).

4   The best source of information and statistics on the National Wilderness Preservation System is the website http://www.wilderness.net, which is managed by the College of Forestry and Conservation's Wilderness Institute at the University of Montana, the Arthur Carhart National Wilderness Training Center, and the Aldo Leopold Wilderness Research Institute.

5   Thomas Cole, "Essay on American Scenery," in *The Collected Essays and Prose Sketches*, ed. Marshall Tymn (St. Paul, MN: John Colet Press, 1836, repr., 1980), 3–19.

6   Henry David Thoreau, *The Maine Woods* (New York: Penguin, 1864; repr., 1988), 212.

7   Frederick J. Turner, "The Significance of the Frontier in American History," in *Rereading Frederick Jackson Turner: The Significance of the Frontier in American History, and Other Essays*, ed. John Mack Faragher (New Haven, CT: Yale University Press, 1893, repr., 1999), 31–60.

8   Aldo Leopold, "Wilderness as a Form of Land Use," *Journal of Land and Public Utility Economics* 1, no. 4 (1925): 400.

9   Wallace Stegner, "Wilderness Letter," in *Marking the Sparrow's Fall: The Making of the American West*, ed. Page Stegner (1960, repr. 1998), 111–17.

10   For scholarship that highlights the importance of a broad conceptualization of

what is "nature" and approaches to environmental activism, see Michael Bess, *The Light Green Society: Ecology and Modernity in France, 1960–2000* (2003); William Cronon, *Uncommon Ground: Rethinking the Human Place in Nature* (1995); Robert Gottlieb, *Forcing the Spring: The Transformation of the American Environmental Movement*, 2nd ed. (2005); Finis Dunaway, *Natural Visions: The Power of Images in American Environmental Reform* (2005); Matthew Klingle, *Emerald City: An Environmental History of Seattle* (2007); Nancy Langston, *Toxic Bodies: Hormone Disruptors and the Legacy of* DES (2010); Jennifer Price, *Flight Maps: Adventures with Nature in Modern America* (1999); Thomas B. Robertson, "The Population Bomb: Population Growth, Globalization, and American Environmentalism, 1945–1980," (PhD dissertation, 2005); and William Shutkin, *The Land That Could Be: Environmentalism and Democracy in the Twenty-first Century* (2000).

11 J. Baird Callicott, "That Good Old-Time Wilderness Religion," in *The Great New Wilderness Debate*, ed. Callicott and Nelson (1991; repr., 1998), 387–94; William Cronon, "The Trouble with Wilderness," *New York Times Magazine*, August 13, 1995, 42–43.

12 Richard White, "'Are You an Environmentalist or Do You Work for a Living?' Work and Nature," in *Uncommon Ground*, ed. William Cronon (1996), 171–85.

13 Shutkin, *The Land That Could Be* (2000).

14 Giovanna Di Chiro, "Nature as Community: The Convergence of Environment and Social Justice," in *Uncommon Ground*, ed. William Cronon (1995), 300.

15 For examples of such responses, see Dave Foreman, "The Real Wilderness Idea," in *The Wilderness Debate Rages On*, ed. J. Baird Callicott and Michael P. Nelson (2008), 378–97, and David Orr, "The Not-So-Great Wilderness Debate . . . Continued," in ibid., 423–34.

16 Where these conditions have not been met, such as in the potentially petroleum-rich Arctic National Wildlife Refuge's coastal plain, the task of protecting wilderness has been much more difficult.

17 The history of the wilderness movement has been a focus of environmental history, but many of those studies examine earlier periods of wilderness history, focus on local or regional wilderness debates, or do not situate the wilderness movement in the broader context of American environmental politics. The classic work in the field is Roderick Nash, *Wilderness and the American Mind*, 4th ed. (2001). More recent scholarship includes Paul S. Sutter, *Driven Wild: How the Fight against Automobiles Launched the Modern Wilderness Movement* (2002); Daniel Nelson, *Northern Landscapes: The Struggle for Wilderness Alaska* (2004); Mark Harvey, *Wilderness Forever: Howard Zahniser and the Path to the Wilderness Act* (2005); Kevin R. Marsh, *Drawing Lines in the Forest: Creating Wilderness Areas in the Pacific Northwest* (2007); Skillen, *The Nation's Largest Landlord* (2009); John Miles, *Wilderness in the National Parks: Playground or Preserve*

(2009); and James Feldman, *A Storied Wilderness: The Rewilding of the Apostle Islands* (2011). For an insightful history of recent American environmental policy which considers public lands issues, see Christopher McGrory Klyza and David Sousa, *American Environmental Policy, 1990–2006: Beyond Gridlock* (2008). For an excellent introduction to the history of modern wilderness advocacy, see Doug Scott, *The Enduring Wilderness: Protecting Our Natural Heritage through the Wilderness Act* (2004).

18 Studies on the history of the modern environmental movement are numerous and include Gottlieb, *Forcing the Spring* (2005); Samuel P. Hays, *Beauty, Health, and Permanence: Environmental Politics in the United States, 1955–1985* (1987); Adam Rome, *Bulldozer in the Countryside: Suburban Sprawl and the Rise of American Environmentalism* (2001); Hal K. Rothman, *The Greening of a Nation? Environmentalism in the United States since 1945* (1998); Victor B. Scheffer, *The Shaping of Environmentalism in America* (1991); Philip Shabecoff, *Earth Rising: American Environmentalism in the 21st Century* (2000); and Thomas Wellock, *Preserving the Nation: The Conservation and Environmental Movements, 1870–2000* (2007).

19 For the distinction between "old" conservation issues and "new" environmental issues, or "first-" and "second-" generation issues, see Robert Cameron Mitchell, Angela A. Mertig, and Riley E. Dunlap, "Twenty Years of Environmental Mobilization: Trends among National Environmental Organizations," in *American Environmentalism: The U.S. Environmental Movement, 1970–1990*, ed. Dunlap and Mertig (1992), 13–14; Kirkpatrick Sale, *The Green Revolution* (1993), 14, 18; Stephen Fox, *The American Conservation Movement: John Muir and His Legacy* (1981), 291–92; Hays, *Beauty, Health, and Permanence* (1987), 13–39; Shabecoff, *Earth Rising* (2000), 3–7; and Scott Hamilton Dewey, *Don't Breathe the Air: Air Pollution and U.S. Environmental Politics, 1945–1970* (2000), 1.

20 "Fighting to Save the Earth from Man," *Time*, February 2, 1970, 56.

21 Adam Rome, "The Genius of Earth Day," *Environmental History* 15, no. 2 (April 2010): 194–205.

22 For the full taxonomy of liberalism drawn on here, see Alan Brinkley, *The End of Reform: New Deal Liberalism in Recession and War* (1996), 8–11. On the environmental movement and the Great Society, see Adam Rome, "'Give Earth a Chance': The Environmental Movement and the Sixties," *Journal of American History* 90, no 2 (Sept. 2003), 527–34.

23 People for the West! "Grassroots Activism Tells Rural America's Story," 1993, TWSR, box 12:3, folder 7.

24 Studies which give attention to the opposition to environmental reform include R. McGreggor Cawley, *Federal Land, Western Anger: The Sagebrush Rebellion and Environmental Politics* (1993); James McCarthy, "Environmentalism, Wise Use, and the Nature of Accumulation in the Rural West," in *Remaking Reality: Nature at the Millennium*, ed. Bruce Braun and Noel Castree (1998), 126–49; Jacqueline

Vaughn Switzer, *Green Backlash: The History and Politics of Environmental Opposition in the United States* (1997); David Helvarg, *The War against the Greens: The "Wise-Use" Movement, the New Right, and Anti-environmental Violence* (1994); and James Morton Turner, "'The Specter of Environmentalism': Wilderness, Environmental Politics, and the Evolution of the New Right," *Journal of American History* 96, no. 1 (July 2009): 123–48.

25   For arguments that "environmental issues seldom shape individual vote preference" and that the environment is rarely an "important 'swing' issue" for most voters in federal elections, see Deborah Lynn Guber, "Voting Preferences and the Environment in the American Electorate," *Society and Natural Resources* 14 (July 2001): 455–69. See also Michael E. Kraft, "Environmental Policy in Congress," in *Environmental Policy: New Directions for the Twenty-first Century*, ed. Norman E. Vig and Kraft (2006), 132–33.

26   Mark Dowie, *Losing Ground: American Environmentalism at the Close of the Twentieth Century* (1995), xii–xiii.

27   Klyza and Sousa, *American Environmental Policy* (2008).

I Why a Wilderness Act?

1   Much of my account of Howard Zahniser's role is drawn from Mark Harvey, *Wilderness Forever: Howard Zahniser and the Path to the Wilderness Act* (2005), xii.

2   The quote is from Roderick Nash, *Wilderness and the American Mind* (1982), xii. See also "Wilderness and Recreation," editorial, *New York Times*, March 8, 1964. On the significance of the Wilderness Act, see Craig W. Allin, "The Triumph of Politics over Wilderness Science," in McCool et al., eds., *Wilderness Science in a Time of Change Conference*, vol. 2, *Wilderness within the Context of Larger Systems* (2000), 180–85; Stephen Fox, *John Muir and His Legacy: The American Conservation Movement* (1981); Michael Frome, *The Battle for the Wilderness* (1997); and Doug Scott, *The Enduring Wilderness: Protecting Our Natural Heritage through the Wilderness Act* (2004).

3   Howard Zahniser, "The People and Wilderness," *Living Wilderness* 29, no. 86 (Spring–Summer 1964): 41.

4   Dan Freedman, "Feuds with Feds Make West Wild," *Times-Picayune*, June 11, 1995; Daniel Goldstein, "Obama to Sign Major Public-Lands Bill That Bars Wyoming Oil and Gas Drilling," *Inside Energy*, March 30, 2009, 14; Tom Kenworthy, "U.S. Judge Upholds Clinton Plan to Manage Northwest Forests," *Washington Post*, December 22, 1994; Cass Peterson, "Tempers Rise over Desert Conservation," *Washington Post*, July 22, 1987; Philip Shabecoff, "Bush Is Asked to Ban Oil Drilling in Arctic Refuge," *New York Times*, January 25, 1989.

5   On the contested origins of the public lands, see Karen R. Merrill, *Public Lands*

and Political Meaning: Ranchers, the Government and the Property between Them (2002).

6   See Mark David Spence, *Dispossessing the Wilderness: Indian Removal and the Making of the National Parks* (1999).

7   Bureau of Land Management, *Public Land Statistics* (1980).

8   John Muir, "The American Forests," *Atlantic Monthly* 80, no. 8 (1897): 157.

9   Nash, *Wilderness and the American Mind*, chap. 9.

10   Samuel P. Hays, *Conservation and the Gospel of Efficiency* (1959).

11   Other land agencies with significant land holdings include the Department of Defense, the Department of Energy, and the Bureau of Indian Affairs.

12   On the postwar West, see Michael P. Malone and Richard W. Etulain, *The American West: A Twentieth-Century History* (1989), 239.

13   Bernard DeVoto, "The West against Itself," in *The Easy Chair* (1955).

14   Harvey, *Wilderness Forever* (2005), 198–99.

15   Michael McCloskey, *In the Thick of It: My Life in the Sierra Club* (2005), chap. 3.

16   Malone and Etulain, *American West* (1989), chap. 6.

17   Thomas Michael Power and Richard N. Barrett, *Post-Cowboy Economics: Pay and Prosperity in the New American West* (2001); Gundars Rudzitis, *Wilderness and the Changing American West* (1996), chap. 1.

18   On the hazards of drawing distinctions between an "old" and a "new" West see Joseph E. Taylor III, "The Many Lives of the New West," *Western Historical Quarterly* 35 (Summer 2004); and Timothy J. LeCain, *Mass Destruction: The Men and Giant Mines That Wired America and Scarred the Planet* (2009), 219–30.

19   On Echo Park, see Mark W. T. Harvey, *A Symbol of Wilderness: Echo Park and the American Conservation Movement* (1994). On Hetch Hetchy, see Robert Righter, *The Battle over Hetch Hetchy: America's Most Controversial Dam and the Birth of Modern Environmentalism* (2006).

20   On the importance of Three Sisters Primitive Area to launching the campaign for the Wilderness Act, see Kevin Marsh, *Drawing Lines in the Forest: Creating Wilderness Areas in the Pacific Northwest* (2007), chap. 1.

21   See Harvey, *Wilderness Forever* (2005), chap. 7; Scott, *Enduring Wilderness* (2004), chap. 3.

22   The Wilderness Society, *Annual Report* (2008).

23   On the origins of the Wilderness Society, see Paul S. Sutter, *Driven Wild: How the Fight against Automobiles Launched the Modern Wilderness Movement* (2002).

24   See Neil M. Maher, "A New Deal Body Politic: Landscape, Labor, and the Civilian Conservation Corps," *Environmental History* 7, no. 3 (July 2002): 435–61.

25   This government report was likely authored by Yard, who borrowed language from Leopold. See U.S. Congress, Joint Committee on Recreational Survey of Federal Lands, *Recreation Resources of Federal Lands* (1928), 90.

26   See Robert Marshall, "The Problem of the Wilderness," *Scientific Monthly* 30, no. 2 (February 1930).

27   See Benton MacKaye, "An Appalachian Trail: A Project in Regional Planning," *Journal of the American Institute of Architects* 9 (October 1921).

28   Leopold published several articles explaining the value of wilderness in the 1920s and 1930s that reflect the shifts in his own thinking. See Aldo Leopold, "A Plea for Wilderness Hunting Grounds," in *Aldo Leopold's Wilderness: Selected Early Writings by the Author of A Sand County Almanac*, ed. David E. Brown and Neil B. Carmony (1925, 1990), 155–65; "The Wilderness and Its Place in Forest Recreational Policy," in *Aldo Leopold's Wilderness*, ed. David Earl Brown and Neil B. Carmony (1921, repr. 1990), 146–54; "Wilderness as a Form of Land Use," *Journal of Land and Public Utility Economics* 1, no. 4 (1925), 398–404; and "Wilderness as a Land Laboratory," *Living Wilderness*, (July 1941). On Leopold's approach to wilderness, see Susan L. Flader, *Thinking Like a Mountain: Aldo Leopold and the Evolution of an Ecological Attitude toward Deer, Wolves, and Forests* (1974); Daniel J. Philippon, *Conserving Words: How American Nature Writers Shaped the Environmental Movement* (2004), 190–207; and Sutter, *Driven Wild* (2002), chap. 3.

29   Leopold, "Wilderness as a Form of Land Use," 1925, 400.

30   Sutter examines this rich conversation over the many, and sometimes conflicting, values of wild lands that informed the genesis of the Wilderness Society. See Sutter, *Driven Wild* (2002).

31   Scott provides the most succinct account of these efforts. See Scott, *Enduring Wilderness* (2004), chap. 3.

32   Harvey, *Wilderness Forever* (2005), chap. 14.

33   Surveys revealed a high degree of confidence in the federal government. See Gabriel A. Almond and Sidney Verba, *The Civic Culture: Political Attitudes and Democracy in Five Nations* (1963), 82, 102.

34   On the history of American politics in the 1960s, see Terry Anderson, *The Sixties* (2003); Terry Anderson, *The Movement and the Sixties* (1995); Irving Bernstein, *Guns or Butter: The Presidency of Lyndon Johnson* (1996); David Farber, *The Age of Great Dreams: America in the 1960s* (1994); Todd Gitlin, *The Sixties: Years of Hope, Days of Rage* (1987); and Maurice Isserman and Michael Kazin, *America Divided: The Civil War of the 1960s* (2004).

35   *Wilderness Act* (1964).

36   Stegner, "Wilderness Letter," 1960.

37   Clinton P. Anderson, "Protection of the Wilderness," *Living Wilderness* 27, no. 78 (Autumn–Winter 1962): 14.

38   Zahniser, "The People and Wilderness," 1964, 41.

39   Stewart L. Udall, "Wilderness," *Living Wilderness* 80 (Spring–Summer 1962): 6–7.

40   *Wilderness Act* (1964).

41   Such concerns were raised in testimony before Congress regarding the Wilder-

ness Act. See U.S. Congress, Subcommittee on Public Lands of the Committee on Interior and Insular Affairs, *Wilderness Preservation System*, 87th Cong., 1st sess., October 30–31, 1961.

42   Wilderness advocates emphasized the Wilderness Act's value for protecting a national recreational resource. As a result, Congress delayed acting on the bill until a national recreation review conducted by the ORRRC was completed in 1962. On the role of the ORRRC review and the Wilderness Act, see Harvey, *A Symbol of Wilderness* (1994), 198, 231. See the original report, ORRRC, "Outdoor Recreation for America: A Report to the President and the Congress by the Outdoor Recreation Resources Review Commission" (January 1962).

43   *Wilderness Act* (1964).

44   Howard Zahniser, "The Need for Wilderness Areas," in *Where Wilderness Preservation Began*, ed. Edward Zahniser (1964, repr. 1992), 65.

45   Theodore Roosevelt, "The American Wilderness: Wilderness Hunters and Wilderness Game," in *The Great New Wilderness Debate*, ed. J. Baird Callicott and Michael P. Nelson (1897, repr. 1998), 63–86; Sigurd Olson, "Why Wilderness?" in ibid. (1938, repr. 1998), 97–102.

46   Marshall, "The Problem of the Wilderness," 1930, 147.

47   William O. Douglas, *A Wilderness Bill of Rights* (1965). For a careful analysis of Douglas's wilderness activism, see Adam M. Sowards, "William O. Douglas's Wilderness Politics: Public Protest and Committees of Correspondence in the Pacific Northwest," *Western Historical Quarterly* 37, no. 1 (2006).

48   Stewart L. Udall, "To Save the Wonder of Wilderness," *New York Times Magazine*, May 27, 1962, 12.

49   Stegner, "Wilderness Letter," 1960.

50   Zahniser, "The Need for Wilderness Areas," 1964, 61.

51   Rachel Carson, *Silent Spring* (1962), 1.

52   On the arguments for the scientific value of wilderness made in the context of the campaign for the Wilderness Act, see Udall, "To Save the Wonder of Wilderness," 1962; and Zahniser, "The Need for Wilderness Areas," 1964, 64.

53   On the breadth of political support, see Harvey, *Wilderness Forever* (2005), 205–6.

54   For a summary of the political opposition, see Henry Dworshak et al., "Minority Views on S.174," *Living Wilderness* 26, no. 78 (Autumn–Winter 1962). See also Harvey, *Wilderness Forever* (2005), 204–12; and Steven C. Schulte, *Wayne Aspinall and the Shaping of the American West* (2002), chap. 4.

55   Schulte, *Wayne Aspinall* (2002); Stephen C. Sturgeon, *The Politics of Western Water: The Congressional Career of Wayne Aspinall* (2002).

56   Harvey offers insight into Zahniser and Aspinall's relationship, and he quotes their correspondence. Harvey, *Wilderness Forever* (2005), 234–36.

57   Twenty-five percent payments from the Forest Service to states, which were based

on sales, leases, rentals, and other fees on the national forests, began to decline in the 1990s due to decreased logging in the national forests. In 2000, Congress passed legislation authorizing an alternative payment system to stabilize the payments. That legislation expired in 2006 and has not been renewed by Congress. Ellis T. Williams, "National Forest Contributions to Local Governments," *Land Economics* 31, no. 3 (August 1955): 206. Ross Gorte, "The Secure Rural Schools and Community Self-Determination Act of 2000: Forest Service Payments to Counties," Congressional Research Service (January 24, 2007), 1.

58   The lockup argument was raised frequently in congressional testimony. See *Wilderness Preservation System* (1961).

59   On these compromises, see Harvey, *Wilderness Forever* (2005), chap. 14; and Schulte, *Wayne Aspinall* (2002), chap. 4.

60   Howard Zahniser, "'Of Course, Conservationists Support It!'" *The Living Wilderness* 27, no. 79 (Winter–Spring 1962).

61   Dworshak et al., "Minority Views on S.174," 1962.

62   Ibid., 35.

63   Udall, "To Save the Wonder of Wilderness," 1962.

64   These visitation statistics are for the national forests only and can be found in John Hendee ed., *Wilderness Management* (1990), 380.

65   Stegner, "Wilderness Letter," 1960.

66   Carolyn Merchant, "Shades of Darkness: Race and Environmental History," *Environmental History* 8, no. 3 (July 2003): 381.

67   Craig W. Allin, *The Politics of Wilderness Preservation* (1982), 123.

68   R. C. Gordon-McCutchan, *The Taos Indians and the Battle for Blue Lake* (1991), 122, 60; Andrew Graybill, "'Strong on the Merits, and Powerfully Symbolic': The Return of the Blue Lake to Taos Pueblo," *New Mexico Historical Review* 76, no. 2 (2001).

69   Holmes Rolston, "The Wilderness Idea Reaffirmed," in *The Great New Wilderness Debate*, ed. J. Baird Callicott and Michael P. Nelson (1991, repr. 1998), 379.

70   On this point, see Harvey, *Wilderness Forever* (2005), 237–38; and Schulte, *Wayne Aspinall* (2002), 143.

71   Stewart M. Brandborg, "Executive Director's Report to the Council," 1964–1965, TWSR, box 1:202, folder "Minutes: Governing Council, 1965."

72   U.S. Department of Agriculture, United States Forest Service, *Roadless Area Conservation: Final Environmental Impact Statement* (2000), 3–237.

73   Phillipon argues that several of the Wilderness Society's founders, at the urging of Leopold, came to envision "a system of interconnected wilderness areas representing distinct ecosystems." Such a well-developed vision for the wilderness system is not reflected in later internal correspondence within the Wilderness Society, however, nor did such logic define the organization's agenda during the campaign for the Wilderness Act. See Philippon, *Conserving Words* (2004), 206–7.

74   Howie Wolke, Earth First!, "Memo to Wilderness Leaders," December 8, 1983, SCNLOR, box 132, folder 9.

75   Roderick Frazier Nash, *The Rights of Nature* (1989), 41.

76   The philosopher Andrew Light has written provocatively on the need to reconsider why humans take action to protect the environment. See Andrew Light, "Contemporary Environmental Ethics: From Metaethics to Public Philosophy," *Metaphilosophy* 33, no. 4 (July 2002): 426–69.

77   Marsh, *Drawing Lines in the Forest* (2007).

78   Howard Zahniser, "Guardians Not Gardeners," *The Living Wilderness* 27, no. 83 (Winter–Spring 1963): 2.

79   Ibid.

80   *Wilderness Act* (1964); emphasis mine.

81   Dworshak et al., "Minority Views on S.174," 1962, 35.

82   *Wilderness Act* (1964).

83   Stewart M. Brandborg, "Letter to Conservationist Friends in Utah," April 13, 1965, TWSR, box 7:175A, folder "Utah: Correspondence, 1959–1966"; Michael Nadel, "The Wilderness Act's Land Requirements," *Living Wilderness* 27, no. 78 (Autumn–Winter 1962); Udall, "To Save the Wonder of Wilderness," 1962.

84   Lyndon B. Johnson, "Remarks upon Signing the Wilderness Bill and the Land and Water Conservation Fund Bill," *The American Presidency Project* (online), September 3, 1964.

85   Arthur Schlesinger Jr., "Where Does the Liberal Go from Here?" *New York Times Magazine*, August 4, 1957, 4.

86   This argument draws heavily from Adam Rome, "'Give Earth a Chance': The Environmental Movement and the Sixties," *Journal of American History* 90, no. 2 (September 2003). See also Andrew Hurley, *Environmental Inequalities: Class, Race, and Industrial Pollution in Gary, Indiana, 1945–1980* (1995), 8–10; and Martin Melosi, "Environmental Justice, Political Agenda Setting, and the Myths of History," *Journal of Policy History* 12, no. 1 (2000).

87   Udall, *The Quiet Crisis* (1963), viii.

88   William Cronon makes this argument most forcefully in an op-ed aimed at George W. Bush's incoming administration. See "When the G.O.P. Was Green," *New York Times*, January 8, 2001. For a more detailed examination of the role of Republicans in environmental politics, see J. Brooks Flippen, *Conservative Conservationist: Russell E. Train and the Emergence of American Environmentalism* (2006); Flippen, *Nixon and the Environment* (2000); and Thomas G. Smith, *Green Republican: John Saylor and the Preservation of America's Wilderness* (2006).

89   See Riley E. Dunlap and Michael Patrick Allen, "Partisan Differences on Environmental Issues: A Congressional Roll-Call Analysis," *Western Political Quarterly* 29, no. 3 (September 1976); and Julius Turner and Edward V. Schneier Jr., *Party and Constituency: Pressures on Congress* (1970).

90   Bernstein, *Guns or Butter* (1996), chap. 10.

91   For a good example of this argument, see Scott Hamilton Dewey, *Don't Breathe the Air* (2000), 1.

92   Johnson, "Remarks upon Signing the Wilderness Bill," 1964.

93   Bernstein, *Guns or Butter* (1996), 266.

94   Dave Foreman, "Wilderness Areas Are for Real," in *The Great New Wilderness Debate*, ed. J. Baird Callicott and Michael P. Nelson (1998), 398.

2 Speaking for Wilderness

1   Henry David Thoreau, *The Writings of Henry David Thoreau: Excursions, Translations, and Poems* (1906), 224.

2   John Muir, *My First Summer in the Sierra* (1911), 354.

3   Aldo Leopold, *A Sand County Almanac and Sketches Here and There* (1949; repr., 1968).

4   Stewart Brandborg, interview, January 22, 2002.

5   Mark Harvey, *Wilderness Forever* (2005), 218.

6   In 1966, the Wilderness Society estimated there were 34, 56, and 65 areas to be reviewed by the Forest Service, National Park Service, and Fish and Wildlife Service, respectively.

7   Brandborg, interview, January 22, 2002.

8   "Total Membership: 1962–1972," 1972, TWSR, box 2:4, folder "Administration: Membership Reports and Statistics, 1950s–1960s."

9   Clif Merritt, interview, July 31, 2001.

10   Rupert Cutler, interview, December 20, 2001.

11   There were eight such trips in 1962 and 112 such trips in 1974. "A Way to the Wilderness," *The Living Wilderness* 38, no. 127 (Autumn 1974): 27.

12   Stewart M. Brandborg, "Letter to Members," May 9, 1966, TWSR, box 7:173, folder "Tennessee: Great Smoky Mountains National Park, May 1966."

13   Wilderness Society, "New Challenges for Wilderness Conservationists," 1968, SCMP, box 223, folder 19, "Wilderness Act of 1964, 1967," 8.

14   Wilderness Society, "1969 Work Plans and Program Reviews," August 1969, TWSR, box 1:203, folder "Minutes: Governing Council Minutes, 1969."

15   There are other federal agencies with large holdings, including the Bureau of Indian Affairs and the Department of Defense.

16   Gifford Pinchot, *The Fight For Conservation* (New York: Doubleday, 1910), 48.

17   Paul W. Hirt, *A Conspiracy of Optimism* (1994), 187–188.

18   For careful analysis of the Three Sisters debate and the relationship between the U regulations and the Wilderness Act, see Marsh, *Drawing Lines in the Forest* (2007), 23–37.

19   David A. Clary, *Timber and the Forest Service* (1986), chap. 6; Hirt, *A Conspiracy of Optimism*, chap. 6.

20   The U regulations did require public hearings, but the Wilderness Act created stronger and more opportunities for public involvement.

21   *National Park Service Organic Act*, Public Law 235, 64th Cong., 1st sess. (Aug. 25, 1916.)

22   On the role of tourism in the national parks, see Stanford E. Demars, *The Tourist in Yosemite, 1855–1985* (1991), chap. 6; Alfred Runte, *National Parks: The American Experience* (1997), chap. 8; and Richard West Sellars, *Preserving Nature in the National Parks: A History* (1997), chap. 6.

23   Quoted in Harvey, *Wilderness Forever* (2005), 189.

24   Edward Abbey, *Desert Solitaire: A Season in the Wilderness* (1968), 131.

25   For a concise history of the wildlife refuge system, see Steve Chase and Mark Madison, "The Expanding Ark: 100 Years of Wildlife Refuges," *Wild Earth* 13, no. 4 (Winter 2004): 18–27.

26   Stewart M. Brandborg, "Memo re: Interior Wilderness Review Schedule," September 16, 1966, SCPNWP, box 2678-1, 6, folder "Wilderness Classification"; Michael Nadel, "Executive Committee Meeting Minutes," February 13, 1965, TWSR, box 1:202, folder "Minutes: Executive Committee, 1963–1965."

27   For a detailed study of the transformation of the BLM, see Skillen, *The Nation's Largest Landlord* (2009).

28   Charles S. Watson Jr., "The Lands No One Knows," *Sierra Club Bulletin* 58, no. 8 (September 1973).

29   Marsh, *Drawing Lines in the Forest* (2007), 141.

30   Bill Worf, interview, February 7, 2001.

31   Richard J. Costley, Division of Recreation, "Memo to Edward P. Cliff, Chief, USFS re: Personal Statement on National Forest Wilderness," August 27, 1971, TWSR, box 8:100, folder "RARE I and II: Roadless Inventory—General."

32   "Proposed Regulation of the Secretary of Agriculture Governing the Administration of National Forest Wilderness," July 12, 1965, FSR, MUAC (1960–1966), box 1, folder "Dec., 1965 Meeting."

33   W. J. Lucas, Rocky Mountain Region, regional forester, Forest Service, "Letter to Ed Connors, Colorado Open Space Council," August 18, 1971, CECP, box 4:32, folder "Wilderness Training Workshops, 1970–1971."

34   Brock Evans, interview, November 28, 2001.

35   U.S. Senate, Interior and Insular Affairs Committee, *San Rafael Wilderness Hearings*, 90th Cong., 1st sess., April 11, 1967.

36   Peter S. Alagona, "Biography of a 'Feathered Pig': The California Condor Controversy," *Journal of the History of Biology* 37 (2004): 557–83.

37   Fred Eissler, "Condors and Wilderness," *Sierra Club Bulletin* 49, no. 3 (March 1964): 10.

38   U.S. Senate, *San Rafael Wilderness Hearings*, 1967, 38.

39   Ibid., 114–18.

40   Worf staunchly defended that position during his career with the Forest Service, and he acted upon it at retirement. He cofounded Wilderness Watch, the first citizens' group to watchdog the management of the wilderness system in 1991. See http://www.wildernesswatch.org/.

41   For an excellent overview of the National Park Service's administrative policies and the tensions underlying it, see Sellars, *Preserving Nature* (1997).

42   Wilderness Society, "Special Memo re: Isle Royale," January 12, 1967, HCP, box 2:7, folder "Wilderness: Isle Royale, 1967."

43   George Hartzog Jr., director, National Park Service, "National Park Wilderness Planning Procedures," August 8, 1966, TWSR, box 2:9, folder "Land Management Policies of the Depts. of Interior and Agriculture."

44   George Hartzog Jr., "The Impact of Recent Legislation on Administrative Agencies," in *Wilderness in a Changing World*, ed. Bruce Kilgore (1966), 176.

45   Wilderness Society, "Special Memo re: Isle Royale," 1967.

46   Cutler to James A. O. Crowe, outdoor editor, *Detroit News*, January 17, 1967, HCP, box 2:7, folder "Wilderness: Isle Royale, 1967."

47   Gordon C. Haber, Dept. of Biology, Northern Michigan University, "Statement on Behalf of Complete Wilderness Act Protection for Isle Royale National Park," February 10, 1967, HCP, box 2:7, folder "Wilderness: Isle Royale, 1960–1966."

48   Doug Scott, e-mail to author, December 17, 2001.

49   Doug Scott to Cutler, February 3, 1969, HCP, box 2:7, folder "Wilderness: Isle Royale, 1968–1969."

50   Cutler to Haber, January 24, 1969, HCP, box 2:7, folder "Wilderness: Isle Royale, 1968–1969."

51   Scott to Haber, May 17, 1971, HCP, box 2:8, folder "Wilderness: Isle Royale, 1971."

52   Cam Cavanaugh, *Saving the Great Swamp: The People, the Power Brokers, and an Urban Wilderness* (1978).

53   Gottlieb, *Forcing the Spring* (2005), chap. 6; Rome, "'Give Earth a Chance,'" 2003.

54   Biographical history drawn from the finding aid to Harry Crandell Papers.

55   Crandell to Jack Berryman, chief, Division of Wildlife Services, Bureau of Sport Fisheries and Wildlife, December 15, 1967, HCP, box 1:1, folder "Correspondence, 1960s."

56   Helen C. Fenske, interview, May 18, 2000.

57   U.S. Congress, Senate Committee on Interior Insular Affairs, *Great Swamp, Pelican Island, Monomoy, Seney, Huron, Michigan Islands, Gravel Island, Green Bay, and Moosehorn Wilderness Areas*, 90th Cong., 2nd sess., June 20, 1968, 100.

58   U.S. Congress, House Committee on Interior and Insular Affairs, *Designating Certain Lands in the Great Swamp National Wildlife Refuge, Morris County, New Jersey as Wilderness*, 90th Cong., 2nd sess., July 26, 1968.

59   John S. Gottschalk, director, Fish and Wildlife Service, "Statement before Public Lands Subcommittee, Department of the Interior," June 3, 1968, GSNWRP, box 11.820 "Wilderness."

60   U.S. Congress, Senate Committee on Interior Insular Affairs, *Great Swamp, Pelican Island, Monomoy, Seney, Huron, Michigan Islands, Gravel Island, Green Bay, and Moosehorn Wilderness Areas* (1968), 49.

61   Refuge Manager, Great Swamp NWR, "Narrative Report: Great Swamp National Wildlife Refuge, 1970," December 1970, Great Swamp National Wildlife Refuge, Annual Reports, Basking Ridge, NJ.

62   Wilderness Society, "New Challenges for Wilderness Conservationists," 1968. The Sierra Club offered a similar publication, but the organization never made facilitating such citizen activism a centerpiece of its outreach. See Sierra Club, "How to Work under the Wilderness Act," April 1967, SCMP, box 132, folder 21.

63   Wilderness Society, "New Challenges for Wilderness Conservationists," 1968, 5.

64   For an excellent article on the unique campaign for French Pete in Oregon, which foreshadows important developments in wilderness advocacy in the 1970s, see Kevin R. Marsh, "'Save French Pete': Evolution of Wilderness Protests in Oregon," in *Natural Protest: Essays on the History of American Environmentalism*, ed. Michael Egan and Jeff Crane (2009), 223–44.

65   The earliest membership survey is Tom I. Eggleston, "Report to Council and Staff on Membership Questionnaire," September 14, 1968, TWSR, box 1:7, folder 17.

66   Terry Anderson, *The Sixties* (2003), chap. 3; Alice Echols, "Nothing Distant about It: Women's Liberation and Sixties' Radicalism," in *The Sixties: From Memory to History*, ed. David Farber (1995), 154–55; David Farber, *The Age of Great Dreams: America in the 1960s* (1994), chap. 9.

67   Anderson, *Sixties* (2003), 95.

68   Brandborg to Van Waganen, May 1, 1968, TWSR, box 1:7, folder 3.

69   U.S. House of Representatives, *San Rafael Wilderness*, 1967, 124.

70   Brandborg, "The Wilderness Act in Practice: The First Three Years," April 7, 1967, SCNLOR, box 136, folder 10, 5.

71   On the Sixties liberalism and the origins of the environmental movement, see Rome, "'Give Earth a Chance,'" 2003; Dewey, *Don't Breathe the Air* (2000); and Milazzo, *Unlikely Environmentalists* (2006).

72   Stewart Brandborg, "The First Ten Years," *The Living Wilderness* 38, no. 127 (1974): 43.

73   "Total Membership: 1962–1972," 1972, TWSP, box 2:4, folder "Administration: Membership reports and statistics, 1950s-1960s."

3 The Popular Politics of Wilderness

1   Theodore J. Kaczynski, "Letter to the Wilderness Society," February 26, 1969, TWSR, box 7:107, folder "States/California: Correspondence."

2   Ibid.

3   Virginia C. Carney, "Letter to Kaczynski," July 21, 1969, ibid.

4   David Johnston, "Judge Sentences Confessed Bomber to Four Life Terms," *New York Times*, May 5, 1998.

5   Michael P. Cohen, *The History of the Sierra Club, 1892–1970* (1988), chap. 6.

6   Michael McCloskey, "Sierra Club Executive Director: The Evolving Club and the Environmental Movement, 1961–1981," an oral history conducted in 1981 by Susan R. Schrepfer, Sierra Club History Series, Regional Oral History Office, The Bancroft Library, University of California, Berkeley, 1983.

7   The most obvious exception to this assertion is the publication of *Ecotactics: The Sierra Club Handbook for Environment Activists*, edited by John G. Mitchell and Constance L. Stallings (1970). In the preface McCloskey asserts the centrality of grassroots leadership to the Sierra Club's goals. The internal files of the Sierra Club, however, suggest a disconnect between the staff's commitment to grassroots involvement and its actions in regard to its membership. This is especially clear in the papers of the Sierra Club's Wilderness Classification Study Committee, SCP, box 2, folder 27. The writings and oral history with Michael McCloskey offer further testimony on this point: McCloskey, "Wilderness Movement at the Crossroads," *Pacific Historical Review* 41 (1972); "The Wilderness Act of 1964: Its Background and Meaning," *Oregon Law Review* 45 (June 1966); and "Sierra Club Executive Director, 1961–1981," 1983. Note, however, that the Sierra Club's Pacific Northwest Office, headed up by Brock Evans, focused more on citizen activism.

8   Chuck Clusen, interview, November 30, 2001.

9   Francis J. Walcott, chairman, Wilderness Classification Study Committee, Sierra Club, to Peter Borrelli, December 23, 1972, SCNLOR, box 133, folder 7; "Wilderness, Why, What and How?" approx. 1970, SCMP, box 222, folder 29.

10   Gottlieb, *Forcing the Spring* (2005); Hal K. Rothman, *The Greening of a Nation?* (1998).

11   Francis J. Walcott, Wilderness Classification Study Committee, "Sierra Club Policy for Wilderness Management and Preservation," November 25, 1969, SCPNWP, accession 2678–09, box 6, folder "Wilderness Management."

12   The final version of the Wilderness Manifesto does not reflect many of the early concerns regarding the manifesto and the club's wilderness policy. See Francis Walcott, "A Wilderness Manifesto from the Sierra Club," December 13, 1969, SCMP, box 222, folder 24, and accompanying correspondence.

13   Ansel Adams to Walcott, January 31, 1970, SCMP, box 222, folder 24.

14   Brock Evans, Sierra Club, to Walcott, December 12, 1969, SCPNWP, accession 2678-1, box 6, folder "Wilderness Management"; Brock Evans, interview, November 28, 2001; Walcott to Evans, December 18, 1969, SCPNWP, accession 2678-1, box 6, folder "Wilderness Management."

15   George Marshall to Walcott, March 26, 1970, SCMP, box 222, folder 24.

16   U.S. Department of Agriculture, Forest Service, *Final Environmental Statement on a Recommended Land Use Plan for the Alpine Lakes Area in the State of Washington* (1974).

17   Brock Evans, interview, November 28, 2001.

18   For additional information about the "limited area" designation unique to Region 6 of the Forest Service, see Kevin Marsh, "'This Is Just the First Round': Designating Wilderness in Central Oregon Cascades, 1950–1964," *Oregon Historical Quarterly* 103, no. 2 (2002), 210–33.

19   Clary, *Timber and the Forest Service* (1986); Hirt, *A Conspiracy of Optimism* (1994); Christopher McGrory Klyza, *Who Controls Public Lands? Mining, Forestry, and Grazing Policies, 1870–1990* (1996).

20   Multiple Use Advisory Committee, Forest Service, "Meeting Minutes," December 7–8, 1965, FSR, MUAC, box 1, folder "Dec. 1965 Meeting."

21   Brock Evans to Holly Jones, Sierra Club Wilderness Committee, approx. 1972, SCPNWP, accession 2678-1, box 6, folder "Wilderness Correspondence, 1972–1973."

22   James R. Turnbull, National Forest Products Association, to Charles W. Colson, White House, August 5, 1970, JWP, box 68, folder "Forest Service—1971."

23   Wendell B. Branches, Western Wood Products Association, to Neal Rahm, USFS, July 22, 1970, NFPAR, box 192b, folder "Magruder Corridor."

24   Marsh, *Drawing Lines in the Forest* (2007), 87; Samuel P. Hays, *Wars in the Woods: The Rise of Ecological Forestry in America* (2006).

25   Brock Evans to Eileen Ryan, December 5, 1967, BEP, box 23, folder "Washington, Alpine Lakes, 1963–1972."

26   Brock Evans to Chris and Jim Powers, May 3,1968, ibid.; Evans, interview, November 28, 2001.

27   Marsh, *Drawing Lines in the Forest* (2007), 90.

28   David G. Knibb, ALPS, "Non-Wilderness Backcountry: An Alpine Lakes Issue with National Implications," 1970, SCPNWP, accession 2678-09, box 6, folder "Wilderness Management."

29   L. O. Barrett, Snoqualmie National Forest, USFS, to Ben Hayes, president, Alpine Lakes Protection Society, January 30, 1970, SCPNWP, accession 2678-09, box 6, folder "Wilderness Management."

30   Ibid.

31   W. E. Ragland, Snoqualmie National Forest, "Letter to David G. Knibb, Alpine

Lakes Protection Society," February 13, 1970, SCPNWP, accession 2678–09, box 6, folder "Wilderness Management."

32 Brock Evans to Holway R. Jones, Sierra Club, February 27, 1973, SCNLOR, box 132, folder 1; Doug Scott, Wilderness Society, "Letter to David Corkran," December 27, 1972, SCPNWP, accession 2678–1, box 6, folder "Wilderness Correspondence, 1972–1973."

33 William A. Worf, chief, Recreation and Lands, USFS, "The Commercial Outfitter and Wilderness, Remarks before the Montana Wilderness Guides Association," January 3, 1970, ACWTCP, document #161.

34 William A. Worf, C. Glen Gorgensen, and Robert C. Lucas, "Wilderness Policy Review Committee Report," May 17, 1972, USFS Region 1 Archives, "Wilderness Primitive Areas," 50.

35 Gerald Williams, "Oral History Interview of Bill Worf," May 1, 1990, USFS Region 1 Archives, Oral History Collection; Bill Worf, interview, February 7, 2001.

36 http://www.wildernesswatch.org/.

37 Marsh, *Drawing Lines in the Forest* (2007), 86.

38 Quoted in ibid., 67.

39 Richard J. Costley to Edward P. Cliff, chief, USFS, "Re: Personal Statement on National Forest Wilderness," August 27, 1971, TWSR, box 8:100, folder "RARE I and II: Roadless Inventory—General," 7.

40 Evans's handwritten notes are found on the following document: Francis Walcott, "Criticism of the Region Five Multiple Use Management Guides for Wilderness," November 24, 1969, SCPNWP, accession 2678–09, box 6, folder "Wilderness Management."

41 Brock Evans to Francis Walcott, December 12, 1969, ibid.

42 Ibid.

43 Brock Evans to Harry Crandell, December 15, 1972, HCP, box 2:5, folder "Wilderness Management—Guidelines / Jurisdiction / Classification."

44 Ibid.

45 Brock Evans, letter to the editor, *New York Times*, January 7, 1972.

46 Brock Evans to Holly Jones, November 10, 1972, SCPNWP, accession 2678–1, box 6, folder "Wilderness Correspondence, 1972–1973," 2.

47 As quoted in Marsh, *Drawing Lines in the Forest* (2007), 91.

48 Ibid.

49 "Alpine Lakes Coalition Plan Announced," October 2, 1973, BEP, box 84, folder "Alpine Lakes, 1973–1976."

50 "Special Study Provision for Wildland Corridors within the Alpine Lakes Wilderness," October 28, 1975, SCPNWP, accession 2678–2, box 4, folder "Alpine Lakes, reports, Misc."

51 Dick Fiddler, "Letter to Alpine Lakes Study Team," February 28, 1973, BEP, box 84, folder "Alpine Lakes Correspondence, 1971–74."

52   Evans to Hayes, June 8, 1973, ibid.

53   Doug Scott to Brock Evans and George Alderson, "Re: Alpine Lakes," April 22, 1975, TWSR, box 7:183, folder "Washington: Alpine Lakes, 1975"; Evans, interview, November 28, 2001.

54   The actual acreage of the Alpine Lakes Wilderness Area is complicated by private inholdings which were included in the designation. The Forest Service listed the size of the wilderness area as 391,988 acres in 2010.

55   For an excellent analysis of the Alpine Lakes campaign, see Marsh, *Drawing Lines in the Forest* (2007), chap. 4.

56   Sara M. Gregg, "From Farms to Forest: Federal Conservation and Resettlement Programs in the Blue Ridge and Green Mountains" (PhD diss., Columbia University, 2004).

57   Evans, interview, November 28, 2001.

58   Sutter, *Driven Wild* (2002), 3–5.

59   Rupert Cutler, interview, December 20, 2001.

60   Rupert Cutler to Grover C. Little, November 1, 1967, TWSR, box 7:189, folder "Western Virginia: General Correspondence, 1955–1967."

61   John R. McGuire, "Wilderness Report," September 24, 1971, FSR, box 1, entry #30B.

62   T. A. Schlapfer and Jay H. Cravens, USFS, "Memo to Chief, USFS," September 3, 1971, TWSR, box 4:410, folder "Wilderness — Eastern, 1971–1973."

63   Leon S. Minckler, "Wilderness East? — Yes," *American Forests* 78 (December 1972): 3.

64   Peter Borrelli, eastern representative, Sierra Club, "Memo re: Eastern Wilderness Meeting," January 19, 1972, SCNLOR, box 133, folder 7.

65   Francis Walcott to Shirley Taylor, Florida chapter, Sierra Club, December 13, 1972, SCNLOR, box 133, folder 7, 1.

66   Jay H. Cravens, "New Hampshire's Great Gulf . . . a Wilderness Area in Trouble," *American Forests* 77, no. 9 (September 1971): 30–32.

67   Peter Borrelli to Ted Snyder, "Re: Testimony on S. 3699," July 12, 1972, SCNLOR, box 133, folder 7, 3.

68   Peter Borrelli, "Memo re: Eastern Wilderness Meeting," January 19, 1972, SCN-LOR, ibid.

69   Ibid., 2.

70   Wilderness Society, "Eastern Wilderness Flash," March 24, 1972, SAFR, box 11, folder "Wilderness, 1971–1977."

71   U.S. Congress, Senate Committee on Agriculture and Forestry, *Wild Areas in the National Forests*, 92nd Cong., 2nd sess., June 20, 1972, 136.

72   Ibid., 135.

73   James E. Ficke to Dr. Paul V. Ellefson, director, Environmental Programs, Society of American Foresters, June 14, 1972, SAFR, box 11, folder "Wilderness, 1971–1977."

74 Ernest P. Dickerman, Wilderness Society, "Letter to Attendee at the Eastern Wilderness Coordinating Committee," November 10, 1972, TWSR, box 8:100, folder "Eastern Wilderness Coordinating Conference."

75 Helen McGinnis, "Notes on the Eastern Wilderness Coordinating Conference in Knoxville, TN," December 2–3, 1972, ibid.

76 Shirley Taylor to Michael McCloskey, December 8, 1972, SCNLOR, box 133, folder 7.

77 Sierra Club, "Text of Sierra Club Resolution on Eastern Wilderness," January 21, 1973, TWSR, box 4:410, folder "Wilderness—Eastern, 1971–1973."

78 John C. Whitaker to Nat Reed, January 18, 1973, JWP, box 118, folder "Wilderness." Testimony of John McGuire, chief of the U.S. Forest Service, in U.S. Congress, House, Committee on Interior and Insular Affairs, *Eastern Wilderness Areas*, 93rd Cong., 1st sess., February 21, 1973, 32.

79 Richard J. Costley, "An Enduring Resource," *American Forests* 78 (June 1972): 8.

80 Testimony of Ernest P. Dickerman and Doug Scott in *Eastern Wilderness Areas*, 1973, 49–50.

81 Ibid., 46.

82 It is worth noting that this was among the first laws to include congressionally legislated "wilderness study areas." Such study areas were to be managed in accordance with the Wilderness Act until Congress could determine if they deserved formal wilderness protection. Such "wilderness study areas" have become central to debates over wilderness, especially on the public domain managed by the Bureau of Land Management.

83 In the last stages of the legislative process, the title "Eastern Wilderness Areas Act" was omitted from the legislation. The law, as passed by Congress, has no title. Public Law 93–622, 93rd Cong., 1st. sess. (January 3, 1975).

84 Harvey Manning, "Where Did All These Damn Hikers Come From?" *Backpacker*, Summer 1975, 38.

85 Timothy P. Connor, "The Brainard Lake Report," Summer 1974, FSADOF.

86 David Brower, ed., *The Sierra Club Wilderness Handbook*, 2nd ed. (1971), 55.

87 John Hart, *Walking Softly in the Wilderness* (1977), 230.

88 Gear descriptions drawn from Colin Fletcher, *The New Complete Walker*, 2nd ed. (1974). Regarding Gore-Tex®, see "Rainwear," *Backpacker*, April 1979, 69. Gore-Tex is a trademark of W. L. Gore & Associates.

89 Gary Braasch, "You & Your Head," *Backpacker*, Spring 1974; William Kemsley Jr., "Editorial: A New Voice for Backpackers," *Backpacker*, December 1976, 5.

90 James W. Whittaker to James Haley, chairman, House Interior Committee, January 23, 1976, SCPNWP, accession 2678–2, box 3, folder "Alpine Lakes, General Correspondence, January 1976."

91 Dick Sill, Sierra Club, "Memo re: Wilderness Entry Permits," June 12, 1972, SCR, box 53, folder 38.

92 Stewart Brandborg's handwritten notes can be found on Harry Crandell, "Memo

to All Reviewers re: Initial Draft—Wilderness Management Policies," April 27, 1972, TWSR, box 2:1, folder "Wilderness Management Policy."

93   John B. Nutter, "Towards a Future Wilderness: Notes on Education in the Mountains," *Appalachia*, December 1973, 89.

94   See the cover of *The Living Wilderness* 33, no. 107 (Autumn 1969).

95   Bob Howes to Stewart M. Brandborg, February 16, 1969, TWSR, box 1:100–200, folder "Governing Council Correspondence, 1966–1969."

96   George Marshall to Governing Council, November 11, 1969, TWSR, box 1:18, folder 13.

97   Wilderness Society, "Minutes of the Executive Committee," January 10, 1969, TWSR, box 1:15, folder 14, 7.

98   Marshall, "Memo to Governing Council," November 11, 1969.

99   Steve Cotton, ed., *Earth Day: The Beginning* (1970).

100   Wilderness Society, "Minutes of the Executive Committee," March 18, 1970, TWSR, box 1:15, folder 16.

101   "ECOS," *Living Wilderness* 34, no. 109 (Spring 1970): 14.

102   Barry Commoner, *The Closing Circle: Nature, Man, and Technology* (1971). For an excellent biography of Commoner, see Michael Egan, *Barry Commoner and the Remaking of American Environmentalism* (2007).

103   Carson, *Silent Spring* (1962).

104   A. J. Haagen-Smit, "Man and His Home," *Living Wilderness* 34, no. 110 (Summer 1970): 38–46.

105   Cotton, *Earth Day* (1970).

106   Ibid., preface, 71, 73.

107   Ibid., 86.

108   Mitchell and Stallings, *Ecotactics* (1970).

109   Wilderness Society, "Minutes of the Executive Committee," March 18, 1970.

110   Marshall, "Memo to Governing Council," November 11, 1969.

111   Wilderness Society, "Minutes of the Executive Committee," March 18, 1970.

112   Margaret E. Murie, "Wilderness Concept," *Living Wilderness* 34, no. 110 (Summer 1970): 63.

113   Rupert Cutler to Kent A. Shirley, November 5, 1968, TWSR, box 4:410, folder "Wilderness—Management, 1968–1979."

114   Kaczynksi, "Letter to the Wilderness Society," February 26, 1969, TWSR.

4 New Environmental Tools for an Old Conservation Issue

1   Michael McCloskey, "Is the Wilderness Act Working?" in *Action for Wilderness*, ed. Elizabeth R. Gillette (1972), 22.

2   Michael McCloskey, "Wilderness Movement at the Crossroads," *Pacific Historical Review* 41 (1972): 346.

3   McCloskey, "Is the Wilderness Act Working?" 1972.

4   McCloskey, "Sierra Club Executive Director," 1983.

5   McCloskey, "Is the Wilderness Act Working?" 1972, 26.

6   McCloskey, "Wilderness Movement at the Crossroads," 1972, 354.

7   Ibid., 352.

8   Ibid., 361.

9   Ibid.

10   Richard Nixon, "Remarks on Signing the National Environmental Policy Act of 1969," *The American Presidency Project* (online), January 1, 1970.

11   Dewey, *Don't Breathe the Air* (2000); Flippen, *Nixon and the Environment* (2000); Judith A. Layzer, *The Environmental Case: Translating Values into Policy* (2002), chap. 2; Milazzo, *Unlikely Environmentalists* (2006).

12   *National Environmental Policy Act*, Public Law 91-190, 91st Cong., 1st sess. (January 1, 1970). Lynton Caldwell, who drafted NEPA, gives an overview of the law's origins in *The National Environmental Policy Act: An Agenda for the Future* (1998).

13   "Environmental Impact Statement," *Code of Federal Regulations*, Title 40, Pt. 1502 (2010) and "Commenting," *Code of Federal Regulations*, Title 40, Pt. 1503 (2010).

14   On the importance of different pathways toward policy making, see Klyza and Sousa, *American Environmental Policy* (2008).

15   Robert Gillette, "National Environmental Policy Act: Signs of Backlash Are Evident," *Science* 176, no. 4030 (April 7, 1972): 30–33.

16   John D. Ehrlichman, "Memorandum for John N. Mitchell, Attorney General," September 24, 1971, JWP, box 26, folder "Trans Alaska Pipeline, 2nd Series (3 of 4)."

17   Peter Coates, *The Trans-Alaska Pipeline Controversy* (1991), 164; Nelson, *Northern Landscapes* (2004), 69–70.

18   For a succinct overview of the discovery of oil on the North Slope, see Daniel Yergin, *The Prize: The Epic Quest for Oil, Money, and Power* (New York: Touchstone, 1991), 569–74.

19   Robert B. Weeden, "Arctic Oil: Its Impact on Wilderness and Wildlife," in *Wilderness: The Edge of Knowledge*, ed. Maxine E. McCloskey (1969), 164.

20   On the complex history of the Alaska Native Claims Settlement Act, see Donald Craig Mitchell, *Take My Land Take My Life: The Story of Congress's Historic Settlement of Alaska Native Land Claims, 1960-1971* (2001).

21   Walter R. Borneman offers an engaging history of Alaska and debates over its land in *Alaska: Saga of a Bold Land* (2003).

22   John C. Whitaker, "Memorandum for the Secretary of the Interior," February 24, 1970, JWP, box 25, folder "Alaska Pipeline (1 of 4)."

23   Rogers C. B. Morton, chairman, Republican National Committee, "Memorandum to President Richard Nixon re: Political Significance of the Alaskan Situation and the Alaskan Pipeline," March 12, 1970, JWP, box 25, folder "Alaska Pipeline (4 of 4)."

24   Brock Evans, Sierra Club, "Memo to Alaska Oil Files," November 16, 1969, BEP, box 7, folder "Alaska, Outgoing Letters, 1969–1972."

25   Nelson, *Northern Landscapes* (2004), 76–78.

26   See Coates, *Trans-Alaska Pipeline Controversy* (1991).

27   Ehrlichman to Mitchell, September 24, 1971, JWP.

28   Coates, *Trans-Alaska Pipeline Controversy* (1991).

29   John C. Whitaker, "Memorandum for John D. Ehrlichman re: Alaska Pipeline Statement," September 24, 1971, JWP, box 25, folder "Alaska Pipeline (4 of 4)."

30   For an excellent overview of the NEPA process for the pipeline, see Nelson, *Northern Landscapes* (2004), 108–18.

31   On the pipeline and the Nixon administration, see Flippen, *Nixon and the Environment* (2000), chap. 6.

32   On the maneuvering important to the national interest review, see Nelson, *Northern Landscapes* (2004), 101–7.

33   Citizens for America's Endangered Wilderness, "RARE II: The Results," January 1979, CECP, box 4:30A, folder "Issues: Memos—Wilderness Areas, 1979–1984."

34   Clary, *Timber and the Forest Service* (1986), 125.

35   Ibid., 173.

36   Hays, *Wars in the Woods* (2006).

37   Evans to Roger Mellem, May 24, 1973, BEP, box 84, folder "Alpine Lakes Correspondence, 1971–74."

38   Flippen, *Nixon and the Environment* (2000), 94.

39   John C. Whitaker, "Memorandum to John D. Ehrlichman Regarding Possible Presidential Executive Order," July 27, 1971, JWP, box 118, folder "Wilderness Areas 4."

40   Brock Evans, interview, November 28, 2001.

41   U.S. Department of Agriculture, Forest Service, *New Wilderness Areas: Roadless Area Review and Evaluation* (1973).

42   United States Forest Service, "A Method for Wilderness Quality Determination," 1971, HCP, box 2:5, folder "Wilderness Management, 1960s-1970s."

43   Michael McCloskey, Sierra Club, to John McGuire, USFS, February 1, 1972, TWSR, box 8:100, folder "RARE I and II: Roadless Inventory—General."

44   " . . . a Voice, Crying in the Wilderness" advertisement, *Idaho Statesman*, April 9, 1972.

45   "Club Wins 'Stunning Victory' as Forest Service Agrees to NEPA," *Sierra Club Bulletin* 58, no. 1 (January 1973): 15.

46   T. K. Cowden, assistant secretary, Department of Agriculture, to Donald Rumsfeld, Cost of Living Council, August 25, 1972, JWP, box 21, folder "USDA 3 of 4."

47   Wendell Wyatt, representative, Oregon, to Earl Butz, secretary of agriculture, September 8,1972, JWP, box 21, folder "USDA 3 of 4."

48   U.S. Department of Agriculture, Forest Service, *New Wilderness Areas* (1973).

49   R. L. Glicksman, "Traveling in Opposite Directions: Roadless Area Management

under the Clinton and Bush Administrations," *Environmental Law* 34 (2004): 1143–1208.

50   Watson, "Lands No One Knows," September 1973.

51   Bureau of Land Management, *Public Land Statistics* (1980), table 9.

52   On the efforts to reform the BLM in the 1960s, see Skillen, *Nation's Largest Landlord* (2009), 81–87.

53   *Federal Land Policy and Management Act*, Public Law 94–579, 94th Cong., 2nd sess. (October 21, 1976).

54   On the political interests that shaped FLPMA and the implications of the legislation, see Skillen, *Nation's Largest Landlord* (2009), 103–11; and Klyza, *Who Controls Public Lands?* (1996), 116–26.

55   Watson, "Lands No One Knows," 1973, 21.

56   Chuck Clusen, Sierra Club, "Memo to Public Lands Conservation Coalition," February 10, 1975, SCNLOR, box 103, folder 23.

57   McCloskey, "Wilderness Movement at the Crossroads," 1972, 361.

58   William E. Cone, Shelley McIntyre, and John W. Harbuck to Raymond Sherwin, president, Sierra Club, October 27, 1971, SCMP, box 103, folder 15.

59   The Wilderness Society's membership was 26,467 in 1966, 58,445 in 1970, and 65,157 in 1972. The Wilderness Society, "Total Membership: 1962–1972," 1972, TWSR, box 2:4, folder "Administration: Membership Reports and Statistics, 1950s-1960s."

60   Constance Holden, "Environmental Action Organizations Are Suffering from Money Shortages, Slump in Public Commitment," *Science* 175, no. 4020 (January 28, 1972): 394–95.

61   Flippen, *Conservative Conservationist* (2006).

62   John C. Whitaker to Richard Fairbanks, October 1971, JWP, box 150, folder "Wilderness Proposals 1 of 3."

63   William A. Morrill, Office of Management and Budget, "Memorandum to John Whitaker regarding Eastern Wilderness/Wild Area Policy," July 18, 1972, JWP, box 118, folder "Wilderness Areas 1," 1–7.

64   Colorado Open Space Coalition, "Wilderness Workshop Minutes," May 18, 1965, CECP, box 4:32, folder "Wilderness Workshop of COSC, 1965–1980."

65   "Draft Recommendation for the Eagles Nest Wilderness Area," April 1968, CECP, box 4:13, folder "Eagles Nest Primitive Area, 1967–1968."

66   This suit was an important precursor to the Sierra Club's strategy for challenging the roadless area review in 1972. Malcolm Rupert Cutler, "A Study of Litigation Related to Management of Forest Service Administered Lands and Its Effect on Policy Decisions" (1972).

67   The product of that work is apparent in Colorado Open Space Coalition, "Letter to Representative Floyd Haskell, Colorado," January 22, 1975, CECP, box 4:32, folder "Wilderness Training Workshops, 1975."

68   W. J. Lucas, regional forester, Rocky Mountain Region, USFS, to Ed Connors, Colorado Open Space Council, August 18, 1971, CECP, box 4:32, folder "Wilderness Training Workshops, 1970–1971."

69   Clifton R. Merritt, Wilderness Society, "Statement in Support of Eagles Nest Wilderness," October 9, 1970, TWSR, box 7:120B, folder "Colorado: Eagles Nest Primitive Area, 1970."

70   Doug Scott to Gordon C. Haber, June 28, 1971, HCP, box 2:8, folder "Wilderness: Isle Royale, 1971."

71   Robert A. Hanson, Northern Michigan Wilderness Association, to Senator Robert P. Griffin, Michigan, April 22, 1971, HCP, box 2:8, folder "Wilderness: Isle Royale, 1971."

72   Scott to Haber, June 28, 1971, HCP.

73   Stewart Brandborg, interview, January 22, 2002.

74   Evans, interview, November 28, 2001

75   Wilderness Society, "Washington Wilderness Seminar," January 31–February 5, 1971, TWSR, box 2:4, folder "Washington Wilderness Seminar, 1971."

76   Ibid.

77   Brandborg, interview, January 22, 2002.

78   Wilderness Society, "Washington Wilderness Seminar," January 31–February 5, 1971, TWSR.

79   Stewart M. Brandborg, "The Wilderness Act in Practice: The First Three Years," April 7, 1967, SCNLOR, box 136, folder 10.

80   Frank Church, senator, Idaho, "Statement before Senate Public Lands Committee," 1972, TWSR, box 7:157, folder "Oregon: Mt. Hood NF, 1970–1972."

81   Doug Scott, interview, July 31, 2001.

82   Nathaniel P. Reed, Department of the Interior, to Stewart Brandborg, August 22, 1972, HCP, box 1:1, folder "Correspondence, 1972."

83   Thomas C. Bailey to Nathaniel P. Reed, 1973, TWSR, box 7:141, folder "Michigan: Isle Royale, 1973."

84   Doug Scott to Clay Peters, staff consultant, Committee on Interior and Insular Affairs, House of Representatives, March 7, 1974, TWSR, box 7:141, folder "Michigan: Isle Royale, 1974."

85   The lack of protection for such well-known national parks should not be surprising. Instead of focusing on protecting already well-protected parks, wilderness advocates instead chose to focus on less well-protected lands, such as the national forests, Alaska, and the BLM public domain.

86   Roth, *Wilderness Movement and the National Forests* (1984), chap. 3.

87   Suzanne Weiss, "Water Board Loses out as Wilderness Bill Ok'd," *Rocky Mountain News*, December 13, 1975.

88   Dick Joy, USFS, to Bill Worf, USFS, November 8, 1971, ACWTCP, document #111.

89   Stewart M. Brandborg, "Director's Annual Report, 1974," 1974, TWSR, box 1:204, folder "Minutes: Executive Committee, 1974."

90   Ibid.

91   All of these measures are detailed in ibid.

92   "Memo to Officers and Governing Council of TWS," October 2, 1974, TWSR, box 1:204, folder "Minutes: Executive Committee, 1974."

93   Virginia C. Carney, "Executive Committee Minutes," May 11, 1974, ibid.

94   Fundraising efforts and related concerns are addressed in ibid., 5.

95   Brandborg, "Director's Annual Report, 1974," 1974, TWSR.

96   Carney, "Executive Committee Minutes," May 11, 1974, TWSR, 2.

97   Stewart M. Brandborg, "Memo to Council of TWS," September 22, 1975, TWSR, box 1:204, folder "Minutes: Executive Committee, 1975"; Wilderness Society, "Minutes of the 30th Annual Meeting of the Council of the Wilderness Society," October 5–10, 1975, ibid.

98   Harry Crandell to Stewart M. Brandborg, July 3, 1975, HCP, box 2:4, folder "Correspondence from the Wilderness Society, 1975–1988"; Rebecca McGinnis to Crandell and Ernest P. Dickerman, June 17, 1975, HCP, box 1:1, folder "Correspondence, 1975"; Sheila Kehoe to Brandborg, June 20, 1975, ibid.; "Petition to the Governing Council," June 18, 1975, ibid.

99   Kehoe to Brandborg, June 20, 1975, HCP.

100   Wilderness Society to Harry Crandell, August 1, 1975, HCP, box 2:4, folder "Correspondence from the Wilderness Society, 1975–1988."

101   Kittleman Associates, "Kittleman Report, 1975," December 15, 1975, TWSR, box 5:1, folder "Kittleman Report, 1975."

102   Gottlieb, *Forcing the Spring* (2005), 155.

103   Dewey, *Don't Breathe the Air* (2000); Hays, *Beauty, Health, and Permanence* (1987).

104   Fox, *John Muir and His Legacy* (1981); Gottlieb, *Forcing the Spring* (2005); Bruce J. Schulman, *The Seventies: The Great Shift in American Culture, Society, and Politics* (2001); Shabecoff, *Earth Rising* (2000).

105   Cronon, "When the G.O.P. Was Green," January 8, 2001; Milazzo, *Unlikely Environmentalists* (2006); Hal K. Rothman, *The Greening of a Nation?* (1998).

106   League of Conservation Voters, Past National Environmental Scorecards, http://lcv.org/scorecard/past-scorecards/.

107   Turner and Schneier Jr., *Party and Constituency* (1970), 103–4. Dunlap and Allen, "Partisan Differences on Environmental Issues" (1976). Historians have also given attention to this persistent partisanship. See Hays, *Beauty, Health, and Permanence* (1987), chap. 2.

108   William A. Turnage, Wilderness Society, "Confidential Special Report on Alaska Lands Legislation," February 27, 1979, TSP, box 3, folder "Conservationist Involvement in Alaska."

5 Alaska: "The Last Chance to Do It Right the First Time"

1   Beula Edmiston to Celia M. Hunter, executive director, TWS, March 29, 1976, TWSP, box 2:2, folder "Resignation Notices, 1976."

2   J. Frederick Bell to Hunter, March 16, 1976, ibid.

3   Arlo I. Smith to Hunter, April 1, 1976, ibid.; Jack Lorenz, executive director, Izaak Walton League of America, to Hunter, March 4, 1976, ibid.

4   Bernard Shanks to Hunter, March 8, 1976, ibid.; Dorothy Gumaer to Hunter, March 1976, ibid.

5   Clifford F. Messinger to Hunter, March 1, 1976, ibid.

6   Chuck Clusen, Sierra Club, "Confidential Memo to Mike McCloskey and Brock Evans," April 5, 1976, TWSP, box 12:300, folder "ANILCA: Correspondence—General, 1976."

7   Roderick Nash, Wilderness and the American Mind (1982), 299.

8   U.S. Department of the Interior, Bureau of Land Management, Public Land Statistics (1971), 10.

9   Regarding the role of the Federal/State Planning Commission, which proposed a new system of state and federal co-management of Alaska's lands, and environmentalists' efforts to protect lands not included in the d(2) selections under section d(1) of ANILCA, see George F. Williss, "Do Things Right the First Time": The National Park Service and the Alaska National Interest Lands Conservation Act of 1980 (1985), chap. 3; and Nelson, Northern Landscapes (2004), 118–29.

10 Harry Crandell to Celia Hunter, February 1, 1976, HCP, box 1:1, folder "Correspondence, 1976."

11 Chuck Clusen, personal communication, August 20, 2010.

12 The deck had been stacked in part by the national environmental community. Environmental leaders played an important role in lobbying for top appointments in the Carter administration and helping to restructure the House Interior Committee in favor of the Alaska lands issue. Chuck Clusen, interview, November 30, 2001.

13 Statistics on historical representation in the Senate are available at http://www.senate.gov.

14 Alaska Coalition, "Newsletters," February 1978, SCMP, box 224, folder 9, "Alaska Coalition."

15 Joel B. Hagen, An Entangled Bank: The Origins of Ecosystem Ecology (1992), 122–33; Donald Worster, Nature's Economy: A History of Ecological Ideas (1977, 1994), chap. 16.

16 Eugene P. Odum, Fundamentals of Ecology (1959).

17 Within the wilderness community, these new concerns were broached most forcefully and publicly at the Sierra Club's Biennial Wilderness Conference in 1968, when speakers raised farsighted questions about wilderness as "biotic

reserves," "stable ecosystems," and having value in protecting "dynamic range[s] of species." See Maxine McCloskey, *Wilderness: The Edge of Knowledge* (1969).

18   On tensions among ecology, policy, and activism, see Stephen Bocking, *Ecologists and Environmental Politics: A History of Contemporary Ecology* (1997), chap. 8; and Worster, *Nature's Economy* (1994), chap. 17.

19   Williss, *"Do Things Right the First Time"* (1985), chap. 3.

20   Note, this December 10, 1978, deadline was set in the Alaska Native Claims Settlement Act.

21   The scope of the original H.R. 39 proposal was a conscious decision on the part of the Alaska Coalition. Starting big allowed more room for negotiation. Clusen, interview, November 30, 2001.

22   On Seiberling's personal commitment to and instrumental role in protecting the public lands, see Daniel Nelson's biography, *A Passion for the Land: John F. Seiberling and the Environmental Movement* (2009).

23   Ibid.

24   Alaska Coalition, "Alaska National Interest Lands Hearing Alert," April 1977, SCMP, box 224, folder 8.

25   These quotes are drawn from the lower forty-eight hearings in U.S. Congress, House of Representatives, Subcommittee on Oversight and Alaska Lands, Committee on Interior and Insular Affairs, *Inclusion of Alaska Lands in National Park, Forest, Wildlife Refuge, and Wild and Scenic Rivers Systems*, 95th Cong., 1st sess., 1977.

26   "Alaska Slide Show Script," ACP, box 4, folder "Grassroots—Slide Shows Scripts."

27   Susan Kollin, *Nature's State: Imagining Alaska as the Last Frontier* (2001).

28   U.S. House of Representatives, *Inclusion of Alaska Lands* (1977).

29   Alaska Coalition, "Grassroots Primer on Fundraising," TWSR, box 12:301, folder "Alaska Coalition: Campaign Work Program and Research."

30   Alaska Coalition, "Report of the Second Alaska Coalition Meeting on the National Interest Lands," TWSR, 1976, 1.

31   For an overview of the hearings, see Nelson, *Passion for the Land* (2009), 133–36.

32   Nelson, *Northern Landscapes* (2004), 199.

33   On the history of the campaign to establish the Arctic National Wildlife Range in the 1950s, see Roger Kaye, *Last Great Wilderness: The Campaign to Establish the Arctic National Wildlife Refuge* (2006).

34   Fish and Wildlife Service, "Arctic National Wildlife Range," May 1971, TWSR, box 12:317, folder "ANILCA: ANWR, 1960s."

35   "Arctic Wildlife Range Bill," *Living Wilderness* 23 (1959), clipping.

36   Regarding early controversy over oil development in ANWR, see John D. Findlay, "History and Status of the Arctic National Wildlife Range," *University of British Columbia Law Review* 6, no. 1 (June 1971): 15–20; John P. Milton to Dr. Harold Coolidge, president, ICUN, February 18, 1969, SCMP, box 224, folder 5; and

Walter J. Hickel, governor of Alaska, to Stewart Udall, secretary of the interior, September 27,1967, TWSR, box 12:317, folder "ANILCA: ANWR, 1960s."

37 U.S. Department of the Interior, Fish and Wildlife Service, *Proposed Arctic National Wildlife Refuge, Alaska; Final Environmental Statement* (1974).

38 On the history of Native Americans and the public lands, see Spence, *Dispossessing the Wilderness* (1999); and Louis S. Warren, *The Hunter's Game: Poachers and Conservationists in Twentieth-Century America* (1997), chap. 5.

39 Harry K. Hugo, mayor, Anaktuvuk Pass, Alaska, to Representative John Seiberling, June 10, 1977, HCP, box 3:5, folder "U.S. House / Alaska: ANILCA Research Papers, 1977."

40 See letters from Alaska Natives in Fish and Wildlife Service, *Proposed Arctic National Wildlife Refuge* (1974).

41 Jim Kowalsky, Friends of the Earth, "Memo to Alaska Coalition People," December 18, 1976, TWSR, box 12:300, folder "ANILCA: Correspondence—General, 1976."

42 Harry Crandell, staff, Committee on Interior and Insular Affairs, "Background Brief: Subsistence," January 5, 1978, HCP, box 3:5, folder "U.S. House / Alaska: ANILCA, 1978."

43 U.S. Congress, House Committee on Interior and Insular Affairs, *Alaska National Interest Lands Conservation Act of 1979*, hearings. 96th Cong., 1st sess., 1979, 1199.

44 William A. Turnage, Wilderness Society, "Confidential Special Report on Alaska Lands Legislation," February 27, 1979, TSP, box 3, folder "Conservationists Involvement in Alaska."

45 Kathie Durbin, *Tongass: Pulp Politics and the Fight for the Alaskan Rain Forest* (1999), chap. 3.

46 Ibid.; Kenn Ross, *Environmental Conflict in Alaska* (2000), chap. 15.

47 Nelson, *Northern Landscapes* (2004), 83–85.

48 Southeast Alaska Conservation Council, "Rocky Pass Alert," October 25, 1976, TWSR, box 12:324, folder "Tongass National Forest, 1970s."

49 Alaska Center for the Environment to Chuck Clusen, Alaska Coalition, January 7, 1977, TWSR, box 12:301, folder "Alaska Coalition: Internal Memos." For a detailed account of environmental activism in southeast Alaska, see Nelson, *Northern Landscapes* (2004), 141–48.

50 U.S. House of Representatives, *Inclusion of Alaska Lands* (1977), 21.

51 As quoted in Nelson, *Northern Landscapes* (2004), 135.

52 Daniel G. Johnson, Kootznoowoo, Inc., to John Seiberling, July 6, 1977, TWSR, box 12:324, folder "Tongass National Forest #2, 1970s."

53 U.S. House of Representatives, *Inclusion of Alaska Lands* (1977), 110.

54 Theodore Catton, *Inhabited Wilderness: Indians, Eskimos, and National Parks in Alaska* (1997), 168.

55 Ted Woodbury, chairman, Great Lakes chapter, Sierra Club, "Subsistence

Hunting—Threat to Alaskan Wildlife," June 21, 1978, TWSR, box 12:300, folder "ANILCA: Correspondence—General Jan.–Jul. 1978."

56   Michael McCloskey, executive director of the Sierra Club, used the term "hell-bent." He explains his reasoning in correspondence with Gary Snyder in 1974. McCloskey to Snyder, December 6, 1974, TWSR, box 12:300, folder "ANILCA: Correspondence—General, 1971–1975."

57   Alaska Center for the Environment to Chuck Clusen, Alaska Coalition, TWSR, 1977.

58   Jim Rearden, "Say Goodbye to Hunting? Alaska's Year of Decision," *Outdoor Life*, July 1978, 62–63.

59   Crandell to Hunter, HCP, February 1, 1976.

60   Alaska Coalition, "Alaska," April 26, 1978, SCPNWP, accession 2678-2, box 11, folder "Alaska, Outgoing Letters."

61   Clusen, interview, November 30, 2001.

62   Gottlieb, *Forcing the Spring* (2005).

63   Comprehensive financial information is unavailable. I estimate the Alaska Coalition controlled one million dollars, and other member organizations contributed one to three million dollars more toward the campaign. Alaska Coalition, "Financial Statement for 1979," March 6, 1980, SCMP, box 224, folder 11; Mark Fisher, "Lobbyists Hold No Weapons Back in Multimillion Dollar Land Fight," *Fairbanks Daily News Miner*, July 25, 1980; Todd Oppenheimer, "Development Forces Outspend Environmentalists on d-2," *Alaska Daily News*, July 28, 1980.

64   Clusen, interview, November 30, 2001.

65   Alaska Coalition, Finance Committee, "Minutes of Meeting," April 19, 1978, TWSR, box 12:301, folder "Alaska Coalition: Budget, 1977–1978."

66   Specific numbers are available for the campaign's grassroots structure in 1980. Alaska Coalition, "Grassroots Capabilities," March 24, 1980, TWSR, box 12:302, folder "ANILCA: Grassroots, Folder #2."

67   John McComb, "Memo to Chuck Clusen re: Costs of Alaska Mailing (Senate Campaign)," September 27, 1978, TWSR, box 12:300, folder "ANILCA: Correspondence—General Aug.–Oct. 1978."

68   Doug Scott and Sandy Turner, "Memo to Alaska Coalition Steering Committee re: Preliminary Draft Proposal, House Floor Campaign," March 14, 1978, TWSR, box 12:300, folder "ANILCA: Campaign—1977–1980."

69   Ibid.

70   Representative Mo Udall to Senator Henry M. Jackson, August 1, 1978, HCP, box 3:5, folder "U.S. House / Alaska: ANILCA, 1978."

71   Chuck Clusen, director, Alaska Coalition, "Letter to Senator," September 13, 1978, ibid.

72   Alaska Coalition, "Memo to Alaska Coordinators," October 15, 1978, SCMP, box 224, folder 9.

73   Ibid.

74 Nelson, *Northern Landscapes* (2004), 219.

75 Charles M. Clusen to Anne Wexler, assistant to the president, October 31, 1978, TWSR, box 12:310, folder "ANILCA: Administration Action, 1978."

76 Schulman, *Seventies* (2001), 128–29.

77 Clusen to Wexler, October 31, 1978, TWSR.

78 On Alaska's efforts to block such presidential action, see Nelson, *Northern Landscapes* (2004), 221–23.

79 *Antiquities Act of 1906*, Public Law 59–209, 59th Cong. 1st sess. (June 8, 1906).

80 White House press secretary, "Press Briefing by Cecil D. Andrus, secretary of the interior, and Rupert Cutler, assistant secretary of agriculture," December 1, 1978, RCP.

81 Edgar Wayburn to Chuck Clusen, December 28, 1978, TWSR, box 12:300, folder "ANILCA: Correspondence—General Dec. 1978."

82 Citizens for Management of Alaskan Lands, "Memo to All Members and Supporters," May 23, 1978, TWSR, box 12:304, folder "ANILCA—Opposition—Citizens for the Management of Alaska [CMAL], 1977–1978."

83 Klyza and Sousa, *American Environmental Policy* (2008), 112–13.

84 "The Big Federal Land Grab," *Conservative Digest* 4 (December 12, 1978): 7–11.

85 "Marching Again," *Fairbanks News-Miner*, December 18, 1978.

86 June Allen and Matt Hammer, "Free Alaska [Song]," 1979, HCP, box 3:6, folder "U.S. House / Alaska: Alaska State Legislature, 1979."

87 Nelson, *Northern Landscapes* (2004), 227.

88 Tony Motley, CMAL to Gregg O'Clarey, April 24, 1977, TWSR, box 12:304, folder "ANILCA—Opposition—Citizens for the Management of Alaska [CMAL], 1977–1978."

89 REAL Alaska Coalition, "Unacceptable Sections in Senate Energy Committee Bill," 1979, HCP, box 3:6, folder "U.S. House / Alaska: Sport Hunting, 1979–1980."

90 Dave Carpenter, "State's Land Lobbying Worth It, Director Says," *Anchorage Times*, August 20, 1980.

91 Bill Horn, minority staffer, Committee on Interior and Insular Affairs, "Briefing Paper: HR 39 Impact on Sport Hunting," approx. 1978, HCP, box 3:5, folder "U.S. House / Alaska: Horn Briefing Paper, 1977."

92 David Levine to Clusen, December 7, 1978, TWSR, box 12:300, folder "ANILCA: Correspondence—General Dec. 1978."

93 "Monument Trespass Scheduled for Friday," *Ketchikan Daily News*, August 9, 1979.

94 Neal Knox, NRA Institute, "Letter to Congressman," April 26, 1979, TWSR, box 12:304, folder "ANILCA—Opposition Materials and Arguments."

95 Alaska Coalition, "And Miles to Go Before We Sleep . . . ," May 1979, HCP, box 3:5, folder "U.S. House / Alaska: ANILCA, 1979."

96 Statistics on the Trans-Alaska Pipeline are available from Alyeska's website,

http://www.alyeska-pipe.com. Statistics on domestic U.S. production are available from British Petroleum, *BP Statistical Review of World Energy* (2009).

97   For information on Alaska's Permanent Fund, see its website, https://www.pfd. state.ak.us/dividendamounts/index.aspx.

98   Jimmy Carter, "Proclamation 4611—Admiralty Island National Monument," *The American Presidency Project* (online), December 1, 1978.

99   Williss, *"Do Things Right the First Time"* (1985).

100   Alaska Coalition, "Huckaby Substitute," February 26, 1979, HCP, box 3:6, folder "U.S. House / Alaska: Huckaby Substitute, 1979"; Harry Crandell, Committee on Interior and Insular Affairs, "Acreage Summary," May 16, 1979, HCP, box 3:5, folder "U.S. House / Alaska: Acreage Comparisons in Pending Legislation, 1978–1980."

101   Dee Frankfourth, "Memo to Out-of-Town Core Lobbyists re: Alaska Lands Update," April 8, 1979, TWSR, box 12:301, folder "Alaska Coalition: Campaign Work Program and Research."

102   Crandell, "Acreage Summary," May 16, 1979, HCP.

103   Alaska Coalition, "Memo to Alaska Coordinators," February 12, 1979, SCMP, box 224, folder 10.

104   Sierra Club, Wilderness Society, and Friends of the Earth, "Confidential Memo on National Forest Wilderness," June 1979, CECP, box 4:30A, folder "Issues: Memos—Wilderness Areas, 1979–1984."

105   Harry Crandell, Staff, Committee on Interior and Insular Affairs, "Memo to Seiberling re: Alaska Lands," July 9, 1980, HCP, Box 3:5, Folder "U.S. House / Alaska: ANILCA Research Papers, 1980s."

106   Ibid.

107   Alaska Coalition, "Memo to Sierra Club Leaders re: Alaska Lands Campaign," January 25, 1980, SCMP, box 224, folder 11.

108   Peter J. Bernstein, "Whatever Happened to the Ecology Movement?" *San Francisco Chronicle*, April 20, 1980; "Hard Times Come to Environmentalists," *U.S. News & World Report*, March 10, 1980, 49.

109   Ellen Knox, Ohio chapter, Sierra Club, "What a Grass Root Needs from the Club," 1980, SCR, box "Sierra Club Regional Conservation Committees," box 245, folder 15. A less acerbic reference to the same problem can be found in Brock Evans, "Memo to McCloskey re: Selected Activists," March 19, 1980, SCMP, box 121, folder 28.

110   Brock Evans, "Memo re: 'Assessment and Direction Session' of Certain Environmentalists, Harpers Ferry," January 11, 1980, SCR, box 246, folder 7.

111   Doug Scott, Sierra Club, "Memo to RCC re: Meeting with RCCs," March 28, 1980, SCR, box 245, folder 15.

112   Carpenter, "State's Land Lobbying Worth It," August 20, 1980.

113 Doug Scott to Cranston, April 18, 1980, TWSR, box 12:301, folder "Alaska Coalition: Correspondence, 1980–1981."

114 Williss, "Do Things Right the First Time" (1985), 235.

115 The Alaska Coalition blamed Stevens in their memo, but Senator Jackson (WA) also played an important role in moving debate off the Senate floor. Alaska Coalition, "Alaska Status Report: Three Test Votes Won New Senate Agreement Forged," August 8, 1980, HCP, box 3:7, folder "U.S. House / Alaska: Correspondence on d-2 lands, 1979–1980." Note, it was at this time that the Senator John Melcher (D-MT) introduced an amendment into the Alaska lands act that relaxed restrictions on vehicular access to inholdings in national forests and public domain lands.

116 Doug Scott, "Urgent, Confidential Memo to Ed Wayburn, Michael McCloskey," July 31, 1980, SCMP, box 224, folder 11.

117 Chuck Clusen, personal communication, e-mail, August 20, 2010.

118 Southeast Alaska Conservation Council to Stan Sloss and Harry Crandell, staff, House of Representatives, June 12, 1977, TWSR, box 12:324, folder "Tongass National Forest, 1970s."

119 "Bill Comparison," September 1980, HCP, box 3:12, folder "Tongass National Forest, 1977–1978."

120 SEACC Board of Directors to Alaska Coalition, October 26, 1980, TWSR, box 12:301, folder "Alaska Coalition: Correspondence, 1980–1981."

121 Theodore Swem, Wilderness Society, "Notes on Turnage Call," September 26, 1980, TSP, box 2, folder "Notes on AK Meetings and Telephone Calls."

122 Ibid.

123 John McComb, Doug Scott, and Chuck Clusen, Alaska Coalition, "Memo to Udall and Seiberling," September 26, 1980, HCP, box 3:5, folder "U.S. House / Alaska: Alaska Coalition Folder 1, 1978–1980."

124 Schulman, The Seventies (2001), chap. 5.

125 On the final legislative deliberations toward ANILCA, see Nelson, Northern Landscapes (2004), 225–48.

126 Alaska Coalition, "Alaska Status Report," December 5, 1980, SCMP, box 224, folder 11.

127 Harry Crandell, staff, Committee on Publics Lands and National Parks, to Tom Watkins, January 30, 1984, HCP, box 1:1, folder "Correspondence, 1983–1986."

128 Comptroller General of the United States to U.S. Senate, Committee on Energy and Natural Resources, July 18, 1980, HCP, box 3:10, folder "U.S. House / Alaska: Arctic National Wildlife Refuge, 1980–1984."

129 Betty Mills, "Natives Swap Park Land for Subsurface Drilling Rights," Fairbanks Daily-News Miner, August 9, 1983. The Arctic Slope Regional Corporation swapped 100,000 acres of inholdings in the Gates of the Arctic National Park for 92,000 acres of land in ANWR. Note, those lands cannot be developed for energy without congressional approval.

130   Nelson, *Northern Landscapes* (2004), 251–56.

131   Durbin, *Tongass: Pulp Politics* (1999), epilogue. Nelson, *Northern Landscapes* (2004), 256–61.

132   When the Alaska lands act was implemented, the Reagan administration interpreted these exceptions for motorized use in the conservation units and wilderness areas as liberally as possible. The so-called "Melcher amendment" substantially eased restrictions on access to private inholdings surrounded by lands managed by the Forest Service and Bureau of Land Management, regardless of any special designations, such as wilderness, much to the disappointment of wilderness advocates. See note 115 above.

133   Regarding the purity policies, see chapters 2 and 3.

134   Wilderness Society, *The Alaska Lands Act, a Broken Promise: The Wilderness Society Report on the Historic Alaska Lands Act Ten Years after Passage* (1990).

6   National Forests: The Polarization of Environmental Politics

1   Tom Fitzpatrick, "Dave Foreman," *Phoenix New Times*, June 14, 1989. Foreman's arrest is also detailed in Susan Zakin, *Coyotes and Town Dogs: Earth First! and the Environmental Movement* (1993), 1–2 and 339.

2   Dave Foreman, *Confessions of an Eco-Warrior* (1991), 17.

3   Ibid., 199.

4   Dave Foreman, Wilderness Society, "Letter to Wilderness Leaders," April 1, 1975, TWSR, box 2:4, folder "Wilderness Leaders Conference, 1975."

5   Dave Foreman, "Memo to: Sally Ranney, TWS," April 13, 1977, TWSR, box 12:300, folder "ANILCA: Correspondence—General, 1977."

6   Foreman, *Confessions of an Eco-Warrior* (1991), chap. 2.

7   As quoted in Molly Ivins, "New Mexico Town Sees Battle on Wilderness Area as Fight to Survive," *New York Times*, January 28, 1981.

8   Foreman, *Confessions of an Eco-Warrior* (1991), 16.

9   A fuller account of the organization of Earth First!, including details of the trip to Pinacate Peak, and the role of Bart Koehler and Ron Kezar, can be found in Susan Zakin's *Coyotes and Town Dogs* (1993).

10   Foreman, *Confessions of an Eco-Warrior* (1991), 19.

11   Rupert Cutler, interview, December 20, 2001.

12   Rupert Cutler to Theodore Snyder, March 27, 1975, SCR, box 53, folder 38.

13   Foreman, *Confessions of an Eco-Warrior* (1991), 13.

14   Cutler, interview, December 20, 2001.

15   Hirt, *Conspiracy of Optimism* (1994).

16   For a detailed account of legislation important to the Forest Service in the 1960s and 1970s, see Clary, *Timber and the Forest Service* (1986), chap. 7; and Hirt, *Conspiracy of Optimism* (1994), chap. 11.

17   Hays, *Wars in the Woods* (2006).

18   Clary, *Timber and the Forest Service* (1986), 193.

19   Specifically, Mahoney confined his appeals to Forest Service Region 2, which included Colorado. Tim Mahoney, "Timber Appeal," June 22, 1976, TWSR, box 7:118, folder "States / Colorado: Colorado Timber Management, 1976."

20   Clifton R. Merritt to Governing Council member, June 8, 1977, TWSR, box 7:118, folder "States / Colorado: Colorado Timber Management, 1977."

21   The Sierra Club dissuaded the Wilderness Society from filing suit for strategic reasons. It already had a legislative strategy underway, which it feared a legal suit would interrupt. Michael McCloskey to George Davis, November 16, 1976, SCMP, box 133, folder 21; McCloskey to Brock Evans, September 30, 1976, SCNLOR, box 132, folder 1.

22   Dave Foreman to Debbie Sease, Sierra Club, September 3, 1976, SCPNWP, 2678–2, accession box 4, folder "EAWA, General Correspondence, Sept.–Oct., 1976"; Foreman, "Memo re: Endangered Wilderness Areas Bill," July 28, 1976, SCPNWP, 2678–2, accession box 5, folder "EAWA, Internal Correspondence, 1976."

23   Dave Foreman, "Shipwrecked Environmentalism," *Earth First! Journal*, March 20, 1984.

24   This argument was made throughout the Endangered American Wilderness Act campaign. The data are drawn from a publication released after the act became law and RARE II was underway: National Forest Products Association, "Wilderness Withdrawals and Timber Supply," July 20, 1978, SAFP, box 3, folder "RARE II," 10.

25   Statistics on total timber sales and average prices are available from the United States Forest Service, Forest Management, http://www.fs.fed.us/forestmanage-ment/reports/sold-harvest/index.shtml.

26   This is also mentioned in a separate letter in Cutler's papers: John M. Bradley Jr., president, Resource Management Services, to John Randolph, president, Alabama Conservancy, April 25, 1979, RCP.

27   U.S. Congress, House, Committee on Interior and Insular Affairs, Subcommittee on Indian Affairs and Public Lands, "Testimony by M. Rupert Cutler, Assistant Secretary of Agriculture, on the Endangered American Wilderness Act, H.R. 3454," 95th Cong., 1st sess., May 6, 1977.

28   Robert Smith, "French Pete Wilderness Gains Administration Favor," *Eugene Register-Guard*, May 7, 1977.

29   Rupert Cutler, "Policy for Management of Wildernesses within the National Forests," November 2, 1977, FSR, entry #30B / A1, box 9, folder "University of Idaho Symposium."

30   John Hendee et al., "A Wilderness Attribute Rating System for RARE II," November 1977, TWSR, box 8:100, folder "RARE I and II: General, 1977–1978."

31   U.S. Department of Agriculture, Forest Service, *RARE II: Final Environmental Statement* (1979), 12.

32   Ibid., appendix W.

33   Jimmy Carter, "Statement by the President," April 16, 1979, TWSR, box 8:101, folder "RARE I and II: Roadless Inventory, General, 1979."

34   Citizens for America's Endangered Wilderness, "RARE II: The Results," January 1979, CECP, box 4:30A, folder "Issues: Memos—Wilderness Areas, 1979–1984."

35   Allin, Politics of Wilderness Preservation (1982), 162–65.

36   See note 25.

37   Southern Oregon Resource Alliance, "Uncle Sam Wants Your Job!" September 20, 1978, TWSR, box 8:103, folder "RARE I and II: Oregon, 1977–1978."

38   Fred Huff, Las Cruces Jeep Club, "The Creeping Wilderness Is About to Run over You!" December 1978, RCP.

39   Scholars have most often considered the Sagebrush Rebellion a specific reaction to BLM public lands issues, especially grazing. My analysis suggests the Sagebrush Rebellion is better understood as a response to the expanding role of the federal government and environmental regulations on the national forests, in Alaska, and on the public domain (see chap. 7). For an excellent history of the Sagebrush Rebellion, see Cawley, Federal Land, Western Anger (1993).

40   "Wilderness Proposals Draw Protest in Macon County," Asheville Times, July 12, 1977.

41   "RARE Hearing Draws Heavy Turn-Out," The Missoulian, October 5, 1977.

42   U.S. House of Representatives, Committee on Interior and Insular Affairs, Sagebrush Rebellion: Impacts on Energy and Minerals, testimony of Congressman Jim Santini, 96th Cong., 2nd sess., 1980, 2–3.

43   "Montana Wilderness Hearing Draws Emotional Testimony," The Missoulian, July 17, 1977.

44   Cawley, Federal Land, Western Anger (1993).

45   The opposition, itself, made this argument. See James R. Craine, Federal Timber Purchasers Association, "Letter to Members re: RARE II Responses," November 13, 1978, WTAR, box 47, folder "RARE II, Oct.–Dec., 1978."

46   James Morton Turner, "Conservation Science and Forest Service Policy for Roadless Areas," Conservation Biology 20, no. 3 (June 2006): 713–22.

47   Despite its success, the American Plywood Association alleged early on in the process that the whole endeavor gave "top priority" to wilderness classification. American Plywood Association, "With Fast, Fair Resolution . . . RARE II Means Padlocked Resources," 1977, FSR, box 1, folder "RARE II."

48   U.S. Forest Service, RARE II (1979), chap. 3.

49   George A. Craig, Western Timber Association, to Rupert Cutler, assistant secretary of agriculture, November 22, 1978, WTAR, box 47, folder "RARE II, Oct.–Dec. 1978."

50   Atlantic Richfield Company, "A Statement by Atlantic Richfield Company regard-

ing RARE II," 1978, TWSR, box 8:100, folder "RARE I and II: Atlantic Richfield Company."

51   Richard Reid, Western Timber Association, "Handwritten Notes on the Roadless Area Review and Evaluation II Symposium Sponsored by the National Outdoor Coalition and the Far West Ski Association," August 19–20, 1978, WTAR, box 47, folder "RARE II, Oct.–Dec. 1978."

52   Malcolm Epley Jr., Western Wood Products Association, "Letter to AFI Western Communications Committee re: RARE II," November 2, 1978, ibid.

53   Ibid.

54   Richard Reid to George Craig, executive vice president, Western Timber Association, "re: RARE II Announcement," January 12, 1979, WTAR, box 46, folder "RARE II, Jan.–Feb. 1979."

55   As quoted in Philip Shabecoff, "Issue and Debate Easing Federal Control of Public Land," *New York Times*, February 10, 1981.

56   As quoted in Curtis Wilkie, "In West, Liberals Fight Back," *Boston Globe*, October 20, 1980.

57   Doug Scott, Sierra Club, "Memo to Mike McCloskey, Paul Swatek, Chuck Clusen re: RARE II and Endangered Wilderness Bill in Senate," August 30, 1977, TWSR, box 12:300, folder "ANILCA: Correspondence—General July/Sept. 1977."

58   Other wilderness advocates, however, acknowledged that the summer hearings had been "overwhelmed" by industry. For instance, see Dave Foreman, "Confidential Memo to Regional Representatives," April 3, 1978, TWSR, box 8:100, folder "Eastern Wilderness Leaders Conference"; and Mike and Linda Comola, Northwest Citizens for Wilderness, "Memo to Environmental Leaders," December 27, 1977, SCPNWP, box 5, folder "RARE II."

59   Tim Mahoney, interview, November 29, 2001.

60   Foreman, "Confidential Memo to Regional Representatives," April 3, 1978, TWSR.

61   Robert A. Jones, "Computer to Play Part in Fate of Forests," *Los Angeles Times*, November 7, 1978.

62   Colorado Open Space Coordinating Council, "Take a Hike to Save Your Favorite Wilderness," approx. 1978, CECP, box 4:31, folder "Issues: RARE II—Roadless Area Inventory."

63   Citizens for America's Endangered Wilderness, "RARE II: The Results," January 1979, CECP.

64   Roger Beers and Trent Orr, Natural Resources Defense Council, "Memo to NRDC Board of Trustees re: California RARE II Suit," September 7, 1979, TWSR, box 13:106, folder "Litigation: RARE II, No. 3."

65   The most detailed discussion of the release legislation can be found in Harry Crandell's papers, which contain correspondence among Crandell, Andy Wiessner, John Seiberling, and the wilderness groups. See HCP, box 4:1, folder "U.S. House / Public Lands: Memos—Wilderness, 1980."

66 John Hooper, Wilderness Society, "Memo to Bill re: TWS Intervention in CA RARE II Suit," September, 21, 1979, TWSR, box 13:106, folder "Litigation: RARE II, No. 1, 1979–1980."

67 Andy Wiessner, "Memo to Seiberling re: Background on River of No Return," June 19, 1979, HCP, box 4:1, folder "U.S. House / Public Lands: Memos—Wilderness, 1979."

68 On efforts to avoid such a compromise, see John Hooper, Wilderness Society, "Memo to Chuck re: Proposed 'Release' Language of H.R. 5487," October 21, 1979, TWSR, box 7:118, folder "Colorado: Colorado Wilderness Bill, 1979."

69 Mahoney, interview, November 30, 2001.

70 Al Sample, forester, Wilderness Society, "Memo to Rebecca Gordon, TWS, re: 9th Circuit Decision on California," n.d./1982, TWSR, box 10:107, folder "RARE III."

71 Tim Mahoney, Sierra Club, "Memo re: Status of the National Forest Wilderness Campaign," August 18, 1981, TWSR, box 7:108, folder "States/California: Roadless Areas, 1980s."

72 Mahoney, interview, November 29, 2001.

73 Foreman, Confessions of an Eco-Warrior (1991), 14.

74 On the legislative maneuvering behind these bills, see Nelson, Passion for the Land (2009), 164–76.

75 Mahoney, "Memo re: Status of the National Forest Wilderness Campaign," August 18, 1981, TWSR.

76 The Alaska Coalition acceded to compromise legislation at the close of the 96th Congress, rather than face the incoming Reagan administration and a Republican Senate in 1981.

77 Tim Mahoney, Sierra Club, "Anti-Wilderness Bill S. 842," April 6, 1981, TWSR, box 8:101, folder "RARE II Review Act of 1981."

78 Rothman, The Greening of a Nation? (1998), chap. 7; Jeffrey K. Stine, "Natural Resources and Environmental Policy," in The Reagan Presidency: Pragmatic Conservatism and Its Legacies, ed. W. Elliot Brownlee and Hugh Davis Graham (2003).

79 Mahoney, interview, November 29, 2001; Zakin, Coyotes and Town Dogs (1993), 84–85.

80 William A. Turnage to George H. Taber, Richard King Mellon Foundation, August 8, 1979, TSP, box 6, folder "Mellon Foundation Proposal."

81 William Turnage, "Letter to Harry Crandell," June 17, 1980, HCP, box 2:4, folder "Correspondence from the Wilderness Society, 1975–1988."

82 Chuck Clusen, interview, November 30, 2001.

83 Information on these new staffers and their credentials can be found in William Turnage to David Freeman, Scherman Foundation, May 15, 1980, TWSR, box 1:100, folder "Governing Council: Correspondence, 1980–1985"; and Turnage,

"Memo to Governing Council re: Year-End Report," January 23, 1980, SCR, box 246, folder 22.

84   Wilderness Society, "Minutes of the Executive Meeting of the Governing Council," April 27, 1979, TWSR, box 1:205, folder "Minutes: Governing Council and Executive Committee, 1979."

85   Wilderness Society, "Minutes of the Executive Meeting of the Governing Council," April 14–15, 1982, TWSR, box 1:205, folder "Governing Council: Committees, 1983."

86   These statements are included in an unedited draft of the Development Committee's meeting minutes. They were later deleted from the final minutes. Sarah Muyskens, "Development Committee Meeting Minutes," September 26, 1981, TWSR, box 1:205, folder "Development Commitee Reports and Briefings, 1980."

87   Wilderness Society, "Minutes of the Executive Meeting of the Governing Council," April 27, 1979, TWSR.

88   William A. Turnage to William S. Beinecke, May 7, 1979, TWSR, box 1:100, folder "Governing Council: Correspondence, 1978."

89   Turnage to Taber, August 8, 1979, TSP, box 6, folder "Mellon Foundation Proposal."

90   William Turnage, "Memo to Executive Committee re: Gulf Oil Stock," February 23, 1981, TSP, box 9, folder "Executive Committee."

91   Sarah Muyskens, "Memo to Governing Council re: Quarterly Report on Development," October 20, 1980, TWSR, box 1:205, folder "Minutes: Governing Council and Executive Committee, 1980."

92   Clusen, interview, November 30, 2001.

93   Zakin, *Coyotes and Town Dogs* (1993), 117; James Eaton, telephone interview, September 22, 2007; Dave Foreman, interview, November 1, 2005.

94   William Turnage to Bernard Shanks, August 14, 1979, TSP, box 7, folder "TWS Correspondence—Swem, etc. on Field Reps, etc."

95   Cutler, interview, December 20, 2001.

96   Clusen, interview, November 30, 2001.

97   Theodore Swem, "Notes on Meeting of Special Committee," March 26, 1979, box 9, folder "Followup Action!!!"

98   Bernard Shanks to Ted Swem, December 5, 1979, TSP, box 7, folder "TWS Correspondence—Swem, etc. on Field Reps, etc." These sentiments were echoed by Wilderness Society staffer Debby Sease. See Theodore Swem, "Notes on Call with Turnage," November 11, 1979, TSP, box 7, folder "Telephone Calls."

99   Turnage to Shanks, August 14, 1979, TSP.

100   Turnage made this comment in regards to an early reorganization plan. William A. Turnage, "Implementation of the NRAG Recommendations," February 21, 1979, TWSR, box 1:205, folder "Minutes: Governing Council, Executive Committee,

1979." Although Turnage publicly supported grassroots organizing, he never matched those words with actions.

101 Turnage to Charles Foster, president, W. Alton Jones Foundation, May 2, 1983, TWSR, box 3:601, folder "Members: William A. Turnage, W. Alton Jones Foundation, 1980s."

102 Charles H. Stoddard to Harry Crandell, June 18, 1980, HCP, box 2:4, folder "Correspondence from the Wilderness Society, 1975–1988." James Marshall, Wilderness Society founder Robert Marshall's relative, also raised similar concerns. See James Marshall to Harry Crandell, June 16, 1980, ibid.

103 George Marshall to Harold Jerry, May 28, 1981, TWSR, box 1:100, folder "Governing Council: Correspondence, 1980–1985."

104 Harry Crandell to Theodore Swem, June 12, 1980, HCP, box 2:4, folder "Correspondence from the Wilderness Society, 1975–1988." In 1986, Crandell started another bout of criticism, which drew even more support from the Wilderness Society's old guard; see chap. 7.

105 Richard W. Van Wagenen, Wilderness Society, "Confidential Annex Attached to Original Minutes," December 19, 1979, TSP, box 9, folder "Executive Committee, Staff and Governing Council."

106 Ibid.

107 Theodore Swem to Harry Crandell, July 23, 1980, HCP, box 2:4, folder "Correspondence from the Wilderness Society, 1975–1988."

108 Foreman, *Confessions of an Eco-Warrior* (1991).

109 Zakin, *Coyotes and Town Dogs* (1993), 117.

110 "Group Vows to Dismantle Glen Canyon Dam," Associated Press, March 24, 1981.

111 As quoted in Zakin, *Coyotes and Town Dogs* (1993), 143.

112 Ibid.

113 "Show Over, EF! Roadies Unwind," *Earth First! Journal*, December 21, 1981.

114 Zakin describes "The Speech" in some detail; *Coyotes and Town Dogs* (1993), 194.

115 "Deep Ecology," *Earth First! Journal*, December 1981.

116 Dave Foreman, "Memo to Wilderness Leaders," September 21, 1983, SCNLOR, box 132, folder 9.

117 Foreman, "Around the Campfire," *Earth First! Journal*, August 1, 1984.

118 Foreman calls Earth First! the "real grassroots." Foreman, "Around the Campfire," *Earth First! Journal*, August 1, 1984.

119 The best summary of these events is in Zakin, *Coyotes and Town Dogs* (1993), 231–38.

120 Ibid.

121 Dave Foreman, "Around the Campfire," *Earth First! Journal*, June 21, 1983.

122 As quoted in Zakin, *Coyotes and Town Dogs* (1993), 151.

123 Ibid.

124 Cheryl Sullivan, "Environmental Militancy Is Alive and Thriving in the U.S.,"

Christian Science Monitor, October 21, 1988; "Tree Climbing Hero," *Earth First! Journal*, June 21, 1985.

125 Dave Foreman, *Ecodefense: A Field Guide to Monkeywrenching* (1985).

126 Ibid., 17.

127 Edward Abbey, "Forward!" in Foreman, *Ecodefense: A Field Guide to Monkeywrenching* (1985).

128 Foreman, *Ecodefense* (1985), 4.

129 Christopher Manes, *Green Rage: Radical Environmentalism and the Unmaking of Civilization* (1990), chap. 1.

130 "Wilderness Preserve System," *Earth First! Journal*, June 21, 1983.

131 Smaller bills for Indiana, Missouri, and Florida (the latter vetoed by Reagan) passed Congress in 1982, but bills for large western states were all stalled. Doug Scott, "Memo re: FS Response to *California vs. Block*," January 20, 1983, SCPNWP, Accession 2678-09, box 4, folder "RARE II."

132 Mahoney, interview, November 29, 2001; Mahoney, "Confidential Memo re: Individual Wilderness Campaigns and Overall Strategy Ideas for 97th Congress," February 17, 1981, SCR, box 261, folder 15.

133 Andy Wiessner, "Memo to Rep. Seiberling re: Further Wilderness Actions," May 2, 1984, HCP, box 2:5, folder "Wilderness: Release Language, 1984"; Wiessner, "Memo to Seiberling," April 12,1984, ibid.; Harry Crandell to Wiessner, April 12, 1984, ibid.; Mo Udall to James A. McClure, April 10, 1984, ibid. For an excellent history of these legislative campaigns, see Nelson, *Passion for the Land* (2009), 192–205.

134 William A. Turnage, Wilderness Society, "Quarterly Report to the Governing Council," April 27, 1984, TWSR, box 1:205, folder "Minutes and Reports: Executive Committee / Governing Council / Departments, 1984."

135 Charles M. Clusen, Wilderness Society, "Memo to Governing Council," April 17, 1984, TWSR, box 1:205, folder "Minutes and Reports: Executive Committee, 1984."

136 Don Tryon, Sage Association, to Jim Blomquist, Northwest Representative, Sierra Club, March 4, 1983, SCPNWP, box 2678-8, 25, folder "BLM Wilderness—Don Tryon."

137 Dave Foreman, "Memo to Wilderness Leaders," September 21, 1983, SCNLOR, box 132, folder 9.

138 "House Democrats Succeed in Passing a Wilderness Bill," *New York Times*, March 23, 1983. For California, the acreage was reduced from 2.5 to 2.0 to 1.7 million acres from the original proposal to the House-passed bill to the final Senate bill.

139 Peter Kirby and Wilma Frey, Wilderness Society, "Memo re: White Mountain Wilderness," August 3, 1983, TWSR, box 7:153, folder "States/New Hampshire: New Hampshire Wilderness Act of 1983."

140 Turnage's comment on Peter Kirby, Wilderness Society, "Memo to Chuck Clusen

re: NH Trip," April 4, 1983, TWSR, box 7:153, folder "States/New Hampshire: New Hampshire Wilderness Act of 1983."

141 Feinstein had won a special election in 1992, requiring another election campaign in 1994.

142 Wilderness Society, "Minutes of the Executive Meeting of the Governing Council," May 1, 1984, TWSR, box 1:205, folder "Minutes and Reports: Executive Committee / Governing Council / Departments, 1984"; William A. Turnage, "Memo re: NH Wilderness," July 5, 1983, TWSR, box 7:153, folder "States/New Hampshire: New Hampshire Wilderness Act of 1983."

143 This figure is tabulated from the 1979 RARE II recommendations and subsequent congressional legislation for each state.

144 Bill Devall, "Editorial," *Earth First! Journal*, December 1, 1984.

145 EarthFirst!, "National Forest Strategy Outline," December 8, 1983, SCNLOR, box 132, folder 9.

146 Ibid.

147 Foreman, "Shipwrecked Environmentalism" (1984).

148 J. Michael Scott et al., "Nature Reserves: Do They Capture the Full Range of America's Biological Diversity?" *Ecological Applications* 11, no. 4 (2001): 999–1007.

149 Howie Wolke, Earth First! "Memo to Wilderness Leaders," December 8, 1983, SCNLOR, box 132, folder 9.

150 Tim Peckinpaugh, Republican Study Committee, "Special Report: The Specter of Environmentalism," 1982, SCR, box 267, folder 52.

151 Foreman's conviction was reduced to a misdemeanor after he abided by the terms of his plea agreement for five years. "Man Gets 6 Years in Plot to Damage A-Plants," *New York Times*, September 8, 1991. Zakin, *Coyotes and Towndogs* (1993), 439–41.

152 Peckinpaugh, "Special Report: The Specter of Environmentalism," 1982, SCR.

1 The Public Domain: Environmental Politics and the Rise of the New Right

1 Senator Ted Stevens, "Speech before League for Advancements of States' Equal Rights," 1980, SCMP, box 224, folder 11.

2 For a more detailed account of the political trends in the postwar American West, see Malone and Etulain, *American West* (1989), chap. 7.

3 The Senate's historical party representation can be tallied from data available on the United States Senate's website, http://www.senate.gov (accessed June 23, 2006). In my analysis, I defined the West to include Alaska, Arizona, California, Colorado, Idaho, Montana, Nevada, New Mexico, Oregon, Utah, Washington, and Wyoming.

4 James Morton Turner, "'The Specter of Environmentalism': Wilderness, Environ-

mental Politics, and the Evolution of the New Right," *Journal of American History* 96, no. 1 (June 2009): 123–48.

5   Bureau of Land Management, *Public Land Statistics* (1980), table 9.

6   On the institutional history of the Bureau of Land Management, see Paul J. Culhane, *Public Lands Politics* (1981); Klyza, *Who Controls Public Lands?* (1996); Merrill, *Public Lands and Political Meaning* (2002); Skillen, *Nation's Largest Landlord* (2009); and Charles F. Wilkinson, *Crossing the Next Meridian: Land, Water, and the Future of the American West* (1992).

7   Initially the agency was required to produce 212 environmental impact statements; that number was reduced to 144 in 1975. Culhane, *Public Lands Politics* (1981), 95; Wilkinson, *Crossing the Next Meridian* (1992), 99. For an excellent overview of the challenges the agency faced from NEPA-related suits, see Skillen, *Nation's Biggest Landlord* (2009), 87–100.

8   Klyza, *Who Controls Public Lands?* (1996), chap. 5.

9   Karl Hess, *Visions upon the Land: Man and Nature on the Western Range* (1992), 107.

10 Cawley, *Federal Land, Western Anger* (1993), chap. 3; Rothman, *The Greening of a Nation?* (1998), 174–80.

11 Bruce Hamilton to Russ Shay and John McComb, Sierra Club, March 19, 1979, SCNLOR, box 138, folder 20, "Bureau of Land Management Interim Management Policy, 1979."

12 Brant Calkin, Sierra Club, "Memo to Southwest Sierra Club Leaders," April 27, 1979, SCR, box 233, folder 8.

13 "BLM Wilderness: A Citizen's Handbook," October 1981, SCR, box 261, folder 19; Philip Shabecoff, "Wilderness Study Announced by U.S.," *New York Times*, November 15, 1980.

14 Cawley, *Federal Land, Western Anger* (1993), 113–18; Klyza, *Who Controls Public Lands?* (1996), 9.

15 On the Carter administration's efforts to implement FLPMA and the Sagebrush Rebellion, see Skillen, *Nation's Largest Landlord* (2009), 111–23.

16 As reported by William Endicott, "'Sagebrush Revolt' Is On; Federal Lands Is the Prize," *Los Angeles Times*, August 5, 1979.

17 Cawley, *Federal Land, Western Anger* (1993), chap. 5; Switzer, *Green Backlash* (1997), chap. 7.

18 When each western state entered the union, each forfeited claims to unclaimed lands within its borders to the federal government.

19 Fred Huff, Las Cruces Jeep Club, "The Creeping Wilderness Is About to Run over You!" December 1978, RCP; "Marching Again," *Fairbanks News-Miner*, December 18, 1978.

20 Endicott, "'Sagebrush Revolt' Is On," August 5, 1979.

21   John Greeley, "House Votes to Study Secession," *Alaska Daily News*, April 30, 1980.

22   Orrin Hatch, "Questions and Answers regarding Public Lands Reform Act of 1981," 1981, AKS, box 273, folder 11.

23   Bert Smith, quoted in "People vs. The Feds," *Greybull Standard*, March 6, 1981.

24   Curtis Wilkie, "In West, Liberals Fight Back," *Boston Globe*, October 20, 1980.

25   On the New Right, see Kevin M. Kruse, "The Politics of Race and Public Space: Desegregation, Privatization, and the Tax Revolt in Atlanta," *Journal of Urban History* 31, no. 5 (July 2005): 610–33; Matthew D. Lassiter, *The Silent Majority: Suburban Politics in the Sunbelt South* (2006); and Lisa McGirr, *Suburban Warriors: The Origins of the New American Right* (2001). On the New Right and the Sagebrush Rebellion, see C. Brant Short, *Ronald Reagan and the Public Lands* (1989).

26   Kevin Michael Kruse, *White Flight: Atlanta and the Making of Modern Conservatism* (2005), 9.

27   Charles Roos, "Sagebrush Rebellion Leaders Gather, Eager to Acquire U.S. Lands," *Rocky Mountain News*, November 21, 1980.

28   Ronald Reagan, "Telegram to the Sagebrush Rebellion Conference," November 20, 1998.

29   Mountain States Legal Foundation, "Second Annual Report, 1978–1979," 1979, JGWP, box 7, folder 4.

30   For a sympathetic profile of Watt, see Ron Arnold, *At the Eye of the Storm: James Watt and the Environmentalists* (1982).

31   Evarts Graham, editorial, "Watt, the Journalism Teacher," *St. Louis Post-Dispatch*, June 18, 1981.

32   James Watt, "Address to Conference of National Park Concessioners," March 9, 1981, TWSR, box 5:36, folder 19.

33   James Watt, "Remarks before the 45th North American Wildlife and Natural Resources Conference," March 23, 1981, JGWP, box 11, folder 9.

34   Wilderness Society, "Statement of Reasons for Opposition to Nomination of James G. Watt," 1981, TWSR, box 12:3, folder 23.

35   Joseph Coors, "Letter to Concerned Coloradoan," November 1980, TWSR, box 12:3, folder 29.

36   Terry Martin, Amoco, "Letter to James Watt," January 8, 1981, JGWP, box 9, folder 6.

37   James Watt, "Interview on CNN," 1982, TWSR, box 5:36, folder 29.

38   Ibid.

39   On the Reagan administration and the BLM, see Skillen, *Nation's Largest Landlord* (2009), 124–31.

40   *Wilderness Act* (1964).

41   It is worth noting that Aspinall, a Democrat, lost his congressional seat in 1972;

but, in the late 1970s, he threw his allegiances in with the Republicans and the
Sagebrush Rebels. Schulte, *Wayne Aspinall* (2002), 285–86.

42   James Watt, "Remarks before the National Petroleum Council," December 3, 1981,
JGWP, box 11, folder 9.

43   Chris Oldham, "Memo re: Privatizing of Public Lands," June 14, 1982, AKS, box
273, folder 5.

44   Ibid. For a detailed account of the administration's plans for disposing of the
public domain, see Cawley, *Federal Land, Western Anger* (1993), chap. 6; and
Short, *Ronald Reagan and the Public Lands* (1989), 63–65, 85–91.

45   Dave Foreman, Wilderness Society, "Memo re: Sagebrush Rebellion and Public
Land Grazing Issues," August 30, 1979, CECP, box 4:30B, folder "Issues: Sagebrush
Rebellion, 1979–1980"; Wilderness Society, "Proceedings of Sagebrush Rebellion 'Counterinsurgency' Conference, Denver," October 26–27, 1979, TWSR, box
3:702, folder "Richard W. Van Wagenen, BLM Organic Act, 1970s-1980s."

46   Doug Scott, Sierra Club, "Status of Major Conservation Campaigns," August 31,
1981, SCR, box 257, folder 16.

47   Sierra Club, "Watt Petition," 1981, TWSR, box 20:101, folder "Petition to Replace
Watt, 1981."

48   Mitchell et al., "Twenty Years of Environmental Mobilization" (1992), 13.

49   Peter J. Bernstein, "Whatever Happened to the Ecology Movement?" *San Fran-
cisco Chronicle*, April 20, 1980; "Hard Times Come to Environmentalists," *U.S.
News & World Report*, March 10, 1980, 49; Robert A. Jones, "U.S. Environmental
Efforts Face Erosion," *Los Angeles Times*, November 25, 1979.

50   William Symonds, "Washington in the Grip of the Green Giant," *Fortune*, October 4, 1982, 136–38.

51   Wilderness Society, "The Watt Book," 1981, TWSR, box 20:100, folder "The Watt
Book, vol. 1, 1981."

52   Gaylord Nelson, "Statement re: Watt," February 23, 1982, TWSR, box 11:15, folder
"James Watt and Wilderness Issues." Privately, Watt complained: "I continue to be
surprised that the newspapers will print the type of garbage that Gaylord Nelson
and his sidekick, Turnage, pump out. There is too much work to be done to lower
myself to his level. We have to trust that, in the long run, truth will prevail." James
Watt, "Letter to Mitchell Melich, Esq.," June 24, 1981, JGWP, box 3, folder 9.

53   William A. Turnage, Wilderness Society, "Draft Letter to R. K. Mellon Foundation," 1982, TWSR, box 3:601, folder "Members: William A. Turnage, Hewlett
Foundation, 1980s."

54   Ibid.

55   While I cannot verify Turnage's claim, clips at the Wilderness Society and
searches of newspaper indices indicate that oil and gas leasing in wilderness was
a frequent topic of editorial comment in the winter of 1982.

56 James Watt, "Memo to the President (Attn: James Baker) re: Withdrawal of Wilderness," February 16, 1982, JGWP, box 10, folder 6.

57 "The Wilderness Protection Act of 1982" passed 340 to 58 in the House. "Factsheet: S. 2801, the Wilderness Protection Act," 1982, TWSR, box 25:2, folder "Conservation Issues: S.2801 Wilderness Protection Act, 1982." For a fuller account of the complexities of the Reagan administration, oil and gas leasing, and the nation's energy demands, see Klyza, *Who Controls Public Lands?* (1996), chap. 3.

58 Extensive materials on Watt's resignation can be found in JGWP, box 10, folder 16.

59 James Watt, "Memo re: Monday Morning Group," September 12, 1983, JGWP, box 7, folder 3.

60 "Report of BLM Wilderness Task Force, SC," June 18, 1979, SCNLOR, box 139, folder 6.

61 Abbey, *Desert Solitaire* (1968).

62 A. Durand Jones, "Cool Islands in the Desert," *The Living Wilderness* 38, no. 129 (Spring 1975): 18.

63 Sease and Foreman divorced in the early 1980s. See Zakin's profile of Sease in *Coyotes and Town Dogs* (1993).

64 Debbie Sease, Wilderness Society, "Memo to BLM Leaders re: Intensive Inventory," December 20, 1979, SCPNWP, accession 2678-8, box 25, folder "Wilderness—BLM"; Russ Shay and Nick Van Pelt, "Memo to John McComb re: BLM Interim Management Policy," January 25, 1979, SCNLOR, box 138, folder 19; Sierra Club, "BLM Wilderness: A Citizen's Handbook," October 1981, SCNLOR, box 138, folder 20.

65 Dave Foreman and Linda Lewis, "Letter to BLM Wilderness Leader," March 24, 1980, SCPNWP, accession 2678-8, box 25, folder "BLM—General Memos."

66 Sease, "Memo to BLM Leaders re: Intensive Inventory," December 20, 1979.

67 BLM, "Status of Wilderness Review of Public Lands," *Federal Register* 45 (December 17, 1980): 83028. Note, subsequent appeals of the agency's 1980 inventory would increase the acreage of wilderness study areas to more than 26 million acres.

68 *Federal Land Policy and Management Act* (1976).

69 Shay and Van Pelt, "Memo to John McComb re: BLM Interim Management Policy," January 25, 1979.

70 Regarding the agency's Interim Management Guidelines and Policy for Land Under Wilderness Review, see H. Michael Anderson and Aliki Moncrief, "America's Unprotected Wilderness," *Denver University Law Review* 76, no. 2 (1999): 413–47; and U.S. Congressional Research Service, *Bureau of Land Management Wilderness Reviews*, Ross Gorte and Pamela Baldwin (August 20, 2004).

71 Anderson and Moncrief, "America's Unprotected Wilderness," 1999, 432; Bureau of Land Management, *Public Land Statistics* (1990), 6.

72   Myron Struck, "BLM Acts to Speed Release of Potential Wilderness Lands," *Washington Post*, February 26, 1982.

73   Philip Shabecoff, "Potential Areas for Wilderness Sharply Reduced," *New York Times*, December 28, 1982.

74   "U.S. Judge Says Watt Erred in Wilderness Decision," *New York Times*, April 20, 1985.

75   See Turnage's notes on Director Terry Sopher, BLM Program, Wilderness Society, "Memo to Bill Turnage re: BLM Wilderness Campaign Themes," November 1, 1984, TWSR, box 11:9, folder "BLM: Media Ideas—BLM Wilderness."

76   "BLM Wilderness Campaign Concept Paper, 1986–1991," March 1986, TWSR, box 11:9, folder "BLM: TWS Campaign Concept re: BLM Wilderness Review Program, 1980s"; "Memo re: BLM Wilderness Campaign," March 11, 1986, TWSR, box 19:29, folder "BLM Wilderness Campaign"; Wilderness Society, "BLM Wilderness Campaign Concept Paper, 1986–1991," March 1986, TWSR, box 11:9, folder "BLM: TWS Campaign Concept re: BLM Wilderness Review Program, 1980s."

77   Southern Utah Wilderness Alliance, "BLM Wilderness Alert #1–5," Summer 1986, TWSR, box 11:9, folder "Utah BLM Wilderness Review, 1985."

78   Debbie Sease, "Memo to Key BLM Contacts re: Intensive Inventory Appeals," May 22, 1980, SCPNWP, accession 2678-8, box 25, folder "BLM—General Memos"; Tony Ruckle, Sierra Club Legal Defense Fund, "Memo re: BLM Wilderness Review Process," August 6, 1980, SCR, box 249, folder 4.

79   Utah Wilderness Coalition, "BLM Wilderness Proposal," July 13, 1985, TWSR, box 11:9, folder "Utah BLM Wilderness Review, 1985."

80   Ibid.

81   Mike Medberry, Wilderness Society, "Memo re: Utah Wilderness Bill," June 27, 1988, TWSR, box 11:9, folder "Utah BLM Wilderness Review, 1988"; Utah Wilderness Coalition, "Memo to BLM Wilderness Supporters," August 12, 1988, ibid.

82   Lee Davidson, "Owens, Republicans Divided on Size for Proposed Wilds Areas," *Deseret News*, March 1, 1989.

83   Jay Evensen, "Utah Says Bush Vowed to Veto Plan for Wilds," *Deseret News*, March 25, 1990.

84   Joseph Bauman, "BLM Submits Report Urging 1.9 Million Acres of Wilderness in Utah," *Deseret News*, February 4, 1992.

85   As quoted in John Lancaster, "Drawing the Line on West's Wilderness," *Washington Post*, April 23, 1991.

86   Brant Calkin, Southern Utah Wilderness Alliance, et al., "Letter to Wayne Owens," August 28, 1991, TWSR, box 19:31, folder "Wilderness Conference—Utah, 1991."

87   These activists were thinking not just of the Alaska lands act, but the Tongass Timber Reform Act too.

88   Stephen Castagnetto, "Mojave Spring," *Sierra Club Bulletin* 59, no. 6 (June 1974): 17.

89   U.S. Department of the Interior, BLM, *California Desert Conservation Area: Final Environmental Impact Statement and Proposed Plan* (1980).

90   On the campaign for California desert wilderness, see Frank Wheat, *California Desert Miracle: The Fight for Desert Parks and Wilderness* (1999).

91   Wilderness Society, "Why the Plan Fails to Do the Job," 1986, TWSR, box 11:9A, folder "CDPA—Failure in the Desert, 1986–1987."

92   Tom Goerold, Wilderness Society, "Memo re: CDCA Mineral Resources," May 18, 1987, TWSR, box 11:9A, folder "CDPA—The California Desert Mineral Report, 1987."

93   Patricia Schifferle, Wilderness Society, "Memo re: Desert Campaign Field Notes," April 22, 1987, TWSR, box 11:9A, folder "CDPA—Campaign Plan, 1980s."

94   "Memo re: Conservation Vice President," March 19, 1987, TWSR, box 19:1, folder "Field Programs, Monthly Reports, 1987."

95   Pro-Desert Coalition, "Publicity Brochure," 1987, TWSR, box 11:9A, folder "CDPA—Pro-Desert Coalition."

96   Ibid.

97   Schifferle, "Monthly Memo," November 2, 1989, TWSR, box 19:1, folder "Field Programs, Monthly Reports, 1987."

98   Joan Reiss, TWS, "Monthly Memo," September 5, 1991, ibid.

99   Wilderness Society, "BLM Wilderness Program," November 1, 1990, TWSR, box 11:9, folder "BLM: Wilderness Campaign Issues, 1988."

100   Wilderness Society, "Dear Journalist," January 23, 1991, TWSR, box 5:45, folder 44.

101   Harry Crandell, "Letter to Edward A. Ames, Mary Flagler Cary Charitable Trust," March 20, 1987, HCP, box 2:4, folder "Correspondence from the Wilderness Society, 1975–1988."

102   Ernest P. Dickerman to Harry Crandell, April 27, 1987, HCP, box 2:4, folder "Correspondence from the Wilderness Society, 1975–1988."

103   Wilderness Society, "Summary of the Planning and Budget Committee Meeting," November 6, 1983, TSP, box 8, folder "Field Rep Study."

104   Michael Scott, regional director, Wilderness Society, "Memo re: Conservation Vice President," March 5, 1987, TWSR, box 19:1, folder "Field Programs, Monthly Reports, 1987."

105   James S. Burling, Pacific Legal Foundation, to colleague, August 10, 1988, TWSR, box 19:38, folder "Wilderness Opposition, Folder #2."

106   Thomas Michael Power and Richard N. Barrett, *Post-Cowboy Economics: Pay and Prosperity in the New American West* (2001), 54.

107   Lancaster, "Drawing the Line on West's Wilderness," April 23, 1991.

108   People for the West! "Grassroots Activism Tells Rural America's Story," 1993, TWSR, box 12:3, folder 7.

109   Ralph Noyes, Western States Public Lands Coalition, "Three Steps We Can Take to Help Save Public Lands Multiple Use," 1993, TWSR, box 12:3, folder 7.

110 People for the West! "New Chapters in Denver, Colorado Springs," 1993, TWSR, box 12:3, folder 7; People for the West!, "The Rush Is On!" 1994, ibid.

111 People for the West! "The Campaign for the Western Mining Community," 1989, TWSR, box 19:38, folder "Wilderness Opposition #1."

112 Heidi Walters, "People for the USA! Disbands," *High Country News*, December 18, 2000.

113 People for the West! "Wise Use Leadership Conference," 1992, TWSR, box 12:3, folder 39.

114 Alan Gottlieb, *The Wise Use Agenda* (1989), "The Top Twenty-Five Goals."

115 Ibid., 10–15.

116 Ron Arnold, Introduction to *The Wise Use Agenda*, ed. Alan Gottlieb (1989), ix–xiii.

117 Gottlieb, *Wise Use Agenda* (1989), xvii–xx.

118 Michael Kazin, *The Populist Persuasion: An American History*, 2nd ed. (Ithaca, NY: Cornell University Press, 1998).

119 On the politics of the New Right, see Chip Berlert and Matthew N. Lyons, *Right-Wing Populism in America: Too Close for Comfort* (2000); Jean V. Hardisty, *Mobilizing Resentment: Conservative Resurgence from the John Birch Society to the Promise Keepers* (1999), chaps. 1 and 2; and Michael Kazin, "The Grass-Roots Right: New Histories of U.S. Conservatism in the Twentieth Century," *American Historical Review* 97, no. 1 (February 1992): 136–55.

120 Oregon Lands Coalition, "The OLC Network—It's Working," 1990, TWSR, box 19:38, folder, "Wilderness Opposition #1."

121 James McCarthy, "Environmentalism, Wise Use, and the Nature of Accumulation in the Rural West," in *Remaking Reality: Nature at the Millennium*, ed. Bruce Braun and Noel Castree (1998).

122 Chuck Cushman, "Roundtable at the Society of Environmental Journalists on Wise Use," 1992, TWSR, box 5:10, folder 16.

123 Keith Schneider, *New York Times* reporter and roundtable participant, emphasized the significance of Wise Use to the media. Keith Schneider, "Roundtable at the Society of Environmental Journalists on Wise Use," 1992, TWSR, box 5:10, folder 16.

124 As quoted in Jon Christensen, "Nevada's Most Rebellious," *High Country News*, October 30, 1995.

125 Fly-In for Freedom, "Press packet: Fly-in for Freedom," 1992, box 3:12, folder 13, TWSR.

126 Blue Ribbon Coalition, "Don't Be Locked Out, Fight Back!" 1991, ibid.

127 Fly-In for Freedom, "Press packet: Fly-in for Freedom," 1992.

128 As quoted in Christensen, "Nevada's Most Rebellious," 1995. Hage develops this point in his book *Storm over Rangelands: Private Rights in Federal Land* (1989).

129 On the importance of property rights to the New Right more generally, see McGirr, *Suburban Warriors* (2001), 185.

130 Anonymous, "Memo re: Wise Use Leadership Conference," 1992, TWSR, box 12:3, folder 39.

131 Scott Allen, "Wise Use Groups Move to Counter Environmentalists," *Boston Globe*, October 20, 1992, 1.

132 The historian Jacqueline Switzer has studied the county supremacy and property rights movements. See *Green Backlash* (1997), chaps. 8–10.

133 T. H. Watkins, "Wise Use: Discouragements and Clarifications," in *Let the People Judge: Wise Use and the Private Property Rights Movement* (1995).

134 Tricia, Wilderness Society, "Memo re: Wise Use Movement," March 9, 1992, TWSR, box 19:38, folder "Wilderness Opposition, #2."

135 Wilderness Society, "Sample Letter to TWS Members re: Wise Use," 1992, TWSR, box 2:5, folder 3.

136 Jim Baca, "Memo to TWS Governing Council re: People for the West!," October 1, 1991, TWSR, box 19:38, folder "Wilderness Opposition #1."

137 Laurie Sullivan, "Clinton May Veto Utah Wilderness Bill," *Salt Lake Tribune*, June 30, 1995.

138 U.S. House of Representatives, Committee on Natural Resources, *California Desert Lands: Hearing on H.R. 518*, 103rd Cong., 1st sess., June 15, 1993, 209.

139 Trent Sanders, "Who Benefits from Desert Protection?" *Christian Science Monitor*, March 31, 1993.

140 Nobby Riedy, Wilderness Society, "Memo to Frank Wells," May 19, 1993, TWSR, box 11:9A, folder "CDPA — TWS Media Initiatives."

141 U.S. House of Representatives, *California Desert Lands*, June 15, 1993.

142 Carolyn Lochhead, "House Passes Plan to Protect States' Desert," *San Francisco Chronicle*, July 28, 1994.

143 "An Incomplete Victory," editorial, *San Francisco Chronicle*, July 28, 1994.

144 "GOP Ganging Up to Knock Down Desert Park Bill," *San Francisco Chronicle*, October 6, 1994.

145 "Drama behind Desert Bill's Triumph," *San Francisco Chronicle*, October 10, 1994.

146 *California Desert Protection Act*, Public Law 103–433, 103rd Cong., 2nd sess., October 31, 1994.

147 Carolyn Lochhead, "Senate Panel OKs California Desert Bill," *San Francisco Chronicle*, October 6, 1993.

148 Helvarg, *War against the Greens* (1994); Carl J. Thurgood, "Wilderness Zealots Aren't Rational," April 25, 1990, TWSR, box 19:38, folder "Utah Wilderness, Folder 2."

149 Ross W. Gorte, *Utah Wilderness Legislation in the 104th Congress*, 1995.

150 Julie Lindquist, "S. Utah Residents Urge Lots of Wilderness," *Salt Lake Tribune*, March 26, 1995; Jim Woolf, "Rural Counties to Be Heard on Wilderness," *Salt Lake Tribune*, April 12, 1995; Jim Woolf, "Proponents Speak Loudly for Wilder-

ness," *Salt Lake Tribune*, April 14, 1995; Jim Woolf, "Crowd Rips Republicans on Wilderness," *Salt Lake Tribune*, June 25, 1995.

151   The mid-1990s debate over Utah's public lands is taken up in chapter 10.

152   Klyza and Sousa, *American Environmental Policy* (2008).

153   Wilderness acreage is available from http://www.wilderness.net (accessed September 17, 2009).

154   Wilderness Society, "FY94 Action Priorities, in Order of Rank," n.d., 1993, TWSR, box 11:8, folder 30.

8 From Wilderness to Public Lands Reform

1   George T. Frampton Jr., president, Wilderness Society, "Conservation Up Front," Wilderness, Summer 1988, 2.

2   My analysis focuses on the Wilderness Society's role in advancing this agenda, but its efforts relied heavily on the NRDC. On NRDC's crucial role in advancing a broader public lands reform policy agenda, see John H. Adams and Patricia Adams, *A Force for Nature: The Story of NRDC and the Fight to Save Our Planet* (2010).

3   *Wilderness Act* (1964).

4   Foundation for Public Affairs, *Public Interest Group Profiles 1988/89* (Washington, D.C.: CQ Press, 1990), 509–11.

5   George Frampton to Harry Crandell, April 14, 1987, HCP, box 2:4, folder "Correspondence from the Wilderness Society, 1975–1988."

6   Roger A. Sedjo, *Marion Clawson's Contribution to Forestry* (1999), 1–6.

7   Marion Clawson, *The Economics of National Forest Management* (1976), ii.

8   Peter D. Coppelman, Wilderness Society, "Memo re: TWS's Forest Planning Agenda," January 18, 1985, SCPNWP, accession 2678-10, box 5, folder "Forest Planning Strategy (National)."

9   George Marshall to Harold Jerry, president, Wilderness Society, May 28, 1981, TWSR, box 1:100, folder "Governing Council: Correspondence, 1980–1985."

10   The Wilderness Society, *America's Vanishing Rain Forest: A Report on Federal Timber Management in Southeast Alaska* (1986); Dennis C. Le Master, Barry R. Flamm, and John C. Hendee, *Below-Cost Sales: Proceedings of a Conference on the Economics of National Forest Timber Sales* (1987); H. Michael Anderson et al., *National Forests: Policies for the Future* (1988).

11   Worster, *Nature's Economy* (1994), 414.

12   On tensions between the science of ecology and environmental activism, see Dorothy Nelkin, "Scientists and Professional Responsibility: The Experience of American Ecologists," *Social Studies of Science* 7, no. 1 (February 1977); Sara

Tjossem, "Preservation of Nature and Academic Respectability: Tensions in the Ecological Society of America, 1915–1979" (1994); and Bocking, *Ecologists and Environmental Politics* (1997), 201.

13 Michael E. Soulé and Bruce A. Wilcox, "Conservation Biology: Its Scope and Challenge," in *Conservation Biology: An Evolutionary-Ecological Perspective*, ed. Soulé and Wilcox (1980), 7.

14 Ibid., 2.

15 Ibid., 1.

16 E. O. Wilson, ed., *Biodiversity* (1988).

17 On the history of conservation biology, see Timothy J. Farnham, *Saving Nature's Legacy: Origins of the Idea of Biological Diversity* (2007); David Takacs, *The Idea of Biodiversity* (1996); and Curt Meine, Michael Soulé, and Reed F. Noss, "'A Mission-Driven Discipline': The Growth of Conservation Biology," *Conservation Biology* 20, no. 3 (June 2006): 631–51.

18 Elliott A. Norse, et al., *Conserving Biological Diversity in our National Forests* (Washington, D.C.: Wilderness Society, 1986).

19 "Habitats in Peril: Biodiversity and the Public Lands," *Wilderness,* Spring 1987.

20 George Frampton, "Conservation Up Front," *Wilderness,* Summer 1990, 2.

21 Robert H. MacArthur and Edward O. Wilson, *Theory of Island Biogeography* (1967). Mark L. Shaffer, "Minimum Population Sizes for Species Conservation," *BioScience* 31 (February 1981): 131–34; David Wilcove, Charles H. McLelland, and Andrew P. Dobson, "Habitat Fragmentation in the Temperate Zone," in *Conservation Biology: The Science of Scarcity and Diversity* (1986): 237–256.

22 Jared M. Diamond, "Island Biogeography and Conservation: Strategy and Limitations," *Science* 193, no. 4257 (September 10, 1976): 1027–28; Daniel Simberloff and Lawrence G. Abele, "Refuge Design and Island Biogeographic Theory: Effects of Fragmentation," *American Naturalist* 120, no. 1 (July 1982): 41–50.

23 Reed Noss, "Sustainability and Wilderness," *Conservation Biology* 5, no. 1 (March 1991): 120–22.

24 Alagona, "Biography of a 'Feathered Pig'" (2004).

25 *National Forest Management Act*, Public Law 94–588, 94th Cong., 2nd sess., October 22, 1976.

26 On the timing of the reviews, see Hirt, *Conspiracy of Optimism* (1994), 265.

27 Dan Heinz, "Memo to Forest Planning Activists," April 5, 1985, SCPNWP, accession 2678–10, box 5, folder "Forest Planning Strategy (National)."

28 Bruce Hamilton, Sierra Club, "Memo re: Draft Summary of Sierra Club Campaign on Forests," January 3, 1984, SCPNWP, accession 2678–10, box 5, folder "Forest Planning Strategy (National)."

29 "Trails '85 Program," November 24, 1985, REIP, binder 2.

30 Kathleen Beamer to Carsten Lien, REI, December 30, 1984, REIP, box "85 Trails Campaign."

31   Bruce Hamilton, Sierra Club, "Memo re: Next Steps in Forest Campaign," April 25, 1985, SCPNWP, accession 2678–10, box 5, folder "Forest Planning Strategy (National)."

32   Dan Heinz and Bruce Hamilton, "Memo to Forest Planning Activists," April 5, 1985, ibid.

33   Peter M. Emerson et al., *Wasting the National Forests: Selling Timber Below Costs* (1984), 7. For evidence of NRDC's work on this issue, see Thomas J. Barlow et al., "Giving Away the National Forests: An Analysis of the U.S. Forest Service Timber Sales Below Cost," 1980.

34   Ibid., 4.

35   Peter Emerson, Anthony T. Stout, and Deanne Klopfer, "The Feds Can't See Their Losses in the Trees," *Wall Street Journal*, November 14, 1984.

36   See testimony by Max Peterson, chief of the Forest Service, and Peter Kirby, Wilderness Society, in U.S. House of Representatives, Committee on Agriculture, *Economics of Federal Timber Sales*, 99th Congress, 1st. sess., October 22, 1985. See also U.S. Department of Agriculture, *Below-Cost Timber Sales: An Overview of the Issue*, by Peter C. Myers (1986).

37   Barlow, *Giving Away the National Forests* (1980); Emerson et al., "The Feds Can't See Their Losses in the Trees" (1984).

38   Richard E. Rice, "Testimony re: Progress on National Forest Timber Sales Cost Accounting," November 21, 1989, TWSR, box 5:45, folder 12.

39   Wells Associates, *National Forest Trails: Neglected and Disappearing* (1985).

40   "Tongass Reform Act Passes," Wilderness, Summer 1988, 3.

41   *The Washington Post*'s editorial focused on grazing issues in particular. See "User Fees," editorial, *Washington Post*, February 3, 1986.

42   Thomas L. Fleischner, "Ecological Costs of Livestock Grazing in Western North America," *Conservation Biology* 8, no. 3 (September 1994): 629.

43   "Government Grass," editorial, *Washington Post*, July 23, 1985.

44   Hage, *Storm over Rangelands* (1989); Merrill, *Public Lands and Political Meaning* (2002).

45   Timothy Egan, "Wingtip 'Cowboys' in Last Stand to Hold On to Low Grazing Fees," *New York Times*, October 29, 1993. Bernard DeVoto, "The West against Itself," in *The Easy Chair* (1955).

46   Klyza, *Who Controls Public Lands?* (1996), chap. 5.

47   Bureau of Land Management, "Press Release: Grazing Fee for BLM Lands Set at $1.86 for 1982," December 1, 1982, HCP, box 2:5, folder "Wilderness: Grazing on Public Lands, 1980"; Ronald A. Michieli to John Seiberling, December 1, 1981, HCP, box 2:5, folder "Wilderness: Grazing on Public Lands, 1980."

48   Cass Peterson, "OMB Urges Freezing Fees for Grazing Federal Land," *Washington Post*, January 28, 1986; T. R. Reid, "Western Grazing Fees Slip Out of Budget Noose," *Washington Post*, February 2, 1986.

49   Klyza, *Who Controls Public Lands?* (1996), 135.

50   As quoted in "User Fees," editorial, *Washington Post*, February 3, 1986.

51   As quoted in Klyza, *Who Controls Public Lands?* (1996), 135.

52   Alan K. Simpson, "Note re: Grazing Issues," December 20, 1985, AKS, box 271, folder 15.

53   "Talking Points on Metzenbaum Grazing Fee Amendment," April 29, 1986, ibid.

54   As quoted in Klyza, *Who Controls Public Lands?* (1996), 137.

55   Peterson, "OMB Urges Freezing Fees for Grazing Federal Land" (1986).

56   Simpson, "Note re: Grazing Issues," (1985).

57   Syd Butler, Wilderness Society, "Memo re: Grazing in Wilderness Policy Issue," April 22, 1991, TWSR, box 11:9, folder "BLM: Wilderness Campaign Issues, 1988."

58   Nancy Green, Wilderness Society, "Memo re: House Passes Synar Grazing Fee Amendment," October 16, 1990, TWSR, box 19:29, folder "Utah/BLM—grazing, Folder #2, 1980s–1990s."

59   George Frampton, Wilderness Society, "Memo re: Grazing Study," June 7, 1990, TWSR, box 19:29, folder "Utah/BLM—grazing, Folder #2, 1980s–1990s."

60   Michael Scott, Jim Norton, and Darrell Knuffke, "Memo to Syd re: OHDPA Statement, TWS Position on Grazing," April 24, 1991, TWSR, box 11:9, folder "BLM: Wilderness Campaign Issues, 1988."

61   Klyza and Sousa, *American Environmental Policy* (2008).

62   Debra D. Warren, *Harvest, Employment, Exports, and Prices in Pacific Northwest Forests, 1965–2000* (2002).

63   Peter H. Morrison, *Ancient Forests on the Mt. Baker-Snoqualmie National Forest: Analysis of Forest Conditions* (1990).

64   For a more detailed analysis of the Forest Service's commitment to ecological science, the role of agency scientists, and the importance of the NFMA, see Thomas R. Wellock, "The Dickey Bird Scientists Take Charge: Science, Policy, and the Spotted Owl," *Environmental History* 15 (July 2010): 381–414.

65   Other scientists who pioneered research on the spotted owl included Gordon Gould Jr., Charles Meslow, and Howard Wight.

66   This anecdote about Forsman raising "Fat Broad" is drawn from correspondence with Forsman and coverage of the owl's induction into the Owl Hall of Fame in 2006 (after her death at the age of 31). http://www.globalowlproject.com/reports.php?f=2006-03-13_hall_of_fame.

67   Eric David Forsman, "Habitat Utilization by Spotted Owls in the West-Central Cascades" (1980).

68   As quoted in William Booth, "New Thinking on Old Growth," *Science* 244, no. 4901 (April 14, 1989): 141–43.

69   U.S. Department of Agriculture, *Forest Service, Ecology and Management of the Spotted Owl in the Pacific Northwest*, ed. Ralph J. Gutierrez and Andrew B. Carey (1984), 100.

70   Brock Evans to Wendell Wood, Oregon Natural Resources Council, July 16, 1985, BEP, box 17, folder "Ancient Forest / Spotted Owls—1985."

71   Brock Evans, "Memo to Files re: Looking Beyond the SEIS: Where from There?" October 23, 1986, BEP, box 17, folder "Ancient Forest / ANC Strategy—1986–1988."

72   Brock Evans, "Minutes of the Ancient Forest Alliance Steering Committee Meeting," December 16, 1988, TWSR, box 23:12, folder "Ancient Forests—Memos, 1991."

73   Daniel Simberloff, "The Spotted Owl Fracas: Mixing Academic, Applied, and Political Ecology," *Ecology* 68, no. 4 (1987): 766–72.

74   William R. Dawson et al., "Report of the Scientific Advisory Panel on the Spotted Owl," *The Condor* 89, no. 1 (February 1987): 205–29.

75   Jack Ward Thomas et al., *A Conservation Strategy for the Northern Spotted Owl* (Portland, OR: The Committee, 1990), appendix Q.

76   Ibid; Philip L. Lee, "History and Current Status of Spotted Owl (*Strix occidentalis*) Habitat Management in the Pacific Northwest Region," in *Ecology and Management of the Spotted Owl in the Pacific Northwest*, ed. Ralph J. Gutierrez and Andrew B. Carey (1984), 5–9.

77   Fish and Wildlife Service, "90-Day Petition Finding and Initiation of Status Review, Northern Spotted Owl," *Federal Register* 52, no. 176 (September 11, 1987): 34396–97.

78   For a full analysis of the legal history of the spotted owl debates, see Brendon Swedlow, "Scientists, Judges, and Spotted Owls: Policymakers in the Pacific Northwest," *Duke Environmental Law & Policy Forum* 13, no. 2 (Spring 2003): 187–278.

79   Chad Roberts, Redwood Region Audubon Society, "Memo to Pacific Northwest Forest Activists re: Wildlife Considerations and the Forest Service," October 23, 1988, BEP, box 17, folder "Ancient Forest / ANC Strategy—1986–1988."

80   As quoted in Swedlow, "Scientists, Judges, and Spotted Owls" (2003), 204.

81   "A New Improved Strategy for Spotted Owl Issue," November 4, 1986, BEP, box 17, folder "Ancient Forest / Spotted Owls—1986."

82   Ibid.

83   Swedlow, "Scientists, Judges, and Spotted Owls" (2003).

84   Warren, *Harvest, Employment, Exports* (2002).

85   As quoted in John de Yonge, "A Forest of Trucks Loggers Bring a Message to Town," *Seattle Times*, June 3, 1989.

86   As quoted in William Allen and Tom Uhlenbrock, "Two Sides Discuss Owl Issue," *St. Louis Dispatch*, November 10, 1991.

87   Fly-In for Freedom, "Press Packet: Fly-in for Freedom," September 21, 1992, TWSR, box 12:3, folder 13.

88   Oregon Lands Coalition, "The OLC Network—It's Working," October 30, 1990, TWSR, box 19:38, folder "Wilderness Opposition, #1."

89   Dianne Dumanoski, "In Reversal, U.S. Agency to Propose Listing Spotted Owl as 'Threatened,'" *Boston Globe*, April 27, 1989.

90   Swedlow, "Scientists, Judges, and Spotted Owls" (2003), 265–66.

91   Karin Sheldon, Wilderness Society, "Status of Ancient Forest Legislation," July 31, 1991, TWSR, box 23:13, folder "Ancient Forest Team, 1992."

92   This argument is advanced most effectively by Swedlow, "Scientists, Judges, and Spotted Owls" (2003), 277–78.

93   Shaffer, "Minimum Population Sizes for Species Conservation" (1981); Mark L. Shaffer, "The Metapopulation and Species Conservation: The Special Case of the Northern Spotted Owl," in Ecology and Management of the Spotted Owl in the Pacific Northwest, ed. Ralph J. Gutierrez and Andrew B. Carey (1984), 86–99.

94   David Wilcove and Dennis D. Murphy, "The Spotted Owl Controversy and Conservation Biology," editorial, Conservation Biology 5, no. 3 (September 1991): 262.

95   T. H. Watkins, "Forests and Butter," Wilderness, Spring 1990, 12–13.

96   Jeff Olson, "Environmental Action Saves Timber Jobs," Seattle Times, July 8, 1991.

97   Larry Tuttle, Wilderness Society, "Memo re: Post-Listing Blues," June 26, 1990, TWSR, box 23:12, folder "Ancient Forests—Memos, 1991."

98   The resolution of the spotted owl debates is taken up in chapter 10.

99   Karin Sheldon, "Memo re: Department Priorities and Structure," January 8, 1992, TWSR, box 6:1, folder 9.

100   The controversy surrounding this and other proposed land exchanges was the subject of testimony in the Subcommittee on Water and Power Resources of the Committee on Interior and Insular Affairs, Oversight Hearing, 100th Cong., 2nd sess., June 9, 1988.

101   Department of the Interior, Arctic National Wildlife Refuge: Coastal Plain Resource Assessment (1987).

102   U.S. House of Representatives, Subcommittee on Water and Power Resources of the Committee on Interior and Insular Affairs, Oversight Hearing, 100th Cong., 2nd sess., May 28, 1987.

103   Exxon Valdez Oil Spill Trustee Council, http://www.evostc.state.ak.us (July 6, 2009).

104   Douglas Scott, "The Next Campaign," Sierra, January 1991, 130–35.

105   Matthew L. Wald, "Gulf Victory: An Energy Defeat?" New York Times, June 18, 1991.

106   George H. W. Bush, "Remarks at a Briefing on Energy Policy," in The American Presidency Project (online), eds. John T. Woolley and Gerhard Peters (February 20, 1991).

107   "Bush Digs In on Arctic Drilling Plan," editorial, New York Times, March 13, 1991.

108   George T. Frampton Jr., "Possible Alaskan Oil That No One Needs," op-ed, New York Times, February 11, 1987.

109   George Frampton Jr., "Memo re: Price Gouging," November 8, 1990, TWSR, box 6:2, folder 9.

110 Mary Hanley, Wilderness Society, "Memo to Paul Fleming re: Energy Bill/ANWR Campaign," July 10, 1991, TWSR, box 5:6, folder 40.

111 George Frampton Jr., "Memo re: Energy and Group of Ten," October 18, 1990, TWSR, box 6:2, folder 9; Jay Hair, National Wildlife Federation, "Memo to Other Environmental Group re: Meeting with Congressional Leaders on Energy Policy," September 7, 1990, TWSR, box 6:2, folder 11.

112 Sarah Chasis and Lisa Speer, Natural Resources Defense Council, "How to Avoid Another Valdez," op-ed, *New York Times*, May 20, 1989.

113 Senator Richard D. Bryan, "Let's Get Serious about Gas Mileage," op-ed, *Christian Science Monitor*, September 21, 1990.

114 Sierra Club, "The Oil Companies vs. The Rest of Us," advertisement, *New York Times*, August 20, 1990.

115 Senator J. Bennett Johnston, "Last Chance for an Energy Policy," op-ed, *Washington Post*, October 31, 1991.

116 Sarah James, "Oil in an Arctic Refuge," op-ed, *Seattle Times*, November 14, 1991.

117 Estimates of petroleum reserves and Horn's statement can be found in Bill Horn, assistant secretary of the interior, testimony, Committee on Interior and Insular Affairs, Subcommittee on Water and Power Resources, *Arctic National Wildlife Refuge Oversight Hearing*, 100th Cong. 1st sess., April 1987, 9.

118 Mobil, "Boy We Wish We'd Said That," advertisement, *New York Times*, April 9, 1992.

119 George Frampton Jr., "Memo to VPs and Program Directors re: Johnston-Wallop Energy Bill," July 5, 1991, TWSR, box 5:6, folder 40.

120 George Frampton Jr., "Letter to Editorial Writer," July 5, 1991, TWSR, box 12:1, folder 9.

121 Senator Paul Wellstone, "Stop This Flawed Energy Bill," op-ed, *Washington Post*, October 31, 1991.

122 "Energy Bill, 1991–1992 Legislative Chronology," in *Congress and the Nation*, 1989–1991 (1993).

123 "President Obama Announces National Fuel Efficiency Policy," the White House, May 19, 2009. Available at http://www.whitehouse.gov/the_press_office/President-Obama-Announces-National-Fuel-Efficiency-Policy. Note, the Obama policy also raised the fuel efficiency standard to 35.5 miles per gallon.

124 Mark Dowie, *Losing Ground: American Environmentalism at the Close of the Twentieth Century* (1995), 45; Michael Shellenberger and Ted Nordhaus, *The Death of Environmentalism: Global Warming Politics in a Post-Environmental World* (2004), 17–18.

125 See Dowie, *Losing Ground* (1995), xii-xiii; Gottlieb, *Forcing the Spring* (2005), 117–61; Shutkin, *The Land That Could Be* (2000), 89–120. The mainstream environmental movement's shrillest critic was Alexander Cockburn, writing in *The*

Nation. See his article with Jeffrey St. Clair: "Death and Life of America's Greens," *The Nation* 259 (December 19, 1994): 760–65.

126 Sarah A. Binder, *Stalemate: Causes and Consequences of Legislative Gridlock* (2003), 42.

127 David W. Brady and Craig Volden, *Revolving Gridlock: Politics and Policy from Jimmy Carter to George W. Bush* (2006), 3–4.

128 Jonathan Rauch, *Demosclerosis* (1995), 60.

129 Klyza and Sousa, *American Environmental Policy* (2008).

130 Jon Roush, testimony, U.S. House of Representatives, Committee on Natural Resources, 103rd Cong., 2nd sess., February 1, 1994.

9 The New Prophets of Wilderness

1 Tim Hermach, "From the Executive Director," *Forest Voice* 1, no. 2 (1993): 2.

2 "Yes! I Want to Help Save the Last of America's Virgin Forests," *Forest Voice*, August 1990, 12.

3 Mat Jacobson, "Matty's Manifesto," August 23, 1994, TWSR, box 9:4, folder 17.

4 Dave Foreman, "The New Conservation Movement," *Wild Earth* 1, no. 2 (Summer 1991): 6–12.

5 Christopher J. Elliman to Jeff B. Swartz, Timberland, January 3, 1993, TWSR, box 5:1, folder 56.

6 Christopher J. Bosso, *Environment, Inc.: From Grassroots to Beltway* (2005), 7; Baumgartner and Jones, *Agendas and Instability in American Politics* (1993), 184–188; Klyza and Sousa, *American Environmental Policy* (2008), 27–30.

7 Wilderness Society, "Minutes of the Governing Council," April 22–23, 1993, TWSR, box 21 (unprocessed).

8 Zahniser, "The People and Wilderness," 1964, 39–42.

9 Stegner, "Wilderness Letter," 1960; Udall, "To Save the Wonder of Wilderness," 1962.

10 Anonymous, "Memo re: Wise Use Leadership Conference," June 15, 1992, TWSR, box 12:3, folder, 39.

11 Ibid.

12 Di Chiro, "Nature as Community," *Uncommon Ground*, 1995, 300.

13 Dave Foreman, "Around the Campfire," *Wild Earth* 1, no. 2 (Spring 1991): 2.

14 Arne Naess, "The Shallow and the Deep Long-Range Ecology Movement: A Summary," *Inquiry* 16 (1973): 95–100.

15 Ibid.

16 "Deep Ecology," *Earth First! Journal*, December 1981.

17 Dave Foreman, "Earth First! California Wilderness Plan," *Earth First! Journal*, August 1, 1987.

18   Dave Foreman, Howie Wolke, and Bart Koehler, "Earth First! Wilderness Preservation System," *Earth First! Journal*, June 1983.

19   Reed Noss, "A Regional Landscape Approach to Maintain Diversity," *BioScience* 33 (1983): 700–6.

20   Reed Noss, "Protecting Natural Areas in Fragmented Landscapes," *Natural Areas Journal* 7 (1987): 2–13.

21   Michael Soulé, "What Is Conservation Biology?" *Bioscience* 35 (December 1985): 731.

22   Arne Naess, "Deep Ecology and Conservation Biology," *Earth First! Journal*, March 20, 1990; Naess, "Intrinsic Value: Will the Defenders of Nature Please Rise?" in *Conservation Biology: The Science of Scarcity and Diversity* (1986), 504–15.

23   Dave Foreman, "Deep Ecology Vision Passion Courage," *Earth First! Journal*, March 20 1987.

24   Feral Curmudgeon, "California Desert: A Vision of Wilderness," *Earth First! Journal*, June 21, 1987; Philip Knight, "An Earth First! Proposal for a Greater Yellowstone Wilderness Preserve," *Earth First! Journal*, September 22, 1988; Rod Mondt, "EF! Vision for California Desert," *Earth First! Journal*, March 20, 1987.

25   Kirkpatrick Sale, "The Cutting Edge: Deep Ecology and Its Critics," *The Nation* 246 no. 19 (May 14, 1988): 670–74.

26   Brian Tokar, "Social Ecology, Deep Ecology, and the Future of Green Political Thought," *The Ecologist* 18, no. 4/5 (1988): 135.

27   Bruce Hamilton, a Sierra Club staffer, made handwritten notes on a memo from Dave Foreman to Wilderness Leaders, September 21, 1983, SCNLOR, box 132, folder 9.

28   Foreman, "Around the Campfire," *Wild Earth* (Spring 1991), 2.

29   John Davis, "It's What We Do . . . ," *Wild Earth* 3, no. 2 (Fall 1993): 2.

30   "The New Conservation Movement," *Wild Earth* 1, no. 3 (Summer 1991): 12.

31   Jim Eaton, "Wilderness: From Aesthetics to Biodiversity," *Wild Earth* 1, no. 3 (Summer 1991): 1.

32   Foreman, "Around the Campfire," *Wild Earth* 1, no. 4 (Fall 1991): 2.

33   Howie Wolke, "Bad Science Lacks the Visceral Connection," *Wild Earth* 2, no. 4 (Winter 1992): 5–9.

34   Dave Foreman et al., "The Wildlands Project Mission Statement," *Wild Earth*, Special Issue, December 1992.

35   Larry D. Harris, ed., *The Fragmented Forest* (1984); C. Margules, A. J. Higgs, and R. W. Rafe, "Modern Biogeographic Theory: Are There Any Lessons for Nature Reserve Design?," *Biological Conservation* 24 (1982): 115–28; Noss, "Regional Landscape Approach" (1983); John Terborgh, "The Big Things That Run the World—A Sequel to E. O. Wilson," *Conservation Biology* 2, no. 4 (December 1988): 402–3; Wilcove, McLelland, and Dobson, "Habitat Fragmentation in the Temperate Zone" (1986).

36 Charles C. Mann and Mark L. Plummer, "The High Cost of Biodiversity," *Science* 260, no. 5116 (June 25, 1993): 1868–1871.

37 Philip M. Hocker, "Yellowstone: The Region Is Greater Than the Sum of Its Parts," *Sierra Club Bulletin* 64 (July 1979): 8–13.

38 For an excellent history of the relationship between scientific research and conceptions of the Greater Yellowstone Ecosystem, see James A. Pritchard, *Preserving Yellowstone's Natural Conditions: Science and Perceptions of Nature* (1999), 251–306.

39 W. D. Newmark, "Legal and Biotic Boundaries of Western North American National Parks: A Problem of Congruence," *Biological Conservation* 33 (1985): 197–208.

40 Charles E. Little, "Yellowstone and the Holistic Imperative," *Wilderness*, Summer 1987; T. H. Watkins, "The Challenge of Greater Yellowstone," *Wilderness*, Summer 1987.

41 Craig Gehrke, Wilderness Society, "Memo re: Monthly Memo," June 11, 1990, TWSR, box 19:1, folder "Field Programs, Monthly Reports."

42 Rob Eure, "'Wise Use' Movement Gains Foothold," *Oregonian*, November 3, 1994; Bruce Hamilton, "Sierra Club Public Lands Campaign," *Sierra*, September 1989.

43 Michael Scott, Wilderness Society, "Memo re: Monthly Memo," July 5, 1990, TWSR, box 19:1, folder "Field Programs, Monthly Reports, 1987."

44 Mike Bader, "Northern Rockies Ecosystem vs. Washington D.C. Political System," *Wild Earth* 1, no. 4 (Fall 1991): 57–58.

45 Dave Foreman, "The Northern Rockies Ecosystem Protection Act and the Evolving Wilderness Area Model," *Wild Earth* 3, no. 4 (Winter 1993): 57–62.

46 Margaret Hays Young and Mitch Friedman, "Legislative Corner," *Wild Earth* 1, no. 1 (Spring 1991): 50.

47 Hart Schaefer, "Legislative Corner," *Wild Earth* 1, no. 2 (Summer 1991): 41–42.

48 Foreman, "Northern Rockies Ecosystem Protection Act," 1993.

49 Craig Gehrke, Wilderness Society, "Memo re: Monthly Memo," September 9, 1991, TWSR, box 19:1, folder "Field Programs, Monthly Reports."

50 "Redfish Meeting, Highlights of the Morning," May 15, 1992, TWSR, box 23:3, folder "USFS: Idaho Wilderness Bills, 1992."

51 Bart Koehler, "Memo re: Big Picture Meeting," December 31, 1992, TWSR, box 23:3, folder "USFS: Montana Wilderness Bill, 1993."

52 "For a Wilder Rockies," editorial, *New York Times*, July 7, 2009.

53 Young and Friedman, "Legislative Corner," 1991.

54 Lance Olsen, "How to Save the Nationals from Themselves without Really Trying," *Wild Earth* 2, no. 3 (Fall 1992): 3–4.

55 Wilderness Society, "Minutes of the Governing Council," April 23, 1992, TWSR, box 5:2, folder 3.

56 Andy Mahler, "Heartwood," *Wild Earth* 1, no. 2 (Summer 1991): 24.

57 "It's 95% Gone, and It Will Never Be Back," *Forest Voice* 1, no. 1 (1989), 3.

58   Hermach, "From the Executive Director," *Forest Voice* 1, no. 2 (1993): 2.

59   Jody Suhanek, "Native Forest Council," *Wild Earth* 1, no. 2 (Summer 1991): 24–25.

60   "It's 95% Gone," *Forest Voice*, 1989.

61   "How Can This Happen?" *Forest Voice* 2, no. 2 (1990): 4.

62   Tim Hermach, "The Great Tree Robbery," *New York Times*, September 17, 1991.

63   "Lighthawk," *Forest Voice* 5, no. 2 (1992), 4.

64   For a sample of the Native Forest Campaign's rhetoric, see *Forest Voice* 4, no. 1 (Special Edition 1991).

65   U.S. House of Representatives. *National Forest Protection and Restoration Act of 1997*. 105th Cong., H.R. 2789, October 31, 1997.

66   George T. Frampton Jr., Wilderness Society, "Does a New Age Now Begin?" *Wilderness*, Winter 1992.

67   Save America's Forests, "Memo re: Longer-Term Issues and Objectives," November 19, 1992, TWSR, box 8:1, folder 6.

68   Pew Charitable Trusts, *Annual Report* (1994), 19.

69   Scott Allen, "Environmental Donors Set Tone," *Boston Globe*, October 20, 1997.

70   Regarding the early campaigns, see Pew Charitable Trusts, *Annual Report* (1994).

71   Ibid., 17.

72   Shabecoff, *Earth Rising* (2000), 39.

73   Victor Rozek, "A Gathering of Warlords or Can't See the Forest for the Grassroots," February 18, 1994, TWSR, box 9:4, folder 13.

74   Correspondence regarding the proposal to the Pew Charitable Trusts can be found in TWSR, box 9:4, folder 13.

75   Jacobson, "Matty's Manifesto," August 23, 1994.

76   Chad Hanson, "Memo re: Ned Fritz's May 27 Criticism of My May 20 Comments on the Pew Proposal," June 5, 1994, TWSR, box 9:4, folder 13.

77   Ned Fritz, "Memo re: Comments on Berck's Fax," July 6, 1994, TWSR, box 9:4, folder 17.

78   James Montieth, "Memo re: Scheduling First Campaign Governing Board Meeting," September 14, 1994, TWSR, box 9:4, folder 17.

79   Victor Rozek, "The Incredible Shrinking Forest Protection Campaign," *Forest Voice* 7, no. 2 (Spring 1994): 14.

80   Phil Berck, "Memo re: Current Drafting Process," July 4, 1994, TWSR, box 9:4, folder 17.

81   Allen, "Environmental Donors Set Tone," 1997.

82   Brock Evans, "Memo re: Meeting with Pew," August 7, 1995, TWSR, box 9:4, folder 14.

83   TWS Steering Committee, "Memo re: Minutes from June 2, 1993 Meeting," June 4, 1993, TWSR, box 11:8, folder 30.

84   Craig Gehrke, Wilderness Society, "Memo re: Monthly Report," December 20, 1992, TWSR, box 19:1, folder "Field Programs, Monthly Reports."

85   Gregory Aplet et al., "Draft Proposal: The American Lifelands Trust: A Tool for

Landscape Conservation," March 1993, TWSR, box 9:39, folder 19; Wilderness Society, "Minutes of the Governing Council," April 22–23, 1993, TWSR.

86   Darrell Knuffke, "Wilderness and the 21st Century," *George Wright Forum* 10, no. 2 (1994): 25.

87   Victor Rozek, "I'm Just One Person, What Can I Do?" *Forest Voice* 9, no. 2 (1996), 8–9.

88   Bruce Hamilton, "An Enduring Wilderness?" *Sierra*, September 1994.

89   Reed Noss, "The Wildlands Project: Land Conservation Strategy," *Wild Earth*, Special Issue, 1992, 10.

90   Ramachandra Guha, "Radical American Environmentalism and Wilderness Preservation: A Third World Critique," in *The Great New Wilderness Debate*, ed. J. Baird Callicott and Michael P. Nelson (1989; repr. 1998), 240.

91   Roderick Nash, *Wilderness and the American Mind* (1982).

92   Arturo Goméz-Pompa and Andrea Kaus, "Taming the Wilderness Myth," in *The Great New Wilderness Debate*, ed. J. Baird Callicott and Michael P. Nelson (1992; repr. 1998), 299.

93   William M. Denevan, "The Pristine Myth: The Landscape of the Americas in 1492," in ibid., 414–42.

94   J. Baird Callicott, "That Good Old-Time Wilderness Religion," in ibid., 387–94.

95   Guha, "Radical American Environmentalism," 1989; repr. 1998, 239.

96   William Cronon, "The Trouble with Wilderness," *New York Times Magazine*, August 13, 1995.

97   William Cronon, "The Trouble with Wilderness; or, Getting Back to the Wrong Nature," in *Uncommon Ground* (1995), 85.

98   Ibid., 80.

99   Bosso, *Environment, Inc.* (2005), 6.

18 The Paths to Public Lands Reform

1   Klyza and Sousa, *American Environmental Policy* (2008), 11.

2   Brooks Yeager, "Memo to Team Leaders of Community Executive Transition Project," November 11, 1992, TWSR, box 5:45, folder 51.

3   Bruce Babbitt, "Remarks to the National Press Club," April 27, 1993, TWSR, box 5:10, folder 47; Tom Kenworthy, "Pragmatic Critic Is Set to Be Interior's Next Landlord," *Washington Post*, January 19, 1993; Francis Wilkinson, "Is He Tough Enough to Save the Environment?" *Rolling Stone*, July 8, 1993.

4   Babbitt, "Remarks to the National Press Club," April 27, 1993.

5   Bruce Babbitt, testimony, U.S. Congress, House, Committee on Science and Technology, Subcommittees on Technology, Environment and Aviation and Investi-

gations and Oversight, *National Biological Survey and H.R. 1845*, 103rd Cong., 1st sess., September 14, 1993.

6   Kenworthy, "Pragmatic Critic," 1993.

7   Clinton won the western states of California, New Mexico, Washington, Oregon, Colorado, Montana, and Nevada in 2002.

8   Taylor, "Many Lives of the New West," 2004.

9   Babbitt quoted in Steve Hinchman, "Turmoil on the Range," *High Country News*, January 24, 1994.

10   Tania Schoennagel et al., "Implementation of National Fire Plan Treatments near the Wildland-Urban Interface in the Western United States," *Proceedings of the National Academy of the Sciences* 106, no. 26 (June 30, 2009): 10706–11.

11   H. Ken Cordell et al., *Off-Highway Vehicle Recreation in the United States, Regions and States* (2005), 6.

12   George Hager, "President Throws Down Gauntlet," *Congressional Quarterly Weekly Report*, February 20, 1993.

13   Andrew Taylor, "President Will Not Use Budget to Rewrite Land-Use Laws," *Congressional Quarterly Weekly Report*, April 3, 1993.

14   Babbitt, "Remarks to the National Press Club," April 27, 1993.

15   Donald Hellmann, "Press Release: TWS on Clinton Administration Plan to Eliminate Federal Subsidies," March 23, 1993, TWSR, box 5:45, folder 26.

16   Klyza and Sousa, *American Environmental Policy* (2008), 58–68.

17   "Democratic Support for Clinton Was Hard-Won, Rarely Certain," *Congressional Quarterly Weekly Report*, December 18, 1993.

18   Babbitt, "Remarks to the National Press Club," April 27, 1993.

19   Department of the Interior, "Administration Announces Sweeping Range Reforms; Grazing Fees Will Move Closer to Market Rates," August 9, 1993, TWSR, box 10:103, folder "Grazing Background."

20   Ralph Noyes, chairman, Western States Public Lands Coalition, "Three Steps We Can Take to Help Save Public Lands Multiple Use," January 1993, TWSR, box 12:3, folder 7.

21   Catalina Camia, "Babbitt and Western Democrats Reach Pact on Grazing Fees," *Congressional Quarterly Weekly Report*, October 9, 1993.

22   Alan K. Simpson, "Talking Points for Meeting with Babbitt," August 15, 1993, AKS, box 271, folder 15.

23   Catalina Camia, "The Filibuster Ends; Bill Clears; Babbitt Can Still Raise Fees," *Congressional Quarterly Weekly Report*, November 13, 1994.

24   William J. Clinton, "Remarks on Opening the Forest Conference in Portland, Oregon," *The American Presidency Project* (online), April 2, 1993.

25   Patricia Byrnes, "Clinton Moves to End Ancient Forest Stalemate," *Wilderness*, Summer 1993.

26   For careful analysis of the Forest Service's internal commitment to this transition, spearheaded by its scientists, see Wellock, "Dickey Bird Scientists Take Charge," *Environmental History*, 2010.

27   Bruce G. Marcot and Jack Ward Thomas, "Of Spotted Owls, Old Growth, and New Policies: A History since the Interagency Scientific Committee Report," 1997, 10.

28   This included 7.4 million acres of new late-successional reserves, 7.3 million acres of existing congressionally withdrawn areas (parks, wilderness areas, etc.), 1.5 million acres of administratively withdrawn areas, and 2.6 million acres of riparian reserves. Figures are drawn from Seattle Aubudon Society et al. *v.* Lyons et al., 871 F. Supp. 1291 (U.S. Dist. 1994).

29   E. Thomas Tuchmann et al., *The Northwest Forest Plan: A Report to the President and Congress* (1996), 52.

30   George Hoberg, "Science, Politics, and U.S. Forest Law: The Battle over the Forest Service Planning Rule," 2003.

31   League of Conservation Voters, *National Environmental Scorecard* (Washington, D.C.: League of Conservation Voters, October 1994), 4.

32   Patricia Byrnes, "Baca Forced Out as BLM Director," *Wilderness*, Spring 1994, 6.

33   Patricia Byrnes, "A Mixed Bag of Reactions to Clinton's First Major Moves," *Wilderness*, Fall 1993, 5.

34   Tim Hermach, "Logging Must End on the Public Lands," op-ed, *Washington Post*, June 13, 1994.

35   Babbitt, *Testimony on H.R. 1845* (1993).

36   Ecosystem management first gained federal sanction when President George W. Bush announced it would be the guiding framework for guiding U.S. forest policy at the 1992 United Nations Conference on the Environment. For analysis of the Forest Service and Bush administration's decision to adopt ecosystem management, see Wellock, "Dickey Bird Scientists Take Charge," 2010, 400–403.

37   Jack Ward Thomas, testimony, Committee on Natural Resources, Subcommittee on National Parks, Forests, and Public Lands, *New Directions for the Forest Service*, 103rd Cong., 1st sess., February 3, 1994.

38   Michael Dombeck, "Thinking Like a Mountain: BLM's Approach to Ecosystem Management," *Ecological Applications* 6, no. 3 (1996): 699.

39   On the "lords of yesterday," see Wilkinson, *Crossing the Next Meridian* (1992), 3–27.

40   People for the West! "Election '94 Presents Opportunities," 1993, TWSR, box 12:3, folder 7.

41   Jack Anderson and Michael Binstein, "'Wise-Use' Movement Likes Foe," *Oregonian*, January 15, 1993.

42   Burns quoted in Joel Connelly, "Republicans Draw Battle Line in Western States," *Seattle Post-Intelligencer*, October 22, 1994.

43   Newt Gingrich and Dick Armey, *Contract with America* (1994), 125.

44   Ibid.

45   Jerry Greenberg, "Memo re: Takings Information," December 29, 1994, TWSR, box 9:17, folder 13.

46   Donna Cassata, "Republicans Bask in Success of Rousing Performance," *CQ Weekly Online*, April 8, 1995.

47   "Wilderness Legislation Preserves Utah for All Americans," *Congressional Record* 141, no. 91 (June 6, 1995): H5611.

48   Quoted in Timothy Egan, "In Utah, a Pitched Battle over Public Lands," *New York Times*, November 13, 1995.

49   *Utah Public Lands Management Act of 1995*, H.R. 1745, 104th Cong., 1st sess. (December 11, 1995). For a careful analysis of the Utah legislation, see Ross W. Gorte, *Utah Wilderness Legislation in the 104th Congress* (1995).

50   U.S. House of Representatives, *Utah Public Lands Management Act of 1995, Dissenting Views*, House Report 104–396, December 11, 1995.

51   Bradley as quoted in Helen Dewar, "Senate Democrats Block Move to Open Utah Federal Lands to Development," *Washington Post*, March 28, 1996.

52   "Environmental Laws Face Revisions," *CQ Weekly Online*, June 17, 1995.

53   "Conservationist Concerns Mark Clinton's Veto of Interior Bill," *CQ Weekly Online*, December 23, 1995.

54   Michael E. Kraft, "Environmental Policy in Congress," in *Environmental Policy: New Directions for the Twenty-First Century*, 6th ed., eds. Norman E. Vig and Michael E. Kraft (2006), 136.

55   Quoted in John H. Cushman Jr., "Growing Argument over Best Treatment for 'Sick' Forest," *New York Times*, March 10, 1995.

56   Neil Lawrence, "Memo re: Assessment of the Salvage Rider Fight," March 25, 1995, TWSR, box 9:19, folder 32.

57   Ross W. Gorte, *Salvage Timber Sales and Forest Health* (1996).

58   John Fitzgerald, Western Ancient Forests Campaign, "National Report—Congress," April 8, 1995, TWSR, box 9:19, folder 33.

59   "Presidential Veto: President Clinton's Veto of Rescissions Bill," *CQ Weekly Online*, June 10, 1995.

60   Ibid.

61   U.S. General Accounting Office, *Emergency Salvage Sale Program: Forest Service Met Its Target, but More Timber Could Have Been Offered for Sale* (1997).

62   Louis Blumberg, "Memo to Mike Francis and Mike Anderson re: Draft Talking Points for Yates," March 8, 1995, TWSR, box 9:19, folder 32.

63   Debbie Sease, Sierra Club, "Memo re: Urgent Opportunity to Get In on NYT Ad," May 19, 1995, TWSR, box 9:19, folder 32.

64   Debbie Sease, "Memo re: Another Opportunity to Tell Clinton How You Feel," July 12, 1995, TWSR, box 9:19, folder 34.

65 Diane Dulken, Natural Resources Defense Council, "Memo re: Friday's Event," July 26, 1995, TWSR, box 9:19, folder 34; Klyza and Sousa, *American Environmental Policy* (2008), 71–77; "The 104th and the Environment," *CQ Weekly Online*, October 12, 1996.

66 Alexander Cockburn, "The Green Betrayers," *The Nation*, February 6, 1995, 157.

67 For a partisan account of this episode, see Alexander Cockburn, "Wilderness Chief in Tree Massacre," *The Nation* 260 (April 24, 1995). For analysis of how this dispute undermined Roush's leadership, see Ronald G. Shaiko, *Voices and Echoes for the Environment: Public Interest Representation in the 1990s and Beyond* (1999), 73–74.

68 Cronon, "Trouble with Wilderness" (1995).

69 On the New Conservation Movement, see chap. 9.

70 "The 104th and the Environment," October 12, 1996.

71 "The G.O.P.'s War on Nature," editorial, *New York Times*, May 31, 1995.

72 Anonymous, "Think Globally, Act Locally: A Pro-Active, Pro-Environment Agenda for House Republicans," August 17, 1995, TWSR, box 9:17, folder 15.

73 As quoted in Allan Freedman, "GOP Trying to Find Balance after Early Stumbles," *CQ Weekly Online*, January 20, 1996.

74 Anonymous, "Think Globally, Act Locally," August 17, 1995.

75 The monument was expanded to 1.9 million acres as a result of the Utah Schools and Lands Exchange Act of 1998.

76 These new wilderness inventory areas were recommended to become wilderness study areas during the agency's land-use planning process under FLPMA. In the interim, they were to be managed for potential wilderness designation. In 2003, however, the Bush administration settled a suit with the state of Utah invalidating the new wilderness inventory areas. Klyza and Sousa, *American Environmental Policy* (2008), 185–87. Administrative action to reverse that settlement was initiated by the Obama administration in December 2010, but was temporarily blocked during the appropriations process in April 2011.

77 George Frampton, interview, August 6, 2009.

78 William J. Clinton, "Remarks Announcing the Establishment of the Grand Staircase-Escalante National Monument at Grand Canyon National Park, Arizona," *The American Presidency Project* (online), September 18, 1996.

79 Paul Larmer, "A Bold Stroke: Clinton Takes a 1.7-Million-Acre Stand in Utah," *High Country News*, September 30, 1996.

80 The wilderness study areas totaled 877,104 acres of BLM land. The agency recommended 362,107 acres for wilderness protection. Bureau of Land Management, *Utah Statewide Wilderness Study Report* (October 1991), volumes 1, 2A, and 3.

81 Julia Duin, "Utahns Bitter over Clinton's Decision; Never Consulted on Monument," *Washington Times*, October 11, 1996. For an overview of the withdrawal, see Skillen, *Nation's Largest Landlord* (2009), 150–56.

82 "Grazing Fees," *CQ Weekly Online*, September 2, 1995.

83 Johanna Wald as quoted in Tom Kenworthy, "Babbitt Drops Increase in Grazing Fees," *Washington Post*, December 22, 1994.

84 "Grazing Fees," September 2, 1995.

85 As quoted in Rick Keister, "Babbitt Begins Range Reform," *High Country News*, September 4, 1995.

86 On grazing reform during the Clinton administration, see Skillen, *Nation's Largest Landlord* (2009), 139–46.

87 Commission on Geosciences, Environment and Resources, National Research Council, *Hardrock Mining on Federal Lands* (1999).

88 Northwest Mining Association, "Abuse of Power: Management of Public Lands by Executive Fiat," *NWMA Bulletin*, July–August 2000.

89 Mineral Policy Center, "MPC Scores Big Win—Stronger Mining Rules," *MPC News*, Winter 2000; Debra W. Struhsacker, "An Overview of the Bureau of Land Management's Rulemaking Efforts for the 43 CFR 3809 Surface Management Regulations for Hardrock Mining," *ABA Section of Environment, Energy, and Resources* 2, no. 1 (June 2003).

90 Dan Beard, National Audubon Society, as quoted in Daniel Lewis, "The Trailblazer," *New York Times*, June 13, 1999.

91 Michael P. Dombeck, Christopher A. Wood, and Jack E. Williams, *From Conquest to Conservation: Our Public Lands Legacy* (2003), 96.

92 In the early 1970s, national environmental groups pressured the Nixon administration in private to issue an executive order protecting all roadless areas in the national forests pending future wilderness reviews. The Nixon administration never followed through on that proposal. See chap. 4.

93 Save America's Forests, "Memo re: Longer-Term Issues and Objectives," November 19, 1992, TWSR, box 8:1, folder 6; "18 Year Blockade Broken!" *Save America's Forests*, Summer 1994; Mark Winstein, "Wildlands, Congress, and You," *Wild Earth*, Winter 1993, 15.

94 Jon Roush, testimony, Committee on Natural Resources, Subcommittee on National Parks, Forests, and Public Lands, *New Directions for the Forest Service*, 103rd Cong., 1st sess., February 1, 1994.

95 Klyza and Sousa, *American Environmental Policy* (2008), 124; Tom Turner, *Roadless Rules: The Struggle for the Last Wild Forests* (2008), 24–25.

96 Michael Dombeck, "Statement regarding the Promulgation of Regulations concerning Roadless Areas within the National Forest System," testimony, United States Senate, Committee on Energy and Natural Resources, Subcommittee on Forests and Public Lands Management, 106th Cong., 1st sess., November 2, 1999.

97 Ken Rait, Oregon Natural Resources Council, "Memo re: Draft Roadless Area Plan," November 7, 1997, TWSR, box 9:19, folder 15.

98 William J. Clinton, "Statement on Signing the Department of the Interior and

Related Agencies Appropriations Act, 1998," in *The American Presidency Project* (online), November 14, 1997.

99   Michael Soulé, "Memo re: Scientists Letter on Roadless Areas," December 3, 1997, TWSR, box 9:19, folder 15.

100   Forest Service, "Administration of the Forest Development Transportation System," *Federal Register* 63, no. 18 (January 28, 1998): 4350–51; Forest Service, "Administration of the Forest Development Transportation System," *Federal Register* 64, no. 29 (February 12, 1999): 7290–7305.

101   Mike Dombeck, chief, U.S. Forest Service, "Protecting and Restoring a Nation's Land Health Legacy," February 3, 1999, TWSR, box 9:18, folder 13.

102   Ken Rait, interview, January 21, 2009.

103   Evidence of the structure of the Heritage Forests Campaign can be found in TWSR, box 9:18.

104   Ken Rait, e-mail to Forest-List forum, "Time to Move On: Protect Heritage Forests Today!" February 12, 1999, http://www.metla.fi/archive/forest/1999/02/msg00068.html.

105   Michael Francis, "Memo to John Podesta re: Lands Legacy," August 4, 1999, TWSR, box 9:18, folder 52.

106   William J. Clinton, "Memorandum on Protection for Forest 'Roadless' Areas," *The American Presidency Project* (online), October 13, 1999.

107   Dombeck, "Letter from the Chief," *Roadless Area Conservation* (online), October 14, 1999.

108   James L. Caswell, forest supervisor, U.S. Forest Service, to Chief Dombeck, December 20, 1999, TWSR, box 9:18, folder 25.

109   Turner, *Roadless Rules* (2008), 37.

110   Dombeck is referring to 860 million visitor-use days. Michael Dombeck, "Letter from the Chief," *Roadless Area Conservation* (online), December 29, 1999.

111   Newspaper advertisement from Heritage Forests Campaign, "3 Out of 4 Americans Agree,"1999.

112   Newspaper advertisement from Heritage Forests Campaign, "You Can't Save the Forests without the Trees," 1999.

113   Newspaper advertisement from Heritage Forests Campaign, "Two Thumbs Up!" 1999.

114   Turner, *Roadless Rules* (2008), 45.

115   Mark Matthews, "Protesters Rock Roadless Area Hearings," *High Country News*, July 3, 2000.

116   People for the USA!, the successor organization to People for the West!, demonstrated little political capability in the late 1990s and decided to disband in October 2000. Heidi Walters, "People for the USA! Disbands," *High Country News*, December 18, 2000.

117 Turner, *Roadless Rules* (2008), 45.

118 U.S. Forest Service, *Roadless Area Conservation: Final Environmental Impact Statement.* Vol. 3, *Agency Responses to Public Comments* (2000), 1.

119 U.S. Forest Service, *Summary of Public Comment: Roadless Area Conservation Proposed Rule and DEIS* (October 6, 2000), x.

120 U.S. Forest Service, *Roadless Area Conservation: Final Environmental Impact Statement.* Vol. 1, (2000), 3–205.

121 U.S. Forest Service, *Roadless Area Conservation: Final Environmental Impact Summary* (2000), S-27.

122 U.S. Forest Service, "Forest Service Offers Preferred Plan for Protecting Roadless Areas in National Forests," news release, November 13, 2000.

123 Ken Rait, "Memo re: Summary of Roadless Call," November 13, 2000, TWSR, box 9:18, folder 43.

124 Klyza and Sousa, *American Environmental Policy* (2008), 120.

125 As quoted in Ken Ward Jr., "Clinton OKs Plan to Protect Forests," *Charleston Gazette*, January 6, 2001.

126 Douglas Jehl, "Road Ban Set for One-Third of National Forests," *New York Times*, January 5, 2001.

127 Associated Press, "Clinton Protects Forest Lands," January 5, 2001.

128 Steven P. Croley, *Regulation and Public Interests: The Possibility of Good Regulatory Government* (2008), 203–12; Klyza and Sousa, *American Environmental Policy* (2008), 133.

129 Daniel T. Rodgers, "Stories, Games, and Deliberative Democracy," *Journal of American History* 88, no. 2 (September 2001): 444–52.

130 George W. Bush and Al Gore, "Transcript of Presidential Debate in Winston-Salem," *The American Presidency Project* (online), October 11, 2000.

131 Jim Motavalli, "Scorched Earth Policy: Environmental Policy of the George W. Bush Administration," *E: The Environmental Magazine*, May 2001; Reed McManus, "Lay of the Land," *Sierra Magazine*, November/December 2001.

132 As quoted in Mike Soraghan, "Watt Applauds Bush Energy Strategy," *Denver Post*, May 16, 2001.

133 George W. Bush, "Remarks at Sequoia National Park, California," *The American Presidency Project* (online), May 30, 2001.

134 George W. Bush, "Remarks Announcing the Energy Plan in St. Paul, Minn.," ibid., May 17, 2001.

135 George W. Bush, "Remarks on the Healthy Forest Initiative," ibid., May 20, 2003.

136 George W. Bush, "Remarks at Ice Harbor Lock and Dam in Burbank, Washington," ibid., August 22, 2003.

137 Luntz Research Companies, "The Environment: A Cleaner, Safer, and Healthier America," 2003.

138   Bush, "Remarks Announcing the Energy Plan in St. Paul, Minn.," May 17, 2001.

139   Rebecca Adams, "Hard-Fought Energy Bill Clears," *CQ Weekly Online*, August 1, 2005.

140   "2005 Legislative Summary: Arctic National Wildlife Refuge Drilling," *CQ Weekly Online*, January 2, 2006.

141   Ann M. Veneman, secretary of agriculture, "Testimony on H.R. 5214 (National Forest Fire Prevention Act)," House Committee on Resources, 107th Cong., 2nd sess., September 5, 2002.

142   Julie R. Hirschfield, "Forest Fires in Western States Ignite Partisan Debate on Hill," *CQ Weekly Online*, September 2, 2000.

143   Robert H. Nelson, "Scorched-Earth Policies," *Wall Street Journal*, November 3, 2003; Linda Platts and Holly Lippke Fretwell, "Why Is the West Always Burning Down?" *Property and Environment Research Center* (online), 2002.

144   The administrative rulemaking procedure was completed in June 2003. "National Environmental Policy Act Determination Needed for Fire Management Activities; Categorical Exclusions; Notice," 40 CFR Part 1505.1, *Federal Register* 68, no. 108 (June 5, 2003).

145   Wilderness Society, "Wildlife Protection Begins near Homes and Towns," May 20, 2003.

146   Natural Resources Defense Council, "Legislation Exploits Fear of Fire to Boost Logging," July 8, 2003.

147   *Healthy Forests Restoration Act*, Public Law 108–148, 108th Cong., 1st sess. (2003). The Senate voted 80 to 14 and the House 286 to 140 in support of the legislation.

148   Tania Schoennagel et al., "Implementation of National Fire Plan Treatments" (2009).

149   Jon Margolis, "The Power of Love, and Its Opposite," *High Country News*, February 12, 2001.

150   U.S. Government Accounting Office, *Oil and Gas Development: Increased Permitting Activity Has Lessened BLM's Ability to Meet Its Environmental Protection Responsibilities* (2005), 1.

151   "Mining Claims," 43 CFR Part 3800, *Federal Register* 66, no. 210 (October 30, 2001).

152   Hoberg, "Science, Politics, and U.S. Forest Law" (2003).

153   "Grazing Administration," 43 CFR Part 4100, *Federal Register* 68, no. 235 (December 8, 2003).

154   For an excellent account of the roadless rule, see Turner, *Roadless Rules* (2008).

155   The Bush administration's strategy on the roadless rule was most successful in Alaska. The Alaska National Interest Lands Conservation Act of 1980 included a clause forbidding future withdrawals of federal land over 5,000 acres in Alaska without congressional authorization. When Alaska challenged the roadless rule in court, making a tenuous argument that the new rule repre-

sented such a withdrawal, the Bush administration quickly settled the suit out of court (over the objections of environmentalists) and, in doing so, exempted the Tongass from the roadless rule in December 2003. The U.S. federal district court in Alaska reversed the subsequent rule exempting the Tongass in March 2011. Ibid., 95–98.

156   Ibid., 117–22.

157   "Idaho Roadless Area Conservation," 36 CFR Part 294, *Federal Register* 73, no. 201 (October 16, 2008). As of 2011, Colorado was the only other state still pursuing a state-specific roadless rule.

158   Wyoming *v.* US Dept. of Agriculture, 570 F.Supp.2d 1309, D. Wyo. (2008).

159   Turner, *Roadless Rules* (2008). Earth Justice, "Major Victory Secures Roadless Rule," *Earth Justice* (online), 2011.

160   Dusty Howitt, Chris Campbell, and Sean Gray, "How Oil and Gas Drilling on the Public Lands Threatens Habitat—and Hunting," *Environmental Working Group* (May 2007).

161   Christina Larson, "The Emerging Environmental Majority," *Washington Monthly*, May 2006.

162   Mark Lubell and Brian Segee, "Conflict and Cooperation in Natural Resource Management," in *Environmental Policy: New Directions for the Twenty-First Century*, 7th ed., ed. Norman J. Vig and Michael E. Kraft, (2009), 172.

163   Klyza and Sousa, *American Environmental Policy* (2008), 296.

164   Richard Lazarus, "Four New Policies, Four Rejections," *Environmental Forum*, March/April 2008, 12.

165   Klyza and Sousa, *American Environmental Policy* (2008), 296.

166   Dowie, *Losing Ground* (1995); Shutkin, *The Land That Could Be* (2000); Shellenberger and Nordhaus, *The Death of Environmentalism* (2004).

167   Klyza and Sousa, *American Environmental Policy* (2008).

Epilogue: Rebuilding the Wilderness Movement

1   See Dickerman's obituary and the tribute to him compiled by Jim and Bess Murray, his longtime friends and associates from the Virginia Wilderness Committee: Holcomb B. Noble, "Ernest Dickerman, Defender of the Wilderness, Is Dead at 87," *New York Times*, August 5, 1998; Elizabeth Murray, ed., *Ernie Dickerman: A Tribute* (1999).

2   "House Wilderness Hearings," 1962.

3   Dickerman, "The National Park Wilderness Reviews (Lost in the Wilderness)," *The Living Wilderness* 34, no. 109 (1970): 41.

4   Rupert Cutler, interview, December 20, 2001.

5   U.S. House, Committee on Interior and Insular Affairs, *Eastern Wilderness Areas* (1973), 46.

6   Dickerman to Harry Crandell, April 27, 1987, HCP, box 2:4, folder "Correspondence from TWS, 1975–1988."

7   Frampton to Crandell, April 14, 1987, HCP, box 2:4, folder "Correspondence from TWS, 1975–1988."

8   Di Chiro, "Nature as Community," *Uncommon Ground*, 1995.

9   Cronon, "The Trouble with Wilderness," *Uncommon Ground*, 1995.

10   Quotes from Mahoney and Dickerman can be found in "Building a Successful Wilderness Campaign: Lessons from the 1998 Wilderness Mentoring Conference," 1999.

11   Arnold, "New Wilderness Land Grab," *Outside Magazine*, 1999; Brian O'Donnell, interview, August 18, 2009.

12   O'Donnell, interview, August 18, 2009; Melyssa Watson, interview, September 1, 2009; Bill Meadows, interview, August 3, 2009.

13   O'Donnell, interview, August 18, 2009; Melyssa Watson, interview, September 1, 2009.

14   Susan Zakin, "Shake-Up: Greens inside the Beltway," *High Country News*, November 11, 1996.

15   Bill Meadows, interview, August 3, 2009.

16   O'Donnell, interview, August 18, 2009; Watson, interview, September 1, 2009; Meadows to O'Donnell, Wilderness Support Center, April 19, 1999, TWSR.

17   "Don't Tread on Me: An Inside Look at the West's Growing Rebellion," *Time*, October 23, 1995.

18   Watson, interview, September 1, 2009.

19   O'Donnell, interview, August 18, 2009.

20   Lynn Scarlett, assistant secretary of the interior, "Moving beyond Conflict: Private Stewardship and Conservation Partnerships," Heritage Foundation Lectures, no. 762, 2002.

21   "2005 Legislative Summary: Arctic National Wildlife Refuge Drilling," *CQ Weekly Online*, January 2, 2006.

22   The settlement stipulated that the BLM's authority to create wilderness study areas under Section 603 of FLPMA, which allowed the agency fifteen years to conduct inventories, expired on October 21, 1993. The settlement denied the agency the discretion to establish new wilderness study areas under Section 202 of FLPMA, its land-use planning program. Natural Resources Defense Council, "Bush Administration Rolls Back Wilderness Protections," press release, April 11, 2003. The Obama administration's efforts to reverse this rule began in December 2010, but were blocked, at least temporarily, during budget negotiations in April 2011. Phil Taylor, "Interior Bites Tongue on Budget Deal to Halt Wilderness Plan," *Energy & Environment Daily*, April 25, 2011, online.

23 Matt Jenkins, "Wilderness Takes a Massive Hit," *High Country News*, April 28, 2003; Norton as quoted in Klyza and Sousa, *American Environmental Policy* (2008), 187.

24 Mike Matz, interview, August 6, 2009.

25 Ibid.

26 *Southern Nevada Public Land Management Act of 1997*, Public Law 105–263, 105th Cong., 2nd sess., October 19, 1998.

27 O'Donnell, interview, August 18, 2009.

28 Adam Chamberlain, "Think Locally, Act Locally," 2009.

29 Roger Scholl and Brian Beffort, "Lincoln County Wilderness," *Call of the Wild*, July 2004.

30 Thomas R. Harris, William W. Riggs, and John Zimmerman, "Public Lands in the State of Nevada: An Overview," 2001.

31 O'Donnell, interview, August 18, 2009.

32 "Nevada's Congressional Delegation Comments on Aspects of the Bill," *Call of the Wild*, July 2004.

33 Friends of Nevada Wilderness proposed 2.5 million acres of wilderness in Lincoln County. Sharon Netherington, "From the Front Lines," *Call of the Wild: Newsletter of Friends of Nevada Wilderness*, July 2004, 2. The soft-release language did not foreclose future wilderness reviews of released areas.

34 *Lincoln County Conservation, Recreation, and Development Act of 2004* (2004).

35 Lisa Kim Bach, "Lincoln County: BLM Auctions 13,300 Acres," *Las Vegas Review-Journal*, September 2, 2005; Launce Rake, "Lincoln County Land Sale Nets $47.5 Million," *Las Vegas Sun*, February 10, 2005.

36 That provision negated a lawsuit filed by environmentalists that objected to such a sale in 2000.

37 In 2000, the Federal Land Transaction Facilitation Act (Public Law 106–248) aimed to expedite sales of public lands already identified for disposal. It allocated 4 percent of the proceeds from such land sales to the state for educational purposes or road construction and the balance to the Federal Land Disposal Account, which could be used for acquiring inholdings in conservation areas.

38 Dansie, "Washington County Growth and Conservation Act," 2008, 199. See also Blaeloch, *Carving Up the Commons* (2009).

39 Meadows to the Governing Council, September, 2006, TWSR, unprocessed.

40 *Washington County Growth and Conservation Act of 2006*.

41 Meadows, interview, August 4, 2009; Groene, interview, July 1, 2010.

42 To Meadows and the Wilderness Society's Governing Council, September 11, 2006, TWSR, unprocessed.

43 "True Wilderness, and False," editorial, *New York Times*, September 4, 2006.

44 Testimony of William H. Meadows, Senate Committee on Energy and Natural Resources, *Miscellaneous Public Lands Bills S.934, S.2833, S.2834, H.R. 1374*, 110th Cong., 2nd sess., 31.

45   *Washington County Growth and Conservation Act of 2008.*

46   Southern Utah Wilderness Alliance, *Statement from SUWA, Sierra Club, and the Wasatch Mountain Club regarding the Washington County Growth & Conservation Act of 2008,* April 22, 2008, http://www.suwa.org/site/News2?page=NewsArticle&id=6621&security=1&news_iv_ctrl=1061

47   *Omnibus Public Land Management Act of 2008.*

48   See Sasha Abramsky, "Blue-ing the West," *The Nation* 284 (January 22, 2007); Robert Saldin, "Democrats Rise Again in the Rockies," *High Country News,* November 11, 2008; "The West: The New South," *New West Politics,* August 13, 2008; and David Sirota, "Drilling for Defeat?" *New York Times,* May 18, 2008.

49   *Omnibus Public Land Management Act of 2009.* The model for handling the allocation of land-use proceeds follows the Federal Land Transaction Facilitation Act. See note 37. See also Blaeloch, *Carving Up the Commons* (2009), 85.

50   Meadows, interview, August 3, 2009.

51   Barack Obama, "Remarks by the President at Signing of the Omnibus Public Land Management Act" (2009).

52   Ray Ring, "A Ghost of the 1970s," *High Country News,* April 13, 2009.

53   For a provoking analysis of the conceptual limits of place-based environmentalism, see Ursula K. Heise, *Sense of Place and Sense of Planet* (2008).

54   George Nickas, "A Promise Broken. . . . " *Wilderness Watcher* 15, no. 4 (2004).

55   Janine Blaeloch and Katie Fite, "Quid Pro Quo Wilderness—A New Threat to Public Lands," 2006.

56   The Wilderness Act of 1964 included language allowing the secretary of agriculture to exempt a portion of the Eagles Nest primitive area in Colorado if it was needed for routing Interstate 70 (it was not).

57   Amy Vedder, Wilderness Society, "Wilderness Legislation Review: Results of the Working Group," September 2006, TWSR, unprocessed.

58   Draft language for the wilderness principles can be found in TWSR. The final principles were provided to the author by Meadows, personal communication, July 25, 2010.

59   Bosso, *Environment, Inc.* (2005).

60   Cockburn and St. Clair, "Death and Life of America's Greens," 1994; Dowie, *Losing Ground* (1995); Shellenberger and Nordhaus, *Death of Environmentalism* (2004).

61   Shutkin, *Land That Could Be* (2000), 122.

62   Although he sees the greatest opportunity in urban areas, Andrew Light makes the important case for public participation as a metric for environmental policy in "The Urban Blind Spot in Environmental Ethics," in *Political Theory and the Environment,* ed. Mathew Humphrey (2001).

63   Juliet Eilperin, "Salazar Voids Drilling Leases on Public Lands in Utah," *Washington Post,* February 5, 2009.

64   Klyza and Sousa, *American Environmental Politics* (2008).

65   Meadows, interview, August 4, 2009.

66   Tom Turner, *Roadless Rules* (2008).

67   Stephen Bocking, *Nature's Experts: Science, Politics, and the Environment* (2004), 24.

68   "For a Wilder Rockies," editorial, *New York Times*, July 6, 2009.

69   Meadows, interview, August 3, 2009.

70   Swedlow, "Scientists, Judges, and Spotted Owls," 2003.

71   Ibid.

72   Cronon, "When the G.O.P. Was Green," *New York Times*, January 8, 2001, A17.

73   Turner and Schneier Jr., *Party and Constituency* (1970); Dunlap and Allen, "Partisan Differences on Environmental Issues" (1976). Data on partisanship since 1973 are based on my review and analysis of the League of Conservation Voters' annual record of votes on environmental issues in the House of Representatives. "Past National Environmental Scorecards," League of Conservation Voters, http://www.lcv.org/scorecard/past-scorecards.

74   Matz, interview, August 6, 2009.

75   *Wilderness Act* (1964).

76   As quoted in a marketing study by Brandgarten, Inc., "Key Findings: TWS" (2007).

77   Muir, *My First Summer in the Sierra* (1911), 211.

78   *Wilderness Act* (1964). Such critiques make clear the problems inherent in drawing a sharp line between humans and nature, which can limit our ability to consider the social causes and consequences of environmental problems. See Cronon, "The Trouble with Wilderness," 1995; Callicott, "Contemporary Criticisms of the Received Wilderness Idea," 2008; and Merchant, "Shades of Darkness," 2003.

BIBLIOGRAPHY

Manuscript Collections

ACP Alaska Coalition Papers, CONS89, Conservation Collection, Denver Public Library, Colorado.

ACWTCP Arthur Carhart Wilderness Training Center Papers, University of Montana, Missoula.

AKS Alan K. Simpson Papers, Collection Number 10449, American Heritage Center, University of Wyoming, Laramie, Wyoming.

BEP Brock Evans Papers, Manuscript Collection No. 1776, University of Washington Libraries, Seattle, Washington.

CECP Colorado Environmental Coalition Papers, CONS137, Conservation Collection, Denver Public Library, Colorado.

FSADOF Forest Service Records, Arapaho and Roosevelt National Forests, Boulder Ranger District Office, Boulder, Colorado.

FSR Forest Service Records, Record Group 95, National Archives and Records Administration, College Park, Maryland.

FWSP Fish and Wildlife Service Papers, Record Group 22, National Archives and Records Administration, College Park, Maryland.

GSNWRP Great Swamp National Wildlife Refuge Papers, Basking Ridge, New Jersey.

HCP Harry Crandell Papers, CONS86, Conservation Collection, Denver Public Library, Colorado.

JGWP James G. Watt Papers, Collection 07667, American Heritage Center, University of Wyoming, Laramie, Wyoming.

JWP John Whitaker Papers, Special Files Unit, Nixon Presidential Materials Project, National Archives and Records Administration, College Park, Maryland.

NFPAR National Forest Products Association Records, Library and Archives, Forest History Society, Durham, North Carolina.

RCP Rupert Cutler Papers, Carter Library, Atlanta, Georgia.

REIP Recreational Equipment Incorporated, Conservation Committee Papers, Corporate Headquarters, Sumner, Washington.

SAFR   Society of American Foresters Records, Library and Archives, Forest History Society, Durham, North Carolina.

SCMP   Sierra Club Member Papers, BANC MSS 71/295 c, Bancroft Library, University of California, Berkeley, California.

SCNLOR   Sierra Club National Legislative Office Records, BANC MSS 71/289 c, Bancroft Library, University of California, Berkeley, California.

SCPNWP   Sierra Club Northwest Office Records, Manuscript Collection No. 2678-1, University of Washington Libraries, Seattle, Washington.

SCR   Sierra Club Records, BANC MSS 71/103 c, Bancroft Library, University of California, Berkeley, California.

TSP   Theodore Swem Papers, CONS91, Conservation Collection, Denver Public Library, Denver, Colorado.

WTAR   Western Timber Association Records, Library and Archives, Forest History Society, Durham, North Carolina.

TWSR*   Wilderness Society Records, CONS130, Conservation Collection, Denver Public Library, Colorado.

* The Denver Public Library reorganized the finding aid and structure of the TWSR in 2004. As a result, two systems of citations are included in the notes. If the name of the folder is written in full, the citation refers to the pre-2004 organizational structure; if a folder number is included, the citation refers to the current organizational structure.

Selected Bibliography

Abbey, Edward. *Desert Solitaire: A Season in the Wilderness.* New York: McGraw-Hill, 1968.

———. "Forward!" In *Ecodefense: A Field Guide to Monkeywrenching,* edited by Dave Foreman, 3–4. Chico, Calif.: Abbzug Press, 1985.

———. *The Monkey Wrench Gang.* Philadelphia: Lippincott, 1975.

Abramsky, Sasha. "Blue-ing the West." *The Nation* 284 (January 22, 2007): 27–30.

Adams, John H., and Patricia Adams. *A Force for Nature: The Story of NRDC and the Fight to Save Our Planet.* New York: Chronicle Books, 2010.

Alagona, Peter S. "Biography of a 'Feathered Pig': The California Condor Controversy." *Journal of the History of Biology* 37 (2004): 557–83.

Allin, Craig W. *The Politics of Wilderness Preservation.* Westport, Conn.: Greenwood Press, 1982.

———. "The Triumph of Politics over Wilderness Science." In *Wilderness Science in a Time of Change Conference,* compiled by Stephen McCool, David Cole, William Borrie, and Jennifer O'Loughlin. Vol. 2, *Wilderness within the Context of Larger Systems,* 180–85. Ogden, Utah: U.S. Department of Agriculture, Forest Service, 2000.

Almond, Gabriel A., and Sidney Verba. *The Civic Culture: Political Attitudes and Democracy in Five Nations*. Princeton, N.J.: Princeton University Press, 1963.

Anderson, Clinton P. "Protection of the Wilderness." *Living Wilderness* 27, no. 78 (1962): 13–14.

Anderson, H. Michael, and Aliki Moncrief. "America's Unprotected Wilderness." *Denver University Law Review* 76, no. 2 (1999): 413–47.

Anderson, H. Michael, Craig Gehrke, David Wilcove, Henry Carey, Jeffrey Olson, and Richard Rice. *National Forests: Policies for the Future*. Washington, D.C.: Wilderness Society, 1988.

Anderson, Terry H. *The Movement and the Sixties*. New York: Oxford University Press, 1995.

———. *The Sixties*. 2nd ed. New York: Pearson, 2003.

Antiquities Act of 1906, Public Law 59–209, 59th Cong., 1st sess. (June 8, 1906).

"Arctic Wildlife Range Bill." *Living Wilderness* 23 (1959): 29.

Arnold, Elizabeth. "The New Wilderness Land Grab." *Outside*, September 1999. http://outside.away.com/outside/magazine/0999/199909wildlands_pol.html.

Arnold, Ron. *At the Eye of the Storm: James Watt and the Environmentalists*. Washington, D.C.: Free Congress Research and Education Foundation, 1982.

Bader, Mike. "Northern Rockies Ecosystem vs. Washington D.C. Political System." *Wild Earth* 1, no. 4 (Fall 1991): 57–58.

Barlow, Thomas J., et al. "Giving Away the National Forests: An Analysis of the U.S. Forest Service Timber Sales below Cost." Natural Resources Defense Council, 1980.

Baumgartner, Frank R., and Bryan D. Jones. *Agendas and Instability in American Politics*. 2nd ed. Chicago: University of Chicago Press, 2009.

Berlert, Chip, and Matthew N. Lyons. *Right-Wing Populism in America: Too Close for Comfort*. New York: Guilford Press, 2000.

Bernstein, Irving. *Guns or Butter: The Presidency of Lyndon Johnson*. New York: Oxford University Press, 1996.

Bess, Michael. *The Light Green Society: Ecology and Modernity in France, 1960–2000*. Chicago: University of Chicago Press, 2003.

"The Big Federal Land Grab." *Conservative Digest* 4 (December 12, 1978): 7–11.

Binder, Sarah A. *Stalemate: Causes and Consequences of Legislative Gridlock*. Washington, D.C.: Brookings Institution Press, 2003.

Blaeloch, Janine. "Carving Up the Commons: Congress & Our Public Lands." Western Lands Project, 2009.

Blaeloch, Janine, and Katie Fite. "Quid Pro Quo Wilderness—A New Threat to Public Lands." Western Lands Project, 2006.

Bocking, Stephen. *Ecologists and Environmental Politics: A History of Contemporary Ecology*. New Haven, Conn.: Yale University Press, 1997.

———. *Nature's Experts: Science, Politics, and the Environment*. New Brunswick, N.J.: Rutgers University Press, 2004.

Booth, William. "New Thinking on Old Growth." *Science* 244, no. 4901 (April 14, 1989): 141–43.

Borneman, Walter R. *Alaska: Saga of a Bold Land.* New York: Harper Collins, 2003.

Bosso, Christopher J. *Environment, Inc: From Grassroots to Beltway.* Lawrence: University Press of Kansas, 2005.

Braasch, Gary. "You & Your Head." *Backpacker,* Spring 1974.

Brady, David W., and Craig Volden. *Revolving Gridlock: Politics and Policy from Jimmy Carter to George W. Bush.* Boulder, CO: Westview Press, 2006.

Brandborg, Stewart. "The First Ten Years." *Living Wilderness* 38, no. 127 (1974): 43.

———. Interview, July 28–29, 2001.

———. Telephone interview, January 22, 2002.

Brinkley, Alan. *The End of Reform: New Deal Liberalism in Recession and War.* New York: Vintage, 1996.

British Petroleum. *BP Statistical Review of World Energy.* June 2009.

Brower, David, ed. *The Sierra Club Wilderness Handbook.* 2nd ed. New York: Sierra Club/Ballantine, 1971.

———. "Wilderness and the Constant Advocate." *Sierra Club Bulletin* 49, no. 6 (September 1964): 2–3.

"Building a Successful Wilderness Campaign: Lessons from the 1998 Wilderness Mentoring Conference." Washington, D.C.: Southern Utah Wilderness Alliance and Alaska Wilderness League, 1999.

Bush, George H. W. "Remarks Announcing the Energy Plan in St. Paul, Minnesota." *The American Presidency Project,* edited by John T. Woolley and Gerhard Peters, University of California, May 17, 2001. http://www.presidency.ucsb.edu/ws/?pid=45617.

———. "Remarks at a Briefing on Energy Policy." *The American Presidency Project,* edited by John T. Woolley and Gerhard Peters, University of California, February 20, 1991. http://www.presidency.ucsb.edu/ws/?pid=19318.

———. "Remarks at Ice Harbor Lock and Dam in Burbank, Washington." *The American Presidency Project,* edited by John T. Woolley and Gerhard Peters, University of California, August 22, 2003. http://www.presidency.ucsb.edu/ws/?pid=64996.

———. "Remarks at Sequoia National Park, California." *The American Presidency Project,* edited by John T. Woolley and Gerhard Peters, University of California, May 30, 2001. http://www.presidency.ucsb.edu/ws/?pid=45923.

———. "Remarks on the Healthy Forest Initiative." *The American Presidency Project,* edited by John T. Woolley and Gerhard Peters, University of California, May 20, 2003. http://www.presidency.ucsb.edu/ws/?pid=910.

Bush, George W., and Al Gore. "Transcript of Presidential Debate in Winston-Salem." *The American Presidency Project,* edited by John T. Woolley and Gerhard Peters,

University of California, October 11, 2000. http://www.presidency.ucsb.edu/ws/?pid=29419.

Byrnes, Patricia. "Baca Forced Out as BLM Director." *Wilderness*, Spring 1994, 6.

———. "Clinton Moves to End Ancient Forest Stalemate." *Wilderness*, Summer 1993, 5–6.

———. "A Mixed Bag of Reactions to Clinton's First Major Moves." *Wilderness*, Fall 1993, 5.

Caldwell, Lynton K. *The National Environmental Policy Act: An Agenda for the Future.* Bloomington: Indiana University Press, 1998.

Callicott, J. Baird. "Contemporary Criticisms of the Received Wilderness Idea." In *The Wilderness Debate Rages On: Continuing the Great New Wilderness Debate*, edited by J. Baird Callicott and Michael P. Nelson, 355–77. Athens: University of Georgia Press, 2008.

———. "That Good Old-Time Wilderness Religion." In *The Great New Wilderness Debate*, edited by J. Baird Callicott and Michael P. Nelson, 387–94. Athens: University of Georgia Press, 1998.

Callicott, J. Baird, and Michael P. Nelson, eds. *The Great New Wilderness Debate: An Expansive Collection of Writings Defining Wilderness from John Muir to Gary Snyder.* Athens: University of Georgia Press, 1998.

———, eds. *The Wilderness Debate Rages On: Continuing the Great New Wilderness Debate.* Athens: University of Georgia Press, 2008.

Carson, Rachel. *Silent Spring.* New York: Houghton Mifflin, 1962.

Castagnetto, Stephen. "Mojave Spring." *Sierra Club Bulletin* 59, no. 6 (June 1974): 17–20.

Catton, Theodore. *Inhabited Wilderness: Indians, Eskimos, and National Parks in Alaska.* Albuquerque: University of New Mexico Press, 1997.

Cavanaugh, Cam. *Saving the Great Swamp: The People, the Power Brokers, and an Urban Wilderness.* Frenchtown, N.J.: Columbia Publishing Company, 1978.

Cawley, R. McGreggor. *Federal Land, Western Anger: The Sagebrush Rebellion and Environmental Politics.* Lawrence: University Press of Kansas, 1993.

Chamberlain, Adam. "Think Locally, Act Locally." Patagonia website, 2005. http://www.patagonia.com/web/us/patagonia.go?slc=en_US&sct=US&assetid=1952 (accessed September 1, 2009).

Chase, Steve, and Mark Madison. "The Expanding Ark: 100 Years of Wildlife Refuges." *Wild Earth* 13, no. 4 (Winter 2004): 18–27.

Clary, David A. *Timber and the Forest Service.* Lawrence: University Press of Kansas, 1986.

Clawson, Marion. *The Economics of National Forest Management.* Baltimore: Johns Hopkins University Press, 1976.

Clinton, William J. "Memorandum on Protection for Forest Roadless Areas." *The American Presidency Project*, edited by John T. Woolley and Gerhard Peters,

University of California, October 13, 1999. http://www.presidency.ucsb.edu/
ws/?pid=56703.

———. "Remarks Announcing the Establishment of the Grand Staircase-Escalante
National Monument at Grand Canyon National Park, Arizona." *The American
Presidency Project*, edited by John T. Woolley and Gerhard Peters, University of
California, September 18, 1996. http://www.presidency.ucsb.edu/ws/?pid=51947.

———. "Remarks on Opening the Forest Conference in Portland, Oregon." *The
American Presidency Project*, edited by John T. Woolley and Gerhard Peters,
University of California, April 2, 1993. http://www.presidency.ucsb.edu/
ws/?pid=46396.

———. "Statement on Signing the Department of the Interior and Related Agencies
Appropriation Act, 1998." *The American Presidency Project*, edited by John T.
Woolley and Gerhard Peters, University of California, November 14, 1997.
http://www.presidency.ucsb.edu/ws/?pid=53556.

Clough, N. K., P. C. Patton, and A. C. Christiansen, eds. *See* U.S. Department of the
Interior.

Clusen, Chuck. Interview, November 30, 2001.

———. Telephone interview, August 24, 2010.

Coates, Peter. *The Trans-Alaska Pipeline Controversy*. Bethlehem, Pa.: Lehigh
University Press, 1991.

Cockburn, Alexander. "Wilderness Chief in Tree Massacre." *The Nation* 260 (April 24,
1995): 556–59.

———. "Wilderness Society: The Saga of Shame Continues." *The Nation* 260 (March
6, 1995): 300.

Cockburn, Alexander, and Jeffrey St. Clair. "Death and Life of America's Greens." *The
Nation* 259 (December 19, 1994): 760–65.

Cohen, Michael P. *The History of the Sierra Club, 1892–1970*. San Francisco: Sierra Club
Books, 1988.

Commission on Geosciences, Environment and Resources, National Research Council.
Hardrock Mining on Federal Lands. Washington, D.C.: National Academy Press,
1999.

Commoner, Barry. *The Closing Circle: Nature, Man, and Technology*. New York: Knopf,
1971.

Cordell, H. Ken, Carter J. Betz, Gary T. Green, and Becky Stephens. *See* U.S.
Department of Agriculture. Forest Service.

Costley, Richard J. "An Enduring Resource." *American Forests* 78 (June 1972): 8–11.

Cotton, Steve, ed. *Earth Day: The Beginning*. New York: Bantam, 1970.

"Cover Art." *Living Wilderness* 33, no. 107 (1969): 1.

Crandell, Harry B., Celia M. Hunter, and Urban C. Nelson. "Discussion, Alaska's
Wilderness Wildlife." In *Wilderness: The Edge of Knowledge*, edited by Maxine E.
McCloskey, 183–92. San Francisco: Sierra Club, 1969.

Cravens, Jay H. "New Hampshire's Great Gulf . . . a Wilderness Area in Trouble." *American Forests* 77, no. 9 (September 1971): 30–32.

Croley, Steven P. *Regulation and Public Interests: The Possibility of Good Regulatory Government*. Princeton, N.J.: Princeton University Press, 2008.

Cronon, William. "The Trouble with Wilderness." *New York Times Magazine*, August 13, 1995.

———. "The Trouble with Wilderness; or, Getting Back to the Wrong Nature." In *Uncommon Ground: Rethinking the Human Place in Nature*, edited by William Cronon, 69–90. New York: Norton, 1995.

———, ed. *Uncommon Ground: Rethinking the Human Place in Nature*. New York: Norton, 1996.

———. "When the G.O.P. Was Green." *New York Times*, January 8, 2001, A17.

Culhane, Paul J. *Public Lands Politics*. Baltimore: Johns Hopkins University Press, 1981.

Curmudgeon, Feral. "California Desert: A Vision of Wilderness." *Earth First! Journal*, June 21, 1987, 18–19.

Cutler, Malcolm Rupert. "A Study of Litigation Related to Management of Forest Service Administered Lands and Its Effect on Policy Decisions." PhD dissertation, Michigan State University, 1972.

———. Interview, December 20, 2001.

Dansie, Daniel. "The Washington County Growth and Conservation Act of 2006: Evaluating a New Paradigm in Legislated Land Exchanges." *Journal of Land Resources and Environmental Law* 28 (2008): 185–221.

Davis, John. "It's What We Do. . . . " *Wild Earth* 3, no. 2 (Fall 1993): 2.

Dawson, William R., J. David Ligon, Joseph R. Murphy, J. P. Myers, Daniel Simberloff, and Jared Verner. "Report of the Scientific Advisory Panel on the Spotted Owl." *Condor* 89, no. 1 (February 1987): 205–29.

"Deep Ecology." *Earth First! Journal*, December 1981.

Demars, Stanford E. *The Tourist in Yosemite, 1855–1985*. Salt Lake City: University of Utah Press, 1991.

Denevan, William M. "The Pristine Myth: The Landscape of the Americas in 1492." In *The Great New Wilderness Debate*, edited by J. Baird Callicott and Michael P. Nelson, 414–42. Athens: University of Georgia Press, 1998.

Devall, Bill. "Editorial." *Earth First! Journal*, December 1, 1984.

Devall, Bill, and George Sessions. *Deep Ecology*. Layton, Utah: Peregrine Smith Books, 1985.

DeVoto, Bernard. "The West against Itself." In *The Easy Chair*, 231–55. Boston: Houghton Mifflin Company, 1955.

Dewey, Scott Hamilton. *Don't Breathe the Air: Air Pollution and U.S. Environmental Politics, 1945–1970*. College Station: Texas A&M University Press, 2000.

Diamond, Jared M. "Island Biogeography and Conservation: Strategy and Limitations." *Science* 193, no. 4257 (September 10, 1976): 1027–28.

Di Chiro, Giovanna. "Nature as Community: The Convergence of Environment and Social Justice." In *Uncommon Ground: Rethinking the Human Place in Nature*, edited by William Cronon, 298–320. New York: Norton, 1995.

Dickerman, Ernest M. "The National Park Wilderness Reviews (Lost in the Wilderness)." *Living Wilderness* 34, no. 109 (1970): 40–49.

Dombeck, Michael. "Letter from the Chief," *Roadless Area Conservation*, October 14, 1999. http://fs.usda.gov/Internet/FSE_DOCUMENTS/fsm8_036118.html.

———. "Letter from the Chief: An Opportunity," *Roadless Area Conservation*, December 29, 1999. http://fs.usda.gov/Internet/FSE_DOCUMENTS/fsm8_035951.html.

———. "Thinking Like a Mountain: BLM's Approach to Ecosystem Management." *Ecological Applications* 6, no. 3 (1996): 699–702.

Dombeck, Michael P., Christopher A. Wood, and Jack E. Williams. *From Conquest to Conservation: Our Public Lands Legacy*. Washington, D.C.: Island Press, 2003.

"Don't Tread on Me: An Inside Look at the West's Growing Rebellion." *Time*, October 23, 1995. Cover.

Douglas, William O. *A Wilderness Bill of Rights*. Boston: Little, Brown, 1965.

Dowie, Mark. *Losing Ground: American Environmentalism at the Close of the Twentieth Century*. Cambridge, Mass.: MIT Press, 1995.

Dunaway, Finis. *Natural Visions: The Power of Images in American Environmental Reform*. Chicago: University of Chicago Press, 2005.

Dunlap, Riley E., and Michael Patrick Allen. "Partisan Differences on Environmental Issues: A Congressional Roll-Call Analysis." *Western Political Quarterly* 29, no. 3 (1976): 384–397.

Durbin, Kathie. *Tongass: Pulp Politics and the Fight for the Alaskan Rain Forest*. Corvallis: Oregon State University Press, 1999.

Dworshak, Henry, J. J. Hickey, Barry Goldwater, and Gordon Allott. "Minority Views on S.174." *Living Wilderness* 26, no. 78 (1962): 35.

Eastern Wilderness Areas Act, Public Law 93–622, 93rd Cong., 2nd sess. (January 3, 1975).

Eaton, Jim. "Wilderness: From Aesthetics to Biodiversity." *Wild Earth* 1, no. 3 (Summer 1991): 1.

Echols, Alice. "Nothing Distant about It: Women's Liberation and Sixties' Radicalism." In *The Sixties: From Memory to History*, edited by David Farber, 149–74. Chapel Hill: University of North Carolina Press, 1995.

"ECOS." *Living Wilderness* 34, no. 109 (1970): 14.

Egan, Michael. *Barry Commoner and the Remaking of American Environmentalism*. Cambridge, Mass.: MIT Press, 2007.

"18 Year Blockade Broken!" *Save America's Forests*, Summer 1994, 1.

Eissler, Fred. "Condors and Wilderness." *Sierra Club Bulletin* 49, no. 3 (March 1964): 10–11.

Emerson, Peter, et al. *Wasting the National Forests: Selling Timber below Costs.*
　　Washington, D.C.: Wilderness Society, 1984.

"Energy Bill, 1991–1992 Legislative Chronology." In *Congress and the Nation, 1989–1992,*
　　vol. 8, edited by Colleen McGuiness, 500–512. Washington, D.C.: CQ Press, 1993.

Evans, Brock. Interview, November 28, 2001.

Farber, David. *The Age of Great Dreams: America in the 1960s.* New York: Hill and
　　Wang, 1994.

Farnham, Timothy J. *Saving Nature's Legacy: Origins of the Idea of Biological Diversity.*
　　New Haven, Conn.: Yale University Press, 2007.

Farrell, Patrick. "Going Big." *High Country News,* September 18, 2006.

Federal Land Policy and Management Act, Public Law 94–579, 94th Cong., 2nd sess.
　　(October 21, 1976).

Feldman, James. *A Storied Wilderness: The Rewilding of the Apostle Islands.* Seattle:
　　University of Washington Press, 2011.

Findlay, John D. "History and Status of the Arctic National Wildlife Range." *University
　　of British Columbia Law Review* 6, no. 1 (June 1971): 15–20.

Fish and Wildlife Service. "90-Day Petition Finding and Initiation of Status Review,
　　Northern Spotted Owl." *Federal Register* 52, no. 176 (September 11, 1987): 34396–97.

Flader, Susan L. *Thinking Like a Mountain: Aldo Leopold and the Evolution of an
　　Ecological Attitude toward Deer, Wolves, and Forests.* Madison: University of
　　Wisconsin Press, 1974.

Fleischner, Thomas L. "Ecological Costs of Livestock Grazing in Western North
　　America." *Conservation Biology* 8, no. 3 (September 1994): 629–44.

Fletcher, Colin. *The New Complete Walker.* 2nd ed. New York: Knopf, 1974.

Flippen, J. Brooks. *Conservative Conservationist: Russell E. Train and the Emergence of
　　American Environmentalism.* Baton Rouge: Louisiana State University Press, 2006.

———. *Nixon and the Environment.* Albuquerque: University of New Mexico Press,
　　2000.

Foreman, Dave. "Around the Campfire." *Earth First! Journal,* June 21, 1983.

———. "Around the Campfire." *Earth First! Journal,* August 1, 1984.

———. "Around the Campfire." *Wild Earth* 1, no. 2 (Spring 1991): 2.

———. "Around the Campfire." *Wild Earth* 1, no. 4 (Fall 1991): 1.

———. *Confessions of an Eco-Warrior.* New York: Harmony Books, 1991.

———. "Deep Ecology Vision Passion Courage." *Earth First! Journal,* March 20,
　　1987, 28.

———. "Earth First! California Wilderness Plan." *Earth First! Journal,* August 1, 1987, 22.

———. *Ecodefense: A Field Guide to Monkeywrenching.* Tucson, Ariz.: Earth First!
　　Books, 1985.

———. "The New Conservation Movement." *Wild Earth* 1, no. 2 (Summer 1991): 6.

———. "The Northern Rockies Ecosystem Protection Act and the Evolving
　　Wilderness Area Model." *Wild Earth* 3, no. 4 (Winter 1993): 57–62.

———. "Shipwrecked Environmentalism." *Earth First! Journal*, March 20, 1984.

———. "Wilderness Areas Are for Real." In *The Great New Wilderness Debate*, edited by J. Baird Callicott and Michael P. Nelson, 395–407. Athens: University of Georgia Press, 1998.

Foreman, Dave, John Davis, David Johns, Reed Noss, and Michael Soulé. "The Wildlands Project Mission Statement." *Wild Earth*, Special Issue, December 1992, 3.

Foreman, Dave, Howie Wolke, and Bart Koehler. "Earth First! Wilderness Preservation System." *Earth First! Journal*, June 1983.

Forsman, Eric David. "Habitat Utilization by Spotted Owls in the West-Central Cascades." PhD dissertation, Oregon State University, 1980.

Fox, Stephen. *John Muir and His Legacy: The American Conservation Movement.* Madison: University of Wisconsin Press, 1981.

Frampton, George T., Jr. "Conservation Up Front." *Wilderness*, Summer 1988, 2.

———. "Conservation Up Front." *Wilderness*, Summer 1990, 2.

———. "Does a New Age Now Begin?" *Wilderness*, Winter 1992, 2–3.

———. Telephone interview, August 6, 2009.

Frome, Michael. *The Battle for the Wilderness.* 3rd ed. Salt Lake City: University of Utah Press, 1997.

Gingrich, Newt, and Dick Armey. *Contract with America.* New York: Times Books, 1994.

Gitlin, Todd. *The Sixties: Years of Hope, Days of Rage.* New York: Bantam Books, 1987.

Glicksman, R. L. "Traveling in Opposite Directions: Roadless Area Management under the Clinton and Bush Administrations." *Environmental Law* 34 (2004): 1143–1208.

Goldstein, Daniel. "Obama to Sign Major Public-Lands Bill That Bars Wyoming Oil and Gas Drilling." *Inside Energy*, March 30, 2009, 14.

Goméz-Pompa, Arturo, and Andrea Kaus. "Taming the Wilderness Myth." In *The Great New Wilderness Debate*, edited by J. Baird Callicott and Michael P. Nelson, 293–313. Athens: University of Georgia Press, 1998.

Gordon-McCutchan, R. C. *The Taos Indians and the Battle for Blue Lake.* Santa Fe, N.M.: Red Crane Books, 1991.

Gorte, Ross. *See* U.S. Congressional Research Service.

Gottlieb, Alan, ed. *The Wise Use Agenda: The Citizen's Policy Guide to Environmental Resource Issues: A Task Force Report.* Bellevue, Wash.: Free Enterprise Press, 1989.

Gottlieb, Robert. *Forcing the Spring: The Transformation of the American Environmental Movement.* 2nd ed. Washington, D.C.: Island Press, 2005.

Graybill, Andrew. "'Strong on the Merits, and Powerfully Symbolic': The Return of the Blue Lake to Taos Pueblo." *New Mexico Historical Review* 76, no. 2 (2001): 125–60.

Gregg, Sara M. "From Farms to Forest: Federal Conservation and Resettlement Programs in the Blue Ridge and Green Mountains." PhD dissertation, Columbia University, 2004.

Groene, Scott. Telephone interview, July 1, 2010.

Guber, Deborah Lynn. "Voting Preferences and the Environment in the American Electorate," *Society and Natural Resources* 14 (July 2001): 455–69.

Guha, Ramachandra. "Radical American Environmentalism and Wilderness Preservation: A Third World Critique." In *The Great New Wilderness Debate*, edited by J. Baird Callicott and Michael P. Nelson, 231–45. Athens: University of Georgia Press, 1998.

Gutierrez, Ralph J., and Andrew B. Carey. *See* U.S. Department of Agriculture. Forest Service.

Haagen-Smit, A. J. "Man and His Home." *Living Wilderness* 34, no. 110 (1970): 38–46.

"Habitats in Peril: Biodiversity and the Public Lands." *Wilderness*, Spring 1987.

Hage, Wayne. *Storm over Rangelands: Private Rights in Federal Land*. Bellevue, Wash.: Free Enterprise Press, 1989.

Hagen, Joel B. *An Entangled Bank: The Origins of Ecosystem Ecology*. New Brunswick, N.J.: Rutgers University Press, 1992.

Hamilton, Bruce. "An Enduring Wilderness?" *Sierra*, September 1994, 46.

———. "Sierra Club Public Lands Campaign." *Sierra*, September 1989, 52–57.

Hardisty, Jean V. *Mobilizing Resentment: Conservative Resurgence from the John Birch Society to the Promise Keepers*. Boston: Beacon Press Books, 1999.

"Hard Times Come to Environmentalists." *U.S. News & World Report*, March 10, 1980, 49ff.

Harris, Larry D., ed. *The Fragmented Forest*. Chicago: University of Chicago Press, 1984.

Harris, Thomas R., William W. Riggs, and John Zimmerman. "Public Lands in the State of Nevada: An Overview." In *Fact Sheet*. Reno: University of Nevada Press, 2001.

Hart, John. *Walking Softly in the Wilderness*. San Francisco: Sierra Club Books, 1977.

Hartzog, George, Jr. "The Impact of Recent Legislation on Administrative Agencies." In *Wilderness in a Changing World*, edited by Bruce M. Kilgore, 172. San Francisco: Sierra Club Books, 1966.

Harvey, Mark. *A Symbol of Wilderness: Echo Park and the American Conservation Movement*. Albuquerque: University of New Mexico Press, 1994.

———. *Wilderness Forever: Howard Zahniser and the Path to the Wilderness Act*. Edited by William Cronon. Seattle: University of Washington Press, 2005.

Hays, Samuel P. *Beauty, Health, and Permanence: Environmental Politics in the United States, 1955–1985*. Studies in Environment and History. New York: Cambridge University Press, 1987.

———. *Conservation and the Gospel of Efficiency*. Forge Village, Mass.: Murray Printing, 1959.

———. *Wars in the Woods: The Rise of Ecological Forestry in America*. Pittsburgh: University of Pittsburgh Press, 2006.

Heise, Ursula K. *Sense of Place and Sense of Planet: The Environmental Imagination of the Global*. New York: Oxford University Press, 2008.

Helvarg, David. *The War against the Greens: The "Wise-Use" Movement, the New Right, and Anti-environmental Violence.* San Francisco: Sierra Club Books, 1994.

Hendee, John C., George H. Stankey, and Robert C. Lucas. *Wilderness Management.* 2nd ed. Golden, Colo.: North American Press, 1990.

Hermach, Tim. "From the Executive Director." *Forest Voice* 1, no. 2 (1993): 2.

Hess, Karl. *Visions upon the Land: Man and Nature on the Western Range.* Washington, D.C.: Island Press, 1992.

Hinchman, Steve. "Turmoil on the Range." *High Country News,* January 24, 1994.

Hirt, Paul W. *A Conspiracy of Optimism: Management of the National Forests since World War Two.* Omaha: University of Nebraska Press, 1994.

Hoberg, George. "Science, Politics, and U.S. Forest Law: The Battle over the Forest Service Planning Rule." Discussion paper. Washington, D.C.: Resources for the Future, 2003.

Hocker, Philip M. "Yellowstone: The Region Is Greater Than the Sum of Its Parts." *Sierra Club Bulletin* 64 (July 1979): 8–13.

Holden, Constance. "Environmental Action Organizations Are Suffering from Money Shortages, Slump in Public Commitment." *Science* 175, no. 4020 (January 28, 1972): 394–95.

"House Wilderness Hearings." *Living Wilderness* 26, no. 80 (1962): 14–15.

Hurley, Andrew. *Environmental Inequalities: Class, Race, and Industrial Pollution in Gary, Indiana, 1945–1980.* Chapel Hill: University of North Carolina Press, 1995.

Isserman, Maurice, and Michael Kazin. *America Divided: The Civil War of the 1960s.* 2nd ed. New York: Hill and Wang, 2004.

"It's 95% Gone, and It Will Never Be Back." *Forest Voice* 1, no. 1 (September 1989).

Jenkins, Matt. "Wilderness Takes a Massive Hit." *High Country News,* April 28, 2003.

Johnson, Lyndon B. "Remarks Upon Signing the Wilderness Bill and the Land and Water Conservation Fund Bill," *The American Presidency Project,* edited by John T. Woolley and Gerhard Peters, University of California, September 3, 1964. http://www.presidency.ucsb.edu/ws/?pid=26481.

Jones, A. Durand. "Cool Islands in the Desert." *Living Wilderness* 38, no. 129 (1975): 18–28.

Kaye, Roger. *Last Great Wilderness: The Campaign to Establish the Arctic National Wildlife Refuge.* Fairbanks: University of Alaska Press, 2006.

Kazin, Michael. "The Grass-Roots Right: New Histories of U.S. Conservatism in the Twentieth Century." *American Historical Review* 97, no. 1 (February 1992): 136–55.

Keister, Rick. "Babbitt Begins Range Reform." *High Country News,* September 4, 1995.

Kemsley, William, Jr. "A New Voice for Backpackers." Editorial. *Backpacker,* December 1976, 5.

Klingle, Matthew. *Emerald City: An Environmental History of Seattle.* New Haven, Conn.: Yale University Press, 2007.

Klyza, Christopher McGrory. *Who Controls Public Lands? Mining, Forestry, and Grazing Policies, 1870–1990*. Chapel Hill: University of North Carolina Press, 1996.

Klyza, Christopher McGrory, and David Sousa. *American Environmental Policy, 1990–2006: Beyond Gridlock*. Cambridge, Mass.: MIT Press, 2008.

Knight, Philip. "An Earth First! Proposal for a Greater Yellowstone Wilderness Preserve." *Earth First! Journal*, September 22, 1988, 26.

Knuffke, Darrell. "Wilderness and the 21st Century." *George Wright Forum* 10, no. 2 (1994): 20–25.

Kollin, Susan. *Nature's State: Imagining Alaska as the Last Frontier*. Chapel Hill: University of North Carolina Press, 2001.

Kraft, Michael E. "Environmental Policy in Congress." In *Environmental Policy: New Directions for the Twenty-First Century*, edited by Norman E. Vig and Kraft, 136–47. 6th ed. Washington, D.C.: C.Q. Press, 2006.

Kruse, Kevin M. "The Politics of Race and Public Space: Desegregation, Privatization, and the Tax Revolt in Atlanta." *Journal of Urban History* 31, no. 5 (July 2005): 610–33.

———. *White Flight: Atlanta and the Making of Modern Conservatism*. Princeton, N.J.: Princeton University Press, 2005.

Langston, Nancy. *Toxic Bodies: Hormone Disruptors and the Legacy of DES*. New Haven, Conn.: Yale University Press, 2010.

Larmer, Paul. "A Bold Stroke: Clinton Takes a 1.7-Million-Acre Stand in Utah." *High Country News*, September 30, 1996.

Larson, Christina. "The Emerging Environmental Majority." *Washington Monthly*, May 2006.

Lassiter, Matthew D. *The Silent Majority: Suburban Politics in the Sunbelt South*. Princeton, N.J.: Princeton University Press, 2006.

Layzer, Judith A. *The Environmental Case: Translating Values into Policy*. Washington, D.C.: CQ Press, 2002.

Lazarus, Richard. "Four New Policies, Four Rejections." *Environmental Forum*, March/April 2008, 12.

LeCain, Timothy J. *Mass Destruction: The Men and Giant Mines That Wired America and Scarred the Planet*. Piscataway, N.J.: Rutgers University Press, 2009.

Lee, Martha. *Earth First!: Environmental Apolcalypse*. Syracuse, N.Y.: Syracuse University Press, 1995.

Le Master, Dennis C, Barry R. Flamm, and John C. Hendee. *Below-Cost Sales: Proceedings of a Conference on the Economics of National Forest Timber Sales*. Washington, D.C.: Wilderness Society, 1987.

Leopold, Aldo. "A Plea for Wilderness Hunting Grounds." In *Aldo Leopold's Wilderness: Selected Early Writings by the Author of A Sand County Almanac*, edited by David E. Brown and Neil B. Carmony, 155–165. Harrisburg, Pa.: Stackpole Books, 1990. First printed in 1925.

———. *A Sand County Almanac and Sketches Here and There.* New York: Oxford University Press, 1968. First printed in 1949.

———. "The Wilderness and Its Place in Forest Recreational Policy." In *Aldo Leopold's Wilderness*, edited by David Earl Brown and Neil B. Carmony, 146–54. Harrisburg, Pa.: Stackpole Books, 1990. First printed in 1921.

———. "Wilderness as a Form of Land Use." *Journal of Land and Public Utility Economics* 1, no. 4 (1925): 398–404.

———. "Wilderness as a Land Laboratory." *Living Wilderness* 6 (July 1941).

Light, Andrew. "Contemporary Environmental Ethics: From Metaethics to Public Philosophy." *Metaphilosophy* 33, no. 4 (2002): 426–49.

———. "The Urban Blind Spot in Environmental Ethics." In *Political Theory and the Environment*, edited by Mathew Humphrey, 7–35. New York: Routledge, 2001.

Lincoln County Conservation, Recreation, and Development Act of 2004. Public Law 108–424, 108th Cong., 2nd sess. (November 30, 2004).

Little, Charles E. "Yellowstone and the Holistic Imperative." *Wilderness*, Summer 1987, 50–55.

Lubell, Mark, and Brian Segee. "Conflict and Cooperation in Natural Resource Management." In *Environmental Policy: New Directions for the Twenty-First Century*, edited by Norman J. Vig and Michael E. Kraft, 171–96. 7th ed. Washington, D.C.: CQ Press, 2009.

MacArthur, Robert H., and Edward O. Wilson. *Theory of Island Biogeography.* Princeton, N.J.: Princeton University Press, 1967.

MacKaye, Benton. "An Appalachian Trail: A Project in Regional Planning." *Journal of the American Institute of Architects* 9 (October 1921): 325–30.

Maher, Neil M. "A New Deal Body Politic: Landscape, Labor, and the Civilian Conservation Corps." *Environmental History* 7, no. 3 (2002): 435–61.

Mahler, Andy. "Heartwood." *Wild Earth* 1, no. 2 (Summer 1991): 24.

Mahoney, Tim. Interview, November 29, 2001.

Malone, Michael P., and Richard W. Etulain. *The American West: A Twentieth-Century History.* Lincoln: University of Nebraska Press, 1989.

Manes, Christopher. *Green Rage: Radical Environmentalism and the Unmaking of Civilization.* Boston: Little, Brown, 1990.

Mann, Charles C., and Mark L. Plummer. "The High Cost of Biodiversity." *Science* 260, no. 5116 (June 25, 1993): 1868–71.

Marcot, Bruce G., and Jack Ward Thomas. *See* U.S. Department of Agriculture.

Margolis, Jon. "The Power of Love, and Its Opposite." *High Country News*, February 12, 2001.

Margules, C., A. J. Higgs, and R. W. Rafe. "Modern Biogeographic Theory: Are There Any Lessons for Nature Reserve Design?" *Biological Conservation* 24 (1982): 115–28.

Marsh, Kevin R. *Drawing Lines in the Forest: Creating Wilderness Areas in the Pacific Northwest*. Seattle: University of Washington Press, 2007.

———. "'Save French Pete': Evolution of Wilderness Protests in Oregon." In *Natural Protest: Essays on the History of American Environmentalism*, edited by Michael Egan and Jeff Crane, 223–44. New York: Routledge, 2009.

———. "'This Is Just the First Round': Designating Wilderness in Central Oregon Cascades, 1950–1964." *Oregon Historical Quarterly* 103, no. 2 (2002): 210–33.

Marshall, Robert. "The Problem of the Wilderness." *Scientific Monthly* 30, no. 2 (February 1930): 141–48.

Matthews, Mark. "Protesters Rock Roadless Area Hearings." *High Country News*, July 3, 2000.

Matz, Matt. Telephone interview, August 6, 2009.

McCarthy, James. "Environmentalism, Wise Use, and the Nature of Accumulation in the Rural West." In *Remaking Reality: Nature at the Millennium*, edited by Bruce Braun and Noel Castree, 126–49. New York: Routledge, 1998.

McCloskey, Maxine, ed. *Wilderness: The Edge of Knowledge*. San Francisco: Sierra Club, 1969.

McCloskey, Michael M. *In the Thick of It: My Life in the Sierra Club*. Washington, D.C.: Island Press, 2005.

———. "Is the Wilderness Act Working?" In *Action for Wilderness*, edited by Elizabeth R. Gillette, 22. San Francisco: Sierra Club, 1972.

———. "Sierra Club Executive Director: The Evolving Club and the Environmental Movement, 1961–1981." An oral history conducted in 1981 by Susan R. Schrepfer, Sierra Club History Series, Regional Oral History Office, Bancroft Library, University of California, Berkeley, 1983.

———. "The Wilderness Act of 1964: Its Background and Meaning." *Oregon Law Review* 45 (June 1966): 288.

———. "Wilderness Movement at the Crossroads." *Pacific Historical Review* 41 (1972): 346–62.

McComb, John. Interview, November 29, 2001.

McGirr, Lisa. *Suburban Warriors: The Origins of the New American Right*. Princeton, N.J.: Princeton University Press, 2001.

McManus, Reed. "Lay of the Land." *Sierra*, November/December 2001.

Meadows, William H. Interview, August 3–4, 2009.

Meine, Curt, Michael Soulé, and Reed F. Noss. "'A Mission-Driven Discipline': The Growth of Conservation Biology." *Conservation Biology* 20, no. 3 (June 2006): 631–51.

Melosi, Martin. "Environmental Justice, Political Agenda Setting, and the Myths of History." *Journal of Policy History* 12, no. 1 (2000): 43–71.

Merchant, Carolyn. "Shades of Darkness: Race and Environmental History." *Environmental History* 8, no. 3 (2003): 380–94.

Merrill, Karen R. *Public Lands and Political Meaning: Ranchers, the Government and the Property between Them*. Berkeley: University of California Press, 2002.

Merritt, Clifton. Interview, July 31, 2001.

Milazzo, Paul Charles. *Unlikely Environmentalists: Congress and Clean Water, 1945-1972*. Lawrence: University Press of Kansas, 2006.

Miles, John C. *Wilderness in National Parks: Playground or Preserve*. Seattle: University of Washington Press, 2009.

Mineral Policy Center. "MPC Scores Big Win—Stronger Mining Rules." *MPC News*, Winter 2000.

Mitchell, Donald Craig. *Take My Land Take My Life: The Story of Congress's Historic Settlement of Alaska Native Land Claims, 1960-1971*. Fairbanks: University of Alaska Press, 2001.

Mitchell, John G., and Constance L. Stallings, eds. *Ecotactics: The Sierra Club Handbook for Environment Activists*. New York: Pocket Books, 1970.

Mitchell, Robert Cameron, Angela A. Mertig, and Riley E. Dunlap. "Twenty Years of Environmental Mobilization: Trends among National Environmental Organizations." In *American Environmentalism: The U.S. Environmental Movement, 1970-1990*, edited by Dunlap and Mertig, 11-25. Philadelphia: Taylor & Francis, 1992.

Mondt, Rod. "EF! Vision for California Desert." *Earth First! Journal*, March 20, 1987, 21.

Morrison, Peter H. *Ancient Forests on the Mt. Baker-Snoqualmie National Forest: Analysis of Forest Conditions*. Washington, D.C.: Wilderness Society, 1990.

Motavalli, Jim. "Scorched Earth Policy: Environmental Policy of the George W. Bush Administration." *E: The Environmental Magazine*, May 2001.

Muir, John. "The American Forests." *Atlantic Monthly* 80 (August 1897): 145-57.

———. *My First Summer in the Sierra*. Boston: Houghton Mifflin, 1911.

Murie, Margaret E. "Wilderness Concept." *Living Wilderness* 34, no. 110 (1970): 63.

Murray, Elizabeth, ed. *Ernie Dickerman: A Tribute*. Washington, D.C.: Wilderness Society, 1999.

Myers, Peter C. *See* U.S. Department of Agriculture.

Nadel, Michael. "The Wilderness Act's Land Requirements." *Living Wilderness* 27, no. 78 (1962): 45.

Naess, Arne. "Deep Ecology and Conservation Biology." *Earth First! Journal*, March 20, 1990, 29.

———. "Intrinsic Value: Will the Defenders of Nature Please Rise?" In *Conservation Biology: The Science of Scarcity and Diversity*, edited by Michael Soulé, 504-15. Sunderland, Mass.: Sinaeur Associates, 1986.

———. "The Shallow and the Deep Long-Range Ecology Movement: A Summary." *Inquiry* 16 (1973): 95-100.

Nash, Roderick Frazier. *The Rights of Nature*. Madison: University of Wisconsin Press, 1989.

———. *Wilderness and the American Mind.* 4th ed. New Haven, Conn.: Yale University Press, 2001.

National Environmental Policy Act of 1969. Public Law 91–190, 91st Cong., 1st sess. (January 1, 1970).

National Forest Management Act. Public Law 94–588, 94th Cong., 2nd sess. (October 27, 1976).

Nelkin, Dorothy. "Scientists and Professional Responsibility: The Experience of American Ecologists." *Social Studies of Science* 7, no. 1 (February 1977): 75–95.

Nelson, Daniel. *Northern Landscapes: The Struggle for Wilderness Alaska.* Washington, D.C.: Resources for the Future Press, 2004.

———. *A Passion for the Land: John F. Seiberling and the Environmental Movement.* Kent, Ohio: Kent State University Press, 2009.

"Nevada's Congressional Delegation Comments on Aspects of the Bill." *Call of the Wild,* July 2004.

"The New Conservation Movement." *Wild Earth* 1, no. 3 (Summer 1991).

Newmark, W. D. "Legal and Biotic Boundaries of Western North American National Parks: A Problem of Congruence." *Biological Conservation* 33 (1985): 197–208.

Nickas, George. "A Promise Broken. . . . " *Wilderness Watcher* 15, no. 4 (2004): 2.

Nixon, Richard. "Remarks on Signing the National Environmental Policy Act of 1969." *The American Presidency Project,* edited by John T. Woolley and Gerhard Peters, University of California, January 1, 1970. http://www.presidency.ucsb.edu/ws/?pid=2446.

Northwest Mining Association. "Abuse of Power: Management of Public Lands by Executive Fiat." *NWMA Bulletin,* July/August 2000.

Noss, Reed. "Protecting Natural Areas in Fragmented Landscapes." *Natural Areas Journal* 7 (1987): 2–13.

———. "A Regional Landscape Approach to Maintain Diversity." *BioScience* 33 (1983): 700–706.

———. "Sustainability and Wilderness." *Conservation Biology* 5, no. 1 (1991): 120–22.

Nutter, John B. "Towards a Future Wilderness: Notes on Education in the Mountains." *Appalachia,* December 1973, 86.

Obama, Barack. "Statement from the President's Signing Statements on H.R. 146, the Omnibus Public Lands Management Act." Office of the Press Secretary, White House, March 30, 2009. http://www.whitehouse.gov/the_press_office/Statement-from-the-Presidents-signing-statements-on-HR-146-the-Omnibus-Public-Lands-Management-Act/.

O'Donnell, Brian. Telephone interview, August 18, 2009.

Odum, Eugene P. *Fundamentals of Ecology.* 2nd ed. Philadelphia: W. B. Saunders, 1959.

———. "The Strategy of Ecosystem Development." *Science* 164 (April 11, 1969): 262–70.

Olsen, Lance. "How to Save the Nationals from Themselves without Really Trying." *Wild Earth* 2, no. 3 (Fall 1992): 3–4.

Outdoor Recreation Resources Review Commission. *Outdoor Recreation for America: A Report to the President and the Congress.* Washington, D.C.: January 1962.

Pederson, Wes. *Public Interest Profiles.* Washington, D.C.: Foundation for Public Affairs, 1982.

Pew Charitable Trusts. *Annual Report.* Philadelphia: Pew Charitable Trusts, 1994.

Philippon, Daniel J. *Conserving Words: How American Nature Writers Shaped the Environmental Movement.* Athens: University of Georgia Press, 2004.

Platts, Linda, and Holly Lippke Fretwell. "Why Is the West Always Burning Down?" *Property and Environment Research Center,* June 26, 2002. http://www.perc.org/articles/article152.php.

Power, Thomas Michael, and Richard N. Barrett. *Post-Cowboy Economics: Pay and Prosperity in the New American West.* Washington, D.C.: Island Press, 2001.

Price, Jennifer. *Flight Maps: Adventures with Nature in Modern America.* New York: Basic Books, 1999.

Pritchard, James A. *Preserving Yellowstone's Natural Conditions: Science and Perceptions of Nature.* Lincoln: University of Nebraska Press, 1999.

Rait, Ken. Interview, January 21, 2009.

Rauch, Jonathan. *Demosclerosis.* New York: Times Books, 1995.

Rearden, Jim. "Say Goodbye to Hunting? Alaska's Year of Decision." *Outdoor Life,* July 1978, 62–63.

Righter, Robert. *The Battle over Hetch Hetchy: America's Most Controversial Dam and the Birth of Modern Environmentalism.* New York: Oxford, 2006.

Ring, Ray. "A Ghost of the 1970s." *High Country News,* April 13, 2009.

Robertson, Thomas B. "The Population Bomb: Population Growth, Globalization, and American Environmentalism, 1945–1980." PhD dissertation, University of Wisconsin–Madison, 2005.

Rodgers, Daniel T. "Stories, Games, and Deliberative Democracy." *Journal of American History* 88, no. 2 (September 2001): 444–52.

Rome, Adam. *Bulldozer in the Countryside: Suburban Sprawl and the Rise of American Environmentalism.* New York: Cambridge University Press, 2001.

———. "The Genius of Earth Day." *Environmental History* 15, no. 2 (April 2010): 194–205.

———. "'Give Earth a Chance': The Environmental Movement and the Sixties." *Journal of American History* 90, no. 2 (2003): 525–54.

Ross, Kenn. *Environmental Conflict in Alaska.* Boulder: University of Colorado Press, 2000.

Roth, Dennis M. *The Wilderness Movement and the National Forests: 1964–1980.* Washington, D.C.: U.S. Department of Agriculture, Forest Service, 1984.

Rothman, Hal K. *The Greening of a Nation? Environmentalism in the United States since*

1945. Edited by Gerald W. Nash and Richard W. Etulain. New York: Harcourt Brace, 1998.

Rozek, Victor. "The Incredible Shrinking Forest Protection Campaign." *Forest Voice* 7, no. 2 (Spring 1994): 14.

Rudzitis, Gundars. *Wilderness and the Changing American West*. New York: John Wiley, 1996.

Runte, Alfred. *National Parks: The American Experience*. Lincoln: University of Nebraska, 1997.

Saldin, Robert. "Democrats Rise Again in the Rockies." *High Country News*, November 11, 2008.

———. "The West: The New South." *New West*, August 13, 2008.

Sale, Kirkpatrick. "The Cutting Edge: Deep Ecology and Its Critics." *The Nation* 246, no. 19 (May 14, 1988): 670–74.

———. *The Green Revolution: The Environmental Movement, 1962–1992*. Edited by Eric Foner. New York: HarperCollins, 1993.

Scarlett, Lynn. "Moving beyond Conflict: Private Stewardship and Conservation Partnerships." Heritage Foundation Lectures, no. 762, 2002.

Schaefer, Hart. "Legislative Corner." *Wild Earth* 1, no. 2 (Summer 1991): 41–42.

Scheffer, Victor B. *The Shaping of Environmentalism in America*. Seattle: University of Washington Press, 1991.

Schoennagel, Tania, Cara R. Nelson, David M. Theobald, Gunnar C. Carnwarth, and Teresa B. Chapman. "Implementation of National Fire Plan Treatments near the Wildland-Urban Interface in the Western United States." *Proceedings of the National Academy of Science* 106, no. 26 (June 30, 2009): 10706–11.

Scholl, Roger, and Brian Beffort. "Lincoln County Wilderness." *Call of the Wild*, July 2004.

Schulman, Bruce J. *The Seventies: The Great Shift in American Culture, Society, and Politics*. New York: Free Press, 2001.

Schulte, Steven C. *Wayne Aspinall and the Shaping of the American West*. Boulder: University Press of Colorado, 2002.

Scott, Doug. *The Enduring Wilderness: Protecting Our Natural Heritage through the Wilderness Act*. Golden, Colo.: Fulcrum Publishing, 2004.

———. Interview, August 2001.

———. "The Next Campaign." *Sierra*, January 1991, 130–35.

Scott, J. Michael, Frank W. Davis, Gavin McGhie, R. Gerald Wright, Craig Groves, and John Estes. "Nature Reserves: Do They Capture the Full Range of America's Biological Diversity?" *Ecological Applications* 11, no. 4 (2001): 999–1007.

Sedjo, Roger A. *Marion Clawson's Contribution to Forestry*. Washington, D.C.: Resources for the Future, 1999.

Sellars, Richard West. *Preserving Nature in the National Parks: A History*. New Haven, Conn.: Yale University Press, 1997.

Shabecoff, Philip. *Earth Rising: American Environmentalism in the 21st Century.* Washington, D.C.: Island Press, 2000.

Shaffer, Mark L. "The Metapopulation and Species Conservation: The Special Case of the Northern Spotted Owl." In *Ecology and Management of the Spotted Owl in the Pacific Northwest,* edited by Ralph J. Gutierrez and Andrew B. Carey, 86–99. Arcata, Calif.: U.S. Forest Service, 1984.

———. "Minimum Population Sizes for Species Conservation." *BioScience* 31 (1981): 131–34.

Shaiko, Ronald G. *Voices and Echoes for the Environment: Public Interest Representation in the 1990s and Beyond.* New York: Columbia University Press, 1999.

Shellenberger, Michael, and Ted Nordhaus. *The Death of Environmentalism: Global Warming Politics in a Post-Environmental World.* Washington, D.C.: Breakthrough Institute, 2004.

Short, C. Brant. *Ronald Reagan and the Public Lands.* College Station: Texas A&M University Press, 1989.

"Show Over, EF! Roadies Unwind." *Earth First! Journal,* December 21, 1981.

Shutkin, William. *The Land That Could Be: Environmentalism and Democracy in the Twenty-First Century.* Cambridge, Mass.: MIT Press, 2000.

Simberloff, Daniel. "The Spotted Owl Fracas: Mixing Academic, Applied, and Political Ecology." *Ecology* 68, no. 4 (1987): 766–72.

Simberloff, Daniel, and Lawrence G. Abele. "Refuge Design and Island Biogeographic Theory: Effects of Fragmentation." *American Naturalist* 120, no. 1 (July 1982): 41–50.

Skillen, James R. *The Nation's Largest Landlord: The Bureau of Land Management in the American West.* Lawrence: University Press of Kansas, 2009.

Smith, Thomas G. *Green Republican: John Saylor and the Preservation of America's Wilderness.* Pittsburgh: University of Pittsburgh Press, 2006.

Soulé, Michael. "What Is Conservation Biology?" *Bioscience* 35 (December 1985): 727–34.

Soulé, Michael E., and Bruce A. Wilcox. "Conservation Biology: Its Scope and Challenge." In *Conservation Biology: An Evolutionary-Ecological Perspective,* edited by Soulé and Wilcox, 1–8. Sunderland, Mass.: Sinauer Associates, 1980.

Sowards, Adam M. "William O. Douglas's Wilderness Politics: Public Protest and Committees of Correspondence in the Pacific Northwest." *Western Historical Quarterly* 37, no. 1 (2006): 21–42.

Spence, Mark David. *Dispossessing the Wilderness: Indian Removal and the Making of the National Parks.* New York: Oxford University Press, 1999.

Stegner, Wallace. "Wilderness Letter." In *Marking the Sparrow's Fall: The Making of the American West,* edited by Page Stegner, 111–17. New York: H. Holt, 1998.

Stine, Jeffrey K. "Natural Resources and Environmental Policy." In *The Reagan*

Presidency: Pragmatic Conservatism and Its Legacies, edited by W. Elliot Brownlee and Hugh Davis Graham, 233–58. Lawrence: University Press of Kansas 2003.

Struhsacker, Debra W. "An Overview of the Bureau of Land Management's Rulemaking Efforts for the 43 CFR 3809 Surface Management Regulations for Hardrock Mining." *ABA Section of Environment, Energy, and Resources* 2, no. 1 (June 2003).

Sturgeon, Stephen C. *The Politics of Western Water: The Congressional Career of Wayne Aspinall*. Tucson: University of Arizona Press, 2002.

Suhanek, Jody. "Native Forest Council." *Wild Earth* 1, no. 2 (Summer 1991): 24–25.

Sutter, Paul S. *Driven Wild: How the Fight against Automobiles Launched the Modern Wilderness Movement*. Edited by William Cronon. Seattle: University of Washington Press, 2002.

Swedlow, Brendon. "Scientists, Judges, and Spotted Owls: Policymakers in the Pacific Northwest." *Duke Environmental Law & Policy Forum* 13, no. 2 (Spring 2003): 187–278.

Switzer, Jacqueline Vaughn. *Green Backlash: The History and Politics of Environmental Opposition in the United States*. Boulder, Colo.: Lynne Rienner Publishers, 1997.

Symonds, William. "Washington in the Grip of the Green Giant." *Fortune*, October 4, 1982.

Takacs, David. *The Idea of Biodiversity*. Baltimore: Johns Hopkins University Press, 1996.

Taylor, Joseph E., III. "The Many Lives of the New West." *Western Historical Quarterly* 35 (Summer 2004): 141–65.

Terborgh, John. "The Big Things That Run the World—A Sequel to E. O. Wilson." *Conservation Biology* 2, no. 4 (December 1988): 402–3.

Thoreau, Henry David. *The Writings of Henry David Thoreau: Excursions, Translations, and Poems*. Boston: Houghton Mifflin, 1906.

Tjossem, Sara. "Preservation of Nature and Academic Respectability: Tensions in the Ecological Society of America, 1915–1979." PhD dissertation, Cornell University, 1994.

Tokar, Brian. "Social Ecology, Deep Ecology, and the Future of Green Political Thought." *The Ecologist* 18, no. 4/5 (1988): 135.

"Tongass Reform Act Passes." *Wilderness*, Summer 1988, 3.

"The Top Twenty-Five Goals." In *Wise Use Agenda: The Citizen's Policy Guide to Environmental Resource Issues*, edited by Alan Gottlieb, 10–15. Bellevue, Wash.: Free Enterprise Press, 1989.

Tuchmann, E. Thomas., Kent P. Connaughton, Lisa E. Freedman, and Clarence B. Mirowaki. *See* U.S. Department of Agriculture. Office of Forestry and Economic Assistance.

Turner, James Morton. "Conservation Science and Forest Service Policy for Roadless Areas." *Conservation Biology* 20, no. 3 (June 2006): 713–22.

————. "'The Specter of Environmentalism': Wilderness, Environmental Politics, and the Evolution of the New Right." *Journal of American History* 96, no. 1 (June 2009): 123–48.

Turner, Julius, and Edward V. Schneier Jr. *Party and Constituency: Pressures on Congress.* Baltimore: Johns Hopkins University Press, 1970.

Turner, Tom. *Roadless Rules: The Struggle for the Last Wild Forests.* Washington, D.C.: Island Press, 2008.

U.S. Congress. Committee on Agriculture. *Economics of Federal Timber Sales.* 99th Cong., 1st sess., June 5, 1985.

U.S. Congress. House. Committee on Interior and Insular Affairs. *Alaska National Interest Lands Conservation Act of 1979.* Hearings. 96th Cong., 1st sess., 1979.

————. *Designating Certain Lands in the Great Swamp National Wildlife Refuge, Morris County, NJ as Wilderness.* 90th Cong., 2nd sess., July 26, 1968.

————. *Eastern Wilderness Areas.* 93rd Cong., 1st sess., February 21, 1973.

————. *San Rafael Wilderness.* 90th Cong., 1st sess., April 11, 1967.

U.S. Congress. House. Committee on Interior and Insular Affairs, Subcommittee on Indian Affairs and Public Lands. "Testimony by M. Rupert Cutler, Assistant Secretary of Agriculture, on the Endangered American Wilderness Act, H.R. 3454," 95th Cong., 1st sess., May 6, 1977.

U.S. Congress. House. Committee on Interior and Insular Affairs. Subcommittee on Oversight and Alaska Lands. *Inclusion of Alaska Lands in National Park, Forest, Wildlife Refuge, and Wild and Scenic Rivers Systems.* 95th Cong., 1st sess., August 20, 1977.

U.S. Congress. House. Committee on Interior and Insular Affairs. Subcommittee on Public Lands. *San Rafael Wilderness.* 90th Cong., 1st sess., June 19, 1967.

————. *Great Swamp, Pelican Island, Monomoy, Seney, Huron, Michigan Islands, Gravel Island, Green Bay, and Moosehorn Wilderness Areas.* 90th Cong., 2nd sess., June 20, 1968.

————. *Wilderness Preservation System.* 87th Cong., 1st. sess., October 30–31, 1961.

U.S. Congress. House. Committee on Interior and Insular Affairs. Subcommittee on Water and Power Resources, Oversight Hearing. 100th Cong., 1st sess., May 28, 1987.

————. Oversight Hearing. 100th Cong., 2nd sess., June 9, 1988.

U.S. Congress. House. Committee on Natural Resources. *California Desert Lands: Hearing on H.R. 518.* 99th Cong., 1st sess., June 15, 1993.

————. "Testimony by Todd Schulke, Center for Biological Diversity, on the President's Healthy Forest Initiative." 107th Cong., 2nd sess., September 5, 2002.

U.S. Congress. House. Committee on Natural Resources. Subcommittee on National Parks, Forests, and Public Lands. "Testimony by Jack Ward Thomas, Chief, United States Forest Service, on New Directions for the Forest Service." 103rd Cong., 1st sess., February 3, 1994.

———. "Testimony by Jon Roush, President of the Wilderness Society, on New Directions for the Forest Service." 103rd Cong., 1st sess., February 1, 1994.

U.S. Congress. House. Committee on Science and Technology, Subcommittees on Technology, Environment and Aviation and Investigations and Oversight. "Testimony by Bruce Babbitt, Secretary of the Interior, on the National Biological Survey and H.R. 1845." 103rd Cong., 1st sess., September 14, 1993.

U.S. Congress. Joint Committee on Recreational Survey of Federal Lands. *Recreation Resources of Federal Lands.* 70th Cong., 1928. Report of the National Conference on Outdoor Education.

U.S. Congress. Senate. Committee on Agriculture and Forestry. *Wild Areas in the National Forests.* 92nd Cong., 2nd sess., June 20, 1972.

U.S. Congress. Senate. Committee on Energy and Natural Resources. Subcommittee on Forests and Public Lands Management. Michael Dombeck. "Statement regarding the Promulgation of Regulations concerning Roadless Areas within the National Forest System." 106th Cong., 1st sess., November 2, 1999.

U. S. Congress. Senate. Interior and Insular Affairs Committee. *San Rafael Wilderness Hearings.* 90th Cong., 1st sess., April 11, 1967.

U.S. Congressional Research Service. *Bureau of Land Management Wilderness Reviews.* By Ross Gorte and Pamela Baldwin. Washington, D.C.: Congressional Research Service, 2004.

———. *Salvage Timber Sales and Forest Health.* By Ross Gorte. Washington, D.C.: Congressional Research Service, 1996.

———. *Secure Rural Schools and Community Self-Determination Act of 2000.* By Ross Gorte. Washington, D.C.: Congressional Research Service, 2007.

———. *Utah Wilderness Legislation in the 104th Congress.* By Ross Gorte. Washington, D.C.: Congressional Research Service, 1995.

U.S. Department of Agriculture. *Below-Cost Timber Sales: An Overview of the Issue.* By Peter C. Myers. Washington, D.C.: Department of Agriculture, 1986.

———. *Of Spotted Owls, Old Growth, and New Policies: A History since the Interagency Scientific Committee Report.* By Bruce G. Marcot and Jack Ward Thomas. General Technical Report. Portland, Ore.: Forest Service, 1997.

U.S. Department of Agriculture. Forest Service. *Ecology and Management of the Spotted Owl in the Pacific Northwest.* Edited by Ralph J. Gutierrez and Andrew B. Carey. Arcata, Calif.: U.S. Forest Service, 1984.

———. *Final Environmental Statement on a Recommended Land Use Plan for the Alpine Lakes Area in the State of Washington.* Washington, D.C.: United States Forest Service, 1974.

———. *Harvest, Employment, Exports, and Prices in Pacific Northwest Forests, 1965–2000.* By Debra D. Warren. Washington, D.C.: Forest Service, 2002.

———. "National Environmental Policy Act Determination Needed for Fire

Management Activities; Categorical Exclusions; Notice." *Federal Register* 68, no. 108 (June 5, 2003): 33814–24.

———. *New Wilderness Areas: Roadless Area Review and Evaluation.* Washington, D.C.: Forest Service, 1973.

———. *Off-Road Vehicle Recreation in the United States and Its Regions and States.* By H. Ken Cordell, Carter J. Betz, Gary T. Green, and Becky Stephens. Internet Research Information Series. Washington, D.C.: United States Forest Service, 2005.

———. *RARE II: Final Environmental Statement.* Washington, D.C.: GPO, 1979.

———. *Roadless Area Conservation: Final Environmental Impact Statement.* Vol. 1. Washington, D.C.: Forest Service, 2000.

———. *Roadless Area Conservation: Final Environmental Impact Statement.* Vol. 3, *Agency Responses to Public Comments.* Washington, D.C.: United States Forest Service, 2000.

———. *Roadless Area Conservation: Final Environmental Impact Summary.* Washington, D.C.: Forest Service, 2000.

———. *Summary of Public Comment: Roadless Area Conservation Proposed Rule and DEIS.* Washington, D.C.: Forest Service, 2000.

U.S. Department of Agriculture. Office of Forestry and Economic Assistance. *The Northwest Forest Plan: A Report to the President and Congress.* By E. Thomas Tuchmann, Kent P. Connaughton, Lisa E. Freedman, and Clarence B. Mirowaki. Portland, Ore.: U.S. Department of Agriculture, 1996.

U.S. Department of the Interior. *Arctic National Wildlife Refuge: Coastal Plain Resource Assessment.* Edited by N. K. Clough, P. C. Patton, and A. C. Christiansen. Report and Recommendation to the Congress of the United States and Final Legislative Environmental Impact Statement. Washington, D.C., 1987.

U.S. Department of the Interior. Bureau of Land Management. *California Desert Conservation Area: Final Environmental Impact Statement and Proposed Plan.* Sacramento, Calif.: California State Office, Bureau of Land Management, 1980.

———. *Public Land Statistics.* Washington, D.C.: GPO, 1971.

———. *Public Land Statistics.* Washington, D.C.: GPO, 1980.

———. *Public Land Statistics.* Washington, D.C.: GPO, 1990.

———. *Utah Statewide Wilderness Study Report.* Washington, D.C.: Utah State Office, Bureau of Land Management, October 1991.

U.S. Department of the Interior. Fish and Wildlife Service. *Proposed Arctic National Wildlife Refuge, Alaska; Final Environmental Statement.* Washington, D.C.: GPO, 1974.

U.S. General Accounting Office. *Emergency Salvage Sale Program: Forest Service Met Its Target, but More Timber Could Have Been Offered for Sale.* Washington, D.C.: United States General Accounting Office, 1997.

———. *Oil and Gas Development: Increased Permitting Activity Has Lessened BLM's*

Ability to Meet Its Environmental Protection Responsibilities. Washington, D.C.: Government Accounting Office, 2005.

———. "Regulatory Review: Delay of Effective Dates of Final Rules Subject to Administration's January 20, 2001." Memorandum. Washington, D.C.: General Accounting Office, 2002.

Udall, Stewart L. *The Quiet Crisis.* New York: Holt, Rinehart and Winston, 1963.

———. "To Save the Wonder of Wilderness." *New York Times Magazine,* May 27, 1962, 12–13+.

———. "Wilderness." *Living Wilderness* 80 (Spring–Summer 1962): 6–7.

Warren, Debra D. *See* U.S. Department of Agriculture. Forest Service.

Warren, Louis S. *The Hunter's Game: Poachers and Conservationists in Twentieth-Century America.* New Haven, Conn.: Yale University Press, 1997.

Washington County Growth and Conservation Act of 2006. S. 3636, 109th Cong., 2nd sess.

Washington County Growth and Conservation Act of 2008. S. 2834, 110th Cong., 2nd sess.

Watkins, T. H. "The Challenge of Greater Yellowstone." *Wilderness,* Summer 1987, 18.

———. "Forests and Butter." *Wilderness,* Spring 1990, 12–13.

———. "Wise Use: Discouragements and Clarifications." In *Let the People Judge: Wise Use and the Private Property Rights Movement,* edited by John D. Echeverria and Raymond Booth Eby. Washington, D.C.: Island Press, 1995.

Watson, Charles S., Jr. "The Lands No One Knows." *Sierra Club Bulletin* 58, no. 8 (September 1973).

Watson, Melyssa. Telephone interview, September 1, 2009.

"A Way to the Wilderness." *Living Wilderness* 38, no. 127 (1974): 27.

Weeden, Robert B. "Arctic Oil: Its Impact on Wilderness and Wildlife." In *Wilderness: The Edge of Knowledge,* edited by Maxine E. McCloskey, 157. San Francisco: Sierra Club Books, 1969.

Wellock, Thomas R. "The Dickey Bird Scientists Take Charge: Science, Policy, and the Spotted Owl," *Environmental History* 15 (July 2010): 381–414.

———. *Preserving the Nation: The Conservation and Environmental Movements, 1870–2000.* American History Series, edited by John Hope Franklin and A. S. Eisenstadt. Wheeling, Ill.: Harlan Davidson, 2007.

Wells Associates. *National Forest Trails: Neglected and Disappearing.* San Francisco: Sierra Club, 1985.

Wheat, Frank. *California Desert Miracle: The Fight for Desert Parks and Wilderness.* San Diego: Sunbelt Publications, 1999.

White, Richard. "'Are You an Environmentalist or Do You Work for a Living?': Work and Nature." In *Uncommon Ground: Rethinking the Human Place in Nature,* edited by William Cronon, 171–85. New York: Norton, 1995.

Wilcove, David, and Dennis D. Murphy. "The Spotted Owl Controversy and Conservation Biology." Editorial. *Conservation Biology* 5, no. 3 (September 1991): 262.

Wilcove, David, Charles H. McLelland, and Andrew P. Dobson. "Habitat Fragmentation in the Temperate Zone." In *Conservation Biology: The Science of Scarcity and Diversity*, edited by Michael Soulé, 237–56. Sunderland, Mass.: Sinaeur Associates, 1986.

Wilderness Act. Public Law 88–577, 88th Cong., 2nd sess. (September 3, 1964).

"Wilderness Preserve System." *Earth First! Journal*, June 21, 1983.

Wilderness Society. *The Alaska Lands Act, a Broken Promise: The Wilderness Society Report on the Historic Alaska Lands Act Ten Years after Passage*. Washington, D.C.: Wilderness Society, 1990.

———. *America's Vanishing Rain Forest: A Report on Federal Timber Management in Southeast Alaska*. Washington, D.C.: Wilderness Society, 1986.

Wilkinson, Charles F. *Crossing the Next Meridian: Land, Water, and the Future of the American West*. Washington, D.C.: Island Press, 1992.

Wilkinson, Francis. "Is He Tough Enough to Save the Environment?" *Rolling Stone*, July 8, 1993.

Williams, Ellis T. "National Forest Contributions to Local Governments." *Land Economics* 31, no. 3 (August 1955): 204–14.

Williss, George F. *"Do Things Right the First Time": The National Park Service and the Alaska National Interest Lands Conservation Act of 1980*. Washington, D.C.: U.S. Dept. of the Interior, National Park Service, 1985.

Wilson, E. O., ed. *Biodiversity*. Washington, D.C.: National Academy Press, 1988.

Winstein, Mark. "Wildlands, Congress, and You." *Wild Earth*, Winter 1993, 15.

Wolke, Howie. "Bad Science Lacks the Visceral Connection." *Wild Earth* 2, no. 4 (Winter 1992): 59.

Worf, Bill. Telephone interview, February 7, 2001.

"Working for Wilderness in D.C." *Call of the Wild*, September 2004.

Worster, Donald. *Nature's Economy: A History of Ecological Ideas*. Edited by Worster and Alfred Crosby. 2nd ed. New York: Cambridge, 1994.

"Yes! I Want to Help Save the Last of America's Virgin Forests." *Forest Voice*, August 1990.

Young, Margaret Hays, and Mitch Friedman. "Legislative Corner." *Wild Earth* 1, no. 1 (Spring 1991): 50.

Zahniser, Howard. "Guardians Not Gardeners." *Living Wilderness* 27, no. 83 (1963): 2.

———. "The Need for Wilderness Areas." In *Where Wilderness Preservation Began*, edited by Edward Zahniser, 59. Utica, N.Y.: North Country Books, 1964.

———. "'Of Course, Conservationists Support It!'" *Living Wilderness* 27, no. 79 (Winter–Spring 1962): 2.

———. "The People and Wilderness." *Living Wilderness* 29, no. 86 (1964): 39–42.

Zakin, Susan. *Coyotes and Town Dogs: Earth First! and the Environmental Movement*. New York: Viking Press, 1993.

———. "Shake-Up: Greens inside the Beltway." *High Country News*, November 11, 1996.

INDEX

WEYERHAEUSER ENVIRONMENTAL BOOKS

Wilderness Forever: Howard Zahniser and the Path to the Wilderness Act
BY MARK HARVEY

On the Road Again: Montana's Changing Landscape BY WILLIAM WYCKOFF

Public Power, Private Dams: The Hells Canyon High Dam Controversy
BY KARL BOYD BROOKS

*Windshield Wilderness: Cars, Roads, and Nature in Washington's
National Parks*
BY DAVID LOUTER

Native Seattle: Histories from the Crossing-Over Place BY COLL THRUSH

The Country in the City: The Greening of the San Francisco Bay Area
BY RICHARD A. WALKER

Drawing Lines in the Forest: Creating Wilderness Areas in the Pacific Northwest
BY KEVIN R. MARSH

Plowed Under: Agriculture and Environment in the Palouse
BY ANDREW P. DUFFIN

Making Mountains: New York City and the Catskills BY DAVID STRADLING

The Fishermen's Frontier: People and Salmon in Southeast Alaska
BY DAVID F. ARNOLD

Shaping the Shoreline: Fisheries and Tourism on the Monterey Coast
BY CONNIE Y. CHIANG

Dreaming of Sheep in Navajo Country BY MARSHA WEISIGER

The Toxic Archipelago: A History of Industrial Disease in Japan
BY BRETT L. WALKER

Seeking Refuge: Birds and Landscapes of the Pacific Flyway
BY ROBERT M. WILSON

Quagmire: Nation-Building and Nature in the Mekong Delta
BY DAVID BIGGS

Iceland Imagined: Nature, Culture, and Storytelling in the North Atlantic
BY KAREN OSLUND

A Storied Wilderness: Rewilding the Apostle Islands BY JAMES W. FELDMAN

The Republic of Nature: An Environmental History of the United States
BY MARK FIEGE

The Promise of Wilderness: American Environmental Politics since 1964
BY JAMES MORTON TURNER

Weyerhaeuser Environmental Classics

The Great Columbia Plain: A Historical Geography, 1805–1910 BY D. W. MEINIG

Mountain Gloom and Mountain Glory: The Development of the Aesthetics of the Infinite BY MARJORIE HOPE NICOLSON

Tutira: The Story of a New Zealand Sheep Station BY HERBERT GUTHRIE-SMITH

A Symbol of Wilderness: Echo Park and the American Conservation Movement BY MARK HARVEY

Man and Nature: Or, Physical Geography as Modified by Human Action by George Perkins Marsh EDITED AND ANNOTATED BY DAVID LOWENTHAL

Conservation in the Progressive Era: Classic Texts EDITED BY DAVID STRADLING

DDT, Silent Spring, and the Rise of Environmentalism: Classic Texts EDITED BY THOMAS R. DUNLAP

Reel Nature: America's Romance with Wildlife on Film BY GREGG MITMAN

The Environmental Moment, 1968–1972 EDITED BY DAVID STRADLING

Cycle of Fire by Stephen J. Pyne

Fire: A Brief History

World Fire: The Culture of Fire on Earth

Vestal Fire: An Environmental History, Told through Fire, of Europe and Europe's Encounter with the World

Fire in America: A Cultural History of Wildland and Rural Fire

Burning Bush: A Fire History of Australia

The Ice: A Journey to Antarctica

LANDSCAPE PHOTOGRAPHY BY GEORGE WUERTHNER

PAGE II: Gold Creek Drainage, Alpine Lakes Wilderness, Mt. Baker-Snoqualmie National Forest, Washington.

PAGE 14: Proxy Falls, Three Sisters Wilderness, Willamette National Forest, Oregon

PAGE 16: Selway River, Selway-Bitterroot Wilderness, Nez Perce National Forest, Idaho

PAGE 44: Great Swamp National Wildlife Refuge, New Jersey

PAGE 70: Alpine Lakes Wilderness, Mt. Baker-Snowqualmie National Forest, Washington

PAGE 100: Gore Range, Eagles Nest Wilderness, White River National Forest, Colorado

PAGE 137: Jacumba Wilderness, Bureau of Land Management, California

PAGE 138: Admiralty Island, Tongass National Forest, Alaska

PAGE 140: Mount McKinley, viewed from Savage River, Denali National Park, Alaska

PAGE 182: Kalmiopsis Wilderness, Rogue River-Siskiyou National Forest, Oregon

PAGE 226: Inyo Mountains Wilderness, Inyo National Forest and Bureau of Land Management, California

PAGE 263: Jacumba Wilderness, Bureau of Land Management, California

PAGE 264: Escalante River, Grand Staircase-Escalante National Monument, Bureau of Land Management, Utah

PAGE 266: Clearcuts below Grizzly Peak, Kootenai National Forest, Montana

PAGE 298: View from Hylite Peak, Gallatin National Forest, Montana

PAGE 330: Lower Calf Creek Falls, Grand Staircase-Escalante National Monument, Utah

PAGE 374: Dark Hollow Falls, Shenandoah National Park, Virginia

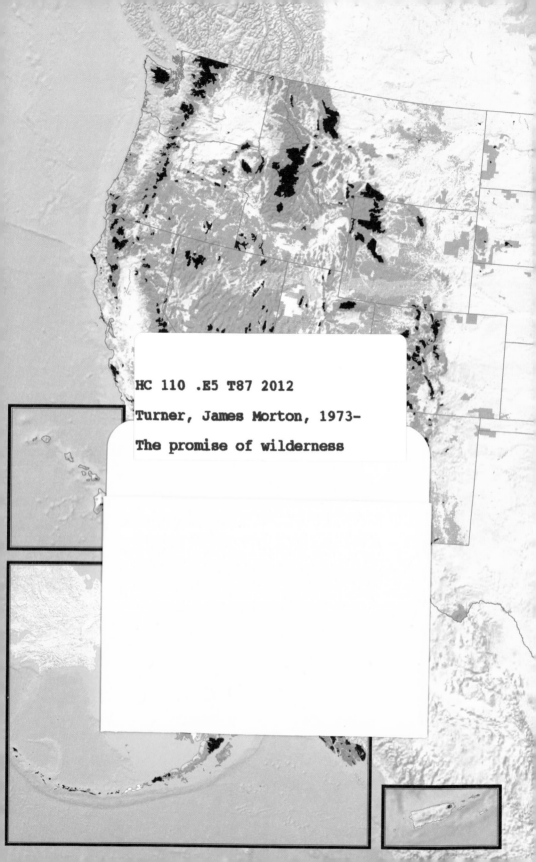